ALSO BY UCADIA

De Dea Magisterium

Five Worlds

Yapa

Waiata

Tara

Lebor Clann Glas

Volume I
10,830 BCE to 365 CE

**OFFICIAL ENGLISH
FIRST EDITION**

BY

UCADIA

Ucadia Books Company

Lebor Clann Glas (Volume I). Official English First Edition. Copyright © 2012-2020 UCADIA. All Rights reserved in Trust.

No part of this book may be reproduced, or stored in a retrieval system, or transmitted in any form or by any means electronic, mechanical, photocopying, recording or otherwise, without the express and authentic written permission of the Publisher.

The Publisher disclaims any liability and shall be indemnified and held harmless from any demands, loss, liability, claims or expenses made by any party due or arising out of or in connection with any differences between previous non-official English drafts and this Official English First Edition.

A party that threatens, makes or enacts any demand or action, against this publication or the Publisher hereby acknowledge they have read this disclaimer and agree with this binding legal agreement and irrevocably consent to Ucadia and its competent forums as being the original and primary Jurisdiction for resolving any such issue of fact and law.

Published by Ucadia Books Company, a Delaware stock corporation (File Number 6779670) 901 N Market St #705 Wilmington Delaware 19801.
First edition.

UCADIA® is a US Registered Trademark in trust under Guardians and Trustees Company protected under international law and the laws of the United States.

ISBN 978-1-64419-009-8

Preface

Comes, divine light. Comes, sacred dream. The mouth at rest. The body still. The ears silent. The mind as water. That your eyes and ears be opened by the fire of the Holly. Your mind be awakened by the wisdom of the Cuilliaéan. That you might see all that was, all that is, and all that might yet come.

Born of earth, all shall return. This is the binding of life, that none can escape. High or low, all physical form becomes as dust. Thus ages past, great kings and queens did battle. Empires of stone and gold, iron and marble. Who were the greatest? The richest? The most powerful? The bones and ruined stones reveal, their secrets.

The Isle, sacred named by all the ancients, from times remotest in the womb of the gods. The ancient exile of the great horned gods and the birthplace of the Prometheus. As Ireland today, as Éire to the Irish. As Hibernia to the Romans. As Hibiru, to the ancient Egyptians and Phoenicians. As Ibbi-Éri to the ancients Akkadians, Sumerians and first tribes of Civilisation.

This Isle that rises over the waves of ocean and birthplace of the Green Gods. Of a people that journeyed far and wide. The founders of the first cities, the seeders of the first fields. No cowardly word, no thieving hand can blight one spoken word of truth. Alas, where once great king priests stood proud, now only weeds and meadow.

Come the redemption Of all that is spirit. More than memory, more than fable, a sacred covenant did the Holly first make for humanity with earth, with fire with water and with spirit. A pact not broken by death or forgetfulness. For the memory of the land outlives the ignorance of sleepy children, knowing not from whence they came, nor who they really are.

It is no shame to tell the truth. Neither a tally, nor footnote. Neither strength of sword, nor loud voice. Far from the finery of greedy hands, nor to be found in the words of those who protest too much. Truth is and always a knowing more than telling, a feeling more than seeing. Thus those who proclaim by reason of folly are blind leading blind. An arrogant spirit stands higher than a mountain at the sound of his own name, yet confidence and ignorance rarely survive the glare of truth. They are bedfellows of those who claim all history is theirs alone.

Fables then, the cowards work, after seeking to defile and murder the truth. To seek to consign the Holly to dust, to thieve their ensigns and arms. To curse the head of Ireland, the kill the body. Verily, without Holly, without proof of the Cuilliaéan, without memory truth and wisdom, they sought to make all Irish and all Celts as but orphans.

Yet nothing is ever truly lost and every thing is revealed in time. The Feara Cualann, the most ancient of leaders, of the region at the heart of the birth of Ireland. These men of the Wicklow Hills. The great road known as Slighe Cualann to the first city of Ireland known as Ath Cliath Cualann, now as Dublin. All be revealed in the Book of the Green Race (Lebor Clann Glas).

Arise then does the spirit of humanity, through a mighty strength and blesses you and each and everyone who opens their ears and eyes and minds to the truth of the Book of the Green Race (Lebor Clann Glas). Remember who and what you are. Remember the truth of your ancestors. Count your blessings and never permit forgetfulness or doubt to return.

May you journey and life be filled with rich blessings of love, joy and and wisdom.

The True Origins of Human History

What is the true story of human history? How did the present world on Planet Earth come to be as it is? And why? How have places, events, people and times been altered in various accounts of history over the years? And why does it matter to unlock these hidden stories at all?

There is a famous saying: *History is Written by the Victors* – and given the way that history has been carefully crafted and shaped over the past two hundred years, such a saying holds true. In other words, there are whole periods of events, people, places and times that have not simply been altered within official history but have been erased entirely. Whole dynasties and civilisation, kings and queens. As for the history that is presented as official doctrine, many events are listed as occurring without logical consequence, as characters enter and leave the stage of history with neither a clear motive, nor a deeper understanding of context.

It is worth remembering then that before a few hundred years ago, there was no such thing as either true history or fiction. Instead, there were just stories. Some popular and interesting stories and many that were not. Some stories had special significance because of their age, or because they belonged to a particular religion or culture. Yet all stories could be measured by the reader or listener according to their subject matter, their continuity and common sense.

The trilogy of books known as Lebor Clann Glas, beginning with Volume I, is such a good story. A story that plots the history of human intellect and civilisation from 13,000 years ago through many of the major events that shaped our history and existence.

Lebor Clann Glas stands for "Book of the Green Race" in the context of a group known variously as "The Holly", "The Cuilliaéan", "The Green Gods", "The Medicine Men of the Woods" and "The Sangreal (Holy Blood or Grail)". In ancient times, there is much evidence that this bloodline dominated human knowledge and influenced the course of many major events and civilisations, as evidenced by the many original symbols and standards once attributed to them.

Yet over time, such symbols as the lion, the harp, the foundation stone and the swan and pelican have all been seized and proclaimed by others and their names and history has become as dust.

Why were the Holly originally born from Ireland extinguished so violently from history? Why was the very origins of Ireland herself scorched and her lands salted with the blood of so many martyrs? What knowledge resided with these Holly Priest Kings and Queens? What could it tell us about today?

There is another famous saying: *Those who cannot remember the past are condemned to repeat it* – as the shores of the Mediterranean Sea and the fields of Europe and Asia testify as true to many who deliberately and willingly suppressed and corrupted such lessons of history.

Yet reading Lebor Clann Glas is not easy. It will challenge you. Yet if you persist then you will see that Lebor Clann Glas is a methodical, consistent and contextual story that is able to account for major events and explain why they happened - or even continue to keep happening.

What then is the greatest story? The one that you are told must be believed? or the story that provides the best context and answers?

Contents

Book 1	The Beginning...	1
Book 2	Great Age of the Horse [10,830-7690 BCE]................................	5
Book 3	Great Age of the Queens [7690-4420 BCE]...............................	11
Book 4	Great Age of Hound and Bull [4420-4030 BCE]........................	15
Book 5	Great Age of Ebla [4030-3180 BCE]..	19
Book 6	Great Age of the Poets [3180-2700 BCE]...................................	25
Book 7	Great Age of the Sign [2700-2680 BCE].....................................	29
Book 8	Great Age of Civilizations [2680-2012 BCE]..............................	35
Book 9	Great Age of Babylon [2012-1627 BCE].....................................	41
Book 10	Great Age of Hyksos [1627-1353 BCE].......................................	47
Book 11	Age of Akhenaten [1353-1323 BCE]...	53
Book 12	Age of the False Pharaohs [1323-1245 BCE].............................	61
Book 13	Great Age of Darkness [1245-925 BCE].....................................	69
Book 14	Great Age of the Prophets [925-594 BCE]................................	79
Book 15	Great Age of the Celts [594-508 BCE]..	93
Book 16	Great Age of Persia [508-430 BCE]..	105
Book 17	Great Age of Eliada [430-323 BCE]..	119
Book 18	Great Age of Empires [323-204 BCE]..	139
Book 19	Great Age of Rome [204-39 BCE]...	163
Book 20	Age of Messiahs [39 BCE - 22 CE]..	193
Book 21	Age of the Nazarenes [22-69 CE]..	221
Book 22	Age of Judaism [69-117 CE]...	285
Book 23	Age of the Gnostics [117-194 CE]...	313
Book 24	Age of Dark Cults [194-277 CE]..	349
Book 25	Great Age of Constantine [277-337 CE]....................................	387
Book 26	Great Age of the Christian Tetrachy [337-365 CE]...................	453

Lebor Clann Glas Volume I

Book 1

The Beginning

C. 1

To chart a course, all must know: 2 the place at hand; 3 by name and hour; 4 by star and day; 5 by season and year, 6 by the heavenly gods, 7 companions of the Ancients, 8 the Great Ages lost. 9 To know thyself, one must know: 10 a great story; 11 by place and figure; 12 by civilisation and age; 13 by darkness and light; 14 by reason and character, 15 there can be no doubt.

C. 2

1 To ancients were known such mysteries: 2 the first of names, by destiny abound; 3 the truth of our story, long forgotten; 4 the reason for being. 5 We beseech thee and our ancestors, 6 to remember.

C. 3

1 Long before cleaving of reason and sense, 2 there be no such things as fact or fiction. 3 It be well known that Truth be its own witness, 4 by a clear mind and open heart. 5 Falsity be exposed by its own weaknesses. 6 Thus belief matters not; 7 proof matters not; 8 for the greatest story is.

C. 4

1 First that be revealed: 2 all be connected; 3 all be dependent and independent; 4 all be similar and different; 5 all be balance and chaos; 6 all be cycle and life; 7 all be mind and reason. 8 A mind orphaned from reason and sense has no means to discern and is cursed to madness. 9 A mind open to reason be free to discover and discern.

C. 5

1 Thus looking outward, the ancients reveal, 2 the wheels of fortune: 3 two seasons, and three of reason in operation. 4 The first (wheel) be that of (E)YAH (EL-A), 5 the Gleaming One, 6 protector of hunters, 7 guide and light of wisdom, 8 first and most sacred, 9 to the ancients. 10 The second (wheel) be that of AUN (ON), 11 the Shining One, revealer of truth, 12 that nothing may be hidden, 13 the God of the new age. 14 The third (wheel) be that of IOR (ANU), 15 the everlasting, 16 great wheel of the heavens, 17 and all the gods. 18 The eternal, 19 the unutterable name. 20 Keeper of all worlds in balance.

C. 6

1 Such (this be) is the sacred three: 2 Trinity, Secret and Mystery. 3 When one is known, 4 may all three be (understood). 5 When the outer is known, 6 the inner be revealed. 7 To the seasons, 8 the man, 9 the stag, 10 the fish and bird, 11 the cycles of the Gods of the Earth E-RE (MU).

C. 7

1 By the first (wheel), (E)YAH, 2 the Gleaming One, 3 begins with full face, 4 is divided equally, at (point of) departure. When YAH does return, to full view, is one cycle (of the wheel).

C. 8

1 The Gleaming One, 2 is particular. 3 To the horizon YAH is 27 days, 4 yet shorter by measure than to the stars. 5 By 29 days is complete.

C. 9

1 There be twelve cycles of (E)YAH. 2 The first be Samonios (October/ November), 3 upon which (time), 4 the leaves and seeds fall. 5 The second be Dumannios (November/ December), 6 upon which (time), 7 darkness opens. 8 The third be Riuros (December/ January), 9 upon which (time), 10 the land returns to ancient times. 11 The fourth be Anagantios (January/ February), 12 upon which (time), 13 the animals and house do stay secure. 14 The fifth be Ogronios (February/ March), 15 upon which (time), 16 cold rain brings ice. 17 The sixth be Cutios (March/ April), 18 upon which (time), 19 the wind and waves to rise. 20 The seventh be Giamonios (April/ May), 21 when the gods of the Earth awaken, 22 and new growth springs. 23 The eighth be Simivisonios (May/ June), 24 when the Shining One AUN (ON), 25 does bring warmth. 26 The ninth be Equos (June/ July), 27 upon which (time), 28 the best foals and calves are born. 29 The tenth Elembiuos (July/ August), 30 upon which (time), 31 men do harvest their crops and market their wares. 32 The eleventh be Edrinios (August/ September), 33 upon which (time), 34 all disputes of the year are discussed. 35 The twelfth be Cantlos (September/ October), 36 upon which (time), 37 the table is full, the stories are sung. 38 Upon every third cycle (of the 1st wheel), 39 there be a thirteenth (added), 40 named Mid Samonios, 41 between Cutios and Giamonios. 42 One who gains such knowledge, 43 and knowledge of the cycles of (E)YAH, the Gleaming One, 44 shall be Eastrolach.

C. 10

1 By the second (wheel) of AUN (ON), 2 the Shining One, 3 ruler of E-RE (Earth) by Day, 4 by rule of five (days), 5 to 72 (weeks), 6 does AUN (ON) return. 7 Divided by two (36 weeks of 5 days), 8 does AUN (ON) stand still, 9 a single cycle (year). 10 The first shall be Yu(le), 11 at the start, near Samonios. 12 The Most Holy of days. 13 The Birth of AUN (ON). 14 The second shall be Ba(al). 15 Count thirty six (weeks of five days) 16 from Yu(le).

C. 11

1 By the great third (wheel) of IOR (ANU), 2 the everlasting, 3 the Great Wheel of the heavens and all the Gods, 4 be divided into eight houses, 5 and two sacred cross(es). 6 (So) no portion greater or less, 7 do the Gods travel through each House. 8 The first (House) be Re the Ram (Aries) (November/ December). 9 The second (House) be Cú the Hound and Young Bull (Canis and Orion) (December/ January/ February). 10 The third (House) be Eala the Swan (Leo) (February/ March). 11 The fourth (House) be Cap-El the Horse (Virgo) (March/ April). 12 The fifth (House) be Tar the Bull (old Taurus/ Arcturus) (May/ June). 13 The sixth (House) be Muc the pig (Boar) (Scorpio) (June/ July). 14 The seventh (House) be Poc the Stag (Capricorn) (August/ September). 15 The eighth (House) be Dága the Fish (Pisces) (September/ October). 16 The ninth is the hidden (House) of IOR as the Great speckled serpent Si (Amen) (Milky Way). 17 The one that travels through all Houses, 18 the one not named, but all (Houses); 19 belongs to the Great speckled serpent (Milky Way).

C. 12

1 The eight and the ninth be the Houses of the heavens, 2 to the first two (Houses) is given, 3 46 cycles of the Shining One. 4 To the second two (Houses), is given 45 cycles. 5 To the third (pair), as the first. 6 To the final (pair) as the second. 7 So the heavens may balance.

C. 13

1 By the Houses, 2 the Great Gods be known. 3 Within the same equal divide of the Heavens, 4 by Nine years and five days, 5 the Shining One shall blacken and glow, 6 and the Gleaming One shall follow soon thus.

C. 14

1 (E)YAH, the Gleaming One, 2 shall visit each house, 3 235 cycles shall it be. 4 19 cycles (years) of AUN, the Shining One, 5 6940 Days, 6 take (away) one day in four cycles (of AUN).

C. 15

1 AUN (ON), the Shining One, 2 shall visit each house. 3 33 cycles (years) of AUN shall it be.

C. 16

1 Each House of the heavens of the eight 2 shall host the Gods, 3 and AUN (ON), the Shining One, 4 shall stand, 5 each being a Great age, 6 3210 cycles (year) of AUN (ON). 7 All eight Houses shall be seen, 8 before a Grand Epoch (origin) is complete. 9 One who gains such knowledge, 10 and the cycles of the three, 11 shall be Fisatóir.

C. 17

1 It is to the lesser Gods of the heavens, 2 the five plus two, 3 we owe the hour and time at night. 4 CYB-EL the Bright One does rise and fall five times, 5 within eight lives of AUN (ON), Shining One, 6 and by thirteen cycles does complete, 7 104 lives (years) of the Shining One. 8 This be a Great Cycle of the Bright One. 9 One who gains such knowledge 10 of the movement of the lesser gods of the heavens, 11 shall be Rollagedagh.

C. 18

1 Nothing be lost in the Universe, 2 only transformed. 3 No memory be forgotten, 4 but for the appointed time of remembrance. 5 This be that time, 6 to remember, 7 to honour, 8 to awaken the Green Race.

Book 2

Great Age of the Horse

[10,830 – 7,690 BCE]

C. 1

In the Great Age of the Horse (10,830 BCE), 2 by one thousand, nine hundred and fifty Great Cycles of the Bright One (8880 BCE), 3 came the warming. 4 The land was freed from slumber. 5 By the awakening of AUN, the Shining One, 6 he revealed all things with his great power. 7 The hills and plains (became) sweeping open meadows. 8 Then came the flowers and the seeds. 9 Then the birds, the fox and the hare. 10 The age of the great Stags. 11 The giants of old, 12 and ancient hunters did follow. 13 To the land of the low clouds.

C. 2

1 These were the best of times. 2 Before law of man; 3 before trickery of mouth and hand; 4 the two faced word. 5 The hunter and his spear, 6 travelled far and fast. 7 A plentiful peace, 8 under the watchful gaze of YAH (the Gleaming One).

C. 3

1 North from ice, 2 south from land, 3 did the ancients come. 4 The ages of our land, 5 without complication, but sign; 6 without moans, but song. 7 For ancient hunters did sing in joy, 8 across the great meadows; 9 a green heaven, 10 calling (out) the Stag to their end.

C. 4

1 In this age, 2 the Gods did smile, 3 upon honest men. 4 The heavens be their roof, 5 the trees by stream their walls, 6 the leaves their beds. 7 Tribes did swell, 8 to all corners of the Isle, 9 until no land was without man.

C. 5

1 The dawn of the Great Age of the Swan (7620 BCE), 2 (Did) Herald great change and calamity. 3 The omen of the Gods. 4 By one cycle of the Bright One, 5 came the Great Flood, 6 of the tribes of the flatlands of man. 7 The great ice lakes of the north did swell, 8 the bridges did break, 9 and many did drown in the flatlands and valleys, 10 even unto the shores of the Black Lake; 11 save one tribe, 12 the tribe of NOA(H); 13 who foretold of doom. 14 And by legend, 15 were saved by their boats. 16 Never again, shall we drown, 17 the tribe of NOA(H) proclaimed. 18 They built then their

new home with high walls, 19 fearing flood, fearing rain. 20 A rocky place, 21 by the River ARI-EN (Jordan). 22 So high did they build their walls, 23 upon the rumbling of the earth, 24 they did fall upon themselves, 25 at a place called YAH-EA (Jericho).

C. 6

1 Of the land of ER-E, MU, 2 the sea God LIR (LUGH) did swallow the bridge of the south. 3 Of the north, 4 AUN did melt the ice into the sea. 5 Born then an island. 6 All birds, 7 all stag and boars, 8 all wild horse and hare, 9 all men, 10 ringed by the sea god LIR.

C. 7

1 In the Great Age of the Swan, 2 at the first third, 3 about nine hundred and thirty Great Cycles of CYB-EL the Bright One (6690 BCE), 4 came the cooling. 5 AUN, the Shining One did retreat from view, 6 so did all the gods of the heavens. 7 Not even YAH, the Gleaming One did show herself. 8 The darkest of times. 9 Of Man alone. 10 Ice and snow did cover the meadows. 11 The great Stag could not find food, 12 nor the animals of the open field. 13 The land did return to sleep. 14 A cold blanket upon it. 15 The hunter did draw lean and fearful.

C. 8

1 The Tribes of men, did rush in haste. 2 To the south, the snow and ice was deep, 3 but LIR (LUG(H)) had swallowed the path. 4 To the west and to the east, 5 no beasts were to be found. 6 To the north the tribes did become hungry. 7 Yet north towards Lough Neagh, 8 men did flee, 9 for food. 10 But LIR the sea god had smashed the ice path. 11 Cold wind tore skin and flesh. 12 Nothing but tumult, 13 as the ravens did feast upon the dead.

C. 9

1 Some made camp beside the waters, 2 along the sacred Shannon, 3 along the Lough Neagh, 4 only to be set upon by hungry tribes. 5 The exiles of the south and west. 6 Spear no longer for beast, but man. 7 Spear upon spear. 8 Blood upon blood. 9 A hundred spear. 10 A thousand spear. 11 Only MU (the earth) shall know.

C. 10

1 In these dark times, 2 stirred blackness of heart. 3 Why the retreat of the gods? 4 What terrible curse? 5 When old ways, 6 of cold and cave long forgotten. 7 Men set upon men, 8 not for war but offering. 9 Women upon their children, 10 sons upon fathers. 11 To seek a cure of darkened curse.

C. 11

1 Beastly, barbaric acts befell. 2 Sacrifice of blood flowed freely. 3 Men cut at their limbs, 4 to nourish their lips. 5 Eating the flesh of kin, 6 to satisfy a whim.

C. 12

1 A chief, bathed in blood and human flesh, 2 did rise in the north. 3 MOT be his name. 4 No longer a hunter of boar, 5 but the flesh and bones of men. 6 United in death, 7 his warriors lie (in wait), 8 for hungry exiles from the south. 9 Feasting on their flesh, 10 MOT claimed himself a god. 11 The old gods gone are no more he proclaimed.

12 The greatest of gods was A-ED, 13 of the underworld he said. 14 A place underneath the ground. 15 Fearful, hungry, 16 MOT united the tribes. 17 Killing and eating the weak. 18 Roasting children in fire like pigs. 19 Enslaving all.

C. 13

1 The tribes of the east, 2 did hear of MOT, 3 and his deeds. 4 They (east tribes) did hide in the mountains, 5 once known as the land of the Holly Men, 6 the Feara Cuileann.

C. 14

1 By the stream known as Lilley, 2 young warriors of a tribe of the east, 3 were set upon by beasts of MOT. 4 None but one did escape. 5 His name is Anainmbaiste, 6 as the first. 7 Hungry and fearful, 8 he leads away from the hiding place of his tribe. 9 For the men of MOT having become accustomed, 10 to the hunt of men, 11 did smell living flesh for many a mile. 12 Into the blackness he climbs. 13 Higher until his fingers torn, 14 his body weakened, 15 near to give up the ghost.

C. 15

1 Upon a grove he comes. 2 Nine Elms (trees), 3 upon a bubbling pond. 4 Around it be strange shrubs, 5 with prickly leaves, 6 fruit red as blood. 7 Anainmbaiste weakened from hunger, 8 did eat the sacred fruit, 9 upon which he fell into deep sleep and sickness. 10 Awaking he did see, 11 a Great White Swan upon the pond. 12 Beside him he did reach for spear. 13 But before his thrust, 14 the swan did speak. 15 Anainmbaiste be still it called. 16 Anainmbaiste be wise it sighed. 17 The spear did loosen from his hold. 18 Upon what magic did he behold? 19 The Swan did call him to see into the pond. 20 By the shallows were countless rocks of golden brilliance. 21 And salmon fat and slow, 22 too many to count. 23 The Swan did say the salmon live, 24 for the bubbling pond that never freezes, 25 and the sacred berries as they drop. 26 Eat one fish called out the swan. 27 And Anainmbaiste did eat a fish, 28 whereupon he gained awareness. 29 You shall be called A-DA-MU, meaning first born of Earth, 30 the Swan did speak. 31 And A-DA-MU did call this place 32 CUILI-EALA-EAN or CUILLEAIN, 33 the sacred healing (knowing) woods of the swan (spirit).

C. 16

1 A-DA-MU did return to his tribe, 2 in the mountains by the stream of the Lilley. 3 To tell of his find. 4 The Tribe do not believe. 5 They cast him out, 6 with his companion E-AN. 7 They cursed his name. 8 To the Cuilleain he returned. 9 To the Salmon the sacred golden rocks and Swan. 10 At the Cuilleain with his companion E-AN, 11 A-DA-MU did learn to remember from the Swan, 12 and the sacred Salmon, 13 to remember the name of plants, 14 the name of animals, 15 the operation of the Gods, 16 the wisdom of law and prophecy. 17 Upon attaining awareness, 18 A-DA-MU named his companion E-VA, 19 meaning first, 20 first amongst women. 21 (The) first priestess. 22 Within one cycle of the shining one, 23 E-VA bore a son named E-(A)L, 24 meaning a god amongst men. 25 There at the

Cuilleain, they lived, 26 for twelve more cycles of the shining one.

C. 17

1 The men of MOT did come, 2 and scatter the tribe of A-DA-MU. 3 Along the Lilley, 4 some did escape. 5 And A-DA-MU did nurse them to life, 6 at the Cuilleain. 7 Soon they will smell us, 8 called the survivors. 9 The men of MOT growing hungry for new flesh, 10 to eat and sacrifice. 11 A-DA-MU did eat the berries, 12 and ask the sacred Swan for (a) sign. 13 Leave this place the Swan spoke, 14 to the coast, 15 the Swan did say. 16 There Build a raft to LIR, the God of the Sea. 17 Leave this Isle, 18 and you shall save your race. 19 The Swan did peck a glistening golden pebble, 20 from the shore of the pond. 21 Take these stones into fire, 22 fashion a band, 23 the same for your arms. 24 These shall ward off all evil.

C. 18

1 A-DA-MU did as the Swan had commanded. 2 He collected the golden rocks. 3 He left the Hollywood and travelled to the coast. 4 To a place called Ath Cliath Cuilleain. 5 A name meaning the sacred (Holly) hurdled ford (of the river Lilley). 6 There he put the rocks into a fire. 7 And they did melt. 8 He fashioned golden bands, 9 one for each member of the tribe. 10 And arm bands, 11 for each hunter of the tribe. 12 There A-DA-MU commanded his tribe to chop down young saplings, 13 to fashion a raft.

C. 19

1 The getting of wisdom. 2 The young are fearful, 3 the MOT shall come. 4 We shall be eaten (they say). 5 Yet A-DA-MU did not yield. 6 The first raft is launched. 7 But LIR (the sea) consumed it. 8 A-DA-MU commands a second raft to be built, 9 it is smaller and lighter, 10 with lashings and beams to hold. 11 But no one dared sail, 12 until E-(A)L the son of A-DA-MU, 13 the strongest and bravest. 14 He takes the raft far from shore. 15 But LIR, (was) jealous of the hero for himself, 16 snatches the raft, 17 and the son of A-DA-MU and brave men drown.

C. 20

1 A-DA-MU deep in grief, 2 returns to Cuilleain. 3 He calls out to the Swan, 4 but none appear. 5 He eats of the berries, 6 but no wisdom comes. 7 He curses the Gods for their wisdom, 8 but not their power. 9 To change the seasons. 10 To give life over death.

C. 21

1 A-DA-MU returned to Ath Cliath Cuilleain. 2 As he approached he did see the Men of MOT. 3 The tribe captured. 4 But fearing the gold around their necks, 5 and their arms, 6 They spear not one. 7 To the north they are herded. 8 To the Land of MOT, 9 his lair to the east of Lough Neage, 10 at where the streams of Farset and Lagan meet.

C. 22

1 MOT himself does inspect the tribe of A-DA-MU. 2 But upon A-DA-MU he does not look up. 3 Fearful a god has come to strike him. 4 He demands by what magic they survive the long winter? 5 Why they dress so? 6 What meaning the gold? 7 A-DA-MU tells him he has been commanded by the

gods, 8 to build a raft and leave the Isle. 9 MOT proclaims to all who watch himself a god. 10 That only E-AD is God and all must worship death. 11 A-DA-MU laughs, 12 for his companion is E-VA, 13 a daughter of the gods, 14 and no harm may befall his tribe. 15 Enraged, MOT prepares for slaughter. 16 A-DA-MU makes a pledge, 17 to most powerful MOT. 18 Build me a raft and release my tribe, 19 and within one cycle of the Shining One, 20 (I) shall return with food for all of the tribe of MOT. 21 Crafty MOT agrees to A-DA-MU. 22 But on the condition, 23 that only four of his warriors to accompany the chief. 24 With a party of men from MOT. 25 E-VA and the tribe as hostage, 26 MOT does command the trees to be cut, 27 and a great raft is made. 28 A-DA-MU and his band do depart.

C. 23

1 Upon the sea and the will of LIR (LUG(H), 2 whereupon a great wind takes hold of them, 3 upon rolling waves, 4 south and south not upon landfall, 5 until they see land east, 6 just before the mouth of the River known as Severn. 7 A-DA-MU and his band to travel inland, 8 to the east in search of animals. 9 None they find. 10 Darkness greater than MU is this land across the sea. 11 In the blackness only shadows, 12 follow them. 13 On the sixth night of landfall, 14 the shadows come. 15 They take A-DA-MU and the band. 16 They kill the men of MOT. 17 But on the five and the gold, 18 are fearful. 19 They take them to a place. 20 A great bare Earth ring upon a plain called SARU(M), 21 surrounded by mountains of bones. 22 Too many to count. 23 Here men are hacked to pieces night and day, 24 by the shadows. 25 To call the Gods to return. 26 Upon this place A-DA-MU does cry. 27 Upon this place I curse, 28 before this night, 29 you shall not last. 30 Before the end of this Age, 31 and by the Gods, 32 my (blood) return, 33 to rid this place of blackness.

C. 24

1 The shadows grunt as horses and dogs. 2 They know not knowledge, 3 not even they are human, 4 wild beasts become the men of Brit. 5 A storm approaches, 6 heavy rain and thunder. 7 The shadows run in fear, 8 A-DA-MU and the five flee. 9 To their raft they return and set adrift. 10 To face fate. 11 But the gods direct the wind against them, 12 not north but south and south east they travel.

C. 25

1 A-DA-MU and the brave come to a land known as Galicia, 2 where they find meadows and warmth, 3 trees and birds, 4 deer and boars. 5 A-DA-MU and the five, 6 come upon a tribe, 7 who having seen them land. 8 Witness upon their finery and gold, 9 praise them as Gods. 10 A-DA-MU did stay with the people of the Galicia for a time. 11 Knowing that before the end of a cycle, 12 honour bound to return, 13 or lose his companion and tribe. 14 As the gods of the Galatians, 15 the men being their subjects, 16 A-DA-MU commissions three stronger raft. 17 Now with thatched sail, 18 to guide the winds of the Gods. 19 Now with oar to steer, 20 to reason with LIR (sea). 21 And hasten their return. 22 The Galicia bestow the bravest of their warriors, 23

to return to the land of the Gods. 24 The Sea Peoples they were first called. 25 The Ibiru and gods of sea, 26 and forever more known.

C. 26

1 A-DA-MU returned triumphant. 2 Inside the cycle, 3 to the lair of MOT. 4 At where the streams of Farset and Lagan meet. 5 His sails Red. 6 Red with the blood of slain animals, 7 did glow in the sea mist. 8 Like the belly of a dreadful beast, 9 a fearful sight for the men of MOT. 10 His raft boats full of bounty. 11 Upon the sight of three boats, 12 the mighty men of MOT flee. 13 E-AN seeing the return of her husband, 14 thrust a spear into MOT. 15 A-DA-MU lands triumphant to his word. 16 First King and High priest of the Gods.

Book 3

Great Age of the Queens

[7690 - 4420 BCE]

C. 1

1 In the Great Age of the Swan (7630 BCE), 2 within one thousand four hundred and thirty Great Cycles of CYB-EL, 3 the Bright One (6200 BCE), 4 the land of our ancestors did awaken, 5 upon the arrival of the god DAGA (DAGNU), 6 the good god, of earth and fertility, 7 DAGA did defeat ADA(D), 8 the god of storms and rain, 9 releasing MU (Earth) from the darkness. 10 First again came the flowers and young bushes, 11 then with pine, elm and tree, 12 the land did raise up forests, 13 the animals returned in numbers, 14 wild boar and red squirrels, 15 wolves and foxes, 16 red deer and eagles, 17 but the giant stag was never again seen.

C. 2

1 The descendants of ADAM (A-DA-MU), 2 made good their land, 3 with mud, they did make walls, 4 wood and reeds their cover (roof). 5 The Gods of MOT and the underworld, 6 banished from the Isle. 7 With the wisdom of the gods messenger, 8 by the sacred Holly, 9 they did make a rule. 10 Never again shall man eat flesh of man. 11 To learn the wisdom of the gods. 12 Respect the ancient gods. 13 To never usurp the gods.

C. 3

1 By the bones of ADAM laid, 2 near the sacred curve of the serpent stream, 3 known by the name Boyn. 4 A most sacred place called GNO, 5 meaning divine wisdom. 6 A city of stone, his everlasting rest. 7 The elders of the tribe of AD-A-MU, 8 did observe and respect the ancient gods. 9 Thus they did name them as spoken, 10 they did write symbols and meaning, 11 they did learn to count, 12 to understand the pattern, 13 and nature of the Gods, 14 by the first wheel of YAH (EL), 15 by the second wheel of AUN(ON), 16 by the third wheel of IOR (ANU).

C. 4

1 The bravest of the tribe, 2 did return by boats of red sails, 3 to the land of Galicia, 4 and return. 5 (So) That by blood, 6 by bond and custom, 7 they became as if one land, 8 but not near the Isle of the shadows, 9 did they sail. 10 The beasts of MOT, 11 exiled to this place. 12 A place of darkness, 13 and barbarity. 14 Many cycles till, 15 the

prophecy of A-DA-MU fulfilled, 16 on the plain of SARU(M).

C. 5

1 Upon the eight Great Cycle of CYBELE, 2 the tribal elders, 3 keepers of the wisdom of the gods, 4 did call a council. 5 For the seed of A-DA-MU, 6 no longer produced a male heir, 7 but three girl child. 8 HA-M(U), the old king, 9 did witness the miracle birth. 10 Before his death, 11 blessing the sacred trinity as his heirs. 12 All three to reign, 13 as one. 14 Each named BRID. 15 Too young to rule, 16 SHEM(U) their kin, 17 did rule as protector and steward.

C. 6

1 A crafty nature was SHEM(U), 2 for upon the twelfth of age, 3 the little BRIGHID, he did challenge them, 4 to resolve a dispute, 5 in ancient ways. 6 Knowing the three girls had not hunted, 7 nor spear, nor seen blood. 8 The three little girls were set out, 9 to seize a boar or deer. 10 For without blooding of the ancient ways, 11 none could claim Kingship. 12 Crafty SHEM(U) and a band, 13 did lie in wait, 14 by a thicket, 15 as the girls did approach. 16 But the old and young gods, 17 did favour the BRIGHID. 18 ADA(D) hid YAH from view. 19 In the darkness, 20 SHEM(U) did stumble. 21 Whereupon DAGA did sent a heard of wild deer, 22 through the thicket, 23 Trampling SHEM(U) and his band. 24 One deer, its neck broken, 25 at the feet of the three. 26 Triumphant, the BRID return, 27 as Queens.

C. 7

1 At twenty, such fearsome warriors the three Queen, 2 no man of E-RE (MU), 3 worthy as companions. 4 The Queens resolved that one should stay, 5 and two should travel, 6 with the blessing of LIR, 7 to find husbands worthy. 8 For their journey, 9 the elders and protectors of the Cuilleain, 10 did fashion each Queen, 11 with a sword of gold and bronze, 12 and a troop of the finest warriors, 13 with bronze tipped spears, 14 that no beast, 15 nor man may harm even a hair, 16 of the warrior Queens.

C. 8

1 First, they travelled to the land of Galicia, 2 and to the King. 3 But not one man was found worthy, 4 of the hand of a sacred Queen. 5 Overland they travelled, 6 unto the shores of the great eastern sea. 7 There they set (out) onwards, 8 in smaller boats, 9 eastward they sailed, 10 to lands not yet seen. 11 The first men they encountered, 12 from the land of yellow hills. 13 Too frightened to come to the shore, 14 where the Brids did rest, 15 the Queens did travel past the coast, 16 of the blackened land of Latin tribes. 17 A land of fire in those days, 18 to the Isle of the Sicani. 19 But these men did not yield, 20 and the Queens cleaved, 21 many a warrior, 22 till they made their escape, 23 to the safety of boats.

C. 9

1 But LIR grew restless. 2 He did conspire with ADA(D), 3 to each take a Queen, 4 to be their consort. 5 LIR threw the Queens up. 6 Upon great waves, 7 while ADA(D) did bring upon

them, 8 great darkened clouds and rain. 9 The Queens did pray for delivery, 10 to the ancient Gods. 11 And CY-BELE did hear their call. 12 Upon the rocks of an Isle, 13 they did come to rest. 14 The Queens did name this place, 15 CYBE-MU, land of the goddess, the Bright One. 16 And a solemn oath. 17 To bring a band Of the finest, 18 to honour the goddess. 19 And so it was such honour was true, 20 for many a year. 21 Even when the Goddess became known, 22 as Aphrodite.

C. 10

1 The two Brids, 2 did each make an oath. 3 One to travel to the north, 4 The other to the south, 5 and to make this Isle a new home, 6 for the tribe of A-DA-MU. 7 The first Brid, known as Mem, 8 did travel south, 9 to the land of the great River, 10 and the tribe known as Badari. 11 These peaceful and noble people, 12 were in awe of Mem, 13 with her sword of gold and bronze, 14 and her honey words, 15 the Chief of the Tribe, 16 did claim her a Goddess, 17 and implored her to stay. 18 There, with her warrior guard, 19 Mem, did teach the Badari, 20 using the shapes, 21 and signs of the Ancients. 22 The keepers of the Cuilleain, 23 the ways of the tribe, 24 the wise laws of the gods, 25 and the names and operation, 26 of the gods themselves. 27 The Badari in turn did show Mem, 28 the flooding of fields, 29 the planting of crops, 30 the use of the cow, 31 but no husband worthy found.

C. 11

1 The second Brid, known as Mam(a), 2 did travel north, 3 towards the mountains of the Bull, 4 to the plain of Konya, 5 and the village of Katal. 6 There the Queen did use, 7 her signing ways, 8 her singing voice, 9 the wisdom of the gods. 10 And the might of her gold and bronze sword. 11 The people of Katal, 12 in turn did show Mama. 13 The making of garments, 14 from the hair of animals, 15 and the skilled use of fire and clay. 16 But the people of Katal, 17 did make Mam(a) their goddess. 18 Refusing her passage, 19 she did escape. 20 With the help of the ancient gods. 21 When YAH did hide AUN, 22 and the people fled.

C. 12

1 The Queen Mem, 2 did travel south with the Badari, 3 and her warrior guard, 4 along the Great Serpent River, 5 to the land of the Pwen (Punt), 6 there the Queen again showed, 7 the wisdom of the Gods, 8 the magic of sign. 9 And the dark skinned Pwen, 10 did show her, 11 the wonder of spices, 12 soft tender fruits, 13 the nature of weaved cloth. 14 And the Pwen did make her their goddess, 15 but amongst the Pwen, 16 no husband was found.

C. 13

1 Queen Mam(a), 2 did travel east, 3 along the mighty river, 4 to the land of the Assur, 5 and the Ubaid. 6 The site of this Queen, 7 with her golden sword, 8 her warrior guard, 9 and caravan of many miles, 10 did amaze the villagers. 11 Before she had even arrived, 12 they called Mam(a) a Goddess, 13 I-MAMA (Inaana) they called her.

C. 14

1 Queen Mem, 2 did leave the tribe of Pwen, 3 and travelled north–east, 4 to the great village of the Ubaid, 5 at the mouth of the great rivers. 6 There she did unite with her sister. 7 Two Queens, 8 two great warriors, 9 and countless worshippers, 10 the village was named in honour, 11 of their sacred homeland. 12 E-RI (E-RE), 13 and in a later age to E-RI-DU. 14 There the Queens did teach their signs, 15 the wisdom of the gods, 16 the wonder of their travels, 17 and all the world did come to know of E-RI.

C. 15

1 Yet for all their journey, 2 and all the tribes, 3 no husbands worthy, 4 had been found. 5 The Queens did return to the inner sea, 6 where the Badari, 7 did make them a great boat of lashed reeds, 8 so LIR could not sink it.

C. 16

1 Upon the return, 2 both Mem and Mam(a) had a vision. 3 Their captains by their side, 4 CAL-MU the brave, 5 who had stood by the side of Mem, 6 since departing MU. 7 UAS-EL, the worthy, 8 who had protected Mam(a), 9 all the while. 10 Upon awakening, 11 the Queens did call to their captains. 12 For worthy men, 13 for worthy husbands, 14 no greater (had) been. 15 Brave, loyal men and true. 16 All the while, 17 from E-RE herself.

C. 17

1 Return home, 2 triumph behold. 3 The wonders of the world, 4 brought to sacred lands. 5 The cow, the weave, 6 the wisdom of clay and fire, 7 all manner of wisdom.

Book 4

Great Age of Hound & Bull

[4420 - 4030 BCE]

C. 1

1 Upon the dawn of the Great Age, 2 of the Hound, 3 and of the Young Bull (4420 BCE), 4 the land of E-RE (MU), 5 had become fat with grace, 6 wonders from all the world. 7 Clothes and peace, 8 civilised men, 9 long lost the art of the hunter, 10 become the crafty trader.

C. 2

1 Since the time of the three BRID, 2 fame had spread across the tribes. 3 Each embracing them as their own, 4 a thirst for the wisdom, 5 of the Isle of Mu. 6 And the strength of women, 7 without respite. 8 The swords of Brid, 9 did each King seek, 10 and power of sacred gold, 11 fashioned by priestly elders. 12 So that the tribe of ADAM, 13 had become fractured, 14 no longer the bravest, 15 nor fiercest reigned, 16 but women of crafty disposition.

C. 3

1 In this age, 2 women did rule strong, 3 and men grew distracted. 4 In the way of the gods, 5 an ancient line of Queens raised. 6 From the time, 7 of the triple goddesses.

C. 4

1 The Gods had seen, 2 what men had become. 3 No rule no law, 4 but pleasure and corrupt, 5 without restraint. 6 DAGAN and (H)ADAD did consort, 7 over the lands. 8 Rain and warmth, 9 unending. 10 Within three Great Cycles of CYBELE, 11 from the dawning, 12 of the new Great Age of the Hound, 13 the land became like bog. 14 So deep and thick, 15 it swallowed many a man, 16 and tree.

C. 5

1 But crafty Queens, 2 did not head the gods, 3 and took to boats, 4 and far places, 5 free from the rains and bog, 6 to Islands in the inland sea, 7 they came, 8 and grew their trade and power. 9 New gods of earth, 10 and passions they formed, 11 Goddesses of love and hate, 12 Goddesses of war and fire, 13 the male gods of old no more.

C. 6

1 To the great lands of the Amratians, 2 the Queens of E-RE (MU) did trade, 3 their city of Nut, the goddess of sky. 4 And further north, 5 along the great Serpent river, 6 did the Maadi worship the powerful Queens. 7 As MA-AT

goddess of truth and law, 8 to the lands of the east, 9 of the people of UR-UK, 10 the great goddess EL-NANA (INAANA), 11 daughter of the moon, 12 Goddess of love, fertility and war, 13 the Queens of MU were worshipped.

C. 7

1 Of one great in age and knowledge of men, 2 was the Queen MA-EVE (MAB), 3 who ruled the land, 4 four hundred cycles of the AUN (Shining One), 5 from the Dawn of the new Great Age of the Hound. 6 It was Queen MA-EVE that banished, 7 the priests and ancient wisdom of the Cuilleain, 8 till time forgotten their ways, 9 to the hills most sacred they were. 10 Exiled from the sacred land of ADAMs rest, 11 by the river BOY(NE).

C. 8

1 Only sons then born to MA-EVE. 2 ARU, the eldest and SETU. 3 Cursed by the gods, 4 no daughter to rule. 5 For in those days, 6 no more did men hold spear, 7 nor hunt on MU, 8 upon penalty of death. 9 The first born of the Queen, 10 ARU the strong, 11 is favoured a while. 12 To learn the way of the ancients, 13 the priests of the Cuilleain. 14 SETU, the second born, 15 displeases the Queen. 16 But SETU is crafty in feminine strength, 17 and survives the wrath, 18 of the warrior Queen.

C. 9

1 The Queen did summons the Head Priest, 2 to divine upon what curse, 3 she had no female child? 4 The priest consult the sacred grove, 5 had a vision of some clarity. 6 He returned and did say to the great Queen. 7 If she be a goddess, 8 then she must find a worthy mate, 9 in the ways of the Brids, 10 a king of great note.

C. 10

1 But crafty Mab did have a plan. 2 To trick the gods, 3 and not leave the throne. 4 She commanded, 5 her most fearsome female warrior guard, 6 to travel across the sea, 7 and return with hostages, 8 Kings worthy, 9 of producing a warrior Queen. 10 The most skilled women warriors, 11 guards of the ancients, 12 did sail across to land. 13 In the south and east, 14 to Battle armies one hundred to one. 15 No match were any man or beast, 16 to these deadly sirens. 17 To capture five, 18 of the greatest kings, 19 of the ancient tribes of man. 20 Five kings captured, 21 rivers of blood. 22 For a Queen's desire.

C. 11

1 Upon their return the Queen did consort, 2 with each hostage King. 3 The first was from the land of the Sahar. 4 Fertile plains of vast wealth and plenty. 5 But no seed did fall. 6 Within three cycles of YAH (the Gleaming One). 7 The second (King) was from the land of Amratians. 8 But no seed did fall. 9 Within the three cycle of YAH. 10 The Third (King) was from the land of Uruk. 11 Again with no seed did fall the Queen. 12 The fourth (King) was from the land of the bull mountains. 13 And with seed she took hold. 14 But could not keep. 15 The Queen did summons the head priest. 16 Consult the gods as to why. 17 She did honour their pledge, 18 and find men worthy. 19 But no Queen

heir, 20 did she bear. 21 The Priest, wary his word might be his doom, 22 did remind the Queen, 23 but one King remained. 24 And so the Queen did consort with the fifth King, 25 a great King, 26 from the Kingdom of Arabu (Arabia). 27 A place of rich and fertile forest and lands, 28 and precious stones. 29 Within two cycles of the Gleaming One, 30 the Queen did proclaim herself in seed. 31 Rejoicing, she did command the Kings returned. 32 By the skilled female warriors.

C. 12

1 By the ninth cycle Queen MAB, 2 did give birth. 3 But not to a Queen Heir, 4 but to a third son. 5 In birth rage, 6 she did curse all the gods, 7 and seized the child, 8 tearing its limbs apart, 9 and eating its flesh. 10 Upon seeing his mother and Queen, 11 SETU did seize the Queens sword, 12 and cleave his genitals, 13 onto the floor. 14 The enraged Queen MAB, 15 upon seeing his act, 16 did proclaim: 17 Not upon the gods, 18 but blood of men, 19 I have found my Queen heir! 20 From this point, 21 SETU shall be my successor.

C. 13

1 The Queen then did order, 2 her Women warriors, 3 to find the priests of the Cuilleain, 4 and kill them all. 5 But ARU upon hearing what had transpired, 6 did rush ahead to warn them. 7 When the captain of the women warriors told the Queen, 8 she did curse the name of ARU. 9 That from this moment, 10 he shall be known as ARYO, 11 meaning stranger in his own land, 12 and none shall give him aid. 13 Upon penalty of death, 14 she did order one thousand men, 15 to be slaughtered like cattle, 16 bathing in their blood. 17 And upon each year, 18 a new born child, 19 to be slaughtered, 20 and eaten, 21 upon the altars of the ancient gods, 22 as curse to their (the gods) treachery, 23 in honour of ancestor MOT, 24 the God of the underworld and shadows.

C. 14

1 For saving the priests, 2 and honouring the Gods, 3 the Cuilleain did train ARYO, 4 in the way of war and battle, 5 in the way of wise counsel. 6 And the smiths of the priests, 7 did fashion a great sword, 8 greater than any in all the ages, 9 for this sword was blessed by the gods, 10 and this sword was made by living gods, 11 a sword for a king of kings.

C. 15

1 Upon his twentieth year, 2 ARYO did leave hiding in the south of the Isle, 3 with a band of priests, 4 to the eastern lands. 5 Queen MAB had sent word, 6 to each King, 7 in each land, 8 that but one who gives aid to Aryo, 9 shall be slaughtered. 10 And so Aryo found no rest, 11 nor quarter. 12 Battle after battle, 13 land after land he came, 14 in peace but to find only war. 15 The ranks of his camp grew in number, 16 till no army, not even the great woman warriors of MAB, 17 could match their fighting skill. 18 They became known as the Aryan, 19 strangers from their own lands, 20 but conquerors of all.

C. 16

1 Queen MAB upon hearing, 2 of the campaigns of ARYO, 3 she did send SETU and her woman army, 4 to seize him. 5 She made SETU swear an oath,

6 that ARYO not be harmed. 7 For in her dark heart, 8 a pinch of pride, 9 at the bravery and blood spilled by Aryo. 10 But SETU grieved at her change of heart, 11 did hatch his own plan for his brother's doom. 12 He did send him a sword of Brid, 13 the sword of Queens, 14 that his mother was greatly ill, 15 and that he had earned his birth right. 16 ARYO agreed to meet SETU, 17 under great cedars, 18 in the land of the white cliffs, 19 upon the Eastern Gulf of the Inland Sea. 20 But SETU did trick his brother, 21 and did break his solemn oath to a sacred Queen, 22 and did thrust a secret blade into his brother. 23 ARYO, did cleave SETU, 24 with one stroke of his sword, 25 that the head of SETU, 26 did fly from his body and over the cliff, 27 to never be found. 28 But before ARYO gave up the ghost, 29 to his captain ARYO did give his sword, 30 and made him swear, 31 to bury him at this place of his doom. 32 For this was now his home. 33 And Upon this place, 34 to make a great city, 35 of knowledge and wisdom, 36 for all the world. 37 The captain did so swear. 38 And ARYO did name him AB-RA-MU.

C. 17

1 In honour of ARYO, AB-RA-MU did found a city, 2 by the white rocks and the cedar forest. 3 The resting place of his King. 4 And did name it Ebla. 5 No greater city of ancient times, 6 did wisdom shine more, 7 than the great towers of Ebla.

C. 18

1 Upon hearing of the death of her sons, 2 the treachery of SETU, 3 the Queen did tear her clothes, 4 and wail through empty rooms. 5 She summonsed the head priest, 6 of the Cuilleain, 7 and pledged he bind a high curse, 8 that her son SET shall never rest. 9 To be cast out, 10 forever in the underworld. 11 And with the curse done, 12 Queen MA-EVE (MAB) did take her own ancient sword, 13 and cut open her breast. 14 Thus the last of the Great Queens, 15 the goddesses of the ancients was no more.

Book 5

Great Age of Ebla

[4030 - 3180 BCE]

C. 1

Upon the death of the last Queen of ER-E (MU), 2 some three hundred and ninety cycles of AUN (4030 BCE), 3 from the dawn of the Great Age, 4 of the Hound and Bull, 5 the holly priests did form a council. 6 Eight of the finest and wisest, 7 eight of the most worthy, 8 to rule the sacred Isle. 9 To Protect rule of law. 10 To Respect and seek wisdom. 11 The gods to keep the balance.

C. 2

1 To hold in check the darkness of men, 2 the Holly did banish, 3 all weapons of death, 4 from the sacred Isle. 5 So no King, nor captain, 6 no guard nor smith, 7 could hold sword nor spear, 8 on most sacred of soil, 9 without incurring the most high of curses.

C. 3

1 Upon the death of ARYO, 2 AB-RA-MU did become a great king. 3 Upon founding of Ebla, 4 from all the known world, 5 came trade and wealth, 6 knowledge and skill. 7 Ebla did become the centre of the world. 8 But AB-RA-MU was exceedingly old, 9 and had not yet fulfilled his final oath. 10 He did make his eldest son swear, 11 a pledge to the gods, 12 that a great tower of learning, 13 be built in Ebla. 14 That all the tribes of man, 15 may speak with one tongue. 16 He named his son ISH-MU-EL, 17 a light of a new covenant. 18 And ISH-MU-EL did honour, 19 his fathers' word. 20 A great tower of learning he made.

C. 4

1 Of the languages of Shem, 2 all come from but one end. 3 The city of the white rock. 4 The city of Ebla, 5 the spoken language of the (H)U-MAN, 6 and the written language of Eblaite. 7 From Eblaite came Cuniform and Hieroglyph. 8 From the tongue of (H)U-MAN came Saharan, Egyptian and Uritic. 9 From Eblaite, came Akkadian, Urgaritic and Caananite, 10 and the tongue of the ancients of the (H)Ibiru. 11 Then came the languages of Hatti, Cythian, Dravidian and Aramaic. 12 From Aramaic came languages of Syriac, Ge'ez and Safaitic. 13 From the Safaitic came Sabaean and Hasaitic. 14 From Aramaic and Akkadian came Moabite and Edomite

and ancient Persian. 15 For none of the languages of Gnosis were yet borne, 16 The languages of Gno of Greek, Etruscan, Gael, Catalian, Lydian, Phoenician and Sanskrit. 17 Nor did the language of Latin yet exist, 18 until the Persians and Yahudi exiles did corrupt Etruscan. 19 Nor did the language of Hebrew yet exist, 20 until the Persian priests sought power over all languages. 21 Thus, from Ebla is borne the release of wisdom, 22 and from Memphis under Ramses and then Babylon came corruption.

C. 5

1 Of all the languages of the sons of Aryo, 2 the (H)U-MAN by one name. 3 But one deep well exists. 4 From the motherland of Éire the first tongue, 5 to the lands from which came the Gaul, 6 to the lands from which came the Anatolians, 7 then the lands of Indus and the Brahma Brehons, 8 then the lands of the Galatians, the Persians and Greeks, 9 to Rome herself and all her childrens' tongues, 10 heritage to the Cuillean once was sung. 11 In truth, you see, 12 all has but one history.

C. 6

1 Yet the covenant of ISH-MU-EL, 2 was not in agreement, 3 with the Council of the Holly, 4 upon the sacred Isle. 5 For the elders, 6 prideful and intoxicated with power, 7 did see such wisdom, 8 as reserved for worthy men, 9 and the gods. 10 So priests did send warning, 11 that such a tower of learning, 12 would tempt the gods, 13 and bring our doom.

C. 7

1 But ISH-MU-EL did not sway. 2 For in his heart, 3 all knowledge was for men, 4 not a few chosen. 5 Yet upon this time that all the tribes, 6 had heard and learnt one tongue, 7 the gods of the heavens, 8 did conspire to scatter man, 9 back to stone and fire.

C. 8

1 Upon nine hundred and forty cycles of AUN(ON) (3480 BCE), 2 from the dawning of the Great Age, 3 of the Hound and young Bull, 4 a new God came into the sky. 5 Usurping all but the most ancient gods, 6 a terrible tail did it reveal. 7 The crows claw of death. 8 For upon this unearthly omen in the heavens, 9 came great death. 10 The lands of the mighty Sahar did shake. 11 A mighty ball of fire, 12 did cleave the land known as Fezzan. 13 Fire, smoke and dust. 14 All the forests burnt. 15 From the Seas of the West to the East, 16 water turned to poison. 17 Land turned to sand, 18 sand turned to glass. 19 Men and animals alike, 20 turned to ash. 21 Across the lands of the great Araba (Arabs), 22 great thunderbolts and fire. 23 Forests and all living things to ash, 24 the mighty river of KUWA(IT), 25 drained of life. 26 The mighty river of KAR(UN), 27 reduced to dust. 28 And all around black rock fell to earth, 29 from the heavens of the gods. 30 Across the lands of the bull, 31 all but dust. 32 The Great culture of the Anatolians, 33 destroyed in one instance. 34 The inland sea did burst its shore. 35 The great serpent river did overflow. 36 The MA-AT and Amratians scattered. 37 The cities of URUK destroyed. 38

Great warrior kings, 39 without a people or a city.

C. 9

1 Not a land or a people touched, 2 but for the sacred city of Ebla, 3 and the sacred Isle herself. 4 The gods spared no fire and smoke, 5 nor darkness that followed. 6 For within a single cycle of the Gleaming One, 7 day was night, all was black. 8 Men once who were sculptor and scribe, 9 became like shadows. 10 Tearing and clasping for a few crumbs, 11 the gods of the underworld did roam once more.

C. 10

1 The exiles of the once great tribes of the Sahar, 2 descended into the lands of the Ma-at and Amratians. 3 All men were like wild beasts. 4 The men of Ma-at could not compete. 5 With the power of the Sahar, 6 the men of the great Serpent river, 7 did move east.

C. 11

1 The exiles of the Anatolians, 2 travelled east, 3 to the lands of Ebla, 4 and south to the great lands of cedars.

C. 12

1 The exiles of the once great, 2 and fertile lands of the Araba (Arabs), 3 moved north and east, 4 into the ancient lands of the Ubaid, 5 and war ensued. 6 The scattered tribes of the Uruk and Ubaid, 7 did not have the fighting strength of the Araba, 8 they themselves were pushed further east, 9 and took the lands of the Indus. 10 Making themselves a new home. 11 While the Araba settled into their new homeland, 12 which they called AK-ADIA, new lands.

C. 13

1 Upon the great darkness, 2 came the great forgetfulness. 3 Men forgot how to be builders, 4 forgot how to be farmers. 5 Robbers and thieves they did become. 6 No order of law. 7 In their stead came merchants of doom, 8 men of trickery and fables. 9 A thousand superstitions, 10 arose amongst the exiles, 11 most strongly, 12 that this was punishment. 13 For man obtaining the wisdom of the gods, 14 untouched, the tower of Ebla, 15 was taken stone by stone, 16 to rubble. 17 For ignorant men, 18 feared the wrath of gods, 19 upon such wisdom, 20 as knowledge and writing.

C. 14

1 Some rejected the gods of the heavens, 2 as the gods of the underworld, 3 of ancient times arose. 4 Human sacrifice, 5 the eating of human flesh abounded. 6 Wherever a scribe or a teacher, 7 did survive the darkness. 8 Beastly men and women, 9 did seek them out. 10 Tearing and Eating their flesh, 11 to appease their gods, 12 of ignorance and fear.

C. 15

1 The Holly Ones of the sacred Isle, 2 spared by the Gods, 3 did see such sign, 4 as proof divine. 5 Such wisdom held tightly, 6 to precious few. 7 Their temples secure, 8 by countless slaves. 9 Initiation chambers made, 10 by willing hands. 11 No need then to save, 12 widow nor orphan.

C. 16

1 Upon the darkness, 2 and return to winter, 3 a single priest named E-SUS, 4 did brave the journey, 5 from Ebla

and the land of Levi, 6 to the sacred Isle, 7 into the chamber of high priests, 8 to Appeal to reason, 9 and kind of heart, 10 to old wizards corrupted by power, 11 bathed in priceless tribute. 12 DE-DANA most senior priest, 13 did reject the young priest. 14 The plea of E-SUS, 15 not to intervene, 16 with the gods quarrel with man. 17 For what heaven has started, 18 let no man withstand. 19 A priestly plan of no account.

C. 17

1 DE-DANA forbid E-SUS to speak of the world afar, 2 on fear of exile and banishment as Cuilleain. 3 A most grievous curse, 4 and no more for four years, 5 did he speak, 6 until a night of restless sleep, 7 a vision came of a serpent, 8 eating itself without restraint. 9 Troubled he sought counsel, 10 from GAU-EL an old master smith and priest, 11 who fashioned the sacred metals. 12 He did tell E-SUS of great portent, 13 such vision held. 14 But E-SUS ignored and returned to study. 15 Yet upon the darkened night, 16 set up on hill, 17 the wind did whip a howl, 18 as if to call him by name, 19 and why E-SUS did not follow, 20 the call of the gods. 21 But again the priest did ignore the wind, 22 the gods quarrel, 23 not his to contest.

C. 18

1 Then upon the great day of Yule, 2 E-SUS did stand for prose. 3 Upon ancient temple stones under darkened sky. 4 And before he could but utter a word, 5 a break in the blanket exposed, 6 a ray of light upon his face. 7 The great council yelled in awe and fear, 8 As E-SUS did proclaim a duty. 9 To take the wisdom of the holly men, 10 and save the tribes of man. 11 But hardened hearts these old priests, 12 with such wonder they did reject, 13 and called E-SUS into exile, 14 at southern shores.

C. 19

1 But GAU-EL upon hearing the signs, 2 did set a course, 3 within six cycles of YAH(EL). 4 The greatest artisans and smiths, 5 of the Cuilleain did work, 6 until GAU-EL called for E-SUS. 7 Upon the presence of E-SUS, 8 GAU-EL did speak. 9 For no more shall weapons of war, 10 be the tools of Holy men, 11 but the power of word. 12 No more shall shadows of the underworld, 13 rule by blood and death, 14 but great monuments to the gods. 15 By which man shall ever know, 16 the covenant of gods. 17 By what magic E-SUS called? 18 For ignorant men have eyes. 19 Whereupon GAU-EL produced eight young priests, 20 all with shaven heads in white robes, 21 upon their heads a white skullcap, 22 and upon their white skullcaps, 23 each a Great cylindrical cone of gold, 24 upon which was guilded all the wisdom of the Holly, 25 the most ancient of priests, 26 discerned for all time. 27 Around their necks hung an ornamental cartouche, 28 of the finest gold and jewels, 29 on which the great gods and wheel displayed, 30 and in their right hand, 31 staffs of wood and gold. 32 These be your sword, 33 the finest artisans, 34 masons and scribes of the Holly. 35 No army, no king, 36 shall withstand the power of divine truth. 37 With these words, 38 E-SUS did shave his head

and beard, 39 and did adopt the robes and cone hat of the eight. 40 Thereafter the nine left the sacred Isle, 41 upon their journey.

C. 20
1 Upon hearing of what GAU-EL had done, 2 the council did banish him, 3 to the great hill of YAH in the sacred BOY(NE). 4 And did decree that E-SUS, 5 henceforth shall be excommunicated, 6 from his sacred homeland, 7 never to return.

C. 21
1 The first lands that E-SUS did see, 2 were the ancient brothers of the Iberians. 3 Upon seeing the sacred Nine, 4 their white robes, 5 their golden cone hats, 6 all men embraced and cried for joy. 7 For the gods as saviours had arrived. 8 Not one stone, axe, or weapon, 9 was held in anger. 10 Prostrate in fear and awe, 11 within short time, 12 order returned. 13 A small band raised, 14 and three new boats.

C. 22
1 The second lands that the sacred Nine did see, 2 were the Islands of the Great Eastern Sea. 3 The Isles of the triple goddesses Brid, 4 upon seeing the three ships, 5 and the great priests, 6 all men dropped their clubs, 7 and bowed to the gods. 8 There, great monuments to the gods were erected.

C. 23
1 The third lands the sacred Nine did see, 2 were the ancient lands of the Maat. 3 Upon seeing the priests, 4 the people did prostrate (themselves), 5 and ceased war. 6 Order was restored, 7 in each land, in each place. 8 Great monuments were made, 9 to honour the gods, 10 and remind man, 11 of a divine covenant.

C. 24
1 But not all the gods were pleased. 2 While their names were honoured, 3 their knowledge, 4 most sacred knowledge, 5 was given unto all men. 6 Upon leaving the land of the great serpent river, 7 to travel east, 8 DAGDA and LIR did consort, 9 and a howling storm did scatter the boats. 10 And blow the priests westward, 11 one boat did land upon the shores of the yellow land, 12 to the east of the Iberians, 13 and the priests did bring the people into order. 14 Travelling inland to the land of great forests. 15 The other two boats were blown out of the eastern sea, 16 into the great sea. 17 E-SUS and his boat was blown, 18 upon the shore of the land of the shadows, 19 a land of savagery. 20 The ancient lands of the exiles of MOT. 21 The other boat was blown for days westward, 22 until the priests near giving up the ghost, 23 did land upon fertile shores, 24 of the crescent gulf, 25 and did bring order, 26 to the lands of the OLME and MAY(A).

C. 25
1 Seeing E-SUS and two priests, 2 the shadows were fearful, 3 But as beasts, 4 their hunger overpowered their fear. 5 They did not submit to the priests, 6 herding them to their most sacred place. 7 The plain of SAL.U(M). 8 And the mountain of bones of man. 9 There, muddy men of great superstition, 10 eyed upon the priests.

11 The priests with their cones were pushed, 12 to the centre of the ring of dirt and ageless blood, 13 as a fire was lit to consume. 14 But at the point which was to be their doom, 15 a crack in the darkness did appear, 16 and the rays of AUN did shine upon E-SUS. 17 And the priests to his side, 18 and upon striking their golden cone hats, 19 did send blinding rays out to the shadows. 20 Never before had these men seen such magic, 21 they scattered and fell. 22 Submitting to a power greater than death. 23 E-SUS and the priests did establish order, 24 to the land of the Britanni, 25 and upon this ancient place of blood and sacrifice, 26 did commence the greatest monument, 27 to the ancient gods, 28 so that no human of this Isle or any other. 29 Upon its gaze, 30 could be in doubt, 31 of the power of the gods.

C. 26

1 But for all that E-SUS had accomplished, 2 for all that he saved, 3 E-SUS never again, 4 rested upon the land of his fathers. 5 For an ancient priests word ushered, 6 is a sacred bond. 7 Never broken. 8 So he passed, 9 some say, 10 in the new land of the ancient Ubaids, 11 upon the streams of the Indus, 12 revered even as a new god to the end.

Book 6

Great Age of the Poets

[3180 - 2700 BCE]

C. 1

Within twelve hundred and forty cycles of AUN (3180 BCE), 2 from the beginning of the Great Age, 3 of the Young Bull, 4 men had returned, 5 to civilised ways. 6 Great monuments begun, 7 with E-SUS strong, 8 stood proud throughout. 9 The great lands of man, 10 in the new lands of the Sahar, 11 upon the Serpent River, 12 a giant monument to the man-gods. 13 The Cuileann, known then as Cu, 14 as the guiding ones, 15 some mistaken for young whelp/dog. 16 For the descendants of the Sahar, 17 did honour the Cu as a giant Dog-god, 18 known as Anubis, 19 upon the ancient plain of Giza, 20 watching over the heavens, 21 ever vigilant, 22 guarding mankind, 23 from the will of the gods.

C. 2

1 As time forgot terrible afflictions, 2 kingdoms formed, 3 with faded memory. 4 The Ubaid of the great fertile plains, 5 now of the Indus valley, 6 did raise themselves. 7 Cities of light and wisdom, 8 language and art, 9 that rivalled Ebla. 10 Ebla herself gained in strength. 11 A jewel of fine work. 12 The Araba (Arabs), 13 now of the old lands of the Ubaid, 14 who called themselves sag-giga, 15 did build many cities. 16 Each to a God of their names. 17 Each with a king and a priest, 18 some versed, 19 in the knowledge of the ancients.

C. 3

1 Upon the Isles, 2 of the great goddesses of Brid, 3 did flourish new villages and trade. 4 Many a novice spending time, 5 in the mountains of the ancient Queens. 6 Even upon the sacred Isle, 7 change had come. 8 The Council redeemed, 9 from the trials of ESUS, 10 to bring forth knowledge, 11 and wisdom to man.

C. 4

1 The gods of the heavens, 2 restless in intent, 3 had not yet spared, 4 fire nor dust, 5 death nor ash, 6 from the realm of man. 7 For upon a night came, 8 twelve hundred and seventy five years (3145 BCE), 9 from the dawning of the Great Age of the Bull, 10 the God Raven, 11 in the night sky, 12 the omen of doom, 13 no brighter had been such sign.

C. 5

1 The Holly men, 2 had foretold this day would come, 3 and did divine its Arrival. 4 The Holly, adorned now with white skull caps, 5 ones who sounds out judgements, 6 with a rod and robes, 7 did warn the kings of impending, 8 doom upon their land. 9 To the kings of the fertile lands of the east, 10 the Holly did come. 11 But the kings did ignore their omen. 12 To the Kings of the Indus lands, 13 the Holly did come. 14 And the kings did heed their woe. 15 And did build great stores and, 16 pens for all manner of beast. 17 To the kings of the north of the Great Inland sea, 18 the Holly did come. 19 But none would listen. 20 To the kings of the south and the serpent river, 21 the Holly spoke, 22 and they did heed the warnings of the gods, 23 and did build mighty stores and walls.

C. 6

1 Brighter, brighter, 2 the god did come. 3 Men of short memory, 4 did ignore it. 5 Some even spoken as a good omen, 6 the men of MOT. 7 Relishing chaos, 8 the pleasure of gods, 9 and the superior man.

C. 7

1 In the year, twelve hundred and eighty years (3140 BCE), 2 from the dawning of the Great Age of the Bull, 3 in the southern sky, 4 beyond the horizon, 5 it was told, 6 to the east of the great lands, 7 of the black people, 8 was an island kingdom, 9 there the gods did cleave the land. 10 Not one life. 11 Not one living thing spared. 12 And further still to the south and east, 13 the gods did cleave, 14 great lands and islands, 15 so that no living thing, 16 did remain. 17 To the north, 18 the east, the west, 19 and south, 20 the Earth did shake. 21 Buildings did fall, 22 and rivers rise, 23 the seas bubbled, 24 and burst the shore.

C. 8

1 Then within one cycle of YAH(EL), 2 the blackness came. 3 So dark it blotted all the gods, 4 so thick, it choked the air. 5 Crops withered and died. 6 Animals gave up the ghost. 7 And people returned to savages.

C. 9

1 The powerfull King Is-rae-lu of Ebla, 2 a poet of skill, 3 had pleaded upon the signs, 4 that the Holly help all races. 5 Though he passed before the time, 6 his words were not forgotten. 7 For fifty cycles of Aun, 8 the finest poets of the Cuileann, 9 did devise, 10 a great song of wisdom, 11 the law of laws, 12 of wise kings, 13 and counsel, 14 of property and citizenry, 15 of trade and honour.

C. 10

1 It was to the son of King Is-rae-lu of Ebla, 2 the poets did first sing. 3 King Da-ud-um (David), 4 a poet of some note. 5 Upon hearing, 6 the Historic cycle of poems, 7 King Da-ud-um did offer, 8 his greatest architect and smith, 9 Ka-sha-lu (Kothar), 10 to accompany the Holly on their journey. 11 The Holly agreed. 12 For the name of Kothar Preceded him, 13 a man of high skill, 14 even the art of science and craft. 15 Upon hearing the poem for himself, 16 Kothar did declare before his end, 17 man will stand without fear, 18 for he determine his destiny. 19 He did then shave his skull, 20

Adorning a skull cap, 21 in the manner of the Holly, 22 and did shave his beard, 23 to a weave upon his chin.

C. 11

1 The Holly did depart to the lands, 2 to the Kings of the Indus, 3 whereupon they did proclaim, 4 Here is abundance greater than gold, 5 the wheel of Kothar, 6 of brick and craft, 7 and to the poems of the law. 8 For we shall build a mighty civilisation, 9 upon these pillars. 10 And the Holly shall be known, 11 as The Bra(h)man, 12 the Ones who sound out (Bra), 13 carrying the stick of the divine (man). 14 And Kothar himself they did honour, 15 as a god amongst the Bra(h)man. 16 They named him Krishna, 17 which means saviour of mankind.

C. 12

1 To the lands of Šumeru they did travel, 2 and their new name as the Bra(h)man, 3 did precede them. 4 There, the kings and people, 5 who had survived the great floods, 6 did rejoice and proclaimed, 7 that they would take the wisdom of the Bra(h)man, 8 and the gifts of Kothar (Krishna), 9 a civilisation greater than all before.

C. 13

1 In the year, thirteen hundred cycles of AUN (3120 BCE), 2 from the dawning of the Great Age of the Bull, 3 and ten cycles after the great Darkness had begun. 4 To the new lands of the Sahar, 5 and the serpent river, 6 did Kothar (Krishna) come. 7 Upon hearing the poems of law, 8 and the wonders of science of Kothar, 9 exiles of Sahar did rejoice, 10 and proclaimed, 11 Kothar, living god, 12 your name shall become, 13 KA-MAT (NAR-MAR) the MAN-ES (Great man), 14 the God who unified the lands, 15 and heals the river. 16 Here we shall build with your wisdom, 17 the greatest culture of all of mankind.

C. 14

1 Kothar did stay a while in these lands, 2 of the Aegyptus (Egyptians). 3 So when he did come to the time to depart, 4 all the nation were in mourning. 5 For their living god, 6 who united them Was departing. 7 Kothar promised within ten cycles of AUN, 8 he would return. 9 Then did he depart to an ancient isle of the goddesses Brid. 10 Upon arriving on the ancient Isle of Brid, 11 his fame had preceded him. 12 Overjoyed, the people did proclaim, 13 him E-SUS returned. 14 Upon this day our land is yours, 15 we shall name our Isle Kaftor, 16 which was their way of his name, 17 an Isle we know today as Krete.

C. 15

1 Kothar did agree to stay. 2 And upon reflecting upon, 3 the same lands as the triple goddesses, 4 did declare that all men, 5 do die and be reborn, 6 that a life honouring Bra(h)man Law, 7 of the most ancient Holly Ones. 8 A man might be immortal, 9 that all men have but one father, 10 he called PE-TAH (PETER).

C. 16

1 With his vision he did return, 2 to his second new home Aegyptus. 3 And upon the serpent river, 4 did architect a mighty capital, 5 in honour of the father of all things, 6 PE-TAH

(PETER/ PTAH), 7 HAT-KA-PETAH, 8 home of the KA (soul) of Ptah, 9 known as Memphis.

Book 7

Great Age of the Sign

[2700 - 2680 BCE]

C. 1

1 In the Great Age of the Hound and Young Bull, 2 at one thousand, seven hundred and twenty cycles of AUN, 3 past the dawn of the Great Age (2700 BCE), 4 great prosperity had been made. 5 Civilisations of all name, 6 honouring man and the gods. 7 The Šumeru excelled in the building of cities, 8 in the education of men. 9 The good government of life, 10 the people of the Indus (Harappa), 11 excelled in the crafts, 12 of intricate design. 13 The people of Ebla, 14 in the crafting of wood and smith of metal. 15 The Aegyptus in the carving of stone. 16 The songs (poems) of Kothar, 17 were sung in all the great halls, 18 and chambers of man, 19 the Bra(h)man revered.

C. 2

1 But upon the season of the rain gods, 2 Dagan (god of rain/ fertility) did not come. 3 The peoples of the river valleys did grow thirsty, 4 the crops began to wither. 5 The kings of man did consult, 6 the Most high Bra(h)man of the sacred Isle.

C. 3

1 The King of the Aegyptus, 2 named Pharaoh Khasekhemwy, 3 did send his young son Djoser, 4 to ERI(U), to plead with the head of the Holly. 5 DON, the most senior of the Cuileann, 6 did first welcome the young prince. 7 For the priests of Aegyptus had spoken, 8 of the bright young prince. 9 But Djoser did protest, 10 not to learn had he come, 11 but to save his people. 12 The high priests of the council, 13 did consult for five days, 14 and then returned, 15 proclaiming that they shall prepare, 16 the greatest of all songs, 17 to help bring order. 18 That such a poem, 19 would be prepared, 20 within ten cycles of YAH (the Gleaming One).

C. 4

1 Djoser did tear his clothes. 2 for such delay, 3 and more prose, 4 would not feed the bellies, 5 of his hungry land. 6 He did depart the sacred Isle, 7 vowing never to regard, 8 such men as gods again.

C. 5

1 Yet even a curse, 2 of good conscience, 3 does not pass unheard, 4

by the gods. 5 And upon his return journey, 6 LIR did pound his boat, 7 with fierce aggression, 8 till it broke in two, 9 upon the rocks of the Latins coast. 10 In the tempest, 11 but two did live. 12 The young prince was saved by Cú, 13 the tiller man of the sacred boat.

C. 6

1 The old king, 2 of the Aegyptus, 3 upon hearing the news, 4 from the other boats, 5 did give up the ghost, 6 believing his son doomed. 7 Without an heir, 8 it was Nimaethap, 9 the wife of the King, 10 and mother of the prince, 11 who ruled in his stead. 12 Not first without fighting a brief rebellion, 13 the second wife and sons scratched out, 14 from the book of life.

C. 7

1 Upon their shipwreck, 2 Cú implored the young prince, 3 to remove his princely clothes, 4 and dress in rags. 5 In those days the Latins, 6 knew no civilised ways, 7 and did treat all strangers, 8 as meat for their dogs. 9 But held special feast, 10 upon the bones of kings, 11 and holy men.

C. 8

1 The Latins did bind and take them, 2 to their Camp, 3 and prepared to cleave them, 4 as was their custom. 5 Whereupon Cú did speak in their tongue, 6 he did call them not to end them, 7 but that they might serve as slaves. 8 The Latins amazed this man could speak, 9 called if he might be a holy priest, 10 for sweet the flesh of doomed poets. 11 Cú did reply that he was no priest, 12 but a mere slave of priests, 13 who happened to gain their favour, 14 by serving them. 15 Upon the sincerity of Cú, 16 the Latins did bind them, 17 and made them slaves.

C. 9

1 Away from the gaze, 2 of the uncivilised Latins, 3 the young prince did ask, 4 knowing the ancient promise, 5 of the Holly since the beginning of time, 6 to never utter an untruth, 7 how then Cú knew such wisdom, 8 if he indeed was not a priest? 9 Cú replied that he once was a novice, 10 of the Holly and destined to shine, 11 but did reject the singing of songs, 12 preferring to write using sign, 13 to commit to memory the knowledge. 14 The Cuilleain had rejected his ways, 15 and condemned him to be a ferryman, 16 upon the seas.

C. 10

1 For five years the Latins kept them bound. 2 For five years Cú and the prince did speak. 3 And Cú did reveal the great wisdom, 4 of the most holy and ancient. 5 The greatest of law of kings, 6 the finest of science and custom. 7 Then upon a night of great storm, 8 the Latins fearful did run from their camp. 9 Seizing the moment, 10 Cú did find a strong young tree and rock, 11 and released them from their bonds. 12 At the coast, 13 Cú and Djoser did lash a raft, 14 and depart the shores of the Latins. 15 First to Krete, 16 and then by boat and crew to his land Aegyptus.

C. 11

1 Upon Memphis, Queen Nimaethap, 2 wept for joy. 3 For her son lost, had returned. 4 Within one cycle of YAH, 5 Djoser was crowned Pharaoh. 6 His first act was to call Cú to his throne,

Book 7 Great Age of the Sign

7 Whereupon Djoser did proclaim: 8 I name thee IM-HATAP (Imotep), 9 meaning the one who comes in peace, 10 I shall make Chancellor of all Lower Egypt, 11 First after the King, 12 Administrator of the Great Palace, 13 Hereditary Nobleman, 14 High Priest, 15 Builder, Chief Carpenter, 16 Chief Sculptor and Maker of Vessels in Chief. 17 To save our kingdom, 18 you shall first make a language, 19 that all men may read, 20 and understand. 21 That they may be literate, 22 in the way, 23 and knowledge of the gods.

C. 12

1 IM-HATAP (Imotep) rose and asked the Pharaoh, 2 how can such things be done, 3 when the most sacred and ancient of high priests forbid it. 4 For all knowledge then was prose, 5 sung from ancient times. 6 The Pharaoh did reply, 7 that wisdom without purpose is nought. 8 Men without culture are animals. 9 No good priest may ransom his King or his people.

C. 13

1 And so, within less than one cycle of AUN, 2 IM-HATAP (Imotep) did give his king and people, 3 a language for all to read and understand. 4 He did use the pressed reeds of the river, 5 and the inks to make sign, 6 and handsome in art. 7 That by carved stone and paint, 8 they might be the same. 9 And within two cycles of the AUN, 10 the kingdom of the Aegyptus, 11 did have knowledge for fields, 12 for law and fair rights, 13 for learning and for taxes, 14 for trade and reason.

C. 14

1 The high priests of the sacred Isle, 2 did hear word of what IM-HATAP had done. 3 They summonsed him to return, 4 on his priestly oaths. 5 But Pharaoh refused to release him. 6 Instead, Pharaoh Djoser sent word, 7 to each and every great King, 8 to meet at the sacred city of Memphis. 9 Upon the question of the writing of signs (written language), 10 such was the question of many Kings, 11 that they did agree, 12 an event to rival the gods of the heavens.

C. 15

1 For the first time, 2 so grave the threat, 3 to their sacred wisdom, 4 the High Priests of the Cuilleain, 5 the High Council of priests, 6 did leave ERI(U), 7 and to the court of Pharaoh. 8 There Pharaoh erected thrones equal in stature, 9 for the great council of the most ancient priests, 10 and a throne equal to each King. 11 Never before had such a scene come, 12 the great and noble King Ebrium (Abrum) of Ebla, 13 the great and noble King Emmaberagesi of Kish, 14 and even the great and noble King GILGAMESH of Uruk. 15 Did all attend. 16 The King of Mari of the Amurru (Amorites), 17 was not invited, 18 on account of their wicked, 19 and dark acts, 20 worse than even the most ancient MOT and MAB.

C. 16

1 Upon the arrival of the Holly Ones, 2 DON, the most senior priest, 3 did speak first, 4 as was most ancient custom. 5 He did remind Pharaoh, 6 that all knowledge was from the gods, 7 and it was the priests who

represented them. 8 That by the priests and the Holly ones alone, 9 did such knowledge reside. 10 Only to noble men worthy should it be spoken in prose, 11 and only spoken and sung, never written. 12 For written signs, 13 such as Pharaoh had designed, 14 was blasphemy to the gods.

C. 17

1 Pharaoh remained as cold a stone. 2 While the words of DON, 3 did boil his blood. 4 He stood up from his throne, 5 and stepped down to the throng. 6 Attendants scattered from his path, 7 men and noble gasped in horror, 8 that Pharaoh may lower himself, 9 in view of great kings and ancient priests. 10 The wise king did let the throng subside, 11 and spoke with purpose. 12 Nearly twelve cycles ago of the great Gods, 13 I did stand before you as a man. 14 For my people starving, 15 and throughout your lands, 16 fields and plough, 17 and all manner of science employed. 18 But in your wisdom you saw fit to offer me but song, 19 now that my people can feed themselves, 20 and can divine science and learn, 21 you threaten all culture, 22 and you threaten all men, 23 that such rights are not ours.

C. 18

1 Upon hearing the Pharaoh's speech, 2 Don did rise from his chair and did yell, 3 Blasphemy! 4 You shall have no more priests, 5 nor divination of the gods. 6 You shall be cut off, 7 and food for the wolves.

C. 19

1 Upon this burst, 2 the Pharaoh did proclaim: 3 Let it be known, 4 as my word bonded, 5 from this day forth, 6 no priest of the Holly, 7 shall step foot in my lands. 8 No song of the Bra(h)man shall be sung, 9 no gods of the ancient names be honoured. 10 For upon your ways, 11 we shall write our own wisdom, 12 we shall sing our own songs, 13 we shall worship our own Gods.

C. 20

1 The old priest and the High Council did cry in horror. 2 DON did rend his sacred robes, 3 smashing his sacred staff upon the floor, 4 of the Pharaohs hall. 5 He did cry out, 6 I curse thee, 7 the highest curse, 8 and all men who follow thee. 9 For fickle will be your wisdom, 10 shallow and without unity. 11 You shall be damned to war, 12 you shall be beguiled by darkness, 13 and this shall be your doom.

C. 21

1 Upon hearing the High Curse uttered, 2 against humanity, 3 by such a powerful and ancient priest, 4 IM-HATAP did speak weeping. 5 In cursing man, 6 you have cursed our kind. 7 Within a Great Age, 8 we will be ghosts. 9 No more of the history of man, 10 doomed as the unremembered.

C. 22

1 Thus the priests departed back to ERI(U). 2 And the great kings each did commission their own writing signs. 3 And each did create their own gods. 4 And each did create their own songs and wisdom. 5 And true to the words of IM-HATAP, 6 before the end of the next Great Age, 7 the most sacred and

ancient of all priests, 8 were long forgotten.

Book 8

Great Age of Civilisations

[2680 - 2012 BCE]

C. 1

1 In the Great Age of the Hound and Young Bull, 2 from one thousand, seven hundred and forty cycles of ATUN (SUN), 3 and the years that followed (2680 BCE), 4 the Civilisations of mankind did prosper. 5 Not only by the grace of the gods, 6 but their written wisdom. 7 Since the rebellion, 8 against the ancient priests of the gods, 9 men had mastered the field. 10 Masons had mastered stonework. 11 Judges did exact fair rule of law. 12 Artisans did make all kinds of wonders, 13 and scribes did record all manner of science. 14 Story and sacred observance. 15 New gods created, 16 with their own temples and priests, 17 some being the men of the ancients. 18 E-SUS did become more than one god. 19 Krishna to some, Jesus to others, 20 Jesus Krishna to more, 21 Horus to the Aegyptians, 22 Zeus to the Greeks. 23 Great myths and stories of their births, 24 reflecting the life of men. 25 The needs of men, 26 not ancient priests of reason, 27 and arrogance.

C. 2

1 In the land of the Aegyptus, 2 under the rule of Pharaoh Djoser, 3 and the wisdom of blessed Imhotep (IM-HATAP), 4 new gods and temples adorned. 5 The greatest of the new gods, 6 was Ra, the sun, 7 and Imhotep as High Priest, 8 did Preside at a city built for the new god, 9 at Heliopolis. 10 Never before, 11 in the mysteries of man, 12 had the Sun risen above the Moon. 13 For all civilisations, 14 by the ancient priests, 15 had respected the Moon above all other Gods. 16 Now even the lands of Ebla did make EL the sun, 17 while YAH and YAHWEH remained the moon.

C. 3

1 Imhotep did make a calendar, 2 in honour of Ra, the sun God. 3 365 days, with the beginning in the Summer, 4 not the winter of the ancient Holly Ones. 5 Thus Aegyptus did make themselves, 6 their own gods, 7 and men as gods, 8 and so hope for all men.

C. 4

1 Yet Pharaoh Djoser, 2 and his most wise and blessed priest Imhotep, 3 did

one more mighty act, 4 to shame the ancient priests, 5 of their folly, 6 and their High Curse. 7 For they commissioned, 8 for the new priests of Ra, 9 the greatest initiation chambers, 10 the world has ever seen, 11 or will ever see. 12 Not caves of stone, 13 like the most sacred valley of the Boyne, 14 but tributes to the genius of men, 15 and the gods they made.

C. 5

1 So precise these ancient caves, 2 for the living initiates of Ra, 3 so massive of scale and perfection, 4 they were wonders from the day, 5 Imhotep and Djoser did conceive them. 6 Their gleaming surfaces so finely finished. 7 No mason mark, 8 no imperfection, nor groove seen, 9 nor the entrance (concealed) to these wondrous temples. 10 The kings of many lands did honour, 11 Imhotep and Djoser and their temples, 12 upon the Giza plain. 13 So that countless of the best masons, 14 artisans, and mathematicians did come. 15 For no better beacon to the age of man, 16 by the hands of free men, 17 by the will of educated men, 18 not slaves, 19 these miracle mountains stand.

C. 6

1 In the Great Age of the Hound and Young Bull, 2 at two thousand and eighty cycles of ATUN (SUN), 3 past the dawn of the Great Age (2340 BCE), 4 the Cuilleain had been abandoned, 5 their singing poems rejected, 6 by the greatest civilisations. 7 Only sung in the nearby lands, 8 in the land of the Britanni, 9 the lands of Espain, 10 and the sacred Isle itself. 11 All but one civilisation had kept relations, 12 the Great kings of Ebla, 13 did show due respect. 14 And all gold and ready-made bronze, 15 from the earth of the Isle of the gods, 16 did come to Ebla first and no other. 17 But for all others, 18 nothing but contempt, 19 for ancient prose and priests.

C. 7

1 No more were the ancient priests revered as most high, 2 Bra(h)man called no more. 3 Instead upon the curse of DON, 4 a new title they had become, 5 the DRU(V)ID. 6 The ones immersed, 7 in knowledge (VID/VEDA). 8 A title while respected, 9 was no more a god. 10 Nor indeed a Holly (holy) man, 11 but a wise man, 12 a mortal man.

C. 8

1 Yet upon these times did come hardship, 2 to the lands of the Akkad, 3 the lands of the Aegyptus, 4 and the lands of the Amurru (Amorites). 5 Even the fresh gods did not help men, 6 when famine came to their lands. 7 So it was for the northern cities of the Akkadians. 8 Their storehouses empty, 9 the well dry. 10 Treaties did not stand, 11 King Iblul-Il, King of Mari and dark priest, 12 of a city of human sacrifice and darkness, 13 did seize this moment as a sign, 14 that their daemon gods had returned. 15 He did send his greatest commander, 16 whose name was Enna-Dagan, 17 on account of the daemon god worshipped. 18 To attack Ebla unprepared, 19 with great haste Enna-Dagan did move, 20 until his army was at the walls of Ebla, 21 but bringing no supplies for siege, 22 and on account of the destruction of the land, 23 the men

of Enna-Dagan, 24 did fall from thirst and hunger.

C. 9

1 But Iblul-Il was a crafty King, 2 and had a plan. 3 He did order his empty stores and empty yards to be burned. 4 He then did send word to Sargon the Great, 5 the most powerful leader of the Akkadians. 6 That in such troubled times, 7 King Ibbi did deliberately attack, 8 and try to burn down his capital, 9 of the wicked city of Mari. 10 Upon this news, 11 Sargon did pitch a rage. 12 The might of the Akkadians did rally, 13 upon the walls of the great city of Ebla. 14 King Ibbi did call for help, 15 but no ally could he find. 16 A city of scholars and trades, 17 no match for such an army,

C. 10

1 But King Ibbi was a crafty King, 2 and had a plan. 3 As the Akkadians approached, 4 he did send his best scribes, 5 and most valued scrolls, 6 of all the written languages of the known world, 7 of stories and science, 8 of trade and measure (mathematics), 9 to the coastal port. 10 There he ordered ships be sailed, 11 with these (written) treasures, 12 from all the great civilisations, 13 to the Isle of the Druids.

C. 11

1 As Sargon the Great approached the capital, 2 his army did shake the ground. 3 Ibbi did offer Sargon an agreement, 4 that he may have the city and its stores, 5 all its temples and wealth of bronze, 6 if he permit the people enough food to eat, 7 and allow the city in peace. 8 Sargon upon such terms agreed. 9 He offered the king safe passage, 10 and Sargon the Great did capture Ebla, 11 without blood nor fire, nor one life lost.

C. 12

1 King Ibbi, 2 the last true King of Ebla, 3 did then take a ship unto the shores, 4 to the most sacred Isle, 5 where awaited his offering, 6 to the most ancient priests. 7 The most senior of the High Council of the Druids, 8 who met King Ibbi, 9 was YO-SAP (Yôsep/ Joseph), 10 his names meaning one who reveres learning. 11 Since the times of the great curse, 12 the High Council had debated, 13 how might they restore, 14 the ancient respects of man. 15 Now upon the arrival, 16 of King Ibbi and his gift, 17 the Council still debated.

C. 13

1 Ibbi did not bring a single sword, 2 nor spear to the most sacred Isle. 3 To do so would be to break, 4 a sacred oath to the gods themselves, 5 that had existed for thousands of years. 6 Instead he did request an audience, 7 with the High Council and YO-SAP. 8 When he arrived he did find the priests, 9 discussing the contents of the scrolls, 10 and the nature of stories and fables, 11 written since the great curse.

C. 14

1 Ibbi did wait until the priests did cease, 2 as was most ancient custom. 3 Then he did proclaim: 4 Most ancient and revered Bra(h)man, 5 most Holy Cuileann, 6 I am a King without a land, 7 you are the most sacred priests without entry, 8 to the very sacred

places you founded. 9 Together we are united in circumstance. 10 Man now writes his own story. 11 And many a King knows not whether you, 12 are true or myth, 13 too late to change the writing of men. 14 But harness it to better ends, 15 let me stay a while, 16 so that I may learn and respect your ways, 17 that I may find wisdom to reclaim, 18 my throne of Ebla.

C. 15

1 As crafty as Ibbi was, 2 the priests did not entertain him, 3 without first a plan. 4 YO-SAP did thank Ibbi for his gift, 5 and did agree to his request to stay, 6 on three conditions, 7 first, that the most sacred land of the Isle, 8 be priests who reign supreme, 9 that no king nor noble may usurp, 10 the will of the gods. 11 Second, that the most learned scribes of Ebla, 12 did teach the Holly the writings of mankind. 13 The third, that Ibbi respect the rights of the priests, 14 upon conquering the lands once more. 15 For this, YO-SAP did say all the riches, 16 of the sacred Isle, 17 be at the command of Ibbi as King.

C. 16

1 So it was, 2 Ibbi became the first King of the sacred Isle, 3 in two thousand years. 4 Near the sacred Ath Cliath Cuilleain, 5 the sacred (holly) hurdled ford (of the river Lilley), 6 Ibbi did found a new home and city, 7 called Eblana, 8 the new Ebla. 9 So it was the most sacred Isle, 10 came to be known as Ibbi-Éri, 11 and the name Ibiru, 12 the land of Ibbi.

C. 17

1 In the Great Age of the Hound and Young Bull, 2 at two thousand two hundred and twenty cycles of ATUN, 3 past the dawn of the Great Age (2200 BCE), 4 a great calamity befell the ancient lands of the Aegyptus, 5 the Akkadians, 6 and as far as the Indus.

C. 18

1 Great balls of fire and black metal, 2 from the gods of the heavens, 3 without warning, 4 did cleave the earth. 5 Across the eastern half, 6 of the Great Inland sea, 7 to the east of the River Jordan, 8 all was laid to waste. 9 To the west, 10 all trees were uprooted. 11 The ancient and mighty forests of pines, 12 turned to kindling, 13 beautiful lakes turned to salt. 14 A Dead Sea, 15 where nothing has lived since. 16 Even the southern lands of the Akkadians and the Aegyptians, 17 did not escape the wrath of the old gods.

C. 19

1 On the other side of the world, 2 the mighty culture of the Aztlan was shook, 3 high in the Antis (Andes) Mountains, 4 the tribe of Atl had built a city of the gods, 5 the Island city of ATL-ANTIS (Atlantis), 6 the walls and city and temples were covered with gold, silver and copper. 7 And metals that sparkled like red fire. 8 The city did gain its wealth. 9 Sets of channels and streams of men. 10 Unlike anything of ancient times, 11 upon the Lake of the Rectangle (Lake Poopo), 12 great canals 100 ft wide and some as wide as 600 ft, 13 crossed the grain plains. 14 Making use of the rains from Heaven in the winter, 15 and waters

that issued from the earth in summer. 16 But in a single night, 17 upon these times, 18 the city did sink below the waters, 19 a great civilisation lost.

C. 20

1 Widows and children cried. 2 For all the knowledge of man, 3 did not spare them from the violence. 4 Of the most ancient of gods, 5 and the great city Ebla, 6 burnt and destroyed. 7 Not by man, 8 but by the gods themselves.

C. 21

1 Darkness, as before, 2 did envelope for three hundred years, 3 while the races of men, 4 did fight and war among themselves, 5 to survive. 6 The descendants of Ibbi, 7 the exiled scribes of Ebla, 8 and the sacred priests, 9 did form a bond of unity and knowledge, 10 unleashing the power of written wisdom, 11 of science and mathematics. 12 Priests did become proficient, 13 with but one purpose, 14 new inventions, 15 for war.

C. 22

1 So it was, 2 despite an oath to the gods, 3 that no weapons of war, 4 may be on the most sacred soil, 5 by hidden design, 6 the priests and the scribes, 7 of the land of Ibiru, 8 did devise the most terrible, 9 weapons of battle, 10 waiting for the time to strike.

Book 9

Great Age of Babylon

[2012 - 1627 BCE]

C. 1

1 In the Great Age of the Hound and Young Bull, 2 within the last quarter of the Great Age (2012-1900 BCE), 3 the darkness that swept the world, 4 carried with it new beliefs, 5 founded in the temples, 6 of the Amurru (Amorites) of Mari, 7 worshipping the gods of the underworld, 8 immortality for a chosen few. 9 Ghastly rituals did they make, 10 condition of salvation from damnation, 11 the sacrifice of first born child, 12 eating of the flesh of children, 13 making of eunuch men, 14 frenzy of blood orgies. 15 These dark priests made mischief.

C. 2

1 Beguiling and powerful, 2 the Amurru did corrupt, 3 a way through the dark soul into light, 4 with darkened curses, 5 and symbols of malcontent. 6 At first the Akkadians, 7 extending their reach, 8 to the ancient lands of the Sumer, 9 their twisted gods of Ishtar/ Inaana, 10 and Dagan were worshipped, 11 with The moon god Sin, 12 and the god himself called Amurru, 13 upon which the city was formed, 14 the hermaphrodite god, 15 and his consort Asherah (Ashtoreth). 16 Such sickness of daemon gods, 17 that rule the world from the underworld, 18 had travelled as far as Egypt. 19 Obsessed they had become, 20 with the occult of the dark forces.

C. 3

1 Upon the exodus, 2 Sargon allowed the Amurru (Amorites), 3 to rule Ebla. 4 Their gods and practices they did install. 5 Puppet kings did rule, 6 pretending the greatness of Ebla did continue, 7 until the great destruction of the lands, 8 the gods, not Naram-Sin did destroy Ebla.

C. 4

1 The darkness did bring great ignorance. 2 Savage superstitions, 3 and forgetfulness to the lands, 4 and constant war as prophesied, 5 by the ancient High Curse, 6 did come to mankind. 7 Ibiru, the land of Ibbi, 8 in the time of forgetfulness, 9 had become (H)Ibiru, 10 the land of the sea peoples, 11 the feared strangers, 12 from which the name Hebrew comes. 13 The memory of Ibbi and Ebla, 14 gone from the memory, 15 the most ancient priests now as myth.

C. 5

1 Yet the Druids had not vanished. 2 Nor had their memory for ancient grievance. 3 For while the world of man turned wild, 4 they did perfect such weapons of war. 5 The cart had become the chariot. 6 A horse drawn device light and fast. 7 The spear had become the reinforced bow. 8 A spear that could be thrust fast. 9 The long bronze sword, 10 that could cut a man in two, 11 with one strike. 12 But for all the weapons, 13 the most fearsome was, 14 their plan. 15 For the ancient Holly, 16 would no longer bow, 17 to kings who claimed rights, 18 from mythical gods. 19 For through Ibbi they had bred, 20 a race of great priest kings, 21 messiah kings to rule the world.

C. 6

1 In the Great Age of the Hound and Young Bull, 2 two thousand five hundred and ninety five cycles, 3 since the dawn of the Great Age (1825 BCE), 4 upon the thaw, 5 a mighty warrior king did unify, 6 the Cities of the Amorites. 7 His name was Shamshi-Adad I. 8 And by blood and crafty ways, 9 he did briefly hold the kingdom, 10 of the Assyrians. 11 Soon after came King Sin-muballit, 12 of Babylonia. 13 He too did seek to unify his kingdom, 14 as the land did return to life. 15 In Egypt, 16 came Pharaoh Khutawyre Wegaf, 17 founding a new dynasty. 18 In all the lands heralded the return, 19 of strong Kings, 20 and powerful armies.

C. 7

1 Such news was returned, 2 by the (H)Ibiru ships of trade. 3 The most trusted seafarers, 4 since most ancient times. 5 The priests of the Holly did confer, 6 with the Great King MELIN (MIL), 7 on most auspicious time, 8 to launch the fleet built for war. 9 MELIN agreed it be best to wait, 10 until one King had killed another. 11 But his sons, 12 Eber the brave, 13 and Emon the wise, 14 called for haste.

C. 8

1 To the chamber of the King did come, 2 the powerful druidess and seer MOR-RE-GAN. 3 She did warn MELIN against war, 4 that to meddle now in the affairs, 5 of the tribes of men, 6 would bring no good to the sacred Isle. 7 But the King was deaf to prophecy. 8 Twenty cycles of YAHWEH (the moon), 9 did the Druids foretell as the rekoning. 10 But Eber and Emon did, 11 refuse to hold fast. 12 They ordered the ships to depart. 13 But at the shore MOR-RE-GAN, 14 did hold her staff, 15 and warn the young messiahs, 16 she did cry: 17 Honour broken, 18 upon the sacred Isle, 19 tools of death, 20 not for souls, 21 never rest, 22 shall sword nor shield, 23 a curse returned (to the Isle), 24 all shall yield (be lost). 25 And so upon the prophecy, 26 the mightiest fleet of ships, 27 for war, 28 did leave the most sacred shores, 29 of (H)Ibiru, 30 bound for the ancient lands of Ebla, 31 to first regain the last lost.

C. 9

1 In the Great Age of the Hound and Young Bull, 2 two thousand six hundred and thirty years, 3 since the dawn of the Great Age (1790 BCE), 4 the ships of the (H)Ibiru did land, 5 upon the levant coast. 6 No force of the

Amarru could withstand, 7 such science of war. 8 Within short time, 9 the city Ebla, 10 returned to the (H)Ibiru.

C. 10

1 Upon hearing of the fall of Ebla, 2 Shamshi-Adad did curse the sky. 3 In rage he tore his attendants to pieces, 4 and did feast upon one sacrificed child, 5 as were the ways, 6 to daemon gods. 7 Shamshi-Adad sent spies, 8 to see what marvels the (H)Ibiru (Hebrews) did possess. 9 His Viziers did proclaim, 10 only defeat would Shamshi-Adad face, 11 midst the chariots of the (H)Ibiru.

C. 11

1 Eber commanded the chariot force, 2 moving south he captured the coastal Amorite cities, 3 Ugarit fell, Byblos, fell, 4 Dimašqa (Damascus) fell, Baalbek fell, 5 and the prize of Ye-ru-sa-lu-um (Jerusalem). 6 Even the trade routes did fall, 7 but not all war did move to favour. 8 The (H)Ibiru (Hebrews), 9 for all their science and war craft, 10 the gods of rain and storm, 11 did hold fast their chariots, 12 on soft ground, 13 equal match then, 14 for ferocious warriors.

C. 12

1 Emon did take the (H)Ibiru fleet to Egypt, 2 unto the great gulf of the Nile, 3 the most ancient serpent river. 4 There Pharaoh Sekhemre Khutawy, 5 the son of Pharaoh Khutawyre Wegaf, 6 did make a stand against Emon, 7 but to no avail. 8 In forgetful curse, 9 for no knowledge of history, 10 other than myth, 11 Sekhemre Khutawy did curse Emon, 12 and the (H)Ibiru as strangers, 13 the Hyksos. 14 The land too soft for chariot, 15 during rains, 16 Emon did make a strong fort, 17 upon the Island of Mokattam, 18 naming it Cui-Re (Cairo), 19 which means the place of the Holly King. 20 Emon did make a second strong fort, 21 upon the great island of Geneffeh, 22 next to the great straights of Esus (Zeus), 23 naming it Avaris, 24 Which means, 25 the place of the (H)Ibiru. 26 The place of the Hebrews, 27 the druids Did forbid Emon, 28 to attack and destroy Memphis. 29 Instead, they did hold, 30 and wait for the end, 31 of the season of rain.

C. 13

1 Eber did also wait for a moment to strike. 2 Upon the death of Shamshi-Adad I, 3 the gods seemed to favour him, 4 and when the King of Babylonia, 5 Sin-muballit did also pass, 6 his viziers did call for war. 7 But the druids urged the Messiah King, 8 for Caution. 9 Better to let the sons, 10 bury the father and mourn, 11 for forty days, 12 than to enrage a fearsome foe. 13 Eber did heed the words of the druids, 14 and before forty days was done, 15 storms did come making the land soft for chariots, 16 as the cities of the Amarru (Assyrians), 17 were at war with each other.

C. 14

1 The young new King of Babylonia, 2 named Hammurabi, 3 was not long on the throne, 4 when the kingdom of Elam, 5 did attack and destroy the Eshnunna. 6 A wise king Hammurabi, 7 he did make peace with Ishme-Dagan I, 8 the son of Shamshi-Adad I. 9 He did make peace with Elam, 10 he

did make peace with Ebla, 11 and did learn from his enemy. 12 For no more prized to the warrior, 13 was bronze from the sacred Isle.

C. 15

1 In the Great Age of the Hound and Young Bull, 2 two thousand seven hundred and sixty six years, 3 since the dawn of the Great Age (1766 BCE), 4 the King of Elam/ Eshnunna and, 5 Ishme-Dagan I of the Assyrians, 6 urged by Zimri-Lim King of Mari, 7 did conspire against Hammurabi. 8 Zimri-Lim had grown powerful, 9 as a dark priest of the occult. 10 A palace temple of obscene dimensions, 11 had he made. 12 Filled with the souls, 13 of sacrificed innocents. 14 Zimri-Lim, the crafty King, 15 did send into the court of Eber, 16 the finest beauty of all the lands, 17 whose name was Mara, 18 a sorceress of great power. 19 Beguiled, Eber did ignore the druids, 20 and let her stay in his chamber, 21 whereupon she did poison the old king. 22 But before the Messiah King, 23 did give up the ghost, 24 he did send word to his druid, 25 the great IPIT-AMU (Spitama), 26 to seek out the young Hammurabi, 27 and build him a civilisation, 28 to end the reign of Mari sorcery.

C. 16

1 So IPIT-AMU (Spitama), 2 the wise druid, 3 did travel to Babylonia, 4 unto the King Hammurabi. 5 There he did speak the last wishes of Eber, 6 great and noble King (Hammurabi), 7 to your east the jackals call, 8 to your west the crocodiles open their mouths, 9 but all around you the hills have daggers. 10 For as long as men to sacrifice men, 11 undo daemon gods of earth, 12 your kingdom shall never be secure. 13 A solemn oath, 14 as is our ancient custom, 15 to build you then a mighty faith, 16 to rid your lands of evil. 17 A mighty code of law defined, 18 of science and civilisation. 19 Upon these words, 20 IPIT-AMU (Spitama) did reveal, 21 his offering of sixty chariots, 22 three thousand bronze spear tips, 23 and five hundred bows.

C. 17

1 Upon the words of the mighty druid, 2 Hammurabi did rejoice. 3 He did embrace IPIT-AMU (Spitama), 4 and spoke to the assembled: 5 A great day this be to Babylon, 6 to all who hold true an oath. 7 For I have been blessed, 8 by the ancient gods themselves, 9 who see worthy to prophecy my victory. 10 I shall rid all lands of wickedness. 11 I shall restore the rule of law. 12 And you shall be my High Priest. 13 Whereupon Hammurabi did name, 14 IPIT-AMU the name ZARA(T)-USTRA (Zoroaster), 15 which means from the heavens (stars) on high.

C. 18

1 Hammurabi did honour his word. 2 He did use the gifts of Ebla, 3 and did defeat both the King of Elam/ Eshnunna, 4 and did defeat the Assyrians. 5 With bronze and weapons of science From Ebla, 6 he did write a new code of law, 7 and bring to an end, 8 the sacrifice of men. 9 Thereupon, on oath to the druids, 10 he did siege Mari, 11 and destroy it. 12 Never again to wield such evil, 13 the survivors did travel north, 14 to become the high priests of the Hittites.

C. 19

1 Emon, a heavy heart, 2 upon the news of his brothers end, 3 did reach into the heart of Egypt. 4 At Thebes on the bank of the Nile, 5 where a channel did exist to the Red Sea, 6 he did found first a fort, 7 and then a compound for the druids. 8 He did then establish a temple in honour, 9 of the old gods, 10 and the great gods of the heavens, 11 not the underworld. 12 He did name it Amen-Ra, 13 the hidden One, 14 in honour of the great speckled serpent, 15 of the heavens (the milky way), 16 and Ra the god of the sun, 17 there, he did give up the ghost.

Book 10

Great Age of Hyksos

[1627-1353 BCE]

C. 1

1 In the Great Age of the Hound and Young Bull, 2 two thousand seven hundred and ninety three years, 3 since the dawn of the Great Age (1627 BCE), 4 a terrible calamity befell, 5 all the civilisations of the north and eastern shores 6 of the Inland Sea. 7 The Great mountain upon the Isle of Thera (Santorini), 8 did erupt with such violence and fire. 9 Great earthquakes it caused, 10 buildings did fall as far as Ebla. 11 Great waves of water did come, 12 swamping all cities by the shore. 13 Countless numbers did the sea claim. 14 All the ancient cities of the Greeks, 15 were lost. 16 Civilisations such as the sacred Isle of Krete, 17 all were lost. 18 Many of the cities of the Hittites were lost. 19 Then came the rocks of fire, 20 and scorching ash. 21 It burnt the cities, 22 it turned fields and cattle into dust.

C. 2

1 Then came the dust and blinding ash, 2 so that day was pitch night, 3 blanketing everything for hundreds of miles. 4 To the north as far as Hattusa, 5 and Zalpa on the Black inland sea. 6 To the south from Dimašqa (Damascus), 7 and even to Ye-ru-sa-lu-um (Jerusalem), 8 to the east as far as Assur, 9 and even to Babylon. 10 Ebla was utterly destroyed, 11 the (H)Ibiru of the north, 12 the sons and daughters of Eber, 13 under Shalik, 14 did travel south and then west, 15 bringing with them, 16 the foundation stone of Ebla, 17 the white rock of limestone. 18 To seek union with the (H)Ibiru Of Egypt, 19 the sons and daughters of Emon, 20 now the priest class of Thebes.

C. 3

1 King Mursili I of the Hittites, 2 a creative king with truth, 3 did abandon his people and his court, 4 like rats, 5 east and then south towards the ruins of Ebla, 6 to escape the doom of the gods, 7 later to claim that he and not the gods, 8 did level Ebla. 9 And he did vanquish, 10 the descendants of Hammurabi. 11 Like crows the Hittite remnants, 12 picked the empty temples of Babylonia, 13 and scavenged for shelter, 14 driven out by the descendants of the Elam, 15 as the Kassites from the Zagros mountains.

C. 4

1 King Samsu-Ditana of Babylonia, 2 did witness the consuming darkness, 3 the withering of crops, 4 the looting of towns. 5 The King did take his scribes, 6 his artisans and masons, 7 his magi druid priests, 8 and did abandon his cities, 9 abandoning his temples, 10 a great exodus, 11 to the Valleys of the India, 12 to form the great Vedic Civilisation.

C. 5

1 In the Great Age of the Hound and Young Bull, 2 two thousand seven hundred and ninety six years, 3 since the dawn of the Great Age (1624 BCE), 4 King Shalik of the abandoned (H)Ibiru Empire of the levant, 5 did meet his cousin, 6 A-NUN, son of Emon, 7 first High Priest of Amen-Ra, 8 Priest-King of the (H)Ibiru (Hebrew), 9 of the most sacred Isle. 10 His name meaning, 11 son of the primordial gods of the heavens. 12 For since the great calamity, 13 and midst the war within Egypt, 14 A-NUN had risen in power. 15 Greatly superstitious were the people. 16 He did tell them, 17 the calamity was punishment, 18 from the Gods, 19 for not following Ra, 20 on orders sent by Nun.

C. 6

1 Upon their meeting, 2 A-NUN and Shalik did embrace. 3 A-NUN did proclaim: 4 Upon the mercy of our ancestors, 5 the great HORUS (E-SUS), 6 the mighty PE-TAH (PETER), 7 the blessed IM-HATAP, 8 united we be. 9 Upon this day I shall crown you, 10 Pharaoh over all Egypt. 11 Your name shall be AL-ATTIS, 12 which means the sole (only) Saviour of Humanity, 13 and the Good Shepherd. 14 And I shall be your priest. 15 Shalik then did kneel, 16 upon the white limestone rock, 17 the foundation stone of Ebla, 18 and A-NUN did anoint him, 19 AL-ATTIS.

C. 7

1 Thus the age of the Shepherd Kings, 2 the HYKSOS age was born. 3 For three hundred years, 4 they reigned supreme. 5 Such fables that do contest this truth, 6 born from malice, 7 and crafty hands, 8 of the Ramesses, 9 and later kings. 10 The pretenders and false Pharaohs, 11 who did loot the tombs of the ancient Pharaohs, 12 for their own ends, 13 and blamed the most ancient and sacred blood, 14 cursing the land. 15 Akhenaten was the last, 16 of the real Pharaoh. 17 Ahmose a mere boy. 18 The Thebians a careless ruse, 19 for they were always Hyksos. 20 To strengthen a Dynasty, 21 without noble blood.

C. 8

1 Within Twenty years, 2 the sons of the King, 3 and the sons of the High Priest, 4 had regained all that had been lost. 5 Science had returned to Egypt. 6 Crops and land tilled with skill, 7 an army undefeated.

C. 9

1 The mighty Hyksos Pharaoh KHAY-AN, 2 did prepare a throne, 3 the greatest of all lands, 4 inlaid with fine detail, 5 of Green marble and gold. 6 The Throne of Amen-Ra it be, 7 and only those of most ancient blood, 8 had right to be seated. 9 The High Priest did refine their craft, 10 HO-SHUA (Joshua), son of A-NUN, 11 to

protect the new Pharaoh, 12 and increase his power, 13 did fashion an Ark, 14 and such an Ark was named, 15 the Breath of Ra. 16 For within the Ark did reside, 17 the living spirit of the living God, 18 and no army could withstand its power. 19 At the head of the army did it travel, 20 for wherever the Ark of the Pharaoh Did go, 21 all enemies would be vanquished.

C. 10

1 And the priests of Amen-Ra, 2 did fashion for each Pharaoh, 3 a second standard, 4 on which a likeness, 5 of the most ancient Anubis (DogGod), 6 upon the ancient plain of Giza, 7 as the living protector of Egypt, 8 and servant of Amen-Ra. 9 And HO-SHUA (Joshua), son of A-NUN, 10 did replace the wooden staff, 11 of most ancient Holly, 12 and Druid, 13 with a Gold encrusted staff, 14 with a head in the shape of a two headed serpent, 15 in honour and power, 16 as the representative of, 17 the hidden serpent, 18 the great speckled serpent (Milky Way), 19 of the heavens.

C. 11

1 And the priests of Amen-Ra, 2 did fashion for each Pharaoh, 3 a third standard, 4 in the Deed (Djed), 5 as a living embodiment of illumination, 6 and the backbone of the divine, 7 and the tree of life, 8 being the eleven centres of priests, 9 of the east and life, 10 of the middle of the waters and intercessors, 11 of the west bank and the afterlife. 12 From the island of elephant, 13 also named Yei-Hu, 14 to the temple of Isis. 15 The Ka, 16 the vital spark of life. 17 The Ba, 18 the soul and unique Character. 19 The La, 20 the spirit of heart and virtue. 21 The Ah, 22 of ultimate wisdom and immortality.

C. 12

1 Such was their power, 2 their science and wisdom, 3 the Hyksos Kings were unchallenged, 4 trading with all the known powers, 5 the lands of Egypt unsurpassed. 6 An Empire when Egypt was at her greatest, 7 treaties with the rulers of Assyria, 8 with the Mitanni (northern Syria), 9 the Vedic lands (India), 10 to the Hittites and Babylonians.

C. 13

1 Under the Hyksos, 2 the Holly, the druids, 3 did regain their glory. 4 In all the great capitals, 5 of all the great civilisations, 6 they did build their own temples. 7 The first embassies, 8 and upon the floor of each embassy, 9 they did forge a mighty seal, 10 being the wheel of life (symbol of Heaven), 11 the symbol of the (H)Ibiru, 12 and the sacred Isle. 13 The druids did become, 14 the first ambassadors, 15 wearing astoundingly bright coloured cloaks, 16 with all the colours of the rainbow, 17 including the colours only reserved, 18 for Royalty and most sacred priests. 19 No other men and women, 20 did wear such colour, 21 not even kings, 22 not even high priests of Amen-Ra.

C. 14

1 In the Great Age of the Hound and Young Bull, 2 three thousand and nineteen years, 3 since the dawn of the Great Age (1401 BCE), 4 shepherd King of the Hyksos, 5 Pharaoh Amenhotep II, 6 did give up the ghost. 7 The Kingship did then fall to his son,

8 Pharaoh Thutmoses IV, 9 his name meaning, 10 Thut, Thoth, the god of truth. 11 Moses meaning son, 12 so Son of truth.

C. 15

1 As was custom then, 2 with druids as ambassadors, 3 they did rotate to a new court. 4 Upon the death of a king or Queen, 5 within one year of the Anointment, 6 of Pharaoh Thutmoses IV, 7 a great and mighty druid, 8 known as YO-YAH (Joseph), 9 which means lover of Yah (God), 10 did arrive to the court of Thutmoses IV. 11 His cloak and vestments, 12 of all the colours of the rainbow, 13 were particularly bright. 14 A man of tall stature, 15 and fine mind, 16 who had served the courts of many great kings. 17 At first the priests of Thebes were fearful, 18 but soon gained trust, 19 as YO-YAH (Joseph) did speak, 20 of many wisdoms, 21 and the stars of the heavens.

C. 16

1 In the court of Thutmoses IV, 2 YO-YAH (Joseph) did meet all the royal family. 3 One who was in awe, 4 of his robes of many colours, 5 and his stories of the world, 6 was the young crown prince Nibmu-areya. 7 He did follow YO-YAH (Joseph), 8 and ask him questions, 9 which YO-YAH (Joseph) did reply. 10 When Nibmu-areya the young prince was four, 11 his mother Mutemwiya did have YO-YAH appointed, 12 Chief Tutor to the prince. 13 A great and rare honour. 14 YO-YAH (Joseph) did meet with the crown prince, 15 many days, 16 and speak of all manner of things, 17 from the time of the ancients, 18 to the meaning of the heavens.

C. 17

1 Upon his visits to Thebes, 2 YO-YAH (Joseph) did come across, 3 a beautiful daughter of Amen-Ra, 4 named Tjuyu. 5 He did fall in love with her. 6 But as was custom of the druids, 7 as an ambassador, 8 he was forbidden to marry, 9 with a foreigner, 10 even of noble birth.

C. 18

1 In the Great Age of the Hound and Young Bull, 2 three thousand and eighty nine years, 3 since the dawn of the Great Age (1391 BCE), 4 shepherd King of the Hyksos, 5 Pharaoh Thutmoses IV, 6 did give up the ghost. 7 The Kingship did then fall to his son, 8 Nibmu-areya, 9 a child of only eight years, 10 when anointed Pharaoh Amenhotep III.

C. 19

1 As was custom YO-YAH (Joseph), 2 was to be recalled from service, 3 and leave Egypt forever. 4 But he called upon the High Priest of Amen-Ra, 5 and request permission, 6 to wed his daughter Tjuyu. 7 The High Priest did agree, 8 and ask to the most sacred druids, 9 that YO-YAH (Joseph) stay in court. 10 But the Druids of the most sacred Isle, 11 would not be moved. 12 So the priests of Amen-Ra did provide, 13 YO-YAH (Joseph) with sanctuary and an ample estate, 14 near the town of Akhmin, 15 where Tiye was born.

C. 20

1 Within eight years of his regency, 2 the mother of Amenhotep III, 3 named

Mutemwiya ceased as stewardess. 4 Amenhotep III then called for YO-YAH (Joseph), 5 to return to court. 6 The priests of Amen-Ra, 7 urged the Pharaoh to reconsider, 8 for the word of the druids, 9 of the most sacred isle, 10 since the beginning of time, 11 was stronger than stone, 12 and never broken. 13 But Amenhotep III Would not be moved, 14 he refused to acknowledge, 15 the current druid ambassador, 16 and ordered him sent away. 17 Again the priests did warn him, 18 for a druid curse was a mighty omen, 19 but Amenhotep III was even more determined. 20 He did then come up with a plan. 21 He announced his first Great Royal Wife, 22 to be Tiye, 23 the daughter of YO-YAH (Joseph). 24 The Pharaoh did greatly anger, 25 the priests of Amen-Ra. 26 For the first great wife, 27 during the days of the Hyksos, 28 was usually reserved for a princess, 29 of the royal line of priests of Thebes, 30 not to a foreigner, 31 even if of most ancient noble blood. 32 But Amenhotep III would not be moved, 33 so he did wed Tiye, 34 and YO-YAH (Joseph) returned to court a noble.

C. 21

1 Within three years, 2 of marriage to Tiye, 3 Amenhotep III was blessed, 4 with a son, 5 which he named, 6 crown prince Thutmoses, 7 the Son of Truth. 8 Within a further year, 9 Amenhotep III was blessed, 10 with a second son, 11 which he named Naphu-rureya (Akhenaten). 12 As had he been raised, 13 Amenhotep III Called upon YO-YAH (Joseph), 14 to be Chief Tutor to the two royal princes, 15 a mighty and rare honour.

C. 22

1 Within the 30th year of the reign (1361 BCE), 2 of Amenhotep III, 3 after the mountains of the north, 4 did erupt, 5 in the lands of Ice (Iceland), 6 the rain did not come of Egypt, 7 the sun did not shine as bright, 8 the crops did wither and die. 9 Throughout the empire, 10 people grew weak and hungry. 11 The towns became restless and angry. 12 The Pharaoh did call his chief viziers, 13 the chiefs of the treasury, 14 the chiefs of the stores and water, 15 all of whom called it a sign, 16 of the displeasure of the gods. 17 They could offer no solution, 18 except to pray to the gods. 19 The Pharaoh did send for the chief priests, 20 of the Temple of Thebes, 21 of the Temples of Memphis, 22 and most ancient Heliopolis, 23 all of whom called it a sign, 24 of the displeasure of the gods. 25 The Pharaoh dismissed them all, 26 he then sent for his old tutor, 27 his second father, YO-YAH (Joseph). 28 YO-YAH told him, 29 that it be but a season of the heavens, 30 that no god did cause such action, 31 but one god, the lord of all gods- Aten. 32 To feed the hungry, 33 and save the empire, 34 the Pharaoh must re-organise the treasury, 35 and the grains, 36 ridding them of ancient superstitions, 37 that stops work, 38 and devote better effort, 39 to the use of water and channels, 40 to expand good land, not reduce it. 41 The Viziers of the Treasury and the Grainery, 42 upon hearing these words, 43 cursed such blasphemy against the gods, 44 who guided every decision, 45 and every act of every day, 46 to expand land in time of famine, 47 they called utter madness.

C. 23

1 But Pharaoh trusted YO-YAH, 2 more than any of them. 3 In his court he declared: 4 I appoint you (YO-YAH) my one and only official, 5 to you I bestow the greatest of titles, 6 you shall hold the ring of Upper Egypt, 7 you shall manage the grainery, 8 you shall be my Treasurer, 9 you shall be my highest vizier. 10 And upon these words, 11 YO-YAH did set about ridding, 12 the minor gods that ruled, 13 every decision of every day. 14 He did change the waters, 15 and increase fertile land, 16 and Egypt was abundant with food, 17 while the rest of the world was in famine. 18 Such was the greatness of his work, 19 that great numbers of refugees, 20 from all parts of the world, 21 did flood into Egypt, 22 and YO-YAH did set about tasking them, 23 with great public works.

C. 24

1 Day and night, 2 YO-YAH did toil, 3 without rest, 4 for his adopted land. 5 Confidant of the King. 6 Day and night, 7 YO-YAH did plan and direct, 8 without rest. 9 The Wise One, 10 the Pharaoh, 11 did praise him, 12 and reward him great title, 13 and YO-YAH did apply himself, 14 even harder, 15 so that every field was named, 16 every road measured, 17 every store accounted, 18 every person fed.

C. 25

1 In the Great Age of the Hound and Young Bull, 2 three thousand one hundred and twenty four years, 3 since the dawn of the Great Age (1356 BCE), 4 YO-YAH (Joseph) did suddenly give up the ghost. 5 A great mourning befell all of Egypt, 6 and all the Empire. 7 Even neighbouring Empires, 8 did send princes and Kings to mourn. 9 The death of YO-YAH (Joseph), 10 for the kingdom saved. 11 Amenhotep III had lost his father, 12 his teacher, 13 his friend. 14 His sons did leave the royal court, 15 Thutmoses to Memphis, 16 Akhenaten to Thebes. 17 Amenhotep III shut his court. 18 He refused visits. 19 His kingdom saved, 20 he became recluse. 21 No doctor did he see, 22 though Sickness wracked his body, 23 and within 3 cycles of the sun, 24 of the death of YO-YAH, 25 the Pharaoh gave up the ghost.

Book 11

Age of Akhenaten

[1353 - 1323 BCE]

C. 1

1 In the Great Age of the Hound and Young Bull, 2 three thousand one hundred and twenty seven years, 3 since the dawn of the Great Age (1353 BCE), 4 upon the death of Pharaoh Amenhotep III, 5 the High Priest AY(E) of Amen-Ra did come to Memphis, 6 to collect Thutmoses to prepare him, 7 and anoint him new pharaoh. 8 Since the death of his grandfather, 9 Thutmoses had dedicated himself, 10 to being a great priest, 11 to study and learn, 12 the ancient stories of the druids, 13 to learn and understand, 14 the wisdom of the ancients, 15 and the wisdom of YO-YAH, 16 in the nature of the Aten (universal God). 17 In the great hall of Memphis, 18 the High Priest AY(E) called upon Thutmoses, 19 to leave the priests, 20 and his study, 21 and take up his role as Pharaoh, 22 to oversee the funerary procession, 23 of His father, 24 as new pharaoh, 25 according to custom.

C. 2

1 But Thutmoses would not be moved. 2 In the presence of his mother Queen Tiye, 3 he did present to the High Priest, 4 the former coloured robe of YO-YAH, 5 for which he was refused to wear, 6 on account of his excommunication, 7 by the druids. 8 He did proclaim: 9 I have no rest in my loins, 10 so long as a great hero of Egypt, 11 may not rest. 12 High Priest AY(E) did tell him, 13 that as Pharaoh, 14 he would be ruler over a great empire, 15 stretching far east to Asia, 16 far west of all of Africa, 17 north and the whole of the inland sea and islands, 18 a god to his people, 19 that he could build great temples, 20 in honour of YO-YAH. 21 Thutmoses did reply, 22 that his father had fought long and hard, 23 to clear the name of YO-YAH, 24 but the most ancient druids had refused, 25 even upon the edicts of a Pharaoh. 26 There is but one thing, 27 the stubborn ancient druids (holly), 28 revere more than power, 29 is knowledge, 30 and knowledge flowing within the blood. 31 He did then proclaim his abdication, 32 as crown prince, 33 that he would travel, 34 to the most sacred Isle of (H)Ibiru, 35 of his ancestors, 36 carrying with him the greatest scrolls, 37 of Science and mathematics and culture, 38 and himself as a vessel of priestly and royal blood. 39 Upon his sons declaration, 40

Queen Tiya did speak: 41 My sons heart is true, 42 I shall accompany him to the island, 43 of my father, 44 to implore the druids, 45 for the mercy of the soul, 46 of my father, 47 as a Queen.

C. 3

1 Yet soon after, 2 Queen Tiye did give up the ghost 3 so Thutmoses with the heart of his mother, 4 did travel to the sacred Isle, 5 carrying the greatest scrolls of mathematic, 6 of wisdom and culture to the druids, 7 with the robes of YO-YAH, 8 for his redemption, 9 in the eyes, 10 of stubborn druids. 11 There upon the most sacred of all isles, 12 Thutmoses did remain, 13 and Thutmoses did marry into the Holly, 14 and the wisdom of scrolls he carried, 15 did impress the druids. 16 Yet it was his blood they most revered. 17 Now folded into the oldest, 18 and most sacred of priests and messengers, 19 the priests and kings from the beginning of time. 20 For the name YOYAH as YOSEF (Joseph), 21 became a most revered name, 22 reserved only for the greatest druids.

C. 4

1 With the rejection by Thutmoses, 2 AY(E) the High Priest, 3 did return to Thebes, 4 where Naphu-rureya (Akhenaten) was studying. 5 Upon his arrival AY(E), 6 did tell Naphu-rureya, 7 that upon the abdication of his brother, 8 in the presence of a noble and priestly court, 9 Naphu-rureya (Akhenaten) would now be Pharaoh.

C. 5

1 In the Great Age of the Hound and Young Bull, 2 three thousand one hundred and sixty seven years, 3 since the dawn of the Great Age (1353 BCE), 4 Naphu-rureya at age of 25, 5 was anointed Pharaoh Amenhotep IV, 6 which means Amen is satisfied. 7 At the suggestion of the priests, 8 that had tutored him, 9 and the place that had been his home, 10 for some years, 11 Amenhotep was first to make Thebes, 12 his new Royal Capital. 13 A strange and melancholy King, 14 was Pharaoh Amenhotep IV. 15 No wife by his side, 16 he did immerse himself in writing, 17 in wisdom, law and poems.

C. 6

1 AY(E) the High Priest of Amen-Ra, 2 did arrange for him a wife, 3 called Kiya, 4 the daughter of a Thebian Priest, 5 and daughter of Amen-Ra, 6 as was custom. 7 But after one year no heir was conceived, 8 to an older King. 9 As Pharaoh Amenhotep IV, 10 had not consummated their marriage, 11 fearing the end of an age, 12 two royal lines, 13 one of King-Pharaohs, 14 the other of King-Priests, 15 the priests of Amen, 16 debated and prayed a solution. 17 Some considered appointing, 18 the High Priest as Pharaoh, 19 for their blood did contain the same, 20 noble and sacred path. 21 But older and wiser priests, 22 considered such action may cause, 23 rebellion and an end to all the Hyksos blood. 24 Others considered appointing a puppet, 25 or a strong warrior, 26 capable of defending the empire, 27 but loyal to the priests. 28 Then AY(E) struck upon an idea, 29 they would search the known world, 30 to find the most beautiful princess, 31 in all the lands. 32 Strong and faithful, 33 she would give the Pharaoh, 34

strong heirs, 35 and the melancholy of the line, 36 would be overcome.

C. 7

1 The priests did come across but one princess, 2 her name was Tadukhipa (Tadu-Hepa), 3 the daughter of Tushratta, 4 the king of Mitanni. 5 It was said that so beautiful she be, 6 that men were spelled, 7 and would willingly die, 8 just for the chance to gaze upon her beauty once. 9 So strong in combat she be, 10 that she would easily dispatch the best warrior. 11 So wise she be, 12 she was known to correct the priests of Mitanni. 13 The High Priests did make an agreement, 14 with King Tushratta, 15 and brought Tadukhipa, 16 to the court of Amenhotep, 17 at Thebes, 18 where the Pharaoh spent his days, 19 writing wisdom and poems. 20 Upon gazing the most beautiful woman, 21 the world had ever seen, 22 her strength and wisdom, 23 the Pharaoh declared: 24 Upon the Universal God, 25 above all others, 26 I am blessed. 27 For here is my Queen, 28 my companion for life. 29 Within short time, 30 they were married, 31 and Tadukhipa, 32 was given the royal name, 33 Nefertiti.

C. 8

1 Within one year of marriage, 2 the first daughter of Amenhotep IV, 3 and Nefertiti was born. 4 Her name was Meritaten. 5 Within two years and by Year 3, 6 of the reign of Amenhotep IV, 7 his second daughter was born, 8 her name was Meketaten. 9 The Pharaoh was entranced, 10 by his Queen, 11 he did lavish upon her all manner, 12 of praise and reward. 13 She in turn did learn, 14 of his Knowledge and teachings, 15 and revelations, 16 since the time of YO-YAH (Joseph).

C. 9

1 At first, the High Priests of Amen-Ra, 2 were joyous upon their plan. 3 The Pharaoh no longer a lonesome poet, 4 but a strong Pharaoh, 5 supported by a beautiful Queen. 6 Yet as time continued, 7 no male heir did she bring. 8 AY(E) grew more insistent, 9 and scheming upon Nefertiti, 10 demanding she tell them of his intentions. 11 At the beginning of year 4, 12 the Queen did declare to Amenhotep: 13 My king my husband, 14 are you not lord of all the world? 15 He did agree. 16 Nefertiti did reply: 17 My Lord my teacher, 18 why do you permit the usurpation, 19 of the lesser gods, 20 and priests upon your reign? 21 The Pharaoh replied: 22 For time and tradition honoured. 23 The crafty and beautiful Queen, 24 did reply: 25 Which then is greater? 26 The Universal God of Aten, 27 or the superstitions of men? 28 The Pharaoh answered Aten. 29 The Queen then did divulge, 30 the scheming of the priests of Amen-Ra, 31 upon which the Pharaoh, 32 enraged did forbid, 33 the priests from his court. 34 Within three cycles of the Moon, 35 he did declare a new Capital shall be made, 36 not Thebes, 37 but upon fresh ground, 38 free of ancient superstitions, 39 he named this place Akhetaten (Armana). 40 Which means "horizon of Aten (God)". 41 With support of his Queen, 42 Amenhotep IV did commence, 43 the building of a great new capital.

C. 10

1 By the fifth year of the reign of Amenhotep IV, 2 Queen Nefertiti did give birth, 3 to their third daughter, 4 called Ankhesenpaaten. 5 The Pharaoh overjoyed with his new capital, 6 did declare to his court: 7 On this day I speak the truth, 8 there is no god but one God, 9 and I am but his humble servant, 10 Aten is both mother and father, 11 Ra in spirit, 12 and Horus the saviour, 13 are but aspects of the same supreme God. 14 The trinity is but one, 15 all other gods are mere plaster and dust, 16 to their greatness. 17 The court of Amenhotep, 18 were aghast at these words, 19 for since the earliest of days, 20 the greatest of the gods, 21 was the moon, 22 and all gods of nature were respected. 23 The Pharaoh did then declare: 24 Henceforth this day, 25 I declare myself Akhenaten, 26 which means servant of Aten, 27 servant of the one Divine Creator.

C. 11

1 By year six of the reign of Akhenaten (1347 BCE), 2 Queen Nefertiti, 3 did give birth to their fourth daughter, 4 named Neferneferuaten Tasherit, 5 while his new capital was still being built. 6 In this year, 7 the Pharaoh did take his court to Armana, 8 to oversee its completion.

C. 12

1 By year nine of the reign of Akhenaten (1344 BCE), 2 Queen Nefertiti, 3 did give birth to their fifth daughter, 4 named Neferneferure. 5 In the same year, the new Capital Akhetaten (Armana), 6 was completed. 7 It was a year of great plenty, 8 with rain and good harvest. 9 To celebrate his capital, 10 and the birth of his daughter, 11 Akhenaten did declare a holiday to Aten, 12 and new laws of Aten, 13 that all minor gods be banished, 14 and the temples closed. 15 This greatly disturbed the people, 16 for they believed their gods protected them. 17 So it was in the next year (1343 BCE), 18 the first of ten great plagues, 19 did befall upon Egypt, 20 the rain did stop. 21 The wind did stop. 22 The days were hot and dry. 23 The water of the Nile, 24 and great lakes did turn red with Algea, 25 that made the people sick. 26 Many saw this as a bad omen from the Gods.

C. 13

1 By year eleven of the reign of Akhenaten (1342 BCE), 2 Queen Nefertiti Did give birth, 3 to their sixth and final daughter, 4 named Setepenre. 5 In the same year, 6 the priests of Amen and AY(E) did conspire, 7 upon the omens. 8 They called Kiya. 9 Dear Queen, 10 the Great Wife has taken age, 11 now is the time for duty, 12 to give Egypt an heir. 13 The Priests did make Kiya, 14 into the likeness perfect of Nefertiti. 15 They did give her a drug, 16 to place in his meal. 17 The priests then did call for Nefertiti, 18 who left the court to attend. 19 That night in the Pharaoh's bed chamber, 20 Kiya dressed as Nefertiti did enter, 21 with the potion. 22 She did intoxicate the Pharaoh, 23 and their marriage was finally consummated, 24 however upon awakening, 25 the Pharaoh did discover the trickery, 26 and he banished Kiya from his court, 27 back to Thebes. 28 Within the year, however, 29 Kiya did give birth to a

boy, 30 his name was Tutankahmun. 31 Fearing the powerful Queen Nefertiti, 32 the Priests did keep the crown prince, 33 hidden from view. 34 Queen Nefertiti enraged another did take her form, 35 ordered by her husband's seal, 36 for all mention of Kiya, 37 to be struck out across the Empire, 38 replaced by the likeness of her daughters.

C. 14

1 By the beginning of Year twelve, 2 of the reign of Akhenaten (1341 BCE), 3 the rains returned, 4 now with flood and heat. 5 Everything was damp, 6 crops were spoiled, stores rotted. 7 All manner of pest, 8 did ravage the land. 9 From frogs and mosquitoes, 10 to abundant numbers of rats, 11 the second of the great plagues.

C. 15

1 By year twelve, 2 of the reign of Akhenaten (1340 BCE), 3 the warmth and wetness did continue, 4 now Egypt was afflicted, 5 with the rise of lice, 6 that affected livestock and people, 7 people scratched at their clothes, 8 till their skin was red, 9 cursing the blasphemy, 10 against the minor gods.

C. 16

1 By year thirteen, 2 of the reign of Akhenaten (1339 BCE), 3 the rain eased, 4 and all the land and deserts were green, 5 but then Egypt was afflicted, 6 with the rise of locusts, 7 and the sickness of animals.

C. 17

1 By year fourteen, 2 of the reign of Akhenaten (1338 BCE), 3 the weather greatly cooled, 4 and the rains returned, 5 it was then that the great black sickness first appeared. 6 Great horrible boils and blood, 7 people began to die in great numbers. 8 The black sickness even travelled to Armana, 9 where three of the daughters of Pharaoh, 10 got sick and died. 11 The Pharaoh Akhenaten was in deep melancholy, 12 for he believed his destiny favoured Aten (God). 13 Now these ten plagues had ravaged the land, 14 cursing his people.

C. 18

1 By year fifteen, 2 of the reign of Akhenaten (1337 BCE), 3 Egypt was in turmoil. 4 It was then that Akhenaten had a vision, 5 he would take the sick people, 6 out of the cities and towns, 7 and restore the favour of Aten, 8 and the people. 9 First, not to cause riot, 10 he ordered his troops, 11 under the command of Paatenemheb (Horemheb), 12 to check every city and town, 13 for households with the plague, 14 then to mark their doors with a sign. 15 Second, upon a single night, 16 he ordered all the sick and diseased, 17 to be rounded up, 18 and to be taken out into the desert, 19 with Pharaoh and his personal guard, 20 commanded by Paatenemheb (Horemheb), 21 at the head. 22 For one year, 23 Pharaoh and the dead and diseased, 24 did walk through the Sinai. 25 For one year, 26 and still many did not die from the plague, 27 yet Pharaoh himself did get sick, 28 with his face contorted from the disease, 29 he took to wearing a veil, 30 to cover his face. 31 Upon the end of the year (1336 BCE), 32 Akhenaten did take the survivors, 33 to the distant military outpost of Jerusalem.

C. 19

1 By year sixteen of the reign of Akhenaten (1336 BCE), 2 Queen Nefertiti did leave Egypt, 3 and travel to Jerusalem, 4 to see her husband and King. 5 But as she entered the court, 6 the Pharaoh wearing a veil, 7 did command her not to step closer, 8 for fear of his face. 9 There amongst the assembled, 10 Akhenaten himself did declare, 11 Nefertiti as Pharaoh, 12 and named her Neferneferuaten (Smenkhkare). 13 Akhenaten did then implore her to return, 14 and rule the Empire, 15 while he would live out his days, 16 as High Priest of Aten (God). 17 In the Temple he did make in Jerusalem, 18 upon the ancient marble throne, 19 of Hyksos Pharaohs now in Jerusalem, 20 the most sacred white (limestone) rock of Ebla, 21 as his rest, 22 his serpent sceptre as his staff, 23 his (Pharaoh's) Ark now the sacred Ark, 24 of a new covenant, 25 he did commission it to be encased with gold, 26 with Seraphim placed on its corners.

C. 20

1 Pharaoh Neferneferuaten (Neferetiti) left Jerusalem, 2 with Paatenemheb (Horemheb), 3 as her Commander of the Army, 4 and returned to Armana, 5 where she did reign for two years. 6 Upon her second year, 7 she did discover the existence, 8 of Crown Prince Tutankhamun, 9 at which time she ordered his capture, 10 and the murder of Kiya. 11 Kiya was killed, 12 but Tutankhamun was spared, 13 a mere boy of eight. 14 Upon hearing the treachery, 15 of Neferneferuaten (Neferetiti), 16 the High Priests of Amen-Ra, 17 did call Paatenemheb (Horemheb), 18 whereupon AY(E) did promise, 19 that upon the dispatch, 20 of the Queen Pharaoh, 21 he would rule a great dynasty. 22 Paatenemheb (Horemheb) did organise, 23 a secret rebellion upon the Queen, 24 causing all to leave Armana, 25 abandoned by her court, 26 without power or authority, 27 Neferneferuaten (Neferetiti), 28 left again to find her husband. 29 But High Priest AY(E), 30 did have support amongst her guard, 31 and upon a lonely stretch, 32 far from sight, 33 the Great Queen met her end, 34 at the sword of Pa-ra-mes-su (Ramesses), 35 a trusted captain of Paatenemheb (Horemheb), 36 who defiled the body, 37 of the most beautiful of all women. 38 That even though he did return her body for burial, 39 as a Queen and Pharaoh, 40 the wickedness of Pa-ra-mes-su (Ramesses) cursed himself, 41 and all his descendants and heirs, 42 as cowards and necromancers without spirit, 43 empty vessels without authority, 44 and living ghosts wracked by lunacy.

C. 21

1 In the Great Age of the Hound and Young Bull, 2 three thousand and eighty seven years, 3 since the dawn of the Great Age (1333 BCE), 4 upon the death of the powerful Queen, 5 and Pharaoh Neferneferuaten (Neferetiti), 6 AY(E) did anoint the son of Kiya and Akhenaten, 7 the new Pharaoh Tutankhamun, 8 Shepherd King of the Hyksos. 9 The boy who had never met his father, 10 nor his father known of him. 11 Upon the anointing of the new Pharaoh, 12 Akhenaten Did receive word, 13 of the trickery of Kiya and

AY(E), 14 the death of Kiya, 15 and the death of his beloved Queen, 16 Akhenaten grew even more melancholy, 17 and kept himself hidden in Jerusalem, 18 contemplating his own end.

C. 22

1 The boy Pharaoh Tutankhamun, 2 did rule as the puppet of AY(E), 3 the prisoner of Paatenemheb (Horemheb). 4 A court of fear. 5 During the same time, 6 Akhenaten did emerge from the cave of the rock, 7 and pronounced he would cease to use, 8 his royal name of Akhenaten. 9 Henceforth, to be known as Aharon-Moses, 10 which means Son of conception, 11 of a new covenant, 12 also known as Zadok, 13 which means righteous. 14 His fame now did spread, 15 no longer as the deposed Pharaoh, 16 no longer as a god-king, 17 but as an anointed Messiah and Christ, 18 and true prophet of the Divine Creator.

C. 23

1 At this small military outpost, 2 called Jerusalem, 3 of no significance until this moment, 4 Moses (Akhenaten) proclaimed the true name, 5 of the Divine Creator to be Yahu, 6 not as the sun like Aten, 7 nor as the earth like Mat, 8 nor as the soil like Kum, 9 or even the waters like Nun, 10 but as a Holy Spirit between all things, 11 and in all things, 12 and beyond all things. 13 Thus Yahu be the spirit of all existence. 14 Without being bound by existence, 15 except in mind. 16 The God of all gods. 17 The one and only true Divine Creator.

C. 24

1 In the Great Age of the Hound and Young Bull, 2 three thousand and ninety six years, 3 since the dawn of the Great Age (1324 BCE), 4 when Aharon-Moses (Akhenaten) was fifty-six, 5 Pa-ra-mes-su (Ramesses), 6 the trusted captain of Horemheb, 7 did arrange for the death of Pharaoh Tutankhamun, 8 by way of accident. 9 Upon the news of the murder of his son, 10 Moses (Akhenaten) was enraged, 11 and gathered forth an army to march on Egypt. 12 Horemheb then did stake his claim to AY(E), 13 who warned him a non-HYKSOS as Pharaoh, 14 would result in civil war, 15 whereupon AY(E) the old priest, 16 appointed himself Pharaoh. 17 To claim himself rightful heir to the throne, 18 Horemheb cursed the forces of Moses, 19 as the Infants, 20 meaning the ones who worship chaos and evil (Infant), 21 and the ones who are wicked and unclean. 22 Never were they called the Israelites, 23 for there be no word in Egyptian, 24 nor there be no true term in history. 25 The forces of Moses (Akhenaten) on water, 26 were invincible as the priests of the navy, 27 known as the Sons of Zion, 28 remained loyal to the Hyksos. 29 Yet Horemheb commanded the loyalty of the army. 30 Thus as the forces of Moses advanced to cross the Red Sea, 31 they were routed by the forces of Horemheb, 32 and forced to flee north, 33 avoiding the stronghold of Kadesh, 34 unto the lands of the last Amorite Kingdom, 35 of King Ammurapi III of Ugarit, 36 who called his kingdom the Pharasi, 37 which in Amurru meant, 38 the ancient and spiritual leaders (Par), 39 of heaven and spirit world (Asi). 40

The Amurru (Amorites), 41 the wicked and once all powerful priests, 42 of Amurru and before then of Mari, 43 and before of Mari, then of Ur. 44 The worshippers of the Ub (Pentagram), 45 the worshippers of power, 46 also known as the Phoenicians. 47 For the forces of King Ammurapi III, 48 were no match for Moses (Akhenaten), 49 and the Yahudi did then take up residence, 50 while also controlling Kepra (Cyprus) and Kefti (Crete).

C. 25

1 In the Great Age of the Hound and Young Bull, 2 three thousand one hundred years, 3 since the dawn of the Great Age (1320 BCE), 4 when Moses (Akhenaten) was himself sixty, 5 Pharaoh AY(E) gave up the ghost, 6 and Horemheb, 7 the treacherous general, 8 of three Pharaohs, 9 did assume the throne. 10 The dynasty of Shepherd-Kings, 11 was at an end. 12 Gravely ill, 13 Moses (Akhenaten), 14 did instruct his loyal court, 15 and his remaining daughters, 16 fearing the hand of Horemheb, 17 and the loyal General Pa-ra-mes-su (Ramesses), 18 Moses did command, 19 that the most ancient sacred throne, 20 of Hyksos Kings, 21 the Stone of Destiny, 22 the Foundation Stone of Ebla, 23 the Sword of Heaven, 24 and his most sacred Ark, 25 to be taken to the most sacred Isle, 26 of the (H)Ibiru, 27 to present to the ancient Druids, 28 that the Hyksos are no more, 29 whereupon Akhenaten, 30 known as Aaron, 31 known as Moses, 32 known as Zadok, 33 did give up the ghost.

Book 12

Age of the False Pharaohs

[1323 - 1245 BCE]

C. 1

In the Great Age of the Hound and Young Bull, 2 three thousand one hundred and ninety seven years, 3 since the dawn of the Great Age (1323 BCE), 4 was the year in which Moses (Akhenaten) did expel, 5 the Pharasi (Phoenician) and King Ammurapi III, 6 from their city of Ugarit. 7 Powerful mercenaries, 8 traders and pirates, 9 had the (H)Apiru (Pharasi) become, 10 that few travelled the Inland sea, 11 without first paying a Parasite, 12 for safe passage.

C. 2

1 Upon their expulsion by Akhenaten, 2 King Ammurapi III and his Queen Tharyelli, 3 sought safe harbour, 4 in the sea city of Tyre. 5 But the people of Tyre, 6 fearing the Egyptians, 7 did not grant them safe passage. 8 So the King and his Queen, 9 were again cast adrift. 10 Next they travelled to Kefu (Cyprus), 11 but were defeated by the sons of Zion, 12 so the Pharasi travelled to Kepra (Crete), 13 and again were fought off, 14 as the island was heavily protected, 15 and had changed its name to Ionia. 16 Such wandering did take its toll, 17 upon the exiled King. 18 They travelled further West, 19 upon the Inland Sea, 20 to the Isle of Sardinia. 21 Again they were denied haven, 22 whereupon the King gave up the ghost. 23 Grieving the Queen did pitch her boats, 24 upon the shore of Africa, 25 in the narrowest passage, 26 of the Inland sea. 27 She did cremate the remains of the King, 28 and seven small children (burnt alive) as kindling. 29 There the Queen did declare: 30 By the Kings of our ancestors, 31 by my dead husband, 32 we shall have our revenge, 33 none shall pass East or West, 34 upon this sea, 35 without being held to account. 36 There she founded the city, 37 of Qart-hadašt (Carthage), 38 and the Queen became known with Kybele (Cybele), 39 and with Athena to the Greeks, 40 the great warrior Queen. 41 The great mother to all Parasites, 42 the one to whom first born were to be sacrificed.

C. 3

1 In the Great Age of the Hound and Young Bull, 2 three thousand one hundred years, 3 since the dawn of the Great Age (1320 BCE), 4 when Akhenaten (Aharon-Moses) did give up the ghost, 5 the priests at Urgarit

did elect Aaron the ArkAlba, 6 as their new king, 7 and the legitimate Pharaoh, 8 as the remains of the great Pharaoh, 9 the great messiah prophet of Yahu, 10 were taken for burial to the necropolis of kings. 11 Once Horemheb, the treacherous general, 12 took the Pharaoh's throne, 13 Queen Tharyelli did call upon him, 14 to help return their city and lands, 15 but Horemheb for all his deeds, 16 was a superstitious man, 17 and upon the lack of an heir, 18 he did not seek to tempt the spirits, 19 of murdered Queens, 20 and deposed kings, 21 by his hand. 22 So Queen Tharyelli did conquer Sardinia, 23 executing all the royalty, 24 that denied her hospitality. 25 The warrior Queen did conquer, 26 the south of Spain, 27 making strong forts, 28 but gave up the ghost, 29 before seeing her own lands returned. 30 Soon after, 31 Pharaoh Horemheb, 32 did also give up the ghost, 33 without child, 34 and without heir.

C. 4

1 In the Great Age of the Hound and Young Bull, 2 three thousand one hundred and twenty eight years, 3 since the dawn of the Great Age (1292 BCE), 4 general Pa-ra-mes-su, 5 became Pharaoh Ramesses. 6 His first act, 7 was to order his son Seti, 8 as crown prince, 9 to take the army into the Levant and Syria, 10 and crush the religion of Akhenaten, 11 and erase their memory, 12 the cursed name called Infants, 13 the people of Ugarit, 14 now known as the Yahudi, 15 to seize the treasures of the Hyksos, 16 that he might claim legitimacy, 17 upon the white stone of destiny. 18 Yet the ancient Hyksos priests of Amen-Ra, 19 did reject the claim of Pa-ra-mes-su, 20 that he be Pharaoh. 21 So Pa-ra-mes-su as Ramesses, 22 broke the most sacred covenant of heaven, 23 Ramses slaughtered the Hyksos priests of Thebes, 24 then destroyed the ancient pantheon of gods. 25 Instead of Osiris, Ramses created Ptah, 26 also spoken as Peter, the false god. 27 Instead of Isis, Ramses created Sekhmet, 28 Ramses replaced Horus with Thoth, 29 and even replaced Amen with Hathor. 30 Ramses then did appoint his own priests, 31 who like their master, 32 knew nothing of the Divine, 33 nor heaven or honour.

C. 5

1 The son of Queen Tharyelli, 2 whose name was King Milk-Qart, 3 whose name is also known as Moloch, 4 sought and was granted an audience, 5 with the Pharaoh Ramses. 6 On account that the fleet of the Hyksos, 7 the sons of Zion, 8 remained loyal to heaven. 9 King Moloch did pledge the Pharaoh his master fleet, 10 to share the spoils, 11 of all cargo seized upon the Inland sea, 12 in exchange for granting them back their ancient land. 13 The false Pharaoh Ramses did agree, 14 to grant the (H)Apriu (Pharasi), 15 the city of Tyre, 16 as replacement for Ugarit, 17 but as for Ugarit, 18 the false Pharaoh stood firm. 19 For he wished it to be wiped from the earth. 20 To be forgotten like the Yahudi.

C. 6

1 In the Great Age of the Hound and Young Bull, 2 three thousand one hundred and thirty years, 3 since the dawn of the Great Age (1290 BCE), 4

Crown Prince Seti and twenty thousand soldiers, 5 did descend upon Ugarit, 6 destroying the city and capturing King Aaron, 7 and scattering the inhabitants. 8 The most senior Yahudi priests and prophets fled west, 9 unto the land and many islands of the Dorians, 10 where they founded a new city along the Pontus (Pineois), 11 through the Vale of Temple called Elios (Larissa), 12 as others travelled further west into the inland sea. 13 Yet, nowhere in the city of Urgarit, 14 did Seti or King Moloch find the treasure of Akhenaten, 15 nor the stone of destiny, 16 nor the sword of heaven, 17 nor the marble throne. 18 Enraged, Seti did slaughter the children of Aaron, 19 until the king told him of the secret journey, 20 to the sacred Isle of (H)Iberu, 21 Seti did then order Urgarit destroyed, 22 to its foundations, 23 that no memory of Moses remain. 24 He did then take the remaining priests, 25 and their families back to Egypt, 26 and King Aaron as captives, 27 in the hope that such tribute, 28 would satisfy the quest of his father.

C. 7

1 Upon his return to Egypt, 2 Seti did arrange a great tribute march, 3 attended by Ramses his father. 4 All the inhabitants of Memphis came to watch, 5 as the most senior of priests of the Hyksos, 6 and their families now as slaves, 7 the Yahudi, cursed as the Infants, 8 were paraded through the streets in chains. 9 At the end of the tribute march, 10 Seti presented the deposed king Aaron, 11 to the false Pharaoh Ramses. 12 Ramses did inquire as to the treasures, 13 which he expected to see, 14 to which Seti replied that the treasures, 15 had been returned to the Holly. 16 Enraged and in despair, 17 Ramses yelled out: 18 Verily, I have murdered Queens, 19 I have butchered kings for the throne, 20 I have cursed heaven and the divine, 21 I have defiled the gods, 22 and all for naught. 23 Let then my successors, 24 and my descendants be my retribution, 25 for I issue a high curse, 26 upon the Hyksos and their descendants, 27 and upon heaven itself. 28 Let them be wiped from history, 29 let their memory be destroyed, 30 for my hatred of their divine commission. 31 Whereupon, Ramses himself thrust a sword, 32 into the heart of Aaron, 33 and in such haste and rage, 34 caused his own heart to burst, 35 whereupon he then gave up the ghost.

C. 8

1 In the Great Age of the Hound and Young Bull, 2 three thousand one hundred and thirty three years, 3 since the dawn of the Great Age (1287 BCE), 4 King Moloch (Milk-Qart), 5 also known as MIL of the Pharasi (Phrygians), 6 did land at Inver Sceni, 7 in Bantry Bay, 8 upon the sacred Isle and did seek, 9 to take control. 10 But the descendants of Tuth-Moses, 11 the brother of Akhenaten, 12 now folded within the blood of the Cuilleain, 13 the Holly ones as kings, 14 had foretold this day might come. 15 They had built a new fort inland, 16 from Eblana (New Ebla), 17 as their capital, 18 and had made the road, 19 difficult from the north. 20 The forces of MIL, 21 were trapped in the North, 22 and could not break out. 23 King Moloch

(Milqart) escaped to Spain, 24 and then to Carthage, 25 where he called upon Seti, 26 to send more ships.

C. 9

1 The exiled fleet, 2 of the Yahudi of Ugarit, 3 the great priests of the sea, 4 known as the Sons of Zion, 5 had word of the plan of Seti. 6 From their haven, 7 in the Southern cities, 8 of Elios (Larissa) in the islands of the Dorians and Crete, 9 they did follow the second fleet, 10 as it made its way to invade, 11 the most sacred Isle. 12 In the Sea between the sacred Isle and Britanni, 13 the Egyptian and Pharasi (Phoenician) fleet was trapped, 14 between the ships of the sacred Isle, 15 and the sons of Zion that followed them. 16 Some of the Phoenicians escaped, 17 and joined their colleagues in the North. 18 Others of the Egyptians escaped south, 19 to land on Britanni, 20 while much of the fleet was sunk. 21 Of the Egyptian and Pharasi (Phoenician) fleet that did land, 22 in the south of Brittani, 23 they established a city, 24 upon the river Lee.

C. 10

1 In the Great Age of the Hound and Young Bull, 2 three thousand two hundred and forty one years, 3 since the dawn of the Great Age (1279 BCE), 4 Seti did give up the ghost, 5 a broken and hollow man. 6 It was then his son Ramesses II, 7 also known as Ramses the Great, 8 became the next pretender to the throne. 9 Thus the word went out, 10 that Ramses did seal a solemn high curse, 11 against heaven and all gods, 12 as has his father had done, 13 and as his grandfather had done. 14 No line of kings had come before, 15 with such hatred of the divine, 16 or such insanity. 17 His contempt for all things sacred, 18 knew no bounds, 19 that he would gladly bathe in the blood, 20 of slain Hyksos children, 21 until the ancient treasures of the Hyksos 22 finally be surrendered unto his grasp.

C. 11

1 Upon word of an impending invasion, 2 the High Priest of the Druids, 3 whose name was ESA-MU (Esau), 4 did call a council, 5 as to how to save, 6 the sacred Isle. 7 Cursed by constant war, 8 all the druids did agree, 9 that the treasure of Akhenaten, 10 had cursed the land, 11 and for it to be safely returned, 12 to the Yahudi. 13 ESA-MU did call upon his Brother, 14 and prophet of visions, 15 named YAH-COB (Jacob), 16 a wise druid, 17 skilled in the history of the world, 18 and the beliefs of YAH, 19 and Akhenaten, 20 to command a small fleet, 21 of the exiles, 22 to see the safe return, 23 of the treasure, 24 and unite the scattered tribe of Moses.

C. 12

1 The fleet from the sacred Isle did leave, 2 to the fortress and port city of Philo, 3 at the mouth of the Pontus (Pineois), 4 at the foot of the Olympus Mountains, 5 then along the Vale of Temple, 6 to Elios (Larissa) the Yahudi city of illumination, 7 that fled the fall of Ugarit. 8 There, YAH-COB (Jacob) did present, 9 the treasures of Akhenaten, 10 the most sacred Ark of the Covenant, 11 the Ark of the Pharaoh Akhenaten, 12 the Sword of Heaven, 13 the Stone of Destiny, 14 the Green Marble Throne of the Hyksos,

15 the White Stone of Kings, 16 the Pharaohs Serpent Sceptre as his staff. 17 The Yahudi of Elios (Larissa) then took the treasures, 18 except the Stone of Destiny, 19 and built a grand temple at the foot of Mount Olympus, 20 called Ella (Hella) as the new home for the Divine Creator, 21 and spiritual home of the Yahudi. 22 YAH-COB (Jacob) did then depart, 23 with the Stone of Destiny, 24 to the hills south of Lake of Galilee, 25 and the valley of the Jordan, 26 to find the remaining lost Yahudi, 27 not imprisoned by the Ramses, 28 the false pharaohs.

C. 13

1 In the Great Age of the Hound and Young Bull, 2 three thousand two hundred and seventy five years, 3 since the dawn of the Great Age (1275 BCE), 4 Ramesses II upon hearing the return, 5 of what he believed as the treasure to the Levant, 6 did order a massive army to march north, 7 unto the Levant, 8 and secure the treasure. 9 King Muwatalli II of the Hittites upon hearing, 10 of the intention and haste of Ramesses, 11 did withdraw his forces, 12 leaving the lands of its vassals, 13 the lands of Mittani and Kadesh exposed. 14 Jacob did then entreat the new King of Kadesh, 15 whose name was Shalmaneser (Solomon), 16 that he give safety to the Stone of Destiny, 17 and the Yahudi upon the impending hoard of Ramses. 18 Yet when Ramses and his men approached, 19 King Shalmaneser announced, 20 that by the Stone of Destiny, 21 he be chosen as a great king, 22 against a false pharaoh. 23 In the ensuing battle, 24 the forces of Ramses were routed, 25 and Ramses almost killed. 26 Upon the defeat of such a great enemy, 27 the fame of King Shalmaneser (Solomon), 28 soon spread and he soon after conquered, 29 the whole lands from Taidu to Irridu, 30 and from Mount Kashiar to Eluhat. 31 King Shalmaneser (Solomon) then founded a new city, 32 he called Kanah (Nimrod), 33 as the Capital of the Kananites. 34 To celebrate his great victory, 35 King Shalmaneser (Solomon) commissioned, 36 the mighty temple to Ba'el, 37 within the Beka valley. 38 The site known as Baalbek. 39 As for Ramses, 40 never again did a Pharaoh, 41 raise an army so far North again.

C. 14

1 Upon his defeat at the hands of the Kananites, 2 the false Pharaoh Ramses began a grand plan, 3 for a new city upon the ruins, 4 of the ancient Hyksos capital of Avaris, 5 within the Delta of the Nile. 6 Ramses did spare no expense nor resource, 7 naming the city Pi-Ramses, 8 and the City of a Thousand Years, 9 his arrogance and greed, 10 having no bounds.

C. 15

1 Ramses did then declare himself alone, 2 the sole protector of Egypt, 3 as he claimed the old gods, 4 had abandoned Egypt, 5 to the hands of its enemies. 6 Ramesses then did take it upon himself, 7 to deface the most ancient and sacred monuments, 8 the Great Anubis of Heaven, 9 and ancient protector of all Egypt. 10 He ordered the monument to be desecrated, 11 and remade into his own likeness, 12 a horrible monster, 13 with the head of an imposter, 14 and the body of a lion.

15 Ramses then did order thousands, 16 of the sacrilegious sculptures, 17 to be made and populated throughout Egypt, 18 known today as the Sphinx. 19 The claim that the Hyksos themselves, 20 did desecrate Anubis, 21 a terrible lie, 22 to hide one of the many great curses, 23 that the Ramses befell upon himself, 24 and his descendants.

C. 16

1 In the Great Age of the Hound and Young Bull, 2 three thousand one hundred and sixty six years, 3 since the dawn of the Great Age (1254 BCE), 4 a great drought gripped the lands of Egypt. 5 Even the life giving waters of the Nile slowed, 6 until the water turned red as blood. 7 People became sick and ill, 8 from the poisoned water. 9 The viziers of Ramses accused the Hyksos slaves, 10 of wicked sorcery against the people. 11 Ramses then summonsed the Sons of Zadok, 12 who had been for many generations, 13 the chief doctors and healers of the Hyksos. 14 The Sons of Zadok refused to confess, 15 saying to the false Pharaoh, 16 let our people go, 17 and we shall tend to the sick and ill. 18 Ramses refused and instead, 19 had the most senior priests executed. 20 Soon after a great plague of frogs arose, 21 whereby the frogs infested every house and temple, 22 every business and every source of water. 23 The viziers of Ramses, 24 again accused the Hyksos slaves, 25 saying this time that it was the sons of Udah, 26 the Hyksos priests who for hundreds of years, 27 oversaw all the royal works and waters. 28 But when they too refused to confess, 29 Ramses had their leaders executed. 30 Soon after the frogs died, 31 and the air was full of flies, 32 and the people tortured by lice. 33 Ramses accused the sons of Gad, 34 who had held the treasury and supplies, 35 and had their leaders tortured to death. 36 Soon after the animals began to die, 37 and the sons of Benjamin, 38 who under the Hyksos had managed the animals, 39 were blamed and their leaders tortured to death. 40 Now the people of Egypt began to rebel, 41 including the army. 42 Yet soon after came great rains and floods, 43 causing a plague of locusts, 44 and great storms and darkness. 45 Ramses demanded the sons of Dan, 46 who had been the Royal Judges, 47 cease the plagues, 48 yet they refused to admit, 49 and called for their people to be released, 50 so Ramses killed their leaders as well. 51 But now the young children and animals, 52 also began to die upon eating bad grain, 53 so Ramses accused the sons of Yusef, 54 of sorcery and witchcraft, 55 and had them wickedly murdered. 56 Now the people were in revolt, 57 and the army itself was ripe for rebellion. 58 So Ramses came upon a plan. 59 He sent out word to every criminal in the land, 60 to every murderer and butcher in the ancient world, 61 that if they pledge loyalty to Ramses the Great, 62 they would be rewarded with riches beyond their dreams. 63 Whereupon Ramses soon raised a militia army, 64 of hundreds of thousands of bandits and murderers, 65 who gleefully butchered his own people, 66 and the army for their prize. 67 Ramses then summonses the sons of Asher, 68 the most ancient priests of the Hyksos, 69 who prepared and buried the noble dead, 70 and demanded that they open

the tombs, 71 that such treasures then be disbursed, 72 to the criminal hoard of Ramses. 73 The sons of Asher refused saying, 74 better to die a terrible death, 75 than curse every generation to come, 76 with the millions of high curses, 77 if one disturb the remains of a king or queen. 78 Whereupon Ramses enraged ordered every slave, 79 of the sons of Asher to be put to death. 80 Finally, Ramses turned to the sons of Levi, 81 who had been the honourable tax collectors, 82 of the Hyksos and threatened them the same, 83 whereupon the sons of Levi agreed. 84 Thus, the tombs were looted by Ramses, 85 and the house of Levi cursed, 86 by millions of curses, 87 for disturbing their own ancestors, 88 and breaching the trust of heaven.

C. 17

1 Within three years of the dawning, 2 of the Great Age of the Ram (1213 BCE), 3 Ramesses The Great, 4 did give up the ghost. 5 No ancient tomb had he not plundered, 6 no sacred scroll had he not altered, 7 no temple had he not desecrated, 8 to honour himself and his clan. 9 Upon his end, 10 a new Pharaoh, 11 Son of Ramesses, 12 known as Merneptah, 13 was crowned King, 14 as an old man.

C. 18

1 The first pledge of Merneptah, 2 was to send forces north, 3 to find the Yahudi in Galilee, 4 which he called the Infants, 5 as a name of curse. 6 For the House of Ramses and their viziers, 7 ignorant of history and bereft of spirit, 8 believed the treasures of Akhenaten, 9 be the source of supernatural power. 10 Yet search as he did, 11 he did not find the treasures, 12 nor destroy the Yahudi, 13 in spite of his false boast, 14 upon a Stele (monument). 15 Not wise to counsel, 16 Pharaoh Merneptah, 17 did end the treaty with the Pharasi (Phrygians), 18 attacking their cities of Tyre, 19 and Carthage. 20 The Parasites in turn, 21 did starve Egypt of vital trade.

C. 19

1 In the Great Age of the Ram, 2 seven years, 3 since the dawn of the Great Age (1203 BCE), 4 the old pharaoh Merneptah, 5 did give up the ghost. 6 The battles of the old king, 7 had weakened Egypt, 8 so that great rivals arose, 9 even with the High Priests of Amen-Ra. 10 For twenty years, 11 was great upheaval, 12 within the dynasty of Ramesses, 13 while the power of the Phoenicians grew. 14 Upon such time, 15 so arrogant the sea people had become, 16 they sought to invade Egypt herself, 17 only to be driven back, 18 by Ramses III. 19 Thus began the great battle between the Parasites (Pharasi), 20 to capture the Island of Ionia (Kefti/ Crete). 21 The legendary battles between Ascianias of the Pharasi, 22 and Priamos of the Ionian Yahudi.

Book 13

Great Age of Darkness

[1245 - 925 BCE]

C. 1

₁ Forty five years before the dawn, ₂ of the Great Age of the Ram (1245 BCE), ₃ the great King Solomon (Shalmaneser), ₄ of the Kananites did give up the ghost. ₅ A wise but brutal king, ₆ Solomon completed his Great Temple at Baalbek. ₇ A site of such power and magnificence, ₈ it defies even today how men did build, ₉ without the aid of demons. ₁₀ The great city of Kanah (Nimrod), ₁₁ a wonder of the world, ₁₂ and the new language of Aramaic, ₁₃ the language of the Kananites. ₁₄ His son named Tukulti-Ninurta, ₁₅ then did take over the throne. ₁₆ Soon after, King Tukulti-Ninurta, ₁₇ achieved a great victory over the Hittites, ₁₈ and the death of King Hattusili, ₁₉ at Nihriya. ₂₀ Thereafter, the Hittites remained in power, ₂₁ for but fifty more years, ₂₂ before they ceased to exist.

C. 2

₁ Upon the dawn of the Great Age of the Ram (1210 BCE), ₂ the dawn of a new age, ₃ the Parasites (Phoenician), ₄ of pirates and traders, ₅ had greatly profited, ₆ from their arrangement, ₇ with the dynasty of Ramesses. ₈ Wealthy cities had they made in Libya, ₉ and upon the Isle of Scicilia, ₁₀ and Sardinia, ₁₁ to the coast of Spain. ₁₂ Yet their most profitable city, ₁₃ was the Island fortress of Tyre. ₁₄ There, the tyrant King Termeg, ₁₅ did ensure all the inhabitants were branded, ₁₆ with tattooed numbers, ₁₇ and a giant ledger of slaves, ₁₈ whereby noble families would use such labour, ₁₉ to manufacture their goods for trade. ₂₀ The most horrible and evil of cities.

C. 3

₁ In the Great Age of the Ram, ₂ seven years since the dawn of the Great Age (1203 BCE), ₃ Pharaoah Merneptah did give up the ghost. ₄ The claim to the throne under the Ramses dynasty, ₅ then fell to his son who called himself Seti, ₆ in honour of his great grandfather. ₇ However, the priests of Amen-Ra, ₈ elected their own Hyksos Pharaoh, ₉ naming him Amenmesse, ₁₀ as the Chosen One of Ra. ₁₁ Civil War once again erupted within Egypt. ₁₂ Once again the Yahudi were punished, ₁₃ and the Ramses used their stolen treasures, ₁₄ to fund a campaign against Elios (Larissa), ₁₅ the great fortress city of Yahudi illumination, 16 whose symbol was now the sixteen point sun, 17 and was protected from all sides by severe mountains. 18 Within five years, 19 Amenmesse was killed, 20 and Seti reigned for four more thereafter, 21 before giving up the ghost. 22 Once again, the priests of upper Egypt, 23 elected one of their own, 24 and named him AkhenRa (Siptah). 25 Once again, Upper and Lower Egypt were at war.

C. 4

1 In the Great Age of the Ram, 2 sixteen years since the dawn of the Great Age (1194 BCE), 3 King Ascanias of Carthage, 4 did come to power upon the death of his father, 5 King Asias, the son of King Zebul. 6 As has become tradition of the Pharasi of Carthage, 7 to worship their kings and queens as demon gods, 8 two hundred and twenty two slave children, 9 were bundled into sacks and thrown from the walls, 10 in honour of Queen Tharyelli as Kybele, 11 the Mother of the Underworld. 12 In honour of King Baal Moloch, 13 sixty six children were burnt alive in ovens. 14 In honour of King Baal Zebul, 15 twelve children were ritually slain. 16 Upon such murder and madness, 17 King Ascanias did utter a high curse, 18 that he would seize the Island of Ionia (Crete), 19 and destroy the Yahudi. 20 With the aid of Tyrant King Termeg of Tyre, 21 King Ascanias did then launch wave after wave, 22 of attack against the Yahudi, 23 who bravely defended the Island, 24 until the Pharasi used spies to weaken, 25 the defences of Knossos, 26 and cause the city to be ablaze. 27 King Priamos then rallied his troops, 28 to defend and die to the last man, 29 that the survivors of the Yahudi did escape. 30 Some went and found refuge to form Argos and Pylos. 31 Others went to found the settlements of Iolos and Spardos, 32 and with Elio (Larissa), 33 came to be known as the Elia, 34 meaning the People of the Divine (Covenant), 35 and many centuries later under Alexander, 36 as the empire known as Eliada, 37 as the land of the Divine and other lands, 38 never as the Greeks nor ever as the Macedonians. 39 As for King Ascanias of Carthage, 40 he declared the new name for Ionia (Crete), 41 to be called Kanadia, 42 meaning a place without spirit, 43 and the dwelling house of demons.

C. 5

1 While the Yahudi, 2 Continued to learn and embrace life, 3 the philosophy and insanity of the Parasites (Pharasi), 4 did also grow. 5 Powerful warlords beguiled by such violence and fear, 6 saw strength in patronage to commercial religion. 7 The merchants and craftsmen saw profit in patronage, 8 even if all virtue be surrendered, 9 to a culture founded on lies, 10 existing for nothing but power itself, 11 the control of money and trade, 12 using poor magic to trick the ignorant, 13 and power and fear to enforce its rule.

C. 6

1 In the Great Age of the Ram, 2 twenty five years since the dawn of the Great Age (1185 BCE), 3 the Tyrant King Termeg of Tyre, 4 did give up the ghost. 5 The control of the largest factory prison city, 6 the world had ever seen, 7 did then fall to his son

Remeg, 8 equally cruel and wicked. 9 Within two years, the Kananite King Enlil, 10 did give up the ghost, 11 and the Great King Dan, 12 did come to power, 13 pushing the Pharasi back to their coastal forts. 14 In Africa, a tribe of Yahudi exiles of Ugarit, 15 now known as the Berbers, 16 had themselves grown strong, 17 and threatened Carthage to the west, 18 while the Parasite alliance of pirate states, 19 threatened all trade in the Inland Sea. 20 Even upon the sacred Isle, 21 the Pharasi did spread their madness, 22 erecting some temples for their gods. 23 The Pharasi (Phrygians) did succeed, 24 in taking control of some of the Isle of Britanni, 25 from the east and the south, 26 but never the west and the north, 27 erecting great numbers of shrines, 28 and centres of sacrifice to their Gods. 29 And sacrificing children day and night. 30 But never the plain of SALUM, 31 for while the Parasites cursed the earth, 32 they greatly feared the physical gods, 33 who built such shrines as Stonehenge.

C. 7

1 In the Great Age of the Ram, 2 seven years since the dawn of the Great Age (1163 BCE), 3 the Tyrant King Remeg of Tyre, 4 did give up the ghost. 5 The control of the most awful site of depravity, 6 that was ancient Tyre, 7 did then befall to his son Pummay. 8 Within a year, King Tantalias of Kanada (Crete), 9 did land a force and capture Tarsos (Tarsus), 10 declaring this to be the new capital, 11 of a great age of magic.

C. 8

1 In the Great Age of the Ram, 2 fifty one years, 3 since the dawn of the Great Age (1159 BCE), 4 appeared a bright and terrible omen. 5 The men of the far east, 6 did record its approach. 7 The men of the Pharasi, 8 did call it Phaete (Fate). 9 All war stopped upon its nearing. 10 The ball of burning iron, 11 came south of east, 12 into pieces as it travelled. 13 It boiled the sky above The Levant, 14 and unto the land of the Arabia, 15 destroying the meadow fields, 16 and their grazing lands, 17 into dust and sand, 18 south and east, 19 to the great sea of the Indus, 20 whereupon mighty waves, 21 came and destroyed the Vedic lands. 22 By the shore, 23 salty rain did fall, 24 poisoning the crops, 25 and turning the land sour. 26 The Earth did shake, 27 buildings did fall. 28 Cities burned across the land. 29 The Earth did erupt, 30 from the mounts of Hekla, 31 and the land of Ice, 32 to the Isles of the Nihon, 33 and the mounts of Fuji, Oyama and Kamiyama, 34 to the Isles as the centre of the Great Sea, 35 and the mounts of Kea, Taupō and Pinatubo, 36 the sky was filled with ash and dust, 37 as every land did erupt, 38 day turned to night, 39 the wind became cold, 40 and winter did not cease.

C. 9

1 As people come to the coast, 2 in times of great cold, 3 that the men of the sea become our light, 4 great empires of the land wither and die. 5 As crops failed and ash fell, 6 Hattusa was destroyed. 7 As wicked men who took chaos as their ally, 8 the Kananites fell. 9 Without a central

leader, 10 the Yahudi were fragmented. 11 Mygdias, the son of Tantalias, 12 expanded the hold on Asia of the Parasites, 13 as they enslaved tens of thousands of the starving. 14 Men who for the safety of a meal, 15 were willing to condemn themselves. 16 Many froze and died without food, 17 outside the walls of their forts. 18 Many more offered themselves, 19 as willing sacrifice, 20 only to save their children, 21 all men became beasts.

C. 10

1 A great forgetfulness, 2 came across the lands. 3 Those who had survived, 4 the wrath of the earth, 5 abandoned the cities. 6 Scholars became mercenaries, 7 merchants became farmers. 8 Fearful and superstitious, 9 robbers and thieves abounded. 10 Yet midst the chaos of doom, 11 the bravest of the brave, 12 of the Yahudi of the Argonauts, 13 from Argos, Ilios, Pylos and Spardos, 14 were chosen at a contest at Elios (Larissa), 15 to recover those lost treasures, 16 granted to the Kananites, 17 by Jacob centuries before. 18 The leader of these men chosen, 19 whose name was Jason, 20 the bravest of all. 21 First to Urgarit they travelled, 22 to find only ruins, 23 and a colony of soothsayers, 24 who cursed their journey to be arduous. 25 From Urgarit, the men travelled to Kadesh, 26 where they did have to fight for their lives. 27 From Kadesh they travelled to Kanah, 28 where the city was in chaos and ruin. 29 They learned that the treasures had been taken, 30 to hell itself at Tarsus, 31 the kingdom of Mygdias, 32 where the monster king did slay children, 33 for their skin and flesh. 34 Yet when the men left by boat to Cyprus, 35 they were ensnared by the women of the island, 36 who implored they stay and make good husbands. 37 Finally, the Argonauts entered the lair of Mygdias, 38 and seized the Stone of Destiny, 39 and the Sword of Heaven, 40 cutting off the head of Mygdias, 41 before making their escape. 42 Thus the bravest and noblest, 43 restored all the treasures of Moses, 44 to their protected home at Mount Olympus.

C. 11

1 Upon the most sacred Isle of the holly, 2 the great forgetfulness extended, 3 across the land. 4 Men abandoned old respects, 5 and took up the new gods, 6 of the Pharasi (Phoenicians), 7 in worship of sacrifice and blood. 8 Many of the druids abandoned all reason, 9 to become priests of sacrifice, 10 and fear of daemon gods, 11 who punished the world. 12 The celebration of Baal (Beltaine), 13 the burning of children. 14 Yet the sacrifices, 15 and worship of daemon gods, 16 the forgetfulness of druids, 17 did not halt the darkness, 18 that enveloped the sacred Isle. 19 For within one hundred years, 20 of the Dark Age, 21 one in three had given up the ghost. 22 Within two hundred years, 23 of the coming of the Dark Age, 24 two in three of all of the sacred Isle, 25 had given up the ghost.

C. 12

1 In the Great Age of the Ram, 2 one Hundred and thirty three years, 3 since the dawn of the Great Age (1077 BCE), 4 Ramesses the Eleventh, 5 the Last of the pretender Pharaohs, 6 did give up the Ghost. 7 Pharaoh

Nesbanebdjed, 8 also known as Smendes was made king, 9 of lower Egypt, 10 while the High Priests of Amen-Ra, 11 the most ancient Hyksos blood, 12 made themselves Kings, 13 of Upper Egypt, 14 beginning with Pinedjem I. 15 A message was sent then to the priests of Elios (Larissa), 16 by the Priests of Amen-Ra, 17 that they return to their ancient homeland, 18 and heal heaven and earth, 19 and restore the balance of the world.

C. 13

1 In the Great Age of the Ram, 2 one Hundred and thirty six years, 3 since the dawn of the Great Age (1074 BCE), 4 the priests of Elios (Larissa), 5 did meet with all the priests and leaders, 6 of the Yahudi in Greece, 7 at a temple of Gaia in the valley of Phocis. 8 There, the Yahudi did declare this place, 9 be a sacred site of union and debate and destiny, 10 and named it Delphi from Gaia, 11 as the womb to the earth. 12 There, the priests and priestesses debated the dangers, 13 of returning the treasures of Moses, 14 to their ancient homeland of Egypt 15 then, the most senior of priestesses, 16 did prophecy before all present, 17 we be custodians of truth, 18 not keepers of treasures. 19 The power be not in gold or stone, 20 but in the knowledge of divine. 21 Thus, let all men know thyself, 22 that he live not in excess, 23 and live according to law, 24 that his word be his bond. 25 Upon these words all agreed, 26 that the treasures of Akhenaten, 27 be returned to Egypt, 28 and a quest returned, 29 to unite the Yahudi, 30 and heal heaven and earth. 31 The priestess was then named Pathia, 32 the first priestess of Delphi, 33 and scryer of fortune and condition.

C. 14

1 In the Great Age of the Ram, 2 one Hundred and forty two years, 3 since the dawn of the Great Age (1068 BCE), 4 a group of high priests of the Yahudi, 5 the bloodline of Akhenaten, 6 the most ancient Hyksos Kings, 7 led by Aaroniah of Elios (Larissa), 8 did have an audience with Pinedjem I, 9 and were granted a site to build a sacred temple, 10 upon the Isle of Yeb (Elephantine Island), 11 the dwelling place of Khnum, 12 the ram-headed god, 13 who guarded and controlled, 14 the waters of the Nile. 15 The ancient birthplace of Maat, 16 the goddess of the primordial waters. 17 The ancient site of the Temple, 18 of the First Prophets of the Hyksos. 19 The cornerstone of the Tree of Life, 20 the Ka-Ba-La-Akh. 21 There, the priests did build their temple. 22 A most sacred temple for the Yahudi, 23 as the spirit home of YAHUWAH (YAHU). 24 The Temple was 20 cubits (9 m) in width, 25 and 60 cubits (27m) in length, 26 being 30 cubits (14m) in height, 27 from the base of the temple, 28 to the roof of the Holy Place. 29 The Temple was made of double walls, 30 and inside those walls were three sections, 31 the entrance (Vestibule), 32 the Holy Place, 33 and then the Holy of Holies. 34 Inside the Holy of Holies, 35 the Ark of Akhenaten (Moses), 36 now venerated as the Ark of the Covenant, 37 of Yahu was placed, 38 along with the treasures of Akhenaten. 39 Thus for the first time, 40 in three hundred years, 41 the two bloodlines of Hyksos, 42 united once more in Egypt.

C. 15

1 In the Great Age of the Ram, 2 one Hundred and sixty nine years, 3 since the dawn of the Great Age (1041 BCE), 4 the first Prophet of Yahuveh (YHVH), 5 the Divine Creator of all things, 6 did give up the ghost. 7 The title of first Prophet of the Yahudi, 8 did then fall to his son Enochiah. 9 The Prophet Enochiah (Enoch), 10 was a great and powerful scryer, 11 who greatly expanded the Temples of Elephantine, 12 that there be a large scriptorium. 13 There he ordered a great manifesto of history, 14 be commissioned that all Yahudi may know, 15 their history and provenance. 16 Enochiah then did give up the ghost, 17 two hundred and eleven years, 18 since the dawn of the Great Age (999 BCE). 19 The office of First Prophet of the Yahudi, 20 then befell to his son Zadokiah, 21 a gifted and tormented messenger. 22 One night in dream, 23 Zadokiah received a vision where he was instructed, 24 that all the tribes of the Yahudi, 25 the former houses of the government of Akhenaten, 26 be freed from servitude and taken to Palestine, 27 as their promised land. 28 His eldest son U'vid (Da'vid) did share the same vision, 29 upon the same night. 30 Thus Zadokiah did issue an edict, 31 that all the Yahudi were to be freed of obligation, 32 that they be forgiven for any transgression, 33 and that those who chose to go, would be given safe passage, 34 to be resettled in Palestine, 35 with Jerusalem as their capital. 36 There at Elephantine Island, 37 Chief prophet Zadokiah, anointed his son, 38 U'vid (Da'vid) as first king and messiah, 39 as first Christ and saviour of the Yahudi.

C. 16

1 In the Great Age of the Ram, 2 two hundred and eighteen years, 3 since the dawn of the Great Age (992 BCE), 4 Christ King U'vid (Da'vid) did lead the Yahudi, 5 out of bondage and slavery in Egypt, 6 to their promised land of Palestine. 7 The priests known as the Sons of Zadok, 8 who had been the royal doctors and healers of the Hyksos, 9 the priests known as the sons of Udah, 10 who had been the overseers of royal works and waters, 11 the priests known as the sons of Gad, 12 who had been the overseers of the royal treasury, 13 the priests known as the sons of Benjamin, 14 who had been the overseers of the animals, 15 the priests known as the sons of Dan, 16 who had been the royal judges, 17 the priests known as the sons of Yusef, 18 who had been the overseers of the royal granaries, 19 the priests known as the sons of Asher, 20 who had been the overseers of the royal tombs and burials, 21 the priests known as the sons of Isis, 22 who had been the royal scribes and teachers, 23 the priests known as the sons of Simeon, 24 who had been the royal viziers that turned against the Hyksos, 25 but since the end of the Ramses, 26 had sworn allegiance to the Yahudi, 27 the priests known as the sons of Levi, 28 who had been the royal tax collectors, 29 and who since the time of Ramses the Great, 30 had been shunned on account of the millions of curses, 31 they brought upon their own as looters of tombs, 32 and metal workers of cursed metals, 33 and now money

lenders of cursed articles. 34 As for the priests as sons of Reuben, 35 who had betrayed Moses (Akhenaten), 36 and betrayed heaven, 37 the former royal army leaders were exiled, 38 to Zafar in the south of Arabia, 39 and some years later to Kambar, 40 at the straights of Ormuz.

C. 17

1 In the Great Age of the Ram, 2 two hundred and twenty two years, 3 since the dawn of the Great Age (989 BCE), 4 Messiah King U'vid (Da'vid) did confront the Moabites, 5 and their powerful King Mesha, 6 who worshipped child sacrifice. 7 Yet King Esau of the Edomites granted safe passage, 8 and the city of Jerusalem back to the Yahudi, 9 on account of Moses (Akhenaten). 10 Thus King U'vid (Da'vid) did declare the new kingdom, 11 the Kingdom of Yahudah (Judah), 12 as the first kingdom of the Yahudi. 13 Never called Israel, 14 for such a false word of magic, 15 never existed in such times. 16 King U'vid (Da'vid) did then commission, 17 the building of a new Temple, 18 for the sacred Ark, 19 and treasure of Akhenaten, 20 for which he did copy, 21 the dimensions of the sacred temple, 22 upon the Isle of Yeb (Elephantine). 23 Within four cycles of the Sun, 24 he did send word, 25 to the High Priests of YAHU (Yahuwah), 26 on the Isle of Yeb (Elephantine), 27 to come to Jerusalem.

C. 18

1 In the Great Age of the Ram, 2 two Hundred and fifty years, 3 since the dawn of the Great Age (960 BCE), 4 Iram (Hiram) of Tyre became the new king. 5 Upon news of the coming return of the treasures, 6 of Akhenaten to Jerusalem, 7 he did make peace with Zimri, 8 the leader of the sons of Levi, 9 and the sons of Simon (Simeon), 10 that if they pledge alliance, 11 King Iram and King Curtias of Phrygia, 12 would recognise their own kingdom. 13 In the same year, 14 a great day for the healing of heaven, 15 upon the return, 16 of the Ark of Akhenaten, 17 the Ark of the Covenant, 18 the Foundation Stone of Ebla, 19 the white (limestone) rock, 20 the Stone of Destiny, 21 the Sceptre of Pharaoh, 22 and the Sword of Heaven, 23 to their new home, 24 the second temple, 25 in Jerusalem.

C. 19

1 In the Great Age of the Ram, 2 two Hundred and fifty five years, 3 since the dawn of the Great Age (955 BCE), 4 upon the return of the treasures of Moses, 5 to Jerusalem, 6 King Imri of the Levites, 7 aided by the Simonites, 8 declared an independent Kingdom called Sumeria (Samaria), 9 with its capital Sumer. 10 King Imri then immediately lay siege upon Jerusalem, 11 aided by King Iram (Hiram) of Tyre, 12 and King Curtias of Phrygia. 13 Facing certain defeat, 14 King U'vid (Da'vid) sent word, 15 to all the Kananite tribes, 16 that if they united against the common enemy, 17 then once more they would be blessed, 18 through the anointing of their leaders, 19 by the sacred treasures and rights of the Yahudi. 20 Thus the Edomites agreed and came from the south, 21 under the new King Bela, son of Esau, 22 the Ammonites came from the north-east, 23 and the Arameans came

from the north. 24 King Curtias and the Phrygians were pushed back, 25 by King Dan of the Arameans, 26 and King Imri was killed in retreat, 27 who sought refuge in the land of the Moabites, 28 and was confronted and killed by King Meshe. 29 The leader of the Sumerians (Samaritans), 30 now King Omri, 31 hiding as bandits without land. 32 True to his word, 33 King U'vid (Da'vid), 34 allowed the kings of the Kananites, 35 to meet at Jerusalem and be anointed, 36 according to the sacred artefacts of the Yahudi. 37 Yet no single king could the Kananites agree, 38 and an uneasy truce remained.

C. 20

1 In the Great Age of the Ram, 2 two Hundred and sixty two years, 3 since the dawn of the Great Age (948 BCE), 4 Zadokiah the third great prophet, 5 of the Yahudi did give up the ghost. 6 The office of great prophet did then befall, 7 to King U'vid (Da'vid) as first and only son. 8 Yet King U'vid (Da'vid) did not see himself fit, 9 for such great honour on account of his deeds. 10 Yet when King U'vid (Da'vid) sought to leave to Yeb, 11 the forces of the Levites and Simonites, 12 under King Omri sought to attack again. 13 King Dan of the Arameans, 14 and King Bela of the Edomites, 15 helped push King Omri back, 16 and like his father, 17 King Omri was killed by the Moabites. 18 King U'vid (Da'vid) did then issue a sacred decree: 19 Let all heaven and earth be witness to truth, 20 that the sons of Levi no more be priests, 21 and that the sons of Simon (Simeon) follow. 22 Nor shall henceforth either have claim, 23 to the sacredness of the Yahudi, 24 nor the patronage of the Divine. 25 They be cast out, ejected, and doomed. 26 To wander the earth as the cursed, 27 as those that rejected eternal life. 28 King U'vid (Da'vid) did then anoint the Edomites, 29 as a new tribe of the Yahudi, replacing the Simonites. 30 He then anointed the Arameans of Dan, 31 replacing the Levites. 32 The captured Levites and Simonites were then exiled, 33 on ships from the sons of Zion, 34 to the Island of the Horse (Euboea) in Greece, 35 where the Levites named their settlement Sumer (Chaldis), 36 and the Simonites named their settlement Sulumer (Eritrea). 37 King U'vid (Da'vid) did then anoint, 38 his cousin Obadiah as his adopted brother, 39 as the fourth great prophet of Yeb. 40 Upon being honoured as one of the twelve houses of the Yahudi, 41 King Bela of the Edomites, 42 did declare to King U'vid (Da'vid): 43 As you honour our people and all Kananites, 44 so I honour the house of U'vid (Da'vid), 45 behold I am blessed with two sons, 46 whose names are Boam (Job) and Saul. 47 Before heaven and earth as my witness, 48 I give Boam (Job) my first born, 49 to Yahuvah and to you as your son. 50 Thus King U'vid (Da'vid) was blessed with an heir.

C. 21

1 In the Great Age of the Ram, 2 two Hundred and seventy nine years, 3 since the dawn of the Great Age (931 BCE), 4 the great King U'vid (Da'vid), 5 of the Kingdom of Yahudah, 6 did give up the ghost. 7 The anointed crown of messiah kings, 8 did then fall to his adopted son Boam (Job), 9 also the

crown prince of the Edomites, 10 who took the name Yahuboam. 11 In the Great Age of the Ram, 12 two hundred and seventy nine years, 13 since the dawn of the Great Age (929 BCE), 14 Obadiah the fourth great prophet, 15 of the Yahudi did give up the ghost. 16 The position then befell, 17 to the son of Obadiah, 18 whose name was Elijiah (Elijah), 19 as the fifth of the Great Prophets of Yahuweh. 20 Elijiah (Elijah) did then come to Jerusalem, 21 as did all the leaders of the Kananites, 22 to meet the messiah king Yahuboam, 23 who was both a Kananite and a Yahudi. 24 Elijiah (Elijah) did also tutor, 25 the eldest son of Yahuboam, 26 whose name was Yahab (Ahab), 27 on the history of the world, 28 and his future obligations. 29 In the Great Age of the Ram, 30 two Hundred and eighty four years, 31 since the dawn of the Great Age (926 BCE), 32 the great King Bela of the Edomites, 33 did give up the ghost. 34 While King Yahuboam of Yahudah, 35 was also the rightful heir of the throne, 36 he did not object to his younger brother, 37 whose name was Saul, 38 to become King of the Edomites.

Book 14

Great Age of the Prophets

[925 - 594 BCE]

C. 1

1 In the Great Age of the Ram, 2 two Hundred and eighty five years, 3 since the dawn of the Great Age (925 BCE), 4 King Saul of the Edomites, 5 did invite the priests deposed of Baalbek, 6 known as the priests of Baal Hanan, 7 to build a temple at his new capital of Selah (Petra). 8 The Great Prophet Elijiah of the Yahudi, 9 did complain to King Yahuboam, 10 yet King Saul ignored him and instead forbid, 11 the worship of Yahuweh in the lands of the Edomites. 12 In the Great Age of the Ram, 13 two Hundred and eighty seven years, 14 since the dawn of the Great Age (923 BCE), 15 King Yahuboam did defeat the Phrygians to the west, 16 capturing the fortress cities of Ekron and Gath. 17 Yet rather than congratulate his brother, 18 King Saul sided with the Phrygians, 19 demanding the cities be returned. 20 When his brother King Yahuboam of Yahudah refused, 21 King Saul did then cut off supplies, 22 from the ports of Elah (Eilat) and Geber (Aqaba). 23 When King Yahuboam did change from trade, 24 along the River Jordan, 25 to the slower use of land, 26 King Saul attacked the caravans, 27 killing the Yahudi. 28 Finally, King Yahuboam had to act. 29 He confronted his brother and the rebellious forces. 30 But when the forces met in the Jezreel Valley, 31 the Edomites abandoned Saul, 32 and sided with King Yahuboam and the true king. 33 Defeated and humiliated King Saul and his sons, 34 refused to surrender and instead climbed Mount Gilboa. 35 There above the valley Saul proclaimed: 36 Before you oh mighty Baal, 37 strike the seed of my brother, 38 that the house of the Yahudah be cursed, 39 with conflict and malevolence. 40 For such is this religion, 41 that it did kill my own house. 42 With the curse been spoken, 43 Saul did kill each of his sons, 44 then took his own life. 45 King Yahuboam did then declare: 46 The Kingdom of heaven of my father, 47 be cleaved by such tragedy. 48 Henceforth, the name of Edom be the whisper of history. 49 Behold all land granted to me by my fathers, 50 be one united Kingdom of Yahudah.

C. 2

1 In the Great Age of the Ram, 2 two Hundred and ninety nine years, 3 since the dawn of the Great Age (911

BCE), ₄ King Yahuboam of Yahudah, ₅ did give up the ghost. ₆ The crown did then fall to his son Yahab (Ahab). ₇ In the same year a powerful king emerged, ₈ from the lands of the Kananites, ₉ called King Adad (Nadab), ₁₀ who defeated the Phrygians (Pharasi) to the north, ₁₁ and established the city of Damascus as his capital. ₁₂ During the third year of Yahab (Ahab), ₁₃ the Great Prophet Elijah, ₁₄ did warn Ahab and his Queen Jezebel, ₁₅ who had taken herself to be a Priestess of Asherah, ₁₆ the Queen of Heaven, ₁₇ and Mother of God, ₁₈ that the murder of innocent children, ₁₉ and the worship of daemon gods, ₂₀ be an abomination, ₂₁ unto the universal God, ₂₂ of Yahu (Yahuweh). ₂₃ Yet Aha would not be moved saying, ₂₄ that though Elijah (Elijah), ₂₅ be the great prophet and teacher, ₂₆ the Universal god Yahuweh, ₂₇ had brought nothing but misery, ₂₈ while it be Ba'al and Asherah, ₂₉ who had protected and brought prosperity, ₃₀ for generations of Kananites. ₃₁ Thus King Adad (Nadab) and Queen Jezebel, ₃₂ did roast little innocents, ₃₃ drinking their blood, ₃₄ and feeding upon their flesh, ₃₅ in High Mass as was custom, ₃₆ since the time of the darkness.

C. 3

₁ Upon such evil, ₂ Elijah did issue a Great Curse, ₃ to Ahab and his wife. ₄ So superstitious and fearful, ₅ of the Great Curse of a Chief Seer, ₆ and Great Prophet of the Yahudi, ₇ the King and his Queen did lock themselves away. ₈ Elijah then did take in disguise, ₉ the treasures of Akhenaten, ₁₀ from the second temple of Jerusalem, ₁₁ to return them to the Isle of Yeb (Elephantine). ₁₂ When King Yahab (Ahab) then discovered, ₁₃ the treasures of Moses (Akhenaten), ₁₄ had been taken by Elijiah (Elijah), ₁₅ he summonsed his army and best chariots, ₁₆ to seize Elijiah (Elijah) and the treasures. ₁₇ Within sight of the canals of Zion (Zeus/ Seuz), ₁₈ the forces of the Berber Pharaoh, ₁₉ of the Yahudi Mazalyi Tribe, ₂₀ known as Pharaoh Osorkon, ₂₁ did see the chariots of Yahudah approach. ₂₂ They did lower the waters of the canal, ₂₃ that Elijiah (Elijah) and the treasures, ₂₄ could safely pass. ₂₅ But when the chariots and army of Yahudah, ₂₆ did follow into the canal, ₂₇ the Egyptians released the water, ₂₈ and the forces of Yahab (Ahab) drowned. ₂₉ Elijiah (Elijah) did then stand, ₃₀ with the sceptre of Moses, ₃₁ by the side of the canal, ₃₂ and did declare in front of King Yahab (Ahab), ₃₃ upon the other side: ₃₄ Verily before all heaven and earth, ₃₅ let the angels and spirits be my witness, ₃₆ for never again shall the Kingdom of Yahudah, ₃₇ be the Chosen People of the Divine Creator. ₃₈ Until one is found to be worthy, ₃₉ the treasures of Akhenaten (Moses), ₄₀ shall remain at Yeb (Elephantine Island).

C. 4

₁ In the Great Age of the Ram, ₂ three hundred and nineteen years, ₃ since the dawn of the Great Age (891 BCE), ₄ King Adad (Nadab) of the Assyrians, ₅ and of the Yahudi tribe of Dan, ₆ did give up the ghost. ₇ The crown then did fall to his son, ₈ whose name was Tukulti. ₉ In the Great Age of the Ram, ₁₀ three hundred and twenty one years, 11 since the dawn of the Great Age (889 BCE), 12 Elijiah (Elijah) the fifth great prophet, 13 of the Yahudi did give up the ghost. 14 The position then befell, 15 to his son whose name was Ahijiah, 16 as the sixth Great Prophet of the Thirty Three. 17 Within two years of the death of Elijiah, 18 Pharaoh Osorkon of the Berber Yahudi, 19 also known as the Mazalyi tribe, 20 did give up the ghost. 21 King Ahab did then rally a great army, 22 of Yahudah and Kananite conscripts, 23 to invade Egypt, 24 and seize the sacred treasures of Moses. 25 Yet word of his plans were given to the priests, 26 and the son of Osorkon, 27 whose name was Pharaoh Shoshenq, 28 who was forewarned of the attack. 29 When King Yahab (Ahab) did strike, 30 the Egyptians did destroy the army of Yahudah. 31 Never again did King Ahab rally an army, 32 to try and seize the treasures of Moses. 33 In the Great Age of the Ram, 34 three hundred and twenty six years, 35 since the dawn of the Great Age (884 BCE), 36 King Tukulti of the Assyrians, 37 did give up the ghost. 38 The crown then did fall to his son, 39 whose name was King Assur (Asa). 40 In the Great Age of the Ram, 41 three hundred and forty years, 42 since the dawn of the Great Age (870 BCE), 43 King Yahab (Ahab) of Yahudah gave up the ghost. 44 The crown did then fall to his son, 45 whose name was Yahushaphat.

C. 5

1 In the Great Age of the Ram, 2 three hundred and twenty one years, 3 since the dawn of the Great Age (861 BCE), 4 Ahiah the seventh great prophet of Yeb, 5 the son of Ahijiah and the grandson of Elijiah, 6 did give up the ghost. 7 The position then befell, 8 to his son whose name was Azariah, 9 as the eighth Great Prophet of the Yahudi. 10 In the Great Age of the Ram, 11 three hundred and twenty six years, 12 since the dawn of the Great Age (859 BCE), 13 Yahudi Kananite King Assur (Asa), 14 of the tribe of Dan, 15 and leader of the Assyrians, 16 did give up the ghost. 17 The crown then did fall to his son, 18 whose name was King Sulmanu (Solomon). 19 Since the fall of the Yahudah under Yahab, 20 King Assur (Asa) had paid homage, 21 to the Great Prophets of Yeb, 22 asking for their atonement, 23 and favour return to the Kananites. 24 Under the tribe of Dan, 25 Law had been restored across the lands, 26 the Kananites united, except for the Yahudah. 27 The great temple of Baalbek had been restored, 28 the wicked kingdoms of Tyre and Biblos destroyed, 29 the Isle of Cyprus retaken, 30 the city of Tarsus destroyed. 31 King Sulmanu (Solomon) did then travel to Egypt, 32 to pay homage and plead, 33 that unless the signs of Moses return, 34 to the gaze and honour of men, 35 no peace can be brought to the lands, 36 nor evil extinguished. 37 For only the illumination of Divine Sacredness, 38 can rid the earth of transgression. 39 Upon hearing the plea of Sulmanu (Solomon), 40 prophet Azariah agreed and the treasures of Moses, 41 did then return to Palestine and to Baalek, 42 renamed the Holy Temple of Sulmanu (Solomon), 43 as the site of a new covenant, 44 with the tribe of Dan the new messiah kings.

C. 6

1 King Sulmanu (Solomon), 2 of the Yahudi and Kananite tribe of Dan, 3 King of Assyria, 4 now anointed as the messiah kings, 5 continued the work of his grandfather, 6 in making Ninevah, the revival of Kanah, 7 his capital and the centre of the world. 8 The tribe of Dan returned the rule of law, 9 that all are equal under the law, 10 to Babylonia under King Za-Kir-Mu, 11 to Elam under King Indash, 12 to the Urartu, Gutium, Arameans, 13 the Philistia, Moabites, Nabateans, 14 the Arabians, the Shutu and Hamathites. 15 Even King Yahushaphat of Yahudah, 16 paid homage to the great Sulmanu (Solomon). 17 In the Great Age of the Ram, 18 three hundred and fifty seven years, 19 since the dawn of the Great Age (853 BCE), 20 King Sulmanu (Solomon) amassed the largest army, 21 ever to be seen in more than five hundred years, 22 against the fortresses of the Phrygians, 23 and the allies of King Midias (Midas). 24 In the Orontes Valley at the fortress of Qarqar, 25 King Sulmanu (Solomon) defeated the Phrygians, 26 and freed Palestine and Syria of the tyranny, 27 of the parasites, who were forced to retreat. 28 Upon such a great victory, 29 King Sulmanu (Solomon) declared: 30 Let this place be remembered as sacred, 31 for here, we shall build a great temple to Yahu. 32 This place became known as the city of light, 33 later also Heliopolis, 34 and later falsely as Antioch on Orontes. 35 In the Great Age of the Ram, 36 three hundred and fifty eight years, 37 since the dawn of the Great Age (852 BCE), 38 King Sulmanu (Solomon) of Assyria, 39 did invade Phrygia with a mass army, 40 capturing the Phrygian capital of Gordium, 41 and its wicked King Midias (Midas). 42 King Midias (Midas) offered Sulmanu (Solomon), 43 the greatest treasure of gold of jewels, 44 stolen and plundered by the parasites, 45 over hundreds of years, 46 as petition to spare his life. 47 To which King Sulmanu (Solomon) ordered that Midias (Midas), 48 be sealed in his own treasure vaults, 49 that if he loved gold and precious gems above life, 50 then let him survive upon them. 51 Upon the death of King Midias (Midas), 52 wise King Sulmanu (Solomon) then divided the treasure, 53 amongst his vassals in recompense of what had been taken, 54 when the parasites (Pharasi), 55 had been in power. 56 He then ordered Gordium to be razed to the ground, 57 and covered in soil, 58 that the Phrygians (Parasites) be wiped from memory. 59 Thus any claim the Phrygians survived, 60 be a wicked untruth.

C. 7

1 In the Great Age of the Ram, 2 three hundred and fifty one years, 3 since the dawn of the Great Age (851 BCE), 4 the King of Argos in Greece, 5 whose name was Perseus, 6 and King Aegis of Sparta, 7 did lead a fierce army of fighters, 8 that captured Kanadia, 9 butchering every last Pharasi (Parasite). 10 The Island was renamed Knossos, 11 and claimed by King Aegis of Sparta. 12 The fleet then sailed to the former lands of Phrygia, 13 and invaded from the sea, 14 capturing the cities of the Phrygians, 15 and renaming the whole region, 16 and their new capital as Troy, 17 claimed

by King Perseus, 18 who granted the kingdom to his son, 19 known as Attis (Atys). 20 With the control of Knossos (Crete), 21 the Spartans soon became famously wealthy, 22 as did the people of Argos. 23 Yet the two cities of Yahudi, 24 did resolve themselves of the wealth, 25 in opposite manners. 26 As the Spartans sought communal wealth, 27 administered by trusted priests, 28 whilst the people lived to perfect, 29 their strength and skill at all forms of war, 30 while the people of Argos, 31 lavished themselves in finery and good living.

C. 8

1 In the Great Age of the Ram, 2 three hundred and sixty five years, 3 since the dawn of the Great Age (845 BCE), 4 King Yahushaphat of Yahudah gave up the ghost. 5 The crown Did then fall to Yahuram. 6 In the same year the Prophet Azariah, 7 did give up the ghost. 8 The position then befell, 9 to his son whose name was Ananiah, 10 as the ninth Great Prophet of the Yahudi. 11 For sixty six years, 12 the Kings of Yahudah, 13 forbidden to be known as Messiah Kings, 14 cast out as the Chosen People, 15 had cursed and schemed, 16 and partaken in the most abominable acts, 17 In the invention of the ritual of Eucharist, 18 by the eating of flesh and drinking of blood, 19 of innocent children murdered to demon gods, 20 that the Yahudi of Jerusalem, 21 had come to believe in nothing, 22 but power for itself. 23 A great and deep insanity had befallen, 24 these once great houses of priests, 25 of the court of Pharaoh Akhenaten. 26 No longer any sign of wisdom, 27 but the madness of men who curse heaven, 28 and sacrifice to spirits they do not believe. 29 The Yahudi of the kingdom of Yahudah, 30 had come to believe only that they were victims. 31 And in such madness of mind, 32 even if an enemy could not be found, 33 the priests of Jerusalem would invent their own, 34 so that the young ones be taught the insanity, 35 They be persecuted by mankind and heaven.

C. 9

1 In the Great Age of the Ram, 2 three hundred and seventy three years, 3 since the dawn of the Great Age (837 BCE), 4 King Yahuram of Yahudah gave up the ghost. 5 The crown of the king of Yahudah, 6 did then fall to Yahuahaz. 7 In the Great Age of the Ram, 8 three hundred and eighty six years, 9 since the dawn of the Great Age (824 BCE), 10 King Sulmanu (Solomon) of the Assyrians, 11 did give up the ghost. 12 The Messiah crown then did fall to his son, 13 whose name was King Shamshi (Sampson), 14 as the leader of the tribe of Dan, 15 the Chosen People of the Divine, 16 the Kananite Yahudi, 17 and the Assyrian Empire. 18 In the Great Age of the Ram, 19 three hundred and ninety seven years, 20 since the dawn of the Great Age (813 BCE), 21 Ananiah the ninth great prophet of Yeb, 22 did give up the ghost. 23 The position then befell, 24 to his son whose name was Amoziah, 25 as the tenth Great Prophet of the Yahudi. 26 In the Great Age of the Ram, 27 three hundred and ninety nine years, 28 since the dawn of the Great Age (811 BCE), 29 King Shamshi (Sampson) of the Assyrians, 30 did give up the ghost. 31 The crown then did fall to his son, 32 whose name

was King Narari. 33 In the Great Age of the Ram, 34 four hundred and nine years, 35 since the dawn of the Great Age (801 BCE), 36 King Yahuahaz of Yahudah gave up the ghost. 37 The crown of Yahudah, 38 did then fall to his son Yahuash.

C. 10

1 In the Great Age of the Ram, 2 four hundred and twenty six years, 3 since the dawn of the Great Age (784 BCE), 4 Amoziah the tenth great prophet of Yeb, 5 did give up the ghost. 6 The position then befell, 7 to his son whose name was Isaiah, 8 as the eleventh Great Prophet of the Yahudi. 9 The Great Prophet Isaiah went to Ninevah, 10 and warned King Narari, 11 that his failure as Messiah king of the Yahudi, 12 would cause the ruin of the empire, 13 and the House of Dan. 14 King Narari ignored the great prophet, 15 and for a brief time forbid him, 16 to attend to the treasures of Moses, 17 at Baalbek the Temple of Solomon. 18 Instead, the priests of Ba'al Hanon 19 were granted control and proceeded to construct, 20 a large golden bull that enclosed, 21 the Ark of the Covenant. 22 Thus, all who came to Baalbek, 23 to worship the Divine Creator, 24 now worshipped Baal Hanon, 25 as the Golden Calf. 26 In the Great Age of the Ram, 27 four hundred and thirty seven years, 28 since the dawn of the Great Age (773 BCE), 29 King Narari of the Assyrians, 30 did give up the ghost. 31 The crown then did fall to his son, 32 whose name was King Ashur. 33 Yet when the Great Prophet Isaiah, 34 came to Ninevah to see the new king, 35 he refused to grant him an audience. 36 Two years passed and again the king refused. 37 Five years passed and again King Ashur, 38 refused to grant Isaiah an audience, 39 to which Isaiah did reply, 40 that soon a day will come, 41 when there will be a weeping in the House of Dan, 42 for nothing shall extinguish, 43 the pain and torment, 44 upon the wrath of the Divine Creator.

C. 11

1 In the Great Age of the Ram, 2 four hundred and forty four years, 3 since the dawn of the Great Age (766 BCE), 4 a great cold did descend upon the world, 5 rivers did freeze, crops did die, 6 and animals did perish. 7 The priests of Baal Hanon, 8 did blame the god Yahu, 9 and so King Ashur summonsed Isaiah to court. 10 Isaiah did then warn King Ashur, 11 to cease the defiling of the treasures of Moses. 12 That if the House of Dan, 13 as the Assyrian Empire, 14 did not repent, 15 then they would be stripped of authority. 16 To which King Ashur responded, 17 it was the treasures of the Yahudi, 18 that had caused the curse on the lands, 19 the great cold and famine, 20 and that he would be granted passage to leave, 21 but be forbidden to return. 22 Upon Isaiah gaining the word of the King, 23 he proceeded to Baalbek and seized the treasures, 24 returning to Egypt, 25 under the protection, 26 of the Berber Yahudi Pharaoh Userken. 27 Yet when King Ashur realised, 28 what Isaiah had done, 29 he ordered the largest army yet assembled, 30 to invade Egypt and return the treasures. 31 Pharaoh Userken sought to defend Egypt, 32 but was overwhelmed. 33 Isaiah then called out, 34 to the King of

the Napata, 35 promising if they protect the sacredness, 36 of the covenant of the Divine Creator, 37 then they would become the messiah kings, 38 of the Yahudi. 39 King Alara of the Napata (Kush), 40 did then enter into Egypt, 41 and defend Yeb (Elephantine), 42 against King Ashur, 43 of the Assyrians, 44 and House of Dan, 45 defeating them and pushing them back. 46 King Alara then became Pharaoh Kashta. 47 The Great Prophet Isaiah then declared: 48 Henceforth, before all heaven and earth, 49 the tribe of Dan no more be the Chosen People, 50 nor may they be called the Messiah Kings. 51 For such honour goes unto the House of Napati (Kush), 52 as the sacred protectors of the covenant. 53 Thus, for the first time the treasures of Akhenaten, 54 did travel south to Napati, 55 until it was deemed safe for their return to Yeb.

C. 12

1 In the Great Age of the Ram, 2 four hundred and thirty seven years, 3 since the dawn of the Great Age (745 BCE), 4 King Ashur of the Assyrians, 5 did give up the ghost. 6 The commander of the Army, 7 whose name was General Turtanu, 8 did immediately seize the throne, 9 and execute the whole royal family, 10 of the House of Dan, 11 thus fulfilling the prophecy of Isaiah, 12 that the House of Dan, 13 would be wiped from the earth. 14 Turtanu then declared himself King Pileser. 15 Turtanu as King Pileser declared war, 16 upon all who opposed him. 17 King Pileser greatly increased the army, 18 conscripting hundreds of thousands. 19 First, King Pileser did brutally put down rebellion, 20 across Palestine and Syria. 21 When the kingdom of Yahudah, 22 refused to pay tribute, 23 King Pileser attacked and conquered Jerusalem, 24 taking all the key people of Jerusalem, 25 as prisoners back to Ninevah, 26 and leaving King Yahuam the king of a ghost city. 27 Rebellion after rebellion he crushed. 28 When he reached Babylon, 29 King Pileser then declared himself king, 30 crowning himself King Pulu of Babylonia. 31 Yet for all his greatness, 32 and all his brutality, 33 King Pileser could not defeat, 34 the son of Pharaoh Kashta, 35 the Messiah Pharaoh, 36 of the Yahudi Napati (Kush), 37 whose name was Pharaoh Pi.

C. 13

1 In the Great Age of the Ram, 2 four hundred and sixty seven years, 3 since the dawn of the Great Age (743 BCE), 4 as Sparta and Argos had become wealthy, 5 Sparta kept its control over Knossos, 6 and became the most powerful of all Greek states, 7 while Argos lost its Trojan Empire, 8 upon the western Anatolia, 9 to internal revolt, 10 and the birth of a federation of cities, 11 that renamed themselves, 12 the Ionian League in honour of the ancient ideal. 13 Yet when the Melites, 14 also known as the Helots (Zealots), 15 of the Island of Pegasus (Euboea), 16 and the city of Sumer (Chaldis), 17 of the ancient Yahudi exiles of Levites, 18 and the city of Sulumer (Eretria), 19 of the ancient Yahudi of Simonites, 20 continued to entrap trade and demand payment, 21 King Pheidon of Argos did enlist, 22 the help of King Alcamenus of Sparta, 23 to launch an invasion. 24 The Levites and Simonites were captured, 25 eight thousand from

Sumer (Chaldis), 26 and ten thousand from Sulumer (Eretria). 27 Yet instead of being executed, 28 the Argeans took their prisoners to Italy, 29 and to their colonies at Cronos (Croton), 30 at Siris and Tartatus (Tarentum), 31 in the Calabrian lands. 32 The Spartans took their Levite slaves 33 to Italy and their colonies, 34 of Zarcle (Messina) and Apoleon (Syracuse), 35 and Heraclea (Hercules), 36 on the isle of Sicilia, 37 and to Hera (Paestum) and the far north Vulcan (Vulci), 38 and to Poseidonia (Olbia), 39 upon the Isle of Sardinia. 40 The sons of Sulumer and Sumer did vow, 41 one day they would be freed, 42 and exact their revenge, 43 upon losing Pegasus their island home. 44 Within one hundred years, 45 their prophecy came true, 46 as both the Spartans and Argeans, 47 released their slaves.

C. 14

1 In the Great Age of the Ram, 2 four hundred and seventy eight years, 3 since the dawn of the Great Age (732 BCE), 4 Isaiah the eleventh great prophet of Yeb, 5 did give up the ghost. 6 The position then befell, 7 to his son whose name was Ezekiah, 8 as the twelfth Great Prophet of the Yahudi. 9 In the Great Age of the Ram, 10 four hundred and eighty eight years, 11 since the dawn of the Great Age (722 BCE), 12 Pileser (Pekah) of the Assyrians, 13 did give up the ghost. 14 The crown then did fall to his son, 15 whose name was King Shallum (Sargon). 16 In the Great Age of the Ram, 17 four hundred and eighty nine years, 18 since the dawn of the Great Age (721 BCE), 19 Pharaoh Pi of the Yahudi house of Napati (Kush), 20 did give up the ghost. 21 The title of Messiah Pharaoh, 22 did then befall to his son, 23 whose name was Shabaka. 24 Yet upon word reaching King Shallum (Sargon), 25 of the death of the great Pi, 26 he ordered a mass invasion of Egypt, 27 catching the Egyptians and Kush by surprise. 28 Unable to reinforce Yeb and Thebes in time, 29 King Shallom (Sargon) surrounded the temple, 30 and forced Ezekiah to yield the treasures, 31 on the promise that the temple, 32 and all the lives of the priests be spared. 33 Thus King Shallom (Sargon) secured, 34 the treasures of Moses (Akhenaten), 35 as the Ark of the Covenant, 36 the Sword of Heaven, 37 the Serpent Sceptre, 38 the Stone of Destiny, 39 and the Standard of the Lion. 40 Yet Shallom (Sargon) did execute Shabaka, 41 and installed his own Pharaoh, 42 by the name of Taharqa. 43 King Shallom (Sargon) did then return to Ninevah, 44 with the treasures of Moses (Akhenaten), 45 his great prize.

C. 15

1 In the Great Age of the Ram, 2 four hundred and forty nine years, 3 since the dawn of the Great Age (705 BCE), 4 King Shallum (Sargon) of the Assyrians, 5 did give up the ghost. 6 The crown did then fall to his son, 7 whose name was Sinherib (Sin). 8 The Yahudi still as prisoners at Ninevah, 9 the treasures of Akhenaten returned to Baalbek, 10 and the control of the priests of Baal-Hanon, 11 who no longer desecrated the artefacts, 12 but instead ensured their proper veneration, 13 as strength had been returned to the Assyrians. 14 In the time that the Assyrians had seized,

Book 14 Great Age of the Prophets

15 the treasures of the Yahudi, 16 and returned them to Baalbek, 17 the great prophet and priests of Yeb, 18 had reconciled themselves to becoming, 19 the greatest tutors of knowledge, 20 of the ancient world. 21 Thus the sons of kings and leaders, 22 from all the ancient world came to Yeb, 23 to be taught and trained in history. 24 Even as a sign of truce, 25 King Sinherib (Sin) even sent his youngest son, 26 whose name was Asaraddon (Esarhaddon), 27 to be taught by Ezekiah. 28 There at Yeb, 29 Ezekiah reminded Asaraddon, 30 of the obligations of a good king, 31 And the consequences of wicked decisions. 32 In the Great Age of the Ram, 33 five hundred and twenty nine years, 34 since the dawn of the Great Age (681 BCE), 35 King Sinherib (Sin) of the Assyrians, 36 was murdered by his older sons. 37 The crown of Assyria did then befall, 38 to his youngest son named Asaraddon (Esarhaddon), 39 above the claims of his older brothers, 40 on account of ancient prophecy, 41 that he would bring healing to the land. 42 Yet upon his rise to the throne, 43 civil war broke out across Assyria. 44 With the guidance and learning acquired at Yeb, 45 King Asaraddon (Esarhaddon) defeated his brothers. 46 He then ordered the release of the Yahudi, 47 permitting them to return to Jerusalem. 48 He further permitted his tutor Ezekiah, 49 and the Yahudi priests of Yeb, 50 to tend to the treasures at Baalbek. 51 Yet he refused permission for their return. 52 Nor did the Yahudi priests seek to grant consent, 53 as to the legitimacy of the house of Turtanu. 54 In the Great Age of the Ram, 55 five hundred and fourteen years, 56 since the dawn of the Great Age (696 BCE), 57 Ezekiah the twelfth great prophet of Yeb, 58 did give up the ghost. 59 The position then befell, 60 to his son whose name was Amariah, 61 as the thirteenth Great Prophet of the Yahudi.

C. 16

1 In the Great Age of the Ram, 2 five hundred and twenty nine years, 3 since the dawn of the Great Age (681 BCE), 4 Amariah the thirteenth great prophet of Yeb, 5 did give up the ghost. 6 The position then befell, 7 to his son whose name was Edaliah, 8 as the fourteenth Great Prophet of the Yahudi. 9 In the Great Age of the Ram, 10 five hundred and thirty eight years, 11 since the dawn of the Great Age (672 BCE), 12 Edaliah the fourteenth great prophet of Yeb, 13 did give up the ghost. 14 The position then befell, 15 to his son whose name was Zephaniah, 16 as the fifteenth Great Prophet of the Yahudi. 17 In the Great Age of the Ram, 18 five hundred and sixty five years, 19 since the dawn of the Great Age (645 BCE), 20 Zephaniah the fifteenth great prophet of Yeb, 21 did give up the ghost. 22 The position then befell, 23 to his son whose name was Ilikiah, 24 as the sixteenth Great Prophet of the Yahudi. 25 Of all the students of Ilikiah. 26 Apart from his own son, 27 the greatest be the crown prince of the Chaldeans, 28 the most ancient Yahudi priests, 29 known as the House of Reuben. 30 Upon the weakening of the Medians, 31 the Chaldean Yahudi of Reuben, 32 had formed a united house known as the Menes. 33 In the Great Age of the Ram, 34 five hundred and eighty four years, 35 since the dawn of the Great Age (626 BCE), 36 King

Teispes (Nebupolassar) of the ancient Yahudi tribe of Reuben, 37 also known as the Chaldeans and Persians, 38 did conquer Babylon and declare himself king, 39 following the death of Assyrian King Ashurbanipal. 40 The Great Prophet Ilikiah did then come to Babylon, 41 and make a fateful speech there, 42 saying that as the Divine be his witness, 43 that all miracles are possible, 44 for the last has become the first, 45 in the restoration of the House of Reuben (Wolf), 46 as the Yahudi House of Menes. 47 Thus, all the world shall recognize, 48 the House of Reuben and the House of Menes, 49 as Messiah Kings of the world. 50 Whereupon Ilikiah blessed the Menesheh army, 51 as it departed to Syria, 52 to recapture the treasures of Moses (Akhenaten).

C. 17

1 In the Great Age of the Ram, 2 five hundred and ninety years, 3 since the dawn of the Great Age (620 BCE), 4 Ilikiah the sixteenth great prophet of Yeb, 5 did give up the ghost. 6 The position then befell, 7 to his son whose name was Jeremiah, 8 as the seventeenth Great Prophet of the Yahudi. 9 While Messiah King Teispes (Nebupolassar), 10 continued to fight towards Ninevah, 11 his son called Cambyses (Nebuchadnezzar), 12 became the star pupil of Jeremiah, 13 tutoring him in all manner of knowledge, 14 and religion and history of the world. 15 In the Great Age of the Ram, 16 five hundred and ninety six years, 17 since the dawn of the Great Age (614 BCE), 18 King Teispes (Nebupolassar) had finally subdued, 19 all enemies in Palestine, Syria and Mesopotamia, 20 and now lay siege to Ninevah itself. 21 Careful that the treasures of Moses (Akhenaten), 22 be not damaged or stolen or destroyed, 23 King Teispes (Nebupolassar) remained patient in siege for five years, 24 until the people themselves rose up, 25 and killed the defenders. 26 Thus King Teispes (Nebupolassar) succeeded in regaining, 27 the sacred treasures of Moses (Akhenaten), 28 and spared the people of Ninevah, 29 but ordered the city of such wickedness to be destroyed, 30 that such a place no longer raise itself, 31 against the call of heaven. 32 King Teispes (Nebupolassar) did then return the treasures of Moses, 33 to Babylon under his protection.

C. 18

1 In the Great Age of the Ram, 2 six hundred and five years, 3 since the dawn of the Great Age (605 BCE), 4 King Teispes (Nebupolassar) did give up the ghost. 5 Cambyses (Nebuchadnezzar) was then crowned, 6 Messiah King of Babylonia and the Yahudi. 7 He then did call his teacher to court. 8 There Cambyses (Nebuchadnezzar) did greet him warmly, 9 as a brother and spoke to the assembled, 10 Great Magi Jeremiah, 11 how might we change the hearts, 12 of the men of the Yahudi, 13 who worship demons, 14 and eat the flesh and blood, 15 of their sons and daughters? 16 Must I turn Jerusalem, 17 and every other wicked city into dust? 18 To rid us of this evil? 19 Jeremiah did reply: 20 Indeed they be abominations, 21 and evil without seeming end, 22 that priests act outwardly with piety, 23 but in hiding

do practice all manner of wickedness, 24 yet they are a people without memory, 25 and without knowledge of history, 26 who know not from where they came, 27 nor of the ancient covenant of the Divine. 28 Jeremiah did then ask Cambyses (Nebuchadnezzar), 29 that before he lay waste to Jerusalem, 30 he grant Jeremiah one year on his word, 31 that he allow Jeremiah to travel to Jerusalem, 32 and plead with King Yahuiakim, 33 that the Yahudi be convinced to change their ways. 34 Cambyses (Nebuchadnezzar) asked how might this be? 35 To which Jeremiah replied, 36 he would employ the best scribes and priests, 37 to work day and night, 38 and within six months shall have a history, 39 worthy of the history of the Yahudi, 40 that they might believe in the truth, 41 and cease practicing their evil ways. 42 Cambyses (Nebuchadnezzar) did agree and give his oath, 43 and for six months the scribes and priests, 44 worked day and night to write the history, 45 so that the Yahudi might remember who they are, 46 and stop such evil and worship of demons.

C. 19

1 In the Great Age of the Ram, 2 six hundred and six years, 3 since the dawn of the Great Age (604 BCE), 4 the High Priest of Yeb, 5 the mighty and wise Jeremiah, 6 did travel to Jerusalem, 7 with the new sacred texts, 8 to the court of King Yahuiakim. 9 But Jeremiah refused the trappings of court, 10 and spoke plainly, 11 a solemn oath did your ancestors give, 12 to honour the covenant of Yahu, 13 which brought you out of the wilderness. 14 I do come now with sacred scripture, 15 faithful to the covenant, 16 for your priests and your court, 17 to end the worship of foreign gods, 18 but King Yahuiakim the son of Yahuhaz, 19 the grandson of Yahuah, 20 and the great grandson of Yahuamon, 21 would not be moved. 22 He ordered the scriptures be seized, 23 and destroyed as a supreme act of evil. 24 King Yahuiakim then ordered Jeremiah imprisoned. 25 All the priests and nobles did defile, 26 and insult Jeremiah except one, 27 whose name was Princess Tamar, 28 also known as Tea Tephi, 29 who tended and fed Jeremiah, 30 and ensured he had enough blankets, 31 when he was imprisoned. 32 Upon hearing the wickedness of the Yahudah, 33 King Cambyses (Nebuchadnezzar) ordered his Generals, 34 to march on Jerusalem and spare no one, 35 but Jeremiah and return his teacher unharmed. 36 For two months the army of King Cambyses (Nebuchadnezzar), 37 lay siege to Jerusalem until finally, 38 the walls of the city could no longer hold, 39 and the city fell.

C. 20

1 In the Great Age of the Ram, 2 six hundred and seven years, 3 since the dawn of the Great Age (603 BCE), 4 Jeremiah and his scribes, 5 were freed by the Persian troops of Cambyses (Nebuchadnezzar), 6 and his finest General Zaradan. 7 King Yahuiakim and all his sons were then executed. 8 But before the Chaldean Yahudi, 9 did touch Princess Tephi, 10 Jeremiah proclaimed that she be his adopted daughter, 11 and no harm was to come

to her. 12 As for the city and its leaders, 13 Jeremiah made General Zaradan swear, 14 that no harm would come until he met, 15 with King Cambyses (Nebuchadnezzar) and sought clemency. 16 Thus Jeremiah, with his scribes, 17 and now his adopted daughter, 18 the last of the line of the Messiah of Edom, 19 the last bloodline of the House of Da'vid, 20 the last of the royal Kananites, 21 did go to Babylon to the court of (Cambyses) Nebuchadnezzar. 22 Jeremiah did then speak of his second plan, 23 that he would bring forth his trusted nephew, 24 from Yeb, named Zedekiah, 25 to be the new King of Jerusalem, 26 and that the ancient treasures of Moses (Akhenaten), 27 be brought also to Jerusalem, 28 that the people of Yahudah might remember, 29 their sacred covenant and end their ways. 30 King (Cambyses) Nebuchadnezzar agreed on the condition, 31 that a Babylonian garrison remain in Jerusalem, 32 and that Jeremiah not travel without guard, 33 and if by seven years, the Yahudi of Jerusalem, 34 had failed to change, the city would be raised. 35 Jeremiah agreed and summonsed Zedekiah to Jerusalem, 36 soon after, the most sacred treasures of Moses came. 37 And the people of Jerusalem were jubilant. 38 Yet Jeremiah warned Zedekiah, 39 that in six years, if the people had not changed, 40 (Cambyses) Nebuchadnezzar would destroy the city. 41 Yet within five years Jerusalem had become a brothel, 42 of money and vice, superstition and magic, 43 as people across the world flocked to worship the ark. 44 Jeremiah again warned Zedekiah and Yahudah, 45 to change their ways and stop accepting such false money, 46 yet they refused. 47 With just two years to go before the end of the time, 48 Jerusalem had returned to the sacrifice of children, 49 and Zedekiah had defiled his sacred oaths, 50 to become a high priest of Baal Moloch. 51 Jeremiah warned him and all the priests, 52 that this was the last straw, 53 and seized the sacred treasures, 54 whereupon the Persian guard did fight to the last man, 55 to enable the escape of Jeremiah and the treasures.

C. 21

1 In the Great Age of the Ram, 2 six hundred and thirteen years, 3 since the dawn of the Great Age (597 BCE), 4 Nebuchadnezzar ordered General Nebuzaradan, 5 and the army to capture Jerusalem and destroy it, 6 killing every living thing. 7 Soon after the Babylonians recaptured the city. 8 Jeremiah pleaded with the General, 9 that he at least spare one hundred of the brightest, 10 and their children and families, 11 from each of the ancient Yahudi tribes, 12 of Jerusalem, lest their knowledge and skills, 13 be consigned to waste, 14 that they be taken to Babylon as slaves. 15 General Nebuzaradan replied that he would only grant, 16 clemency to just forty of the brightest of each tribe, 17 whereupon just four thousand Yahudi, 18 from Jerusalem were taken back to Babylon as slaves. 19 On a day to become known as Tisha B'Av, 20 six hundred and thirteen years, 21 since the dawn of the Great Age (597 BCE), 22 every other man, woman, child, 23 and living thing was killed. 24 General Nebuzaradan then demolished the

walls of the city, 25 burning and destroying every building and temple, 26 and ordered that no man or woman be permitted to live, 27 amongst the ruins of Jerusalem.

C. 22

1 Upon the destruction of Jerusalem, 2 to rubble and ghosts, 3 Jeremiah returned to Babylon, 4 and spoke to King (Cambyses) Nebuchadnezzar, 5 verily, no matter what remedy we seek, 6 men who desire nothing more than power, 7 be ignorant to the greatest of forces, 8 that is knowledge and wisdom, 9 instead coveting the symbols of power, 10 which has no more power than a rock or tree. 11 If such treasures then remain, 12 I fear such madness will tear apart, 13 the house of Menes. 14 Thus, I shall return the sacred artefacts, 15 to their temporary home at Mount Olympus, 16 and travel then to Ireland, 17 that the most ancient of priests and kings, 18 whose name means the sacred stone of heaven, 19 be awakened and humanity be saved. 20 King (Cambyses) Nebuchadnezzar did approve, 21 and permitted the sacred treasures, 22 to be removed and taken to Greece.

C. 23

1 In the Great Age of the Ram, 2 six hundred and fourteen years, 3 since the dawn of the Great Age (597 BCE), 4 Jeremiah did depart Palestine, 5 with all the sacred treasures of Moses (Akhenaten), 6 back to Greece and the Port of Philo, 7 at the mouth of the sacred Pontus (Pineois) River, 8 then along the Vale of Temple, 9 to the Temple Complex of Ella (Hella), 10 at the foothills of Mount Olympus, 11 as the ancient resting place of the Divine (Ella). 12 At Elios (Larissa) Jeremiah did have a prophetic vision, 13 where he believed the Divine Creator did speak to him, 14 and call him to free all men of the darkness of mind, 15 that had plagued the men of Yahudah, 16 and so many of the Yahudi, 17 and cursed the ancient most sacred isle, 18 of the Cuilliaéan. 19 Jeremiah did then summons the Spartan, 20 and then the Argeans of Argos, 21 and told them of the vision, 22 that no man who honours heaven, 23 may call another a slave. 24 That no man who honours the sacred covenant, 25 worship any form of human sacrifice. 26 He did then tell them, 27 that he would depart to the sacred Isle, 28 with his daughter Princess Tephi, 29 and his son Baruciah, 30 and the Stone of Destiny, 31 And the Sword of Heaven, 32 to re-awaken the Green Race, 33 the sleeping gods.

Book 15

Great Age of the Celts

[594 - 508 BCE]

C. 1

Six hundred and six years, 2 since the dawn of the Great Age (594 BCE), 3 Jeremiah, Baruciah and Princess Tephi, 4 did land at a place, 5 known as Carrickfergus, 6 in the north of the most sacred Green Isle. 7 From there they did travel south, 8 to the court of King Eochaid, 9 a descendant of the Holly, 10 and the bloodlines of the Hyksos, 11 who had united, 12 the warring tribes. 13 There in the court of King Eochaid, 14 Jeremiah did anoint him, 15 upon the most ancient and sacred Stone of Destiny, 16 the foundation stone of Ebla, 17 the white (limestone) rock. 18 King of the Isle, 19 and the new messiah king, 20 Jeremiah did hand him, 21 the sword of heaven (Ex Caeli Bur), 22 and the standard of the House of Yahudah, 23 that upon a sacred marriage with Princess Tephi, 24 a union of the most ancient bloodlines, 25 of the Holly, 26 the bloodlines of Ebla, 27 the Hyksos, 28 and now the House of Yahudah. 29 Jeremiah did then declare: 30 Let the descendants of this sacred union, 31 unite the world and rid it of evil. 32 Thus the Red Lion upon the yellow field, 33 became the standard of the court, 34 of the High King of Ireland, 35 of the House of the Holly, 36 and the title Ha Rama Theo, 37 which means His Divine Highness, 38 wrongly written as Arimathea. 39 King Eochaid did then show Jeremiah, 40 the great treasures of Ireland, 41 saved and hidden for millennia, 42 the memorial of great and ancient cities, 43 and the Hyksos kings themselves. 44 King Eochaid did present to Jeremiah, 45 the ancient poems of wisdom of Ebla, 46 and the ancient commandments of Akhenaten, 47 the books of mathematics of the Hyksos, 48 the spell books of Ur, 49 the lexica of the first languages, 50 the astronomy tables of the Holly. 51 At such wonder of wisdom, 52 Jeremiah did declare: 53 Let us end evil, 54 by lighting an eternal flame, 55 in the soul and mind of every man, 56 that through knowledge of truth, 57 all madness cease. 58 That once more the sacred isle, 59 be the foundation stone, 60 of divine revelation.

C. 2

1 In the Great Age of the Ram, 2 six hundred and four years, 3 since the dawn of the Great Age (596 BCE), 4 the Spartans released their Levite prisoners, 5 now more than thirty

thousand their colonies in Italy. 6 From Apoleon (Apollo also Syracuse), 7 the Levites now calling themselves Sabians, 8 did found Mars (Katania) to the north, 9 and Mercuria (Kamarina) to the south-west. 10 From Zarcle (Messina) the Sabians, 11 did found Satania (Reggio) across the straits, 12 and Cerberus to the west of Sicily. 13 From Heraclea (Hercules), 14 the Sabians did travel east, 15 and found Diana (Gela). 16 In the lands of Calabria the Argeans freed the Simonites, 17 numbering more than fifty thousand. 18 From Cronos (Croton), 19 the Simonites travelled north, 20 to found Sybilaris (Sybaris), 21 from Tartatus (Tarentum), 22 the Simonites travelled south, 23 and founded Calipolis. 24 From Sisis the Simonites travelled north, 25 and founded Metapolis (Metapontum). 26 To the north in Italy, 27 from Hera (Paestum) the Simonites founded, 28 Pixolis (Pixous) to the south. 29 From Cumae, the Simonites founded Neopolis. 30 To the far north from Vulcan (Vulci), 31 the Spartans freed the Sabians, 32 who then founded Ceres (Caere), 33 and Venus (Veius). 34 Within twenty five years, 35 the Sabians (Levites) to the north, 36 had founded a federation of cities, 37 called Rusna or Chosen People, 38 also known as the Etruscans. 39 By the same period, 40 the Sabians and Simonites had formed, 41 an alliance in the south, 42 to create the federation called Graecia (Greece).

C. 3

1 Upon the most ancient green throne, 2 of Amen-Ra of the Hyksos, 3 which had been in Ireland, 4 for many centuries, 5 and upon the Foundation stone of Ebla, 6 the sacred singing stone of kings, 7 and with the sword of heaven (ex caeli bur), 8 a new bloodline of Messiah-Kings was formed. 9 Jeremiah did issue a new sacred law, 10 called Tara and later corrupted to Torah, 11 of five sacred texts, 12 the first being Genasis (genesis), 13 meaning to start and seek and search for knowledge, 14 the second being Eacturas (exodus), 15 meaning the example and parable of knowledge, 16 the third being Diatuair (deuteros), 17 meaning the laws of heaven (divine law), 18 the fourth being Nome (nomos), 19 meaning the laws of name (natural law), 20 the fifth being Anacánain (anakineos), 21 meaning to move and converse (trade) upon water (positive law). 22 Above all Jeremiah did decree: 23 The Law of Moses and the Yahudi be, 24 that no man shall be above the law. 25 For if one claims to be above the law, 26 there be no rule of law. 27 That if the law be not followed, 28 in good faith and without prejudice, 29 there be no justice. 30 King Eochaid with his Queen Tephi, 31 did unite Ireland, 32 under the laws of Moses, 33 as defined by Jeremiah, 34 and renamed the capital to Tara, 35 a sacred city from which five sacred roads, 36 connected the whole of the sacred isle, 37 with Tara being the height of law, 38 and the law of the land. 39 Jeremiah did build, 40 a school and scriptorium, 41 upon the banks of the River Shannon, 42 in the Kingdom of Meath, 43 as the first Academy and University of Knowledge, 44 of the ancient world. 45 As to the division of Ireland to five, 46 the Kingdom of Ulaid (Ulster) be the north, 47 the Kingdom of Cóiced

(Connacht) be the west, 48 the Kingdom of Mumha (Munster) be the south, 49 the Kingdom of Laighin (Leinster) be the east. 50 All four surrounding the kingdom of Míde (Meath), 51 the Kingdom of the High King of Ireland, 52 that no King may rule, 53 for more than seven years, 54 a rule in honour of ancestors of the Holly, 55 from the time of Ebla. 56 Jeremiah did build, 57 a school and scriptorium, 58 upon the banks of the River Shannon, 59 in the Kingdom of Meath, 60 as the first Academy and University of Knowledge, 61 of the ancient world. 62 That all may make pilgrimage to Ireland, 63 and honour the most ancient wisdom, 64 of the Holly and first priests of civilisation. 65 Jeremiah did then spend, 66 the rest of his days, 67 upon the Isle of Ireland, 68 teaching and writing his scriptures, 69 while discovering long lost treasures and scrolls, 70 of thousands of years of history, 71 as his son Baruciah did return, 72 to Elios (Larissa).

C. 4

1 In the Great Age of the Ram, 2 six hundred and twenty eight years, 3 since the dawn of the Great Age (572 BCE), 4 Jeremiah the seventeenth great prophet of Yeb, 5 the son of Ilikiah and the grandson of Zephaniah, 6 the man who saved the bloodline, 7 of the house of Da'vid (David), 8 and the blood of the tribe of Edomites, 9 the man who formed the sacred scripture of Tara, 10 as the five books of Moses to the Celts, 11 did give up the ghost. 12 The position then befell, 13 to his son whose name was Baruciah, 14 as the eighteenth Great Prophet of the Yahudi. 15 Upon his death, 16 a great tomb was erected, 17 upon the Isle, 18 now known as Devenish, 19 in the Lower Lough Erne, 20 and the no man was permitted, 21 to set foot upon such sacred ground.

C. 5

1 Within twenty years, 2 the religion of Jeremiah, 3 known as Celtii, 4 had spread across the known world, 5 in Britannia (Britain), 6 there was the Dumnonii of south-west, 7 the Breton of south-west, 8 the Atrebatii of central Britannia, 9 the Icenii of eastern Britannia, 10 the Cymrii of western Britannia, 11 the Coritani of eastern Britannia, 12 the Otadini of northern Britannia, 13 and the Caledonii of far north Britanni. 14 In Iberia (Spain), 15 there was the Gallaeci of northern Iberia, 16 the Lusitani of western Iberia, 17 the Turduni of southern Iberia, 18 the Bastenii of south eastern Iberia, 19 and the Edetani of eastern Iberia. 20 In Gaul (France), 21 there was the Ausci and Pictonii of south-west Gaul, 22 the Narbonii and Arverni of south-east Gaul, 23 the Aulerci of west Gaul, 24 and the Remi, Parisii and Treveri of northern Gaul. 25 In Saxony (Germany), 26 there was the Sequani and Elvetii, 27 and the Teutonii. 28 In the Anatolia there was the Galatii, 29 and in the Ionian Islands, 30 there was the Spartan and Argeans, 31 who embraced the new religion. 32 Yet those who refused to embrace, 33 the laws of Moses most fiercely, 34 were the Levites and Simonites, 35 who hated rule of law by equality, 36 and remained hateful towards heaven. 37 The Yahudi prisoners of the Persians, 38 as well as the Kananites and Persians, 39 rejected the call for unity

amongst the Yahudi, 40 as they falsely saw themselves superior to all men.

C. 6

1 In the Great Age of the Ram, 2 six hundred and forty one years, 3 since the dawn of the Great Age (559 BCE), 4 King Cambyses (Nebuchadnezzar), 5 of the Persians also known as the Chaldeans, 6 also known as the Yahudi tribe of Menes, 7 also known as the ancient Yahudi of Reuben, 8 did give up the ghost. 9 The messianic right of kings, 10 granted to him by Jeremiah did befall his son, 11 whose name was King Cyrus. 12 The claim that Cyrus and Cambyses (Nebuchadnezzar), 13 were enemies of different tribes, 14 a wicked untruth. 15 The wisdom of Jeremiah, 16 and the power of the most sacred treasures, 17 had awoken the most ancient Druids, 18 from their forgetfulness, 19 and dark rituals. 20 Upon the uniting of Ireland, 21 and a world of warrior priest tribes, 22 no longer through other kings, 23 but an Empire built not on politics, 24 but upon honour, knowledge and law, 25 with no centre that might be crushed or corrupted. 26 Yet such wisdom has also awoken, 27 great hatred and madness, 28 in the form of the false prophet, 29 whose name was Daniah (Daniel), 30 a cousin of Zedekiah, 31 who with several priests were seized, 32 upon the destruction of Jerusalem.

C. 7

1 In the Great Age of the Ram, 2 six hundred and forty two years, 3 since the dawn of the Great Age (558 BCE), 4 false priest Daniah (Daniel), 5 succeeded in an audience with King Cyrus. 6 Whereupon he asked him, 7 if he were a man of science or superstition, 8 King Cyrus was outraged by the insult, 9 and threatened to have him executed, 10 to which Daniel replied, 11 that he would prove, 12 that the demon god of the Yahudah, 13 be more powerful than the god of Jeremiah. 14 Whereupon King Cyrus ordered, 15 that Daniel be burned alive. 16 But before he was set to be cast into the ovens, 17 the Yahudi slaves did coat him in a substance, 18 that he did not burn, 19 to the fear of the court of Cyrus. 20 Yet when they cast Daniah (Daniel) to the lions, 21 again the Yahudi covered him, 22 in the scent of an old lion, 23 and he was spared. 24 The Persians unaware of the deceptions, 25 did believe it to be black magic, 26 whereupon Daniah by using light, 27 and mirrors created the illusion, 28 of a hand writing on a wall before the King. 29 Yet the head vizier of Cyrus, 30 did see the trick, 31 and Daniah was disgraced, 32 for the fraud of writing on the wall. 33 Yet while he remained in prison, 34 Daniah demonstrated profound vision and skill, 35 which the king and the court tested. 36 King Cyrus however remained deeply troubled, 37 by dream and ghosts, 38 to which only Daniah (Daniel), 39 appeared to answer. 40 King Cyrus did say that though he fear heaven, 41 the magic of Daniah (Daniel) was potent, 42 thus the life of Daniah was spared.

C. 8

1 The druids of the Holly did devise new poems, 2 simple and clear. 3 Laws and rules for tribal warriors, 4 they did re-fashion long lost weapons, 5 the return of the chariot, 6 yet with new

science of the road, 7 a respect for knowledge, 8 and the wisdom of nature. 9 Warriors were also poets, 10 and diviners of nature, 11 that they could read the signs, 12 of the enemy, 13 and not waste their lives, 14 upon the errors of generals. 15 In faith they did reveal, 16 secret wisdom, 17 in the reincarnation of the soul, 18 that an honourable death in battle, 19 would return a greater warrior, 20 to respect the gods of nature, 21 to respect a brave enemy, 22 that the head of the enemy, 23 bravely slain, 24 was to be revered not cursed. 25 The druids did know, 26 from ancient curse, 27 when a king dies, 28 the family pick like crows. 29 The Druids did devise, 30 a culture of local belief, 31 in spirits and heroes, 32 and tribes were preserved, 33 that one King might be vanquished, 34 and ten more carry forth. 35 Yet in priests most strict the Holly be, 36 for no one may be named a druid, 37 a Brehom of the law, 38 other than those who did study, 39 for such an honour. 40 Thus for the first time, 41 in all history, 42 a druid no longer be blood, 43 of the Cuilleain, 44 but one who did show honour and truth, 45 for the bonding of word, 46 remained most high, 47 that any oath of a Celt, 48 be honour bound, 49 in this life and the next. 50 But most of all, 51 the Holly did honour the word, 52 to Jeremiah, 53 to the end of human sacrifice, 54 and restore rule of law, 55 that no one be above the law, 56 that good faith and clean hands, 57 prevail the course of justice. 58 In the Great Age of the Ram, 59 six hundred and forty five years, 60 since the dawn of the Great Age (555 BCE), 61 Holly High King Eochaid, 62 the living foundation stone of the Divine, 63 of the most ancient Cuilliaéan, 64 and blood descendant of the priests of Ebla, 65 and blood descendant of the priests of Ur, 66 and blood descendant of the priest-kings of the Hyksos, 67 and blood descendant of the priests of Ugarit, 68 did give up the ghost. 69 the Marble Throne of Amen-Ra, 70 did then fall to his son, 71 whose name was Lugaid mac Eochaid, 72 as the only true blood descendant of Messiah King Da'vid.

C. 9

1 In the Great Age of the Ram, 2 six hundred and fifty years, 3 since the dawn of the Great Age (550 BCE), 4 General Magon of Carthage, 5 did seize the throne. 6 To defeat the Spartans and Argeans, 7 King Magon did entreat the Levites, 8 that as the Rusna (Etruscans), 9 they rise up and expel the Spartans. 10 In the Great Age of the Ram, 11 six hundred and fifty six years, 12 since the dawn of the Great Age (544 BCE), 13 the Etruscans with the Carthaginians, 14 defeated the Spartans at Vulcan, 15 and the other colonies in the north, 16 killing every living thing. 17 The Levites and Catharginians, 18 then did capture Alalia, 19 upon Corsica and declared, 20 a great union between the people of Carthage, 21 and the people of Rusna (Erusca federation). 22 Yet as hard as the Carthagians tried, 23 they could not yet capture Sardinia.

C. 10

1 In the Great Age of the Ram, 2 six hundred and fifty five years, 3 since the dawn of the Great Age (545 BCE), 4 the fame and influence, 5 of Keltoi had spread, 6 so far and wide, 7 that Ireland became, 8 the centre of

learning, 9 and wisdom for the whole world. 10 Only the best students, 11 were chosen to come. 12 Even the Levites and Simonites, 13 did send their royal sons, 14 to Ireland to learn. 15 Thus Damasus of Siris, 16 also known as Pythagorus, 17 and even Smindyrides of Sibylaris, 18 did come to Ireland, 19 unto the school of Jeremiah, 20 on the banks of the River Shannon, 21 to read and learn, 22 the most ancient scrolls of the Egyptians, 23 the science of mathematics, 24 the nature and rule of law, 25 the fair governance of justice, 26 the creation and management of money, 27 the ancient secrets of the priests, 28 and the mysteries of immortality. 29 Upon such knowledge and secrets, 30 that in the hope of the holly, 31 and the legacy of Jeremiah and the priests, 32 that men overcome their base desires, 33 and a new world order be formed, 34 one borne not from fear but logic, 35 a world not crippled by superstition, 36 but empowered by spirit.

C. 11

1 In the Great Age of the Ram, 2 six hundred and fifty seven years, 3 since the dawn of the Great Age (543 BCE), 4 Damasus of Siris did return, 5 to become king of the city. 6 There he did found a new religion, 7 called Pythagorea, 8 based upon the knowledge of the druids, 9 and his knowledge of his ancestors. 10 Damasus proclaimed himself a divine messiah, 11 that all forms of obscene consumption and wealth, 12 be an abomination before the Divine, 13 and that the wise man seek to overcome, 14 the eternal cycle of re-birth and death. 15 Many people from other cities of the Graecia (Greece), 16 did hear of Damasus now as Pythagorus, 17 and came to Siris to hear him speak. 18 Many more came to learn of mathematics, 19 and the knowledge of the world of numbers, 20 and the knowledge of the ancient Holly, 21 and the knowledge of the Hyksos, 22 which Damasus as Pythagorus, 23 did falsely claim as his own inspiration. 24 Those that did follow Pythagorus, 25 began wearing the symbol of the Pentagram, 26 which Pythagorus proclaimed be a talisman, 27 of great power and good fortune, 28 without greater knowledge of its provenance. 29 In the same year, 30 Holly High King Lugaid, 31 son of Holly King Lugaid, 32 and Queen Tephi of Jerusalem, 33 did bequeath his kingdom to his two sons, 34 before he did give up the ghost. 35 To the north and the Kingdoms, 36 of Ulaid (Ulster) and Cóiced (Connacht), 37 he bestowed to his son named Congal. 38 To the south and the Kingdoms, 39 of Mumha (Munster) and Laighin (Leinster), 40 he bestowed to his son named Eochaid Uairches. 41 In the Great Age of the Ram, 42 six hundred and fifty nine years, 43 since the dawn of the Great Age (541 BCE), 44 after the city of Sybilaris becoming fractured, 45 by the new religion of Pythagorus of Siris, 46 Smindyrides did attack Siris, 47 and destroy the city to its foundations. 48 Pythagorus initially sought sanctuary, 49 with the people of Cronos (Croton). 50 Within the year, 51 the people of Kronos and an army of Pythagorea, 52 did attack and utterly destroy Sybilaris. 53 Yet the people of Kronos still rejected Pythagorus, 54 fearing they would be overwhelmed. 55 Thus Pythagorus sought sanctuary at Satanis (Reggio).

56 There the tyrant king known as Anaxilas, 57 did embrace Pythagorea, 58 and Pythagorus anointed him saviour, 59 granting him and all his Levite descendants, 60 the symbol of the swastika, 61 as yet another symbol stolen from the knowledge, 62 from the ancient Cuilliaéan. 63 Supported by the followers of Pythagorus, 64 Anaxilas captured Zarcle (Messina), 65 adopting the name for himself as Iove (Jupiter), 66 as saviour of all Graecia (Greece).

C. 12

1 In the Great Age of the Ram, 2 six hundred and sixty two years, 3 since the dawn of the Great Age (538 BCE), 4 King Cyrus once again summonsed the false prophet, 5 named Daniah (Daniel), 6 to speak to him on terrible visions, 7 of his father King Cambyses (Nebuchadnezzar), 8 as a tormented spirit. 9 Daniah (Daniel) did speak that the king, 10 did suffer for his dishonour of the Divine, 11 upon the total destruction of Jerusalem. 12 That the only means by which the curse, 13 of the house of Menes (Reuben), 14 be lifted be through the restoration of Jerusalem, 15 and the return of the Ark of the Covenant, 16 to a new temple. 17 King Cyrus did speak that he promised an oath, 18 unto his dying father, 19 to honour the covenant with the priests of Yeb. 20 Thus he could no more demand the return of the Ark. 21 Yet it be within his power to free the Yahudah, 22 and restore Jerusalem. 23 Thus it was King Cyrus, 24 fifty nine years after the complete destruction, 25 of Jerusalem to the ground, 26 that he did issue a decree for all the Yahudi, 27 of the Yahudah, 28 to be freed from service and allowed to return. 29 King Cyrus then did give the Yahudi, 30 twenty thousand slaves by which to recommence, 31 the rebuilding of the city of Jerusalem, 32 one stone at a time. 33 Soon after Daniah (Daniel), 34 did give up the ghost, 35 and the claim of false prophet, 36 did befall to his son Haggiah. 37 Haggiah did then speak a solemn oath, 38 that in honour restored, 39 the Yahudah of Jerusalem swear allegiance, 40 unto the House of Reuben, 41 by an eternal blood oath and covenant, 42 before all heaven and the earth, 43 and that this new holy covenant, 44 shall be known as Mitra (blood oath/ blood covenant).

C. 13

1 In the Great Age of the Ram, 2 six hundred and seventy years, 3 since the dawn of the Great Age (530 BCE), 4 King Magon of Carthage, 5 did give up the ghost. 6 The crown did then go to his son Hasdrubal. 7 In the same year, 8 Baruciah the eighteenth great prophet of Yeb, 9 the son of Jeremiah and the grandson of Ilikiah, 10 did give up the ghost. 11 The position then befell, 12 to his son whose name was Osiah (Hosea), 13 as the Nineteenth Great Prophet of the Yahudi. 14 As had now become custom, 15 since the time of his grandfather, 16 Osiah (Hosea) did spend time, 17 in his education in Ireland, 18 and to Yeb (Elephantine Island), 19 before returning to Elios. 20 Thus the Persians and Yahudah spies, 21 remained unclear as to the site of the treasures, 22 and believed them for a time, 23 to be returned to Yeb, 24 and their ancient home in Egypt. 25 In the Great Age of the Ram, 26 six hundred and seventy two years, 27 since the

dawn of the Great Age (528 BCE), 28 King Cyrus of the Chaldeans, 29 also known as the Persians, 30 also known as the Yahudi tribe of Menes, 31 also known as the ancient Yahudi of Reuben, 32 did give up the ghost. 33 The crown did then befall to his son, 34 whose name was Darius.

C. 14

1 In the Great Age of the Ram, 2 six hundred and seventy three years, 3 since the dawn of the Great Age (527 BCE), 4 upon the new reign of Darius, 5 Pythagorus and King Anaxilas (Jupiter), 6 sent tribute to the new Persian King, 7 as a new alliance between the original home, 8 of the Graecians (Greeks), 9 in Sicily, Calabria, Campania and Salento. 10 King Darius agreed and sent a force, 11 of more than 500 ships and 10,000 men, 12 to support and protect the alliance. 13 With the aid of the Persians, 14 the Pythagoreans captured Cumae, 15 and the Isle of Arime (Ischia), 16 which meant the Graecians (Greeks), 17 did then control trade along the coast. 18 King Hasdrubal and the Etruscans, 19 did then attack Cumae and destroy the city. 20 Thus for the first time, 21 the Levites as the Sabians and Etruscans, 22 also known as the people of Sulumer, 23 and the Simonites and the Simones and Greeks, 24 also known as the people of Sumer, 25 were in open war, 26 with Carthage supporting the Levites, 27 and Persia supporting the Simonites. 28 To assist in its struggle, 29 the Graecians (Greeks) agreed to peace, 30 with the Spartan cities of Apoleon (Syracuse), 31 and Heracles (Heraclea) as well as Poseidonia (Olbia), 32 upon the Isle of Sardinia.

C. 15

1 In the Great Age of the Ram, 2 six hundred and seventy three years, 3 since the dawn of the Great Age (527 BCE), 4 and seventy years since the city of Jerusalem, 5 was destroyed to its foundations, 6 the slaves of the Persians, 7 had rebuilt its walls and cleared its wicked markets, 8 and reconstructed a temple, 9 above the ancient Rock and cave of Akhenaten (Moses). 10 The false prophet Haggiah, 11 with thousands of the exiled Yahudi, 12 returned triumphant to Jerusalem, 13 while the main priests remained bound to Babylon, 14 as they had sworn by blood oath they called Mitra. 15 Upon their return, 16 Haggiah, the son of Daniah (Daniel), 17 did swear that upon our sacred city, 18 we shall build an empire of the mind, 19 that will control the world in secret. 20 Never again shall we allow such torment. 21 Our people shall be free of all curse, 22 yet bound to live as if slaves, 23 in close quarters (ghettos), 24 that they never forget their blood oath. 25 Our people shall seize all the wealth, 26 yet shall live in absolute poverty, 27 that no one is wiser who are their masters. 28 We shall sacrifice the innocents of our enemies, 29 and perform unspeakable evils, 30 unto the lord of demon hosts, 31 that he keeps heaven and the Divine at bay, 32 and grants us good fortune. 33 We shall write history as our own, 34 we shall teach even our children falsities, 35 that none can rise above, 36 or divide us again. 37 Where there is no enemy, 38 we shall create them. 39 When our

children are complacent, 40 we shall torment them with fears, 41 that the world forever remain ours, 42 that we be the servants, 43 of the demon lord of hosts, 44 and beyond the hand of heaven.

C. 16

1 In the Great Age of the Ram, 2 six hundred and seventy five years, 3 since the dawn of the Great Age (525 BCE), 4 the Persian King Darius, 5 did defeat Pharaoh Psamtik III, 6 near the east mouth, 7 of the River Nile. 8 The Persian King, 9 upon capture of the Pharaoh, 10 had him executed, 11 declaring himself Pharaoh. 12 Yet when the forces of Darius, 13 did come to Yeb, 14 nowhere did they find the treasures of Moses. 15 Thus they concluded such treasures, 16 must be returned to Elios (Larissa), 17 under the guard of Osiah (Hosea). 18 The false prophet Haggiah, 19 did devise a trick whereby King Darius, 20 could force the true great prophet, 21 to break the bond of Persian Kings, 22 that they might attack and seize, 23 the precious so wanted by the Yahudah. 24 Haggiah did visit and meet with Damasus (Pythagoras), 25 whereupon Pythagoras did reveal his religion, 26 and Haggiah declared that together they would form, 27 a great faith upon the bond of mitra, 28 binding all men to perpetual servitude. 29 Haggiah did then implore Darius to aid, 30 the Graecians (Greeks) with his invasion forces, 31 to crush the Etruscans and Carthaginians, 32 and make the land of the Greeks (Italy), 33 a permanent vassal of Persia. 34 King Darius did agree and within five years, 35 all of Sicily and the south of Italy, 36 was under the control of Persia and the Greeks.

C. 17

1 With aid of Haggai, 2 and the Yahudi priests of Mitra, 3 who now called themselves the Magi (Magicians), 4 Pythagoras did devise a model of a new society, 5 he called the Republic, 6 whereby men rule according to intellect and wisdom, 7 as a benevolent council of dictators, 8 under a fascist state, 9 as a corruption of the Spartan decree of law. 10 Citizens would be divided into three classes, 11 the first being the Patricians, 12 of which would be exclusively those born, 13 of Yahudi priestly houses. 14 The second would be men who through skill, 15 and learning achieved the highest degree, 16 and these would be called Plebians. 17 The third being Municeps, 18 who swore with a straight arm salute, 19 their pledge of allegiance to the Republic. 20 The last would be slaves, 21 who themselves would be emancipated, 22 if they served their masters well, 23 or paid their way to freedom. 24 As to the mysteries of the universe, 25 Pythagoras did take the stolen knowledge, 26 of the Holly priests and the Hyksos, 27 and the stolen knowledge of the Tree of Life, 28 of the HA-KA-BA-LA-AH of Upper Egypt, 29 and devised ten occult degrees. 30 The first degree was the Messenger (Dove) under Mercury, 31 the second degree was the Muse (Kingfisher) under Pleiades, 32 the third degree was the Scribe (Magpie) under Sirius, 33 the fourth degree was the Soldier (Falcon) under Mars, 34 the fifth degree was the Mendicant (Stork) under Jupiter, 35 the sixth

degree was the Martyred Hero (Condor) under Venus, 36 the seventh degree was the Father (Eagle) under Sun, 37 the eighth degree was the Priest (Owl) under the Moon, 38 the ninth degree was the Prophet (Crow) under the Comet, 39 the tenth degree was the Illuminated Man (Gewe) under the darkest night. 40 Thus began the Pythagorean mysteries, 41 and the theft of wisdom to create corruption, 42 the origin of the false mysteries, 43 the source of false knowledge, 44 the cause of the cleaving of all spirit. 45 In the Great Age of the Ram, 46 six hundred and eighty six years, 47 since the dawn of the Great Age (514 BCE), 48 Holly King Congal mac Lugaid, 49 to the north and the Kingdoms, 50 of Ulaid (Ulster) and Cóiced (Connacht), 51 and grandson of Holly High King Eoachaid, 52 did give up the ghost. 53 His kingdom then did befall to his son, 54 whose name was Conaing Bececlach.

C. 18

1 In the Great Age of the Ram, 2 six hundred and ninety years, 3 since the dawn of the Great Age (510 BCE), 4 King Hasdrubal of Carthage, 5 did give up the ghost. 6 The crown did then go to his son Hamilcar. 7 King Darius of Persia, 8 did offer a treaty through his general Mardonius, 9 by a plan conceived by Pythagorus and Haggiah, 10 that if the Levites as Etruscans, 11 and the Simonites as Graecians (Greeks), 12 did cease their feud, 13 then a neutral and sacred place, 14 would be chosen to build a mighty Persian city, 15 as a meeting place and safe sanctuary, 16 protected by an elite Persian Guard, 17 whereby all cities of Levites and Simonites, 18 would be recognised, 19 and the kings of these tribes, 20 honoured as equals known as Patricians, 21 as the fathers of a new world. 22 A leader would be chosen from each side, 23 and co-rule the assembly of Patricians, 24 known as the Senate, 25 as equals without dispute, 26 under the sacred motto, 27 that the Senate are the People who Rule (SPQR). 28 Thus under the patronage of King Darius, 29 of the Yahudi house of Menes (Menesheh), 30 and of the most ancient Yahudi of Reuben, 31 the sons of Sumer of RusNa, 32 and the sons of Sulumer of Graecia (Greece), 33 did found the city of Rama (Roma), 34 meaning sacred and neutral field. 35 Mardonius did leave in camp a garrison, 36 of several thousand Persian soldiers, 37 known as the Persian Guard (Praetorian Guard), 38 to keep the peace between both sides. 39 Pythagorus and Orpheus did present, 40 the sacred Pantheon in which the gods of all cities, 41 of the federation were to be honoured, 42 the sacred cult of priests known as Flamens, 43 would oversee the peace and the laws, 44 and the Senate would be the forum for representatives, 45 of each of the cities. 46 King Anaxilas and the Simonites, 47 agreed that his son who name was Junius (Aeneas), 48 be the first Consul for the Graecians (Greeks), 49 while King Turnus also appointed his son, 50 whose name was Titus as Consul for the Etruscans. 51 In the Great Age of the Ram, 52 six hundred and ninety one years, 53 since the dawn of the Great Age (509 BCE), 54 the sons of Remus (Sumer), 55 and the sons of Remulus (Sulumer), 56 honoured the wolf (Reuben), 57 that brought them together, 58 to form the

eternal sacred Persian city of Rome (Rama), [59] under the religion of Pythagorea and Mitra, [60] an eternal pledge to Persia, [61] as the protectors of the blood covenant (Mitra).

Book 16

Great Age of Persia
[508 - 430 BCE]

C. 1

1 In the Great Age of the Ram, 2 six hundred and ninety two years, 3 since the dawn of the Great Age (508 BCE), 4 one year after the founding of Rama (Rome), 5 King Daemos of Chimaera, 6 did conquer the Spartan city of Heraclea, 7 declaring himself a messiah of the Yahudi. 8 King Daemos did then found a new religion, 9 that it be the will of Yahu the divine creator, 10 that the Levites and Simonites return, 11 to the great island of Pegasus (Euboea), 12 and defeat the Argeans that enslaved them. 13 King Daemos of Chimaera, 14 did commission new scriptoriums, 15 and reading of sciences, 16 that all who swear an oath, 17 to this new religion, 18 be men of science not superstition. 19 King Daemos then did found a city in his name, 20 called Gela as a centre of knowledge. 21 In reply Pythagorus did declare, 22 that the followers of King Daemos, 23 be false believers, 24 who dishonour the Divine Creator, 25 by making false oaths, 26 to ideas they do not comprehend. 27 In the Great Age of the Ram, 28 six hundred and ninety four years, 29 since the dawn of the Great Age (506 BCE), 30 consul Junius (Aeneas) the son of King Anaxilas, 31 did give up the ghost. 32 Pythagorus did convince the Graecians (Greeks), 33 to appoint his son as the new Consul. 34 Consul Titus of the Etruscans, 35 did protest as Orpheus be a priest, 36 and son of Pythagorus, 37 was favoured by the Persians, 38 while the Etruscans then be forbidden, 39 to trade with the Carthagians. 40 In the same year, 41 Holly King Eoachaid Uairches, 42 of the south and the Kingdoms, 43 of Mumha (Munster) and Laighin (Leinster), 44 and grandson of Holly High King Eoachaid, 45 did give up the ghost. 46 His kingdom then did befall to his son, 47 whose name was Lugaid Lamderg.

C. 2

1 In the Great Age of the Ram, 2 six hundred and ninety five years, 3 since the dawn of the Great Age (505 BCE), 4 the religious forces of King Daemos, 5 did conquer the city of Catania, 6 aided by Persian General Artaphernes. 7 yet King Daemos was mortally wounded in battle. 8 His son Gelo did become King, 9 and aided by his brothers, 10 whose names were Hiero (Hero) and Thalo (Thales) and Zeno, 11 did rally forces against Apoleon (Syracuse), 12 and captured the great city. 13 Upon news of the great feats,

₁₄ of the sons and followers of King Daemos, ₁₅ many more Graecians (Greeks) joined the cult. ₁₆ In the Great Age of the Ram, ₁₇ six hundred and ninety seven years, ₁₈ since the dawn of the Great Age (503 BCE), ₁₉ Damasus of Siris, ₂₀ also known as Pythagorus, ₂₁ also known as father and friend of the people, ₂₂ of the sacred Persian city of Rome, ₂₃ did give up the ghost. ₂₄ A great funeral ceremony, ₂₅ was held in Rome. ₂₆ The title of Hiereus or Priest, ₂₇ and Soothsayer did fall to his son, ₂₈ whose name was Orpheus. ₂₉ King Gelo of Syracuse did then demand, ₃₀ that Consul Orpheus order all Yahudi, ₃₁ to give aid to a sacred campaign, ₃₂ to invade and capture, ₃₃ the island of Pegasus (Euboea), ₃₄ and punish the Argeans. ₃₅ Yet Orpheus refused. ₃₆ Thus King Gelo of Syracuse, ₃₇ did appeal directly to King Darius, ₃₈ through Artaphernes, ₃₉ who then agreed to provide troops and ships, ₄₀ under the command of Datus, ₄₁ for the great invasion. ₄₂ King Gelo did then appoint his brother, ₄₃ whose name was Hiero, ₄₄ as leader of the Graecians (Greeks).

C. 3

₁ In the Great Age of the Ram, ₂ six hundred and ninety eight years, ₃ since the dawn of the Great Age (502 BCE), ₄ a great fleet of Graecians (Greeks), ₅ and Persians under the command of Datus, ₆ did attack and invade Pegasus (Euboea), ₇ capturing Chalcis and Eritrea within twelve months. ₈ The Graecians (Greeks) and Persians, ₉ did also attack and destroy Argos, ₁₀ killing the great King Pheidos of Argos, ₁₁ before Datus did establish his capital, ₁₂ upon a high rock outcrop, ₁₃ upon the plain of Attica, ₁₄ protected by four great mountains. ₁₅ He called this fortress the Acropolis. ₁₆ In the Great Age of the Ram, ₁₇ six hundred and ninety nine years, ₁₈ since the dawn of the Great Age (501 BCE), ₁₉ upon the Graecian (Greek) forces, ₂₀ weakened through the war of invasion, ₂₁ of Pegasus (Euboea) and Argea, ₂₂ Consul Titus with the aid of the Veii, ₂₃ and the Volsci to the south of Rome, ₂₄ and the Aequi to the east, ₂₅ did attack the Persian Guard (Praetorian), ₂₆ slaughtering all of them, ₂₇ then did capture and kill Consul Orpheus, ₂₈ tearing his body into pieces, ₂₉ and throwing it into the Tiber. ₃₀ Titus then did declare himself Kaiser (Caesar), ₃₁ and Dictator of Rome. ₃₂ Kaiser Titus then claimed a new treaty, ₃₃ with Hamilcar of Carthage, ₃₄ who then did invade Sicily, ₃₅ and did capture and destroy Chimaera, ₃₆ restoring the ancient Carthage city of Balaam (Palermo).

C. 4

₁ In the Great Age of the Ram, ₂ seven hundred years, ₃ since the dawn of the Great Age (500 BCE), ₄ upon news of the invasion by Carthage, ₅ Aristagoras of Miletus in Anatolia, ₆ did cause the colonies under Persia, ₇ to rebel and destroy the Persian ships. ₈ The rebel forces of Ionian colonies, ₉ then did destroy the Persian city of Sardis. ₁₀ Yet the forces of Artaphernes stood firm, ₁₁ and Artaphernes himself survived. ₁₂ Soon rebellion was across the western Persian Empire. ₁₃ King Darius did then remove General Mardonius, ₁₄ who was exiled in disgrace, 15 and appointed three generals, 16 splitting Persian forces under Daurises, 17 and Hymaes and Octanes. 18 While the Persians were still in defence, 19 Aristagoras of Miletus, 20 and Lakedos of Argos the son of Pheidos, 21 did invade Pegasus (Euboea), 22 and killed Hiero the brother of Gelo, 23 after a prolonged siege of Chalcis. 24 Lakedos and Aristagoras then did siege, 25 Datus at his fortress at the Acropolis. 26 Yet for every attack the Persians defended.

C. 5

1 In the Great Age of the Ram, 2 seven hundred and one years, 3 since the dawn of the Great Age (499 BCE), 4 the Persians under Daurises sought to recapture, 5 the Island of Naxos, 6 to relieve the siege of Datus, 7 upon the plain of Attica. 8 Yet the invasion of the isle of Naxos, 9 was a terrible failure. 10 Instead general Daurisus did attack Ephesus, 11 and then conquering Cyprus. 12 The army of General Hymaes, 13 came north-east through the Propontus, 14 and did attack and reclaim, 15 the regions of Troad and Mysia, 16 in the north of Anatolia, 17 and the cities of Paesus, Abydos and Dardanus. 18 The army of General Octanes, 19 did come west along the Hermes river, 20 and relieved the garrison at Sardis, 21 before heading south towards Marysas, 22 and then finally towards Miletus. 23 Yet General Otanes did not destroy Miletus, 24 but spared the people of the Ionian cities, 25 and sent the rebellious leaders to Persia as slaves. 26 In the Great Age of the Ram, 27 seven hundred and five years, 28 since the dawn of the Great Age (495 BCE), 29 it had not occurred to King Darius, 30 that the forces of Datus at Acropolis, 31 upon the Attica plain, 32 could hold out for such time, 33 against the superior numbers, 34 of Argeans and Ionians. 35 So when the forces of Artaphernes, 36 landed at Marathon, 37 they prepared for battle against the Argeans. 38 Datus and his men did see the invasion fleet, 39 from the great plateau of the Acropolis, 40 and chose his fittest warrior, 41 whose name was Pheidippides, 42 to send word to the rescuers, 43 that the Persian fortress had held. 44 Pheidippides evaded the Argean lines, 45 and ran the 25 miles (40km) to Marathon, 46 to give word to Artaphernes, 47 saying to him that the Acropolis still stands. 48 Joyed at the news Artaphernes, 49 did then order an immediate attack, 50 urging Pheidippides to return and give warning. 51 Pheidippides did return to the Acropolis, 52 and gave word to Datus, 53 saying praise the Divine, we are victorious, 54 whereupon he died from exhaustion. 55 The Persians descended upon the Argeans, 56 like wild beasts, killing every last man. 57 Thereupon King Darius declared, 58 that Datus and his men, 59 be forever known as the Immortals, 60 and their fortress be a sacred sanctuary, 61 known as the Partheo (Parthenon), 62 meaning the place of the immortals. 63 Datus and his men returned to Persia, 64 the greatest of heroes throughout the empire, 65 and with his troops did become, 66 the famous bodyguards to the Persian kings.

C. 6

1 In the Great Age of the Ram, 2 seven hundred and six years, 3 since the dawn of the Great Age (494 BCE), 4 the forces of Persian General Octanes, 5 and Greek King Gelo did face against Kaiser Titus, 6 and his father King Turnus of the RusNa (Etruscans), 7 near the fortress of Tusculum, 8 southeast of Rome. 9 The Levites were no match for the Persians, 10 and the enraged Graecians (Greeks), 11 who destroyed their army and captured Rome, 12 killing both King Turnus and Titus. 13 General Octanes then did summons, 14 the leaders of all the Etruscans tribes and cities, 15 and all the Graecian (Greek) cities and tribes, 16 to the Senate of Rome, 17 whereupon he did issue terms, 18 that the religion of Pythagorus and Orpheus, 19 would be forbidden and suppressed, 20 and that only the religions of Yahudi or Mitra, 21 or the cult of science of King Daemos be permitted. 22 General Octanes then did pledge, 23 that no Etruscan city be destroyed, 24 nor would they lose their lands, 25 despite their dishonour and rebellion. 26 Instead each Etruscan city was to conscript, 27 every second son or any volunteer, 28 into a new military units called Legio, 29 to fight and defend the Persian Empire, 30 for service of ten years, 31 and for the city to levy one tenth, 32 of its wealth to military upkeep. 33 Only those who served in honour of Mitra, 34 be allowed to retain arms, 35 to defend the lands and homes, 36 and no army again be permitted, 37 to march within sight of Rome. 38 Thus the might of Rome, 39 being the cohorts were formed, 40 not by the ancient Simonites, 41 but by the Levites. 42 General Octanes then returned, 43 a Persian Guard to Rome, 44 with absolute power to execute or depose, 45 any Patrician guilty of treason, 46 against Persia or Rome. 47 The Persians then granted King Gelo, 48 to be Kaiser (Caesar) of Rome, 49 while his brother Thalo (Thales), 50 was granted King of Miletus and Euboea, 51 and his brother Zeno as King of Syracuse, 52 and Magna Graecia (Greece). 53 Thus the religious cult of King Deimo, 54 through his sons became, 55 the dominant religion of Rome.

C. 7

1 In the Great Age of the Ram, 2 seven hundred and fourteen years, 3 since the dawn of the Great Age (486 BCE), 4 King Darius of the Persians, 5 also known as the Yahudi tribe of Menes, 6 also known as the ancient Yahudi of Reuben, 7 did give up the ghost. 8 The crown did then befall to his son, 9 whose name was Xerxes (Pericles). 10 A wise and intelligent man, 11 Xerxes as a student was obsessed, 12 by the history of the treasures of Akhenaten (Moses), 13 and the origins of his empire. 14 He travelled to Elia with the immortals, 15 to seek audience with the great prophet Osiah (Hosea). 16 Yet prophet Osiah (Hosea) refused, 17 saying that until Persia acknowledged, 18 the rights of all men under the law, 19 and ended its false ways of the Yahudah, 20 of the false prophets, 21 no Persian king may rightfully hold, 22 the treasures of Akhenaten (Moses). 23 Xerxes Immediately then took control, 24 in suppressing the revolts in Egypt, 25 and travelling to Elephantine Isle

(Yeb). 26 There he met remaining Yahudi priests, 27 who spoke to him of his heritage, 28 and the ancient promise to Yahu, 29 his forefathers did take. 30 Xerxes then appointed his brother, 31 whose name was Achamenese as governor, 32 and returned to Babylon. 33 In the Great Age of the Ram, 34 seven hundred and sixteen years, 35 since the dawn of the Great Age (484 BCE), 36 Xerxes summonsed the false prophet Nehemiah, 37 son of Haggiah and chief priest of Mitra, 38 that he may explain the law. 39 Nehemiah did speak and say: 40 The law be whatever the king wish it to be, 41 that it be effected by might and sword, 42 that men must be ruled by fear and awe, 43 and that men of wealth be drawn to secrets. 44 Xerxes did then ask Nehemiah, 45 the provenance of the golden statue to Baal Moloch, 46 compared to the Ark of the Covenant of Moses, 47 to which the wicked false prophet replied, 48 that the Yahudah possessed knowledge, 49 of both the path of darkness and light, 50 and for most men the only achievement, 51 be wisdom through horror and blood. 52 Xerxes then did order the sacred gold statute, 53 of Baal Moloch be seized and destroyed, 54 that all the false priests of the Yahudah be banished, 55 to which the false prophet Nehemiah, 56 did succeed in causing the people of Babylon, 57 to briefly rise up against Xerxes. 58 Xerxes then did issue a high curse, 59 that Babylon be a whore before heaven, 60 that it be an empty vessel of law. 61 Thus it shall no longer be honoured as a capital, 62 nor residence of the Persian kings, 63 nor any descendant of Xerxes. 64 Instead the city shall be cursed, 65 and all that is created from it shall be cursed, 66 and all those who worship it shall be cursed, 67 and its beauty shall fade, 68 and be destroyed. 69 In the same year, 70 Holly King Conaing Bececlach, 71 of the north and the Kingdoms, 72 of Ulaid (Ulster) and Cóiced (Connacht), 73 did give up the ghost without heir. 74 His kingdom then did befall to Art, 75 the son of Holly King Lugaid Lamderg, 76 of the south and the Kingdoms, 77 of Mumha (Munster) and Laighin (Leinster).

C. 8

1 In the Great Age of the Ram, 2 seven hundred and seventeen years, 3 since the dawn of the Great Age (483 BCE), 4 Xerxes (Pericles) moved his entire court, 5 and his administration west to Sardis, 6 proclaiming it to be his new capital. 7 Thus a great migration, 8 of nearly one million people, 9 of warriors and military, 10 of scribes and priests, 11 of artisans and masons, 12 of stores and merchants all came, 13 to the lands of the Anatolians. 14 Xerxes then did send word, 15 to the great prophet Osiah (Hosea), 16 that the rule of law be restored, 17 that he had issued an edict against false idols, 18 that he had abandoned the whore of Babylon, 19 and that the rights of men, 20 be recognised before heaven. 21 The great prophet Osiah (Hosea) replied, 22 that no man be the judge of heaven, 23 and that if it be the will of the divine, 24 then let the divine give such sign. 25 Xerxes then was enraged by such refusal, 26 and upon Sardis being less suitable, 27 resolved himself to build a great city, 28 upon the foundations of Partheo, 29 upon the Attica plain, 30 where the Yahudi

priests shall come to him, 31 and not be prostrate before old men. 32 In the same year, 33 Holly King Lugaid Lamderg, 34 of the south and the Kingdoms, 35 of Mumha (Munster) and Laighin (Leinster), 36 did give up the ghost. 37 His kingdom then did befall to Art, 38 and the most sacred isle was again united, 39 under one living foundation stone of the Divine, 40 of the most ancient Cuilliaéan, 41 and blood descendant of the priests of Ebla, 42 and blood descendant of the priests of Ur, 43 and blood descendant of the priest-kings of the Hyksos, 44 and blood descendant of the priests of Ugarit, 45 and the only true blood descendants of King Da'vid, 46 and the Messiah Kings of Yahuda.

C. 9

1 In the Great Age of the Ram, 2 seven hundred and nineteen years, 3 since the dawn of the Great Age (481 BCE), 4 Xerxes did cross the Hellespont, 5 and pour into the north, 6 towards the lands of Elia, 7 and the great city of light, 8 known as Elios. 9 The great prophet Osiah (Hosea), 10 did then call out to all Yahudi, 11 to defend the sacred city of Elios, 12 and protect he most sacred treasures, 13 at the temple to heaven at Elea, 14 Along the Vale of the Temple. 15 Yet neither did Xerxes (Pericles) immediately attack, 16 nor did the Yahudi quickly respond, 17 to the entreats of Osiah (Hosea). 18 King Leonides of Sparta called a meeting, 19 of the Spartan and Dorian cities, 20 whereupon they all requested, 21 he swear to obey the Oracle of Delphi, 22 not the prophet of Yeb at Elios (Larissa), 23 who had insulted Xerxes, 24 and caused the invasion.

25 Leonides agreed and did speak to the Oracle, 26 who replied thus: 27 Oh strong and noble Sparta, 28 be there two streams, 29 which fate demands you must choose, 30 either to the death of your cities, 31 or to the destruction of your pride, 32 for no man be perfect, 33 but one who be king, 34 yet sacrifice himself for his people.

C. 10

1 In the Great Age of the Ram, 2 seven hundred and twenty years, 3 since the dawn of the Great Age (480 BCE), 4 Osiah (Hosea) the nineteenth great prophet of Yeb, 5 the son of Baruciah and the grandson of Jeremiah, 6 did give up the ghost, 7 at an advanced age. 8 The position then befell, 9 to his son whose name was Osanniah (Hosanna), 10 also known as Socrates, 11 as the twentieth Great Prophet of the Yahudi. 12 In the same year, 13 King Leonides and 300 of his finest warriors, 14 supported by other small groups of the Dorians, 15 did confront the Persians, 16 at Philo and the mouth of the Pontus, 17 that the Persians shall not pass through the Vale. 18 Xerxes implored that King Leonides stand aside, 19 and that he pledged not to destroy Elios, 20 nor take the treasures from the lands, 21 yet Leonides refused to yield, 22 and on the third day, 23 the Persians attacked. 24 Yet the Spartans held at the narrowest part, 25 where the Vale of the Temple, 26 possess the highest of cliffs, 27 and the narrowest of approach. 28 Wave after wave of Persians, 29 were defeated and slaughtered, 30 until Xerxes implored that a pathway be found, 31 to outflank the Spartan defenders, 32 whereupon

the finest Persian soldiers, 33 were shown the long path and surrounded Leonides, 34 and the brave Spartans were killed to the man. 35 Upon entering Elios, 36 Xerxes did take Osanniah (Hosanna), 37 also known as Socrates prisoner. 38 Upon the bravery of King Leonides, 39 King Xerxes (Pericles) did decree, 40 that no Spartan city be harmed, 41 thus fulfilling the sacred prophecy, 42 of the Oracle of Delphi.

C. 11

1 In the Great Age of the Ram, 2 seven hundred and twenty years, 3 since the dawn of the Great Age (480 BCE), 4 following the conquest of Elia, 5 by the forces of Xerxes, 6 and the heroic death of Leonides, 7 a massive fleet under the control of Mardonius, 8 did invade the lands and islands of the Argeans. 9 Capturing Melos, Sifnos, Serifos, Kythnos, Salamis, 10 then Megara Corinth and finally Argos. 11 The Persians did begin work immediately on a great channel, 12 opening the Saronic Gulf to the Corinthian Gulf, 13 while the Argeans planned their counter attack. 14 The Argeans sought to engage the Persians, 15 by splitting their fleet and pushing them, 16 into the narrow waters beside Salamis Isle. 17 Yet the forces of Mardonius were too skilled, 18 and the entire Argean fleet was destroyed. 19 Thus the ancient state of Argos was no more. 20 In the Great Age of the Ram, 21 seven hundred and twenty years, 22 since the dawn of the Great Age (480 BCE), 23 King Hamilcar of Carthage, 24 did seek the invasions of Xerxes, 25 as a pretext to launch his own great invasion, 26 of Graecia (Sicily), 27 on the assumption that the Greek forces, 28 were in support of Xerxes. 29 Yet the Carthaginians under estimated Rome. 30 Kaiser (Caesar) Gelo of Rome, 31 was able to raise the support of the Levite cohorts, 32 and his own reserves to counter attack. 33 Thus King Hamilcar of Carthage, 34 was killed at the Battle of Himera, 35 ending the Magonid line. 36 The Carthaginians did face such a terrible defeat, 37 the people rose up and elected a cartographer, 38 whose name was Hanno as their new king. 39 Carthage did not seek any further expeditions, 40 for many decades to come. 41 Xerxes did then commission his finest masons, 42 to build the greatest temple upon the Acropolis, 43 known simply as The Temple, 44 later known as the Parthanon, 45 and a fine palace atop the Acropolis, 46 all of which was finished in less than ten years.

C. 12

1 In the Great Age of the Ram, 2 seven hundred and thirty years, 3 since the dawn of the Great Age (470 BCE), 4 King Xerxes of Persia, 5 also known as the famous one (Pericles), 6 also known as the King of Kings, 7 did enter triumphant to the Acropolis, 8 and the new Temple of the Covenant, 9 in which the Treasures of Akhenaten, 10 and the Ark were placed in honour. 11 Osanniah (Hosanna) the twentieth great prophet of Yeb, 12 also known as Socrates did accompany Xerxes. 13 Xerxes did then boast to Osanniah (Socrates), 14 that no finer Temple be there to the Divine, 15 to which Socrates (Osanniah) did say, 16 all wealth and power fades, 17 but

wisdom is eternal. 18 Xerxes did then declare, 19 he would make the city his new capital, 20 and named it Athena, 21 meaning the place of flowering of all wisdom. 22 Socrates did then reply: 23 Let him who would move the world first move himself, 24 and Xerxes did pledge himself and his household, 25 as his students that he might teach them, 26 to which Socrates (Osanniah) did say, 27 then let this be the first lesson, 28 all I know, is that I am wise, 29 for I know that all I know is nothing.

C. 13

1 In the Great Age of the Ram, 2 seven hundred and thirty one years, 3 since the dawn of the Great Age (469 BCE), 4 a summons went out to the brightest minds, 5 to come to Athena where no amount be spared, 6 to build a paradise to wisdom and the best of men. 7 Xerxes ordered a great theatre to be constructed, 8 and three men of profound talents, 9 whose names were Sophocles, Aeschylus and Euripides, 10 did come and begin to write plays. 11 Great historians did also come, 12 such as Heroditus and Thucydides, 13 whose works were later corrupted. 14 To encourage debate and fraternity, 15 Xerxes constructed the great Agora (forum). 16 When Xerxes showed his tutor Socrates (Hosannah), 17 the accomplishments of his city, 18 Socrates did reply: 19 Wonder is the beginning of wisdom, 20 yet men who seek only wealth and pleasure are still slaves. 21 To which Xerxes in frustration, 22 did call upon his teacher to guide him, 23 by what means he may do more? 24 To which Socrates did reply: 25 One can forgive a child who is afraid of the dark, 26 yet the greatest tragedy, 27 is when good men are afraid of the light.

C. 14

1 In the Great Age of the Ram, 2 seven hundred and thirty two years, 3 since the dawn of the Great Age (468 BCE), 4 Xerxes did rename all the lands, 5 and all the islands known as Eliada, 6 to the sacred name of Acadia, 7 meaning all men are equal under the Divine, 8 as Paradise (Heaven) on Earth, 9 where no man be a slave, 10 or less than another. 11 Upon seeing the proclamation of Xerxes, 12 Socrates (Hosannah) did say, 13 if one is still not free, 14 then none are free. 15 Xerxes did then refuse to speak with Socrates, 16 enraged by his uncompromising wisdom, 17 yet permitted his son to continue as his student. 18 In the Great Age of the Ram, 19 seven hundred and thirty four years, 20 since the dawn of the Great Age (466 BCE), 21 a league of cities of Asia Minor, 22 who called themselves the Delian League, 23 led by Simon of Perga, 24 who declared himself the king of Pamphyloi, 25 did launch an attack against Athena, 26 destroying the Persian fleet. 27 Yet Socrates (Hosannah) did succeed, 28 in calling King Pleistarchus of Sparta, 29 to the aid of the Persians. 30 Upon the arrival of the Spartans, 31 the fleet of Simon of Perga retreated. 32 Xerxes thus declared a sacred bond, 33 that the Spartans be sacred allies, 34 never again to be challenged. 35 Xerxes then demanded that not only Athena, 36 but the entire port of Piraeus, 37 be protected by the largest walls of ancient times. 38 Within the year the

Persians defeated Simon of Perga, 39 raising the city to dust, 40 declaring Perga to be a cursed place, 41 where no soul may leave. 42 Within fifteen years, 43 the great walls of Athens and its port, 44 were finally completed.

C. 15

1 In the Great Age of the Ram, 2 seven hundred and thirty seven years, 3 since the dawn of the Great Age (463 BCE), 4 a great earthquake struck the Peloponnese, 5 devastating Sparta and many of its cities. 6 Athena itself was also damaged, 7 yet neither Xerxes (Pericles) nor Socrates, 8 or the royal household, 9 or the priests were harmed. 10 News of the great earthquake of Sparta, 11 and the devastation and deaths of tens of thousands, 12 swirled like thick mist across the empire. 13 Xerxes instead chose to ignore such rumours, 14 as his claimed death or murder, 15 But pledged to oversee the repair of Athena, 16 and to visit King Pleistarchus of Sparta, 17 the son of the Great Leonidas, 18 and offer the finest resources of Persia, 19 in rebuilding Sparta as a city of magnificence. 20 Yet the rumours of the death of Xerxes, 21 persisted until they spawned rebellion, 22 in Egypt and Asia Minor, 23 in parts of Mesopotamia and even Rome, 24 where the Senate appointed, 25 Gaius Aemilius Mamercus as dictator. 26 Xerxes ordered his generals to put down the rebellions, 27 then summonsed his old teacher Socrates, 28 that he might answer why people, 29 to whom he had given so much, 30 in ending poverty and corruption, 31 in permitting local worship and customs, 32 would still rebel against Persian rule. 33 Socrates (Hosannah) did reply, 34 that a man who is not free to consent, 35 to his own form of rule of law, 36 is neither free nor bound to obey the law, 37 for the laws of a tyrant, 38 are still by force or fear and not consent, 39 no matter how benevolent be the tyrant.

C. 16

1 In the Great Age of the Ram, 2 seven hundred and thirty nine years, 3 since the dawn of the Great Age (461 BCE), 4 the rebellion of Egypt was crushed, 5 the uprisings of Asia and Mesopotamia, 6 had been put down, 7 and the Spartan cities were under repair, 8 as the great city of Athena, 9 itself was restored to higher brilliance. 10 Whereupon Xerxes did command, 11 henceforth the lands of Acadia, 12 the kingdom of heaven on earth, 13 be according to the Golden Rule, 14 that all men be borne equal, 15 that no man is above the law, 16 this be the Rule of Law. 17 In honour of the wisdom of Socrates (Hosannah), 18 Acadia was to be forever more, 19 the first state of heaven and the people, 20 according to the rule of Democratia, 21 which means Rule by the Consent of the People. 22 Xerxes ordered that Athena be a Polis, 23 in which all men who declare an oath, 24 be citizens and possess the right to elect, 25 the government of the city and state, 26 which was then called the Aristocratia, 27 or simply the Council (Committee) of 300. 28 Xerxes then ordered the Aristocratia, 29 perfect a civil law for all the people, 30 to be displayed in the Agora, 31 that all men may know the law. 32 Thus upon this year and

moment, 33 athena became the birthplace of Democracy.

C. 17

1 In the Great Age of the Ram, 2 seven hundred and forty years, 3 since the dawn of the Great Age (460 BCE), 4 King Hanno of Carthage, 5 did give up the ghost. 6 The crown did then go to his son Himilco. 7 In the Great Age of the Ram, 8 seven hundred and forty five years, 9 since the dawn of the Great Age (455 BCE), 10 upon the success of Democracy, 11 and the State of Acadia, 12 Xerxes ordered that all cities of the Empire, 13 form their own civil law and constitution, 14 that no place be a city (polis), 15 without law, 16 that no land be a state, 17 without a constitution. 18 All cities from Rome to Babylon, 19 from Gortyn to Jerusalem, 20 were granted the right to form their own law, 21 providing no man be considered greater, 22 that the Golden Rule be honoured, 23 and all be equal under the law. 24 The false prophet Ezriah, 25 son of Nehemiah, 26 did use the edict to travel to Jerusalem, 27 where he created the scriptures of Mithra, 28 declaring the 14 Nisan (14th March), 29 the birthday of Mithra, 30 the birthday of the universe, 31 and the day of eternal sacrifice and redemption. 32 The Roman Senate promulgated its own laws, 33 called the Twelve Tables.

C. 18

1 In the Great Age of the Ram, 2 seven hundred and forty nine years, 3 since the dawn of the Great Age (451 BCE), 4 as celebration of ten years, 5 since Xerxes granted the men of Athena, 6 self-rule under Rule of Law, 7 the Oligarchy of the Council of 300, 8 did commission Phidias, 9 to construct a massive statue of Xerxes, 10 upon the Acropolis, 11 near the great gates known as the Propylaea. 12 Within three years the statue was complete, 13 measuring more than 60 ft in height, 14 so that from its base, 15 it was higher than the Temple (Parthenon), 16 with Xerxes in full armour, 17 holding the torch of liberty high in his right hand, 18 and a great spear low in his left hand. 19 The bronze effigy was so large, 20 that its reflection could be sighted by crews on ships, 21 as they rounded Cape Sounion, 22 more than forty miles in distance. 23 The members of the Oligarchy, 24 both fearful and jealous of Socrates, 25 called upon him to dedicate the monument, 26 to which Socrates declined and said: 27 No man be deserving as to be worshipped a god, 28 for all the minds of men are immortal, 29 yet only the minds of the virtuous, 30 are both immortal and divine. 31 Yet the great statute of Xerxes, 32 captured the hearts and awe of all, 33 so that within a few years, 34 pilgrims from all over the world, 35 came to Athena not only to pay homage, 36 but to worship at the feet of the colossus. 37 In the Great Age of the Ram, 38 seven hundred and fifty nine years, 39 since the dawn of the Great Age (441 BCE), 40 the Oligarchy did order, 41 that the Constitution of Athena be changed, 42 that Xerxes be immortalised, 43 as the living god and saviour of the city, 44 not as Esus but as Zeus. 45 Again the Oligarchy sought division, 46 between Xerxes and Socrates, 47 from their eternal discourse, 48 atop the Acropolis, 49 to which Socrates did reply: 50 Great

minds discuss ideas, 51 average minds discuss events, 52 weak minds discuss people.

C. 19

1 In the Great Age of the Ram, 2 seven hundred and sixty seven years, 3 since the dawn of the Great Age (433 BCE), 4 Holly High King Art did give up the ghost. 5 The throne of Amen-Ra did then befall to his son, 6 whose name was Ailil mac Art. 7 In the Great Age of the Ram, 8 seven hundred and sixty nine years, 9 since the dawn of the Great Age (431 BCE), 10 Acadia and the Athenians had become exceedingly wealthy, 11 no more so than the Aristocratia, 12 that they sought to diminish the power and authority, 13 of the Holly priests of the Covenant. 14 Anytus of the Oligarchy of thirty, 15 of the Aristocracy (Council) of three hundred, 16 did issue the decree that upon the thirty year anniversary, 17 of the dedication of the great colossus of Zeus, 18 and in recognition of the deification of Xerxes, 19 that all men must attend the feast, 20 and pledge a sacred oath to the living god of the city, 21 as this was now the law of the people, 22 and the Rule of Law. 23 Socrates declined to participate, 24 and so the Oligarchy petitioned Xerxes, 25 that Socrates (Hosannah) be handed to them for trial, 26 on the charges of disrespecting the patron deity of the city, 27 and introducing new deities. 28 Xerxes declined and warned the Council, 29 that if they should harm one hair of Socrates, 30 then he would surely render them all to dust, 31 whereupon Socrates pleaded with Xerxes, 32 that he swear a sacred oath to harm no man, 33 who bear false witness against him, 34 for if men were to rise above ignorance, 35 the law itself must be sacred, 36 even if wicked men seek to abuse it. 37 Xerxes gave his word and Socrates left the Acropolis, 38 to be arrested and taken by the Council of 300. 39 Anytus assisted by Meletus and others of the Oligarchy, 40 brought Socrates before the Council of 300, 41 and presented the charges, 42 to which they were astounded when Socrates admitted, 43 that if this truly be the law of the people, 44 then he be culpable. 45 The Council then was deeply worried, 46 for they feared a vote of capital punishment, 47 and had yearned instead, 48 that the power of the priests be weakened. 49 Socrates (Hosanna) replied that if the law demands death, 50 then justice be done, 51 or the Council be unfit to rule. 52 Thus the Council ordered Socrates be put to death, 53 for this be the punishment by rule of law. 54 A poison of gentle action by fatal consequence, 55 was prepared and given to Socrates, 56 who upon consuming his sentence did speak: 57 Flesh to earth, garments to ashes, wealth to dust. 58 All men die, 59 but blessed are those who may choose, 60 the hour and nature of departure, 61 that such act may strengthen not harm the law.

C. 20

1 In the Great Age of the Ram, 2 seven hundred and sixty nine years, 3 since the dawn of the Great Age (431 BCE), 4 Osanniah (Hosanna) the twentieth great prophet of Yeb, 5 the son of Osiah (Hosea) and the grandson of Baruciah, 6 also known as Socrates, 7 did give up the ghost. 8 The position

then befell, 9 to his son whose name was Eliah, 10 as the twenty first Great Prophet of the Yahudi. 11 Xerxes upon the execution of his teacher, 12 at the hands of the Aristocratia, 13 without a single Athenian in protest, 14 caused the old king to fall into a deep malady. 15 He ordered Socrates be embalmed, 16 and then placed in state atop the Acropolis, 17 that all may pay homage, 18 whereupon Xerxes (Pericles) gave his last speech, 19 that if any man call himself a man, 20 let him measure himself not by what he knows, 21 but how he acts with humility and respect. 22 For if a man seeks high office, 23 then let him come as a pauper, 24 that none may say he seeks fortune, 25 let him come as a servant of law, 26 that none may say he seeks corruption, 27 let him come upon his sacred oath, 28 that none may question his good faith. 29 If a king truly be a king, 30 let him be measured by his honour of the law, 31 that he would sacrifice himself, 32 than see the justice fail. 33 For what man is truly a man, 34 if he does not seek to make a better world? 35 Let all ages call out the name, 36 Hosanna (Socrates), 37 Hosanna (Socrates), 38 Hosanna in the highest. 39 For no greater love a man have, 40 than to give himself to save our virtue, 41 and the dream of our new world.

C. 21

1 In the Great Age of the Ram, 2 seven hundred and seventy years, 3 since the dawn of the Great Age (430 BCE), 4 King Xerxes (Pericles) of Persia, 5 the King of Kings, 6 the King honoured as Zeus, 7 a God amongst men, 8 also known of the Yahudi tribe of Menes, 9 also known of the ancient Yahudi of Reuben, 10 did give up the ghost. 11 The crown did then befall to his son, 12 who was named the Son of God, 13 the King of Kings, 14 and Artaxerxes, 15 also known as the foreign voice (Xenophon).

C. 22

1 Artaxerxes called upon his troops, 2 aided by the Spartans, 3 to surround Athena, 4 as he ordered his court and household, 5 to establish his new capital as Elios (Larissa), 6 where he pledged to rebuild, 7 a great city of illumination, 8 of free and equal men, 9 honouring rule of law and justice, 10 upon the wisdom of knowledge and virtue, 11 not the hubris and arrogance of Athena. 12 Artaxerxes then addressed the Council of 300, 13 and the citizens of Athena, 14 who had manipulated the laws, 15 to cause the death of Socrates, 16 and the unhappy death of his old father. 17 To the Athenians he said: 18 You desire wealth over virtue, 19 and false praise over life, 20 then let the city be sealed, 21 that no living thing enter, 22 and no living thing leave. 23 Acadia no longer be a garden of the divine, 24 but a cursed place of wickedness and evil, 25 where shadows of ghosts and demons, 26 shall be bound and imprisoned. 27 That if such false gods have real power, 28 then let the gold and jewels of Athenians, 29 become food and water, 30 then let them eat and drink of its sustenance. 31 Whereupon Artaxerxes departed, 32 and all the entrances and exits of Athens were sealed, 33 with guards placed all around so that none could leave, 34 and none could enter. 35 Within the first few days, 36 the people of the city

ignored the curse, 37 but by the seventh day the people did kill the council, 38 by the tenth day the people became like animals, 39 for the city never cared for making provisions, 40 by the thirtieth day the city was silent, 41 by the ninetieth day no living thing remained, 42 and Athena became the most cursed city of the dead.

Book 17

Great Age of Eliada

[430 - 323 BCE]

C. 1

In the Great Age of the Ram, 2 seven hundred and seventy years, 3 since the dawn of the Great Age (430 BCE), 4 as Athena remained surrounded and sealed as punishment, 5 Artaxerxes issued a decree to all satraps, 6 from Indus to the east, 7 to Armenia in the centre, 8 to Arabia in the south, 9 and Italia to the west, 10 that the name of the Empire, 11 was to now be known as Eliada, 12 meaning the states of the Illuminated Divine, 13 on account of Elios (Larissa) as the new capital, 14 meaning the city of illumination, 15 and the city of the divine sun. 16 Yet smaller city states around the Peloponnese, 17 began to rebel in defiance and fear, 18 of the fate of Athena. 19 The first of these was Megara, 20 followed by Pylos. 21 Other cities and islands quickly followed, 22 such as Eretria on Euboea, 23 and the isles of Chios and Lesbos. 24 Artaxerxes immediately ordered the rebellion put down, 25 which in turn sparked a greater uprising, 26 of the satraps of Thrace, Ionia, Phrygia, Karia and Graecia (Sicily). 27 With the trade of the Aegean threatened by wider revolt, 28 Artaxerxes chose to put down the revolt in Thrace first, 29 followed by Phrygia, Ionia and then Karia. 30 His generals then dealt with the rebel Peloponnese cities, 31 destroying Megara and Pylos to its foundations, 32 and emptying the island of Euboea of people, 33 then sent eastward as forced labourers, 34 into Parthia and Hyrcania. 35 In the Great Age of the Ram, 36 seven hundred and seventy nine years, 37 since the dawn of the Great Age (421 BCE), 38 the forces of Artaxerxes invaded Graecia (Sicily), 39 to seek to re-establish order. 40 Yet the Eliada (Persian) fleet was destroyed, 41 by a united fleet from Graecia, 42 led by Syracuse.

C. 2

1 In the Great Age of the Ram, 2 seven hundred and eighty years, 3 since the dawn of the Great Age (420 BCE), 4 Artaxerxes (Xenophon) had completed the restoration of Elios, 5 and the creation of the great gardens temples and libraries, 6 known as the Academie (Academy), 7 as a new centre of learning for the world. 8 The Ark of the Covenant and the artefacts of Akhenaten, 9 placed in a new Temple complex at the centre of the city. 10 In the Great Age of the Ram, 11

seven hundred and eighty three years, 12 since the dawn of the Great Age (417 BCE), 13 Eliah the twenty first great prophet of Yeb, 14 also known as Eli, 15the son of Osanniah (Hosanna) and the grandson of Osiah (Hosea), 16 did give up the ghost. 17 The position then befell, 18 to his son whose name was Oadiah, 19 as the twenty second Great Prophet of the Yahudi.

C. 3

1 In the Great Age of the Ram, 2 seven hundred and ninety one years, 3 since the dawn of the Great Age (409 BCE), 4 King Artaxerxes of Eliada (Persia), 5 also known as the King of Kings, 6 also known as the Son of God, 7 also known as the foreign voice (Xenophon), 8 also known as the Yahudi tribe of Menes, 9 also known as the ancient Yahudi of Reuben, 10 did give up the ghost. 11 The crown did then befall to his son, 12 whose name was Arxenes, 13 also known as Plato, 14 and also known as Artaxerxes II. 15 Upon Arxenes (Plato) becoming King, 16 the Satrap of Hyrcania of the House of Ochus, 17 did Rebel against Artaxerxes, 18 aided by the Parthians. 19 Ochus did then seize the most sacred city of Persepolis, 20 the ancient home of the Menes, 21 and then declared himself anointed by Ahura Mazda, 22 as the reincarnation of King Darius the Great, 23 in opposition to the Divine Creator known as Theos (God), 24 and the teachings of equality amongst men, 25 as the Golden Rule of Law. 26 Ochus as the Imposter Darius claimed divine right, 27 that some men are born greater than others, 28 and that the divine permits different laws, 29 for the elite of society compared to slaves.

30 His message combined with traditional beliefs, 31 caused many of the satraps of the east to pledge loyalty, 32 and the empire was now divide in two, 33 and the stage for civil war.

C. 4

1 In the Great Age of the Ram, 2 seven hundred and ninety one years, 3 since the dawn of the Great Age (409 BCE), 4 upon news of the death of Artaxerxes, 5 navigator Himilco of Carthage, 6 led an invasion force to Graecia (Sicily), 7 seeking first to capture Selinus to the west. 8 The Greeks did ferociously defend their city, 9 and while Himilco was victorious, 10 it was at the expense of many men. 11 Upon news of the fall of Selinus, 12 the elders of Syracuse quickly appointed Dionysus as tyrant, 13 that he defend the city against attack. 14 Dionysus then sought alliances with smaller cities, 15 that he be capable of holding the Carthaginians, 16 from direct siege. 17 Himilco soon had reinforcements, 18 that Dionysus and Syracuse were outnumbered. 19 Yet Dionysus appealed to all the people of Syracuse directly, 20 declaring he be the son of the god Zeus (Xerxes), 21 and the son of the Semele the daughter of Kadmos, 22 the true name of Baal. 23 That if any man or woman or slave pledge absolute obedience, 24 and fight for him then he be free. 25 Dionysus then created a ritual whereby men and woman, 26 died to themselves and suffered symbolic trial, 27 to be reborn and possessed by spirits and demons, 28 claiming they then had great strength and wisdom. 29 When the

Carthaginians attacked, 30 they were overwhelmed by the frenzied forces of Dionysus, 31 until Himilco himself was under siege. 32 In the Great Age of the Ram, 33 seven hundred and ninety four years, 34 since the dawn of the Great Age (406 BCE), 35 navigator Himilco of Carthage, 36 the first amongst equals, 37 of the Carthage Council of Elders, 38 did give up the ghost, 39 during his failed campaign in Sicily. 40 The office did then go to Mago, 41 who agreed to terms with Dionysus. 42 To celebrate victory, 43 Dionysus declared himself patron god of Graecia (Sicily), 44 commencing a week of celebrations, 45 where people consumed wine and other drugs, 46 and obscene orgies of lust went unchecked, 47 while Dionysus introduced a new secret ritual, 48 to the leaders of all the cities of Sicily, 49 who pledged their loyalty to him, 50 in the sacrifice of a new born baby, 51 slaughtered and eaten in a cave, 52 as a symbol of eternal loyalty to Zeus (Xerxes), 53 who gives and can take away eternal life.

C. 5

1 In the Great Age of the Ram, 2 seven hundred and ninety two years, 3 since the dawn of the Great Age (408 BCE), 4 King Arxenes (Plato), 5 also known as Artaxerxes II, 6 sought first to appeal to the satraps, 7 to pledge their loyalty to the empire, 8 from common love of wisdom and culture, 9 than the shallow lust for power and wealth. 10 Yet the appeal to reason was taken as a sign, 11 not of strength of character but weakness, 12 and Alcibiades the Satrap of Karka (Church), 13 declared from his city at Ephesus, 14 to be the King of Lydia, 15 encompassing the satraps of Ionia, Karka and Phrygia. 16 Never before had Lydia existed, 17 Yet Alcibiades to support his false claim, 18 invented untold frauds and fantasies, 19 of a mythical kingdom emerging from Troy, 20 and kings as heroes who first invented money, 21 that possessed the power of foresight and forethought, 22 to which King Arxenes (Plato) famously cried out in frustration: 23 What does it profit a man to gain the whole world, 24 yet lose his soul?

C. 6

1 Midst the empire of Eliada falling into anarchy, 2 King Arxenes (Plato) of Persia, 3 also known as Artaxerxes II did summons his loyal generals. 4 No more would he appeal to merchants and administrators, 5 but to men of loyalty and honour as soldiers of the Divine. 6 King Arxenes (Plato) then presented the Fasces, 7 being a bundle of wooden rods and a single axe, 8 strapped together by leather, 9 to which King Arxenes (Plato) announced: 10 These sticks and axe held by straps, 11 be the symbol of the perfect state, 12 as the symbol of justice and rule of law, 13 the wooden sticks as corporal punishment, 14 and the axe as the symbol of capital punishment, 15 bound by knowledge and love of law. 16 A king be like a father, 17 and his subjects be like his children. 18 He may speak to them of knowledge, 19 but without disciplines the children cease to learn. 20 That all men who gain self-knowledge are immortal, 21 that life is a dream and all the world is made up of ideas. 22 Thus the pursuit of wealth is futile, 23

as too is the desire for power. 24 But men who pledge themselves to austerity and obedience, 25 to honour and humility can never die. 26 Thus as single sticks, we may be divided and broken, 27 but as Divine Soldiers of the Sons of God, 28 we are unconquerable. 29 King Arxenes (Plato) then issued each general, 30 with the sacred text called Republic, 31 saying that all men who seek self-knowledge are equal, 32 and choose then to be rulers, 33 yet men who choose to live like animals, 34 in the pursuit of wealth and pleasure, 35 choose themselves to be ruled.

C. 7

1 In the Great Age of the Ram, 2 seven hundred and ninety four years, 3 since the dawn of the Great Age (406 BCE), 4 the forces of King Arxenes (Plato) of Eliada, 5 united under the symbol of the fasces (Republic), 6 utterly destroyed the forces of Alcibiades, 7 and captured the city of Ephesus, 8 burning it to the ground as punishment. 9 King Arxenes (Plato) and his army then moved east, 10 to confront the imposter and pretender Darius, 11 capturing Mesopotamia and returning law. 12 In the Great Age of the Ram, 13 seven hundred and ninety nine years, 14 since the dawn of the Great Age (401 BCE), 15 the army of the false King Darius, 16 of the House of Ochos, 17 was defeated at Cunaxa, 18 near the city of Babylon. 19 Ochos himself was killed. 20 Yet his son did escape, 21 and sought refuge in Syria, 22 before being rescued by the priests of Mithra. 23 Ochos the Younger was then brought before Ezra, 24 where Ezra the false High Priest did declare, 25 that if Ochos the Younger did swear obedience to Mithra, 26 and the supremacy of the priests, 27 and the return of the Ark of the Covenant, 28 to the city of Jerusalem, 29 then they would help him create, 30 the greatest empire in history. 31 Ochos the Younger then did become the first king, 32 ordained under the religion of Mithra, 33 and proclaimed himself to be Cyrus.

C. 8

1 In the Great Age of the Ram, 2 eight hundred and one years, 3 since the dawn of the Great Age (399 BCE), 4 the Imposter King Cyrus did declare, 5 under the direction of Ezra, 6 that 14th Nisan (14th March) of the year, 7 seven hundred and forty five years, 8 since the dawn of the Great Age (455 BCE), 9 being the Day and Year Jerusalem was granted, 10 its own constitution and laws by Xerxes, 11 be year zero of a new calendar, 12 of the refined religion of Mithra, 13 to celebrate the birthday of Mithra, 14 and the birth of a new world, 15 Cyrus ordered the old solar calendar to be rejected, 16 to be replaced by a complicated moon based calendar, 17 that Ezra and the priests of Mithra created, 18 the first month being Nisan of March/ April, 19 the second month being called Iyyar of April/ May, 20 the third month being called Siman of May/ June, 21 the fourth month being called Duzu of June/ July, 22 the fifth month being called Ab of July/ August, 23 the sixth month being called Ulul of August/ September, 24 the seventh month being called Tasrit of September/ October, 25 the eighth month being called Ashsam of

October/ November, 26 the ninth month being called Kisilim of November/ December, 27 the tenth month being called Tebet of December/ January, 28 the eleventh month being called Shabat of January/ February, 29 the twelfth month being called Adar of February/ March, 30 and every six years the month of Shaitan (Satan) added, 31 to correct the calendar due to its gross error. 32 Cyrus under orders from Ezra also decreed a new zodiac, 33 ending thousands of years of tradition of eight houses, 34 for twelve houses in the heavens, 35 for which the heavens did not evenly match. 36 Imposter King Cyrus did then declare that the 14th Nisan, 37 be known as the New Year and the Day of Blood, 38 and the Day of Passover, when death was conquered, 39 that Mithra was the light of the world, 40 that he was born from the sacred Rock of Jerusalem, 41 and that all good men must make a pilgrimage to Jerusalem, 42 or else their soul in the afterlife be in peril. 43 Thus despite the falsities and absurdities, 44 of this false religion, 45 many people subscribed to the demand for fear and awe, 46 and for blood atonement, 47 and the fear of divine judgement.

C. 9

1 In the Great Age of the Ram, 2 eight hundred and two years, 3 since the dawn of the Great Age (398 BCE), 4 Dionysus of Syracuse and Graecia (Sicily), 5 broke his peace treaty with Carthage, 6 and attacked the city of Motya in Sicily, 7 killing all its inhabitants and raising it to the ground. 8 The elders of Carthage then ordered Navigator Mago, 9 to take a massive army and retake Motya in Sicily, 10 while a second invasion army under the command of Hanno, 11 landed in the north near Ostia, 12 to stop any reinforcements, 13 and outflank the Graecians. 14 The massive forces of the Carthaginians under Mago, 15 took Dionysus by surprise, 16 recapturing the ruins of Mago, 17 then taking Messina, Catana, Naxos and Lentini, 18 before laying siege to Syracuse and capturing the city, 19 but not its fortress island of Ortygia. 20 Dionysus and his remaining forces escaped for their lives, 21 and headed east to Attica, 22 hiding amongst the abandoned and cursed ruins of Athena, 23 that neither King Arxenes (Plato) or the Spartans, 24 were at first aware of his presence. 25 The Roman tribes quickly formed into Legions, 26 and sought to defend against the Carthaginian invasion. 27 However, the Persian (Praetorian) Guard remained, 28 protectors of the city, 29 while the Romans were pushed back by the Carthaginians. 30 To stop the slaughter of the Romans, 31 the Praetorian broke their sacred oath, 32 and left Rome unprotected to engage the forces of Hanno, 33 putting them into retreat and saving the Roman people. 34 But in a deliberate act of brutality, 35 the Carthaginians burnt and sacked Rome, 36 killing every woman and child. 37 In response the Romans pledged an eternal and unbreakable oath, 38 to the defence of Eliada and to the true kings of Persia, 39 and a high curse that one day, they would wipe Carthage, 40 from the face of the earth. 41 In the same year, 42 Holly High King Ailil mac Art, 43 of the most ancient Cuilliaéan, 44 of the

Messiah bloodline of King Da'vid, 45 did give up the ghost. 46 The throne of Amen-Ra did then befall to his son, 47 whose name was Eochaid mac Ailella.

C. 10

1 In the Great Age of the Ram, 2 eight hundred and three years, 3 since the dawn of the Great Age (397 BCE), 4 the false prophet known as Ezra, 5 of the false Yahudi of Babylon, 6 also known as the High Priest of Mithra, 7 and son of Nehemiah, 8 did give up the ghost. 9 The title of High Priest of Mithra, 10 did then befall to his son, 11 whose name was Habakiah. 12 In the same year, 13 King Arxenes (Plato), 14 also known as Artaxerxes II, 15 ordered King Agesilaus of Sparta, 16 to lead an army to Asia, 17 to defeat Cyrus and rid the world of Mithraism.

C. 11

1 In the Great Age of the Ram, 2 eight hundred and four years, 3 since the dawn of the Great Age (396 BCE), 4 Dionysus and his surviving troops in Athena, 5 had stumbled into the greatest tomb of riches, 6 of the ancient world. 7 For no man dared cross the Persian and Spartan guards, 8 who stood as sentinels to the cursed city of the dead. 9 Yet more feared that a painful death by people, 10 were the demons and ghosts said to inhabit such a place. 11 Dionysus then struck upon an idea. 12 So vast were the treasures of the cursed city, 13 he would use it to fund the greatest militia army in history. 14 To each of his men he gave the most valuable of jewels and artefacts, 15 and ordered them to travel to every city across the world, 16 to proclaim that Dionysus had conquered death, 17 and travelled to the underworld to face the king of souls, 18 who then granted Dionysus the keys to eternal life, 19 and the power to command or ward off spirits, 20 and whosoever he condemned would be tortured forever, 21 in the bowels of the furnaces of Hades. 22 The men of Dionysus were told to say, 23 that upon his resurrection from death, 24 Dionysus then ascended into heaven, 25 to be granted the power to heal and live a prosperous life. 26 That if any man take up arms in the name of Dionysus, 27 so long as he believed in the resurrection, 28 and the truth of Dionysus as saviour of the world, 29 then he shall be granted such riches in this world and the next. 30 So the men of Dionysus followed his orders, 31 and travelled to the cities of the world, 32 and within a few weeks the dead city of Athena, 33 was full of tens of thousands of militia, 34 and the coast with hundreds of warships. 35 Dionysus then declared a new name for Athena, 36 calling it Thebes, 37 and the capital of a new kingdom, 38 the Kingdom of Thebes.

C. 12

1 In the Great Age of the Ram, 2 eight hundred and five years, 3 since the dawn of the Great Age (395 BCE), 4 King Arxenes (Plato), 5 also known as Artaxerxes II, 6 was enraged upon hearing of the acts of Dionysus, 7 and his false spiritual teachings, 8 saying: What kind of madness entrap the world, 9 that a man may utter such falsities, 10 yet people believe them? 11 King Arxenes (Plato) then ordered the Spartans to return, 12 and take Athens from Dionysus and his Theban band.

13 King Agesilaus of Sparta and his forces returned, 14 to be overwhelmed by the numbers of militia, 15 first at Haliartas in the Boeotia region, 16 then at Koronea then Nemea and then at Cnidus. 17 Yet even the superiority of the Spartans, 18 could not replace their ranks, 19 with the numbers of militia and mercenaries, 20 that had come from the four corners of the world, 21 to worship the gold of Dionysus. 22 The false king Cyrus of Persia, 23 had also noted the power of Dionysus now of Thebes, 24 and sent his best general Bardyllis, 25 to meet with Dionysus, 26 so that a treaty might be agreed, 27 and that together King Arxenes (Plato), 28 be defeated. 29 Yet Dionysus had no interest in attacking Plato, 30 nor in engaging with any treaty with Cyrus. 31 Instead he launched a great invasion, 32 to recapture Syracuse and Graecia, 33 from the Carthaginians. 34 Within two years Dionysus had regained Syracuse, 35 and fought Carthage to a standstill, 36 whereby Dionysus controlled the east, 37 and Carthage controlled the west of Graecia (Sicily).

C. 13

1 In the Great Age of the Ram, 2 eight hundred and fourteen years, 3 since the dawn of the Great Age (386 BCE), 4 after ten years of fighting, 5 and wave after wave of Spartans, 6 Dionysus of Thebes and Syracuse agreed to secret treaty, 7 with the imposter King Cyrus of Persia, 8 and to aid in the theft of the most sacred Ark of the Covenant, 9 and the treasures of Moses (Akhenaten), 10 from the custody of King Arxenes (Plato), 11 the true King of Persia and Eliada. 12 Dionysus appointed his most skilled diplomat, 13 whose name was Antalcidas, 14 to seek terms with King Agesilaus of Sparta, 15 and end the ten years of constant war. 16 King Cyrus did then withdraw his forces to the east, 17 towards Parthia and pretending, 18 that his strength was much weakened. 19 King Arxenes (Plato), 20 also known as Artaxerxes II, 21 seeking to end the madness of two false religions, 22 committed his main army to Asia, 23 to finish Cyrus, 24 while Cyrus secretly sent Bardyllis, 25 and his main army and fleet to land at Labeates, 26 and travel east into the mountains of Illyria, 27 to attack from the north. 28 King Agesilaus of Sparta agreed to terms, 29 through Antalcidas to Dionysus, 30 as his forces had been greatly weakened, 31 by constant fighting. 32 In the Great Age of the Ram, 33 eight hundred and fifteen years, 34 since the dawn of the Great Age (385 BCE), 35 the forces of Bardyllis attacked Elios from the north, 36 while Dionysus landed from the east of Epirus, 37 and attacked Elios from the east. 38 King Arxenes (Plato) was taken by surprise, 39 as his Immortals Guard could defend against most attacks, 40 yet a swarm of over one hundred thousand mercenaries, 41 and the professional forces of Bardyllis were overwhelming. 42 King Arxenes (Plato) implored the Great Prophet Oadiah, 43 come with him and escape with the Ark of the Covenant, 44 to which Oadiah did reply, 45 that the King must choose whether blood be more sacred, 46 than a mere box of gold and jewels. 47 It be true that the greatest of empires and kings, 48 had spilled the blood of millions for its control, 49 but always in ignorance and

never in wisdom. 50 For the Ark of the Covenant be nothing more than a symbol, 51 that all Pharaoh of the Hyksos did possess. 52 The true power always be in the knowledge, 53 of a philosopher king or priest, 54 and the blood that honours such ancient wisdom. 55 For if the King seized the Ark then all will surely be lost, 56 yet if the Immortals and the Ark remain, 57 then the King his household and the priests may yet survive. 58 King Arxenes (Plato) bowed to Oadiah and pledged: 59 So long as there be breath in my body, 60 as long as there be heirs to defend my honour, 61 let no man if he truly be a man dishonour your name, 62 let your name and memory be praised forever as Alelujiah (Halelujiah). 63 Verily a hero is born among a hundred, 64 a wise man is found among a thousand, 65 yet a complete man of austerity and honour and virtue, 66 be not found even among a hundred thousand. 67 King Arxenes (Plato) then departed north-east, 68 protected by his closest guard, 69 As the Great Prophet Oadiah (Halelujiah), 70 and only a thousand Immortals remained at Elios, 71 to face the largest army ever assembled, 72 since the times of Xerxes.

C. 14

1 In the Great Age of the Ram, 2 eight hundred and fifteen years, 3 since the dawn of the Great Age (385 BCE), 4 as soon as word of the forces of Cyrus under Bardyllis, 5 and Dionysus were attacking Elios, 6 reached King Agesilaus of Sparta, 7 he dispatched every able bodied Spartan, 8 to defend his lord and sacred ally. 9 Never before had the Spartans moved so swiftly, 10 then or since. 11 Dionysus anticipating the Spartan support, 12 had placed thirty thousand troops, 13 north-east of Corinth. 14 Yet the Spartans cut through the thirty thousand, 15 in half a day and continued to advance northward. 16 Further north at Elios, 17 Oadiah the twenty second great prophet of Yeb, 18 also known forever as Alelujiah (Halelujiah), 19 the son of Eliah and the grandson of Osanniah (Hosanna), 20 remained standing at the entrance of the Great Temple of Elios, 21 as wave upon wave of the marauders of Dionysus army of greed, 22 were cut down by the Immortals. 23 When the buildings of Elios were on fire, 24 and the streets clogged with bodies and blood, 25 Bardyllis committed his troops, 26 killing the last of the Immortal defenders, 27 until confronting Oadiah in the holy of holies. 28 As Bardyllis thrust a mortal blow into Oadiah, 29 Oadiah prophesised that Bardyllis would not leave Eliada, 30 that the sons of Arxenes (Plato), 31 and their legacy of illumination would triumph, 32 the wickedness of liars and frauds. 33 As Oadiah did give up the ghost. 34 The position then befell, 35 to his son whose name was Oananiah, 36 as the twenty third Great Prophet of the Yahudi. 37 Bardyllis then ordered an elite guard of Cyrus, 38 to take the Ark and the treasures of Moses (Akhenaten), 39 back to the King at Babylon, 40 as he advanced northward to seize Arxenes (Plato). 41 The forces of Arxenes (Plato) in retreat set defences, 42 at the north of the great lake of Loudiaka, 43 upon the plain of Pella. 44 as the forces of Bardyllis approached, 45 the army of King Agesilaus of Sparta, 46 reached the

ruins of Elios, 47 and the looting militia of Dionysus, 48 cutting down fifty thousand men in a day, 49 before continuing their advance. 50 Upon news of the Spartans Bardyllis hesitated. 51 And sought his own defences. 52 Yet they were no match for the Spartans, 53 who killed more than forty thousand, 54 of the troops of Cyrus and Bardyllis, 55 saving Arxenes (Plato), 56 and the priests of Yahu. 57 Upon his rescue King Arxenes (Plato) declared: 58 Upon this sacred plain, 59 where the divine ordained we be spared, 60 I shall dedicate a city of light and truth, 61 which shall be called Philipi (Thessaloniki), 62 as my capital. 63 Let it be known to all who come, 64 that no man have the right to be a priest or servant, 65 or judge or officer of law, 66 if he does not pledge his oath and honour, 67 to truth and wise knowledge, 68 to rid this world of superstitions and ignorance, 69 and the falsities of pirates and messiahs.

C. 15

1 In the Great Age of the Ram, 2 eight hundred and seventeen years, 3 since the dawn of the Great Age (383 BCE), 4 the imposter King Cyrus called unto all his loyal satraps, 5 to attend a celebration of the arrival of the Ark of the Covenant, 6 and the sacred treasures of Moses (Akhenaten) to Babylon, 7 yet the satrap of Armenia refused to bear false witness, 8 and was put to death. 9 Habakiah demanded that King Cyrus return the Ark to Jerusalem, 10 as he had pledged before heaven his loyalty to Mithra, 11 to which Cyrus expelled all the priests of Mithra from Babylon. 12 The forces of Dionysus were expelled from Thebes (Athena), 13 and a Spartan garrison established to guard against in habitation. 14 Yet upon the loss against Cyrus, 15 and the deceptions of Dionysus, 16 Arxenes (Plato) sought to build an impregnable defence, 17 while planning a strategy to reclaim the empire. 18 King Agesilaus of Sparta maintained control, 19 of the south and central lands, 20 using the uneasy peace to rebuild his forces. 21 Dionysus in Syracuse then ordered the scribes Homer and Hesiod, 22 to fashion a history for the Graecians, 23 as great and wonderful a story that even the simplest child, 24 be in awe of its mystery and power. 25 Using the vast library of works stolen to Syracuse, 26 of the former inhabitants of Athena, 27 especially the works of Heroditus, 28 Homer and Hesiod set about creating for their master, 29 a wholly fraudulent history, 30 full of fantasy and fables. 31 Homer and his scribes completed the Iliad and the Odyssey, 32 while Hesiod finished Theogony and the Works and Days. 33 When Plato eventually saw extracts of what was written he exclaimed, 34 how could grown men believe such children stories, 35 as if great giants and mythical creatures built our temples, 36 and magic and potions created our sciences and arts. 37 No man could be such a fool to believe a lie that does not hide itself. 38 Yet despite the disbelief of Arxenes (Plato), 39 people all over the world embraced the lies and corruptions, 40 of Homer and Hesiod as epics and true.

C. 16

1 In the Great Age of the Ram, 2 eight hundred and twenty four years, 3 since the dawn of the Great Age (376 BCE), 4 Navigator Mago of Carthage, 5 the first amongst equals, 6 of the Carthage Council of Elders, 7 did give up the ghost. 8 The office did then go to Suniatus. 9 In the same year Dionysus sent his finest general, 10 whose name was Epaminondas, 11 to overpower and secure Thebes (Athena), 12 ahead of a large invasion force. 13 Epaminondas succeeded in defeating the Spartan garrison, 14 yet could not hold the city and escaped back to Syracuse, 15 where he was welcomed as a hero and conqueror, 16 as Dionysus concluded it was better to boast, 17 that the Spartans were not immortal, 18 than to expose his own miscalculation.

C. 17

1 In the Great Age of the Ram, 2 eight hundred and twenty nine years, 3 since the dawn of the Great Age (371 BCE), 4 King Arxenes of Persia, 5 also known as the King of Kings, 6 also known as the Son of God, 7 also known as the broad one (Plato), 8 also known as the Yahudi tribe of Menes, 9 also known as the ancient Yahudi of Reuben, 10 did give up the ghost. 11 The crown did then befall to his son, 12 whose name was Aristoteles, 13 also known as Aristotle, 14 also known as The Philipi, 15 and also known as Artaxerxes III. 16 As was custom from the beginning of time, 17 upon the funeral of a great king, 18 all armies did cease conflict. 19 Thus the Spartans assured no people, 20 be so weak of character to attack, 21 did leave their homeland on mass, 22 to attend the funeral of Plato at Philipi. 23 At that precise moment Epaminondas, 24 and the forces of Dionysus did land at Attica, 25 and seize Thebes (Athena), 26 then did march upon the homeland of the Spartans, 27 killing every woman and child, 28 burning every town and farm, 29 until nothing remained. 30 As the Spartans rushed back to defend their homeland, 31 an army of Cyrus under the leadership of Gorgidas, 32 landed to the north and outflanking the Spartans. 33 Still in shock from such perfidy, 34 never before witnessed in history, 35 and broken upon the murder of their families, 36 the Spartans were given the chance to swear by oath, 37 their surrender or face death. 38 For the first and only time the Spartans chose enslavement, 39 and Dionysus achieved his greatest victory, 40 through the most wicked and insanity of character, 41 not of evil or magic but transgressions of madness, 42 that have stood as the hallmarks, 43 of his religion then and since. 44 Upon news that Cyrus participated in the desecration, 45 of the funeral ceremony of King Arxenes (Plato) of Persia, 46 six satraps rebelled against Cyrus, 47 and declared themselves as allies of King Aristoteles (Aristotle), 48 including Kappodokia, Armenia, Phrygia, Ionia, Lydia and Kilikia. 49 For the next ten years, 50 Cyrus was crippled by the consequences of his actions, 51 and never fully regained the west of his empire. 52 Persian general Gorgidas chose to remain in Thebes, 53 forming an elite bodyguard for Epaminondas as dictator, 54 of 300 pairs of male lovers, 55 called the Sacred Band of Thebes.

C. 18

1 In the Great Age of the Ram, 2 eight hundred and thirty two years, 3 since the dawn of the Great Age (368 BCE), 4 Navigator Suniatus of Carthage, 5 the first amongst equals, 6 of the Carthage Council of Elders, 7 did give up the ghost. 8 The office did then go to Hanno. 9 In the same year, 10 King Aristoteles (Aristotle), 11 and his wife the daughter of Oananiah, 12 also known in history as Olympias, 13 did give birth to an extraordinary son, 14 the true heir to the Persian Empire, 15 and the Great Prophets of Yahu, 16 whose name was Alexandros (Alexander). 17 In the Great Age of the Ram, 18 eight hundred and thirty two years, 19 since the dawn of the Great Age (367 BCE), 20 Dionysus of Syracuse, 21 the wicked tyrant and false messiah, 22 did give up the ghost. 23 Yet to keep the myth alive, 24 his son was also named Dionysus, 25 in an attempt to claim him immortal. 26 Upon the younger son claiming the throne, 27 he ordered Epameinondas to attack Philipi, 28 and bring him the head of King Aristoteles. 29 King Aristoteles (Aristotle) without the trusted defence, 30 of the Spartans under King Agesilaus, 31 who remained bound to their pledge to Epameinondas, 32 entreated Tribune Gaius Licinius Stolo of Rome. 33 Rome then sent general Marcus Furius Camillus, 34 appointing him Caesar (dictator) of a sizeable army. 35 The Romans and the Persian Guard defeated Epameinondas, 36 causing him to retreat. 37 In the Great Age of the Ram, 38 eight hundred and thirty seven years, 39 since the dawn of the Great Age (363 BCE), 40 Epameinondas tried once more to attack the north, 41 and again he was defeated, 42 with the assistance of the Roman Caesar (dictator), 43 whose name was Appius Claudius Crassus. 44 This time Epameinondas did not escape, 45 and was executed. 46 In the same year, 47 Holly High King Eochaid mac Ailella, 48 of the most ancient Cuilliaéan, 49 did give up the ghost. 50 The throne of Amen-Ra did then befall to his son, 51 whose name was Lugaid Laigdech mac Ailella.

C. 19

1 In the Great Age of the Ram, 2 eight hundred and thirty six years, 3 since the dawn of the Great Age (364 BCE), 4 the false prophet known as Habakiah, 5 of the false Yahudi of Babylon, 6 also known as the High Priest of Mithra, 7 and son of Ezra, 8 did give up the ghost. 9 The title of High Priest of Mithra, 10 did then befall to his son, 11 whose name was Zephaniah. 12 In the Great Age of the Ram, 13 eight hundred and forty years, 14 since the dawn of the Great Age (360 BCE), 15 King Agesilaus of Sparta, 16 did give up the ghost. 17 The crown did then befall his son, 18 whose name was Archidamus. 19 Upon the death of the old Spartan king, 20 Dionysus the Younger and his general Damocles, 21 did come to Thebes (Athens), 22 and summonsed Archidamus to his presence, 23 to which Archidamus sent his brave emissary, 24 with the message that Sparta still honours its sacred oath, 25 not to attack Thebes or the king, 26 nor shall Sparta attack Eliada. 27 Dionysus in rage ordered the emissary slowly boiled. 28 In the Great Age of the Ram,

29 eight hundred and forty two years, 30 since the dawn of the Great Age (358 BCE), 31 the false King named Cyrus, 32 of the House of Ochos, 33 who claimed to be king of Persia, 34 did give up the ghost. 35 His son did then choose, 36 the ancient name of Darius.

C. 20

1 In the Great Age of the Ram, 2 eight hundred and forty two years, 3 since the dawn of the Great Age (352 BCE), 4 King Aristoteles (Aristotle) of Eliada, 5 the true King of Kings, 6 the philosopher King, 7 did finally launch his attack. 8 Unable to call upon the Spartans, 9 who remained honour bound to Thebes (Athens), 10 King Aristoteles (Aristotle) placed his faith, 11 in the battled hardened and loyal Romans, 12 and Caesar (dictator) Marcus Fabius Ambustus. 13 Within a few weeks, 14 the forces of King Aristoteles (Aristotle), 15 conquered Thessaly and Molossia, 16 and recaptured Larissa and Pherae, 17 and the key cities of Dodona and Ambracia. 18 In the Great Age of the Ram, 19 eight hundred and forty two years, 20 since the dawn of the Great Age (343 BCE), 21 the loyal Roman legions under the command, 22 of Caesar (dictator) Marcus Valerius Corvus, 23 did conquer for King Aristoteles (Aristotle), 24 the Kingdoms of Thrace and Maronea and Perinthus. 25 In the Great Age of the Ram, 26 eight hundred and fifty nine years, 27 since the dawn of the Great Age (341 BCE), 28 the forces of King Aristoteles (Aristotle), 29 under the command of Marcus Valerius Corvus, 30 succeeded in conquering the Island of Euboea, 31 and the cities of Chalcis and Eretria. 32 Soon after Thebes (Athens) fell, 33 and Dionysus the Younger was forced to flee, 34 back to Graecia (Sicily) and Syracuse. 35 Upon the defeat of Dionysus and the Thebians, 36 King Archidamus and the Spartans rejoiced, 37 upon their freedom from the bond and curse, 38 that they had bound themselves. 39 King Archidamus did proclaim, 40 an eternal pledge to King Aristoteles (Aristotle), 41 and his descendants, 42 and as forever allies to their Roman brothers. 43 Caesar Marcus Valerius Corvus returned to Rome a great hero, 44 to one of the most magnificent triumphs of any Caesar (dictator).

C. 21

1 In the Great Age of the Ram, 2 eight hundred and fifty nine years, 3 since the dawn of the Great Age (341 BCE), 4 Oananiah the twenty third great prophet of Yeb, 5 the son of Oadiah (Halelujiah) and the grandson of Eliah, 6 did give up the ghost. 7 The position then befell, 8 to his grandson whose name was Adiah, 9 also known as Alexandros (Alexander), 10 as the twenty fourth Great Prophet of the Yahudi. 11 Adiah (Alexander) had been prepared for such position, 12 from the moment of his birth. 13 That he would never marry nor have an heir himself. 14 That he would be lord and saviour of the world, 15 and enact the plans of his father and ancestors, 16 to end the reign of false messiahs and kings. 17 In the same year, 18 Navigator Hanno of Carthage, 19 the first amongst equals, 20 of the Carthage Council of Elders, 21 did give up the ghost. 22 The office did then go to Gisco. 23 King Aristoteles

(Aristotle), 24 did then ensure that throughout the world, 25 all peoples did know that Alexandros (Alexander), 26 also known as Adiah was the true heir and prophet, 27 and that all who did humble themselves before him, 28 would be saved and all who dishonoured him, 29 would be punished. 30 In the Great Age of the Ram, 31 eight hundred and sixty two years, 32 since the dawn of the Great Age (338 BCE), 33 King Archidamus of Sparta, 34 did give up the ghost. 35 The crown did then befall his son, 36 whose name was Eumenes.

C. 22

1 In the Great Age of the Ram, 2 eight hundred and sixty four years, 3 since the dawn of the Great Age (336 BCE), 4 King Aristoteles of Persia, 5 also known as the King of Kings, 6 also known as the Son of God, 7 also known as Aristotle, 8 also known as Philippi, 9 also known as the Yahudi tribe of Menes, 10 also known as the ancient Yahudi of Reuben, 11 aid give up the ghost. 12 The crown did then befall to his son, 13 whose name was Alexandros (Alexander), 14 also known as known as Artaxerxes IV as Son of God, 15 also known as the Great Prophet Adiah, 16 also known as the Lord Saviour of the Divine, 17 as the twenty fourth Great Prophet of the Yahudi. 18 Upon the death of Aristoteles (Aristotle), 19 Dionysus the Younger of Graecia (Sicily), 20 through his General Damocles, 21 did hatch a plan to try and destroy Rome, 22 known as the Sword of Damocles, 23 where he did succeed in causing the Samnites, 24 and other powerful tribes of Italy, 25 to rise up in rebellion against Roman rule to the north, 26 and for King Cleitus of Illryia and the Thessalians, 27 as well as the Thracians, 28 to rebel against Alexandros (Alexander). 29 The Romans then would have to choose against their sacred honour, 30 as protectors of the true Persian Kings and lose their homeland, 31 or break their sacred oaths and abandon Alexandros (Alexander). 32 The Roman Senate appointed Lucius Aemilius Mamercinus as Caesar, 33 and the Romans entreated that Alexandros (Alexander) come to their aid. 34 Without hesitation Alexandros (Alexander) split his military forces into four, 35 ordering his cavalry led by Spartan King Eumenes and Langarus, 36 to crush the Thracian uprising, 37 ordering his heavy infantry led by Perdiccas and Leonatus, 38 to crush the Thessaly and Athenian uprising, 39 the infantry then led by Ptolemy, Lysimachus and Pyrrhus of Epirus, 40 to march into Illryia and defeat Cleitus, 41 and the navy led by Craterus under Alexander himself, 42 to set sail to blockade Graecia, 43 and force Dionysus the Younger to withdraw. 44 The strategy of Alexandros (Alexander) worked, 45 and the rebellions of Illryia, Thrace and Thessaly, 46 were fiercely put down. 47 Yet instead of executing the rebellious military, 48 Alexandros (Alexander) ordered the nobility executed, 49 and that the tenth most untrustworthy of the population, 50 be condemned and executed in public, 51 with one tenth of the best men of character to join his army, 52 under the newly formed idea of legions. 53 As to Thebes (Athena) the generals of Alexandros (Alexander), 54 pleaded

that all men be executed, 55 for no good men of character and virtue, 56 could be found within the walls of Thebes (Athena). 57 Alexandros (Alexander) declined executing the people. 58 Instead he ordered that they be bound to servitude, 59 as funerary attendants and baggage handlers, 60 for seven generations, 61 and that the name Thebes be forbidden. 62 Upon news that Alexandros (Alexander) had arrived to Graecia, 63 the people of Syracuse rebelled against Dionysus the Younger, 64 killing him and his court and his generals, 65 then the city immediately surrendered. 66 Lucius Aemilius Mamercinus then defeated the rebellious tribes, 67 and followed the honour set down by Alexandros (Alexander), 68 and offered the tribes to serve as legionnaires, 69 in the greater army of Rome, 70 and in service to the military of Eliada and Persia. 71 Thus the great ethos of the Legions were born, 72 throughout the greater empire of Eliada.

C. 23

1 In the Great Age of the Ram, 2 eight hundred and sixty six years, 3 since the dawn of the Great Age (334 BCE), 4 King Alexandros (Alexander) of Eliada, 5 also known as the Great Prophet Adiah, 6 did cross the Hellespont, 7 with the largest army ever seen, 8 since the time of his ancestor Xerxes (Zeus). 9 Upon stepping onto Phrygian soil, 10 Alexandros (Alexander) did seize a flag of his standard bearers, 11 and thrust it into the soil with the words: 12 That from this moment forward, 13 let the Divine Creator and all spirits of heaven, 14 guide this sacred army to reclaim the Ark (of the Covenant), 15 to rid the world of the evil of ignorance and falsity, 16 and bring Rule of Law to all peoples, 17 respect amongst all true faiths, 18 and democracy to the whole world. 19 Soon after crossing into Asia, 20 a combined army of the satraps of Darius, 21 supported by Graecian (Greek) mercenaries, 22 did attack the forces of Alexandros (Alexander), 23 and the army of Darius was cut to pieces. 24 Alexandros (Alexander) refused to accept the plea of terms, 25 that the satraps could escape along with their nobles. 26 Instead Alexandros (Alexander) ordered, 27 that all the Graecian (Greek) mercenaries be executed, 28 as they be men who fight for money and are without honour. 29 He then ordered the satraps and nobles be taken to Sardis 30 and one tenth of the defeated forces of Darius be executed, 31 with the bravest and most honourable soldiers the choice to join, 32 his great army of Heaven and Earth. 33 At Sardis Alexandros (Alexander) and two other generals, 34 presided over a trial of the satraps, 35 declaring them culpable for crimes against the law, 36 and handed them to the people to be executed. 37 King Alexandros as Adiah then declared, 38 that upon this day, 39 no man may be judged a capital crime, 40 if he not be judged by three tribunes, 41 who pledge their austerity, obedience and humility, 42 to heaven as true and sacred witnesses. 43 That all are equal under the law. 44 That no man be a slave to another. 45 That all are deserving of justice, 46 even the most wicked.

C. 24

1 In the Great Age of the Ram, 2 eight hundred and sixty six years, 3 since the dawn of the Great Age (334 BCE), 4 upon the Edict of Sardis, 5 and the abolition of satraps of Phrygia and Ionia, 6 King Alexandros as Adiah then introduced, 7 the new democratic form of government by Archons, 8 each representing the people of cities and provinces as nomos (name), 9 then collectively making a body politic called a synodos (synod), 10 of a country known then as an eparch. 11 Alexandros (Alexander) then marched on Karia, 12 and at Halicarnassus quickly forced Memnon of Rhodes, 13 and the Darian satrap to flee for their lives. 14 The satraps of Cappadocia and Cilicia quickly followed, 15 until King Alexandros (Alexander) finally met in battle, 16 the full army of King Darius, 17 near the mouth of the Pinarus River. 18 Despite Darius possessing superior numbers, 19 he fled in fear upon the advance of Alexandros (Alexander), 20 and his army collapsed in defeat. 21 Once safely returned to Babylon, 22 Darius sent offer of a treaty to Alexandros (Alexander), 23 and the payment of a ransom for the return of his royal household. 24 Instead Alexandros (Alexander) ordered the safe return, 25 of the royal household to Darius, 26 as well as the treasures. 27 Such was the historic gesture, 28 that news of it spread across the known world. 29 Alexandros (Alexander) then did bring his army south, 30 capturing all of Syria, 31 and laying waste to the cities of Tyre and Gaza, 32 until he entered Jerusalem. 33 At Jerusalem he did not find the Ark (of the Covenant), 34 but was greeted by the old false prophet, 35 and high priest of Mithra known as Zephaniah. 36 High Priest Zephaniah did tell Alexandros as Adiah, 37 that even if he succeeded in reclaiming the Ark, 38 from his son Malachiah at Babylon, 39 he would still fail to win the peace, 40 for ambitious men have always found a way to corrupt, 41 and weak minded people have always believed half-truths, 42 and fanciful tales over truth and their own conscience. 43 King Alexandros (Alexander) as the Great Prophet Adiah, 44 did reply that no matter how many treacherous scribes, 45 sought to corrupt knowledge and wisdom, 46 truth and character always outlasts a hundred generations, 47 whereas hate, revenge and even the ignorance of evil, 48 burns itself out within a few generations. 49 In the Great Age of the Ram, 50 eight hundred and sixty eight years, 51 since the dawn of the Great Age (332 BCE), 52 the false prophet known as Zephaniah, 53 of the false Yahudi of Babylon, 54 also known as the High Priest of Mithra, 55 and son of Habakiah, 56 did give up the ghost. 57 The title of High Priest of Mithra, 58 did then befall to his son, 59 whose name was Malachiah, 60 upon the return of the body of his father, 61 with an honour guard sent by Alexandros (Alexander) to Babylon.

C. 25

1 In the Great Age of the Ram, 2 eight hundred and sixty eight years, 3 since the dawn of the Great Age (332 BCE), 4 King Alexandros (Alexander) and his army, 5 travelled south and then west to Egypt and as far as Libya. 6 Alexandros as the Great Prophet

Adiah, 7 of the ancient Great Seers and Prophets of Yeb, 8 did then travel up the Nile to Karnak, 9 and then to the ruins of the Temple of Yahu, 10 upon the Island of Yeb (Elephantine). 11 At Yeb he met the famed Oracle of Amun, 12 who remained as a solitary witness, 13 to the sanctity of the most holy of places. 14 Upon seeing Alexandros (Alexander) the oracle proclaimed: 15 Verily Amun-Ra has returned to life, 16 as the son of Zeus (Xerxes). 17 Truly he be the Son of Man and Pharaoh, 18 for no man be honourable, 19 unless he comes with good faith and clean hands. 20 And no man be great, 21 unless he humbles himself before the law for all. 22 And no man be divine, 23 unless he pledges himself to the service of heaven. 24 Alexandros (Alexander) did then ask the Oracle, 25 three questions as to the immediate fate, 26 the fate in years and the future against evil and ignorance. 27 To which the Oracle replied: 28 Even the greatest of men die, 29 and the mightiest of cities decay, 30 but the brilliant illumination, 31 of a divine idea outlasts all. 32 To the first you shall be granted your mission, 33 but at fateful cost. 34 To the second the lesser nature of men, 35 shall claim and hide your light. 36 To the third a day shall come, 37 when one like the Son of Man, 38 of the Holly blood, 39 whose name means truth, 40 as witness to your mission, 41 shall cause the end of the war in heaven. 42 Upon the meeting and prophecy of the oracle, 43 Alexandros (Alexander) returned north, 44 to the western delta of the Nile on the coast of the sea, 45 at the site of the city of Rhacotis, 46 where he did declare: 47 Upon this site a great city for all people shall be built, 48 where the Ark of the Covenant shall come to rest, 49 where all true knowledge shall be united, 50 and representatives (diplomats) of all nations shall come, 51 that all disputes shall be resolved peacefully. 52 Alexandros (Alexander) did then announce, 53 the creation of a universal currency, 54 to end the practice of fractioning by moneychangers (bankers), 55 when they rubbed or clipped shavings of coins, 56 and to end the practice of the same moneychangers (bankers), 57 in controlling all trade between markets and cities and regions. 58 The base unit was then called the drachme of silver, 59 minted as either 2.16 grams of silver called a didrachm, 60 or 4.32 grams of silver called a tetradrachm. 61 Tetradrachm were minted according to the ancient principles, 62 of the Celtic smiths whereby the coin had three sides, 63 being an obverse a reverse and a lined edge. 64 Thus if a moneylender (banker) sought to ply their trade, 65 the coin would clearly be damaged and replaced. 66 1 Drachme was then equivalent to six oboloi, 67 being small sticks of iron, 68 or eight chalkoi being sticks of copper. 69 24 drachma or 6 tetradrachm or 12 didrachm, 70 were then equivalent to one gold stater, 71 of 8.64 grams of gold and also fashioned with three sides. 72 For no coins were permitted to be minted, 73 except by an official treasury, 74 and no coins were permitted to be circulated, 75 that did not have three sides and a clear serrated edge. 76 Only those kingdoms and places controlled by bankers, 77 continued the practice of two sides coins, 78 With uneven edges that could then be clipped, 79 and fractionalised by the moneychangers (bankers). 80

Alexandros (Alexander) then ordered the arrest of all moneylenders, 81 and moneychangers (bankers) and the forbiddance of their trade, 82 as the actions of a banker be an abomination, 83 before the divine creator and all heaven. 84 That all men may trade freely amongst each other, 85 that none be forced to exchange currency, 86 that no man be charged compound interest upon a debt. 87 In the same year, 88 Holly High King Lugaid Laigdech mac Ailella, 89 of the most ancient Cuilliaéan, 90 did give up the ghost. 91 The throne of Amen-Ra did then befall to his son, 92 whose name was Eochaid Buadach mac Lugaid.

C. 26

1 In the Great Age of the Ram, 2 eight hundred and sixty nine years, 3 since the dawn of the Great Age (331 BCE), 4 Alexandros (Alexander) departed Egypt, 5 and travelled north into Syria, 6 and then east into Mesopotamia, 7 crossing first the Euphrates and then Tigris, 8 before heading south-west towards Arbela. 9 There Darius had assembled a massive army, 10 of several hundred thousand, 11 and even practised upon the battlefield, 12 to give himself the greatest advantage. 13 The combined forces of Alexander did not yield, 14 and the army of Darius was greatly slaughtered, 15 before once again Darius fled eastward, 16 this time to Persepolis to avoid capture. 17 Alexandros (Alexander) chose not to pursue him, 18 but instead moved quickly to take Babylon, 19 and secure the Ark of the Covenant. 20 Upon reaching Babylon the people celebrated his arrival, 21 as the true king and liberator. 22 But when he entered the main temple, 23 he discovered that Malachiah, 24 the high priest of Mithra, 25 had escaped with the Ark of the Covenant, 26 and the treasures of Moses (Akhenaten), 27 to Persepolis and the protection of Darius. 28 In frustration Alexandros (Alexander) ordered, 29 that every priest and follower of Mithra, 30 be publicly executed as heretics against heaven, 31 and henceforth that to worship Mithra, 32 forever be a capital crime and transgression, 33 against the divine creator. 34 Alexandros (Alexander) and his forces departed eastward, 35 first to Susa and then across the Zagros Mountains, 36 to siege Persepolis. 37 Upon the arrival of Alexandros (Alexander), 38 the guard of Darius rebelled and the city fell. 39 In the Great Age of the Ram, 40 eight hundred and seventy years, 41 since the dawn of the Great Age (330 BCE), 42 the false King named Darius, 43 of the House of Ochos, 44 who claimed to be king of Persia, 45 did give up the ghost, 46 thus ending the line of the false claimants. 47 Yet when Alexandros (Alexander) entered the city, 48 he found that High Priest Malachiah, 49 had once again fled with the Ark, 50 north to the mountains on the edge of the Caspian Sea, 51 in the ancient homeland of the Hyrcanians, 52 and the city of Ray.

C. 27

1 In the Great Age of the Ram, 2 eight hundred and seventy years, 3 since the dawn of the Great Age (330 BCE), 4 Alexandros (Alexander) as the Great Prophet Adiah, 5 reached the city of Ray that immediately surrendered. 6 Yet when Alexandros (Alexander)

entered the population attacked, 7 and Alexandros (Alexander) was badly wounded. 8 Upon such treachery of the city and home of the false kings, 9 Alexandros (Alexander) ordered every living thing to be killed, 10 and every building to be destroyed, 11 that Ray become dust, 12 and no longer offend heaven. 13 After a brief recovery Alexandros (Alexander), 14 continued his pursuit of High Priest Malachiah, 15 into Parthia and then Aria and Drangiana. 16 At each city the king and Great Prophet, 17 became less tolerant of the people and nobles, 18 who gave aid to Malachiah and the Mithraic guard. 19 Finally Alexandros (Alexander) crossed the Hindu Kush, 20 to Kabul then Taxila and finally to the Kingdom of Paurava, 21 where Malachiah had pledged an unholy oath, 22 that the descendants of the King Porus, 23 and the tribes of Mongols, 24 would one day rule the world, 25 through treachery and deception and bloodshed, 26 in honour of the true nature of the god of Mithra. 27 King Porus then did summons a great army, 28 to challenge Alexandros (Alexander). 29 Yet upon the sight of a living god, 30 the Mongols and Pauravanians fled, 31 and King Porus and Malachiah, 32 as well as the Ark of the Covenant, 33 were finally captured. 34 In the Great Age of the Ram, 35 eight hundred and seventy four years, 36 since the dawn of the Great Age (326 BCE), 37 the false prophet known as Malachiah, 38 of the false Yahudi of Babylon, 39 also known as the High Priest of Mithra, 40 and son of Zephaniah, 41 did give up the ghost, 42 upon being executed, 43 along with King Porus and his household, 44 except his daughter Roxanna, 45 who all agreed possessed such beauty, 46 that to destroy such light would be a sacrilege. 47 The title of High Priest of Mithra, 48 was then abolished and none ever held it again. 49 As the false religion they followed. 50 Exhausted and exulted King Alexandros (Alexander), 51 travelled south along the Indus River to Pattala, 52 where a fleet under Nearchus did take him west, 53 into the Persian Gulf and then back to Babylon, 54 where the Ark of the Covenant was returned.

C. 28

1 In the Great Age of the Ram, 2 eight hundred and seventy six years, 3 since the dawn of the Great Age (324 BCE), 4 Alexandros (Alexander) as the Great Prophet Adiah, 5 called for Oniah his cousin and great grandson of Oananiah. 6 At Babylon Alexandros (Alexander) as Adiah, 7 adopted Oniah as his son and successor, 8 as the twenty fifth great prophet of the Yahuda. 9 Alexandros (Alexander) as Adiah then entrusted, 10 the Ark of the Covenant and the sacred treasure of Akhenaten, 11 to Oniah and the priests of the Yahudi. 12 Alexandros (Alexander) then entrusted his general Lysimachus (Ptolemy), 13 as Guardian of Heliopolis (Alexandria), 14 and the Lands of Oniah, 15 that he protect the city the Ark and the priests, 16 whereupon they did depart Babylon. 17 In the Great Age of the Ram, 18 eight hundred and seventy seven years, 19 since the dawn of the Great Age (323 BCE), 20 upon ill health of Alexandros (Alexander), 21 the great king summonsed his generals, 22 and court and priests to bear witness, 23 whereby he bestowed his signet ring to

Book 17 Great Age of Eliada

Perdiccas, 24 declaring that Perdiccas be the patros (father), 25 of all men as protector and guardian of the law, 26 never to be known as king or emperor, 27 for only men elected by their peers may claim, 28 the right to rule according to justice. 29 Alexandros (Alexander) then summonsed Craterus, 30 who he appointed his executor, 31 and reader of his Testament, 32 in whom he did entrust for perpetual memory, 33 the great trust of all the civilised world, 34 all the true knowledge of wisdom and spirit, 35 all the rights and claims of sacred office, 36 according to such sacred instrument. 37 That none may claim to be his heir. 38 That none may claim to be a messiah. 39 That all men may be equal before the law forever. 40 Alexandros (Alexander) then summonsed Pyrrhus of Epirus, 41 to take his armour and personal effects back to Philipi, 42 along with Roxanna and his attendants safely. 43 In the Great Age of the Ram, 44 eight hundred and seventy seven years, 45 since the dawn of the Great Age (323 BCE), 46 King Alexandros of Persia, 47 also known as the King of Kings, 48 also known as the great prophet Adiah, 49 also known as the Son of God, 50 also known as the Saviour of the Divine, 51 also known as the Yahudi tribe of Menes, 52 also known as the ancient Yahudi of Reuben, 53 did give up the ghost, 54 as the last of the Wise Kings of Persia. 55 Upon his death Craterus did read his Testament, 56 which did become known as the Testament of Babylon, 57 and the trust for the whole world, 58 by which all men are created equal, 59 that no one is above the law, 60 that no one may be condemned a slave, 61 or any man worshipped as a god alone, 62 that all have the right to choose their government, 63 under the rule of democracy and free will, 64 that never again shall false teachers and scriptures, 65 be permitted to stand in defiance of true history, 66 nor moneylenders (bankers) interpose themselves, 67 for only one currency exists in truth for the world, 68 and if the world faces evil and danger, 69 it be the duty of the holy father (patros), 70 to defend the laws of heaven, 71 and for men of honour to stand against tyranny, 72 for any law that does not agree cannot be law.

Book 18

Great Age of Empires

[323 - 204 BCE]

C. 1

In the Great Age of the Ram, 2 eight hundred and seventy seven years, 3 since the dawn of the Great Age (323 BCE), 4 upon news of the death of the great Alexandros (Alexander), 5 the city of Athens and the island of Euboea and the Ionian coast rebelled. 6 Pyrrhus who was due to return the personal effects of Alexandros (Alexander), 7 as well as deliver Roxanna to Olympias, 8 the priestess and mother of Alexandros, 9 was ordered by the holy patros Perdicass to strike at Athens, 10 and cut the heart out of the rebellion. 11 The Athenians had aligned themselves, 12 with a coalition of powerful merchants, 13 under the authority of Demosthenes, 14 who pledged themselves against the rule of Eliada, 15 and against the destruction of their moneylending (banking) trade. 16 Thousands of mercenaries had been purchased, 17 that the forces against Pyrrhus were overwhelming. 18 Upon Pyrrhus viewing the mercenary army of the Athenians, 19 and facing almost certain defeat and death, 20 Pyrrhus also known as Antipater did devise a plan, 21 whereby he adorned the armour of Alexandros (Alexander), 22 and rode out with his cavalry in front of his forces. 23 When the mercenaries and Athenians saw the image of Alexandros (Alexander), 24 they immediately surrendered and opened the gates, 25 that Pyrrhus appearing as Alexandros (Alexander), 26 accompanied by Roxanna and his forces entered Athens. 27 When the Athenian leader Demosthenes saw Roxanna, 28 he fell down at her feet claiming the sight of Hestia the goddess herself. 29 Demosthenes then pledged the loyalty of Athens and all forces, 30 that had rebelled unto Pyrrhus as Alexandros (Alexander), 31 by which Pyrrhus did say to Demosthenes and the Athenians: 32 On this fateful day heaven bestows Athena a great gift, 33 of the goddess Hestia personified as Athena, 34 and the most beautiful virgin of the world. 35 She shall be your queen, 36 and upon the self-sacrifice of Demosthenes, 37 as all shall only make sacrifice to the goddess Athena, 38 she shall protect you and lead you, 39 and give birth to a saviour for all mankind. 40 Upon these words Demosthenes grabbed a knife, 41 and plunged it into his chest, 42 falling down dead before the other leaders. 43 Thus Athens pledged itself to Roxanna now the goddess Athena, 44 and Pyrrhus still pretending as Alexandros (Alexander), 45 did depart and return some days later without armour, 46 as Pyrrhus and servant of the goddess Athena. 47 Upon news that Alexandros (Alexander) had risen from the dead, 48 and descended from heaven with the goddess Hestia, 49 installing her at Athens, 50 the Island of Euboea as well as the Ionian cities, 51 also pledged their loyalty and service.

C. 2

1 In the Great Age of the Ram, 2 eight hundred and seventy eight years, 3 since the dawn of the Great Age (322 BCE), 4 Lysimachus (Ptolemy) continued to oversee, 5 the greatest construction force, 6 since the time of Holly Hyksos, 7 of two hundred thousand workers building Heliopolis. 8 Lysimachus (Ptolemy) appealed to Perdiccas, 9 to resolve the Cult of Alexandros (Alexander), 10 born from the actions at Athena, 11 as the stories had affected the entire west of Eliada. 12 Holy Father (Patros) Perdiccas refused at first, 13 the entreats of Lysimachus (Ptolemy), 14 and instead ordered Eumenes of Sparta from the south, 15 Cassander from the north, 16 and Craterus from the south-east, 17 to crush the rebellion and new cult. 18 Yet Perdiccas had greatly underestimated, 19 the power of the story of the death and resurrection, 20 of Alexandros (Alexander) as the Son of God, 21 and the virgin goddess Athena (Roxanna), 22 who now claimed an immaculately conceived child, 23 with the spirit of Alexandros (Alexander). 24 King Eumenes of Sparta with all his might, 25 was unable to break through from the south. 26 Craterus from the south-east could not breach, 27 the defences of Athens, 28 and the forces of Cassander continued to be outflanked, 29 by reinforcements from both Epirus and Ionia. 30 Even with further reinforcements, 31 the forces of Pyrrhus grew stronger, 32 as they were inspired to fight to the death, 33 believing this to be a Holy War. 34 In the Great Age of the Ram, 35 eight hundred and eighty one years, 36 since the dawn of the Great Age (319 BCE), 37 the forces of Cassander finally broke the lines of Athens, 38 forcing Pyrrhus and Roxanna and his son Alexander Aegus, 39 to flee east to Phrygia, 40 and the care of Philetaerus of Pergamon. 41 At Pergamon King Philetaerus welcomed Roxanna, 42 naming her Cybele instead of Athena, 43 and naming her son as Attis instead of Aegus, 44 pledging his undying loyalty, 45 to the Queen of Heaven and her infant messiah. 46 Pyrrhus as a man was not unaware, 47 of the extreme beauty of Roxanna, 48 thus he had already established the doctrine of devotees, 49 sacrificing their genitals to become eunuchs, 50 lest any devotee succumb to the power of the goddess. 51 Pyrrhus then offered King Philetaerus, 52 to be the first high priest of Cybele, 53 to which the king gladly agreed, 54 and upon the same day marked as the birthday of Mithra, 55 being the 14 Nisan (14 March), 56 he led a procession of devotees to the temple, 57 where they sacrificed several first born children, 58 and then participated in a gross orgy, 59 in the manner of Dionysus, 60 and the rituals of cannibalism, 61 before hacking off

their genitals, 62 to become celibate priests, 63 of the Queen of Heaven.

C. 3

1 In the Great Age of the Ram, 2 eight hundred and eighty two years, 3 since the dawn of the Great Age (318 BCE), 4 Holy Father (Patros) Perdiccas ordered, 5 that the remains of Alexandros (Alexander), 6 be removed from his mausoleum, 7 and that they be displayed at major cities, 8 firmly within control of the empire, 9 on their route and final resting place, 10 in Egypt and first to Memphis, 11 until Heliopolis (Alexandria) was finished. 12 Great crowds gathered to see the sight, 13 of the body of the great Alexandros (Alexander), 14 and Perdiccas had arranged that at each site, 15 the Testament of Babylon would be recited, 16 that all myth and tales be dismissed. 17 Yet a new phenomena arose, 18 in place of the worship of supernatural tales, 19 in the form of icon devotees, 20 who abandoned their posts and fields, 21 in vast numbers, 22 to follow the remains of Alexandros (Alexander), 23 even into Egypt. 24 In the same year Pyrrhus left Pergamon, 25 accompanied only by his best guard, 26 and secretly returned to Epirus, 27 and then travelled to Carthage, 28 where he met King Gisco and his son Hamilcar, 29 and announced that Roxanna as the Phrygian goddess, 30 be the reincarnation of Queen Tharyelli, 31 also known as Queen Elissa and founder of Carthage. 32 That no longer the wars against the Graecians or Spartans, 33 be commercial or political but a Sacred War, 34 and that Carthage be called by heaven and their gods, 35 to take a stand against those who wish to corrupt, 36 the destiny of the world. 37 Upon hearing the speech by Pyrrhus, 38 all the wealth of Carthage to the Sacred War. 39 King Gisco of Carthage did pledge, 40 all the wealth of Carthage to the Sacred War. 41 Pyrrhus did then return briefly to Pergamon.

C. 4

1 In the Great Age of the Ram, 2 eight hundred and eighty three years, 3 since the dawn of the Great Age (317 BCE), 4 Pyrrhus of Epirus also falsely known as Polyperchon, 5 also falsely known as Antipater and Agathocles, 6 did invade Graecia (Sicily) from the east, 7 with a great army from Epirus, 8 as Hamilcar the son of Gisco of Carthage, 9 did invade Graecia (Sicily) from the south. 10 The Graecian cities were overwhelmed, 11 by the speed and force of the attack, 12 and Pyrrhus achieved a great victory in securing Syracuse, 13 with Messina and Rhegium falling to the Carthaginians soon after, 14 that within two years of war, 15 Pyrrhus had achieved what not even Alexander had done, 16 in conquering and uniting Graecia (Sicily). 17 In the Great Age of the Ram, 18 eight hundred and eighty six years, 19 since the dawn of the Great Age (314 BCE), 20 Pyrrhus declared himself King of Sicily, 21 before returning to Pergamon, 22 to the court of King Philataerus, 23 where he retrieved Roxanna as Cybele, 24 the Queen of Heaven, 25 and Alexander Aegus as Attis. 26 Pyrrhus then set sail to Carthage. 27 Upon reaching Carthage, 28 news of the coming of the living goddess, 29 and the arrival of her

son, 30 caused excitement amongst the people of Carthage. 31 Pyrrhus was welcomed by King Gisco as a hero, 32 and Roxanna as Cybele and the personification of Queen Dido, 33 and the patron goddess Tanit of Carthage. 34 In honour of the visit the people of Carthage, 35 made Pyrrhus and his court all honorary citizens. 36 King Gisco then did sign and seal a sacred treaty, 37 to recognise the sacred kingdom of Sicily, 38 and Pyrrhus and his heirs and successors, 39 as rightful kings and perpetual allies. 40 Upon news of the treaty between Pyrrhus and Gisco, 41 and the threat of such a treaty to the existence of Rome, 42 the Roman Senate appointed Quintus Fabius Maximus, 43 as Roman Caesar (dictator) at the head of a massive army, 44 to destroy Sicily and capture or kill Pyrrhus. 45 The claims that Rome was at war with the Etruscans, 46 an absurd lie as the Romans themselves were Etruscan.

C. 5

1 In the Great Age of the Ram, 2 eight hundred and eighty seven years, 3 since the dawn of the Great Age (313 BCE), 4 Roman Caesar Quintus Fabius Maximus, 5 applied his maximum forces against Messina, 6 and the Carthaginians soon faulted. 7 Quintus Fabius Maximus then captured Rhegium, 8 and then Catania with Hamilcar killed. 9 Confident of the defences of Syracuse, 10 King Pyrrhus split his forces into two, 11 and sought to cut off Quintus Fabius Maximus, 12 as he entreated his sacred ally King Gisco, 13 to send reinforcements as the body of Hamilcar, 14 was returned under military honours to Carthage. 15 Upon seeing the body of his only son, 16 Gisco fell into a deep melancholy, 17 and did not respond to the requests of his generals, 18 to support Pyrrhus against the Romans. 19 Without the expected support from Carthage, 20 Pyrrhus could only disrupt the Romans, 21 and after two years (310 BCE) Syracuse did briefly fall, 22 as some of the men of Quintus Fabius Maximus, 23 breached the defences of the royal quarters, 24 killing both Roxanna and Alexander Aegus. 25 Upon the murder of Roxanna and Alexander Aegus, 26 the troops of Pyrrhus and the king, 27 became like madmen and the Romans, 28 were forced to retreat to Messina, 29 on account of the ferocity of the forces of Pyrrhus. 30 Upon witnessing the body of his beloved Roxanna, 31 and his son Alexander Aegus, 32 King Pyrrhus did utter a high curse, 33 that with every fibre of his being, 34 and through every descendant he would spawn, 35 he would dedicate every waking moment, 36 to the complete and utter destruction of Rome. 37 In the Great Age of the Ram, 38 eight hundred and eighty eight years, 39 since the dawn of the Great Age (312 BCE), 40 Holy Father (Patros) Perdiccas, 41 did give up the ghost. 42 The position of holy father (Patros) of the world, 43 and the Universal Ecclesia did befall to Seleucus. 44 Upon news of the death of Perdiccas, 45 Aeschines briefly tried to lead a rebellion in Athens, 46 and the forces of King Eumenes of Sparta, 47 quickly captured the rebels and executed them. 48 In the same year, 49 the great lighthouse of Heliopolis (Alexandria), 50 also known as the Phaoros, 51 was completed at over 450 ft in height. 52 So bright the light and

so tall the lighthouse, 53 that it could be seen for many miles at sea.

C. 6

1 In the Great Age of the Ram, 2 eight hundred and ninety years, 3 since the dawn of the Great Age (310 BCE), 4 Pyrrhus quit Syracuse and eastern Sicily to the Romans, 5 and arrived with his army to Carthage, 6 where the population began a month of mourning, 7 upon the arrival of the body of Roxanna as Cybele, 8 and Alexander Aegus as Attis. 9 King Gisco who had remained in hiding, 10 and who had failed to provide reinforcements, 11 was arrested with his court and brought before Pyrrhus, 12 whereby Pyrrhus held a public trial, 13 of Gisco before the people of Carthage. 14 Gisco demanded that Pyrrhus and his generals, 15 be arrested and killed as invaders, 16 yet the Carthaginian generals reminded Gisco, 17 that Pyrrhus be a citizen and sacred ally, 18 whereupon Pyrrhus spoke to the city saying: 19 If any man love freedom and heaven, 20 if any man love his children and the world, 21 then he must choose either to take up arms, 22 and rid the world of Rome, 23 or be an agent for such evil. 24 For any man or general or king, 25 that ignores such evil approves of such evil. 26 Upon the speech by Pyrrhus, 27 the people demanded that Gisco, 28 and all the nobles who supported him, 29 be put to death, 30 and Pyrrhus was made the new king of Carthage, 31 with the support of the united forces. 32 In the Great Age of the Ram, 33 eight hundred and ninety one years, 34 since the dawn of the Great Age (309 BCE), 35 King Eumenes of Sparta, 36 did give up the ghost. 37 The crown did then befall his son, 38 whose name was Areus.

C. 7

1 In the Great Age of the Ram, 2 eight hundred and ninety two years, 3 since the dawn of the Great Age (308 BCE), 4 the Mausoleum of Alexander, 5 and the Great Serapheum of Heliopolis (Alexandria), 6 were finally completed. 7 The body of Alexander was then brought up from Memphis, 8 and placed in state within the Mausoleum. 9 The Ark of the Covenant, 10 being the ancient Ark of Pharaoh Akhenaten, 11 itself was brought to pride of place within the Serapheum. 12 Within one year the Great Museum of Heliopolis (Alexandria), 13 in which the famed Library was located, 14 was also completed. 15 Lysimachus (Ptolemy) then appointed the scholar Euclid, 16 as the first Master of the Museum, 17 and to celebrate the text known as Elements by Euclid, 18 was promulgated to all corners of the empire. 19 In the same year, 20 King Pyrrhus of Carthage, 21 did wed Alcia the daughter of deposed King Gisco. 22 In later years they did have two sons, 23 the first was named Alexander, 24 also known as Hamilcar Barakas, 25 and the other known as Heracles (Herocles), 26 also known as Hasdrubal. 27 In the Great Age of the Ram, 28 eight hundred and ninety three years, 29 since the dawn of the Great Age (307 BCE), 30 King Pyrrhus of Carthage, 31 sought friendly relations with Ophelas of Cyrene, 32 that they might form a sacred alliance. 33 To seal the union King Ophelas of Cyrene, 34 gave his daughter Berenice

to Pyrrhus in matrimony. ₃₅ It was their son known as Mara (Magas) of Cyrene, ₃₆ who became king twenty years later. ₃₇ In the Great Age of the Ram, ₃₈ Eight hundred and ninety four years, ₃₉ since the dawn of the Great Age (306 BCE), ₄₀ King Pyrrhus of Carthage, ₄₁ sought friendly relations with Bardylis of Illyria, ₄₂ that they might form a sacred alliance. ₄₃ To seal the union King Bardylis of Illyria, ₄₄ gave his daughter Bircenna to Pyrrhus in matrimony. ₄₅ It was their son known as Heracles, ₄₆ also known as Mytilus of Illyria, ₄₇ who became king twenty five years later. ₄₈ King Pyrrhus of Carthage, ₄₉ also wed with Lanassa of Athena. ₅₀ It was their son known as Alexander of Epirus, ₅₁ that dominated Epirus and Macedonia. ₅₂ In the Great Age of the Ram, ₅₃ eight hundred and ninety five years, ₅₄ since the dawn of the Great Age (305 BCE), ₅₅ King Pyrrhus of Carthage, ₅₆ sought friendly relations with Gala of Numidia, ₅₇ that they might form a sacred alliance. ₅₈ To seal the union King Gala of Numidia, ₅₉ gave his daughter to Pyrrhus in matrimony. ₆₀ It was their son known as Masinissa, ₆₁ also known as Massena of Numidia, ₆₂ who became king thirty years later. ₆₃ Thus within five years from the death, ₆₄ of Roxanna and Alexander Aegus, ₆₅ King Pyrrhus did seal five sacred treaties, ₆₆ through five matrimonial unions, ₆₇ to sow the seeds, ₆₈ to try and end Rome. ₆₉ The Carthaginians had begun to worship, ₇₀ Pyrrhus as their new living god, ₇₁ as Ba'al Moloch, ₇₂ to which children were burnt as offering.

C. 8

₁ In the Great Age of the Ram, ₂ nine hundred and two years, ₃ since the dawn of the Great Age (298 BCE), ₄ Holly High King Eochaid Buadach mac Lugaid, ₅ the king of all priests and prophets, ₆ and blood descendant of the priests of Ebla, ₇ and blood descendant of the priests of Ur, ₈ and blood descendant of the priest-kings of the Hyksos, ₉ and blood descendant of the priests of Ugarit, ₁₀ and the founding bloodlines of the prophets of Yeb, ₁₁ and the only true blood descendants of King Da'vid, ₁₂ did give up the ghost. ₁₃ The throne of Amen-Ra did then befall to his son, ₁₄ whose name was Ugaine Mor. ₁₅ By the same year, ₁₆ King Pyrrhus of Carthage, ₁₇ since the dawn of the Great Age (297 BCE), ₁₈ had concluded friendly trade treaties, ₁₉ with the Amorican tribes of Brittany for tin, ₂₀ and the Iberian tribes (south-east Spain), ₂₁ also for tin, lead, copper and silver, ₂₂ establishing the colonies of New Carthage, ₂₃ and Malaca and Gades. ₂₄ Carthage also established strategic colonies, ₂₅ within the lands of Numidia, ₂₆ such as Cartenna and Iol and Rusaddir, ₂₇ and the colony of Tingis and Lixus, ₂₈ in the ancient lands of the Mani (Morocco). ₂₉ In the Great Age of the Ram, ₃₀ nine hundred and three years, ₃₁ since the dawn of the Great Age (297 BCE), ₃₂ Cassander the guardian of Macedon and Thessaly, ₃₃ did give up the ghost. ₃₄ The position of guardian of Macedon and Thessaly, ₃₅ did then befall general Demetrius. ₃₆ With support from Pyrrhus, ₃₇ and King Philataerus of Pergamon, ₃₈ two rebel leaders did emerge, ₃₉ the first being named

Peisis, 40 who proclaimed himself King of all Thebes, 41 and the second being Dromichaetes, 42 who proclaimed himself King of Getae (Thrace). 43 With Lysimachus (Ptolemy) facing danger, 44 from King Ophelas of Cyrene, 45 Cassander the guardian of Macedon and Thessaly, 46 called on King Areus of Sparta, 47 and aid from holy father (patros) Seleucis. 48 The war to the north the centre and south, 49 raged for seven years until, 50 Cassander captured Athens, 51 and executed Peisis, 52 as the great walls of Athens, 53 were finally demolished, 54 that no more rebellions could be raised. 55 It would then be ten more years, 56 before King Dromichaetes of Getae (Thrace), 57 was finally defeated and executed.

C. 9

1 In the Great Age of the Ram, 2 nine hundred and three years, 3 since the dawn of the Great Age (297 BCE), 4 upon the chaos of rebellion in the east, 5 of the Inland (Mediterranean) Sea, 6 to the west King Pyrrhus, 7 reinforced his colonies of Iberia, 8 seizing the Islands of Ibiza and the Balearic, 9 before invading and seizing Massila (Marseilles), 10 and then invading and seizing Aleria, 11 upon the Island of Corsica, 12 and the city of Caralis, 13 upon the Island of Sardinia. 14 King Pyrrhus now firmly controlled, 15 all the trade of the west of the Inland (Mediterranean) Sea. 16 Thus Rome found herself, 17 completely cut off from supplies, 18 and allies able to help defend it. 19 The Roman Senate under the leadership, 20 of Appius Claudius Caecus and Quintus Fabius Maximus, 21 did commission the master merchant, 22 whose name was Pytheas of Massalia (Marsailles), 23 to pass through the blockade of Carthage, 24 at the Straits of Gibraltar, 25 and urgently seek friendly sources, 26 with which Rome could treaty, 27 for urgent metals and supplies. 28 Pytheas of Massalia (Marseilles), 29 did sail the same sea ships of the Celts, 30 which permitted them to sail of sea, 31 not like the Carthaginian and Roman ships, 32 which could only sail in calm waters near shore. 33 Pytheas of Massalia (Marsailles) succeeded in passing, 34 upon a windy night past the blockade of Carthage, 35 first unto the Island of Britannia (Britain), 36 and then as far north to the lands of Batavi (Netherlands), 37 then around the Island of Britannia, 38 to the lands of the Dumnoni, 39 and the west of Britannia (Britain). 40 There Pytheas of Massalia (Marseilles), 41 did establish a treaty with the custodians of the lands, 42 the Cuilliaéan tribe known as the Custenin (Constantines), 43 who served the ancient and sacred owner of the lands, 44 being the Cuilliaéan High Kings and Ugaine Mor. 45 Pytheas of Massalia (Marsailles), 46 did leave with metals and some men of the Dumnoni, 47 back to Rome, 48 with news of his journey.

C. 10

1 In the Great Age of the Ram, 2 nine hundred and five years, 3 since the dawn of the Great Age (295 BCE), 4 upon the return of Pytheas of Massalia (Marsailles), 5 the Roman Senate did appoint, 6 not one but two Caesars (dictators), 7 whose names were Appius Claudius Caecus, 8 and Lucius

Aemilius Barbula. 9 Caesar Appius Claudius Caecus, 10 was charged with preparing the armies of Rome, 11 that could be raised and trained in time, 12 against the expected attacks of Pyrrhus. 13 Caesar Lucius Aemilius Barbula, 14 was ordered to accompany Pytheas of Massalia (Marsailles), 15 on a mission for the survival of Rome, 16 past the blockage of Carthage upon the Gibraltar Straits, 17 to the Sacred Isle to obtain an audience, 18 with Cuilliaéan High King Ugaine Mor, 19 and help secure a supply of much needed tin and copper, 20 as well as a supply of trained and armed men, 21 capable of reinforcing the legions of Rome. 22 Upon reaching the most sacred Isle, 23 Caesar Lucius Aemilius Barbula, 24 was granted an audience with High King Ugaine Mor, 25 who spoke first as was custom, 26 and enquired not of the immediate mission, 27 but the deeper intentions of Rome, 28 to which Lucius Aemilius Barbula replied: 29 First to protect our honour our home, 30 second to provide for our people and all who love freedom, 31 third to serve heaven and defend the world against evil. 32 Upon hearing these words and the knowledge and respect, 33 of Lucius Aemilius Barbula to the wisdom of Jeremiah, 34 and the sacred laws of Tara, 35 Cuilliaéan High King Ugaine Mor did issue a decree: 36 Henceforth let it be known to all men, 37 who honour the Rule of Law, 38 who honour Justice and the Divine, 39 that Romans be welcomed as brothers, 40 not confronted as enemies, 41 and that any man who serve the cause of Rome, 42 so long as the spirit of Rome exists, 43 serves the same source of law as Tara. 44 Upon hearing these words, 45 Lucius Aemilius Barbula did declare: 46 Let it be known to all people, 47 as it will be written in the sacred scrolls of Rome, 48 and honoured by its Senators and Consuls, 49 as I hold this baton of authority, 50 I now give it to you most high holly king, 51 that you and your descendants forever more, 52 shall be welcomed as sons of Rome, 53 as honoured tribunes and priests of Rome, 54 and as long as Rome survives, 55 I pledge for Rome that your lands shall be protected, 56 and Rome shall never permit, 57 any force to rise against you. 58 With the sacred pact witnessed and sealed, 59 Cuilliaéan High King Ugaine Mor, 60 granted the Romans the right to mine, 61 in the lands of the Dumnonii to the south-west, 62 and the lands of the Demetae and Silurae, 63 and the Ordovici and Cornovi of the west. 64 The Romans set about expanding the mines, 65 and the building of new metal works, 66 and new port towns at Glevum and Isca, 67 and the training and building of the first legions, 68 raised beyond the shores of Italy.

C. 11

1 In the Great Age of the Ram, 2 nine hundred and eleven years, 3 since the dawn of the Great Age (289 BCE), 4 King Pyrrhus did launch three simultaneous attacks, 5 the first against Macedon, 6 the second against Messina and Syracuse, 7 and the third against Gortyn and Knossos on Crete. 8 Against Macedon Pyrrhus did attack from the west, 9 as King Philetaerus of Pergamon did attack from the east. 10 The forces of Demetrius the Guardian of Macedon, 11 were no match for such an invasion, 12 and even with support

from King Areus of Sparta, 13 Pyrrhus captured Macedonia and Thessaly, 14 placing General Sosthenes as regent, 15 for the son of Pyrrhus by Lanassa of Athens, 16 whose name was Alexander. 17 As to Messina and Syracuse, 18 the Romans were ill prepared with this new warfare, 19 of ferocity and destruction, 20 and the whole of Sicily soon fell again to Pyrrhus. 21 Crete also quickly fell to the forces of Pyrrhus, 22 and for a moment, 23 Pyrrhus controlled the fate of the world in his hands. 24 Holy Patros (Father) Seleucus of Eliada, 25 did send relief armies to Macedon and Thessaly, 26 and for ten years the forces of Carthage and Eliada, 27 fought for control of the lands and islands, 28 at terrible cost and waste. 29 In the Great Age of the Ram, 30 nine hundred and eighteen years, 31 since the dawn of the Great Age (282 BCE), 32 a great battle was fought between the forces, 33 King Philetaerus of Pergamon, 34 and Demetrius and Seleucus of Eliada. 35 So fierce and bloody the battle, 36 that tens of thousands of men died, 37 and the death of Sosthenes and Alexander, 38 and even King Philetaerus of Pergamon, 39 and Demetrius were killed in the battle. 40 The crown of Pergamon did then befall, 41 to his son named Atlas (Attalis), 42 who abandoned the support of Pyrrhus, 43 and instead sought terms with Antagonus, 44 the son of Demetrius. 45 Upon the truce, 46 Antigonus became King of Macedon, 47 and Pergamon an unlikely ally against Pyrrhus. 48 In the same year, 49 Lysimachus (Ptolemy) the Guardian of Heliopolis, 50 did give up the ghost. 51 His position did then befall to his son, 52 whose name was Philadelphos, 53 and the Peter (Ptah and Ptolemy).

C. 12

1 In the Great Age of the Ram, 2 nine hundred and eighteen years, 3 since the dawn of the Great Age (282 BCE), 4 upon news of the death of his son Alexander, 5 King Pyrrhus as Moloch was enraged, 6 and demanded a great holocaust be offered, 7 as the original name of the most sacred ritual, 8 of his cult did name the murder of innocents, 9 to the demon gods as atonement. 10 Pyrrhus as the living god Moloch did issue a high curse, 11 unto Atlas (Attalis) of Pergamon, 12 that his kingdom will crumble into dust, 13 and that Atlas (Attalis) shall be cursed to hold the burdens, 14 of the world forever. 15 To Antagonus he did issue the high curse that Macedon, 16 shall be laid to waste and ruin, 17 and that all the world will forget the truth. 18 Pyrrhus did order his scribes to modify his cult, 19 that all who dishonour his name and do not worship him, 20 shall be forever tormented by flame and fire in the underworld, 21 for he be a jealous god, 22 and no followers be permitted to worship any other deity. 23 But those who worship ignorance and fanaticism, 24 those who worship without question, 25 and sacrifice themselves and their first born, 26 shall have eternal salvation from the flames and torture. 27 Pyrrhus did then form a treaty, 28 with Priest King Menes of Tarsus, 29 who pledged the tribes of Cilicia, 30 and northern Syria to the service of Pyrrhus. 31 In the Great Age of the Ram, 32 nine hundred and nineteen years, 33 since the dawn

of the Great Age (281 BCE), ₃₄ Holy Patros (Father) Seleucus of Eliada, ₃₅ did give up the ghost. ₃₆ The position of the third Holy Patros (Father), ₃₇ in History did befall to his son, ₃₈ whose name was Antiochus. ₃₉ Upon the death of Seleucus, ₄₀ Pyrrhus seized the moment to invade Syria, ₄₁ aided by King Shem of Cilicia, ₄₂ and soon also captured Palestine, ₄₃ making Damascus the Capital, ₄₄ of the Kingdom of Samaria. ₄₅ King Shem then did anoint himself high priest, ₄₆ of the Cult of Mithra, ₄₇ claiming his father to be called Methuseliah, ₄₈ and to be his son as Shemiah (Samuel), ₄₉ as the last High Priest of Mithra, ₅₀ that had been eradicated by Alexander. ₅₁ Menes did then call himself Meneshiah, ₅₂ and then changed the foundation of Mithra religion, ₅₃ to make the supreme deity Ba'al Moloch, ₅₄ as the living god Pyrrhus on earth, ₅₅ and not the Divine Creator. ₅₆ Thus all men who worshipped Mithra, ₅₇ no longer worshipped heaven, ₅₈ but the gods of the underworld through trickery.

C. 13

₁ In the Great Age of the Ram, ₂ nine hundred and nineteen years, ₃ since the dawn of the Great Age (281 BCE), ₄ King Pyrrhus as Moloch, ₅ did land a massive mercenary army of eighty thousand, ₆ including more than five hundred war elephants, ₇ at Tarentum in southern Italy, ₈ and circumventing the massive defences, ₉ built by the Romans to prevent an invasion from Sicily. ₁₀ Publius Valerius Laevinus and his army of forty thousand, ₁₁ moved north from Calabria and confronted Pyrrhus, ₁₂ at the city of Heraclea. ₁₃ Despite the bravery of the Romans, ₁₄ they were completely overrun, ₁₅ losing more than twenty thousand of their forces, ₁₆ and the death of Publius Valerius Laevinus, ₁₇ compared to the loss of ten thousand by Pyrrhus. ₁₈ The army of Pyrrhus then moved north westward, ₁₉ to siege the region of Campania, ₂₀ and a defensive force of Tiberius Coruncanius. ₂₁ Naples quickly fell and Tiberius Coruncanius himself was killed, ₂₂ and Pyrrhus then made Naples his new capital, ₂₃ before sending his best diplomat, ₂₄ whose name was Cineas, ₂₅ to Rome to negotiate the terms of their surrender. ₂₆ At Rome Cineas addressed the Senate and the people, ₂₇ saying that the god Pyrrhus as Ba'al Moloch, ₂₈ did not wish ill upon the city or the people of Rome, ₂₉ and that if they surrender peacefully, ₃₀ he would spare the city and the people. ₃₁ Many of the Senators pleaded with one another, ₃₂ that such generous terms be agreed, ₃₃ while others sought deferral and delay, ₃₄ upon secret prayers that Lucius Aemilius Barbula, ₃₅ may return in haste an army of Holly Celts from Britannia. ₃₆ In the Great Age of the Ram, ₃₇ nine hundred and twenty years, ₃₈ since the dawn of the Great Age (280 BCE), ₃₉ word reached Rome that Lucius Aemilius Barbula, ₄₀ had set sail with a mighty force, ₄₁ of five legions and forty five thousand, ₄₂ Celt warriors from Britannia and Germanica. ₄₃ Upon the return of Cineas to Rome and the Senate, ₄₄ he warned the Senators that time had run out, ₄₅ to which Caesar Appius Claudius Caecus, ₄₆ did reply that while no man may stop time, ₄₇ every man is the architect of his own fortune. 48 Cineas did then return to Pyrrhus, 49 and declared that not even a cow, 50 be so stubborn as Rome, 51 as to ignore its own fate. 52 Before Pyrrhus could move against Rome, 53 the fleet of Lucius Aemilius Barbula, 54 successfully passed through the blockade, 55 at the straits of Gibraltar, 56 and then split into two, 57 with one force of some twenty thousand, 58 of the Holly Legions, 59 under the command of Publicus Decius Mus, 60 landing to the east of Pyrrhus, 61 at the port town of Bari, 62 and was soon joined a second force, 63 of twenty thousand Roman legionnaires, 64 under the command of Publius Sulpicius Saverrio. 65 The second larger fleet landed at Eryx, 66 in western Sicily under Lucius Aemilius Barbula, 67 and began to attack and seize the Carthaginian cities, 68 and destroying their supply lines. 69 Pyrrhus confronted the combined army, 70 of forty thousand Romans and Celts, 71 at Asculum in the Apulia region, 72 with a force of forty thousand of his own, 73 and secured a decisive victory, 74 killing fifteen thousand Romans and Celts, 75 including Publicus Decius Mus, 76 yet losing seven thousand more men. 77 In the Great Age of the Ram, 78 nine hundred and twenty one years, 79 since the dawn of the Great Age (279 BCE), 80 a second fleet of Holly Legions, 81 did pass through the blockades, 82 of the Carthaginians, 83 and land upon Corsica, 84 seizing the city of Aleria, 85 and then onto Sardinia, 86 and the city of Caralis. 87 Pyrrhus in need of supplies, 88 was forced to move his army, 89 back south to Sicily, 90 to confront Lucius Aemilius Barbula. 91 Yet by the time Pyrrhus had arrived, 92 to confront the Romans, 93 Lucius Aemilius Barbula used the Celt ships, 94 to move his forces north to Calabria, 95 to man the original defences, 96 of Publius Valerius Laevinus. 97 With insufficient men, 98 and now with the reinforcements, 99 of the Holly and Germanic Legions, 100 Pyrrhus abandoned his plans against Rome. 101 Instead he ordered the Syrian and Persian mercenaries, 102 to build the defences of the Campania region, 103 and especially the city of Naples. 104 And the mercenaries of Libya, 105 of King Mara (Magas), 106 did reinforce the region of Calabria. 107 Upon saving Rome, 108 Lucius Aemilius Barbula and the generals, 109 of the Holly Legions were awarded, 110 the greatest triumph yet seen.

C. 14

1 In the Great Age of the Ram, 2 nine hundred and twenty two years, 3 since the dawn of the Great Age (278 BCE), 4 upon reinforcing the defences of Sicily cities, 5 Pyrrhus landed a new army of fifty thousand mercenaries, 6 through Campania and Naples and Cumae, 7 to then march against Rome. 8 Consul Gaius Fabricius Luscinus, 9 with a much smaller force met against Pyrrhus, 10 at the high ground of Beneventum (Beneveto). 11 Pyrrhus chose not to by-pass the army of Gaius Fabricius Luscinus, 12 and instead engaged the smaller enemy army, 13 even though the conditions were against him. 14 Yet soon what was a smaller force became a bloody siege, 15 and rolling battles where month after month the forces fought, 16 and more and more men were killed. 17 After a

year of terrible war, 18 more than ten thousand Roman soldiers had died, 19 and more than twenty five thousand of the forces of Pyrrhus. 20 In the Great Age of the Ram, 21 nine hundred and twenty four years, 22 since the dawn of the Great Age (276 BCE), 23 Pyrrhus withdrew his forces back to Campania, 24 to focus on building the walls of Naples, 25 and defences of the Campania cities. 26 Soon after Pyrrhus returned to Carthage. 27 In the Great Age of the Ram, 28 nine hundred and twenty five years, 29 since the dawn of the Great Age (275 BCE), 30 King Pyrrhus also known as Moloch, 31 did divide the Carthaginian Empire, 32 between his two sons, 33 with the eldest son known as Alexander, 34 also known as Hamilcar Barakas, 35 being granted the crown of Carthage and Hispania, 36 and Heracles also known as Hasdrubal, 37 being granted the crown of Sicily. 38 King Hasdrubal (Heracles) immediately departed, 39 to lead invasion of Corsica and Sardinia, 40 to seize back the islands from the Romans, 41 and honour the legacy of his father. 42 Yet the defence of the islands proved formidable, 43 and Hasdrubal was forced to purchase mercenaries, 44 to fill his ranks in Sicily, 45 and support his war against Sardinia. 46 In the same year, 47 Pirate King Mara (Magas) of Marmarica (Cyrene), 48 son of Pyrrhus and Queen Berenice of Cyrene, 49 did wed Cybele (Apama) the high priestess, 50 and daughter of Priest King Shem of Samaria. 51 They did have but one daughter, 52 who they named Berenice. 53 in the Great Age of the Ram, 54 nine hundred and thirty years, 55 since the dawn of the Great Age (270 BCE), 56 King Pyrrhus also known as Moloch, 57 also known as Pyrro the Philosopher, 58 and founder of scepticism against the Divine, 59 and inventor and founder of war as industry, 60 also falsely known as Polyperchon, 61 also falsely known as Antipater and Agathocles, 62 did give up the ghost. 63 His legacy beyond total war, 64 remained in the flesh of his sons, 65 through King Hamilcar Barakas of Carthage and Hispania, 66 King Hasdrubal of Sicily and Sardinia, 67 Pirate King Mara (Magas) of Marmarica (Cyrene), 68 King Alexander of Epirus, 69 King Mytilus of Illyria, 70 and King Massena (Masinissa) of Numidia.

C. 15

1 By the time of the death of Pyrrhus, 2 the light of Heliopolis (Alexandria) shone brighter, 3 as men and women did make the pilgrimage, 4 from the four corners of the world, 5 to honour the man known as the Son of God, 6 to stand in awe at the marvels of such of the City of God, 7 to learn of the wisdoms of the world from its Museum, 8 and to pay homage to the most sacred ark of the covenant, 9 within the most holy of temples. 10 Not only religion but the power of knowledge, 11 and the power of the relics of gods, 12 had captured the imagination of all races of men. 13 Other cities sought to aspire if not to such greatness, 14 then at least in imitation to the city of light. 15 Pergamon had constructed grand temples, 16 and restored its museum after the terrible wars. 17 Even King Shemiah (Samuel) of Samaria had established, 18 a prosperous colony at Campania called Samnia. 19 In

celebration of fifty years since the death of Alexander, 20 Philadelphos the Peter (Ptah and Ptolemy) of Egypt, 21 did order the name of the great city be changed to Alexandria, 22 and that the greatest statue ever conceived, 23 be commissioned to Archimedes, 24 the Chief Curator of the Museum of Alexandria, 25 and the greatest mind of his day, 26 to be constructed upon the island named Rhodes, 27 within the great harbour, 28 and over one hundred and fifty feet in height, 29 yet as high as the great lighthouse (450 ft) on account of its base, 30 so all would see it upon their arrival. 31 The statue known as the Colossus, 32 and the Eternal Flame of Liberty, 33 was a mighty image of Alexander in bronze, 34 in priestly robes and a star crown, 35 holding aloft a mighty torch with his right hand, 36 and holding a great pair of scales by his left hand. 37 Holy Patros (Father) Antiochus, 38 the patron and guardian of Eliada, 39 did not approve of such worship and change, 40 to enlargen the Cult of Alexander, 41 yet his protests were ignored by Philadelphos. 42 Instead the Cult of the Alexandrian Divinities, 43 as knowledge of supreme power and the mind of God, 44 did call the most powerful men of the world, 45 to join a fraternity of the enlightened, 46 upon corrupted knowledge, 47 concerning a Great Architect of the Universe, 48 and a scientific spherical model of the heavens.

C. 16

1 In the Great Age of the Ram, 2 nine hundred and thirty years, 3 since the dawn of the Great Age (270 BCE), 4 upon the death of King Pyrrhus, 5 King Mara (Magas) of Marmarica (Cyrene), 6 and the Pentapolis of Graecian cities of Libya, 7 and son of Pyrrhus and Berenice, 8 did declare himself an ally of Rome, 9 pledging his kingdom and colony of Marsi, 10 in Calabria and southern Italy, 11 to the aid of the Romans. 12 King Shemiah (Samuel) of Samaria, 13 did also pledge his kingdom and colony, 14 of Samnia (Campania) in aid of the Romans. 15 King Mara (Magas) of Marmarica (Cyrene), 16 did then lead swift invasion of Crete, 17 capturing Gortyn and then island of Malta, 18 while all the Carthaginians were slaughtered. 19 Neither King Hasdrubal or King Hamilcar Barakas, 20 had the resources or means to attack the Marmatines (Mamertines). 21 Even Rome itself was without resources or supplies. 22 In the Great Age of the Ram, 23 nine hundred and thirty one years, 24 since the dawn of the Great Age (269 BCE), 25 Rome sent Quintus Ogulnius Gallus to Cyrene then Samaria, 26 where he concluded treaties, 27 with King Mara (Magas) of Marmarica (Cyrene), 28 and then Priest King Shemiah of Samaria. 29 That in recognising the colonies of Samnia (Campania) and Marsi (Calabria), 30 the Marmatines and Samaritans would begin supplies, 31 and help build Rome a great navy of its own. 32 Quintus Ogulnius Gallus returned to Rome, 33 and in the same year the first silver and bronze coins of Romans, 34 were minted by the Samnites at Naples and Marsi at Tarantum, 35 bearing the Head of King Mara (Magas), 36 the silver Denarius had the same weight of a didrachm (3 grams), 37 while the bronze As was three times the weight (of Denarius).

38 In the Great Age of the Ram, 39 nine hundred and thirty two years, 40 since the dawn of the Great Age (268 BCE), 41 General Crino of the Marmatines (Mamertines), 42 did attack and capture Rhegium and Messina from Carthage, 43 further weakening the defences of Carthage. 44 As King Hasdrubal (Heracles) of Sicily, 45 sought aid from his brother King Hamilcar Barakas of Carthage. 46 As Carthage was in retreat in the east of Sicily, 47 the Graecians of Syracuse led by Hiero, 48 then rebelled against the Carthage garrison, 49 and seized the city with Hiero as King, 50 and Syracuse now an ally of Rome. 51 In the Great Age of the Ram, 52 nine hundred and thirty three years, 53 since the dawn of the Great Age (267 BCE), 54 King Hasdrubal (Heracles) of Sicily, 55 did attack Rhegium and crush the Marmatines (Mamertines), 56 before moving to attack Messina. 57 King Mara (Magas) then did appeal to his ally Rome. 58 Yet the Senate of Rome were at first hesitant, 59 upon the great loss of life inflicted, 60 through the wars against Pyrrhus. 61 Upon the hesitation by the Romans and Samnites, 62 King Hasdrubal (Heracles) of Sicily, 63 moved against the Marsi of Tarantum and Locri, 64 destroying both cities, 65 and taking more than thirty thousand prisoners. 66 Within the year they did appoint Appius Claudius Caudex, 67 to command an army to support the Marmatines (Mamertines), 68 by which stage Messina had already fallen. 69 In the Great Age of the Ram, 70 nine hundred and thirty four years, 71 since the dawn of the Great Age (266 BCE), 72 the mercenary army of Appius Claudius Caudex, 73 did confront the forces of King Hasdrubal (Heracles) at Rhegium, 74 destroying the Carthaginians, 75 before driving them out of Marsi (Calabria), 76 and taking Messina at great cost. 77 King Mara (Magas) of Marmacia (Cyrene), 78 then ordered the rebuilding of Tarantum and Locri, 79 with even stronger defences.

C. 17

1 In the Great Age of the Ram, 2 nine hundred and thirty five years, 3 since the dawn of the Great Age (265 BCE), 4 King Areus of Sparta, 5 did give up the ghost. 6 The crown did then befall his son, 7 whose name was Eudamidas. 8 In Athens the leader Chremonides, 9 sought to incite war between Sparta and Macedon, 10 by dressing up his troops as Spartans, 11 and seeking to attack the forces of Antagonus of Macedonia. 12 Yet King Eudamidas and King Antagonus, 13 discovered the plans of the Athenians, 14 and had Chremonides executed, 15 with all responsible for the trickery. 16 In the Great Age of the Ram, 17 nine hundred and thirty nine years, 18 since the dawn of the Great Age (261 BCE), 19 Holy Patros (Father) Antiochus, 20 the patron and guardian of Eliada, 21 did give up the ghost. 22 The position of Holy Father did then befall to his son, 23 whose name was Theos and also Antiochus. 24 In the same year, 25 King Hamilcar Barakas of Carthage, 26 did land a force of fifty thousand in Sicily, 27 to aid his brother Hasdrubal, 28 in the recapture of the eastern cities. 29 A fierce battle then ensued between Rome and Carthage, 30 at the southern city of Sicily of Agrigentum, 31 where the fifty thousand from

Carthage fought, 32 against forty thousand from Rome, 33 and victory went to Rome at terrible cost. 34 In the same year, 35 Guardian Philadelphos Ptolemy of Alexandria, 36 and Holy Patros (Father) Theos Antiochus, 37 defeated Priest King Meneshiah from Palestine, 38 and southern Syria. 39 King Meneshiah was forced to return to his stronghold, 40 of Tarsus in Cilicia.

C. 18

1 In the Great Age of the Ram, 2 nine hundred and forty four years, 3 since the dawn of the Great Age (256 BCE), 4 and after the great victory of Rome, 5 to the south and west of Sicily, 6 King Hamilcar Barakas of Carthage, 7 sought a new force to invade Sicily, 8 as the Romans had commissioned the largest fleet, 9 yet seen in the Inland Sea (Mediterranean), 10 of more than two hundred coastal oared ships, 11 from King Mara (Magas) of Marmarica (Cyrene). 12 As King Hamilcar Barakas prepared an invasion force, 13 of more than sixty thousand, 14 the Romans under Marcus Atilius Regulus, 15 and Lucius Manlius Vulso Longus, 16 prepared the launch of their invasion force of fifty thousand, 17 whereupon both fleets encountered each other, 18 off the southern coast of Sicily near Cape Eknomus. 19 The Carthaginians were overwhelmed, 20 and lost more than a third of their ships, 21 before retreating back to Africa. 22 The Romans continued with their invasion, 23 with Marcus Atilius Regulus and the army, 24 landing at Tunis and defeating the Carthage resistance. 25 Yet Marcus Atilius Regulus did not march on Carthage, 26 and set in camp while peace was negotiated. 27 This gave time to King Hamilcar Barakas, 28 to call for aid from King Masnissa of Numidia. 29 King Masnissa of Numidia did then move east, 30 as King Hamilcar Barakas moved from the south, 31 trapping and surrounding Marcus Atilius Regulus. 32 With King Masnissa of Numidia honoured by Carthage, 33 as the most precious jewel, 34 also known as the Xanthiplus, 35 destroying the Roman army and capturing Marcus Atilius Regulus. 36 King Hasdrubal did then seize Agrigentum in Sicily, 37 totally destroying the city to its foundations. 38 While Rome had suffered a terrible defeat, 39 its new alliance with the Marmatines (Mamertines), 40 enabled the creation of auxiliary legions, 41 of paid mercenaries for hire, 42 as the Holly legions of Britannia, 43 could give no further aid. 44 In the Great Age of the Ram, 45 nine hundred and forty six years, 46 since the dawn of the Great Age (254 BCE), 47 the Romans attacked the Carthage cities of Sicily, 48 capturing Therma then Panorma then Drapna. 49 The Roman fleet and mercenary Legions, 50 also helped secure Sardinia and Corsica for Rome, 51 as Carthage continued to find, 52 such waste of life and materials, 53 impossible to be sustained. 54 In the Great Age of the Ram, 55 nine hundred and forty nine years, 56 since the dawn of the Great Age (251 BCE), 57 ahead of a planned invasion fleet, 58 King Hamilcar Barakas did release, 59 the prisoner general Marcus Atilius Regulus, 60 on his oath and the lives of his remaining men, 61 that he would argue for peace, 62 and if he did fail

that he would return, 63 to meet his fate at Carthage. 64 Marcus Atilius Regulus pledged a sacred oath, 65 that if the last of his men be freed, 66 then as a man of honour he would agree. 67 Thus Marcus Atilius Regulus, 68 and five hundred Roman officers were freed, 69 and returned to Rome, 70 where Marcus Atilius Regulus warned the Senate, 71 to believe nothing honourable could come from Carthage, 72 that a vile and wicked serpent it be, 73 and that if given the chance it would strike again. 74 The Senate implored Marcus Atilius Regulus to remain, 75 that an oath to men without law or honour be void. 76 Yet the general reminded the Senate, 77 that upon the day Rome chooses which laws of the Divine, 78 it wishes to keep and which ones it chooses to break, 79 Rome shall cease to be. 80 Whereupon Marcus Atilius Regulus returned to Carthage, 81 and told King Hamilcar Barakas, 82 that every last Roman would rather die, 83 defending their honour and rule of law, 84 than make peace with such vipers. 85 Marcus Atilius Regulus was then tortured to death, 86 as the Roman Senate mourned his death, 87 and honoured his memory, 88 as one of the greatest of heroes.

C. 19

1 In the Great Age of the Ram, 2 nine hundred and fifty one years, 3 since the dawn of the Great Age (249 BCE), 4 Oniah the twenty fifth great prophet of Yeb, 5 the son of Adiah and the grandson of Oananiah, 6 did give up the ghost. 7 The position then befell, 8 to his son whose name was Eleziah, 9 as the twenty sixth Great Prophet of the Yahudi, 10 at the great Temple of Alexandria. 11 In the Great Age of the Ram, 12 nine hundred and fifty two years, 13 since the dawn of the Great Age (248 BCE), 14 Holly High King Ugaine Mor mac Eochaid, 15 the king of all priests and prophets, 16 the king of all the Celts, 17 did give up the ghost. 18 The throne of Amen-Ra did then befall to his son, 19 whose name was Cobthach Coel Breg.

C. 20

1 In the Great Age of the Ram, 2 nine hundred and fifty four years, 3 since the dawn of the Great Age (246 BCE), 4 Guardian Philadelphos Ptolemy of Alexandria, 5 did give up the ghost. 6 His position as guardian and protector of Alexandria, 7 did then befall to his son, 8 whose name was Eurgetes, 9 aso known as Ptolemy III. 10 In the same year, 11 Holy Patros (Father) Antiochus II Theos, 12 did give up the ghost. 13 The position of Holy Father and Guardian, 14 for the known world did then befall to his son, 15 whose name was Seleucus II Callinicus. 16 Upon the death so soon of the Peter (Ptah) of Egypt, 17 and the Holy Father (Patros), 18 caused great uncertainty across Eliada. 19 Diodotus the Governor of Bactria, 20 did seize the opportunity to declare himself King, 21 and rebel against imperial forces, 22 while Andragoras the Governor of Parthia, 23 also proclaimed himself king, 24 of an independent state. 25 As Seleucus II Callinicus sought to quell rebellion, 26 Shemiah (Samuel) of Tarsus attacked imperial forces in Syria, 27 declaring once again the Kingdom of Samaria, 28 and himself as the High Priest of

Mithra. 29 Eurgetes the Ptolemy then did invade Palestine, 30 and then defeat and kill Shemiah (Samuel), 31 forcing his family and son named Menassiah, 32 to seek protection under Andragoras of Parthia. 33 Yet Seleucus II Callinicus was weak as a general, 34 and failed to bring Parthia or Bactria to submission. 35 Eurgetes the Ptolemy then refused to return, 36 the lands of Palestine and Syria to the stewardship, 37 of Seleucus II Callinicus and for the first time, 38 the Seleucus and the Ptolemy were at enmity. 39 In the Great Age of the Ram, 40 nine hundred and fifty five years, 41 since the dawn of the Great Age (245 BCE), 42 King Eudamidas of Sparta, 43 did give up the ghost. 44 The crown did then befall his son, 45 whose name was Agis. 46 Upon the death of Eudamidas of Sparta, 47 Alexander of Epirus sought to attack Macedon, 48 using Cyrenian and Ionian Mercenaries. 49 Yet Antagonus of Macedon did crush the forces of Alexander of Epirus, 50 and he was killed, 51 thus ending the bloodline of Pyrrhus in Epirus. 52 Upon the death of Priest King Shemiah of Samaria, 53 the colony of Samnia (Campania), 54 did elect a leader named Pontius as their King.

C. 21

1 In the Great Age of the Ram, 2 nine hundred and fifty eight years, 3 since the dawn of the Great Age (242 BCE), 4 a great drying began to grip the north of Africa, 5 as well as the lands of Europe and Asia. 6 The Celts of north and eastern tribes, 7 sought more fertile lands to the south, 8 and people moved closer to the coastline. 9 In the Great Age of the Ram, 10 nine hundred and fifty nine years, 11 since the dawn of the Great Age (241 BCE), 12 King Agis of Sparta, 13 did give up the ghost. 14 The crown did then befall his son, 15 whose name was Eucleidas. 16 In the Great Age of the Ram, 17 nine hundred and sixty years, 18 since the dawn of the Great Age (240 BCE), 19 the great drying of North Africa and Europe and Asia, 20 became a most terrible drought. 21 The kingdom of Egypt under Eurgetes the Ptolemy, 22 grew even more powerful as many nations sought food. 23 Even Rome sought stronger treaties with Egypt, 24 for the valuable supply of grain. 25 In the lands of Cyrene and Carthage and Numidia, 26 crops turned to dust and animals died of thirst. 27 The Marmatines (Mamertines) moved tens of thousands, 28 to Crete and Syracuse and Campania, 29 yet the drought did not relent. 30 Finally Mara (Magas) of Marmarica (Cyrene), 31 turned his massive mercenary army of over one hundred thousand, 32 westward towards Carthage, 33 in the hope of better conditions, 34 and a weakened former ally. 35 At first King Hamilcar Barakas was overwhelmed, 36 by the forces of Mara (Magas) and his cavalry. 37 Yet upon calling for aid from King Masnissa of Numidia, 38 the Numidia horsemen under Micipsa (Naravas), 39 did help defeat and destroy the Marmatines (Mamertines), 40 and Mara (Magas) of Marmarica (Cyrene) was killed, 41 but at great cost to both sides. 42 Upon news of the death of King Mara (Magas), 43 Queen Cybele (Apama) in mortal grief, 44 did throw herself to the royal lions, 45 and was torn to pieces before her guard. 46 The crown of

Marmarica (Cyrene), 47 did then befall to Berenice, 48 the only daughter of Mara (Magas), 49 who travelled east to Alexandria, 50 and the court of Eurgetes the Ptolemy, 51 where she offered herself in marriage, 52 and union of Peace with Egypt, 53 Eurgetes the Ptolemy agreed, 54 on account of her strength and intellect, 55 and they produced five offspring, 56 the eldest being a daughter, 57 who they named Arsinoe, 58 the second being a son named Alexander, 59 also known as Philopater, 60 the second daughter known as Berenice, 61 the second son known as Maras (Magas), 62 and the youngest daughter known as Apama (Cybele). 63 In his honour and treaty with the pirate cities, 64 of Marmarica (Cyrene), 65 Eurgetes the Ptolemy, 66 did change the name of the port of Derna to Philopatos, 67 and the name of the port of Susa to Marsa, 68 and the name of the port of Tauchira to Arsinoe, 69 and the name of the port of Bayda to Berenice, 70 and the name of the port of Boreas to Apama, 71 in honour of the names of his children, 72 and their right to autonomy through Cyrene.

C. 22

1 In the great city of Alexandria, 2 its arrogance continued to grow, 3 as the city itself began to be worshipped, 4 as the Kingdom of Heaven on Earth. 5 Not only the worship of knowledge, 6 much now corrupted to claim greater importance, 7 but the worship of money itself, 8 that men did come and offer to pay huge sums, 9 that may be permitted to learn the secrets of the universe. 10 Thus began several secret societies and cults, 11 throughout the sacred city, 12 as variations of the perversions of Pythagorus, 13 and Orpheus and then the worship of Alexander, 14 as to the death and rebirth of mind, 15 and the worship and creation of messiahs, 16 emerged to claim unique possession, 17 of secret knowledge and illumination. 18 Two such corruptions was the birth of complete fable, 19 and the world of Hades (Hell) and the Ferry-man, 20 where the love of money and the perversion of false knowledge, 21 spawned an afterlife even more corrupt, 22 and insane than the physical world. 23 The second being the corruption of the wisdom of the Hyksos, 24 in the form of Kabalah and magic charms, 25 in the belief that secret charms and spells, 26 and secret symbols and signs, 27 granted the initiate immense power. 28 Thus was born a madness of the academic mind, 29 and an elitism worship to false knowledge.

C. 23

1 In the Great Age of the Ram, 2 nine hundred and sixty two years, 3 since the dawn of the Great Age (238 BCE), 4 the world did seem to be in upheaval, 5 as the positions of the heavens (constellations), 6 changed by a full degree (Small Pole Shift), 7 and the lands of Europe and the Inland Sea (Mediterranean), 8 became noticeably warmer. 9 The ancient priests throughout the world, 10 did speak and prophecy as to the will of the gods, 11 in the changes of Heaven, 12 as many began to question if the gods, 13 were punishing men who had been unfaithful. 14 The great drought had brought such misery, 15 to the lands of

Carthage, 16 that King Hamilcar Barakas ordered his whole court, 17 and army of over three hundred thousand people, 18 depart from Carthage westward to their new homeland, 19 and the city of New Carthage (Cartagena) in Hispania. 20 Yet the ancient priests of Baal Hammon, 21 did refuse to leave and spoke that such signs in the heavens, 22 were a portent to the punishment of the gods against men. 23 And thus did become the priest kings to a city of ghosts. 24 The Numidians to the west, 25 had also suffered through the great drought, 26 so that King Masnissa of Numidia, 27 refused safe passage for such a large force. 28 King Hamilcar Barakas was then forced to fight, 29 whereupon the Numidians were defeated, 30 and King Masnissa of Numidia and his sons were killed, 31 ending the dynasty of Pyrrhus in Numidia. 32 Yet Hamilcar Barakas did not remain in Numidia, 33 and instead crossed the Straits of Gibraltar, 34 and into Hispania. 35 In the same year, 36 upon the great signs (from 24 degree to 23.5 degree angle), 37 Menassiah the son of Shemiah (Samuel), 38 did succeed in causing the army and people of Parthia, 39 to rise up against King Andragorus, 40 saying the gods demanded men return to blood sacrifice, 41 and fearing the gods, 42 and that only he as High Priest could save the people. 43 In the great city of Alexandria, 44 Eurgetes the Ptolemy demanded that Archimedes, 45 conceive a new religion, 46 whereby Eurgetes the Ptolemy be saviour of the world, 47 and that all men must pay homage to him, 48 or be denied eternal life, 49 and be condemned to eternal torment. 50 Archimedes refused such demands saying: 51 Better a tyrant who despises the law, 52 than a priest who defiles the will of heaven, 53 whereupon Archimedes departed back to Syracuse, 54 and to the services of King Hiero of Syracuse.

C. 24

1 In the Great Age of the Ram, 2 nine hundred and sixty nine years, 3 since the dawn of the Great Age (231 BCE), 4 Mytilus of Illyria did give up the ghost, 5 with the crown going to his son named Philip. 6 In the Great Age of the Ram, 7 nine hundred and seventy two years, 8 since the dawn of the Great Age (228 BCE), 9 King Hamilcar Barakas of Carthage and Hispania, 10 did give up the ghost. 11 His brother the former king of Sicily, 12 whose name was Hasdrubal, 13 did then become King of New Carthage. 14 In the Great Age of the Ram, 15 nine hundred and seventy five years, 16 since the dawn of the Great Age (225 BCE), 17 Holy Patros (Father) Seleucus II Callinicus, 18 did give up the ghost. 19 The position of Holy Father and Guardian, 20 for the known world did then befall to his son, 21 whose name was Antiochus III the Great. 22 In the Great Age of the Ram, 23 nine hundred and seventy eight years, 24 since the dawn of the Great Age (222 BCE), 25 Guardian Ptolemy III Euergetes of Alexandria, 26 did give up the ghost. 27 His position as guardian and protector of Alexandria, 28 did then befall to his son, 29 whose name was Philopator, 30 also known as Peter and the Rock, 31 also known as Ptolemy. 32 Philopator the Ptolemy was a weak and immoral leader, 33 controlled by Chief Minister Sosibius, 34 who upon seizing such

position convinced Philopator, 35 that his mother was plotting to overthrow him, 36 and install his younger brother Mara (Magas) as King. 37 Mara (Magas) was warned by his mother of the danger, 38 and fled into exile and sanctuary, 39 to the Marmatine (Mamertine) colony of Rheggio. 40 Upon news of the escape of his brother, 41 Philopator the Ptolemy was enraged, 42 and had his mother Berenice executed. 43 Soon after he fell into brief mourning, 44 ordering that a temple be formed in her honour. 45 Philopator then took his sister Arsinoe, 46 as his reluctant queen. 47 For ten years she lived in terror, 48 and resisted his advances, 49 until she relinquished, 50 and gave birth to Epiphanes.

C. 25

1 In the Great Age of the Ram, 2 nine hundred and seventy nine years, 3 since the dawn of the Great Age (221 BCE), 4 King Hasdrubal of New Carthage, 5 did give up the ghost. 6 The crown of New Carthage did then befall to Hannibal, 7 also known as Hannibal the Great. 8 In the Great Age of the Ram, 9 nine hundred and eighty two years, 10 since the dawn of the Great Age (218 BCE), 11 the Romans did invade Hispania and Massalia. 12 with the Roman legions first attacking Emporion, 13 led by Gnaeus Cornelius Scipio, 14 and his brother Publius Cornelius Scipio, 15 capturing Massalia (Marsailles) within the year. 16 The Carthaginians and Romans met in Hispania, 17 at Cissa near Tarraco, 18 with the first Carthaginian Army led by Hasdrubal Gisco, 19 the brother of Hannibal. 20 When the army of Hannibal then arrived, 21 the forces of Gnaeus Cornelius Scipio were crushed, 22 and Gnaeus Cornelius Scipio was killed. 23 Yet without any respite, 24 the Roman Army of Publius Cornelius Scipio, 25 did then arrive and continue to attack. 26 King Hannibal then conceive of a plan, 27 that if the invasion plans of Rome, 28 could be delayed or halted, 29 then the refugees of Carthage, 30 could complete their integration and new cities, 31 along the Guada River to the south, 32 and the city of Cordoba, 33 and along the Ebro River to the north, 34 and the city of Zaragoza. 35 Hannibal then left the defences, 36 and future of New Carthage, 37 in the hands of his brother Hasdrubal Gisco, 38 and then travelled along the coast, 39 into the lands of the Gaul and around Massalia (Marsailles), 40 then onto the Alps and into North Italy. 41 Upon the arrival of Hannibal and his army, 42 of over forty thousand and three hundred elephants, 43 the Roman army of General Tiberius Sempronius Longus, 44 of over fifty thousand did attack Hannibal, 45 near the Trebbia River. 46 The army of Hannibal succeeded in destroying the army, 47 of Tiberius Sempronius Longus, 48 with more than thirty thousand legionnaires losing their lives, 49 for light casualties for Hannibal. 50 Philip of Illyria did offer fresh troops, 51 in seeking an alliance with Hannibal against Rome, 52 that replaced the men that Hannibal had lost. 53 This gave Hannibal and his army time to rest and regain strength, 54 that within the year a second massive army, 55 of more than sixty thousand Roman legionnaires, 56 led by Gnaeus Servilius Geminus and

Gaius Flaminius Nepos, 57 did attack Hannibal near Lake Trasimene. 58 Yet once again Hannibal succeeded, 59 and this time more than twenty five thousand Romans, 60 were slaughtered by the forces of Hannibal, 61 as well as Gnaeus Servilius Geminus. 62 So great now was the legend of Hannibal and his immortals, 63 that no army stood in his way. 64 Yet Hannibal refrained from attacking Rome, 65 even though momentum was in his favour. 66 In the Great Age of the Ram, 67 nine hundred and eighty four years, 68 since the dawn of the Great Age (216 BCE), 69 Hannibal and his army did gain valuable rest, 70 yet without reinforcements, 71 the army of Hannibal was now thirty thousand, 72 and few elephants still alive. 73 The Roman Senate resolved to defeat Hannibal, 74 in one massive strike and commissioned the largest army, 75 yet seen in Italy of over one hundred thousand mercenaries, 76 under the command of Gaius Terentius Varro, 77 and Lucius Aemilius Paullus. 78 The Romans and Hannibal met at Cannae, 79 where Hannibal let the generals believe, 80 they had broken his lines, 81 yet the forces of Hannibal enveloped the Romans, 82 and in one day the army of Hannibal, 83 slaughtered more than seventy thousand Romans, 84 including Lucius Aemilius Paullus, 85 and more than a third of the senate of Rome, 86 who led units as officers. 87 The army of Hannibal was now down to a strength, 88 of just twenty five thousand men. 89 Yet over the next three years did still defeat, 90 three more formidable armies. 91 In the Great Age of the Ram, 92 nine hundred and eighty five years, 93 since the dawn of the Great Age (215 BCE), 94 King Hiero of Syracuse, 95 did give up the ghost. 96 Upon his death his son named Gelo, 97 did declare himself an ally of Hannibal. 98 Damarata the daughter of Hiero, 99 did then appeal to Mara (Magas), 100 and aided by Antonius the husband of Damarata, 101 succeeded in King Gelo, 102 before the Carthaginians, 103 could take the city. 104 Upon news of the actions of his brother, 105 Philopater declared himself an ally of Hannibal, 106 and promptly launched a sea attack, 107 as Hannibal sought to conquest by land. 108 Yet the great Archimedes, 109 in the service of Syracuse, 110 had anticipated such events, 111 and had invented the most powerful and deadly, 112 of machines against the invaders. 113 The Egyptian ships were smashed to pieces, 114 and Hannibal lost more men than in any other battle. 115 After two years of failed attempts, 116 all that Philopater of Egypt succeeded, 117 was the assassination of Archimedes, 118 by a lone attacker. 119 Upon the failure to take Syracuse, 120 Hannibal escaped back to Africa, 121 with the remainder of his army, 122 as one final stand. 123 The Senate recalled Publius Cornelius Scipio, 124 and his army from Hispania, 125 to go to Africa and defeat Hannibal. 126 Yet Hannibal had failed to find men willing, 127 to make such a final stand. 128 At Zama near Carthage, 129 outnumbered twenty to one, 130 the forces of Hannibal were finally defeated, 131 by Publius Cornelius Scipio, 132 and Hannibal and his surviving army, 133 committed suicide rather than surrender. 134 Ashamed of the terrible dishonour, 135 of how Rome dispatched such a great general, 136 many a historian falsely claimed he lived on. 137 Many a great city now in ruins, 138 and two million lives and four empires lost, 139 such be the waste and futility of war, 140 that no one profits from war, 141 except those that enable such evil. 142 For what Pyrrhus had failed to do in battle, 143 his descendants would soon achieve through money, 144 in the corruption of the spirit of Rome.

C. 26

1 In the Great Age of the Ram, 2 nine hundred and eighty three years, 3 since the dawn of the Great Age (217 BCE), 4 Holly High King Cobthach Coel Breg mac Ugaine, 5 the king of all priests and prophets, 6 the king of all the Celts, 7 did give up the ghost. 8 The throne of Amen-Ra did then befall to his brother, 9 whose name was Loegaire Lorc mac Ugaine. 10 In the Great Age of the Ram, 11 nine hundred and ninety two years, 12 since the dawn of the Great Age (208 BCE), 13 a terrible sign appeared in the heavens, 14 upon the approach of the comet Encke. 15 as tradition since ancient times, 16 a comet signalled bad omens. 17 So Encke did bring hardship, 18 to many cultures yet spared others. 19 The meteorite swarm did come, 20 yet not as destructive to all mankind, 21 as in ancient times. 22 Some hundreds fell across the Levant, 23 and cultures of the Mediterranean, 24 bringing a halt to the campaigns of Antiochus the Great. 25 Many more did smash into the lands of the Celts, 26 of Northern and Central Europe. 27 Upon such signs from heaven, 28 rational men abandoned their reason, 29 and superstitions arose again. 30 In the lands of the Romans, 31 spared from any destruction, 32 their good fortune was heralded as a sign, 33 they be chosen by heaven to lead the world, 34 and rid the world of ignorance and evil.

C. 27

1 In the Great Age of the Ram, 2 nine hundred and ninety one years, 3 since the dawn of the Great Age (209 BCE), 4 King Menassiah of Parthia, 5 did give up the ghost. 6 The crown did then befall to his son, 7 whose name was called Machiah. 8 Upon the death of Menassiah, 9 Holy Patros (Father) Antiochus the Great, 10 did attack Parthia and defeat Machiah, 11 who he then let live on the pledge of loyalty, 12 and renunciation of claims of priesthood. 13 Machiah then changed his name, 14 Machiah then changed his name, 15 as vassal to the Eliada Empire. 16 In the same year, 17 Holy Patros (Father) Antiochus the Great, 18 did defeat King Euthydemus of Bactria, 19 and return it to control. 20 Upon the securing of the Kingdom, 21 Antiochus continued in the building of his new capital, 22 at Heliopolis upon the Orontes River, 23 falsely claimed by the name of Antioch, 24 to hide its provenance. 25 Holy Patros (Father) Antiochus the Great, 26 also secured peace with the Nabateans, 27 the wealthy merchants and kings of north Arabia, 28 and their leader King Rabelas. 29 In the Great Age of the Ram, 30 nine hundred and ninety three years, 31 since the dawn of the Great Age (207 BCE), 32 as Philopator the Ptolemy resumed fighting, 33 against Antiochus the Great in Palestine, 34 he halted shipment of grain to Rome. 35 So important was the grain shipments from Egypt, 36

that the Senate sent a delegation of two Consuls, 37 whose names were Marcus Livius Salinator, 38 and Gaius Claudius Nero, 39 yet Philopator the Ptolemy refused to reason. 40 The Great Prophet Eleziah then confronted Philopator, 41 against his wickedness that Alexandria, 42 had become a place of vice and madness against heaven. 43 In response Philopator the Ptolemy ordered Eleziah, 44 to be executed and declared himself the great prophet.

C. 28

1 In the Great Age of the Ram, 2 nine hundred and ninety four years, 3 since the dawn of the Great Age (206 BCE), 4 Eleziah the twenty sixth great prophet of Yeb, 5 the son of Adiah and the grandson of Oniah, 6 did give up the ghost. 7 The position then befell, 8 to his son whose name was Elkaniah, 9 as the twenty seventh Great Prophet of the Yahudi. 10 The Roman Senate appointed Marcus Livius Salinator, 11 as Caesar (dictator) at the head of an army to seize Philopator, 12 to restore the grain supply to Rome, 13 and rescue Elkaniah and the holly priests. 14 The people of Alexandria who hated the excesses of Philopator, 15 helped the Romans enter the city without conflict, 16 and Philopator the Ptolemy was captured and executed, 17 with Marcus Livius Salinator, 18 installing a garrison of Roman Soldiers, 19 within the city to protect against rebellion, 20 as Epiphanes the young son of Philopator, 21 was made the new Peter (Ptah) and Ptolemy. 22 Marcus Livius Salinator then returned to Rome, 23 with the Ark of the Covenant, 24 the sacred treasures of Moses (Akhenaten), 25 and the most ancient holly priests of Yeb. 26 Thus for the first time in history, 27 the Ark of Akhenaten (Covenant), 28 did come to Rome.

C. 29

1 The arrival of the Ark of the Covenant, 2 and the Holly priests of Yeb, 3 was a moment of great history for Rome, 4 hidden by falsely claiming it be merely the arrival, 5 of a black rock of Cybele, 6 by snakes and assassins of history. 7 For there was no celebration in blood, 8 no worship yet of Magna Mater as Queen of Heaven, 9 no worship of self-mutilation and celibacy, 10 no celebration of human sacrifice and black magic. 11 Yet what is not in dispute, 12 is that such a momentous occasion called for Rome, 13 to build its greatest temple. 14 The Roman Senate did fear the power of the Ark, 15 and that all who had possessed it had fallen, 16 thus they commissioned a separate city and temple, 17 be constructed upon Mount Vaticanus, 18 using a structure of catacombs to level the hill, 19 and support such a grand edifice. 20 Within ten years the great temple was completed, 21 and Elkaniah honoured as the first Pontifex Maximus, 22 meaning the Head Prophet and Seer, 23 as Supreme Pontiff of Yahu, 24 being the Divine Creator of all existence, 25 and the God of all gods. 26 Supreme Pontiff Elkaniah did then usher, 27 a most prophetic prayer, 28 that though the heavens may fall, 29 let justice be done, 30 for men are known to forget, 31 yet nothing is lost to the Divine Creator, 32 thus let the light of Rome, 33 shine forever as a beacon of the Rule of Law, 34 that none are above the law, 35 and every man must give

account, [36] for none be damned but by their own ignorance.

Book 19

Great Age of Rome
[204 - 39 BCE]

C. 1

1 In the Great Age of the Ram, 2 nine hundred and ninety six years, 3 since the dawn of the Great Age (204 BCE), 4 the lands of the great Po valley, 5 which had supported Hannibal, 6 were finally brought to account, 7 as a new Province known as Gallia Citerior, 8 later known as Gallia Cisalpine, 9 commanded by Lucius Scribonius Libo. 10 With the wars against Hannibal and his brothers, 11 finally coming to an end, 12 Rome faced the terrible cost, 13 and the demands of peace, 14 as mercenary soldiers of the Marsi and Samnites, 15 from Sparta to Ionia and Africa, 16 as well as Celts from Britanni and Germanica, 17 sought compensation for their service. 18 The Samnites (Samaritans) did still control, 19 the minting of money through their city of Naples, 20 as they had done well before the wars with Hannibal, 21 and now dominated all trade and supplies. 22 Yet the Senate of Rome still commanded the law, 23 and by law only a Citizen of Rome could hold land. 24 The Roman Senate then did appoint Quintus Caecilius Metellus, 25 as Caesar (Dictator) with a commission of ten Senators, 26 to negotiate with King Mara of the Marmatines (Mamertines), 27 and King Pontius of Samnia and King Antonius of Syracuse. 28 Upon his appointment Caesar Quintus Caecilius Metellus, 29 did consult with the Pontifex Maximus Elkaniah, 30 The Great Prophet of Yeb in Rome. 31 The Supreme Pontiff of the Divine Creator did warn Caesar, 32 that the law does not permit two types of Citizens, 33 that if even one man be above the law, 34 then the Golden Rule be dishonoured, 35 and there be no Rule of Law. 36 Thus Caesar Quintus Caecilius Metellus, 37 failed to resolve the crisis.

C. 2

1 In the Great Age of the Ram, 2 nine hundred and ninety seven years, 3 since the dawn of the Great Age (203 BCE), 4 as the threat of open rebellion grew, 5 amongst the veterans of the great wars, 6 who had settled in the Po and Arno valleys, 7 to the northern province, 8 and across Campania and Sicily, 9 to the southern provinces. 10 The Senate then appointed Publius Sulpicius Galba as Caesar. 11 Caesar Publius Sulpicius Galba then issued, 12 the historic proclamation making all veterans, 13 of the wars against the Carthaginians as Plebian Citizens,

14 as second class Citizens but with the right of land, 15 on condition of their sacred pledge, 16 of loyalty and allegiance to Rome. 17 As a symbol to the Marmatines (Mamertines), 18 Caesar Publius Sulpicius Galba appointed the son of King Mara, 19 who was also known as Mara, 20 as his Magister Equitum (Master of the Horse). 21 Upon such illustrious appointment, 22 the son of King Mara did adopt a Roman Name, 23 calling himself Gaius Marius Servilius, 24 as a loyal and obedient servant to the glory of Rome, 25 and pledged upon his ancestors and his blood, 26 that he and all his descendants be bound, 27 to protect the honour of Rome, 28 and the laws of Rome. 29 As a symbol to the Samnites (Samaritans), 30 of Campania and Naples, 31 Caesar Publius Sulpicius Galba appointed the son of King Pontius, 32 who was also known as Pompus, 33 as his Quastor (Master of mint and finance). 34 Upon such illustrious appointment, 35 the son of King Pontius did adopt a Roman Name, 36 callling himself Gnaeus Pompeius Sterno. 37 As celebration King Pontius of the Samnites (Samaritans), 38 ordered his mint at Naples forge a new coin, 39 made of seven grams of gold, 40 called the Aureus and equal to 25 denarii. 41 King Pontius then sent a thousand coins to each Senator, 42 as a sign of the good will of the Samnites (Samaritans). 43 As a symbol to the Graecians of Sicily and Syracuse, 44 Caesar Publius Sulpicius Galba appointed the son of King Antonius, 45 who was also known as Sempronius, 46 as his Tribune of the Plebs (Supreme Justice). 47 The son of King Antonius did adopt a Roman Name, 48 calling himself Tiberius Sempronius Gracchus. 49 Thus upon the first formation of the Plebian class, 50 in the history of Rome, 51 the connection was forged in the mind, 52 of the pirates and mercenaries, 53 to honour the equis (horse), 54 as the laws of equity instead of equality, 55 as law had become the weapon, 56 for power and privilege at all cost.

C. 3

1 In the Great Age of the Ram, 2 nine hundred and ninety seven years, 3 since the dawn of the Great Age (203 BCE), 4 upon Rome securing an uneasy peace, 5 with Pirate King Mara (Magas) of Marmarica (Cyrene), 6 and King Antonius of Syracuse and Sicily, 7 with Egypt and the regent of Epiphanes the Ptolemy, 8 and King Pontius of Samnia (Campania), 9 King Philip of Illyria and Macedonia, 10 secured an alliance with Holy Patros Antiochus the Great. 11 King Philip did invade Crete and seized it, 12 as Antiochus seized Cyprus. 13 Yet King Philip of Illyria met fierce resistance at Rhodes, 14 and his fleet was destroyed. 15 To protect his kingdom, 16 King Attalis of Pergamon, 17 did conclude a peace treaty with Rome. 18 Thus the ancient alliances since the time of Alexander, 19 were finally broken, 20 and no more did the Empire of conscience, 21 exist in the hearts of men, 22 or the halls of kings.

C. 4

1 In the Great Age of the Ram, 2 one thousand and three years, 3 since the dawn of the Great Age (197 BCE), 4 the Great Temple known as the Vaticanus, 5 atop Mount Vaticanus was

completed, 6 as the new home for the Ark of the Covenant, 7 and the first Pontifex Maximus, 8 the Great Prophet Elkaniah of Yahu. 9 The catacombs did support a giant structure, 10 above the virgin earth of more than two hundred feet in length, 11 nor had such earth been desecrated as a place of burial, 12 until the time of Gaius Marius who called himself Julius Caesar, 13 and the worship of Cybele and Mithra and sacrifice. 14 Upon the completion of the most sacred Temple of all Rome, 15 the Senate instituted two most sacred rituals, 16 united together as the representation, 17 of death and resurrection, 18 with the first being ceremony of Quadragesima (Lent), 19 during the month of late February and March, 20 as forty days of fasting and austerity, prayer and charity, 21 where Romans prayed to their ancestors and household gods, 22 consuming only unleavened bread and unfermented wine, 23 until the celebration of the new festival called Megalesia, 24 led by the Pontifex Maximus Elkaniah, 25 at the beginning of April and celebrating rebirth and new life, 26 at which for fourteen days Romans could celebrate their providence, 27 and thanks to the one Divine Creator. 28 Thus was born the sacred liturgy of Essenoi, 29 meaning those who seek to be enlightened through, 30 purity of spirit and honesty of character.

C. 5

1 In the Great Age of the Ram, 2 one thousand and four years, 3 since the dawn of the Great Age (196 BCE), 4 King Attalis the Lion of Pergamon, 5 did give up the ghost. 6 The crown did then befall, 7 to his son named Eumenes. 8 In the same year, 9 the Roman Senate did divide the lands of Hispania (Spain), 10 conquered from Carthage, 11 into two provinces, 12 the first being the Ebro Valley and called Hispania Citerior, 13 and the second being the Iberian peninsula called Hispania Ulterior. 14 Yet within two years the people of both provinces rebelled, 15 and Rome was forced to accept the services of a mercenary army, 16 led by plebian Marcus Porcius Cato to put down the rebellion. 17 Within a year the mercenary army had destroyed all opposition, 18 and as an offering to Rome and the Senate, 19 Marcus Porcius Cato returned to Rome with a huge bounty, 20 of gold and silver and precious gifts, 21 that were then distributed amongst the Senators and officials, 22 in honour of plebian service to Rome.

C. 6

1 Since the edict of Publius Sulpicius Galba, 2 in the creation of all Plebs as equal, 3 land had been allocated to the former mercenaries, 4 and soldiers as free men, 5 for slavery remained a capital crime under Roman Law, 6 and no man be bound to serve except by their own consent, 7 as surety for their valid debts. 8 Yet Pirate King Mara (Magas) of Marmarica and Crete, 9 did secretly dishonour these laws, 10 by importing slaves to Sicily and Calabria and Campania, 11 to work the larger estates owned by the more powerful. 12 Thus slowly the price of agriculture continued to remain low, 13 as larger farms with slave labour, 14 could charge less than free men, 15 and more and more freemen became indebted and impoverished. 16 Rather than

enforcing the strictness of the law, 17 Senators of Rome increasingly turned a blind eye, 18 as King Mara through his son Gaius Marius Servilius, 19 gifted to key senators the most beautiful girls, 20 and young boys as personal slaves and attendants. 21 Nor did the Plebs themselves rise up, 22 as Gnaeus Pompeius Sterno of the Samnites, 23 gradually built the largest network of brothels, 24 and drug dens and taverns full of enslaved girls and boys. 25 In the history of the known world, 26 never before had such depravity been at so large a commercial scale, 27 as such vices were the stories of conquest and pillage. 28 Yet mercenaries and Plebs could afford to indulge themselves, 29 in opiates and sexual pleasures and alcohol cheaply. 30 In the Great Age of the Ram, 31 one thousand and eight years, 32 since the dawn of the Great Age (192 BCE), 33 Holy Patros Antiochus the Great, 34 did end his war with Ptolemy of Egypt, 35 for Syria and Sinai and his army attacked Pergamon, 36 aided by King Philip of Illyria and Macedonia. 37 King Eumenes of Pergamon did appeal to Rome, 38 who then sent Lucius Cornelius Scipio, 39 and a Samnite mercenary army to his aid. 40 In the Great Age of the Ram, 41 one thousand and ten years, 42 since the dawn of the Great Age (190 BCE), 43 Holy Patros (Father) Antiochus the Great, 44 was soundly defeated upon the plains of Lydia (Anatolia). 45 Lucius Cornelius Scipio then annexed Anatolia, 46 from the Empire of Eliada and renamed it Pontus, 47 appointing Lucius Pompeius Pharnaces as governor, 48 with Amisos the capital of the new Roman province. 49 Lucius Cornelius Scipio then formed a peace treaty, 50 with King Prusias of Bithynia to the west, 51 and King Artaxis of the Armenians to the east. 52 In the Great Age of the Ram, 53 one thousand and thirteen years, 54 since the dawn of the Great Age (187 BCE), 55 Holy Father (Patros) Antiochus the Great, 56 did give up the ghost. 57 The position of holy father (Patros), 58 did befall to his son named Epiphanes. 59 Upon the death of Antiochus the Great, 60 Lucius Pompeius Pharnaces extended the lands of Pontus, 61 by capturing the Crimea (Peninsula), 62 establishing Pontius to the east, 63 and Taurica (Yalta) to the south, 64 and Heraclea (Sevastapol) to the south-east.

C. 7

1 In the Great Age of the Ram, 2 one thousand and eighteen years, 3 since the dawn of the Great Age (182 BCE), 4 King Phriapites of Parthia, 5 formerly known as Machiah, 6 did give up the ghost. 7 His crown did then fall to his son, 8 Phrates who then changed his name to Mithradiah, 9 and proclaimed himself the true and only saviour, 10 and high priest of Mithraism. 11 Mithradiah then proclaimed blood heritage, 12 directly through to the Great Prophet Enochiah, 13 through a mysterious and absurd genealogy, 14 beginning with Methuseliah who he now claimed, 15 did live for hundreds of years, 16 then his claimed son Lameciah, 17 who he also claimed lived for hundreds of years, 18 and then Noiah (Noah) who lived for hundreds of years, 19 before Shem (Shemiah) then Menassiah then Machiah. 20 In the Great Age of the Ram, 21 one thousand and nineteen

years, 22 since the dawn of the Great Age (181 BCE), 23 Holly High King Meilge Molbthach mac Cobthach, 24 the Cuilliaéan king of all the Celts, 25 did give up the ghost. 26 The throne of Amen-Ra did then befall to his son, 27 whose name was Irereo Fathach mac Meilge. 28 Since the tin and silver and gold mines of the Holly High Kings, 29 they had become increasingly wealthy, 30 along with the Constantine (Custenynn), 31 the stewards of the Drumnonii. 32 In the Great Age of the Ram, 33 one thousand and twenty one years, 34 since the dawn of the Great Age (179 BCE), 35 King Philip of Illyria and Macedonia, 36 the Grandson of the Great Pyrrhus, 37 did give up the ghost. 38 The crown then did befall to his son, 39 whose name was Perseus.

C. 8

1 In the Great Age of the Ram, 2 one thousand and thirty three years, 3 since the dawn of the Great Age (167 BCE), 4 Roman Consul Lucius Aemilius Paullus, 5 defeated the army of King Perseus of Illyria and Macedon, 6 at the battle for Pydna in Macedon. 7 King Perseus of Illyria, 8 the great grandson of the King Pyrrhus, 9 was captured and killed, 10 thus the bloodline of Pyrrhus ended in Illyria and Eliada. 11 The Province of Illyricum was then declared for Rome and the Senate. 12 Upon the death of King Perseus, 13 the Cypriots and Syrians and Palestinians revolted, 14 under the leadership of Priest King Mattathiah of Tarsus, 15 who proclaimed himself to be the one true high priest, 16 in opposition to Mithradiah of Parthia. 17 Holy Patros Epiphanes the Antiochus, 18 did restore order to Cyprus, 19 yet Priest King Mattathiah and his sons, 20 did cripple and delay the superior forces, 21 of Epiphanes the Antiochus. 22 In the Great Age of the Ram, 23 one thousand and thirty five years, 24 since the dawn of the Great Age (165 BCE), 25 the city of Tarsus was destroyed by Epiphanes the Antiochus, 26 and Priest King Mattathiah and several of his sons, 27 were killed in defending the city. 28 Iudiah the son of Mattathiah, 29 did flee south to the lands of Rabelas, 30 the warlord of the Nabatean Arabic tribes, 31 who agreed to enter a trade treaty, 32 to control the spice and incense trade, 33 against the Seleucid traders. 34 The army of Epiphanes the Antiochus, 35 was overwhelmed by the Arabic horsemen, 36 and upon the great victory, 37 Iudiah declared himself King of Asmonea (Hasmonea), 38 with Jerusalem as his capital. 39 In the Great Age of the Ram, 40 one thousand and thirty nine years, 41 since the dawn of the Great Age (161 BCE), 42 King Iudiah of Asmonea (Hasmonea), 43 was killed at the Battle of Elasa, 44 by General Bacchides who served, 45 King Demetrius the Antiochus. 46 The crown of Asmonea (Hasmonea) did then befall, 47 to Yehoniah the youngest son of Mattathiah, 48 and brother of Iudiah. 49 In the same year, 50 Pirate King Mara (Magas) of Marmarica and Crete, 51 did give up the ghost. 52 Control of the Marmatine Pirate Empire, 53 of Libya and Calabria and Crete, 54 did befall to his son, 55 Gaius Marius Servilius, 56 who chose not to be named as a king, 57 but who still ruled as a king, 58 as Roman law forbid Romans claiming to be king.

C. 9

1 By the time of the death, 2 of Pirate King Mara (Magas) of Marmarica and Crete, 3 the fabric of Rome and the model of law, 4 was itself under attack. 5 The explosion of cheap drugs and alcohol, 6 of gambling and prostitution, 7 promoted by the pirates and the Samnites, 8 had kept the Plebs satisfied, 9 and the Senate distracted, 10 even if the rate of wars had decreased, 11 and the price of agriculture continued to fall. 12 Yet the trust between men and woman, 13 and the institution of matrimony and household, 14 were diminished by the changes in mind, 15 as women were turned to objects and property. 16 Neighbours no longer trusted neighbour, 17 friends no longer trusted friends, 18 and merchants fought to cheat one another. 19 Thus as trust within communities diminished, 20 so the power of the moneylenders and the private mints, 21 increased in power, 22 as people abandoned the capital of goodwill, 23 for the capital of money. 24 The dependency upon the mints of Naples and Rheggio, 25 grew to the highest levels as money began to control, 26 all aspects of the lives of Romans, 27 whereas a century earlier their ancestors had no need of such coin. 28 People had become addicted to pleasure, 29 and respect for moral values continued to decline. 30 Whereas Rome was once like Sparta, 31 it had become a place devoid of honour and Rule of Law. 32 In the Great Age of the Ram, 33 one thousand and forty one years, 34 since the dawn of the Great Age (159 BCE), 35 King Eumenes of Pergamon, 36 did give up the ghost. 37 The crown of Pergamon did then befall, 38 to his son named Euergertes the Attalus. 39 In the Great Age of the Ram, 40 one thousand and forty two years, 41 since the dawn of the Great Age (158 BCE), 42 Elkaniah the twenty seventh great prophet of Yeb, 43 the son of Eleziah and the grandson of Oniah, 44 did give up the ghost. 45 The position then befell, 46 to his son whose name was Zadokiah, 47 as the twenty eight Great Prophet of the Yahudi, 48 and Pontifex Maximus (Supreme Pontiff) of the Divine Creator.

C. 10

1 In the Great Age of the Ram, 2 one thousand and forty three years, 3 since the dawn of the Great Age (157 BCE), 4 Holly High King Irereo Fathach mac Meilge, 5 the living foundation stone of the Divine, 6 of the most ancient Cuilliaéan, 7 and blood descendant of the priests of Ebla, 8 and blood descendant of the priests of Ur, 9 and blood descendant of the priest-kings of the Hyksos, 10 and blood descendant of the priests of Ugarit, 11 and the only true blood descendants of King Da'vid, 12 and the Messiah Kings of Yahuda, 13 did give up the ghost. 14 The throne of Amen-Ra did then befall to his son, 15 whose name was Connla Caem mac Irereo. 16 In the same year, 17 Pontifex Maximus Zadokiah, 18 the Great Prophet of the Divine Creator, 19 did issue from the Vaticanus, 20 a terrible rebuke against the people of Rome, 21 for accepting the bribery and corruption of money, 22 for turning a blind eye to the return of slavery, 23 for removing the Rule of Law, 24 and allowing the destruction of trust. 25 The Senate did respond by closing the

Vaticanus, 26 and refusing Pontifex Maximus Zadokiah, 27 from attending to the Ark of the Covenant, 28 to which the Great Prophet replied: 29 The Ark be only a symbol of no more spiritual power, 30 than the smallest flower. 31 As both are born and both shall return to dust, 32 but those that live with the spirit of Divine, 33 can never die. 34 The Senate relented in their protest, 35 and begged the Pontifex Maximus for forgiveness, 36 saying that they were powerless against the forces of commerce, 37 and the wealth of the Samnites and Marmatines and Sicilians. 38 Pontifex Maximus Zadokiah did then prophecy: 39 The house shall be empty of spirit, 40 no taste shall satisfy nor drink shall quench thirst, 41 nor wealth or conquest or power. 42 For the spirit of the Divine shall leave this city, 43 and the evil of ignorance and superstition, 44 shall dwell as a false shadow in its place, 45 until the return of one like the son of man, 46 upon the dawn of a new Great Age. 47 The Senate was still greatly troubled, 48 and asked by what signs such events will come, 49 whereupon Zadokiah added to the beliefs of Essenoi, 50 saying: There shall be signs in all forms, 51 of the coming destruction of the present world, 52 by the Divine Creator of all things. 53 The earth shall shake and the mountains roar; 54 the animals shall stop giving birth and the crops wither; 55 men shall tear the flesh from other men, 56 and pray for death; 57 the city shall be destroyed three times; 58 before the Kingdom of Heaven returns. 59 The Divine Creator shall call to judgement, 60 all who corrupted Divine Law and Rule of Law, 61 upon the arrival of a great Messiah, 62 who will cleanse the world of its transgressions, 63 and restore the Rule of Law and Justice, 64 and that those who choose to be of the world, 65 shall be doomed by their own iniquity, 66 yet those who repent and cleanse themselves, 67 of the vices of this world, 68 shall have eternal life. 69 In the Great Age of the Ram, 70 one thousand and forty four years, 71 since the dawn of the Great Age (156 BCE), 72 Pontifex Maximus Zadokiah, 73 the twenty eight Great Prophet of the Yahudi, 74 did depart Rome with all the Yahudi priests, 75 leaving the Ark of the Covenant behind, 76 and the great Vaticanus empty of Holly Spirit, 77 to establish a new temple at Leontopolis (Cairo) in Egypt, 78 with the permission of Philometor the Ptolemy. 79 At the city of the lion (Leontopolis), 80 Pontifex Maximus Zadokiah dedicated the new temple, 81 naming it Chi Rho (Cairo), 82 as the site of a Christ yet to come.

C. 11

1 In the Great Age of the Ram, 2 one thousand and forty five years, 3 since the dawn of the Great Age (155 BCE), 4 upon the departure of the Great Prophet Zadokiah, 5 and the Holly Priests of Yeb from Rome, 6 the Senate called out to all citizens and colonies, 7 that the wisest and skilled priests or philosophers, 8 come to Rome that a Supreme Pontiff, 9 without the fire and controversy of Zadokiah, 10 be selected as custodian over the Ark of the Covenant. 11 Soon all manner of mystic, false messiah and false prophet, 12 did descend upon Rome until the Senate selected three, 13 the

first being Carneades of Cyrene, 14 the second being Diogenes of Tarsus, 15 and the third being Critolaus of Pergamon. 16 The Roman Senate then interviewed each man, 17 especially upon the prophecies of Zadokiah. 18 Carneades of Cyrene who perpetuated the philosophy of Nihilism, 19 and false skepticism of Pyrrhus, 20 did declare that all dogma and law is subject to change, 21 for even justice must be considered relative and not absolute. 22 Carneades of Cyrene then challenged even the reason of the Senators, 23 for the law is whatever the Senate believes it to be, 24 that the might of the sword is right, 25 and the only truth can be measured by probability, 26 for no one can prove Divine law with certainty. 27 Upon such a speech the Senate was terrified, 28 and forbid the teachings of Carneades in Rome. 29 Thus Carneades became glorified by the pirates, 30 and the moneylenders who believed in nothing. 31 Next Critolaus of Pergamon, 32 declared that none of what Zadokiah said could be proven, 33 thus none of it could be true, 34 for only facts gathered through induction, 35 may be argued as true, 36 and all other sayings be mere conjecture. 37 Critolaus of Pergamon then showed the power of logic, 38 and the artful use of dialectics whereby the same subject, 39 may be proven as true or false, 40 or that a man may be found innocent or guilty, 41 through the skilled use of argument and mere words. 42 The Senate was indignant that truth be so technical, 43 as the art of word assembly without strength of rhetoric, 44 and forbid the teachings of Critolaus to be used in law. 45 Yet the skills of word play and dialectics soon became, 46 the secret art of orators and lawyers of the Republic. 47 Next Diogenes of Tarsus, 48 refuted the prophecies of Zadokiah, 49 that the battle is not external, 50 but internal as men are prone to good or evil, 51 that the enemy is emotion and desire of pleasure. 52 To overcome a man must yield to absolute self control, 53 and perfect reason with nature and logic. 54 The Senators were disturbed by such challenge, 55 yet permitted Diogenes to open a school, 56 as such self discipline remained a Spartan tradition, 57 of the founding of Rome. 58 Upon the failure to find the wisest philosopher, 59 to replace the Great Prophet Zadokiah as Pontiff, 60 the Senate called for the most honourable and pious men. 61 Yet after four years of searching, 62 the Senate could find no more honourable or honest, 63 or loyal or pious gens (house) than Cornelia. 64 In the Great Age of the Ram, 65 one thousand and fifty years, 66 since the dawn of the Great Age (150 BCE), 67 the Senate appointed Publius Cornelius Scipio, 68 Pontifex Maximus (Supreme Pontiff), 69 and the first Nasci (Nazi) or Knight, 70 and Protector of the honour of Rome. 71 Thus for all its faults, 72 the Senate of Rome through an act of inspiration, 73 deemed one good and humble and honourable man, 74 to be more deserving than the wisest philosopher.

C. 12

1 In the Great Age of the Ram, 2 one thousand and forty eight years, 3 since the dawn of the Great Age (152 BCE), 4 as more and more Plebians were losing land, 5 and turning to banditry, 6 or being forced into becoming debt

slaves, 7 Gaius Marius Aquillius, 8 Lord of Marmarica and Calabria, 9 sought permission from the Roman Senate, 10 to confront the Carthaginians for compensation, 11 as a means of employing the rebellious mercenaries. 12 Yet the Senate remained unwilling to rekindle war with Carthage. 13 Instead Gaius Marius Aquillius commissioned, 14 Polybius the Liar and infamous creator of fiction, 15 to create a vile history of Carthage and its depravities, 16 that through such leaders as Marcus Porcius Cato, 17 the propaganda might sway the mind of the Senate. 18 In the Great Age of the Ram, 19 one thousand and fifty one years, 20 since the dawn of the Great Age (149 BCE), 21 before Marcus Porcius Cato gave up the ghost, 22 the fictions of Polybius the Liar, 23 succeeded in fermenting war, 24 and Gaius Marius Aquillius was granted permission, 25 to confront Carthage with a sizeable mercenary army. 26 The Carthaginians led by the priests of Baal Hamon, 27 agreed for payment in slaves and gold, 28 yet Gaius Marius Aquillius demanded more. 29 So when the Carthaginians refused, 30 Gaius Marius Aquillius attacked and lay siege to the city, 31 causing the death of tens of thousands, 32 before the city surrendered within three years. 33 In the Great Age of the Ram, 34 one thousand and fifty four years, 35 since the dawn of the Great Age (146 BCE), 36 following defeat of Carthage, 37 Gaius Marius Aquillius took more than fifty thousand, 38 as slaves back to Marmarica, 39 before selling tens of thousands as slaves, 40 to the Gracchi of Sicily, 41 and the Pompeii and Samnites of Campania, 42 openly rebuking the laws of Rome, 43 against direct slavery. 44 Gaius Marius Aquillius then declared, 45 the old lands of Carthage, 46 the Roman province of Africa. 47 The head priest of Baal Hamon, 48 whose name was Sabaoth, 49 did flee the destruction of Carthage with his family, 50 to the lands of the Nabatea, 51 where King Rabelas granted him sanctuary, 52 and Sabaoth anointed him, 53 the blessed of Baal, 54 and rightful king. 55 In the same year, 56 Praetor Quintus Caecilius Metellus did defeat, 57 the rebel leader whose name was Andriscus of Macedon. 58 Rome then established the Province of Macedonia, 59 including Epirus, Thessaly, Paeonia, Thrace and south of Illyria.

C. 13

1 In the Great Age of the Ram, 2 one thousand and fifty nine years, 3 since the dawn of the Great Age (141 BCE), 4 Pontifex Maximus Publius Cornelius Scipio Nasci, 5 the Knight and Protector of Rome did give up the ghost. 6 The Senate upon the influence of the moneylenders (bankers), 7 led by the corrupt Fulvius Flaccus, 8 did then elect a new Pontifex Maximus, 9 of poor character and leadership, 10 whose name was Pontifex Maximus Publius Mucius Scaevola. 11 Publius Mucius Scaevola had no interest in confronting the Gracchi, 12 or Pompeia or Lord pirates of Marmarica, 13 and the influx of tens of thousands of Carthaginian slaves, 14 as some Senators themselves had come to accept the offer, 15 of strong slaves for their own estates. 16 Yet the Plebian farmers continued to become

indebted, 17 and financial slaves to the wealthy families, 18 and even the mercenaries had become indebted and slaves, 19 for the lack of wars and cost of vices. 20 In the Great Age of the Ram, 21 one thousand and sixty five years, 22 since the dawn of the Great Age (135 BCE), 23 a group of Plebians who had become debt slaves, 24 to a wealthy merchant did rebel and kill the lord, 25 seizing the natural fortress city Enna, 26 at the centre of Sicily. 27 News quickly spread of the uprising, 28 and within only a few weeks, 29 the Gracchi and the wealthy land barons, 30 faced the loss of much of Sicily to rebellion. 31 The leader of the rebellion called Eunus, 32 did declare himself a saviour and that no man, 33 has the right to enslave another through debt. 34 The tyrant Tiberius Sempronius Gracchus, 35 appealed for assistance from pirate Lord Gaius Marius Aquillius, 36 who declined on account of the rebellion spreading to Calabria. 37 Nor did the Samnites of Campania assist. 38 Tiberius Sempronius Gracchus in turn appealed to his brother, 39 Gaius Sempronius Gracchus in Sardinia, 40 who advised him to urgently seek a settlement else, 41 all would be lost. 42 Thus tyrant Tiberius Sempronius Gracchus, 43 did declare that all Plebians that pledge allegiance to him, 44 would have their debts forgiven and lands restored, 45 yet those who continued to rebel would be offered no quarter. 46 Upon news of the offer of Tiberius Sempronius Gracchus, 47 the rebel army of Eunus split apart. 48 A new army led by Publius Rupilius then declared loyalty to Gracchus. 49 After two bitter and gruesome years of fighting, 50 the rebel army of Eunus was defeated, 51 and so Publius Rupilius and the loyal mercenaries, 52 gathered at Syracuse to have their reward confirmed. 53 Yet upon the end of the rebellion, 54 the tyrant Tiberius Sempronius Gracchus refused to honour his word, 55 saying that a promise to an infant or an animal, 56 has no importance if broken. 57 Upon such perfidy Publius Rupilius and his best soldiers, 58 seized Tiberius Sempronius Gracchus and killed him, 59 parading the body through Syracuse. 60 Upon news of the death of Gracchus, 61 Gaius Marius Aquillius did launch against Publius Rupilius, 62 defeating him and his army, 63 within two years. 64 Yet the pirate lord did not grant the Gracchi control, 65 over Sicily on account of their failed custody, 66 and risk to all the plebian lords. 67 Instead he appointed Marcus Antonius Orationus, 68 as lord over Sicily, 69 while granting Gaius Sempronius Gracchus keep, 70 the personal estates in Sicily, 71 as well as control over Sardinia. 72 Gaius Sempronius Gracchus, 73 then proclaimed fealty and service, 74 to the pirate lord and his successors.

C. 14

1 In the Great Age of the Ram, 2 one thousand and sixty seven years, 3 since the dawn of the Great Age (133 BCE), 4 King Euergertes the Attalus of Pergamon, 5 did give up the ghost. 6 Pirate King Gaius Marius Aquillius, 7 did then seize Pergamon and proclaim it a donation, 8 to himself and the province of Asia. 9 Yet Aristonicus the brother of Euergertes, 10 revolted against the pirate lord, 11 and for five more years there was conflict, 12 until

Book 19 Great Age of Rome

no more men were left willing to stand against evil. 13 In the Great Age of the Ram, 14 one thousand and eighteen years, 15 since the dawn of the Great Age (127 BCE), 16 King Mithradiah of Parthia, 17 also known as Phraates, 18 did give up the ghost. 19 His crown did then fall to his son, 20 Epiphanes who then changed his name to Mithradiah II. 21 Seizing upon the prophecies and condemnations of Zadokiah, 22 Epiphanes declared that men have a good spirit and bad spirit, 23 and that the wicked world will be destroyed, 24 and the only salvation be through blood, 25 and only those who purge themselves, 26 and believe in him, 27 are free from a cycle of servitude and misery. 28 Upon the message of a wrathful and jealous god, 29 that demands blood sacrifice and atonement, 30 the revival of the religion of Mithra under Mithradiah, 31 grew in followers and influence, 32 even to the west.

C. 15

1 Since the end of the rebellion in Sicily, 2 the condition of the poor and landless plebians, 3 had only grown worse. 4 Second generation bandits in Sicily, 5 and Calabria and even northern Italy threatened travellers. 6 Rome itself had become so awash with unemployed plebians, 7 that even the most corrupt of Senators, 8 prayed for a leader with sufficient strength and character, 9 bemoaning that Rome had become the prisoner of a marauding mob, 10 and it is they (plebians) not the Senate, 11 that did control the destiny of Rome. 12 In the Great Age of the Ram, 13 one thousand and eighty six years, 14 since the dawn of the Great Age (114 BCE), 15 Pontifex Maximus Publius Mucius Scaevola, 16 The Nasci (Knight) and Protector of Rome, 17 did give up the ghost. 18 The Senate then did overwhelmingly agree, 19 to the appointment of Lucius Cornelius Sulla, 20 the son of Publius Cornelius Scipio Nasci, 21 as Pontifex Maximus and Nasci, 22 as the Protector of Rome. 23 Upon his appointment, 24 Pontifex Maximus Lucius Cornelius Sulla, 25 implored the Senate to consider the root cause, 26 for a people that surrender their currency, 27 surrender their energy, 28 and willingly accept being slaves of moneylenders (bankers). 29 That a nation divided where some citizens have all protection, 30 yet none of the burdens of obligations, 31 is a nation of law that cannot stand. 32 For Rome permitted a parasite to rest in its heart, 33 for the sake of survival of what was believed a dream, 34 a dream that died the day the Senate agreed, 35 to make mercenaries and moneylenders who have no loyalty, 36 or honour to Rome as citizens. 37 Thus unless Rome cleanse its spirit of such corruption, 38 and belief in nothing but pleasure and greed, 39 then not even the bravest of citizens can save the city. 40 Upon the speech of Pontifex Maximus Lucius Cornelius Sulla, 41 the Senate implored that he visit their traditional allies, 42 such as the Celt tribes of Germanica, Gaul, Batavi and Britannia, 43 that they would support the Senate in what may become, 44 a Civil War for the soul of Rome. 45 Lucius Cornelius Sulla agreed and soon departed, 46 even with such knowledge already in the hands, 47 of the pirate lord and the moneylenders. 48 In the Great Age of

the Ram, 49 one thousand and eighty six years, 50 since the dawn of the Great Age (114 BCE), 51 King Rabelas the Great of the Nabateans, 52 beloved of Baal Hamon, 53 did give up the ghost. 54 The crown of the Nabatea did then befall to his son, 55 whose name was Aretas. 56 In the Great Age of the Ram, 57 one thousand and eighty seven years, 58 since the dawn of the Great Age (113 BCE), 59 within a few months of the return, 60 of Pontifex Maximus Lucius Cornelius Sulla to Rome, 61 a mass army of more than three hundred thousand, 62 Germanic, Batavi (Dutch) and Scandanavian Celts, 63 did attack and defeat a pirate mercenary army, 64 of pirate lord Gaius Marius Aquillius, 65 in the north of Illyricum, 66 forcing the pirates, bandits and moneylenders to flee. 67 The mass army then moved westward and seized the Po River valley, 68 again forcing the pirates and merchants, 69 to flee for their lives. 70 Pirate lord Gaius Marius Aquillius, 71 protested to the Senate demanding such action cease, 72 as he claimed it a violation of ancient Senate laws, 73 and Rome risked its own annihilation. 74 The Senate replied to the pirate lord, 75 that no general had been given order to head this army, 76 nor did any Senate authorized General lead it now, 77 and that as for Rome then the fiercest army, 78 of fifty thousand trained and decorated men, 79 under the command of Lucius Cornelius Sulla, 80 stood ready to defend the city to the last man. 81 Thus the pirates and moneylenders did not attack Rome, 82 as the Celts now through a second army, 83 did then invade the pirate controlled lands of Pergamon, 84 eliminating the mercenaries and declaring a new name, 85 called Galatia.

C. 16

1 In the Great Age of the Ram, 2 one thousand and ninety years, 3 since the dawn of the Great Age (110 BCE), 4 the High Priest of Baal Hamon, 5 the Spirit of the Nabateans, 6 whose name was Sabaoth, 7 did give up the ghost. 8 The position of High Priest of Baal Hamon, 9 did befall to his son whose name was Seth. 10 Upon becoming the new High Priest, 11 the young Seth declared his father, 12 to have been granted the position, 13 as Lord of the Underworld and Lakes of Fire, 14 and Lord of Hosts, 15 and that whomsoever shall sacrifice their first fruits, 16 or worthy sacrifice to Sabaoth, 17 shall in the same manner to Baal be saved. 18 Yet because all men are sinful, 19 those who do not repent and seek salvation, 20 shall be doomed to eternal torment, 21 in the lakes of Fire of the Underworld. 22 Thus was born the most perverse and insane, 23 religious cult in the history of humanity. 24 In the Great Age of the Ram, 25 one thousand and ninety four years, 26 since the dawn of the Great Age (106 BCE), 27 Holly High King Connla Caem mac Irereo, 28 did give up the ghost. 29 The throne of Amen-Ra did then befall to his son, 30 whose name was Ailill mac Connla. 31 In the Great Age of the Ram, 32 one thousand and ninety six years, 33 since the dawn of the Great Age (106 BCE), 34 Zadokiah the twenty eighth great prophet of Yeb, 35 the son of Elkaniah and the grandson of Eleziah, 36 did give up the ghost. 37 The position then befell, 38 to his son whose name was Barachiah, 39

as the twenty ninth Great Prophet of the Yahudi. 40 Thus upon the time that Zadokiah, 41 did give up the ghost, 42 the ancient world was now dominated by three religions, 43 all claiming that the Divine Creator would destroy the world one day, 44 the first being Yahudism offering salvation through water, 45 the second being Mithraism offering salvation through blood, 46 the third being Baalism through offering salvation through fire (holocaust).

C. 17

1 In the Great Age of the Ram, 2 one thousand and ninety five years, 3 since the dawn of the Great Age (105 BCE), 4 Lord Pirate Gaius Marius Aquillius of the Marmatines, 5 demanded the Senate approve him as consul, 6 that he may defeat the Celts in northern Italy, 7 and reclaim lands under his control. 8 Yet the Senate rejected his demand. 9 Gaius Marius Aquillius then demanded that all food, 10 from Sicily and Gaul be halted, 11 and all minerals from Spain and Sardinia be stopped. 12 The Senate then appointed Lucius Cornelius Sulla, 13 Caesar (Dictator) as well as Nasci (Knight), 14 and Pontifex Maximus (Supreme Pontiff). 15 The Gauls did then revolt against the pirates and money lenders, 16 and a mass army of Celts did form, 17 to move against Massalia (Marsailles), 18 Gaius Marius Aquillius did then take control, 19 of his own mercenary army, 20 at the battle north of Massalia (Marsailles), 21 yet his mercenaries were completely destroyed by the Gaul legions, 22 killing more than one hundred and twenty thousand, 23 near Arausio and the River Rhone. 24 As the lord pirate was distracted in Gaul, 25 Lucius Cornelius Sulla issued an edict, 26 henceforth banning all currency struck and minted, 27 from any pirate city such as Naples or Rheggio, 28 and that currency shall henceforth be minted only in Rome. 29 Furthermore that all valid currency was to be moulded, 30 and never again shall pirates be allowed under any form of law, 31 to claim control of the currency of any city, 32 or people that honour Rule of Law and Justice. 33 Lucius Cornelius Sulla did issue a second edict, 34 abolishing the notion of Plebian citizenship, 35 and that henceforth all moneylender and merchant families, 36 all pirate and bandit families were forbidden to be known as citizens, 37 now and forever and to never hold any position of office, 38 or role or influence in the affairs of Rome, 39 nor hold any form of property according to Roman Law, 40 reinforcing the prohibition of slavery. 41 Instead all cities and towns that declared allegiance to Rome, 42 would be honoured as citizens and as municeps, 43 being citizens under the constitution of their city or community. 44 Thus all the Celt cities and tribes, 45 were granted and recognised as municept citizens, 46 and the pirates and bandits were citizens no more. 47 Gnaeus Pompeius Strabo pledged himself and his family, 48 to the cause of Rome and ceased any hostility, 49 whereas the pirate lord Gaius Marius Aquillius, 50 fled back to his homeland of Marmarica, 51 of Cyrene and the Pentopolis of pirate ports. 52 Caesar Lucius Cornelius Sulla then appointed, 53 Gaius Licinius Verres as Governor of Sicily, 54 and

Quintus Mucius Scaevola as Governor of Sardinia, 55 and Decimus Junius Brutus Callaicus for Hispania Lusitania, 56 and Publius Licinius Crassus as Governor of Hispania Ulterior. 57 Whereupon, with the western provinces secured, 58 and Italy and Sicily secured, 59 Lucius Cornelius Sulla did resign his position as Caesar. 60 In the Great Age of the Ram, 61 one thousand and ninety seven years, 62 since the dawn of the Great Age (103 BCE), 63 King Yehoniah of Asmonea (Hasmonea), 64 the youngest son of Mattathiah, 65 did give up the ghost. 66 The crown did then befall to his son, 67 whose name was Alexander, 68 and then took the false name of Yanniah, 69 in falsely claiming to be a Great Prophet. 70 In the same year, 71 Lucius Pompeius Philadelphus of Pontus, 72 declared Pontus an independent Samnite kingdom, 73 and neutral towards Rome.

C. 18

1 Within ten years of restoring the currency to the people, 2 and clearing all the lands except Campania of the pirates, 3 and bandits and moneylenders (bankers), 4 prosperity had returned to the Roman Republic. 5 Yet Gnaeus Pompeius Strabo and the Samnite merchants, 6 remained relentless liars and cowards and tricksters. 7 King Philadelphus (Lucius Pompeius) of Pontus, 8 had since seized Cappodocia and Bithnyia into his kingdom, 9 growing in strength year by year. 10 The Samnites in Campania had continued in secret treaty, 11 with their former colony of Pontus, 12 now a major kingdom in its own right, 13 and had hatched a plan, 14 to secretly weaken and disrupt trade of Rome. 15 Gnaeus Pompeius Strabo then convinced Marcus Livius Drusus, 16 to attack the confidence and reliability of the new Roman molded coin, 17 by circulating deliberate fake and inconsistent coins, 18 shipped to Campania from Pontus, 19 thus reducing the confidence of eastern and western merchants. 20 Yet the plot of the Samnites was exposed, 21 and the Senate issued an edict forbidding trade or commerce, 22 with a Samnite or a Samaritans as none could be trusted, 23 to possess any honour, good character or quality wares. 24 In the Great Age of the Ram, 25 eleven hundred and eleven years, 26 since the dawn of the Great Age (89 BCE), 27 King Philadelphus (Lucius Pompeius) of Pontus, 28 did invade the province of Asia, 29 and then prepared to invade Macedonia. 30 The Senate called upon Lucius Cornelius Sulla once more, 31 faced with such a growing threat, 32 by appointing him Caesar for a second time. 33 Lucius Cornelius Sulla as Caesar wasted no time, 34 in amassing a great army and instead launched, 35 a siege against Pergamun in the hope, 36 that King Philadelphus (Lucius Pompeius) of Pontus, 37 would be forced into changing his plans, 38 by which time a second army would arrive, 39 and crush the Samnites (Samaritans). 40 Yet as Lucius Valerius Flaccus was preparing to embark, 41 with the second Roman Army, 42 Gnaeus Pompeius Strabo of Campania, 43 and his Samnite mercenary army attacked Rome itself, 44 killing the Praetorian Guard and overwhelming the city, 45 murdering every Senator and noble they could

find, 46 then placing their heads on pikes, 47 before burning down the ancient Senate buildings, 48 known as the Curia Hospitala and Rostra, 49 and all the ancient records and scrolls of laws of Rome. 50 Yet the forces of Gnaeus Pompeius Strabo, 51 failed to penetrate the massive walls of the Vaticanus. 52 Pirate Lord Gaius Marius Aquillius did also attack, 53 Sicily and Calabria seizing the cities in the south, 54 seeking to regain what had been taken from him. 55 The population of Rome was in a panic and many did flee east, 56 to Anatolia in the hope of being saved by Sulla, 57 as the Senate granted Sulla the power of absolute Caesar, 58 and the greatest power ever conceived under Roman law. 59 Faced with Rome burning and in ruins by the Samnite bandits, 60 and the overwhelming forces of King Philadelphus (Lucius Pompeius) of Pontus, 61 Sulla ordered Lucius Valerius Flaccus to restore order to Rome, 62 at all cost and not to yet pursue Pompeius Strabo.

C. 19

1 In the Great Age of the Ram, 2 eleven hundred and twelve years, 3 since the dawn of the Great Age (88 BCE), 4 as Lucius Valerius Flaccus now held Rome secure, 5 Caesar Lucius Cornelius Sulla positioned his army, 6 of forty thousand at Pessimus (Pessinus), 7 on the upper reaches of the Sakarya River, 8 as King Philadelphus (Lucius Pompeius) of Pontus, 9 and King Mithradiah II of Parthia, 10 approached with their mercenary army of two hundred thousand. 11 Yet the position and height of the city and its buildings, 12 and the discipline of the men of Sulla, 13 overcame the forces of King Philadelphus, 14 and King Mithradiah of Parthia, 15 and by the end of a bloody battle, 16 more than one hundred and fifty thousand mercenaries were killed, 17 with few deaths to the men of Sulla. 18 Caesar Lucius Cornelius Sulla then executed both kings, 19 abolishing Pontus and reconstituting the province of Asia, 20 but permitting the son of King Mithradiah II, 21 whose name was Orodes and Mithradiah III, 22 to continue as monarch of Parthia and vassal of Rome. 23 Sulla and most of his army then departed and invaded Libya, 24 where every one of the pirate port cities was utterly destroyed, 25 especially the pirate capital of Cyrene. 26 In the Great Age of the Ram, 27 eleven hundred and thirteen years, 28 since the dawn of the Great Age (87 BCE), 29 upon his return to Italy, 30 and with the fiercest army of Romans, 31 ever conceived in history, 32 every major city of the Samnites of Campania, 33 was destroyed to its foundations, 34 including the city of Naples. 35 Gnaeus Pompeius Strabo, 36 the leader of the Samnites, 37 did give up the ghost. 38 The leadership of the Samnites, 39 did befall to his son named Gnaeus Pompeius Magnus, 40 also known as Pompey the Great, 41 who escaped capture by fleeing to Spain. 42 In the Great Age of the Ram, 43 eleven hundred and fourteen years, 44 since the dawn of the Great Age (86 BCE), 45 Pirate Lord Gaius Marius Aquillius, 46 was finally cornered and defeated and killed. 47 The de facto King of the Marmatines, 48 also known as the Marsi, 49 also known as the Men from Mars, 50 being the ancient Libyan

pirates, 51 did befall to his son named, 52 Gaius Marius Julius, 53 also known by the fraudulent title Julius the Caesar, 54 who ran away from capture, 55 also to Spain.

C. 20

1 In the Great Age of the Ram, 2 eleven hundred and fifteen years, 3 since the dawn of the Great Age (85 BCE), 4 Caesar Lucius Cornelius Sulla, 5 began the rebuilding of Rome, 6 destroyed by the Samnites and Pompeius Strabo, 7 with the creation of the Comitium as a new Place of Assembly. 8 The Pontifex Maximus Lucius Cornelius Sulla, 9 also commissioned the finest scholars to commence, 10 a new Constitution for Rome, 11 where the rights of all men were to be enshrined, 12 to never again permit the scourge of slavery, 13 or the immorality of the Samnites, 14 through their pornography and prostitution, 15 of all music and culture. 16 From the Constitution the Caesar did order, 17 that all law be codified, 18 that the Senate may only pass laws that add to the body, 19 not to annex or deprive the body for the favour of a few. 20 Thus all law was to enshrine the Rule of Law, 21 and Golden Rule that none are above the law, 22 through Code and Statute. 23 The highest law of Rome was to be, 24 known as Ius Divinum as the law of the Divine, 25 and the highest of all law. 26 The second highest law was to become, 27 known as Ius Curia as the power and authority of the Senate, 28 to make laws under Divine Law. 29 The third highest law was to become, 30 known as Ius Gentium as the law of all peoples, 31 to guide the manner in which all people did act. 32 The fourth highest law was to become, 33 known as Ius Civile as the law of all citizens. 34 Thus under the Constitution of Rome, 35 no rights (Ius) could be claimed, 36 unless such rights conformed to Law, 37 and the Rule of Law else they be false. 38 Pontifex Maximus Lucius Cornelius Sulla did also reform, 39 the administration of provinces in the creation of new titles, 40 rector being the new governor of a province, 41 and Censor being an official visitor and overseer of the Senate. 42 In the same year, 43 Holly High King Ailill mac Connla, 44 the king of all priests and prophets, 45 the king of all the Celts, 46 did give up the ghost. 47 The throne of Amen-Ra did then befall to his son, 48 whose name was Labraid Lorc mac Ailill, 49 also known as Eterscel Mor and Cú-Las, 50 meaning the light of the Cuilliaéan.

C. 21

1 In the Great Age of the Ram, 2 eleven hundred and sixteen years, 3 since the dawn of the Great Age (84 BCE), 4 Caesar Lucius Cornelius Sulla, 5 as Supreme Pontiff (Pontifex Maximus), 6 and Nasci (Knight) and Protector of Rome, 7 did order his son Publius Cornelius Spartacus, 8 to take the Ark of the Covenant, 9 and return it to Leontopolis (Cairo) in Egypt, 10 and for a permanent company of Praetorian, 11 to thereafter guard the Great Prophet of Yeb, 12 as the one true and only Pontifex Maximus of Rome, 13 whereupon Caesar Lucius Cornelius Sulla did decree, 14 that never again shall the Senate as a secular body, 15 have the power to decree the will of heaven, 16 in the appointment of the Supreme Pontiff,

Book 19 Great Age of Rome

17 that such high office be the realm of the Great Prophet of Yeb, 18 and their true successors and no other. 19 Upon Barachiah receiving the great honour from Caesar, 20 and the return of the Ark of Akhenaten, 21 he did declare that the light of the Divine, 22 had returned to Rome, 23 and that all who profess the beliefs of Essenoi (Essenes), 24 must likewise respect that the Divine did speak through Caesar, 25 and all men and women must be considered equal under the law. 26 In the Great Age of the Ram, 27 eleven hundred and twenty years, 28 since the dawn of the Great Age (80 BCE), 29 upon the dedication and opening of the Comitium, 30 as a place of Assembly for the Senate of Rome, 31 as a symbol of the equality of all men, 32 Caesar Lucius Cornelius Sulla did resign his post, 33 and did give the title of Nasci (Knight) and Protector of Rome, 34 to his son Publius Cornelius Spartacus. 35 Whereupon the greatest soldier and servant of Rome, 36 did spend his last moments of life in peace. 37 In the Great Age of the Ram, 38 eleven hundred and twenty one years, 39 since the dawn of the Great Age (79 BCE), 40 Lucius Cornelius Sulla did give up the ghost.

C. 22

1 Since the great purges of Sulla, 2 Marcus Licinius Crassus the son of Publius Licinius Crassus, 3 had become the undisputed king of all Hispania (Spain), 4 ruling as the worst of tyrants through a massive mercenary army. 5 Through the enslavement of the whole population, 6 and the ravaging of all the lands for profit, 7 Marcus Licinius Crassus had become one of the wealthiest men in the world, 8 rivalled only by the Holly Kings of Ireland and Kings of the Celts, 9 through their mines and trade. 10 Both Gnaeus Pompeius Magnus and Gaius Marius Julius (the Caesar), 11 had received great patronage from Marcus Licinius Crassus, 12 and in turn both had started to restore their family fortunes, 13 with Gaius Marius Julius (the Caesar) rebuilding the pirate port of Cyrene, 14 and Gnaeus Pompeius Magnus securing trade into Anatolia, 15 and treaty with King Tigranes of the Armenian Empire. 16 In the Great Age of the Ram, 17 eleven hundred and twenty seven years, 18 since the dawn of the Great Age (73 BCE), 19 a mercenary army of thirty thousand, 20 funded by Marcus Licinius Crassus, 21 and led by Gaius Claudius Glaber, 22 did land and invade the territory of Capua in Campania. 23 The Senate did then hastily appoint Publius Cornelius Spartacus, 24 both Caesar in addition to being Nasci (Knight), 25 and Protector of Rome. 26 Sensing further forces and invasion, Caesar Publius Cornelius Spartacus, 27 dispatched a much smaller force, 28 under his cousin Publius Cornelius Varinius, 29 to engage the mercenaries from Hispania. 30 While the Romans sought to engage the Spanish mercenaries, 31 a second invasion force of mercenaries then did land in Sicily, 32 led by Gaius Lucinius Verro, 33 that quickly captured and conquered Sicily for the pirate merchants. 34 A third invasion force did then attack and conquer Calabria, 35 under Quintus Marcius Rufus for the ancient Marmatines. 36 Upon such overwhelming attack, 37 Caesar Publius Cornelius Spartacus

called to all Roman Citizens, 38 to come to the aid of Rome against the pirate merchants, 39 and corrupt moneylenders (bankers) funding such war. 40 In the same year, 41 a mercenary force of Marcus Licinius Lucullus, 42 did attack and invade and conquer, 43 Crete and then the province of Macedonia for the pirate merchants.

C. 23

1 In the Great Age of the Ram, 2 eleven hundred and twenty eight years, 3 since the dawn of the Great Age (72 BCE), 4 King Crixus of the Allobrogi of southern Gaul did land at Ostia, 5 and help reinforce the defence of Rome itself. 6 To the north King Oenomaus (Orgetorix) of the Helvetii, 7 did cross the alps and into the Po River Valley, 8 as a further mercenary invasion force under Gaius Cassius Longinus, 9 did land at the port city of Piso, 10 and engage the Roman legions of the Helvetii, 11 killing King Oenomaus (Orgetorix) in battle. 12 The remaining Helvetii legions did then head south, 13 to help further reinforce the defence of Rome. 14 Facing the inevitable encirclement of Rome, 15 Caesar Publius Cornelius Spartacus ordered, 16 the evacuation of the Senate and records, 17 as well as young women and children, 18 to be transported to sanctuary and safety, 19 by the Allobrogi and Holly Celt ships, 20 to Alexandria under Philadelphos the Ptolemy. 21 In the Great Age of the Ram, 22 eleven hundred and twenty nine years, 23 since the dawn of the Great Age (71 BCE), 24 Marcus Licinius Crassus accompanied by Gnaeus Pompeius Magnus, 25 did land with another force of mercenary pirates and bandits, 26 near the port of Ostia to complete the siege of Rome, 27 and personally command its capture. 28 Gaius Marius Julius also falsely known as Caesar, 29 did not accompany his allies, 30 but remained in command of Hispania, 31 as his true skill never existed in war, 32 but the administration of banking and slaves. 33 Caesar Publius Cornelius Spartacus, 34 and the remaining Praetorian Guard, 35 with the Allobrogi and Helvetii and surviving legions, 36 had prepared their defences as best they could, 37 as Marcus Licinius Crassus unleashed wave after wave, 38 of African mercenaries to their death. 39 In the Great Age of the Ram, 40 eleven hundred and thirty years, 41 since the dawn of the Great Age (70 BCE), 42 after wave after wave, 43 of mercenary bandits had fallen to their swords, 44 after the numbers of brave defenders of Rome, 45 had fallen to less than twelve thousand, 46 Caesar Publius Cornelius Spartacus, 47 called out one last time, 48 to the surviving Praetorian and Patrician, 49 to the bloodied Celt and Roman heroes, 50 that a fate worse than death be, 51 in the hands of the pirate merchants and moneylenders (bankers), 52 who thrive upon the misery and enslavement of others. 53 Better then to die an honourable death, 54 for all good men be immortal, 55 and to live another life than to suffer the tortures, 56 of deranged men who believe in nothing. 57 Thus upon the next wave of attack, 58 the defenders cut down as many of the enemy, 59 before taking their own lives, 60 and depriving Marcus Licinius Crassus, 61 of a single living prisoner, 62 and claiming any honour in victory.

63 Marcus Licinius Crassus then ordered, 64 the burning and destruction of the Comitium, 65 the burning of all records, 66 and the looting of all temples. 67 Before long Rome was in flames. 68 Pirate king Marcus Licinius Crassus then ordered, 69 his bandit army to hang the bodies of the defenders, 70 upon crosses from Rome to Capua, 71 as a perverse and absurdly gruesome curse, 72 against the courage and strength of the defenders. 73 Satisfied with his evil, 74 Marcus Licinius Crassus then returned to Hispania (Spain), 75 after placing Gnaeus Pompeius Magnus in command, 76 of the ruins of Rome and its ghosts.

C. 24

1 In the Great Age of the Ram, 2 eleven hundred and thirty one years, 3 since the dawn of the Great Age (69 BCE), 4 Marcus Licinius Crassus extended his empire, 5 into Anatolia and northern Syria, 6 when King Tigranes of Armenia was defeated, 7 by a mercenary army led by Lucius Licinius Lucullus. 8 In the same year, 9 Gaius Marius Julius the false Caesar, 10 failed to capture the south of Gaul, 11 with his mercenary army of bandits and thieves, 12 against a superior army of Roman legions, 13 led by King Ariovistus of the Suebi, 14 united with Averni and Sequani. 15 So frustrated was Gaius Marius Julius, 16 at the lack of discipline of the bandits, 17 that he ordered all but one in ten, 18 to be spared from brutal execution, 19 to then form a new disciplined army. 20 In the Great Age of the Ram, 21 eleven hundred and thirty two years, 22 since the dawn of the Great Age (68 BCE), 23 at sixteen years of age, 24 Cú-Roi(n) the son of Holly King Labraid Lorc mac Ailill, 25 did request the permission of his father, 26 to leave the sacred Isle, 27 and to travel to Egypt and Alexandria. 28 King Holly King Labraid Lorc mac Ailill, 29 also known as Cú-Las (Light of the Cuilliaéan), 30 did decline his request, 31 for no King nor crown prince of the Holly, 32 had left the sacred Isle, 33 for hundreds of years. 34 In the Great Age of the Ram, 35 eleven hundred and thirty three years, 36 since the dawn of the Great Age (67 BCE), 37 Cú-Roi(n) again requested the permission of his father, 38 to leave the sacred Isle. 39 King Cú-Las initially declined again, 40 saying his son had not yet married, 41 nor did he have an heir, 42 but relented allowing the young prince, 43 to travel to the west territory, 44 of the Dumnonii and Durotriges, 45 to see the mines and property of the Holly. 46 There Cú-Roi(n) did spend one year, 47 and then returned to the Old King. 48 In the same year, 49 Queen Salome of Asmonea (Hasmonea), 50 the last of the undisputed Hasmonean, 51 did give up the ghost. 52 A supremely evil and wicked dynasty had they been, 53 for countless people sacrificed and burned, 54 in demonic rituals to ancient gods, 55 with orgies of wine and depravity. 56 At her death Civil War did erupt in Asmonea (Hasmonea), 57 as Hyrcanus sought support, 58 from Gnaeus Pompeius Magnus, 59 and his brother Aristobulus, 60 sought the support of the Nabatea. 61 In the same year, 62 King Mithradiah III of Parthia, 63 also known as Orodes, 64 did give up the ghost. 65 His crown did then fall to his

son, 66 Sanatruces who then changed his name to Mithradiah IV.

C. 25

1 In the Great Age of the Ram, 2 eleven hundred and thirty four years, 3 since the dawn of the Great Age (66 BCE), 4 King Aretas of the Nabatea, 5 beloved of Baal Hanan, 6 did give up the ghost. 7 The crown of the Nabatea did then befall to his son, 8 whose name was Herodas, 9 also known as Herod the Great. 10 In the same year, 11 Gnaeus Pompeius Magnus witnessed the first fruits, 12 of his commission to Marcus Tullius Cicero, 13 to present a new set of laws for Rome, 14 through the completely fraudulent works, 15 known as De Re Publica on the Republic, 16 and De Legibus on the law. 17 The scribe of lies known as Cicero, 18 paid so handsomely for his fraud, 19 that he became one of the wealthiest men, 20 did weave even a new form of mythos, 21 as to the kingship of Rome, 22 that no longer the role of king, 23 be an abomination to the laws of Rome, 24 but that Rex Romanum be the highest law. 25 Thus Gnaeus Pompeius Magnus declared himself, 26 Rex Romanum and King of Rome, 27 and all citizens be subject to his rule. 28 In the same year, 29 Holly High Prince and Priest, 30 whose name was Cú-Roi(n), 31 also known as Conaire Mor, 32 did again request the permission of his father, 33 the Holly High King of Ireland and King of al Celts, 34 that he be granted leave to travel to Egypt, 35 and to the ancient lands of their bloodlines. 36 But the old King Cú-Las refused again. 37 Whereupon Cú-Roi(n) pledged, 38 that if he did marry and leave an heir, 39 he be permitted to travel as his heart so yearned. 40 Upon such pledge the King agreed, 41 and Cú-Roi(n) did soon marry, 42 and before the end of a year he did have an heir. 43 But before leaving on his journey, 44 the Holly High King Cú-Las, 45 did call upon his son to swear a Sacred High Oath, 46 to return within four years to sacred soil, 47 and no more speak of travel. 48 Upon giving such sacred oath, 49 Cú-Roi(n) did then leave Ireland, 50 as Ha Rama Theo (High Divine Highness), 51 a Messiah prince of the House of Yahudah. 52 In Alexandria Cú-Roi(n) was introduced to the great wonders, 53 and the museum and library of Alexandria, 54 by the respected philosopher Eudorus, 55 the senior student of the head librarian, 56 whose name was Andronicus the great. 57 Cú-Roi(n) spent many weeks at the library and the city, 58 meeting travellers from around the world, 59 including the exiled senators and leaders of Rome, 60 who petitioned him to call upon his father, 61 to rally a mighty Celtic army and end the reign of evil. 62 Next Cú-Roi(n) travelled south unto Leontopolis (Cairo), 63 where he was welcomed by Barachiah and the other priests, 64 including the strong willed and opinionated Zachariah, 65 and where he saw for the first time, 66 the Ark of his blood ancestor Pharaoh Akhenaten. 67 Weeks turned into months as Cú-Roi(n) shared his knowledge, 68 and listened to the Great Prophet Barachiah, 69 who himself was humbled by the extraordinary knowledge, 70 and skill possessed by Cú-Roi(n) and for which he was unaffected, 71 as priests such as Zachariah became more and more jealous, 72 of the time that Barachiah

bestowed to their visitor. 73 Within two years of coming to Leontopolis, 74 the Holly High King of Ireland sent word to his son, 75 that his grandson and the son of Cú-Roi(n) had died, 76 and that stricken with grief and woe, 77 his wife had ended her own life. 78 Yet Cú-Roi(n) did not leave Egypt and instead travelled south, 79 to the most ancient temples of Thebes and Karnak, 80 where he was received and welcomed not only as a great prophet, 81 but a true pharaoh in blood and knowledge of hieroglyph. 82 Upon his return to Leontopolis (Cairo), 83 Cú-Roi(n) did wed the granddaughter of Zadokiah, 84 whose name was Esa, 85 but honoured as Luacháil, 86 whereupon Barachiah did challenge Cú-Roi(n), 87 to consider his own prophetic abilities, 88 and what he consider to be his purpose, 89 for the ultimate destiny of the Cuilliaéan, 90 may rest less in blood than the actions, 91 of one good priest who cares for the world, 92 and be willing to fulfil their intended Divine Commission.

C. 26

1 Upon news of Gnaeus Pompeius Magnus, 2 declaring himself Rex Romanum, 3 and king of all Romans 4 Marcus Licinius Crassus was enraged. 5 Yet under the fraudulent writings of Marcus Tullius Cicero, 6 and the reforms of merchant slavery, 7 men had begun flocking to Italy, 8 on promises of free land and a new world order, 9 of pleasure and liberty and an end to old morality, 10 of a new age of free science and thought, 11 where men could create their own history and own stories. 12 Thus Rome under Gnaeus Pompeius Magnus, 13 had become the new Athens and a centre of new thought, 14 which abandoned the old and sought to form its own truths, 15 yet still based upon the philosophy of pirate merchants, 16 that everything has a price and the law is whatever is convenient. 17 Marcus Licinius Crassus was forced then to prepare carefully, 18 with his best legions from northern Spain, 19 on a course of action to confront Gnaeus Pompeius Magnus. 20 In the Great Age of the Ram, 21 eleven hundred and thirty six years, 22 since the dawn of the Great Age (64 BCE), 23 before embarking with his legions, 24 Marcus Licinius Crassus made known across his empire, 25 that Gaius Marius Julius, 26 also falsely known as Caesar Gaius Julius, 27 was to be his sole lawful heir and successor. 28 Yet such an act did nothing to distract Gnaeus Pompeius Magnus. 29 Instead upon the news of the coming invasion of Marcus Licinius Crassus, 30 he sent word that all men who stand for liberty and equality, 31 all men who seek justice and happiness, 32 shall be forgiven their debts and granted promised land, 33 if they rebel against the yoke of the tyrant Crassus. 34 Thus upon landing in Italy Crassus faced an immediate revolt, 35 of his own generals and army and was seized and killed, 36 with his head presented to Gnaeus Pompeius Magnus. 37 True to his word the King of Rome, 38 did forgive the debts and grant land, 39 on condition that the commanders seize control, 40 of the former lands of Crassus to the east. 41 The powerful governor of Sicily, 42 whose name was Gaius Lucinius Verro, 43 was seized and arrested and brought to Rome, 44 where Cicero chose to conduct the

prosecution. 45 In the Great Age of the Ram, 46 eleven hundred and thirty seven years, 47 since the dawn of the Great Age (63 BCE), 48 the new legions of Gnaeus Pompeius Magnus, 49 did seize Macedonia and Crete from Marcus Licinius Lucullus, 50 before capturing Anatolia from Lucius Licinius Lucullus, 51 and renaming it again the province of Pontus, 52 with Macedonia and Crete and Pontus granted, 53 to the control of Gnaeus Pompeius Iunior, 54 the eldest son of the King of Rome. 55 The forces of Gnaeus Pompeius Magnus, 56 then moved south and defeated Hyrcanus of Asmonea (Hasmonea), 57 as Aristobulos and his court, 58 did then escape to the South of Arabia, 59 and conquer the key cities of the Sabeans, 60 forming the Kingdom of the Himyarite. 61 Gnaeus Pompeius Magnus then did form a treaty, 62 with King Herodas of the Nabateans, 63 also known as Herod the Great, 64 to control all the trade from east Africa and Arabia, 65 by granting him control of Palestine, 66 and the gulf of Aden, 67 while Syria and Lebanon was renamed, 68 the great province of Samaria, 69 under the control of the youngest son of Pompey, 70 whose name was Sextus Pompeius Magnus.

C. 27

1 Upon news of Gnaeus Pompeius Magnus 2 declaring himself Rex Romanum, 3 and the death of Marcus Licinius Crassus, 4 Gaius Marius Julius falsely known as Caesar, 5 did face great rebellion in Hispania. 6 It was this moment more than any other, 7 that transformed the administrator into a leader, 8 as Gaius Marius Julius chose to execute his generals, 9 and permit the men to elect leaders they trusted, 10 and honour the legions with better pay, 11 than the brutality that had existed under Crassus. 12 Thus the legions of Hispania came to pledge, 13 absolute allegiance to Gaius Marius Julius, 14 and rule was restored. 15 In the Great Age of the Ram, 16 eleven hundred and thirty nine years, 17 since the dawn of the Great Age (61 BCE), 18 Pontifex Maximus Barachiah, 19 the Great Prophet of Yeb, 20 did summons all the priests of Leontopolis, 21 where he did call upon Prince Cú-Roi(n), 22 also known as Conaire Mor, 23 the Ha Rama Theo (His Divine Highness) of the Holly, 24 to come forward. 25 There in Egypt the Great Prophet Barachiah, 26 did officially adopt Cú-Roi(n) as his only son, 27 and heir and successor as Pontifex Maximus, 28 and the next Great Prophet of Yeb, 29 naming him Adoniah meaning the Lord and Saviour, 30 and the Messiah of all the World. 31 There was great celebration except for Zachariah, 32 who protested that he and not Cú-Roi(n), 33 deserved to be named the next Great Prophet. 34 In the Great Age of the Ram, 35 eleven hundred and forty one years, 36 since the dawn of the Great Age (59 BCE), 37 Barachiah the twenty ninth great prophet of Yeb, 38 the son of Zadokiah and the grandson of Elkaniah, 39 did give up the ghost. 40 The position then befell, 41 to his adopted son whose name was Adoniah, 42 also known as Cú-Roi(n), 43 and the Holly crown priest-prince of Ireland, 44 as the thirtieth Great Prophet of the Yahudi. 45 Enraged at Adoniah becoming the new Great Prophet, 46 Zachariah did leave for Jerusalem, 47 and seek an audience with Seth, 48 the High Priest

of Baal Hamon and then to Herodas at Aqaba, 49 where he promised to deliver the Ark of the Covenant to Jerusalem, 50 if both the priests of Baal Hamon, 51 and the Nabateans recognise him alone, 52 as the true Great Prophet of Yeb. 53 The priests of Baal and the Nabateans agreed, 54 and soon after Zachariah and his rebel priests, 55 departed Leontopolis with the Ark of the Covenant, 56 to be greeted by a force of Nabateans, 57 who then escorted the Ark back to Jerusalem. 58 Adoniah declined the request for his elite Praetorian, 59 to recover the Ark and punish Zachariah, 60 saying that the Divine Creator has chosen its return, 61 to its ancient resting place after more than a thousand years, 62 for some greater purpose yet to be revealed. 63 At Jerusalem Herodas then declared he would build, 64 the Greatest Temple in all the World, 65 to the greater glory of Baal Hamon as Moloch, 66 and to honour the presence of the Ark. 67 Herodas envisioned a mighty temple more than 110 ft high, 68 and 1600 ft wide and 900 ft wide. 69 Yet it was not to be. 70 After 46 years the project was finished, 71 just eight years before his death (12 BCE). 72 For Zachariah a new community and settlement was constructed, 73 at a site called Qumran near the Dead Sea, 74 protected by Nabatean guard, 75 yet close enough to walk to Jerusalem.

C. 28

1 Upon news of the Ark of the Covenant returning to Jerusalem, 2 the younger son of the King of Rome, 3 whose name was Sextus Pompeius did demand that Herodas, 4 bring the Ark to him at Damascus for his pleasure. 5 Yet the Nabateans and priests of Baal refused, 6 reminding the son of Pompey, 7 that it had been bestowed to Jerusalem as its home. 8 Sextus Pompeius Magnus then ordered his legions, 9 to seize the Ark and bring it to Damascus, 10 and for all the priests of Baal to be executed, 11 and their temples destroyed. 12 Immediately there was revolt throughout Syria, 13 upon the desecration of the ancient temples, 14 as more than two hundred thousand Nabatean warriors, 15 faced against the legions of Sextus Pompeius, 16 until Gnaeus Pompeius Magnus called for truce, 17 and an uneasy peace was restored to Samaria (Syria). 18 Gaius Marius Julius falsely known as Caesar, 19 did hear of the desecration of the most ancient temples, 20 and the murdering of priests, 21 and so did send a secret emissary to Palestine, 22 where he did pledge allegiance to the priests of Baal, 23 if they would aid him in times to come, 24 against the nihilism of the Samnite moneylenders (bankers). 25 Gaius Marius Julius did then reconstitute the pledges, 26 of his legions to Baal and Mithra, 27 replacing their standards with the standard of the bull, 28 that no longer was his army an army of mercenaries, 29 but a religious army embarking upon a crusade, 30 to rid the world of immorality and false worship. 31 In the Great Age of the Ram, 32 eleven hundred and forty two years, 33 since the dawn of the Great Age (58 BCE), 34 Gaius Marius Julius, 35 also falsely known as Caesar Gaius Julius, 36 and his armies marching for Baal and Mithra, 37 did defeat the Allobrogi of southern Gaul, 38 before defeating a

mass army, 39 of the Suebi near the Rhine. 40 Yet instead of permitting the killing of prisoners, 41 or the looting of lands or raping of women, 42 Gaius Marius Julius offered to appoint the senior officers, 43 of the former enemy to the ranks of his generals, 44 if they pledge allegiance and discipline, 45 in the religious war. 46 Thus tens of thousands of Celts did join with Gaius Marius Julius, 47 and soon Gaul was almost within his control. 48 In the same year, 49 Pontifex Maximus Adoniah, 50 also known as Cú-Roi(n), 51 The Ha Rama Theo (Divine Highness) of Ireland, 52 did return to the sacred isles with his elite Praetorian Guard, 53 to the land of the Dumnonii, 54 where Constantine (Custenin), 55 as Chief Steward over the lands for the Holly, 56 did agree to help build him a new fortress, 57 and sacred temple at Glastonbury, 58 as the Praetorian prepared the Holly legions, 59 for defence against the pirates and moneylenders. 60 There the Great Prophet did reside, 61 for upon breaking his word to the Holly High King, 62 he could not yet return to Tara.

C. 29

1 In the Great Age of the Ram, 2 eleven hundred and forty four years, 3 since the dawn of the Great Age (56 BCE), 4 Holly High King Labraid Lorc mac Ailill, 5 also known as Cú-Las (Light of the Cuilliaéan), 6 the king of all priests and prophets, 7 and blood descendant of the priests of Ebla, 8 and blood descendant of the priests of Ur, 9 and blood descendant of the priest-kings of the Hyksos, 10 and blood descendant of the priests of Ugarit, 11 and the founding bloodlines of the prophets of Yeb, 12 and the only true blood descendant of King Da'vid, 13 did give up the ghost. 14 The throne of Amen-Ra did then befall to his son, 15 whose name was Eterscel Mor, 16 also known as Cú-Roi(n), 17 also known as Adoniah the Pontifex Maximus, 18 and the Thirtieth Great Prophet of Yeb. 19 Cú-Roi(n) did then finally return to Tara, 20 with his company of elite Praetorian, 21 to be crowned the Holly High King, 22 and King of kings of all the Celts. 23 In the same year, 24 upon Gaius Marius Julius completing his conquest, 25 and alliances of the whole of Gaul, 26 Gaius Marius Julius did come to Tara, 27 in the winter months, 28 under the flag of hospita and truce, 29 to meet the great Druid High King, 30 and Great Prophet and Pontifex Maximus Adoniah. 31 Into the Great Hall of Tara, 32 Gaius Marius Julius (later the Caesar) did go, 33 unto Cú-Roi(n) seated upon the most ancient throne, 34 of Amen-Ra and the Hyksos kings. 35 Cú-Roi(n) as Adoniah did speak first as was custom, 36 to ask of the purpose of such a strange visit, 37 Gaius Marius Julius did reply that as Adoniah had become, 38 the most famous of all priests and kings in the world, 39 as not only the Holly High King but the Great Prophet of Yeb, 40 he did come to seek counsel and seek amicable terms, 41 to prevent any further war between the Men from Mars, 42 and the honourable tribes of the Celts. 43 Adoniah replied that history did teach, 44 no house founded on evil did last beyond five generations, 45 before becoming consumed by its own madness. 46 Thus all men must be afforded the presumption of virtue and character,

47 even the descendants of Pyrrhus, 48 and so he did grant the general a prophetic reading. 49 Gaius Marius Julius did declare, 50 that it be his solemn and sacred mission, 51 to end the nihilism of the Pompey, 52 and those that discard the lessons of history, 53 to indulge themselves in their own pleasures and intellect. 54 Gaius Marius Julius did then implore, 55 to gain the trust of all Roman citizens, 56 he must be seen as more than a general, 57 and a priest of good character. 58 Adoniah then replied that it was not for himself to grant, 59 Gaius Marius Julius the title of Pontifex Maximus, 60 but the surviving senate residing in exile in Alexandria. 61 Gaius Marius Julius did then warn the Holly High King, 62 to consider carefully his choices for if Britannia was taken, 63 such titles may also fall with Tara, 64 to which Adoniah did bid Gaius Marius Julius safe journey, 65 and that if he travel to the sacred valley of the Boyne, 66 there he shall receive the greatest of all revelations, 67 from the most revered seer of the Holly, 68 her name being Bandraoi, 69 which simply means the witch. 70 Gaius Marius Julius and his guard, 71 did then travel to the sacred valley of the Boyne, 72 where he did meet the Bandraoi, 73 who did then speak as was custom in prophetic riddle saying: 74 That unto you (Gaius Marius Julius) a treasure come, 75 flesh and sword Unite. Glory be your destiny, 76 not King but God, upon the mide of Mars. 77 Gaius Marius Julius then departed the sacred Isle, 78 unto Gaul where he cursed the stubbornness of the Cuilliaéan, 79 where he ordered Marcus Antonius to make haste to Alexandria, 80 and seek if terms be made with the Senate, 81 while invasion plans be prepared first for Britannia (Britain). 82 In the Great Age of the Ram, 83 eleven hundred and forty six years, 84 since the dawn of the Great Age (54 BCE), 85 the first invasion of Gaius Marius Julius (later the Caesar), 86 into Britanni was a terrible failure, 87 with high cost and little gained. 88 An attempt for the second year was equally as pyrrhic, 89 even with five legions of Gaius Marius Julius seeking to hold, 90 just south and east Britain. 91 In the same year, 92 after much costs and pain, 93 Gaius Marius Julius (later the Caesar), 94 did withdraw every last Roman Soldier, 95 from Britain to Gaul. 96 In the Great Age of the Ram, 97 eleven hundred and forty eight years, 98 since the dawn of the Great Age (52 BCE), 99 the High Priest of Baal Hamon, 100 and his Lord of Hosts named Sabaoth, 101 the Spirit of the Nabateans, 102 whose name was Seth, 103 did give up the ghost. 104 The position of High Priest of Baal Hamon, 105 did befall to his son whose name was Anath, 106 later written as Annas the elder, 107 and even Ananias.

C. 30

1 In the Great Age of the Ram, 2 eleven hundred and fifty years, 3 since the dawn of the Great Age (50 BCE), 4 Gaius Marius Julius summonsed Marcus Antonius, 5 to return from Alexandria and give word, 6 if the Senate had agreed to his demands, 7 to be made both Caesar and Pontifex Maximus, 8 before his invasion of Italy. 9 Marcus Antonius protested that he had used all his skill, 10 to force the Roman senate in exile to grant such demands, 11 yet had fallen

under the spell of Queen Cleopatra. 12 In the Great Age of the Ram, 13 eleven hundred and fifty one years, 14 since the dawn of the Great Age (49 BCE), 15 Gaius Marius Julius chose to proclaim himself Caesar, 16 and proceeded to invade Italy from the north, 17 warning in advance that any soldier who did not pledge allegiance, 18 to the greater glory of Rome under Mithra, 19 would be brutally executed including their family. 20 Gnaeus Pompeius Magnus remained supremely confident, 21 that with more than twenty legions of mercenaries, 22 he could defend against any attack from Gaius Marius Julius. 23 Yet upon word of the claim that Gaius Marius Julius had been made Caesar, 24 despite the ferocity of his troops, 25 many of the mercenaries were unwilling to fight, 26 so that the defence of Italy quickly crumbled, 27 and within just twenty eight days, 28 Gaius Marius Julius was upon the outskirts of Rome. 29 In panic Gnaeus Pompeius Magnus and his court escaped, 30 to Macedonia and the court of his eldest son, 31 whose name was Gnaeus Pompeius Iunior. 32 Upon entering Rome Gaius Marius Julius ordered, 33 that the lives of Catallus and Cicero and his students be spared. 34 He then summonsed the greatest writers and flatterers, 35 from the previous court of the Pompey, 36 and presented them a new commission, 37 that their lives be spared if they re-write the history of Rome, 38 that the Men of Mars be of noble Patrician blood, 39 and that Cicero make Gaius Marius Julius, 40 the greatest of heroes and messiahs. 41 Cicero and the scribes set about building the mythos, 42 of Gaius Marius Julius the false Caesar, 43 declaring the day of his birth on December 25th, 44 being the festival of Christmas as a sacred celebration of the saviour, 45 and liberator of Rome. 46 Cicero declared in his work known as Evangelium Marci, 47 known as the Gospel of Mark, 48 that Gaius Marius Julius was born of the virgin goddess Venus, 49 and that the gods granted him the power to forgive transgressions, 50 and that a great comet heralded his birth. 51 In the Great Age of the Ram, 52 eleven hundred and fifty two years, 53 since the dawn of the Great Age (48 BCE), 54 having secured Rome and Italy, 55 and having granted permission for Marcus Antonius, 56 to return to Alexandria and call upon the Senate to return to Rome, 57 Gaius Marius Julius invaded Macedonia, 58 to confront the mercenary forces of Gnaeus Pompeius Magnus. 59 At Pharsalos in southern Thessaly the two armies met, 60 with the forces of Gaius Marius Julius less than twenty thousand, 61 and the mercenary forces of the Pompey more than eighty thousand. 62 Yet despite the numerical superiority it was Gaius Marius Julius, 63 who was victorious and the army of Gnaeus Pompeius Magnus, 64 was utterly destroyed with tens of thousands killed. 65 Gnaeus Pompeius Magnus once again deserted his men, 66 and did travel to Alexandria to the court of Queen Cleopatra, 67 unbeknownst of the relation between Cleopatra and Mark Antony, 68 to seek sanctuary and offer his vast fortune, 69 against Gaius Marius Julius. 70 Cleopatra called upon Gnaeus Pompeius Magnus to bring the treasure, 71 to Alexandria and at the great temples for safe keeping, 72 to which Gnaeus Pompeius Magnus agreed. 73 Yet once the treasure had arrived, 74 Queen Cleopatra handed Gnaeus Pompeius Magnus, 75 to her lover and new husband Mark Antony, 76 who then executed Gnaeus Pompeius Magnus, 77 and sent the head of his former enemy, 78 and a small part of the fortune to Gaius Marius Julius. 79 In the Great Age of the Ram, 80 eleven hundred and fifty three years, 81 since the dawn of the Great Age (47 BCE), 82 the legions of Gaius Marius Julius, 83 led by Marcus Junius Brutus and Gaius Cassius Longinus, 84 did defeat Gnaeus Pompeius Iunior of Pontus, 85 thus reclaiming Anatolia as the Province of Asia. 86 Upon news of the death of his brother, 87 Sextus Pompeius Magnus escaped from Samaria, 88 with his army and took Syracuse and central Sicily. 89 Gaius Marius Julius then did go to Baalbek, 90 and the most ancient Temple of Solomon, 91 where the High Priest of Baal Hamon, 92 whose name was Anath, 93 also known as Ananias did proclaim him Rex Sacrorum, 94 and the living personification of Mithra, 95 as Saviour for the world. 96 In Palestine Gaius Marius Julius did renew his treaty, 97 with Herodas and the Nabatean warriors. 98 Gaius Marius Julius who falsely claimed himself as Caesar, 99 then demanded that Marcus Antonius execute the Senate in exile, 100 for their refusal to pledge allegiance.

C. 31

1 In the Great Age of the Ram, 2 eleven hundred and fifty three years, 3 since the dawn of the Great Age (47 BCE), 4 the Senate in exile led by Lucius Cornelius Balbus did declare, 5 Marcus Antonius as the true Caesar and Nasci (Knight). 6 Enraged at the slight Gaius Marius Julius did attack Alexandria, 7 as Herodas did attack from the west and south. 8 Yet the city held and the fleet of Gaius Marius Julius was destroyed. 9 In retribution Gaius Marius Julius ordered a fire attack, 10 against the city and to destroy it completely, 11 as the most barbaric act of piracy yet seen against Alexandria. 12 Part of the Great Library was lost to the madmen of Mars. 13 Yet Gaius Marius Julius was forced to abandon his siege, 14 upon growing illness and poor health, 15 and did return to Rome, 16 where he proclaimed the old Senate invalid, 17 and proceeded to appoint his most loyal generals and followers, 18 as a new Senate to meet at the Vulcanal Temple to Vulcan, 19 led by Marcus Junius Brutus and Gaius Cassius Longinus, 20 and Marcus Aemilius Lepidus from Leptis Major of Africa. 21 In the Great Age of the Ram, 22 eleven hundred and fifty six years, 23 since the dawn of the Great Age (44 BCE), 24 as Gaius Marius Julius was now gravely ill, 25 he summonsed his two consuls, 26 being Marcus Junius Brutus and Gaius Cassius Longinus, 27 and demanded that they swear no one claim themselves Caesar, 28 and to hunt down and kill Marcus Antonius, 29 for never again shall anyone be permitted to proclaim themselves, 30 King or Caesar of Rome after his death. 31 Gaius Marius Julius then demanded his most loyal generals, 32 prepare a symbolic sacrifice upon the Ides of March (Mars), 33 and the Day of Blood as the birthday of Mithra, 34 whereby Gaius Marius Julius would

sacrifice his blood to Rome, 35 to become its Holy Ghost and perpetual protector as a god, 36 to watch over the Senate and the people of Rome. 37 Thus upon March the 14th and the Ides of March, 38 Gaius Marius Julius was given a strong sedative, 39 before his loyal and devoted followers as the false Senate, 40 did stab Gaius Marius Julius to death, 41 except Marcus Junius Brutus who could not bring himself, 42 to strike at the false Caesar even as he implored him. 43 Thus was born the mythos of the Messiah of Rome, 44 and the fraud of Gaius Marius Julius the Caesar.

C. 32

1 Following the elaborate suicide of Gaius Marius Julius, 2 Marcus Antonius and the true Senate, 3 sought a truce and alliance with the warlord of Leptis Magna, 4 named Marcus Aemilius Lepidus, 5 and Marcus Junius Brutus and Gaius Cassius Longinus. 6 Yet no sooner had the funeral ceremony of Gaius Marius Julius, 7 finished when Marcus Tullius Cicero declared himself, 8 executor of the testament and wishes of Julius the false Caesar, 9 and falsely proclaimed the warlord of Calabria whose name was Octavius, 10 to have been adopted by Julius before his death, 11 and thus possessed the Imperator of Julius Caesar, 12 and the persona of Emperor. 13 Marcus Junius Brutus and Gaius Cassius Longinus did then seize, 14 Marcus Tullius Cicero and have him brutally executed, 15 as an enemy of the state before securing a solemn oath from Octavius, 16 that he repudiate the claims of the dead Cicero. 17 Marcus Junius Brutus then moved to Macedonia and Asia, 18 to confront Marcus Antonius. 19 In the Great Age of the Ram, 20 eleven hundred and fifty seven years, 21 since the dawn of the Great Age (43 BCE), 22 as Gaius Cassius Longinus was engaged with Marcus Aemilius Lepidus, 23 against Sextus Pompeius Magnus in Sicily, 24 assassins for Gaius Marius Octavius did kill Gaius Cassius Longinus, 25 before Marcus Aemilius Lepidus pledged loyalty to Octavius. 26 Sextus Pompeius Magnus did then escape to Ionia, 27 where he was killed by the forces of Marcus Junius Brutus. 28 In the Great Age of the Ram, 29 eleven hundred and fifty eight years, 30 since the dawn of the Great Age (42 BCE), 31 Gaius Marius Octavius and Marcus Aemilius Lepidus, 32 did face against Marcus Junius Brutus, 33 who was defeated and committed suicide. 34 As the forces of the deceased Gaius Marcus Julius, 35 continued to fight themselves, 36 Marcus Antonius successfully invaded Palestine and Syria, 37 forcing Herodas to briefly retreat to Arabia. 38 The disciples of the dead Cicero, 39 supported by Quintus Horatius Flaccus and Publius Vergilius Maro, 40 did petition Octavius and the ancient pirate families, 41 that a new world order be formed known as the Ordo sacrorum arcana, 42 into which the powerful and wealthy be invited, 43 as well as the most intelligent and talented of society, 44 to break the endless cycle of blood and war, 45 where merchant families and moneylenders (bankers) are destroyed. 46 For history did reveal that men would fight to the death, 47 to free themselves from the bonds of slavery, 48 yet given the right for

personal wealth, 49 even the oldest of races would sign themselves into servitude. 50 Thus Octavius and the merchant elite agreed to form a new world, 51 where men would be given the appearance of freedom, 52 where money would become the new god and religion, 53 and ancient ties of trust and good faith be broken, 54 for the worship of power and fame and wealth, 55 yet forever guided by the illusion of liberty, 56 in the hands of the best and brightest, 57 to forever protect the interests of the merchants, 58 as a new class of men of the horse (equestrians). 59 At the same time Marcus Antonius, 60 chose a fateful and failed attempt to invade Parthia, 61 that he did lose much of the land he had captured. 62 In the Great Age of the Ram, 63 eleven hundred and sixty nine years, 64 since the dawn of the Great Age (31 BCE), 65 the forces of Gaius Marius Octavius did invade Egypt, 66 and overwhelmed its defences whereupon Antonius committed suicide. 67 Cleopatra also committed suicide some time later, 68 before she could be taken back to Rome to Octavius. 69 Gaius Marius Octavius then declared himself Imperator (Emperor), 70 and possessed by the Holy Spirit (Julius the false Caesar). 71 Octavius then reformed the Senate, 72 and began to restrict the minting of coin, 73 and the exchange of coin (banking), 74 while declaring that men who pledge themselves to Rome, 75 and be a loyal citizen may own their own land. 76 In the Great Age of the Ram, 77 eleven hundred and seventy three years, 78 since the dawn of the Great Age (27 BCE), 79 at Baalbek Gaius Marius Octavius was crowned, 80 Rex Sacrorum and Divine Son of God, 81 by Anath also known as Annias. 82 The age of the Roman Empire, 83 under the absolute power of merchants and moneylenders, 84 and the worship of money as god had begun.

Book 20

Age of Messiahs

[39 BCE - 22 CE]

C. 1

The rise of Octavius under the guide of the Illuminati, 2 transformed the mind of the pirates and merchants, 3 and along with it the destiny of Rome and the world. 4 Avowed enemies and priest lines became allies, 5 as traditional alliances of pirates and assassins were destroyed. 6 The birth of the concept of private property and portal rights, 7 swept through the ancient world, 8 as young men of talent sought their fortune. 9 In the Great Age of the Ram, 10 eleven hundred and sixty one years, 11 since the dawn of the Great Age (39 BCE), 12 in the same year Herod the Great did marry as his second wife, 13 the last Hasmonean Princess whose name was Mariamne. 14 Acclaimed as the most beautiful woman in all the ancient world, 15 Herodas remained obsessed by her all his life, 16 for no other thing did he love more. 17 His first wife Malthace did bear him two sons, 18 whose names were Archelas and Aenas (Antipas), 19 yet his first wife did hate the beauty of Mariamne, 20 and constantly schemed to end her life. 21 Mariamne did convince Herodas for a time, 22 to keep safe her brother named Aristobulus, 23 but Herod grew tired of him and had him drowned. 24 Mariamne bore him four children of which only one ruled, 25 the greatly handsome Herod Philip. 26 Upon the most sacred Isle (Ireland), 27 since becoming the Holly (holy) King, 28 the Chief Prophet Adoniah, 29 also known as Holly High King Cú-Roi(n), 30 and Pontifex Maximus had failed to raise a new heir. 31 Lucháil had first fallen with child, 32 that failed to reach term. 33 Thereupon some years later, 34 she gave birth to a second child, 35 who died soon after birth. 36 Many of the druids and scribes, 37 believed it was on account, 38 of the curses that Cú-Roi(n), 39 had brought upon himself, 40 on abandoning his first wife, 41 to travel overseas and the breaking of a high oath, 42 to his father the former Holly High King. 43 In the same year Octavius did marry Livia Drusilla, 44 the mother of Tiberius Claudius Nero and Decimus Claudius Drusus. 45 Octavius then appointed Lucius Seius Strabo, 46 the great philosopher and geographer and historian, 47 originally from Amascia (Amasya) in Pontus, 48 to be the tutor of Tiberius and Decimus.

C. 2

1 In the Great Age of the Ram, 2 eleven hundred and seventy two years, 3 since the dawn of the Great Age (28 BCE), 4 Queen Luacháil gave birth to a healthy boy. 5 Holly High King Cú-Roi(n) did name him Cú-Cúileann, 6 as the royal title meaning Holly of Holly and Holy of Holies. 7 The Holly King as Great Prophet and Pontifex Maximus, 8 did also name his son by the name Yasiah also known as Joseph, 9 known in false legend as Cú Chulainn and Cú Ċulainn. 10 Upon news of the birth of Joseph (Yasiah), 11 Emperor Octavius sent his blessings to the Holly King, 12 and Edicts giving in perpetuity the Cuilliaéan, 13 the sole recognised rights of the isle of Britannia, 14 as well as the gift of large estates in Hispania and Gaul (France), 15 and above the Plain of Jezreel in the region of Galilee, 16 and the royal estate upon the Mount of Olives and Gardens of Gethsemane, 17 to the east wall of the city of Jerusalem, 18 as sacred land upon which no mausoleum or necropolis yet stood. 19 Holly High King Cú-Roi(n) did later name this estate Bethesda, 20 meaning the House (Estate) of Holly Grace and Mercy. 21 Upon such a sign of truce and good will, 22 Holly High King Cú-Roi(n) ordered Gaius Cornelius Gallus, 23 to take half of the Praetorian and return to Rome, 24 to the eternal service of the people of Rome, 25 and the protection of the Emperor. 26 Thus Lucius Cornelius Balbus born from Alexandria, 27 did become the new praefectus praetorio pontifex, 28 and protector of the Holly family, 29 while his cousin Gaius Cornelius Gallus, 30 did become the new praefectus praetorio of Rome, 31 under Emperor Octavius Augustus. 32 So it was upon such mutual faith, 33 and the great wealth of the mines of Britannia, 34 the Cuilliaéan continued to become, 35 the wealthiest house of the Roman Empire.

C. 3

1 In the Great Age of the Ram, 2 eleven hundred and seventy six years, 3 since the dawn of the Great Age (24 BCE), 4 the Holly King Cú-Roi(n) did proclaim, 5 his son Cú-Cúileann also known as Joseph (Yasiah), 6 be a gift of the Divine Creator and all heaven, 7 destined to become the greatest of all Holly Kings, 8 while his mother Queen Luacháil also known as Esa, 9 the grand daughter of the Great Prophet Zadokiah, 10 did vision Cú-Cúileann to be a saviour of the world, 11 thus at age four Cú-Cúileann (Joseph) was taken to Glastonbury, 12 to begin his education midst the greatest library of ancient truth, 13 not by ancient poems but the most ancient scrolls of the world. 14 A brilliant student was Cú-Cúileann that by eight years, 15 he could speak and write the major languages of the Empires, 16 and could speak upon the ancient history of man, 17 of science and civil matters, 18 of religions and divination of the stars. 19 His father the Holly King did seek his son to be tested, 20 before he planned to take him upon a great journey, 21 to visit their estates of Hispania and Southern Gaul, 22 and then to Rome and unto Alexandria and Jerusalem. 23 Thus Cú-Cúileann of eight years, 24 was summonsed to stand in the Great Hall of Tara, 25 before a great council of priests and

scribes. 26 There the druids and the court were then amazed, 27 at the knowledge and skill of young Cú-Cúileann, 28 to answer and reason as fine as any master druid. 29 When they had finished examining him, 30 Cú-Cúileann also known as Joseph (Yasiah), 31 did ask and was granted permission for three questions. 32 Cú-Cúileann did then ask his first question, 33 saying father if we be so wise and ancient of priests, 34 why do we not use all our skills to help the world? 35 To which the King replied because we are not gods, 36 and so do not interfere in the affairs of men. 37 In reply Cú-Cúileann did ask his second question, 38 saying if we be men and live and trade as men, 39 why do we not use our wealth to help those who have none? 40 To which the King replied because to give without knowledge, 41 is fruitless for unless a man seeks to better himself, 42 no alms shall better his cause or those of his family. 43 In reply Cú-Cúileann did ask his third question, 44 father are you not the one true pharaoh? 45 are you not the Great Prophet of the Divine Creator? 46 And the Pontifex Maximus of the whole Roman Empire? 47 And the blood of Da'vid and the messiah kings? 48 Why do you not claim your birth right and order men to obey? 49 The King replied that even to heaven no respect is shown, 50 for men who have made themselves gods, 51 yet ignorant of the smallest things, 52 knowing not from whence they come. 53 Alas I fear even now you are formidable, 54 thus never again shall you ask a question in court, 55 until you are king. 56 For the wisdom I fear most, 57 is the truth of such a child.

C. 4

1 In the Great Age of the Ram, 2 eleven hundred and eighty years, 3 since the dawn of the Great Age (20 BCE), 4 Holly High King Cú-Roi(n) also known as Adoniah, 5 the Great Prophet of Yeb and Pontifex Maximus, 6 did travel with his son Cú-Cúileann also known as Joseph (Yasiah), 7 and protected by his Praetorian Guard, 8 to the Provincial Capital of Nimes in southern Gaul, 9 to be received by Marcus Vespanius Agrippa on behalf of Augustus. 10 There, Holly High King Cú-Roi(n) as Pontifex Maximus, 11 did dedicate the new Temple complex in honour of Octavius, 12 before travelling north up the Rhone River to the lands formerly of the Averni, 13 now granted in perpetuity as private property of the Holly. 14 Upon a major fork in the River the Holly High King as Pontifex Maximus, 15 did dedicate a new city to be known as Lucifier (Lyons), 16 meaning in the traditional tongue of the Holly, 17 as the place where good fortune is forged and fired, 18 and a sacred temple city to be administered by the Holly, 19 for the minting of coin for the whole Empire, 20 no longer by merchants and moneylenders, 21 but dedicated priests sworn to a life of austerity. 22 Holly High King Cú-Roi(n) as Pontifex Maximus, 23 and his son accompanied by Marcus Vipsanius Agrippa, 24 with the Praetorian and several legions, 25 did then return to Rome to be greeted by Augustus Octavius, 26 who had overcome grievous illness and was saved, 27 not by the superstitious blood letters of Rome, 28 but the Yahudi Therapeutae of Macedonia. 29 Holly High King Cú-Roi(n) as Pontifex

Maximus in Rome, 30 did then bless and dedicate the Pantheon as the new Temple, 31 for the Divine Creator and all the lesser gods, 32 before then travelling again with Marcus Vipsanius Agrippa, 33 to Alexandria to see its wonders of the world. 34 There in Alexandria Holly High King Cú-Roi(n) implored, 35 the priests and scribes to honour the reign of Augustus, 36 and to support the reform of the Roman Empire, 37 before travelling to the Temple of Leontopolis, 38 to visit Eliah and the priests of Yeb. 39 There at Leontopolis High King Cú-Roi(n), 40 did agree to give the hand of his son Joseph (Yasiah), 41 to the new-born daughter of Eliah and Anna, 42 whose name was Mariah when she come of age. 43 Holly High King Cú-Roi(n) did then travel east to Jerusalem, 44 accompanied again by Marcus Vipsanius Agrippa, 45 unto the court of King Herodas and the Temple of the Ark. 46 While the Great Temple of Herod was not yet complete, 47 Holly High King Cú-Roi(n) as Pontifex Maximus did bless it and dedicate it, 48 as the second great mint for coin of the Roman Empire, 49 to be administered by Yahudi Holly priests and not priests of Baal Hamon, 50 for Herodas was ordered to cease all forms of sacrifice, 51 that the blood of children or animals not desecrate the temple. 52 Holly High King Cú-Roi(n) then granted Herodas, 53 a sizeable treasure as a gift of good will, 54 before commissioning the construction of Bethesda, 55 to the east wall of the city, 56 and the city of Sepphoris to the north, 57 along the great trade routes of Galilee. 58 In response Herodas offered to execute Zachariah, 59 and all his troublesome priests at Qumran, 60 to which King Cú-Roi(n) as Pontifex Maximus, 61 did seek the pledge of Herodas that not a single hair of Zachariah, 62 be injured upon penalty of death to whomever so seek an act, 63 as the punishment for Zachariah from Heaven be a long bitter life, 64 without heir or fortune.

C. 5

1 The plans by Emperor Augustus Octavius, 2 to end the cycle of inflation and poverty and rebellion, 3 that had cursed and plagued Rome under the merchants, 4 by bestowing the forming of coin as a sacred task of Holly priest, 5 did quickly take hold across the Empire. 6 The skill of the Cuilliaéan smith did produce coin, 7 of perfect weight and form and design, 8 that no merchant could fraud or deface without detection, 9 as the powerful merchant families became the only moneylenders (bankers). 10 The alliance of Holly High King Cú-Roi(n) as Pontifex Maximus, 11 and as Adoniah the Great Prophet of Yeb, 12 did bring peace to the many of the great tribes of Celts, 13 and competence to the administration of the Empire, 14 an alliance between the pirates and the priests, 15 destined to be smashed and reformed in many centuries to come, 16 while some tribes still refused to yield to peace with Rome. 17 Even the priests of Baal Hamon, 18 exiled from control of the Temple of Jerusalem, 19 did yield to the grand alliance, 20 and profess themselves as Yahudi, 21 and claim to repudiate their ancient ways to Moloch. 22 Thus a strange and lingering peace did descend for a time,

23 as more men tilled the soil and crafted and traded and prospered. 24 In honour of such peace Holly High King Cú-Roi(n) as Pontifex Maximus, 25 continued to preside upon religious duties and ceremonies, 26 in the restoration of Dies Lentum (Lent), 27 as the great month of fasting and austere reflection, 28 first introduced by Zadokiah, 29 during the month of February beginning with Dies Natalis, 30 as the Days of remembrance of the Birth of Rome, 31 then the Dies Parentalis as the Days of Ancestors, 32 then Dies Manes (Demanes or Demons) as the Days of the honoured dead, 33 followed by Dies Festum as the great month of celebration, 34 of joy and festivity and song and merriment. 35 Thus Cú-Cúileann the son of Holly King Cú-Roi(n), 36 also known as Joseph (Yasiah), 37 the Divine Royal Highness (A-Rama-Theo), 38 falsely written as Arimethea, 39 did witness more of the world, 40 than any Holly Prince had ever done before.

C. 6

1 In the Great Age of the Ram, 2 eleven hundred and eighty three years, 3 since the dawn of the Great Age (17 BCE), 4 upon the birth of Lucius Vipsanius Agrippa, 5 as the second son to Marcus Vipsanius Agrippa, 6 and his wife Julia the only child and daughter of Augustus Octavius, 7 Emperor Augustus Octavius declared Marcus Vipsanius Agrippa, 8 to be his eldest adopted son and only heir, 9 thus depriving his stepson Tiberius Claudius Nero through marriage, 10 and enraging his wife and mother of Tiberius named Livia Drusilla. 11 Upon the attempts by Livia Drusilla to incite rebellion in the Senate, 12 against the granting of co-equal powers to Marcus Vipsanius Agrippa, 13 Emperor Augustus Octavius reluctantly banished her to Capri, 14 and Tiberius Claudius Nero to Spalatum (Split) on the Illryian coast. 15 Marcus Vipsanius Agrippa then set about restructuring the administration, 16 of the empire beginning with Gaul by establishing three new Provinces, 17 the first being Gallia Belgica of the lands of north of Gaul and Netherlands, 18 with its new Capital at Courtorum (Rheims) meaning the origin and arisen, 19 the second being Gallia Aquitania of the lands of western Gaul, 20 with its new Capital at Burdigala (Bordeaux), 21 and the third being Gallia Lucifer of the lands of the centre and south of Gaul, 22 with its Capital at Lucifer (Lyons) meaning the source of good fortune. 23 Holly High King Cú-Roi(n) as Pontifex Maximus, 24 did reform the worship and rituals of Mithra, 25 and Roman liturgy with the first issue of the Missalum (Missal), 26 and the formal ritual and ceremony of Missa (Mass), 27 which forbid actual rituals of sacrifice and cannibalism, 28 and any simulated such rituals of cannibalism, 29 or any worship of blood and flesh, 30 as an abomination against the Divine and the gods. 31 Instead the sacred Missalum (Missal) and Missa (Mass), 32 did celebrate the respect and honour of self-sacrifice, 33 of duty and honour to family and Rome.

C. 7

1 In the Great Age of the Ram, 2 eleven hundred and eighty seven years,

₃ since the dawn of the Great Age (13 BCE), ₄ Cú-Cúileann at fourteen years, ₅ also known as Joseph (Yasiah), ₆ did accompany his father back to Palestine, ₇ to witness the grand construction of Sepphoris, ₈ which Holly High King Cú-Roi(n) as the Great Prophet Adoniah, ₉ had pronounced it to become a city of light, ₁₀ and a restoration of the highest of learning and ideals, ₁₁ in honour of the ancient memory of Eliada and of Alexandria, ₁₂ and to officiate as Pontifex Maximus, ₁₃ the blessing of Caesarea Maritima upon the coast, ₁₄ named in honour of Augustus Octavius, ₁₅ built over ten years by King Herodas. ₁₆ Holly High King Cú-Roi(n) planned to remain at Bethesda, ₁₇ and at Sepphoris for winter before the formal dedication, ₁₈ of the Great Temple Mint of Mithra at Jerusalem, ₁₉ yet was summonsed by Augustus Octavius, ₂₀ to return to Italy and Campania, ₂₁ upon the sudden death of Marcus Vipsanius Agrippa, ₂₂ the beloved named heir and adopted son of the Emperor. ₂₃ Octavius commissioned the greatest funeral, ₂₄ Rome had yet seen and ordered Marcus Vipsanius Agrippa, ₂₅ be placed in his own mausoleum as a rightful Emperor. ₂₆ For months Augustus Octavius was inconsolable, ₂₇ until Holly High King Cú-Roi(n) as Pontifex Maximus, ₂₈ with support of Praetorian Prefect Gaius Cornelius Gallus, ₂₉ did convince the Emperor to allow the return of Livia Drusilla, ₃₀ and her son Tiberius Claudius Nero to Rome, ₃₁ for the sake of Rome, ₃₂ and the fragile peace that still held across the Empire, ₃₃ that it may live a little longer.

C. 8

₁ In the Great Age of the Ram, ₂ eleven hundred and eighty nine years, ₃ since the dawn of the Great Age (11 BCE), ₄ the return of Livia Drusilla and her sons, ₅ Tiberius Claudius Nero and Decimus Claudius Drusus, ₆ created an uneasy tension across Rome, ₇ even if the succession to the Empire appeared more stable. ₈ Livia Drusilla convinced Augustus Octavius to appoint Drusus, ₉ head of the northern Armies in Germania, ₁₀ and that Tiberius Claudius Nero marry Julia the daughter of Augustus, ₁₁ and widow of beloved Marcus Vipsanius Agrippa, ₁₂ that the grandsons of the Emperor, ₁₃ whose names were Gaius Vipsanius Agrippa and Lucius Vipsanius Agrippa, ₁₄ had the protection of a father. ₁₅ Thus Tiberius Claudius Nero and Julia the Elder, ₁₆ were forced into an unhappy marriage. ₁₇ In the same year, ₁₈ Lucius Cornelius Balbus the loyal Praetorian prefect, ₁₉ to the Pontifex Maximus did give up the ghost. ₂₀ The position of Praetorian Prefect and protector of Pontifex Maximus, ₂₁ did then befall to his son whose name was Lucius Cornelius Sulla, ₂₂ in honour of their brave and honourable ancestor. ₂₃ In the Great Age of the Ram, ₂₄ eleven hundred and ninety years, ₂₅ since the dawn of the Great Age (10 BCE), ₂₆ Holly High King Cú-Roi(n) also known as Conaire Mor, ₂₇ the living foundation stone of the Divine, ₂₈ of the most ancient Cuilliaéan, ₂₉ and blood descendant of the priests of Ebla, ₃₀ and blood descendant of the priests of Ur, ₃₁ and blood descendant of the priest-kings of the Hyksos, ₃₂ and blood descendant of the priests of

Ugarit, 33 and the only true blood descendants of King Da'vid, 34 and the Messiah Kings of Yahuda, 35 also known as Adoniah and Great Prophet of Yeb, 36 also known as Pontifex Maximus, 37 did give up the ghost. 38 The crown of Holly High King and the Marble Throne of Amen-Ra, 39 and the title of Great Prophet of Yeb, 40 and the title of Pontifex Maximus, 41 did befall to his son Cú-Cúileann, 42 also known as Yasiah (Joseph), 43 as the thirty first Great Prophet of Yeb. 44 Upon news of the death of Holly High King Cú-Roi(n), 45 Emperor Augustus Octavius again was in mourning. 46 Livia Drusilla then summonsed Yasiah (Joseph) to Rome, 47 where she demanded he surrender the title of Pontifex Maximus, 48 to which Holly King Cú-Cúileann did reply, 49 that such title was granted in perpetuity to the Great Prophets, 50 and not within the power of an Empress to seize. 51 Enraged by such refusal Livia Drusilla did then commission a statue, 52 of Augustus Octavius as Pontifex Maximus, 53 then installed within the Forum, 54 as a symbol to pressure the Senate to request Augustus, 55 to seize the title from the Holly. 56 Upon news of the actions of Livia Drusilla, 57 against the young Great Prophet Yasiah (Joseph), 58 Octavius ordered the statue be destroyed and forbid Livia Drusilla, 59 to discuss religious affairs of the Empire. 60 Instead Livia Drusilla had the statue taken down by her guard, 61 and secretly buried for some future use, 62 which never came again in the lifetime of Augustus.

C. 9

1 In the Great Age of the Ram, 2 eleven hundred and eighty nine years, 3 since the dawn of the Great Age (9 BCE), 4 after untold cruelty and waste, 5 General Decimus Claudius Drusus, 6 did give up the ghost in Germania, 7 when his generals claimed he fell from his horse. 8 Livia Drusilla was overcome with rage, 9 and demanded the execution of every general, 10 of the armies of the north as punishment, 11 yet the tiring Augustus Octavius spared his generals, 12 and elevated Tiberius to co-emperor, 13 to appeal for some peace against the schemes of Livia Drusilla. 14 Yet Tiberius Claudius Nero was not only inept at war, 15 but the very worst of administrators and soon, 16 the supplies and management of Rome was in chaos, 17 causing a crisis and famine for the city and Italy. 18 The people of Rome hated Tiberius and Livia Drusilla, 19 yet feared them and especially Livia Drusilla for her temper and cruelty, 20 yet now in hunger and disgust they openly mocked Tiberius as Oedipus, 21 and his mother as Jocasta of the Graecian myths. 22 Yet rather than addressing the starving and sick of Rome, 23 Tiberius and his mother staged him a lavish entrance to Rome, 24 with Tiberius arriving as if the conquering hero, 25 proclaiming victory against mythical enemies in mythical battles, 26 for which the starving people of Rome knew as fraud. 27 Facing open rebellion and the collapse of Rome from Rome itself, 28 Emperor Augustus Octavius banished Livia Drusilla to Capri again, 29 and demoted Tiberius Claudius Nero to

prefect of the eastern provinces, 30 and to the city of Caesarea Maritima on the Palestinian coast. 31 Augustus Octavius then appointed Praetorian Prefect Gaius Cornelius Gallus, 32 as the first Nasci (Protector of Rome) for fifty years, 33 to repair the damage of Tiberius and Livia Drusilla. 34 Within the year Gaius Cornelius Gallus had restored order, 35 and the safety and regularity of supplies to Rome. 36 Yet worked himself to exhaustion and died soon after. 37 Grief stricken Augustus Octavius appointed Gaius Cornelius Lentulus, 38 the son of Gaius Cornelius Gallus the Praetorian Prefect, 39 as well as Nasci and Protector of Rome, 40 falsely known as Lucius Aelius Sejanus, 41 by the liars and scribes for hire in years to come. 42 Augustus Octavius did then call upon all Praetorian to swear a sacred vow, 43 to protect Rome and the honour of the Senate and Imperial Offices, 44 that no tyrant be permitted to threaten or destroy Rome from within.

C. 10

1 Since the ascension of young Cú-Cúileann as Holly High King, 2 and as Yasiah (Joseph) the Great Prophet of Yeb, 3 and still the Pontifex Maximus, 4 false prophet Zechariah the arch-enemy of his father, 5 single minded in his hatred of all who betrayed his ambitions, 6 and fermented madness and bitterness and falsities, 7 amongst the acolytes of the caves of Qumran, 8 did seek to reach out and seek an audience with Yasiah. 9 Qumran had become the centre site of anti Roman propaganda, 10 carefully coded in Aramaic and Greek to all who could read, 11 yet never in Hebrew a language not yet created, 12 until the Aryan Empire of Persia first formed in centuries to come, 13 nor of the writings of Josephus ben Matthias not yet born. 14 For only the most wicked of liars and merchants, 15 could devise such frauds to claim otherwise. 16 There at Bethesda under the watchful eye of the Praetorian, 17 Zechariah asked the young Cú-Cúileann, 18 of what destiny behold the good priest or wicked priest, 19 when the world comes to an end? 20 Young Cú-Cúileann as the Great Prophet Yasiah (Joseph) replied, 21 that for every calamity claimed as the will of the Divine, 22 one may find equally the mind or hand of Man. 23 Zechariah was enraged by such skill and pushed further, 24 declaring that the Divine Creator will truly destroy the world, 25 and all men will die and be judged, 26 and those found wanting shall be punished for eternity, 27 for the world has become obsessed in the love of money as god, 28 that the world was drowning in evil, 29 and the worship of flesh and pleasure. 30 To which Cú-Cúileann as Yasiah (Joseph) responded, 31 the only true evil is wilful ignorance, 32 for if it be the will of heaven to end the world, 33 and the Divine to reveal itself to be a hateful god, 34 and thus a jealous god and a lesser god, 35 than the one who created all of existence, 36 then there would be signs and prophecies, 37 and a messenger at the last days to speak to such signs. 38 Verily unless such prophecies and messenger be foretold, 39 then all talk of the vengeance of the Divine, 40 must be the musings of bitter men, not the gods. 41 Zechariah screamed against such words of challenge, 42 and again Cú-Cúileann as

Yasiah (Joseph) demanded proof, 43 till Zechariah relented and said that such signs will come in the heavens, 44 that the earth will shake and the crops wither and animals will die, 45 and wells will become poison and neighbour will fight neighbour, 46 and the last messiah to come to the people will be from ancient priests, 47 of the Yahudi lines of Akhenaten and Elijiah and Isaiah and Jeremiah, 48 yet will be from the priests that keep the covenant, 49 and not those that have strayed. 50 Cú-Cúileann as Yasiah (Joseph) did then reply, 51 that it be not for men to decide when the Divine speaks, 52 nor choose the will of Heaven, 53 but the one true Divine Creator who chooses such grace, 54 thus it may well come to pass that by some miracle, 55 the seed of Zechariah emerges as the messiah of such prophecy. 56 Yet no word of prophecy be arbitrary, 57 especially when signs of the heavens be claimed. 58 Cú-Cúileann as Yasiah (Joseph) did then proceed to discuss, 59 the operation of the stars and the heavens, 60 of astronomy and seasons and signs, 61 which angered Zechariah even further, 62 for the false priests of Qumran had lost the knowledge of the stars. 63 Thus Zechariah and the priests departed, 64 even more self convinced they alone, 65 be the saviours of the world, 66 and the final arbiters of the will of God.

C. 11

1 In the Great Age of the Ram, 2 eleven hundred and ninety six years, 3 since the dawn of the Great Age (4 BCE), 4 Herod the Great gave up the ghost, 5 and darkness appeared across Jerusalem. 6 Upon the treachery of Aenas (Antipas) even against his own father, 7 Archelas had been made sole heir to Nabatea, 8 against his older brother Aenas (Antipas) and younger brother Philipas. 9 Yet Philipas Agrippa had already made a close alliance with Cú-Cúileann, 10 as the Great Prophet Yasiah (Joseph) and Pontifex Maximus. 11 Archelas his son did request Cú-Cúileann as Yasiah (Joseph), 12 conduct a lavish funeral for his father, 13 as Aenas (Antipas) sought every stone unturned to impede his brothers. 14 First he sought an alliance with Zachariah, 15 against Cú-Cúileann as Yasiah (Joseph) yet failed to win popular support. 16 Thus at the funeral for his own father, 17 Aenas (Antipas) ordered his own troops to dress as guards of Archelas, 18 to begin slaughtering mourners on false pretences. 19 Chaos and riots quickly ensued as people enraged by such sacrilege, 20 blamed Archelas while the troops of Archelas hunted down, 21 and killed the false assassins. 22 Aenas (Antipas) then retreated to beseech Tiberius Claudius Nero, 23 exiled to Caesarea Maritima by the Emperor, 24 that he urgently send troops to Jerusalem to protect the Roman Mint, 25 and the sacred Ark of the Covenant against the madness of Archelas. 26 Tiberius Claudius Nero then dispatched Publius Quinctilius Varus, 27 on the premise of establishing law and order. 28 Yet Publius Quinctilius Varus was heavy handed and brutal, 29 and slaughtered thousands of people for no good cause, 30 until the troops of Archelas were forced to defend the people, 31 and destroy one of the legions of Varus. 32 Before complete civil war erupted

Holly King Cú-Cúileann, ₃₃ as Yasiah (Joseph) and Pontifex Maximus, ₃₄ demanded that Publius Quinctilius Varus stand down, ₃₅ on account of the intrigue and treachery of Aenas (Antipas). ₃₆ Emperor Augustus Octavius did then summons, ₃₇ Holly High King Cú-Cúileann and Archelaus and Tiberius, ₃₈ to Rome to give account of the uprising, ₃₉ at which time Antipas took the absence of his brother, ₄₀ as a chance to seize Jerusalem until he was forced to retreat. ₄₁ Yasiah (Joseph) and Pontifex Maximus did give account, ₄₂ and exonerated Tiberius and Varus of any blame, ₄₃ as well as Archelas for the actions of his brother Aenas (Antipas). ₄₄ Emperor Augustus Octavius then considered the decision, ₄₅ of war against Aenas (Antipas) located at Petra, ₄₆ and holding the loyalty of the Bedouin tribesmen, ₄₇ and Nabatean arabic militia. ₄₈ Instead Yasiah (Joseph) suggested that Aenas (Antipas) be recognised, ₄₉ while a new kingdom made of the surrounds of Jerusalem, ₅₀ called Idumea and granted to Archelas, ₅₁ while Philipas Agrippa be granted a kingdom called Galilea. ₅₂ Thus the brothers would be separated, ₅₃ while Rome still kept strong allies in Palestine and Arabia. ₅₄ The Emperor impressed as the wisdom of such a king, ₅₅ and Great Prophet and Pontifex Maximus at twenty four years, ₅₆ did agree and Archelas returned as king of Idumea. ₅₇ Thus Yasiah (Joseph) as Pontifex Maximus, ₅₈ remained with his Praetorian in Rome, ₅₉ and conducted his first official ceremonies at the request of Augustus, ₆₀ as Tiberius was reunited with the only love of his life at Capri.

C. 12

₁ In the Great Age of the Ram, ₂ twelve hundred years, ₃ since the dawn of the Great Age (0 BCE), ₄ Holly High King Cú-Cúileann as Yasiah (Joseph) at twenty eight, ₅ the Great Prophet of Yeb and Pontifex Maximus, ₆ did wed Mariah (Mary) aged sixteen, ₇ the daughter of Eliah the High Priest of Leontopolis, ₈ also known as Chi-Rho (Cairo). ₉ An important wedding of great note, ₁₀ Kings, queens and priests of many nations, ₁₁ did come to celebrate at the Temple of Oniah: ₁₂ the Brahman from India, ₁₃ King Archelas from Idumea and King Philipas Agrippa of Galilea, ₁₄ the Magi High Priests from the east, ₁₅ the High Priests of Amen-Ra, ₁₆ and High Druids from Britannia and the sacred Isle, ₁₇ yet none more important than the Prefect of Egypt, ₁₈ being Emperor Augustus Octavius himself, ₁₉ accompanied by his daughter Julia the widow of Marcus Vipsanius Agrippa. ₂₀ All who were invited did come to the wedding. ₂₁ All except one being the false priests and prophet Zecheriah from Qumran, ₂₂ who dishonoured all with no word or explanation for such disgrace. ₂₃ Yet less than six months after the wedding of Joseph and Mary, ₂₄ news came from Jerusalem that Elisabeth the sister of Anna, ₂₅ the mother of Mary (Mariah), ₂₆ who was well beyond the age of children, ₂₇ who had been barren all her life, ₂₈ and the false prophet Zechariah well advanced in age, ₂₉ had miraculously given birth to a boy child. ₃₀ Some of Qumran did say it was a virgin birth, ₃₁ while others revealed the infant to be the son of shepherds, ₃₂ purchased for thirty pieces of silver. 33 They named him Yahuaniah (John), 34 also known as Johanan ben Zakkai and John the Baptist. 35 Despite the production of thousands of papers from Qumran, 36 and the best efforts to ferment the absurdity of a virgin birth, 37 the wicked lie failed to grab hold. 38 False prophet Zecheriah then did declare, 39 his scribes and agents of propaganda write to all Yahudi priests, 40 that this year be the year zero, 41 as the heavens and the prophecies foretold, 42 that rule of law be restored and people united. 43 Thus some temples and priests began to accept the calendar, 44 not for the fantasies protested by Zecheriah, 45 but the appeal to ancient traditions, 46 and the yearning for a new world order. 47 Thus the almanac of the western world, 48 under which the world has lived since, 49 was born not from the birth of a true messiah, 50 but the birth of a wicked lie, 51 by insane and false priests who prayed daily, 52 for the world they could not control to end. 53 Upon the propaganda of Zechariah, 54 and the falsity of the virgin birth and year zero, 55 King Archelas of Idumea was enraged. 56 Whilst Zecheriah was at the Great Temple at Jerusalem, 57 soldiers of Archelaus did seize the priest and end his life. 58 Upon news of such blasphemy on sacred ground, 59 the Essenoi rioted across Jerusalem and Palestine. 60 King Archelas did appeal that his actions be justified, 61 as the Essenoi did ferment sedition against Rome, 62 yet Holly High King Cú-Cúileann as Yasiah (Joseph), 63 the Great Prophet of Yeb and Pontifex Maximus, 64 demanded that Qumran and the family of Zechariah, 65 not be harmed nor any Essenoi that cease rebellion be killed. 66 To protect the Great Temple Mint of Mithra at Jerusalem, 67 Augustus Octavius appointed Titus Coponius Sabinus as Procurator, 68 with three elite cohort of Roman guards for the Great Temple Mint. 69 Never again did the Idumean guard the Temple, 70 as King Archelas and Holly High King Cú-Cúileann, 71 were once again summonsed to Rome to give account. 72 Yet this time before Augustus Octavius, 73 Archelas was forced to cede his kingdom to Philipas Agrippa, 74 before Yasiah (Joseph) as Pontifex Maximus. 75 Thus Archelas was arrested and forced to remain in exile in Rome, 76 as surety for peace with the Nabateans. 77 The ageing Elisabeth did flee with her new purchased child, 78 known as Johanan ben Zakkai and John the Baptist, 79 unto Egypt and the House of Eliah and Anna at Leontopolis, 80 for safety and sanctuary against the Idumeans and Romans. 81 Upon news of the death of Zecheriah and the uprising of the Essenoi, 82 a snake arose from Babylon called Gamaliel the Elder.

C. 13

1 In the year known as 2 CE, 2 twelve hundred and two years since the dawn of the Great Age, 3 Lucius Vipsanius Agrippa died from a terrible fever, 4 at Massalia (Marseilles) in Gaul. 5 Suspected by some as a victim to the poison of a loyal assassin, 6 to the maniacal matriarch Livia Drusilla exiled to Capri. 7 Julia the daughter of Augustus Octavius implored, 8 the Emperor execute Livia Drusilla lest her only remaining son, 9 whose name was Gaius Vipsanius Agrippa, 10 and Commander of the Armies to the East,

11 did also follow the fate of his younger brother. 12 Yet Augustus Octavius refused on account, 13 that as much as the women may despise one another, 14 there be no evidence of foul play. 15 In Galilee and the former lands of Shem, 16 Gamaliel the Elder from Babylon continued to ferment rebellion, 17 and foster support from the Essenoi proclaiming himself messiah, 18 until High Priest Simon of Qumran summonsed Gamaliel. 19 Gamaliel spoke to Simon and declared that as he be without succession, 20 no authority did he possess to question the teachings, 21 of a High Babylonian Priest of Mithra. 22 Simon did reply that no man can demand of another, 23 he worship one god or cease the worship of another, 24 but that he speak the truth concerning that which he knows. 25 To which Gamaliel did reply that the people be sheep, 26 and the priests the shepherds, 27 and that prudence demands the shepherds sometimes dress as wolves, 28 to confuse the predators and to keep the sheep alert. 29 For there be no greater weapons than fear and deception.

C. 14

1 In the year known as 4 CE, 2 twelve hundred and four years since the dawn of the Great Age, 3 King Marbodus of the Marcomanni united several Germanic tribes, 4 to a region later to be known as Silesia, Saxony and Bohemia, 5 as King Segimerus of the Cherusci agreed to a treaty with Augustus Octavius, 6 that his son Arminius lead the Auxillary legions, 7 of the best Germanic troops in defending the Empire. 8 In the same year, 9 Gaius Vipsanius Agrippa the Commander of the Armies to the East, 10 did fall into great sickness and fever, 11 upon his physicians failing to heal a minor wound, 12 sustained during his campaign in Armenia. 13 Upon the death of his second beloved grandson Augustus was inconsolable, 14 as his daughter Julia wept for her loss and what fate now faced the world. 15 After two months of mourning Augustus Octavius, 16 summonsed Tiberius and his mother Livia Drusilla back to Rome, 17 where Augustus Octavius once more announced Tiberius as heir, 18 but upon several solemn conditions before the most senior Senators, 19 where Livia Drusilla and Tiberius were forced to swear, 20 that Tiberius a man who had still produced no heir, 21 on account of his distaste for all but one woman, 22 would adopt Nero Claudius Drusus later known as Germanicus, 23 and his younger brother Tiberius Claudius Drusus later known as Claudius, 24 being the sons of his dead brother Decimus Claudius Drusus, 25 as his own sons and heirs, 26 and that Gaius Cornelius Lentulus would remain Nasci, 27 and Protector of Rome as Praetorian Prefect, 28 and finally that Livia Drusilla would be forbidden to give counsel, 29 as Tiberius would have to be a judge of men and not just an obedient son. 30 In the same year High Priest Simon of Qumran, 31 declared himself messiah of the Essenoi, 32 as Simon Magus and the Great Simon, 33 against Gamaliel the Elder. 34 In the year known as 5 CE, 35 twelve hundred and five years since the dawn of the Great Age, 36 a momentous event was divined in the heavens, 37 and the coming arrival of a great comet. 38 Holly High King

Cú-Cúileann as the highest astrologer, ₃₉ and as Yasiah (Joseph) the Great Prophet of Yeb, ₄₀ and as Pontifex Maximus was called to give account, ₄₁ before the Emperor and the Senate, ₄₂ for fear that such a great sign could spell impending doom. ₄₃ Yasiah (Joseph) replied to Augustus Octavius and Tiberius, ₄₄ that unlike omens of old this great sign be good fortune, ₄₅ of a time of rebirth and renewal. ₄₆ The Emperor asked how Yasiah (Joseph) be so certain, ₄₇ to which Holly High King Cú-Cúileann replied, ₄₈ that his wife whose name was Mariah (Mary), ₄₉ had failed to conceive for five years since their wedding night, ₅₀ yet now be blessed by heaven with conception of a child, ₅₁ who upon full term be due upon the most sacred of days of Dies Festum, ₅₂ and the Ides of March (14th of March), ₅₃ the birthday of Mithra and the day of Blood, ₅₄ upon which the followers of Mithra did observe before the Passover meal. ₅₅ Upon such sign Augustus Octavius did then declare, ₅₆ let Rome and the world celebrate the coming of such events, ₅₇ for my faith and hope be renewed. ₅₈ Whereupon the Emperor pronounced his retirement, ₅₉ and Tiberius be the new leader of the world.

C. 15

₁ In the year known as 6 CE, ₂ twelve hundred and six years since the dawn of the Great Age, ₃ upon triple conjunction of Mars, Jupiter and Saturn, ₄ that created the brightest new star in the heavens, ₅ and the arrival of a great comet, ₆ dignitaries and pilgrims from across the world did come to Jerusalem, ₇ to celebrate the birth of a new Holly Prince and future great prophet. ₈ Thus upon the birthday of Mithra and the eve of Passover of Mithra, ₉ and the Ides of March (14th March) as the Day of Blood, ₁₀ and the eve of the beginning of the celebration of Dies Festum, ₁₁ Queen Mariah (Mary) did give birth to a baby boy, ₁₂ at Bethesda to the east side of Jerusalem upon the famed mount of Olives, ₁₃ within the great hall of the palace that had been converted into a stable, ₁₄ so that the prophecies of the return of Mithra, ₁₅ known throughout the world would be literally fulfilled. ₁₆ There at Bethesda under the watchful eye and protection, ₁₇ of Lucius Cornelius Sulla and the Praetorian, ₁₈ priests and dignitaries did come from all over the known world, ₁₉ bringing priceless treasures as homage to such a momentous birth. ₂₀ Holly High King Cú-Cúileann also known as Yasiah (Joseph), ₂₁ did name his son Esus (Jesus) and Yahusiah and Cú-Laoch, ₂₂ meaning the Hero of the Cuilliaéan, ₂₃ as the living foundation stone of the Divine, ₂₄ of the most ancient Cuilliaéan, ₂₅ and blood descendant of the priests of Ebla, ₂₆ and blood descendant of the priests of Ur, ₂₇ and blood descendant of the priest-kings of the Hyksos, ₂₈ and blood descendant of the priests of Ugarit, ₂₉ and the only true blood descendants of King Da'vid, ₃₀ and the Messiah Kings of Yahuda. ₃₁ In the same year, ₃₂ Tiberius announced the formation of a special treasury, ₃₃ called the Aerarium Militare to pay a reward to veterans, ₃₄ and the loyalty of the troops to Rome and the new Emperor. ₃₅ The tutor and lifelong advisor of Tiberius named Lucius Seius Strabo, ₃₆ had estimated that if

Rome imposed uniform laws of taxes, 37 and the registration of property and goods in provinces not yet taxed, 38 then such a generous offering be well afforded. 39 Tiberius then appointed Publius Sulpicius Quirinius, 40 as the new legate for Syria to form a census and raise taxes, 41 and Valerius Messalla Messallinus to Dalmatia and Pannonia, 42 to also make a census and raise taxes, 43 and Tiberius Quinctilius Varus to Germania to do the same. 44 Yet Tiberius had greatly erred not only in the heavy handed demands, 45 but in the brutal methods of his legates, 46 that Arminus of the Cherusci revolted in Germania, 47 and King Bato of the Daesitiate rebelled in Illyricia, 48 and Gamaliel with Arabian fighters led resistance in Syria. 49 Within a few months rebellion was rising across the Empire, 50 from legions promised their reward not yet paid, 51 and rebel leaders now challenging key provinces. 52 Once again and for the third time Augustus Octavius, 53 was forced from retirement and once again Livia Drusilla, 54 was exiled back to Capri. 55 Yet Augustus Octavius did not send Tiberius away, 56 but instead demanded he repair the damage wrought, 57 by leading the army to restore order beginning with Illyria. 58 Thus Tiberius with Marcus Valerius Messallinus, 59 faced real danger and hostility against forces, 60 of more than one hundred thousand warriors.

C. 16

1 Following the birth of Jesus (Esus) also known as Cú-Laoch in the year 6 (CE), 2 Holly High King Cú-Cúileann also known as Yasiah (Joseph), 3 and Queen Mariah (Mary) did have five other children. 4 The second child was named Matia (Martha), 5 later acquiring the name Salome, 6 when she herself became a Queen of Nabatea. 7 The third eldest was James the brother of Jesus, 8 also known as Yacobiah (Jacob) and James the Just. 9 The fourth child was known as Jose which means Joseph. 10 The fifth child was named Iudas also known as Jude, 11 and Thomas. 12 The last child was known as Miriam also known as Mary. 13 These be the six children of Holly High King Cú-Cúileann, 14 also known as Yasiah (Joseph), 15 and Queen Mariah (Mary).

C. 17

1 In Galilee and into Syria Gamaliel the Elder, 2 found through the Bedouin Tribe known as the Sicari, 3 the perfect terrorists with which to promote his vision. 4 Known as the most ruthless and deadly of assassins, 5 Gamaliel the Elder secured an alliance with their leader, 6 who proclaimed himself Iudiah of Galilee and a prophet to his people. 7 To the Romans the followers of Gamaliel became known as the Zealots, 8 a fanatical and insane cult driven by themselves as victims, 9 who respected nothing of law or honour or culture, 10 and who viewed all form of deception and trickery as their right. 11 Instead of attacking seasoned Roman guards, 12 Gamaliel and the Zealots attacked innocent people, 13 themselves dressed as Romans to ferment division and fear. 14 Gamaliel even arranged for constant attacks against his own people, 15 using elite Sicari dressed as Nabatean and Romans, 16 to

perpetuate the climate of fear of victims, 17 and reinforce the lie of a people cursed by the gods, 18 and unjustly hated by all races of men. 19 Thus the invention of Gamaliel of a people united only in hate and fear, 20 with no history but lies led by leaders who despised them, 21 and tricked them with constant falsities of fear and attack was born, 22 a philosophy of madness that came to be known as Zionism. 23 In the year known as 7 CE, 24 twelve hundred and seven years since the dawn of the Great Age, 25 the danger of the Sicari around Sepphoris and Jerusalem, 26 had become too great for the Holly family. 27 Prateorian prefect Lucius Cornelius Sulla warned, 28 the climate of fear and uncertainty gripped Rome, 29 as Augustus Octavius sought to repair once again the damage of Tiberius. 30 Holly High King Cú-Cúileann as Yasiah (Joseph), 31 and Queen Mariah (Mary) and the baby Jesus (Cú-Laoch), 32 did then return to the Royal House of Glastonbury, 33 to the island of Britannia recognised by Rome in perpetuity to the Holly. 34 There Holly High King Cú-Cúileann did help raise several legions, 35 to aid Rome in its war in Illyria. 36 Despite the skill and forces of Marcus Valerius Messallinus, 37 the war against King Bato and the Daesitiate was failing, 38 as Tiberius proved himself even worse a general than administrator. 39 Augustus Octavius then did appoint the young Nero Claudius Drusus, 40 as commander of the second mass army, 41 raised from Britanni and Gaul to fight independently. 42 The strategy succeeded and within a few months, 43 the rebellion of Illyria was crushed,

44 after more than 200,000 men had lost their lives in the war. 45 In the year known as 9 CE, 46 twelve hundred and nine years since the dawn of the Great Age, 47 Marcus Valerius Messallinus as Governor of Dalmatia and Pannonia, 48 was rewarded for his victory with his son Marcus Valerius Barbatus, 49 as the new Procurator of the Great Temple Mint of Mithra at Jerusalem, 50 as Titus Coponius Sabinus was promoted to Procurator, 51 of the Great Temple Mint of Lucifer (Lyons). 52 There in the sacred city of Lucifer (Lyons), 53 the wife of Titus Coponius Sabinus, 54 whose name was Vespasia Polla, 55 gave birth to a son whose name was Titus Coponius Vespasianus, 56 later known as Titus Flavius Vespasianus and Lucifer. 57 In the same year as Tiberius was forced to Germania, 58 King Arminus of the Cherusci destroyed four Roman legions, 59 led by Publius Quinctilius Varus at Teutoburg Forest. 60 Yet the arrival of Nero Claudius Drusus and his army, 61 rallied the survivors and within two years the Cherusci were defeated. 62 Thereafter Nero Claudius Drusus became known as Germanicus.

C. 18

1 In the year known as 10 CE, 2 twelve hundred and ten years since the dawn of the Great Age, 3 at the Holly Grounds of Sacred Glastonbury, 4 Queen Mariah (Mary) did give birth to her third child, 5 named James also known as Yacobiah (Jacob) and James the Just. 6 Whilst at Glastonbury Holly High King Cú-Cúileann (Joseph), 7 ordered that the finest manuscripts and ancient documents, 8 be brought to Glastonbury for the tutoring of his

son Jesus (Cú-Laoch). 9 Already at aged five Jesus was a brilliant student, 10 natural at languages on account of the travel and people, 11 at the Holly Court of Glastonbury. 12 At the earliest age of six, 13 Jesus could speak no less than five ancient languages, 14 from Greek to Latin and the ancient tongue of the Holly (proto-Gaelic), 15 and the languages of the Aramaic tribes, 16 yet of all the languages that fascinated him the most, 17 Jesus was obsessed in the hieroglyph of the Egyptians. 18 Thus Holly High King Cú-Cúileann (Joseph) summonsed, 19 all the most ancient manuscripts of hieroglyph be brought to Glastonbury, 20 some even as ancient as his ancestors the Hyksos Kings. 21 There at Glastonbury Jesus devoured every hieroglyph manuscript, 22 of the history of his ancestors and the world, 23 from the most ancient times of Ebla and the Poets, 24 the birth of Babel (Babylon) and the Hyksos, 25 and the great works of his ancestor Akhenaten, 26 and the Great Prophets of Yeb (Elephantine), 27 and the destruction of the Yahudi Messiah Kings, 28 whose blood did run through his veins. 29 Even the Holly High King as a man well known for his wisdom, 30 did find debate with his son Jesus (Cú-Laoch) as a great challenge, 31 not for the complexity of subject but simplicity of argument. 32 Like the brilliance of Socrates and Plato and Aristotle before him, 33 Jesus knew the power of the right question and the simplest of queries. 34 As his father and tutors offered answers of history and complexity, 35 Jesus continued to ask why to the mind of men to be their worst enemies, 36 why were civilisations seemingly doomed to repeat the lessons of history, 37 why did priests deem themselves righteous judges, 38 in deciding the mind of the Divine Creator, 39 and what to teach and what to hold secret, 40 when the Rule of Law and Golden Rule speaks of all men being equal. 41 To these and many questions neither his father or tutors, 42 did provide the answers sought by Jesus (Cú-Laoch). 43 In the year known as 12 CE, 44 twelve hundred and twelve years since the dawn of the Great Age, 45 as Augustus Octavius was sick with advanced age and weight of rule, 46 and the Empire had returned to order, 47 the Emperor restored once again Tiberius as his heir. 48 Tiberius then arrived to Rome via a grand triumph, 49 which Livia Drusilla arranged with loyal Senators, 50 to celebrate Tiberius as the victor of Illyria and Germania, 51 at the expense of his adopted son Germanicus.

C. 19

1 In the year known as 14 CE, 2 twelve hundred and fourteen years since the dawn of the Great Age, 3 Emperor Augustus Octavius did give up the ghost. 4 Holly High King Cú-Cúileann as Pontifex Maximus, 5 also known as Yasiah (Joseph) the Great Prophet of Yeb, 6 did return to Rome to oversee the rituals and mourning, 7 of a man that had brought a longer peace, 8 than any leader of Rome for two hundred years. 9 Yet even before the period of official mourning had ended, 10 Livia Drusilla could not contain herself, 11 and Julia the elder the only biological child of Augustus, 12 died suddenly in her sleep, 13 and soon after Vipsania Julia the eldest granddaughter of Augustus. 14 Rome

itself was thrust from mourning to deep panic and fear, 15 as Praetorian Prefect Gaius Cornelius Lentulus, 16 and Nasci and Protector of Rome was helpless to act, 17 unless Livia Drusilla openly moved against the Senate and the people. 18 Livia Drusilla through Tiberius then called upon Publius Sulpicius Quirinius, 19 the Legate of Syria and infamous for his brutal methods, 20 to return to Rome to be promoted as Consul, 21 replaced by Quintus Caecilius Metellus Creticus Silanus. 22 In Rome Livia Drusilla called on Quirinius to move against the Praetorian, 23 to which Quirinius did reply that the Praetorian be too powerful, 24 and held the favour of all the legions the people and the priests, 25 and unless such favour be weakened then the Nasci could not be seized. 26 At the conclusion of the official period of mourning, 27 Tiberius and Livia Drusilla summonsed Holly High King Cú-Cúileann, 28 at a meeting with Senators and loyalists of Livia Drusilla, 29 where Livia Drusilla demanded Yasiah (Joseph) swear a High Oath, 30 of loyalty and allegiance to Tiberius as the Son of God. 31 Yasiah (Joseph) replied that his pledge remained, 32 to the people of Rome as their Pontifex Maximus, 33 and to all Celts as the Holly High King, 34 and to the Divine Creator of all as Great Prophet of Yeb. 35 Thus no greater pledge is needed to be given, 36 for if the people of Rome through the Senate choose Tiberius, 37 then he does still remain a loyal servant. 38 Enraged Livia Drusilla did curse such words as the artful tongue, 39 of a Cuilliaéan Priest known throughout history, 40 as the most arrogant and skilled at inventing words. 41 Yet Lucius Seius Strabo the personal adviser and tutor to Tiberius, 42 warned him that such public attacks by his mother, 43 would give strength to his enemies, 44 upon which Yasiah (Joseph) did leave with his Praetorian guard. 45 Gaius Cornelius Lentulus through Lucius Cornelius Sulla, 46 did then warn Holly High King Cú-Cúileann to leave Italy, 47 for fear that Livia Drusilla did plan to end his life, 48 like so many already through her potions and assassins. 49 Upon the departure of Holly High King Cú-Cúileann, 50 Livia Drusilla through Tiberius issued an edict, 51 that the sanctity and security of Rome, 52 demanded the permanency of sacred orders, 53 thus four colleges would be formed in honour of ancient laws, 54 the highest being the Collegium Pontificum (College of Pontiffs), 55 selected from the most honourable of families, 56 the second being Collegium Sacris Faciundis (College of Sacred Rites), 57 being the priests responsible for performance of sacred rites, 58 the third being Collegium Augurum (College of Augurs), 59 responsible for all prophecy and divinations, 60 and fourth being Collegium Epulonum (College of Festivities) 61 responsible for all feasts and games.

C. 20

1 In the year known as 15 CE, 2 twelve hundred and fifteen years since the dawn of the Great Age, 3 Matthias son of Ananus (Ananias) the High Priest, 4 and former chief priest of Baal Hamon, 5 did have to a son born he named Usias, 6 also known as Joseph and later Josephus, 7 and in history

the name Flavius Josephus. 8 For in all the history of fraud and fiction, 9 no other was as ambitious nor as destructive, 10 in the formation of a history so littered with absurdity, 11 that removed the oldest priests from history, 12 merely to serve his merchant masters at the time. 13 In the year known as 16 CE, 14 twelve hundred and sixteen years since the dawn of the Great Age, 15 King Philipas Agrippa of Idumea and Galilee, 16 and High Priest Ananus (Ananias) did write and plead, 17 to Holly High King Cú-Cúileann also known as Yasiah (Joseph), 18 for his aid against the Procurator Marcus Valerius Barbatus, 19 also known as Valerius the Gratus (exceedingly greedy), 20 who had demonstrated himself to be every bit as cruel, 21 as his former mentor Publius Quinctilius Varus, 22 who had put down the rebellion at the time of the death of Herodas. 23 Jesus (Cú-Laoch) also known as Yahusiah, 24 the son of Holly High King Yasiah (Joseph) and Queen Mariah (Mary), 25 had continued to grow in spirit and intellect, 26 as the dangers from Tiberius and his mother had subsided, 27 and the business of the Holly estates of Britannia and southern Gaul, 28 were as prosperous as at any other time. 29 The richest man and king in the world, 30 Joseph the Divine Royal Highness, 31 falsely written as Arimetheo, 32 did return to the Holly Lands of Idumea and Galilee. 33 In the same year, 34 Nero Claudius Drusus now known as Germanicus, 35 did lead a mass Roman army of more than 60,000 legionaries, 36 to victory against the reformed Germanic army of Arminius. 37 At the same time general Publius Silius Nerva, 38 a loyal ally of Germanicus did put down a revolt in Illyrica. 39 Upon such great victories the Senate implored Tiberius, 40 he reward his son with a triumph, 41 an event denied him from previous campaigns. 42 Yet Tiberius resisted until Lucius Seius Strabo reminded him, 43 that all glory aside the people of Rome need their heroes, 44 as much as their laws to keep the peace. 45 Thus Tiberius agreed and his adopted son Germanicus, 46 returned to Rome the great hero, 47 having rescued the lost standards of Vara, 48 seized by Arminius and his former Germanic army years before.

C. 21

1 In the year known as 17 CE, 2 twelve hundred and seventeen years since the dawn of the Great Age, 3 Holly High King Cú-Cúileann also known as Yasiah (Joseph), 4 did return to Idumea and Galilea with his Queen Mariah (Mary), 5 his Praetorian Guard led by Lucius Cornelius Sulla, 6 and his young family including his eldest son Jesus (Yahusiah). 7 Holly High King Cú-Cúileann as Pontifex Maximus, 8 did then visit Procurator Marcus Valerius Barbatus, 9 also known as Valerius Gratus at Caesarea Maritima. 10 The Procurator unaccustomed to entertaining such position, 11 did speak first and inquire what interest, 12 the Pontifex Maximus did have in the affairs of local priests and kings, 13 to which Yasiah (Joseph) as Holly High King reminded Valerius, 14 that since the time of the ancients before even the founding of Rome, 15 it be custom amongst civilised peoples that the Holly speak first, 16 that even

Gaius Julius Caesar and Gaius Augustus Octavianus, 17 did honour this most important custom. 18 Marcus Valerius Barbatus in deep regret to his offence, 19 did then implore what action he might take to mitigate his error, 20 to which Holly High King Cú-Cúileann replied, 21 that the position of High Priest be restored, 22 to a family of honour through High Priest Ananus (Ananias). 23 Soon after Marcus Valerius Barbatus replaced the high priest, 24 granting the position of high priest of the Great Temple, 25 and Mint of Mithra to Caiaphas the son in law of Ananus (Ananias), 26 who then ruled the position of High Priest for eighteen years, 27 without interruption from a Prefect or Procurator again. 28 In the same year, 29 following the great triumph of his adopted son Germanicus into Rome, 30 Tiberius learnt of the return of Holly High King Cú-Cúileann, 31 to Idumea and Galilea and his intervention on behalf of Ananias. 32 Livia Drusilla then suggested a plan and Tiberius recalled the Syrian legate, 33 whose name was Quintus Caecilius Metellus Creticus Silanus, 34 and replaced him with Gnaeus Calpurnius Piso, 35 of the infamous House of Piso (Pisa) of northern Italy, 36 and an exceedingly violent and cruel and arrogant man. 37 Tiberius then gave Piso an offer that if he could help rid the world, 38 of Germanicus and the Pontifex Maximus, 39 then he would be rewarded with great wealth and gold. 40 Tiberius then announced Germanicus as the new consul of Illyricum, 41 as well as commander of the armies to the east as well as north. 42 Thus Germanicus set off for his new mission and posting, 43 to help rid the empire of any signs of rebellion to the east.

C. 22

1 In the year known as 18 CE, 2 twelve hundred and eighteen years since the dawn of the Great Age, 3 Emperor Tiberius Augustus summonsed King Philipas Agrippa, 4 to come to Rome with Legate Gnaeus Calpurnius Piso of Syria. 5 Gnaeus Calpurnius Piso had already sent his son Marcus Calpurnius Piso, 6 as emissary to King Aenas (Antipas) of Nabatea, 7 with offering of peace and generous new terms. 8 Yet upon approaching Rome King Philipas Agrippa received word, 9 that soldiers loyal to Lucius Calpurnius Piso, 10 had killed his half brother in exile named Archelas, 11 and planned to falsely arrest him for the murder. 12 King Philipas Agrippa then abandoned Italy, 13 and returned to Damascus to receive word, 14 that his half brother King Aenas (Antipas), 15 had been falsely told by Marcus Calpurnius Piso, 16 he had been murdered by his half brother Philipas Agrippa. 17 Upon King Philipas Agrippa fleeing Italy before entering Rome, 18 Emperor Tiberius Augustus ordered his adopted son, 19 Nero Claudius Drusus Germanicus to assist Gnaeus Calpurnius Piso, 20 in defeating King Philipas Agrippa of Idumea and Galilea, 21 and aiding the ally of Rome of King Aenas (Antipas), 22 in exacting revenge for the murder. 23 When Holly High King Cú-Cúileann as Pontifex Maximus, 24 also known as the Great Prophet Yasiah (Joseph) of Yeb, 25 received word of the intrigues of Tiberius and the Pisans, 26 he immediately sent word to Nero

Claudius Drusus Germanicus, [27] that King Philipas Agrippa be innocent of the accusations, [28] and to delay his march until such rumours and falsities, [29] be resolved amongst the Nabatean kings, [30] lest a great region be plunged into war, [31] and hundreds of thousands of brave men die for a lie. [32] Holly High King Cú-Cúileann then sent his Praetorian prefect, [33] Lucius Cornelius Sulla as emissary to Aenas (Antipas), [34] to plead he listen to reason and cease preparing his army, [35] of over three hundred thousand for war. [36] Yet King Aenas (Antipas) would not be moved, [37] even upon the entreats of the highest priest and prophet, [38] as Gnaeus Calpurnius Piso through his son Marcus Calpurnius Piso, [39] had already assured King Aenus (Antipas) that he would recognise, [40] a united Nabatean Kingdom and Aenas (Antipas), [41] as Herod Antipas (Aenas) and great ally of Rome. [42] Upon the news Holly High King Cú-Cúileann, [43] also known as the Great Prophet Yasiah (Joseph) of Yeb, [44] did announce to the whole world that so certain of the innocence, [45] and character of King Philipas Agrippa he be, [46] that he did announce with agreement of Philipas, [47] that his son Jesus (Cú-Laoch) also known as Yahusiah, [48] be betrothed to Princess Mariamne (Mary) also known as Magdalene, [49] the beautiful young daughter, [50] of King Philipas Agrippa of Idumea and Galilea, [51] and that when she come of age then both shall be wed. [52] The news across the world of the betrothal was a shock, [53] for it was the first time the Cuilliaéan had recognised, [54] with such an honour as matrimony the blood of the Nabateans, [55] and the bloodlines of the ancient priests of Baal-Hamon, [56] and the bloodlines of the false prophets of Mithra, [57] through the blood of the Hasmoneans. [58] No greater honour had the Nabatean people been bestowed, [59] to know that one day one of their own become, [60] a King of kings and priest of all priests. [61] Thus King Aenas (Antipas) of Nabatea sent offerings, [62] of peace and goodwill towards such a historic union, [63] and his army ceased its preparations, [64] as Nero Claudius Drusus Germanicus returned to Illyria. [65] Upon news of the plan to incite civil war had failed, [66] Emperor Tiberius Augustus sent word for Holly High King Cú-Cúileann, [67] to come to Rome to assist in sacred duties. [68] Yet Cú-Cúileann as Pontifex Maximus politely declined, [69] saying that such a visit and call to ceremony, [70] risk usurping the works the emperor had already decreed, [71] through the Collegium Pontificum and Collegium Sacris Faciundis, [72] and the Collegium Epulonum and the sacred rites already assigned. [73] Caiphas the High Priest to the Great Temple of Mithra at Jerusalem, [74] and the former priests of Baal-Hamon did then suggest, [75] to celebrate the betrothal of Prince Jesus (Yahusiah), [76] to Princess Mariamne (Mary) also known as Magdalene, [77] that a great ecumenical council of all faiths be called to Jerusalem, [78] to bear witness to the extraordinary talents of Jesus, [79] for the fame and wonder of young Jesus and his knowledge of languages, [80] and particular the ancient hieroglyph wisdom of the Hyksos kings, [81] had already become legendary throughout the halls and libraries of the world. [82] So it was that the greatest ecumenical council of religions, 83 yet assembled in the history of the civilised world, 84 was convened to bear witness to the treasures of Jesus. 85 Caiphas the High Priest of Mithra did commence to proceedings, 86 by asking Jesus (Yahusiah) of his knowledge of Mithraism, 87 and which faith best represent the highest path to truth, 88 to which Jesus did reply that any faith which respects the truth of prophets, 89 and honours the rule of law and justice be worthy, 90 for there are many paths to the Divine but only one true source. 91 Other senior priests from the known world did then ask, 92 to hear the twelve year old prince speak to them in their own tongue. 93 For each question Jesus did reply with great wisdom, 94 that the priests began speaking to themselves that truly he be, 95 the reincarnation of the greatest of all prophets and saviour for the world. 96 Finally the priests of Amen-Ra asked Jesus of the greatest knowledge, 97 that he had deciphered from the texts of the ancient Hyksos kings, 98 to which Jesus did reply to love one another as much as you love the Divine, 99 for we may be many but we also be one and this be the greatest wisdom.

C. 23

1 In the year known as 19 CE, 2 twelve hundred and nineteen years since the dawn of the Great Age, 3 upon the announcement of the betrothal of Prince Jesus (Yahusiah), 4 to Nabatean and Hasmonean Princess Mariamne (Mary), 5 the Sicari leader Iudiah of Galilee pledged a blood oath of his people, 6 to protect the House of Holly High King Cú-Cúileann Yasiah (Joseph). 7 Thus the lands of Galilee around Sepphoris, 8 became impregnable against attack from any force, 9 but the Nabateans themselves. 10 Gamaliel the Elder was enraged at losing all of his Zealot army, 11 and so sought an alliance with his former enemy Simon Magus of Qumran. 12 At Qumran both Gamaliel the Elder and Simon Magus hatched a plan, 13 to counter and confuse the rising fame of Holly Prince Jesus (Yahusiah), 14 with Simon Magus declaring that while priests may be in awe of knowledge, 15 the people as sheep cannot discern truth from lies, 16 nor can they discern miracles from false magic. 17 Gamaliel the Elder agreed that the people be no more than sheep, 18 who yearn to be led by whomever looks to be a good shepherd, 19 even if they be the most bloodthirsty wolf. 20 Let us then create a religion led by wolves in sheep's clothing. 21 Simon Magus did then describe his vision for such a religion, 22 saying that people believe half-truths more than knowledge, 23 and false magic tricks more than true miracles of divinity, 24 thus let us create a religion for the masses, 25 and ignore the ancient priests of Baal and Mithra and Holly. 26 Lets us create our own scriptures and stories, 27 and give the masses the greatest of magic tricks, 28 and the worst of nightmares and fears, 29 for this is what the simplest of sheep seek, 30 and the key to controlling the world. 31 In the same year, 32 upon the failure of Tiberius to entrap Germanicus, 33 and the questioning of his adopted son to the falsities and lies of the Pisans, 34 Emperor Tiberius Augustus ordered Germanicus to Syria, 35 to arrest Gnaeus Calpurnius Piso and Marcus

Calpurnius Piso, 36 at their capital at Heliopolis (Antioch). 37 Yet when Germanicus and his legions entered Syria, 38 Gnaeus Calpurnius Piso sent his son forward to surrender, 39 with word that no resistance would Germanicus meet into Heliopolis. 40 Thus in respect of honourable surrender Nero Claudius Drusus Germanicus, 41 did enter Heliopolis (Antioch) to arrest Gnaeus Calpurnius Piso, 42 yet that night Germanicus did suffer and die from poisoning, 43 and immediately the legions in Syria and throughout the empire, 44 were in revolt at such treachery against a son of Rome. 45 Gnaeus Calpurnius Piso and Marcus Calpurnius Piso, 46 and the whole Pisan family were arrested in Syria, 47 and returned to Rome midst the greatest outcry for years. 48 Yet the night before Gnaeus Calpurnius Piso was due, 49 with his son before the Senate he and his son were poisoned. 50 As no one but the emperor or his mother could have caused the event, 51 the air of Rome was thick with the knowledge of conspiracy.

C. 24

1 In the year known as 20 CE, 2 twelve hundred and twenty years since the dawn of the Great Age, 3 Gnaeus Sentius Saturninus was appointed the new Legate of Syria, 4 as Tiberius Claudius Drusus the stepson of Emperor Tiberius, 5 remained as sole heir to the purple robes. 6 Yet neither Tiberius Augustus or Livia Drusilla were threatened, 7 by Claudius as they had been by his dead brother Germanicus, 8 for since his adoption he had remained afflicted by lunacy, 9 and much mockery was made of his deformed movement and slow wit. 10 Thus Livia Drusilla was happy to place Claudius unto the care, 11 of Praetorian Prefect Gaius Cornelius Lentulus, 12 and the Nasci and Protector of Rome. 13 Gaius Cornelius Lentulus then did cautiously teach Claudius, 14 the knowledge of administration and strategy. 15 For though Rome saw Claudius as the fool, 16 Gaius Cornelius sensed the brilliance of survival, 17 of an intelligent man midst a den of hungry wolves. 18 In the same year, 19 the alliance between Gamaliel the Elder and Simon Magus, 20 brought forth the shepherd son purchased by Zecheriah, 21 whose name was Yahuaniah (John), 22 also known as Johanan ben Zakkai and John the Baptist, 23 now a tall and strong young man dressed in skins, 24 and proclaimed him to be the true messiah of the world, 25 who could cast out demons by his words, 26 and heal the sick through the blessing of the water, 27 and the ritual of Baptism. 28 Soon people throughout the region and even Asia, 29 began flocking to witness the miracles of the Baptist, 30 as hysterical people that claimed to be possessed, 31 appeared to be cured by the words and hands of the Baptist, 32 and people who claimed great illness testified to be healed. 33 Gamaliel the Elder and Simon Magus even promoted further claims, 34 that Yahuaniah (John) could control the weather, 35 and turn dust into gold coins, 36 and a few fish and loaves into a feast for thousands. 37 Thus the people of the region soon forgot the stories of knowledge, 38 and reason and wisdom of Jesus (Yahusiah), 39 and yearned to witness

the daily entertainment of miracles, 40 of John the Baptist (Johanan ben Zakkai), 41 and to be scared and frightened by his sermons, 42 of a coming destruction of the world, 43 by an emotional and spiteful god that loved those that followed the Baptist, 44 but would subject disbelievers to an eternity of torture and hate.

C. 25

1 In the year known as 21 CE, 2 twelve hundred and twenty one years since the dawn of the Great Age, 3 soon after the celebration of her 79th birthday, 4 Livia Drusilla became violently ill. 5 Tiberius Augustus implored that his mother grant him permission, 6 to seek the skill of the Holly Therapeutae to help cure her illness, 7 yet she steadfastly refused and instead sought counsel, 8 from every soothsayer, auger and psychic in Rome and Italy. 9 Yet none could seem to remedy her state. 10 Tiberius Augustus even sought aid from his tutor Lucius Seius Strabo, 11 himself advanced with age yet even he could offer no comfort. 12 Emperor Tiberius Augustus then ordered his mother be moved to Capri, 13 and left Rome himself to be by her bedside. 14 Thus Praetorian Prefect Gaius Cornelius Lentulus, 15 Nasci and Protector of Rome became then for a time, 16 the most powerful man throughout the Roman Empire. 17 Yet many did resent the power of Gaius Cornelius Lentulus, 18 and sought the means and way to reduce his power, 19 without causing the rage of Tiberius. 20 Lucius Calpurnius Piso the wealthy tyrant and governor of Hispania, 21 and brother of the executed Gnaeus Calpurnius Piso, 22 did object to many wealthy Senators, 23 and sought an alliance with Lucius Visellius Varro, 24 and Marcus Licinius Crassus and General Gaius Silius Aulus, 25 for the right time to strike against the Praetorian Prefect.

C. 26

1 In the year known as 22 CE, 2 twelve hundred and twenty two years since the dawn of the Great Age, 3 upon news of the severe illness of Livia Drusilla, 4 and the retirement of Tiberius Augustus to her side at Capri, 5 Holly High King Cú-Cúileann Yasiah (Joseph), 6 and King Philipas Agrippa of Idumea and Galilea, 7 did conduct a lavish feast and celebration, 8 for the matrimony of Prince Jesus (Yahusiah) aged sixteen, 9 to Princess Mariamne also known as Mary at aged thirteen. 10 Jesus (Yahusiah) objected to his father the Holly King, 11 at being forced to marry a young girl he had only met once, 12 and without the choice to determine his own fate and destiny. 13 Yet Holly High King Cú-Cúileann Yasiah (Joseph) reminded him, 14 of the importance of his blood line and the significance of the union, 15 and that their progeny would be the unity of the oldest lines, 16 of priests and kings of all civilisation and history combined. 17 Yet Jesus persisted saying a union without love can produce only thorns, 18 nor can a world be sustained on the strength of blood alone, 19 but only upon the equality of law and truth of heart. 20 Holly High King Cú-Cúileann Yasiah (Joseph) agreed with his wise son, 21 but reminded him of the precarious state of the world, 22 and the necessity for the Holly as

custodians of the mind of the Divine, 23 to renew and strengthen bonds between all priests and prophets, 24 as such men as Gamaliel and Simon Magus use John the Baptist, 25 as a weapon to dispense falsities and errors of law and history. 26 After the ceremonies and matrimonial feast of Jesus and Mariamne, 27 and on account of the age of the bride and groom, 28 being too young to consummate such union, 29 Holly High King Cú-Cúileann Yasiah (Joseph) did order Jesus (Yahusiah), 30 to remain in the hospitality of King Philipas Agrippa at Damascus, 31 that he may become more acquainted with his beautiful new wife. 32 At first Jesus resisted and protested at his father controlling his destiny. 33 Yet after the first week Jesus began to acquaint himself with Mary (Mariamne), 34 and within several weeks they became close friends.

C. 27

1 In the year known as 22 CE, 2 twelve hundred and twenty two years since the dawn of the Great Age, 3 the fame and influence of John the Baptist (Johanan ben Zakkai), 4 had grown even beyond the expectations of his puppet masters, 5 in the formation of a wholly false religion, 6 based on magic tricks of awe and nightmare stories of fear. 7 The speeches and words of a vengeful and jealous god, 8 did appeal to the poor and dispossessed as well as the angry, 9 as they sought vengeance against Rome. 10 The demands that all submit to such an intolerant and mentally ill god, 11 did also hold with the people as the Baptist be the first prophet, 12 in the history of the world to demand that all priests, 13 hold themselves accountable as equal to the people, 14 and not above the law. 15 Yet this did not apply to Gamaliel the Elder nor Simon Magus, 16 for the priests of Qumran now did hide themselves as mendicants, 17 and condemned any priests who possessed wealth and did not submit, 18 to absolute poverty in the service of the people. 19 Thus so great was the popular belief of the masses, 20 assisted by the wickedly false testimony of paid testifiers, 21 that even the priests of Baal-Hamon and Mithra, 22 felt compelled to have themselves baptised by John the Baptist. 23 Even Holly High King Cú-Cúileann Yasiah (Joseph) felt great pressure, 24 that he called upon his eldest son Prince Jesus (Yahusiah), 25 to visit the Baptist and also be baptised. 26 Upon such news Gamaliel the Elder and the priests of Qumran, 27 did spread the news of the arrival of Jesus to meet John, 28 that many tens of thousand lined the banks of the River Jordan, 29 to witness such a historic encounter. 30 Jesus (Cú-Laoch) with a small troop of Praetorian did approach the place, 31 where John the Baptist was blessing midst the waters, 32 and did kneel in respect with head bowed in the river, 33 before the baptist as witnessed by the crowd. 34 Whereupon the Baptist did speak for all to hear saying: 35 Cousin you grace me with your presence, 36 is it not I who should be baptised by you? 37 Behold before me is the great holly messiah. 38 Surely it shall be by your voice and not mine, 39 that the heavens shall open and the angels anoint you themselves. 40 In response Jesus did arise and look

directly at the Baptist saying: 41 I did not come here to dishonour nor be dishonoured, 42 I did not call these people to bear witness, 43 but am here present on account of duty. 44 If this be your will then I shall depart. 45 Yet as Jesus sought to move away the Baptist seized his arm, 46 and grabbed hold of his hand then holding it next to his. 47 The hands of the Baptist were thick and coarse, 48 yet the hands of Jesus were smooth and manicured and as soft as a child. 49 The Baptist then did speak saying: 50 If you truly be the messiah worthy to lead my people, 51 then I shall baptise you and bow before you, 52 for forty nights hence we shall fast, 53 and if you be the anointed messenger of the Divine Creator, 54 then the angels shall give you strength and courage. 55 The Baptist had therefore challenged Jesus. 56 As a Prince of the most sacred and ancient bloodlines of all humanity, 57 Jesus had never before slept in anything less than the softest bed, 58 he had never been without a meal of the finest meats and delicacies, 59 nor had he ever been too cold or too warm, 60 or without devoted attendants to care for his every need, 61 or the fiercest Praetorian to defend him to the death. 62 Yet the Baptist had been forced from the youngest of age, 63 to live like a wild beast and hide from the Nabateans and Romans, 64 to adapt to the harsh sun and wind and even wear animal skins. 65 Yet to decline such a challenge before tens of thousands of witnesses, 66 would disgrace his father and countless ancestors, 67 even as to the dangers and uncertainties of such a challenge. 68 Thus Prince Jesus also known as Yahusiah, 69 did accept the challenge of the Baptist, 70 and the crowd watched as the Baptist and Jesus, 71 departed together across to the East bank of the river Jordan, 72 and into the unknown wilderness and desert.

C. 28

1 The first day in the wilderness the Baptist took Jesus, 2 to a small grove with a fresh water stream surrounded by olive and fruit trees. 3 There they did sit and pray in the manner of the ancient psalms, 4 and venerations for which Jesus was familiar. 5 By the end of the first day the pain of hunger had come. 6 But Jesus did not speak of relief. 7 Only when the Baptist did wet his lips, 8 did Jesus allow himself the touch of the water. 9 The second day the Baptist repeated the same, 10 as the roar of hunger did churn in the belly of Jesus. 11 By the third day the hunger had been replaced by a lightness of head, 12 that made the eyes of Jesus feel heavy. 13 Then John the Baptist did take Jesus to an exposed dusty plain, 14 where only a solitary bush sprung from the earth. 15 There the Baptist sat and began picking the berries from the bush, 16 giving an equal portion to Jesus. 17 Upon consuming the berries Jesus did become violently ill, 18 yet the Baptist also consumed the berries but did not become sick. 19 Thus as the Baptist remained seated in the morning and the evening, 20 to eat the berries Jesus too did eat. 21 By the seventh day the fair skin of Jesus was scorched and blistered, 22 his fine brown hair dirty and matted. 23 Then the Baptist did take Jesus to a high mountain, 24 overlooking the valley of the River

Jordan. 25 When they were seated the Baptist did speak for the first time, 26 asking why Jesus did torture himself so. 27 Jesus replied that if it be the will of the Divine, 28 he be tested then so be it. 29 The Baptist did then reply that he had lived in the desert all his life, 30 and it be four hundred days instead of forty, 31 then on dust alone he could live, 32 but Jesus as a prince had not suffered for any want or desire. 33 Jesus did then agree that his life had been one of privilege, 34 yet everything about his life his teachings and heritage be true. 35 To which the Baptist did reply that indeed it be true, 36 that his father be an unknown shepherd who sold him to Zecheriah, 37 but what right then do the houses of priest claim, 38 they and they alone interpret the mind and will of the Divine? 39 Is it you believe yourself to be the true messiah? 40 To which Jesus replied I am my fathers' son. 41 The Baptist enraged then challenged Jesus that if he think himself a god, 42 then call on the angels of heaven to cushion his fall, 43 and throw himself from the cliff. 44 But Jesus would not be tempted nor bullied by the words of the Baptist. 45 Again the Baptist challenged Jesus that if he think himself a god, 46 and the words of the Baptist be false then call upon the heavens, 47 to strike the Baptist dead. 48 But Jesus would not be tempted nor bullied by the words of the Baptist. 49 Then after two days the Baptist took him to a lush grove, 50 where he tempted Jesus with the fruit trees which Jesus resisted. 51 Finally, the Baptist returned Jesus to the dusty plain and the single bush. 52 As each day passed whatever the Baptist would eat and do, 53 Jesus would do and follow also. 54 As each day passed Jesus grew stronger in mind, 55 and the Baptist grew more frustrated. 56 Finally on the thirtieth day the Baptist enquired of Jesus, 57 cousin, what do you know of the truth of god's wisdom? 58 Jesus did then speak of ancient scripture and custom, 59 of the wisdom of Akhenaten as Moses and Hyksos kings, 60 of Xerxes and Artaxerxes and the Great Prophets of Yeb, 61 to which the Baptist replied, 62 that he respected the discipline and knowledge of such custom, 63 but cousin we both are schooled in deeper wisdom, 64 with you in a history that is not fable, 65 and with my teaching into the nature of men and control. 66 What then is the real truth of god's wisdom? 67 To which Jesus spoke of other cultures scripture, 68 to which the Baptist replied that he too could quote other scripture by rote, 69 but this not be his question for remembering be different to knowing. 70 Jesus did ask then what he meant by his question, 71 to which the Baptist replied that Jesus may be the true Messiah by blood, 72 and as of the Cuilliaéan the Divine Corner stone, 73 but you have experienced nothing of the truth of god's wisdom. 74 The Baptist then remained silent for the final nine days, 75 until the end of the forty days. 76 Out of the wilderness the two men did come, 77 with Jesus unrecognisable as a Crown Prince, 78 on account of his tattered clothes and animal fur for warmth and protection, 79 and his gaunt and dirty frame. 80 Unto the river Jordan the Baptist did take him, 81 and anointed him as promised. 82 Thereupon Jesus vanished into the crowd and disappeared, 83 walking past

Praetorian Lucius Cornelius Sulla who did not recognise him. 84 After three days from emerging from the wilderness, 85 Lucius Cornelius Sulla did demand to know the location of Jesus, 86 to which the Baptist refused to reply. 87 Upon hearing of the disappearance of his son, 88 and the reluctance of the Baptist to speak, 89 Holly High King Cú-Cúileann requested that King Philipas Agrippa, 90 arrest John the Baptist that it not be seen as an attack by Rome. 91 There in the prison of King Philipas Agrippa, 92 the Baptist remained Silent and in prayer 93 as Gamaliel and Simon Magus sought to ferment riots, 94 and until the riddle of the disappearance of Jesus was solved.

Book 21

Age of the Nazarenes

[22 - 69 CE]

C. 1

In the year known as 22 CE, 2 twelve hundred and twenty two years since the dawn of the Great Age, 3 after forty days in the desert with John the Baptist, 4 where Jesus (Yahusiah) had been tempted and tested, 5 the young prince did use his changed appearance, 6 to escape from his guard and travel north along the ancient highway, 7 along the Jordan Valley towards the great city of Damascus, 8 where his young wife and father in law awaited his return. 9 As he walked upon a road he had travelled many times yet never on foot, 10 the words of the Baptist and his challenge continued to haunt him, 11 that for all he knew and all he sensed here for the first time, 12 he did walk amongst the people who accepted him or denied him, 13 not on blood or status or fear or promise but on character and trust alone. 14 Thus upon the road to Damascus Jesus at but sixteen years of age, 15 did resolve to himself to learn of people and of the nature to be a man, 16 to learn of ancient cultures and see the ancient cities, 17 and to witness the lands he had only read about in scripture, 18 before he would accept any further direction from his father. 19 Upon arriving at Damascus Jesus did not return to the palace, 20 as he had originally intended but walked to the markets, 21 where using his natural skills of language and arithmetic, 22 he soon found himself joining a caravan as an interpreter. 23 Thus began a great journey East along the Asian silk road. 24 The caravan made its way first across the Syrian deserts, 25 then South-East along the Euphrates to the famous city of Babylon, 26 through the gates of Ishtar to witness a wonder of the ancient world. 27 There in Babylon Jesus did see the ziggurat of Nebuchadnezzar, 28 and the Hanging Gardens and the great library and temples. 29 The Caravan did then travel along the River Tigris and then east, 30 unto the great city of Susa the capital of Parthia. 31 In Susa Jesus did encounter again the Magi priests. 32 Upon speaking with the priests and sharing his knowledge, 33 of wisdom even the priests of Zoroaster did not know, 34 they recognised this be the famous Holly boy prince of the temple. 35 Jesus pleaded they each swear a solemn oath not to reveal his presence, 36 for he sought on his journey to be his own witness. 37 Upon accepting the entreat to pledge the Magic priests did then share, 38 the truth of how they saw the Holly (Cuilliaéan), 39 as truly the greatest priests of wisdom and revelation, 40 but the worst of tyrants and corruptors of the world, 41 for they saw themselves as gods amongst animals, 42 and judged the gifts of heaven not worthy for the people. 43 Thus the misery and evil of the world, 44 did in part come and thrive because of the Holly, 45 and their arrogance towards mankind. 46 Jesus (Yahusiah) did thank the priests for their honesty, 47 and so agreed to stay with them a while, 48 and teach them all he knew.

C. 2

1 Since the arrest of John the Baptist, 2 Holly High King Cú-Cúileann as Pontifex Maximus, 3 also known as the Great Prophet Yasiah (Joseph) of Yeb, 4 remained distraught at the disappearance of Jesus (Yahusiah), 5 his eldest son and Holly crown prince. 6 Pontifex Praetorian Prefect Lucius Cornelius Sulla, 7 urged caution on account of few knowing the true cause, 8 of the arrest of the Baptist. 9 Holly High King Cú-Cúileann then ordered Lucius Cornelius Sulla, 10 to see that Legate Gnaeus Sentius Saturninus issue orders, 11 that all followers of the Baptist be considered the enemy of Rome, 12 and that such a religion be forbidden as contrary to heaven, 13 thus giving reason for such a public arrest. 14 Yet many tens of thousands of the followers of the Baptists remained in Palestine, 15 and Simon Magus called upon all pilgrims to Qumran, 16 for his protection and a shield against the forces of Rome, 17 as Gamaliel once again fled unto the mountains of Galilee. 18 To console Mariamne (Mary) the daughter of King Philipas Agrippa, 19 and the Virgin wife of Jesus (Yahusiah), 20 Holly High King Cú-Cúileann send his second child Matia (Salome), 21 being of the same age as the Virgin Mary (Mariamne), 22 to the court of King Philipas Agrippa. 23 At the palace in Damascus Matia (Salome) soon became close friends, 24 with the Virgin Mary (Mariamne) and her younger sister, 25 whose name was Anna (Enygeus) and the youngest, 26 and only other child of King Philipas Agrippa, 27 who was already famous for possessing the sight of an oracle. 28 Pontifex Praetorian Prefect Lucius Cornelius Sulla, 29 then sent out thirty five pairs of his most experienced Praetorian, 30 to travel to Egypt and Parthia and beyond, 31 to seek out carefully all knowledge of the whereabouts of Jesus.

C. 3

1 The Magi priests at Susa who had sworn to Jesus (Yahusiah), 2 they would keep his identity and travels hidden, 3 did plead with him to travel east from Susa, 4 into the Great Zagros Mountains, 5 up through to Borujerd then east to Kashan, 6 then north to the most sacred city of Kum (Qom), 7 to meet the most senior of all priests of Zoroaster, 8 that he might share and expound the greatest knowledge of heaven, 9 kept from the world by the Cuilliaéan for thousands of years. 10 Jesus agreed and so did travel in disguise as a Zoroastrian priest. 11 At Kum (Qom) Kum the most senior of the Magi priests celebrated, 12 the

arrival of Jesus (Yahusiah) and the true sharing of divine wisdom. 13 Jesus (Yahusiah) again entreated that the priests swear, 14 to keep his visit and journey a secret, 15 that he may honour his quest to seek and know the truth of divine wisdom. 16 For many days and nights Jesus did share all he knew of Holly wisdom, 17 and the most senior Magi shared all they knew of the wisdom, 18 of Zarathustra (Zoroaster) and his great works with Hammurabi. 19 Jesus also did witness many religions from other parts of the world, 20 the ancient Jains and their enlightened vision of a conscious universe, 21 and the importance of refraining from any harm, 22 the Confucian monks of India and Asia, 23 and their mastery at humility and compassion and rhetoric, 24 yet without negative judgement to happiness and life, 25 the Indian Brahmins with their extraordinary poetry and rich stories, 26 of cosmic battles and constant renewal and rebirth. 27 Jesus then did leave the Zoroastrian priests and travelled north, 28 to the ancient ruins of city of Ray (on Caspian Sea), 29 in the ancient Kingdom of Hyrcania which means land of the wolves. 30 There Jesus did meet a colony of Jains and lived with them for a time, 31 refraining from consuming the flesh of any animal. 32 In the year known as 23 CE, 33 twelve hundred and twenty three years since the dawn of the Great Age, 34 from Ray Jesus did travel east to Meru (city of Mary), 35 a most sacred city for the Brahman poets. 36 At Meru Jesus did spend time with the Brahmans, 37 in learning their poems and discussing the nature of re-birth, 38 and the migration and learning of the soul. 39 Jesus did then travel with the Brahmins, 40 East and then South-East from Meru, 41 into Bagrām and the great valley of Panjsher in Aria, 42 then south-east through the Hindu Kush mountains, 43 to the great city of Gazak (Kabul). 44 From Gazak (Kabul) Jesus did then did travel south-east to the city of Mathura, 45 and the centre of worship of Krishna and the great Temple of Keshav Dev. 46 In Mathura Jesus did spend time with the greatest of Brahman Priests, 47 on the nature of the world and god's wisdom. 48 The senior Brahman priests being well regarded, 49 for their pious ways and frugality of possessions, 50 and the non-harm of any living creature, 51 and the refrain from partaking in the eating of meat, 52 or in any celebration that sacrificed animals or worshipped cannibalism, 53 were amazed at the wisdom and character of Jesus, 54 that word soon spread that Krishna was reborn in the form of Jesus, 55 tens of thousands flocked to see the living Krishna, 56 until fearing his identity would soon be revealed, 57 and he would be forced to return home, 58 Jesus did leave Mathura and travelled south shaving his long hair, 59 to hide and travel with a caravan of monks, 60 on a sacred pilgrimage of fasting and prayer.

C. 4

1 In the year known as 24 CE, 2 twelve hundred and twenty four years since the dawn of the Great Age, 3 Lucius Aelius (Seius) Strabo the famous historian and philosopher from Pontus, 4 and the beloved teacher and life long adviser of Tiberius Augustus, 5 did give up the ghost. 6 Emperor

Tiberius was distraught upon the news of the death of Strabo, 7 and returned briefly to Rome to oversee the funeral, 8 and console his friend and the only son of Strabo, 9 whose name was Lucius Aelius Seianus (Sejanus). 10 Unlike his father Lucius Aelius Seianus was an administrator, 11 and so in honour of his father Tiberius Augustus ordered, 12 the recall of Legate Gnaeus Sentius Saturninus of Syria, 13 and appointed Lucius Aelius Seianus (Sejanus) as Legate, 14 of the Province of Syria and head of the procurator, 15 of the Great Temple Mint of Mithra at Jerusalem. 16 As Lucius Aelius Seianus had also been born in Pontus, 17 the Nabateans and people of Palestine and Syria called him, 18 the Pontus Pilates meaning the pillager and pirate from Pontus, 19 on account of his coldness and lack of care to the people. 20 In the same year, 21 Marcus Licinius Crassus and General Gaius Silius Aulus, 22 supported by Lucius Calpurnius Piso and Lucius Visellius Varro, 23 did move against Praetorian Prefect Gaius Cornelius Lentulus, 24 by seeking to bring legions to Rome to usurp the Praetorian. 25 Yet Tiberius now nursing his dying mother and without his tutor, 26 did trust Gaius Cornelius Lentulus against the rebels, 27 and ordered the plot crushed and the ringleaders executed. 28 Thus Marcus Licinius Crassus and General Gaius Silius Aulus, 29 were executed and all their properties seized so that, 30 neither family survived beyond these last generations, 31 and Praetorian Prefect Gaius Cornelius Lentulus, 32 strengthened his position as the most powerful man of Rome.

C. 5

1 In the year known as 24 CE, 2 twelve hundred and twenty four years since the dawn of the Great Age, 3 Jesus did travel east from Mathura to the Kingdom of Kosala, 4 unto the famed sacred garden city of Saketa (Ayodhya), 5 founded by the revered Lord Rama who claimed to be Vishna, 6 where the most beautiful of gardens full of every species of plant, 7 and animal and beast did live in a perfectly made garden of Eden, 8 in which any man or woman could live happily on its produce alone. 9 King Sihahanu the leader of the Sakya people and King of Kosala, 10 did hear about the young Jesus (Yahusiah) and his remarkable wisdom, 11 and summonsed him to his palace midst the grandest gardens, 12 where he beseeched Jesus be tutor for his eldest son Suddhodana, 13 in exchange for a handsome fortune as he was unaware of the true identity, 14 of Jesus and the truth that as Holly Crown Prince, 15 he stood to inherit the greatest fortune of the ancient world. 16 Jesus declined the wealth but accepted the request, 17 on the conditions that it be for only one year, 18 that he be permitted to live within the royal gardens, 19 that the scribes teach him to read Sanskrit, 20 that he be permitted to read the ancient scrolls or wisdom, 21 and that the king not question his methods of teaching. 22 King Sihahanu agreed and the mind of the young Suddhodana, 23 was placed in the care of his new tutor Jesus (Yahusiah). 24 Jesus took Suddhodana deep into the royal gardens, 25 to an ancient giant fig tree believed to have been planted, 26 by Lord Rama himself upon founding the

gardens. 27 Under the shade and protection of the fig tree Jesus did say, 28 that this be the place where all lessons and knowledge shall be revealed, 29 for the divine does not simply reside in temples, 30 nor in the grandest of libraries and scriptoriums, 31 but in the hearts and minds of those who seek the truth, 32 and the right way and path of life and rebirth. 33 Suddhodana then asked Jesus what be the right way and path, 34 to which Jesus replied that the ancient Hyksos Kings of Egypt believed, 35 all beings who die to their most base spirit or Ha have immortal life, 36 but only those beings that die to base mind of Ka have divine immortality. 37 Suddhodana then asked Jesus what is base mind to which he replied, 38 that base mind be those emotions and urges that weaken men, 39 such as hate or ignorance or dishonesty or depression or hate, 40 or anger or self doubt or fear for all of these lead to pain. 41 Yet the ancient Egyptians believed in an answer to die and be reborn, 42 free from being an animal or base mind or arrogance, 43 they called Ha-Ka-Ba-La-Ah: 44 Ha being the spirit of existence of all things, 45 Ka being the base spirit of animals in body, 46 Ba being the higher soul and mind, 47 La being the highest mind and soul, 48 Ah being the perfected enlightened being. 49 Suddhodana then asked Jesus how one might become enlightened, 50 to which Jesus replied that the Hyksos believed a mind full, 51 cannot think nor a heart silent cannot feel, 52 thus there be eight correct emotions beginning with right attitude, 53 then respect then honesty then courage then enthusiasm then compassion, 54 then good cheer then joy. 55 Suddhodana then asked Jesus that surely with such knowledge, 56 he must be an enlightened god who need not be a humble teacher, 57 but the ruler of great empires and armies. 58 Surely the ultimate power is to know the mind of the gods, 59 to which Jesus replied that to be a king or a god is nothing, 60 nor is enlightenment of the mind of god the ultimate power, 61 but a man who could be a great messiah or god who chooses to be more, 62 being a man of humility and compassion. 63 Suddhodana then asked Jesus saying Master are you a happy man, 64 to which he replied that this is the question for which he could not yet answer. 65 Thus Jesus (Yahusiah) continued to live in the gardens, 66 and Suddhodana continued to become a fine and wise student, 67 until upon the anniversary of the year Jesus did give notice, 68 and departed south toward the ancient city of Mathas Goa, 69 upon the western coast of India.

C. 6

1 After three years of searching for Jesus (Yahusiah), 2 the men of Lucius Cornelius Sulla could find no trace. 3 Holly High King Cú-Cúileann remained deeply melancholy, 4 refusing to accept the worse yet not preparing for the future. 5 Yacobiah (Jacob) also known as James the Just had grown up to be, 6 the most loyal and dedicated of sons, 7 as Matia continued to keep the Virgin Mary and her sister Anna company. 8 John the Baptist remained alive and in prison, 9 as rumours of the disappearance of Jesus had grown in strength, 10 that King Philipas Agrippa urged Holly

High King Cú-Cúileann (Joseph), 11 to act lest the fanatical zealot and other enemies strike, 12 believing weakness through such inaction. 13 Holly High King Cú-Cúileann as Pontifex Maximus, 14 also known as the Great Prophet Yasiah (Joseph) of Yeb, 15 did finally relent and give the order to destroy the Zionists. 16 In the year known as 25 CE, 17 twelve hundred and twenty four years since the dawn of the Great Age, 18 the pilgrims of the Baptist defending Qumran had dwindled to a few, 19 when the forces of the Roman Legate Lucius Aelius Seianus, 20 also known as Pontius Pilates and aided by Pontifex Praetorians, 21 did strike Qumran and destroyed it to its foundations, 22 capturing Simon Magus and a few priests alive. 23 Soon after the forces of King Philipas Agrippa, 24 did utterly destroy the Zionist army of Gamaliel, 25 also capturing him alive after finding him hiding in a grave. 26 Yet Simon Magus and the Baptists had one final act of revenge, 27 by circulating the claim that the Holly High King did falsely claim the Baptist, 28 did murder crown prince Jesus when in fact he did commit suicide. 29 Thus soon such rumours had spread across the ancient world even to Rome, 30 where Praetorian Prefect Gaius Cornelius Lentulus, 31 did ask if such stories be true and when the Pontifex Maximus, 32 would then name his son Yacobiah (Jacob), 33 also known as James the Just as his new heir. 34 Yet when Holly High King Cú-Cúileann did visit Damascus, 35 Mariamne known now as the Virgin Mary refused to yield, 36 and marry Yacobiah (Jacob) recalling the visions of Anna, 37 who protested and proclaimed Jesus was still alive.

C. 7

1 In the beautiful city of Goa upon the coast of India, 2 Jesus (Yahusiah) did first contemplate his time and meditations, 3 midst the greatest gardens of the ancient world at Saketa (Ayodhya). 4 From the many lessons under the ancient fig tree, 5 which King Sihahanu of the Sakya people ordained the Bodhi Tree, 6 as the tree of awakening and enlightenment for his son Suddhodana, 7 and all the people of Kosala and all the princes of the house of Gautama. 8 It was under the Bodhi Tree that Jesus (Yahusiah) came to recognise, 9 the deeper truth of the mystery of the trinity of the Hyksos in the relations, 10 of father, mother and child and in the relation of birth, death and rebirth. 11 For Jesus (Yahusiah) did now see the truth of the wisdom of life as a dream, 12 that the Divine Creator of all depends upon creation for existence, 13 for the Divine Creator be the father and the creation and the spirit of creation, 14 thus the Divine Creator be the one and the many and the sacred trinity. 15 It was then that Jesus did commit himself to the three sacred vows, 16 in the manner of his ancestors the ancient Hyksos kings, 17 of Simplicity and the solemn promise not to be ensnared by the world, 18 of Charity and love of all living beings and knowledge, 19 of Humility in embracing the greatest state of his existence as a man. 20 Soon after Jesus (Yahusiah) began to teach the monks and pilgrims at Goa, 21 where he soon became known as a bodhisattva and great mind, 22 and

many tens of thousands flocked to Goa to witness his teachings. 23 Soon even kings and princes of India and nearby lands did come, 24 to witness the mahasattva and great bodhisattva, 25 who spoke of the end of suffering through the end of attachment, 26 and the sanctity of all life and the purpose of all existence. 27 Yet when a Roman praetor did come to witness the lessons of Jesus, 28 Jesus did fear his identity as a holly prince would soon be discovered, 29 and the next day Jesus left Goa by boat and headed west, 30 unto the city of Aden in the south of the lands of Arabia.

C. 8

1 In the year known as 26 CE, 2 twelve hundred and twenty six years since the dawn of the Great Age, 3 Holly High King Cú-Cúileann as Pontifex Maximus, 4 also known as the Great Prophet Yasiah (Joseph) of Yeb, 5 did announce the mourning of the loss of his son Jesus. 6 A great sadness came across the whole world and even Rome, 7 as many had hoped that Jesus would be the saviour and prophet, 8 that would help restore law and end the tyranny of the bankers, 9 and merchants who continued to enslave so many through debts and bonds. 10 Holly High King Cú-Cúileann Yasiah (Joseph) did then name, 11 his second son Yacobiah (Jacob) also known as James the Just, 12 as the new Holly Crown Prince and heir. 13 Upon the refusal of the Virgin Mary to permit her matrimony to be annulled, 14 King Philipas Agrippa announced that his youngest and only second child, 15 named Anna be betrothed to James (Jacob). 16 Despite the pronouncement the mood of all Palestine remained sombre, 17 as to the tragic loss and death of Jesus, 18 until the wedding feast of James (Jacob) and Anna. 19 Yet the problem remained as to the fate to befall those claimed responsible, 20 in the form of John the Baptist and Gamaliel and Simon Magus. 21 Praetorian Prefect Lucius Cornelius Sulla urged a swift execution, 22 to cut off the rise of the Zionists who still held hope of freeing their leaders, 23 yet Holly High King Cú-Cúileann Yasiah (Joseph) remained hesitant, 24 as both Virgin Mary (Mariamne) and Anna remained firm, 25 that Jesus would return within seven years of his absence. 26 Nor could Holly High King Cú-Cúileann bring himself to condemn such men, 27 despite the loss of his son if not one strip of proof of culpability yet be found. 28 Thus he urged caution until evidence as to life or death present itself.

C. 9

1 In the city of Aden upon the southern Arabian coast, 2 Jesus (Yahusiah) did spend some time with Arab holy men, 3 learning and discussing their beliefs of the gods of the desert, 4 and the divine judge of life and death known as El-Alla (Allah). 5 The Arab holy men also possessed extraordinary knowledge, 6 of the origins of mankind which had been passed down, 7 from the priests of the holy city of Ma'Rab, 8 who claimed to be descended from the first civilisations, 9 that men were formed not by the divine but flesh and blood gods, 10 who made men first to be slaves in the mines, 11 yet when the

first men showed they possessed a soul, 12 the flesh and blood gods then made second man, 13 and filled him with greed and hate and fear, 14 by giving him a home and fields to grow, 15 but forever in fear that it would all be taken. 16 Yet a third race of men were born unlike any other, 17 who came from the west and the sacred isles, 18 and taught men to remember their spirit. 19 This third race of men were giants as were the first, 20 but with red skin and horns and with the greatest mind, 21 for they were created not by the grey gods themselves, 22 but by serpent and reptilian gods banished to the sacred island. 23 By which time the fourth and final race of men were born, 24 who were the most bloodthirsty and cruel and arrogant of all, 25 for the flesh and blood gods made them in their own image, 26 and they were taught to fear and hate the third race of men. 27 After learning the origins of the four races of men, 28 the Arab holy men implored that Jesus (Yahusiah) did travel north, 29 to the most sacred city for all Arabs at Al-Baqa (Mekka), 30 which they called Sacred Altar and the Doorway to Heaven. 31 Jesus (Yahusiah) did travel north to Al-Baqa (Mekka), 32 where he met the Keeper of Time and Celestial Bodies, 33 and was explained the working of the most ancient celestial calendar, 34 called Ka Bakka or the Doorway of the Spirit of Allah, 35 a great circular time piece that through the light of the sun, 36 and light of the moon did record time for thousands of years, 37 using the shadow and shape of the circular Ka Bakka temple. 38 Around the Ka Bakka was then arranged a great wheel of stone ridges, 39 divided into twelve segments so that time could be divided, 40 by the shadows cast from the circular temple. 41 The Keeper of Time and Celestial Bodies then permitted Jesus, 42 to step into the wheel of time and then to visit the sacred Ka Bakka, 43 for the Arab people over thousands of years to step onto such sacred soil, 44 unless one was a priest of the Keepers was the ultimate transgression, 45 against the laws of Allah and to even be an Arab, 46 and even to walk against time was a supreme curse against ones soul, 47 and a curse for hundreds of generations of ones tribe and name. 48 Thus Jesus spent time with the priests of Al-Baqa (Mekka), 49 and then departed westward to the coast, 50 where Arab merchants transported Jesus across to Egypt, 51 and through the ancient channel from the Red Sea, 52 to Karnak and Upper Egypt.

C. 10

1 In the year known as 27 CE, 2 twelve hundred and twenty seven years since the dawn of the Great Age, 3 James the Just also known as Yacobiah (Jacob) and Anna (Enygeus), 4 did give birth to a son they named Bel and Beliah. 5 Holly High King Cú-Cúileann Yasiah (Joseph) was overjoyed, 6 and King Philipas Agrippa and his brother King Aenas (Antipas), 7 declared it a sacred holiday and amnesty as celebration. 8 Simeon the son of Gamaliel and the Zionist leaders then demanded, 9 that John the Baptist, Gamaliel the Elder and Simon Magus, 10 be forgiven and released on account of the promised amnesty, 11 yet King Philipas Agrippa refused saying there be no amnesty for madness. 12 Simeon and the other Zionists leaders then began a

campaign of terror, 13 such that the world had never before seen such insanity and manipulation, 14 where young men and women were encouraged to commit suicide, 15 and seek to kill as many innocent people in the same process, 16 even attacking and disrupting the Great Temple Mint of Mithra at Jerusalem. 17 Roman Legate Lucius Aelius Seianus also known as Pontius Pilates, 18 called upon Praetorian Prefect Lucius Cornelius Sulla, 19 to petition Holly High King Cú-Cúileann Yasiah (Joseph) to act, 20 lest such a threat did grow across the Roman Empire. 21 High Priest Caiaphas did then suggest that as John the Baptist, 22 and Gamaliel the Elder and Simon Magus be not Roman citizens, 23 they be tried according to the laws of Mithra and the Great Temple. 24 In the year known as 28 CE, 25 twelve hundred and twenty eight years since the dawn of the Great Age, 26 and the sixth year since the disappearance of Jesus, 27 Caiaphas summonsed all priests of Syria, Idumea, Galilea and Nabatea, 28 to come to Jerusalem for a great trial and examination, 29 of John the Baptist and Gamaliel and Simon Magus, 30 on the accusations of heresy against the laws of Mithra. 31 The soldiers of King Philipas Agrippa aided by Roman legionnaires, 32 did then parade John the Baptist into Jerusalem, 33 upon a donkey in mockery of his claims of being a messiah. 34 At the temple midst the council of priests Caiaphas called witnesses, 35 yet none could provide substance to the claims of heresy, 36 until finally Caiaphas challenged John the Baptist under oath, 37 that he speak to the claim he did see himself as the true messiah, 38 against the holly and against Crown Prince Yacobiah (Jacob), 39 to which John the Baptist replied that whatever words are spoken they be the words and beliefs of others, 40 for no man can claim another has spoken, 41 when he be silent or that he said the words of another. 42 Thus no man ought to be condemned on the prejudice of the mob, 43 for any forum without good faith or good character or good conscience, 44 cannot be a court of law much less a court of divine law. 45 Caiaphas was enraged and demanded John the Baptist, 46 be handed to the Romans as a terrorist and enemy of the state. 47 Gamaliel the Elder was also resolute that the council, 48 could not convict him on supposition alone. 49 Yet when Simon Magus was brought before the council, 50 he denied on oath three times he knew John the Baptist, 51 even before witnesses who swore they had seen them together. 52 Thus all three prisoners were then sent to Caesar Maritima, 53 to be presented before Roman Legate Lucius Aelius Seianus, 54 as dangerous enemies against Rome.

C. 11

1 Roman Legate Lucius Aelius Seianus also known as Pontius Pilates, 2 did summons John the Baptist to be brought to him, 3 that he may question him first before ruling upon his fate. 4 Lucius Aelius Seianus then asked the Baptist, 5 if he believed himself to be a king or some leader, 6 to which the Baptist replied that these be the words of others. 7 Lucius Aelius Seianus then warned the Baptist that as he be not a Roman, 8 it be perfectly lawful for him

to be put to death even on suspicion, 9 of being an enemy of Rome much less with the need of any proof, 10 to which the Baptist did reply that only heaven knows, 11 the truth within the hearts of men and that if it be his time to die, 12 then the gods have ordained this be the day. 13 Legate Lucius Aelius Seianus also known as Pontus Pilates, 14 was surprised at the frankness of the Baptist and so asked, 15 why he was so sure of the truth of his belief against such ancient priests, 16 of the Holly (Cuilliaéan) and Mithra who have sworn him as an enemy, 17 to which the Baptist did reply, 18 it is not by the will of man or woman to decide when God speaks, 19 it is not to the authority of a church that God submits, 20 but the church that submits to God. 21 Therefore no matter how great the authority of a man, 22 it cannot be greater than the Divine Creator. 23 No matter how ancient a scripture or belief, 24 it cannot be older than the creator the universe. 25 No matter how firm a doctrine of faith, 26 it cannot withstand even the smallest drop of true revelation. 27 It is men, not God who say that only the most esteemed, 28 the most holy elders have right above all others for divine insight. 29 All the words ever written in defence of doctrine cannot change these facts. 30 Roman Legate Lucius Aelius Seianus was horrified and in awe, 31 at the truths spoken by the Baptist that he feared passing judgement, 32 and instead ordered he be returned to King Philipas Agrippa, 33 along with the other two prisoners.

C. 12

1 Upon the return of John the Baptist to Philipas Agrippa, 2 after enduring a great trial of priests, 3 and surviving a personal trial before Roman Legate Lucius Aelius Seianus, 4 word quickly spread of the Baptist being even more powerful, 5 as a prophet and messenger of the Divine than before his imprisonment. 6 Holly High King Cú-Cúileann as Pontifex Maximus, 7 also known as the Great Prophet Yasiah (Joseph) of Yeb, 8 did then suggest that the people of Jerusalem be allowed to decide, 9 to release or condemn the Baptist upon a choice of another prisoner. 10 King Philipas Agrippa then arranged for hundreds of his soldiers, 11 to go to Jerusalem in disguise ahead of the arrival of the Baptist. 12 High Priest Caiaphas then arranged for the arrest of Ananias the younger, 13 a popular and respected young priest of the Temple. 14 Legate Lucius Aelius Seianus also known as Pontus Pilates, 15 then asked the mob whom they wished, 16 at which time there were loud shouts for Ananias (Barabbas). 17 Legate Lucius Aelius Seianus also known as Pontus Pilates, 18 asked the mob again what then be the punishment for the condemned, 19 asked the mob again what punishment shall befall the Baptist and the others, 20 to which the mob then called almost in unison for crucifixion, 21 being a most unusual capital punishment for the cross, 22 that was reserved normally for the hanging of the remains of the condemned. 23 John the Baptist was then released to the Roman Temple Guard. 24 Then the soldiers of the governor took the Baptist into the Praetorium, 25 and

Book 21 Age of the Nazarenes

gathered the whole garrison around him, 26 and then they stripped him and scourged him, 27 before placing a scarlet robe on him and a crown of thorns on his head. 28 And when they had finished mocking him the troops took him, 29 to the western outskirts of the city and the highest point of the Necropolis, 30 for by tradition the dead were always buried to the west, 31 and upon a place called Golgotha they crucified the Baptist, 32 placing a sign above his head saying I.N.R.I. 33 Or Ioannes Natamus Rex Iumentum in Latin, 34 meaning John the Baptist is King of the Donkeys. 35 And then they crucified Gamaliel and Simon Magus on either side. 36 Within a few hours all men were dead from their torture and ordeal. 37 When Holly High King Cú-Cúileann had heard of the manner of the execution, 38 of John the Baptist and Gamaliel and Simon Magus, 39 he was deeply troubled for though the death of Jesus had been atoned, 40 such executions were the most brutal and cruel in memory. 41 He ordered the bodies be immediately taken down, 42 with the body of Gamaliel and Simon Magus released for burial, 43 but the body of John the Baptist to receive royal burial, 44 in the tomb reserved for Holly High King Cú-Cúileann (Joseph). 45 Thus word spread throughout the ancient world, 46 of the courage and events surrounding the death of the Baptist, 47 the brutality of his death and the compassion of the Holly High King, 48 even unto the man he believed killed his eldest son.

C. 13

1 Before the news of the terrible events in Jerusalem, 2 reached the priests of Karnak in Egypt, 3 Jesus (Yahusiah) had immersed himself learning all the wisdom, 4 of the ancient kings and scribes of Egypt, 5 visiting the greatest of temples and shrines. 6 To the priests of Amen-Ra at Karnak, 7 Jesus knew more of the meaning of hieroglyph than any man, 8 for more than a thousand years. 9 The priests marvelled at what he did reveal to them, 10 that they proclaimed him Osiris reborn, 11 the Ptah (Peter and Father) and rock of heaven, 12 and did anoint him the one true Pharaoh and the only Son of God, 13 being the customary title of the true Pharaoh. 14 Yet upon the news of the execution of John the Baptist, 15 and Gamaliel the Elder and Simon Magus, 16 Jesus was distraught and abandoned further teaching in Egypt, 17 and resolved himself to finally return to his father in Palestine, 18 and to beg for his forgiveness for his absence and his failings. 19 In the year known as 29 CE, 20 twelve hundred and twenty nine years since the dawn of the Great Age, 21 after seven years of absence and abandonment of his duties, 22 with the whole ancient world presuming him to be dead or lost, 23 Jesus (Yahusiah) returned to Jerusalem to face the consequences. 24 Yet before he was even at the main gates to Bethesda, 25 Jesus had been sighted and word sent to Holly High King Cú-Cúileann, 26 who ran ahead of his guard to greet his long lost son. 27 Before Jesus could speak Yasiah (Joseph) ordered his servants, 28 for Jesus to be bathed and placed in the finest robes and sandals,

29 Holly High King Cú-Cúileann as Pontifex Maximus, 30 then announced a great holiday and for the greatest feast to be prepared. 31 News quickly spread that Jesus had risen from the dead, 32 to Heliopolis and Roman Legate Lucius Aelius Seianus, 33 and to all corners of the Roman Empire that the prodigal son had returned. 34 News also came to Holly Crown Prince Yacobiah (Jacob) at Sepphoris, 35 of the return of his brother and to Damascus and Virgin Mary (Mariamne), 36 that her husband was resurrected from the dead. 37 Yet when Jesus returned to the court of his father at Bethesda, 38 in the presence of Praetorian Lucius Cornelius Sulla and a great throng, 39 he wore not the finest robes but the simple linen vestments of a servant, 40 and threw himself down before his father saying: 41 Forgive me Father for I have transgressed against Heaven, 42 against the Gods and against your name and the name of my wife. 43 I am no longer worthy to be called your Son. 44 Instead make me a servant in your home and I will honour my duties. 45 His Father then embraced him and said thus: 46 My Son I shall never abandon you nor ever forsake you. 47 Yet Character is nothing if not tested. 48 For in such an act of penance you have proven to the world, 49 you are a greater prophet than I shall ever be remembered. 50 For we celebrate then with this feast your death and rebirth, 51 your loss and your return as a true priest of the Divine. 52 When King Philipas Agrippa and his daughter the Virgin Mary arrived, 53 Jesus did prostrate himself before the king and his wife, 54 and Mariamne the Virgin Mary did forgive him for his transgressions, 55 revealing that her sister Anna now the wife of Yacobiah (Jacob), 56 had prophesised his return and the events that unfolded with the Baptist. 57 Upon the arrival of Prince Yacobiah (Jacob) Holly High King Cú-Cúileann, 58 did announce not only the restoration of Jesus as heir, 59 but that he be now the Pontifex Maximus and the thirty-second Great Prophet. 60 Yacobiah (Jacob) did then complain bitterly in front of the court, 61 that he had done everything his father had asked and never run away, 62 and yet Jesus had brought disgrace upon the name of the Holly, 63 and men had died upon the presumption of foul play, 64 and yet the Holly King did lavish him not only with a great feast, 65 but restore him his fortune and make him the highest. 66 To which Holly High King Cú-Cúileann (Joseph) did reply, 67 that what you Yacobiah (Jacob) did, you did out of duty, 68 yet what your brother (Jesus) did, he did upon a calling from heaven. 69 For my son who was dead has now been resurrected to life, 70 and your brother who was but a child has returned a man, 71 and no priest of the Holly for thousands of years, 72 has more honoured our blood or prepared himself better.

C. 14

1 In the year known as 29 CE, 2 twelve hundred and twenty nine years since the dawn of the Great Age, 3 Livia Drusilla the mother of Augustus Tiberius did finally give up the ghost. 4 Emperor Tiberius was so distraught with grief that his guard had to beg him, 5 that the body be interred for it had already begun to decay. 6 By the

time he left the side of his mother, 7 Praetorian Prefect Gaius Cornelius Lentulus did arrange, 8 a grand funeral and for all of Rome to pay its respects, 9 to the matriarch who had killed so many for so little. 10 In the same year Holly High King Cú-Cúileann sent word, 11 to the four corners of the world for the wisest of priests and holy men, 12 of all the religions to come to Jerusalem and bear witness, 13 to the testimony of his son Jesus returned from the dead, 14 and now Pontifex Maximus and the Great Prophet of Yeb. 15 So they did come from all cities and faiths as far as China and India, 16 from Tibet and Parthia and from Africa and Arabia and the Roman Empire, 17 to hear the wisdom and knowledge revealed by a holly priest, 18 who had travelled much of the known world in search of truth. 19 When the multitude of priests and holy men had assembled at Bethesda, 20 Jesus (Yahusiah) did speak from the lowest point that all might hear. 21 He spoke first in Greek then Latin then Aramaic then Arsacid, 22 then in Egyptian then Sanskrit then finally in Gnosis (Gaelic) of the Holly, 23 the same message that all may hear and understand these words: 24 Blessed are those that possess the right attitude, 25 for theirs are the keys to the wisdom of heaven. 26 Blessed are those who respect life and seek to do no harm, 27 for they are the true custodians of all creation. 28 Blessed are those who are honest in all intentions and actions, 29 for only they speak for heaven and no other. 30 Blessed are those who are courageous in the face of evil, 31 for they are the very best leaders. 32 Blessed are those whose hearts are full with enthusiasm, 33 for they are the ones that change the world. 34 Blessed are those who are compassionate, charitable and forgiving, 35 for they are the best teachers and priests. 36 Blessed are those who show good cheer, 37 for they are truly free. 38 Blessed are the joyful at life and all creation, 39 for they are the Divine Creator made flesh. 40 And Blessed are those of you who are persecuted for speaking the truth, 41 for this is the way of all true prophets born into an age of ignorance. 42 You are the salt of the earth, you are the light of the world. 43 Let then your light so shine before men, that they may see. 44 Let your actions not your words speak for themselves, 45 that all men may come to know the truth of heaven, 46 that we are many but we are also part of the one Divine Creator and Creation, 47 that we can never die nor shall we ever be abandoned or cursed, 48 that we are all fraternal brothers in trust of the one true Universal Ecclesia. 49 Do not think that I come here to destroy the Laws of the Great Prophets, 50 I do not come here to destroy but to restore the Rule of Law. 51 For you have heard it said the worst transgression against heaven be murder, 52 but I say to you that murder be not the worst of all transgressions. 53 Verily the worst transgression be false testimony before heaven, 54 as the falsity of oaths means no office and sacred trust may exist, 55 nor may any judgment or sentence possess any authority unto heaven, 56 and the falsity of vows means the end of trust and trade between people, 57 and a people of a society quickly devours itself. 58 Therefore guard against false testimony and false oaths and vows, 59 lest you sow the seeds for the destruction of your own people and cities. 60 You have heard it said the highest law be divine and that as the priests, 61 you be above the laws of lesser souls and those of trade, 62 for some even quote the ancient laws of Egypt that a priest, 63 must be above all temporal matters such as money and labour. 64 Verily I say to you there was and is and has only ever been one law, 65 that no man is above the law and all are equal before it. 66 For when men seek to use the law as a weapon or a means of enrichment, 67 the Rule of Law ceases to be and the seeds of rebellion are sown. 68 Therefore make just laws for all people and not corrupt the law, 69 lest the day come when your flesh or that of your descendants, 70 becomes the food for worms and dogs. 71 You have heard it said that all debts must be paid, 72 for to deny such obligation is a grave transgression against heaven. 73 Thus when a man cannot pay his debts it be deemed lawful he be bonded, 74 and that even his family be made destitute or slaves. 75 Yet a moneylender that make no provision for the forgiveness of debts, 76 is the worst scoundrel and thief in the eyes of heaven. 77 Verily I say to you that a man is obliged to pay his debts in the same manner, 78 and to the same extent as the moneylender offers forgiveness and good faith. 79 Therefore a man is no more obliged to pay a moneylender as a pirate, 80 for by such acts a merchant or moneylender forfeits protection of the law. 81 Nor does a man have any right to enslave another, 82 nor claim that such act be ordained by heaven, 83 for it be wicked falsity to claim that tax be the inherited debts, 84 and transgressions of our forefathers when such demands be no more than a tribute, 85 to a conquering force that rules more by force and fear than law. 86 No man can serve two masters; for either he will hate one and love the other, 87 or else he will be loyal to the one and despise the other. 88 Verily you must choose whether to serve heaven or the false idol of money. 89 You have heard it said that you shall not commit adultery, 90 for such a transgression be a grave immorality before heaven. 91 Verily I say to you that the worst immorality is a priest dressed in finery, 92 surrounded by the wealth of this world while the people are in distress. 93 There be no greater perversity before heaven than this. 94 Therefore do not bring gifts to your altars, 95 nor slaughter innocent animals in vain glory of favour with the gods, 96 for these are hollow offerings and only offend heaven. 97 Let your gift and your sacrifice be your own lives, 98 to live amongst the people not separate from the people, 99 to live in true poverty and obedience and humility, 100 to be in the world but not of the world, 101 to be the first to give alms and the last to refuse, 102 that men may know the true nature of heaven and the Divine Creator, 103 through your actions than believe the falsity there are no gods, 104 for how could heaven permit such men to be emissaries. 105 Do not desire for yourselves treasures on earth, 106 where decay destroys and where thieves may break in and steal, 107 but make for yourselves treasures in heaven where there be no decay nor thieves. 108 Therefore I say to you cease your worry of fine food and drink and clothing, 109 and tend to your flock as exemplary shepherds before heaven. 110 For nothing be more disgusting to the Divine Creator than false piety. 111 Let then your earnest prayers be in a quiet place without crowds. 112 Verily there is no reward in hollow rituals above true contrition. 113 You have heard that it was said the law be an eye for an eye, 114 and that only through force may peace be assured. 115 Yet the greatest force against tyranny is passive resistance, 116 and the greatest law against evil is forgiveness. 117 Resist peacefully and in honour and heaven be your witness, 118 for even the worst tyrant cannot survive without consent. 119 Forgive those who trespass against you and break the chains, 120 where evil begets evil that a world becomes blinded. 121 Take care against judgment that you be not judged. 122 For with what judgment you judge, you will be judged. 123 And with the measure you use, it will be measured back to you. 124 And consider not the splinter in your brothers eye that blinds him, 125 but first remove the planks from your own eyes. 126 Take care not to give what is sacred to men who behave as dogs, 127 nor cast these pearls from heaven before swine, 128 lest they trample them under their feet, 129 and then turn upon you and tear you to pieces. 130 Ask, and it will be given to you; seek, and you will find, 131 knock, and every door in heaven will be opened to you. 132 For everyone who asks receives, and he who seeks finds, 133 and to him who knocks it will be opened. 134 Verily who among you would deny your own children food and drink, 135 or would cut off your own arm to spite your face. 136 Why then would you permit men to believe that the gods, 137 be hateful and vexatious and spiteful and ignorant as men, 138 or that the Divine Creator would punish and hurt that which he created. 139 Verily the Divine Creator is love and heaven is love, 140 and the truth of all existence is the awareness of the love of life. 141 Be gentle then to one another and do not bear false witness, 142 for you are the rock upon which the kingdom of heaven on earth is built. 143 Therefore, whatever you seek men to do to you, do also to them, 144 for this is the Rule of Law and the Law of the Prophets.

C. 15

1 In the year known as 30 CE, 2 twelve hundred and thirty years since the dawn of the Great Age, 3 Prince Jesus of the Holly and Pontifex Maximus, 4 also the true Pharaoh and thus the Son of Re (God), 5 also known as Yahusiah the thirty second Great Prophet of Yeb, 6 received word that Praetorian Prefect Gaius Cornelius Lentulus, 7 did summons him to meet at Rome and speak to the Senate, 8 and to the most learned jurists and teachers of the eternal city. 9 Pontifex Praetorian Prefect Lucius Cornelius Sulla did warn him, 10 that while Augustus Tiberius be absent Rome still be a danger, 11 and men of high ambition may not respect the words of such a prophet. 12 In reply Jesus did say that though such counsel be sound, 13 and the consequences profound there be a time for all men of conscience, 14 to set aside their doubts and concerns and causes for peace, 15 and trust in the truth and authority of heaven over the schemes of men. 16 For better the holly vanish from the pages of history and

no one remember, 17 than to compromise another day in the face of wilful ignorance. 18 Soon after Jesus with his wife Mariamne (Mary) and his Praetorian Guard, 19 did depart Palestine for Egypt and the city of Alexandria, 20 where Jesus did meet Chief Librarian Hero of Alexandria, 21 and did share with him the sights and inventions and knowledge, 22 of his travels across Asia of wind and steam powered devices, 23 and all manner of pumps and levers for lifting and drawing, 24 in exchange for the Chief Librarian providing his finest scribes, 25 to help write and copy the first sacred scripture of Jesus, 26 called the Evangelicum Sacrum meaning the Holy (Holly) Gospel. 27 When the sacred scripture was completed and its copies, 28 Jesus did then entrust the safety of Mariamne to the Hero of Alexandria, 29 as Jesus and Praetorian Prefect Lucius Cornelius and his guard, 30 did depart for Rome. 31 At Rome Prince Jesus of the Holly and Pontifex Maximus, 32 was warmly greeted by Praetorian Prefect Gaius Cornelius Lentulus, 33 and by many Senators and Claudia Livia Julia the sister of Claudius. 34 Jesus did visit the Vaticanus and Great Temple which had since become, 35 the Temple of Livia Drusilla as Magna Mater of Rome. 36 Jesus did pay his respects and then did prophecy that in times to come, 37 the Temple as a mighty house of the Divine Creator, 38 would be destroyed and restored three times before the end of the great age. 39 Some of the Senators questioned how Jesus could possibly know, 40 when even the most esteemed of oracles fail to give such specificity, 41 to which Jesus did reply that it be not his duty to interpret the mind of God, 42 but merely to speak what is given to him and trust his heart and stomach, 43 that such words spoken be true at the time they come to be. 44 For all men who can see can view the true face of the Divine.

C. 16

1 In the year known as 31 CE, 2 twelve hundred and thirty one years since the dawn of the Great Age, 3 Prince Jesus of the Holly and Pontifex Maximus, 4 also known as Yahusiah the thirty second Great Prophet of Yeb, 5 did address the Senate and the jurists of Rome with these words: 6 May the Divine Creator of all existence continue to shine upon the eternal city, 7 may the gods of heaven continue to bring good fortune to all under its care, 8 may the ancestors and heroes continue to guide our hearts and minds, 9 that we as priests or jurists or leaders of men do honour, 10 the sacred office and obligations entrusted to us, 11 that we never forget nor seek to obstruct the first truth of law: 12 There is, there was, there has only ever been One Law. 13 All law is equal that no one is above it, 14 all law is measured that all may learn and know it, 15 all law is standard that it may always be applied the same. 16 A law is a rule that prohibits or permits certain acts. 17 A rule is a norm, bar, maxim, measure or standard. 18 A rule may be derived by instruction, discovery, custom or consent. 19 The highest law is Divine being a rule given by divine instruction, 20 as nothing may contradict such a rule. 21 The second highest law be the reason of Mind, 22 being an edict given by a

great council of wise elders or jurists, 23 as nothing absurd and without good reason may be considered law. 24 The third highest law be the law of the people, 25 as the consent and will of the people is the source of true authority. 26 The weakest rule is that of a tyrant, 27 as any rule without authority or right of heaven but merely by force, 28 cannot be sustained and the people shall eventually overcome, 29 and render such unjust rule and unjust laws as dust. 30 This be the law of all great civilisations from the beginning of time, 31 and no king or assembly or city has sustained itself in ignorance to such foundation. 32 These then be the foundations of Rule of Law: 33 All law be spoken as it is the spirit of the word that carries the authority. 34 Therefore all action under law be by word of mouth, 35 and writing be only for memory and trade and never be the law. 36 All are equal under the law, 37 all are accountable and answerable under the law, 38 all are without blemish until proven culpable, 39 where there is a law there must be a cause, 40 where there is a law there must be a penalty, 41 where there is a law there must be a remedy. 42 An action in law cannot proceed without first a cause. 43 An action is not granted to one who is not injured. 44 The action of a valid law can do no harm (injury). 45 An action decided in law must reflect cause of such action. 46 No injury to the law means no valid cause for action by law. 47 No action through law can arise from a fraud before heaven and earth. 48 No action through law can arise in bad faith or prejudice. 49 An act does not make one culpable unless there be intent to do wrong, 50 for no one may suffer punishment by valid law for mere intent. 51 No one is punished for the transgression of an ancestor or another. 52 No one can derive an advantage in law from his own wrong, 53 for what is invalid from the beginning does not become valid over time. 54 No one is accused of the same exact cause twice. 55 No man be a judge over his own matter, 56 nor a man possess the authority of heaven to be both judge and executioner. 57 No penalty may exist without a valid law. 58 The immediate cause and not the remote cause be the subject of law. 59 These be the foundations of Rule of Law. 60 As to justice it be the maxim that Justice never contradicts the rule of law, 61 for Justice be the lawful right of use of all that has been defined by law, 62 and Justice be the rights to adjudicate the law itself before heaven and earth, 63 and Justice be a judge under sacred oath and trust granted such rights, 64 as a right being a power or authority or privilege or benefit recognised by law. 65 Divine Law is the law that defines the Divine and all creation, 66 and demonstrates the spirit and mind and instruction of the Divine, 67 and the operation of the will of the Divine Creator through existence. 68 Therefore all valid rights and Justice are derived from Divine Law. 69 Natural Law is the law that defines the operation of the will of the Divine, 70 through the existence of form and sky and earth and physical rules. 71 Thus Natural Law governs the operation of what we can see and name. 72 The laws of People are those rules enacted by men having proper authority, 73 for the good governance of a society under the Rule of Law. 74

The laws of People are always inherited from Natural Law. 75 A law of People cannot abrogate or usurp a Natural Law, 76 nor is it possible for a Natural Law to usurp Divine Law. 77 These then be the foundations of Justice: 78 All possess the Right to be heard even if such speech be controversial, 79 all possess the Right of free will to choose our actions and destiny, 80 all possess the Right of reason that distinguishes them from lesser animals, 81 all possess the Right to informed consent or withdraw consent, 82 all possess the Right over their body that none may claim our flesh, 83 all possess the Right of our divine self that none may claim our soul. 84 Thus no man can make a blood oath on their flesh or vow on their soul, 85 nor may any man claim servitude or obligation under such an abomination, 86 for such Rights are granted solely by heaven to all people, 87 and no man or body of jurists have the authority to usurp heaven or the gods. 88 Verily all true authority and power to rule is inherited from heaven, 89 and to only those men in good faith and good character and good conscience, 90 who then make a sacred oath in trust and form an office, 91 into which such Divine Rights are conveyed for only so long, 92 as they honour their oath and obligations to serve the people. 93 For whenever a man who makes an oath to form a sacred trust of office, 94 then breaks such an oath through prejudice or unclean hands or bad faith, 95 then all such authority and power ceases from them, 96 as the cord between heaven and earth is severed and the trust dissolved. 97 Verily no man may serve the people unless under sacred oath, 98 nor may any man serve heaven unless under solemn vow. 99 Therefore guard your behaviour and actions of office, 100 that though the heavens appear to fall, let justice always be done. 101 These be the foundations of Justice. 102 As to the administration of Justice these be the foundations of Due Process: 103 No valid action in law proceeds without first a valid cause, 104 and no valid cause exists until such claim is first tested. 105 Thus the birth of all action in law must begin with the claim. 106 If a claim be not proven as a valid cause then the accused has nothing to answer. 107 Yet if the claim be proved to have merit as a cause, 108 then all valid causes in law must be resolved. 109 Thus, he who first brings the claim must first prove its merit, 110 as the burden of the proof lies upon him who accuses not he who denies. 111 A heavy obligation then on one who first brings the controversy. 112 For one who brings false accusation is the gravest of transgressors, 113 that it injures not one law, but all heaven and all law. 114 Thus a valid claim in part is one in which an accuser makes a complaint, 115 bringing two witnesses as proof and petitions a forum of law for remedy. 116 If merit of a cause be proved, the one accused must appear to answer. 117 The one accused and any witnesses appear by summons. 118 When anyone be summonsed, he must immediately appear without hesitation. 119 If a man summonsed does not appear or refuses to appear to answer, 120 then let him be seized by force to come and attend. 121 When anyone who has been summonsed seeks to evade, or attempts to flee, 122 let the one who summons lay hands on them to prevent their escape. 123 One who flees fair judgement confesses his culpability. 124 The accused cannot be judged until after the accusations be spoken, 125 and then after the accused exercise or decline their three rights to defence, 126 the first being Prolocution and the right to speak as a matter of law, 127 and why the complaint and investigation should not continue, 128 the second being Collocution as to why the complaint and accusation is false, 129 and upon such proof why the burden should now be placed on the accuser, 130 and the third being Adlocution being a final speech in defence, 131 against a complaint or accusation having been heard. 132 If illness or old age hinder the appearance of the one summonsed, 133 let the one who made the summons provide a basic means of transport. 134 When men wish to settle their dispute among themselves, 135 then they shall have the right to make peace. 136 If a dispute cannot be settled before seeking a judge, 137 then both the accused and the accuser must be granted equal hearing. 138 An accused cannot be found culpable unless three pieces of evidence may be attributed. 139 Judges are bound to explain the reason of their judgement. 140 The setting of the sun shall be the extreme limit of time within, 141 which a judge must render his decision. 142 These be the foundations of Due Process. 143 These be the foundations of Rule of Law and Justice. 144 Any law that is against such truth, cannot be law.

C. 17

1 Upon the speech by Jesus as Pontifex Maximus to the Senate, 2 and to the greatest jurists and minds of Rome, 3 there was uproar as Praetorian Lucius Cornelius Sulla feared. 4 Praetorian Prefect Gaius Cornelius Lentulus arranged for safe escort, 5 to aid Jesus and his Praetorian Guard safe passage to Alexandria, 6 by pledging his own son Gaius Cornelius Gaetulicus at the service of Jesus, 7 with the promise his whole family who also fled would be protected. 8 Yet Apicata Cornelia the wife of Lentulus chose to remain in Rome. 9 Marcus Annaeus Seneca and Lucius Calpernius Piso sought an alliance, 10 with the jurist Marcus Cassius Sabinus of the Sabiniani, 11 and with jurist Publius Iunius Celsus of the Procularii, 12 and with Gaius Suetonius Macro of the Vigiles and night watchman, 13 that upon the demise of Praetorian Prefect Gaius Cornelius Lentulus, 14 Gaius Suetonius Macro would become Praetorian Prefect, 15 and the Senate would press for Gaius Calpernius Piso, 16 the son of Lucius Calpernius Piso to be adopted as heir to Tiberius, 17 as the Procularii and Sabiniani would then write such laws and maxims, 18 to purge and defeat the writings of Jesus and the Evangelicum Sacrum. 19 Marcus Annaeus Seneca did then summons Gaius Cornelius Lentulus, 20 to attend the Senate upon the evening where Seneca and Piso, 21 permitted the discussion to drag well into the night. 22 Once the forces of Gaius Suetonius Macro and the Vigiles were in place, 23 Gaius Iunius Silanus and Titus Cassius Severus did strike, 24 and Praetorian Gaius Cornelius Lentulus was mortally wounded. 25 The men of Gaius Iunius Silanus and Lucius Calpernius Piso, 26 did march upon the home of Apicata Cornelia and murdered her. 27 Word was immediately sent to Augustus

Tiberius at Capri by Macro, 28 that a terrible plot had been averted by the Senate of a plan to kill Tiberius, 29 by Praetorian Prefect Gaius Cornelius Lentulus who it was then claimed, 30 had murdered his wife and planned to wed Claudia Livia Julia. 31 As proof Macro produced the head of Gaius Cornelius Lentulus, 32 at which site the Praetorian Guard raised their swords at Macro, 33 and the men of Macro surrounded the guard and executed them. 34 Upon the appearance of saving the life of Augustus Tiberius, 35 Gaius Suetonius Macro was immediately made Praetorian Prefect, 36 with orders to arrest those of the Senate responsible, 37 for the death of Gaius Cornelius Lentulus without orders from the emperor. 38 Upon his return to Rome and guarded by the men of Suetonius Macro, 39 Augustus presided over the trial of the conspirators beginning with Claudia Livia Julia. 40 A letter was produced purporting to be from Apicata Cornelia and accusing, 41 Claudia Livia Julia of having an affair with Gaius Cornelius Lentulus, 42 and plotting to murder the emperor and name himself emperor. 43 Yet Claudia Livia Julia denied the accusations saying it was Piso and Seneca, 44 who plotted to take power upon the death of all heirs of Tiberius. 45 Gaius Asinius Gallus then spoke to the defence of Claudia Livia Julia, 46 to which Publius Iunius Celsus produced witnesses who testified, 47 that Asinius Gallus was in secret relations with Claudia Livia Julia. 48 At the conclusion of the inquisition Augustus Tiberius, 49 condemned Gaius Asinius Gallus and Claudia Livia Julia to death, 50 as well as Titus Cassius Severus and Gaius Iunius Silanus, 51 for the killing of Gaius Cornelius Lentulus without authority of the emperor. 52 Yet upon the petition of Marcus Cassius Sabinus for Iunius Silanus, 53 and not his own son, the emperor reprieved Iunius Silanus. 54 Gaius Asinius Gallus and Claudia Livia Julia did then commit suicide, 55 as did Titus Cassius Severus for such an act was considered noble. 56 Before his departure back to Capri Augustus Tiberius did then name, 57 Gaius Suetonius Macro as his adopted son and immediate heir, 58 and successor ahead of Claudius who remained in Lucifer (Lyons). 59 The Senate and Praetorian then hailed Macro by the name Caligula, 60 meaning little boots in honour of the great Gaius Cornelius Lentulus. 61 Yet despite his loathing of such a name even Tiberius called him Caligula. 62 In the same year Princess Mariamne (Mary) also known as Virgin Mary, 63 did give birth to the first child of Jesus which they named Iudiah (Judah).

C. 18

1 After the purge of Augustus Tiberius and his return to Capri, 2 and Gaius Suetonius Macro named as Caligula as Praeteorian and heir, 3 the Senate and the intellectual class of Rome resolved themselves, 4 to rid Rome of all vestige of Divine Authority as basis of law. 5 Instead the jurists of Rome declared true law be based on the reality of nature, 6 that men themselves may be their own gods if they possess such reason and skill, 7 and that the original course of rule of law be the consent and will of the people, 8 except for the eternal city which had proven its

superior status over all others. 9 Thus, the Senate glorified the insanity and absurdity against the history of all law, 10 in claiming Imperial Exceptionalism whereby whatever Rome does is lawful, 11 yet what all other people do in law is illegal unless approved by Rome. 12 The Senate did commission a series of monumental works of fraud and propaganda, 13 funded by the wealthiest merchant and mercenary Senators, 14 and those families that possessed the greatest number of slaves, 15 such as Titus Coponius Sabinus of Gaul and Lucius Calpurnius Piso of Hispania. 16 The first task the corrupt Senators did agree was to remove all history, 17 and all trace of the origin of Rome under true Rule of Law, 18 and all memory of the origins of the Pontifex Maximus and the Ark of the Covenant, 19 and all honour to the Great Prophets and the Holly (Cuilliaéan), 20 and all evidence of the war between the merchants and the founders of Rome. 21 Thus a completely false and absurd history of Rome did appear, 22 in which the gens Cassia (Cassius) magically became central to the history of Rome, 23 along with the gens Piso and other wealthy families, 24 through more than 140 books called the "Books from the Foundation of the City", 25 in honour of slain Titus Cassius Severus and Claudia Livia Julia, 26 and falsely claimed to have been written by a single mythical scribe, 27 whose name was Titus Livius and later known as Livy. 28 The second work of deliberate fiction and fraud was even more ambitious, 29 and for this Marcus Annaeus Seneca himself and his son Lucius Annaeus Seneca, 30 and the brilliant Gaius Plinius Secundus known as Pliny the Elder, 31 and many dozens of the best scribes were commissioned and funded, 32 to reside in Ercolanium Campania under the patronage of Lucius Calpurnius Piso, 33 and to construct a complete philosophy of merchant nihilism, 34 to curse heaven and the gods and destroy Divine Law, 35 to repudiate thousands of years of authority of priests and the Cuilliaéan (Holly), 36 to defy the law expressed by Holly Prince Jesus as Pontifex Maximus, 37 to justify slavery and piracy and treachery of the elite merchant families, 38 that might is right and the law be whatever the Senate deems expedient to be, 39 and that there be no good or evil but only pleasure and pain, 40 and that any priest or prophet that claimed moral restraint seeks harm, 41 while Rome and the elite seek only to serve the people, 42 for every man can be a banker or a merchant or general, 43 and pleasure and consumption of goods even unto excess be no transgression. 44 Thus Lucius Annaeus Seneca called himself Philodemus of Cordoba, 45 and with Gaius Plinius Secundus also known as Pliny the Elder, 46 did construct an epic poem attributed to a fictional philosopher named Titus Lucretius, 47 who then quoted a range of philosophers back to a mythical teacher, 48 of complete imagination called Epicurus. 49 Within the fraudulent poem inventing the philosophy of Nihilism, 50 and its twin philosophies of Epicurianism and Secularism, 51 the poem known as De rerum natura (On the Nature of Things), 52 did claim that the unhappiness of mankind be not tyranny, 53 but the unfounded power they attribute to the gods and heaven,

54 for the universe and existence be not by divine intervention but chance, 55 nor be there forces of good or evil in the world but pleasure and pain, 56 for what men perceive as good is only pleasure and what is bad is painful, 57 thus it be the duty of society to promote pleasure and happiness, 58 and remove the constraints of old thinking and old ways, 59 for there be no ultimate truth of law nor rule of law or perfect justice, 60 but what may only be measured and weighed by reason and mind. 61 Thus it was that Marcus Cassius Sabinus completed the third work, 62 known as Ius Civile (Civil Law) in three volumes, 63 in direct opposition to Evangelicum Sacrum and all laws of history, 64 that immunity and segregation and slavery be normal and lawful, 65 that all law issued by the Senate and Rome must be obeyed, 66 for the exceptionalism of the eternal city be without dispute, 67 and all law and crime be then commercial, 68 and no such rules of clean hands or good faith or without prejudice apply, 69 except in steadfast pledge and vow to Rome and no other. 70 For blind ignorance now had become the law and teaching of Rome, 71 and all who were without noble title or wealth were to obey, 72 and the teachings of Holly Prince Jesus were the enemy of real law, 73 and the source of true misery and pain of the people, 74 thus to then question or think then was to be an enemy of the state.

C. 19

1 In the year known as 32 CE, 2 twelve hundred and thirty two years since the dawn of the Great Age, 3 Prince Jesus of the Holly and Pontifex Maximus, 4 also known as Yahusiah the thirty second Great Prophet of Yeb, 5 remained conflicted upon the events in Rome, 6 upon the murder of Cornelius Lentulus and his wife Apicata Cornelia, 7 and the appointment of Prefect Gaius Suetonius Macro (Caligula) as heir. 8 Pontifex Praetorian Cornelius Sulla had warned Jesus of the consequences, 9 and Jesus had replied of the significance of the moment to make a stand against evil. 10 Yet the people of the East and the Yahudi Diaspora and the Celts, 11 continued to be apathetic to the words and teachings of Jesus, 12 with many still hostile as to his actions of abandonment, 13 which they blamed as the cause of the death of the Baptist and Gamaliel and Simon Magus. 14 Even the mass of priests who had come to Jerusalem only a few years earlier, 15 and pledged their solidarity within a sacred and apostolic Universal Ecclesia, 16 had distanced themselves from the Holly for fear of retribution to come from Rome. 17 Far from rejecting the absurdity of nihilism and the falsities concerning Epicurus, 18 many of the wealthy celts and even noble families saw affinity in the message, 19 that the gods of old and especially the Cuilliaéan (Holly) were responsible, 20 for much of the misery and pain of the world and not the merchants and bankers. 21 His father Holly High King Cú-Cúileann also known as Yasiah (Joseph), 22 had been forced to return to Britanni to quell unrest amongst the tribal leaders, 23 as Yacobiah (Jacob) remained estranged to his brother Jesus. 24 Thus Jesus did commission

the construction of a large earthen amphitheater, 25 as well as a therapeutae settlement a few miles south of Sepphoris, 26 he named Nazara (Nazareth) meaning the city of truth. 27 There Jesus chose to listen to the common people and help teach knowledge of healing, 28 as he continued to commission new sacred scripture in response, 29 to the terrible lies of Marcus Cassius Sabinus and Marcus Annaeus Seneca, 30 and the Senate of Rome concerning the purpose of life and society. 31 Within one year of teaching at Nazara, 32 Mariamne And Jesus did give birth to their second child, 33 being a daughter named Mary in honour of the mother of Mary. 34 As Lucius Annaeus Seneca as Philodemus of Cordoba, 35 and Marcus Annaeus Seneca as the fictional philosopher Epicurus, 36 did promote the false doctrines of nihilism against heaven and pain, 37 Jesus began to embrace the symbolism of the cross and the teachings of the Baptist saying: 38 Anyone who does not choose to be reborn through the ritual of baptism, 39 becomes lost to a joyous life on earth and condemns themselves to a life of pain. 40 For no man who seeks to constantly avoid pain can truly live, 41 nor does any man honour the gift of life if he seeks to carry the world upon his shoulders. 42 Verily we are born without transgression or debt or obligation, 43 and so we are all born equal under the laws of heaven, 44 as the law forbids one be punished for the transgression of an ancestor or another. 45 Embrace then the ritual of baptism that all may see your acknowledgement of law, 46 and your rights before heaven as a spirit without blemish a mind without fear and flesh without curse. 47 Verily any man who does not embrace the cross and die to the falsities of this world, 48 becomes lost to the afterlife of heaven and condemns themselves to an otherworld. 49 For men who believe in nothing know nothing and can see nothing, 50 and when death comes upon them as nature demands, 51 they are without knowledge of self or reason but fear and hate. 52 Thus any man who does not believe in the cross or the resurrection of the cross, 53 is ignorant to joy and the emancipation of all our fears. 54 So it was the more Jesus did speak and embrace the knowledge of the Baptist, 55 the more the people did come to listen and bear witness, 56 including many of the rebel leaders and zealots, 57 such as Simon also known as Simon bar Giora and St. Peter the Apostle, 58 and Judas the son of Judas the leader of the Sicari, 59 and Heliodores the High Priest of Eliada also known as John of Patmos and St John. 60 Soon many thousands did come to Nazara to hear Jesus speak and teach, 61 and the respect of Jesus grew amongst the people, 62 and his teachings in opposition to the excesses of greed and avarice.

C. 20

1 In the year known as 34 CE, 2 twelve hundred and thirty four years since the dawn of the Great Age, 3 Mariamne and Jesus gave birth to their third child, 4 a son they named James in honour of the brother of Jesus, 5 who along with Judas had come to Nazara along with many thousands, 6 to listen to the teachings of Jesus as a prophet of the people. 7

Yet while Jesus and James were reconciled tension did continue to rise, 8 as Gaius Suetonius Macro as Caligula and the Senate sought means, 9 of halting the messages of Jesus and promoting a new world of conspicuous consumption, 10 upon the false philosophy of Epicurus as Nihilism. 11 Legate Lucius Aelius Seianus as Pontius Pilates did report, 12 that unless Jesus did depart the lands of Galilea he be untouchable, 13 for not only be he protected by his thousand Praetorian but a strange alliance, 14 of thousands of the deadliest Sicari of Judas and the legions of Nabatea. 15 Yet of all the opportunities for Rome to isolate Jesus and Holly High King Cú-Cúileann, 16 it was the priests of Baal-Hamon and of Alexandria who were most disturbed, 17 for they saw their positions threatened by the new philosophy of Jesus, 18 that demanded priests live amongst the people and help the poor. 19 The priests of Baal-Hamon even agreed that they might lure Jesus to Jerusalem, 20 and help Rome rid themselves of the rebel Cuilliaéan (Holly) prophet. 21 Praetorian Cornelius Sulla warned Jesus of the rising perfidy and dangers from Rome, 22 and that if he did not act soon and decisively against Macro (Caligula), 23 then the people may support him but with little military and strategic support. 24 Prince Jesus of the Holly and Pontifex Maximus, 25 also known as Yahusiah the thirty second Great Prophet of Yeb, 26 did thank Cornelius Sulla and Cornelius Gaetulicus for their concern and said, 27 that soon there will come a time when all good men will be called to stand, 28 some to fight, some to teach and others to bear witness. 29 Yet such a day is not yet at hand nor may the plans of heaven be the privy of men. 30 Verily the mightiest of trees may be born from the smallest of seeds, 31 and the most profound of ideas be the simplest of truths. 32 For even if the Senate be defeated and held to account, 33 even if the mightiest of battles be won, 34 nothing can destroy an idea except a greater inspiration of heaven, 35 nor may a spiritual army be defeated by a temporal one. 36 Thus the seeds we shall plant will grow and the battles we fight will end, 37 and as men we shall all die to flesh and become dust. 38 Yet the ideas we bring from the Divine shall never die, 39 and upon one day at the end of the world of merchants and bankers, 40 all shall know the truth and power of such ideas.

C. 21

1 Jesus was teaching and speaking to people at Nazara, 2 when the High Priest of Eliada named Heliodores (John of Patmos), 3 did ask him of the paradox of prayer and revelation, 4 for Jesus as Yahusiah the thirty second Great Prophet of Yeb, 5 was born into a most ancient and illustrious line of priests, 6 through which the blood of the greatest prophets of history did flow, 7 how then could lesser men do what Jesus said when they did not possess such power. 8 In reply Jesus did say to Heliodores and to the many hundreds present these words: 9 Verily I say to you if a man truly wishes to serve the Divine Creator, 10 then let him be baptised and then let him take up his cross and serve. 11 For no birth right or blood right or title or family can make a man closer to God. 12

Clothes and robes can easily hide wickedness and those who are outwardly pious, 13 only offend the ears and eyes of heaven for their boisterous pleadings. 14 Verily a man who claims to be a prophet or messiah by title is an imposter, 15 for a worker in the field or a cook in the kitchen be closer to the Divine. 16 Indeed a priest be a priest not by anointing or ritual or study or patronage, 17 but by the depth of their moral character and willingness to help others. 18 Verily a man who refuses to teach and clean the feet even of the poor, 19 can never be considered a priest before the eyes of heaven, 20 nor may any priest claim to speak solely for heaven or interpose themselves, 21 between the Divine Creator of all existence and every man and woman. 22 Upon hearing these words Simon bar Jonah also known as the apostle Peter, 23 did protest and say that the people do not know how to pray, 24 for the priests have always accepted such actions for themselves. 25 Upon hearing the entreats of Simon bar Jonah, Jesus did say: 26 When you pray do not rush to a temple or altar for there is no need, 27 the Divine Creator of all existence is all around and through you. 28 Nor dress in simple robes or place ash upon your faces or make such public spectacle. 29 Make your prayer simple and honest and one of thanks and respect. 30 Thus when you pray, let these be your words: 31 Our Father of All Creation, 32 we beseech thee and honour your name, 33 for your Rule be united as One, 34 and your Laws be equal to All, 35 On Earth as it is in Heaven, 36 grant us the means to sustenance, 37 as we shall give alms to those in need. 38 Save us from trickery and false oaths, 39 as our vows and our oaths shall be true. 40 Forgive us our debits and transgressions, 41 as we shall forgive the debits and transgressions of others. 42 Release us from any curse and ills, 43 as we shall not curse nor wish ill upon another. 44 We ask most humbly and with deep gratitude, 45 for let then your will be done. 46 Amen.

C. 22

1 In the year known as 35 CE, 2 twelve hundred and thirty five years since the dawn of the Great Age, 3 and thirty five years since the birth of John the Baptist, 4 prince Jesus of the Holly and Pontifex Maximus, 5 also known as Yahusiah the thirty second Great Prophet of Yeb, 6 did reply to the invitation of Caiaphas and the priests of Baal-Hamon, 7 that he would come to the Great Temple Mint of Mithra at Jerusalem, 8 upon the day of his thirtieth birthday being March the 14th, 9 and the most sacred day of all Mithraism being the Day of Blood, 10 and the traditional ceremony of the Eucharist of bread and wine. 11 Soon the word travelled across the ancient world of the special visitation, 12 and Gaius Suetonius Macro as Caligula did send word, 13 to Legate Lucius Aelius Seianus as Pontius Pilates, 14 that once Jesus was within the walls of Jerusalem, 15 he was to be seized and executed as an enemy of the state. 16 Gaius Suetonius Macro as Caligula did then summons the best assassins, 17 to Jerusalem to blend into the crowds as a surety, 18 that if the priests of Baal-Hamon and Aelius Seianus failed, 19 then the assassins would ensure the death of the Holly Prince. 20 In the year known as 36 CE, 21 twelve

hundred and thirty six years since the dawn of the Great Age, 22 the time had arrived for Jesus to depart the safety of Nazara, 23 to the Great Temple of Mithra at Jerusalem. 24 Pontifex Praetorian Cornelius Sulla warned Jesus of the plots to kill him, 25 and Judas and the leaders of the Sicari and Zealots urged him not to go, 26 yet Jesus would not be moved and bid farewell to his family and children saying: 27 This be the day anointed by heaven when the wickedness upon the earth be cleansed, 28 for destiny be my bride and I shall not leave her in waiting. 29 Upon his arrival to Jerusalem upon a pale horse Jesus was greeted by huge crowds, 30 which overwhelmed the Roman guards to the city and even the guards of the priests. 31 Thus the King Philipas Agrippas did deploy his own troops as pretext to keeping the peace, 32 and neutralising the legionnaires of Lucius Aelius Seianus as Pontus Pilates. 33 Judas the leader of the Sicari and Simon Peter of the Zealots, 34 had already entered the city with thousands of their most deadly assassins and moved door to door, 35 till not one assassin of Rome remained breathing. 36 Thus when Jesus entered the Great Temple and Mint of Mithra to greet Caiaphas, 37 Cornelius Sulla and his Praetorian were unopposed. 38 There in the vast temple courtyard where bench upon bench of clerks and bankers, 39 did count taxes and exact their ledgers of debts, 40 Jesus ordered the ledgers be seized and the bankers arrested, 41 for as Pontifex Maximus he be the supreme priest of Rome, 42 and as the Great Prophet of Yeb he be the supreme priest of all Yahudi.

C. 23

1 In the year known as 36 CE, 2 twelve hundred and thirty six years since the dawn of the Great Age, 3 upon the 14th of March and the birthday of Jesus and Mithra, 4 atop the Great Temple and Mint to Mithra in Jerusalem, 5 Prince Jesus as Pontifex Maximus and the Great Prophet of Yeb, 6 did order criers to call out from the walls, 7 so that the tens of thousands of pilgrims below, 8 could hear these words spoken by Jesus: 9 Fifty years it be since the Great Temple Mint of Mithra here in Jerusalem, 10 and the Great Temple Mint of Lucifer in Gaul were consecrated, 11 by my grandfather the Holly High King Cú-Roi(n) as the Great Prophet Adoniah, 12 and as the Pontifex Maximus and supreme priest of all of Rome. 13 Now I stand before you all upon this most sacred day to Mithra and upon the day of my birth, 14 not only as Pontifex Maximus and the highest priest and custodian of sacred rights of heaven, 15 but as the steward of all the Yahudi diaspora and tribes as the Great Prophet of Yeb, 16 and as the master gold smith and master minter of all Holly (Cuilliaéan) coin. 17 For no lesser priests and their clerks and money lenders (bankers) may claim authority, 18 to bind men to debt and death oaths (mortgages) and servitude in the name of heaven, 19 yet no force on earth can rightfully deny that it is I Jesus the son of Joseph, 20 who holds the keys to the treasury of one heaven and no other. 21 Thus it be the law upon which this Great Temple be founded and the very foundations of Roman Law, 22 that when I speak in matters of rights and property claimed from heaven, 23 what I seal on earth

Book 21 Age of the Nazarenes

shall be sealed in heaven and what I loose on earth shall be loosed in heaven. 24 Therefore may all who have ears hear and all who have eyes see that you may bear witness, 25 to all peoples of all places and all cultures across the lands of Rome and beyond, 26 that no man may bear false witness now or into the future, 27 against what you heard spoken here today as the word of law and the seal of heaven and earth. 28 Verily all men and women are born equal and without transgression or debt or obligation, 29 as the law forbids one be punished for the transgression of an ancestor or another. 30 Nor are men and women bound in death by the transgressions or debts of life, 31 for death is the ultimate settlement of all debts and transgressions. 32 Thus when a man dies so does his debts and obligations, 33 and a merchant or moneylender may not seize any property from the widow and her children, 34 for the merchant and money lender have no right to demand such settlement, 35 and a man have no right to pledge his family as surety. 36 Nor may a people be bound for the transgressions of their ancestors, 37 or the cost of war or the demands for reparations by an invading army or payment for imprisonment, 38 for such false claims be both absurd and abhorrent before heaven. 39 Thus no son can be bound by the transgressions or obligations of the father, 40 for death and heaven have settled such debts that if a merchant or moneylender deny, 41 then seize them for such fraud and offence against all Rule of Law. 42 As for those merchants and money lenders who now follow the false teachings of Rome, 43 in the absurd claims that there be no heaven or gods above us, 44 and that all ever written as to Rule of Law and Justice and Due Process be a myth, 45 for they claim to be men of reason and logic and intelligence, 46 when they are but nihilists and madmen and fools. 47 Woe unto you such purveyors of illness of the mind, 48 who seek to control by trickery and confusion and deception, 49 by promising a life of pleasure and happiness without substance or conscience. 50 Verily such nihilists and tricksters repudiate the existence of the Divine, 51 yet still rely upon the authority of the Divine for their office and law, 52 these madmen and liars deny the existence of heaven, 53 yet depend upon the magic of money and blood curses and false vows, 54 to ply their trade in condemning men to servitude and a life of slavery. 55 Thus do not let those who speak with illness of mind hide from the truth, 56 that the power and authority of the merchants and moneylenders, 57 remains upon the foundations of these temples and its priests. 58 Verily men have made goods and grown food and traded with each other since the first cities, 59 and it be a sacred right of all men to be able to trade and exchange their goods and labour, 60 and it be a right of true law that men receive a fair price for their goods and labour, 61 and money be anything that people be willing to accept as a means of fair exchange, 62 and the most important element to fair trade and price is trust. 63 Verily the only true capital is trust that the vow or oath of a man be true. 64 When trust is strong there be no need for the borrowings of bankers and priests, 65 as men can call upon the deepest supply of capital of good will of others to aid, 66 in helping build and grow and make objects and goods of value, 67 knowing that after the harvest or the market day they shall be paid fairly for their labour. 68 But when men lose trust with one another they turn to the money of priests and bankers, 69 and replace true capital with false capital and bond themselves to curses. 70 Even the greediest of bankers do not know these truths for they seek ways to corrupt, 71 and call for the days when Coin was stamped and not moulded and uneven and not perfect. 72 They do not understand even in times of loss of trust and greater profits, 73 that their hold on power rests upon the sacred foundations of the creators of true coin. 74 A Coin is but a standard of measure and a unit of value and a means of exchange, 75 but when it can be clipped or rubbed (fractionalised) of uneven weight, 76 or metals substituted so that it is not true gold or silver then it becomes worthless. 77 This is why the Cuilliaéan (Holly) invented standards of weight and measure, 78 that a true coin weigh not more or less than 432 grains and have three sides, 79 to end the madness of the bankers in destroying their own source of power, 80 and injuring the people through higher prices and unfair exchange. 81 Yet even the most perfect coin of a mint be worthless if people cannot work and trade. 82 Verily the only true money is the work and effort of men and women using their talents, 83 and the numbers in the ledgers of clerks and bankers be worthless, 84 if men and women refuse to give effort and energy to sustaining such numbers, 85 and if such numbers be written in bad faith or with any form of compound interest. 86 Truly there be few acts more wicked before heaven than a banker who adds his fee upon a debt, 87 or charges interest that the debt owed continues to grow of its own accord. 88 A merchant or banker may demand the fee at the time of the loan and at no other. 89 Thus if a banker or merchant charge any interest or fee on a debt, 90 have him seized as the worst of thieves and transgressors against the Rule of Law. 91 As for the payment of debts and honouring of such obligations, 92 verily I say to you that a man is obliged to pay his debts in the same manner, 93 and to the same extent as the banker offers forgiveness and good faith. 94 Therefore a man is no more obliged to pay a banker as a pirate, 95 for by corrupt acts a merchant or banker forfeits protection of true law. 96 If a man enter into consensus then let there be proper terms and consideration, 97 that if another comes and demands payment he may respond in honour and agree, 98 that if such debt be through proper consensus and in good faith and good conscience, 99 he must pay or find the means to pay but if such proof be not provided, 100 then such demand be that of a pirate or robber and a man be not obligated to pay, 101 nor may he be bound into servitude upon such false premise. 102 Verily a Tax be nothing more than the threats of pirates and robbers, 103 and a Tax be the demands of merchants and bankers who protect themselves by mercenaries. 104 For a people have no obligation to pay the debts of others nor those that enslave them. 105 Truly the very word Tax is abhorrent before all heaven and the

Divine Creator, 106 and no man or woman be bound to pay the ransom and threats of tyrants and thieves. 107 As for those who say such demands are for the common good and for roads and water, 108 I say to these weasels who speak for the corrupt merchants and bankers, 109 that any man or woman who uses the talents given unto them from heaven, 110 who is baptised and takes up their cross to live honourably and respectfully, 111 gives a thousand times more to the welfare of his community than any banker. 112 A society built upon true capital need not demand taxes but the good will of its people, 113 who shall gladly contribute to its aid and benefit. 114 But a community enslaved by mercenaries and thieves and liars can only demand by force in defiance of heaven, 115 that the people pay that which they do not owe. 116 Verily any priest who says taxes are in honour of heaven is a liar and not a priest. 117 Therefore I say to all of you today before all of heaven and the Divine Creator, 118 with the full authority and seals of office that all death pledges (mortgages) are expunged, 119 for such agreements are forbidden before heaven and are repugnant to the Rule of Law. 120 Furthermore I say to you that all debts and bonds upon the demands of taxes are expunged, 121 and the ledgers and registers to be destroyed as sacrilegious books, 122 for no man owe even a single coin of tribute to those that enslave him, 123 as his obligations be first to himself and his family and secondly to his community. 124 To all those many hundreds of thousands enslaved by such false debts and taxes, 125 I say to all of you upon the memory of the true laws of Rome and heaven, 126 that slavery in all its forms and especially by debt is absolutely forbidden. 127 Therefore any man or woman or child bonded into slavery upon the ledgers of the temples, 128 be now discharged and released from all such obligations and debts and emancipated. 129 Any merchant or land owner or banker or priest who then demands these people remain bound, 130 is nothing more than a tyrant and such people nothing more than prisoners, 131 for no law in heaven or on earth permit such false imprisonment or slavery, 132 and when such people find their strength to rise up let them seek justice, 133 and overthrow such tyrants and slave masters for by the Rule of Law of heaven and earth, 134 verily I say to you there was and is and has only ever been one law, 135 that no man is above the law and all are equal before it, 136 that no man or woman or child be bound as a slave, 137 and any such debts used to bind people have been expunged, 138 and all men and women are free to live according to their conscience, 139 knowing they are loved by their Father of all Creation, 140 they are protected by their ancestors and the spirits of heaven, 141 that the world and the land and all its fruits are as much their inheritance. 142 Therefore be good and honourable stewards of the world and fear nothing. 143 For your Father shall never abandon you nor leave you without aid nor condemn you. 144 You are divine immortal spirits carnated in flesh. You can never die.

C. 24

₁ In the year known as 36 CE, ₂ twelve hundred and thirty six years since the dawn of the Great Age, ₃ upon the spreading of the words and edict of Prince Jesus as Pontifex Maximus, ₄ and as Yahusiah and the Great Prophet of Yeb, ₅ the whole Roman world was thrown into upheaval, ₆ as hundreds of thousands of debt bonded slaves rejected their station, ₇ and many more demanded their debts be expunged by the bankers and merchants, ₈ as the words that Jesus had forgiven the debts of the world were spoken. ₉ In Gaul the city of Lucifer (Lyons) was briefly sieged by mobs, ₁₀ who stormed the Great Temple of Lucifer killing Legate Titus Coponius Sabinus, ₁₁ and burning all the records of debts and slaves of the bankers, ₁₂ as Jesus had also ordered be destroyed at the Great Temple of Mithra in Jerusalem. ₁₃ However Titus Coponius Vespasianus (Vespasian) and Claudius did escape, ₁₄ and succeeded in returning order to Lucifer (Lyons) while rebellion spread across the provinces. ₁₅ Lucius Aelius Seianus as Pontus Pilates then stripped Caiphas of the High Priesthood for his failures, ₁₆ but before a replacement was installed, Gaius Suetonius Macro as Caligula ordered him to Rome where he was executed, ₁₇ and the family of Lucius Aelius Seianus fled to Hispania and Hispalis (Seville). ₁₈ Macro as Caligula then appointed Lucius Vitellius Veteris to Syria, ₁₉ supported by General Marcus Asinius Marcellus and a mass army of several legions, ₂₀ to hunt down and kill Jesus and the Holly and any of their supporters, ₂₁ and restore order at the Great Temple Mint of Mithra at Jerusalem. ₂₂ Fearing their doom upon such treachery the priests of Baal-Hamon led by Jonathan, ₂₃ did pledge their loyalty to King Philipas Agrippa and the Nazarene Edicts, ₂₄ and Jonathan was appointed High Priest by Jesus as Pontifex Maximus. ₂₅ As a mass army of the Nabateans led by King Aenas (Antipas) prepared to confront Marcellus, ₂₆ Gaius Cornelius Gaetulicus the son of Cornelius Lentulus did depart to Egypt, ₂₇ with an army of Nabateans and Roman legionnaires and loyalists to support the uprising of Alexandria. ₂₈ Yet before the army of Cornelius Gaetulicus arrived the city of Alexandria fell, ₂₉ and Lucius Aelius Lamia the Legate of Africa did execute Thrasyllus of Alexandria and the rebels. ₃₀ When Cornelius Gaetulicus did arrive his army cut Lucius Aelius Lamia to pieces, ₃₁ as many of the legionnaires of Aelius Lamia defected to Cornelius Gaetulicus, ₃₂ and the strength of the Nazarene philosophy of Jesus of the salvation of all debts of the world. ₃₃ Cornelius Gaetulicus did then move north capturing Crete before landing upon the Peloponnese. ₃₄ In Lebanon the forces of Marcus Asinius Marcellus prepared for battle against King Aenas (Antipas), ₃₅ yet upon the night before the battle Judas and two thousand Sicari entered the camp of the Romans, ₃₆ cutting the throat of Marcus Asinius Marcellus and thousands more that upon day break, ₃₇ the Romans abandoned their camp and no battle was fought. ₃₈ With Holly High King Cú-Cúileann (Joseph) safely upon the Holly Isle of Britanni (Britain), ₃₉ and with the bounty price of Macro as Caligula on his head, 40 Prince Jesus did summons his brother James (Jacob) to Sepphoris, 41 and did call upon King Philipas Agrippa and King Aenas (Antipas) as witness, 42 where in the great temple to Yahu (The Divine Creator) Jesus did say: 43 The truths of heaven have now been unleashed upon the world, 44 that all men and women be saved and forgiven of their debts, 45 that none may deny the truth of the resurrection as none can die, 46 nor may any man or woman be again lawfully claimed as a slave, 47 nor any false teacher or tyrant claim false law as Rule of Law, 48 nor false rights as Justice or false ritual as Due Process. 49 Verily the madness of men who believe in nothing but themselves has been exposed, 50 and no more shall the bankers or merchants claim protection of heaven. 51 Alas such forces unleashed bring with them storms and tempest before the calm, 52 and there be the deeper cause of history to address. 53 For every true revelation of heaven comes through a divine messenger, 54 and thus the Holly have been such messengers from the beginning of time. 55 Yet all men and women are created equal and so unless this history be broken, 56 that none stand between heaven and earth as a messiah and messenger, 57 then no man or woman is truly free and corruption and madness will only return. 58 Verily I say to you most solemnly that unless I die as the only Son of God, 59 unless I die as the Pontifex Maximus and the Great Prophet of Yeb, 60 unless I die as the thirty second Great Messiah and be reborn a man, 61 a man no greater or lesser than the men in the fields or in arms, 62 then all that has been done and said will be for naught. 63 Thus I say to all here present that I was the Christ and now I am the Anti-Christ, 64 for I am the one who was once the only son of God as Pharaoh who rejected the crown, 65 that I become more as a man and restore the Golden Rule that all are equal, 66 and none may be above another and no man be a god but all men be greater than gods, 67 for they be Divine Immortal Spirit carnated in flesh. 68 Therefore one last prophecy I speak and thereafter no more for it shall be my brother James, 69 who be leader of the Universal Ecclesia not as messiah but as its priest and Ptah (father/Peter). 70 One more will come before the final restoration of law and truth as Christ and Anti-Christ, 71 as Holly in blood and character and upon the death to all title and birth as a man, 72 the old world of pain and suffering will end and the Kingdom of Heaven shall be upon the earth. Amen.

C. 25

1 In the year known as 37 CE, 2 twelve hundred and thirty seven years since the dawn of the Great Age, 3 Gaius Suetonius Macro declared himself Emperor Caligula in a grand ceremony in Rome, 4 before even Tiberius had finally given up the ghost. 5 When news of the event reached Capri the invalid and elderly Tiberius suddenly revived through rage, 6 and prepared himself to come to Rome and declare Macro a traitor and have him executed. 7 But news reached Suetonius Macro and he departed to Capri, 8 where he choked Tiberius to death and then waited till he turned

blue, 9 thus ensuring the transition was completed from one tyrant to the next. 10 In the same year news reached Rome of the abdication of Jesus, 11 the appointment of Yacobiah (Jacob) also known as James as heir, 12 and successor to Jesus known as the first Peter (Ptah) meaning Holy Father, 13 of the Universal Ecclesia (Church) of Truth (Nazara), 14 and the release of Pontifex Praetorian Prefect Lucius Cornelius Sulla, 15 who now joined the growing army of Gaius Cornelius Gaetulicus on the Peloponnese. 16 In the Roman provinces of Upper and Lower Germania the Celts revolted, 17 in honour of the edicts and message of Jesus, 18 with Legate Lucius Visellius Varro and his legions destroyed. 19 Emperor Caligula then appointed Lucius Apronius Caesianus as legate of Germania, 20 and Aulus Avillius Flaccus as legate of Africa, 21 and his own son Gaius Suetonius Paulus as Legate of Gaul, 22 to crush the rebellions across the Empire. 23 Yet Gaius Suetonius Paulus was no match for Claudius, 24 and he soon retreated south to Hispania to seek sanctuary with Lucius Calpurnius Piso, 25 whom granted him sanctuary but did give up the ghost soon after, 26 with his son Gaius Calpurnius Piso forming an alliance with Gaius Suetonius Paulus. 27 In the same year Gaius Cornelius Gaetulicus with Cornelius Sulla moved north, 28 and routed the legions of Gaius Calvisius Sabinus of Pannonia, 29 with most of the legions defecting to Sulla as a famous soldier of honour. 30 At the same time the Celtic tribes of Gaul and Hispania began full rebellion against Roman rule, 31 upon the death of the tyrant merchant lord Lucius Calpurnius Piso, 32 such that the forces of Gaius Calpurnius Piso the son of Lucius Calpurnius Piso, 33 and Gaius Suetonius Paulus the son of Caligula (Macro), 34 were no match for the rage of the Celts, 35 and the pirate merchants were forced to abandon their treasures and estates, 36 and flee south to the coast of Africa and the safety of Mauretania. 37 Yet instead of attacking the main tribes of Gaul and Hispania, 38 Claudius declared himself the true Emperor and proclaimed he embraced the teachings of Jesus, 39 concerning the Rule of Law, of Justice and Due Process and that if Caligula be defeated, 40 he would ensure democratic rule for all with the chiefs of the tribes represented in the Senate of Rome, 41 and an end to taxes by census and piracy and robbery of property. 42 Upon news of the announcement by Claudius in favour of the Nazarenes, 43 Emperor Caligula ordered his legions to attack Lucifer (Lyons) in Gaul, 44 and seize Claudius as a traitor while choosing to lead the campaign himself. 45 With the Emperor leaving to the west Gaius Cornelius Gaetulicus moved to Germania, 46 as Cornelius Sulla prepared his army to invade central Italy and take Rome itself.

C. 26

1 In the year known as 38 CE, 2 twelve hundred and thirty eight years since the dawn of the Great Age, 3 Aulus Avillius Flaccus was defeated and killed by the rebels of Egypt, 4 as Lucius Apronius Caesianus was trapped and killed in the low lands (Netherlands), 5 by the army of Gaius Cornelius Gaetulicus. 6 Emperor Caligula did have Lucifer (Lyon) under

Book 21 Age of the Nazarenes

siege as he received word, 7 that Cornelius Sulla and the main army had landed in Italy and defeated Lucius Calpernius Piso, 8 and had now entered Rome to a triumph by the people as liberators. 9 Upon the news Caligula chose to abandon the siege of Lucifer (Lyons), 10 and return to Italy in the hope of devising a plan to eliminate Sulla and win back Rome. 11 In Rome the Praetorian immediately welcomed Cornelius Sulla as their leader, 12 arresting the murderers of Lentulus and the creators of the false histories and laws and philosophies, 13 of Nihilism and grotesque consumerism of the fictional Epicurus. 14 Masurius Sabinus Cassius and many of his followers were publicly executed, 15 with his texts banned and ordered to be destroyed. 16 Marcus Annaeus Seneca was also captured condemned and executed, 17 as a traitor to history and truth and philosophy. 18 Yet many of the rats escaped including Gaius Cassius Longinus, 19 and Lucius Annaeus Seneca the son of the elder, 20 and Gaius Calpernius Piso the son of Lucius Calpernius Piso. 21 The Senate then appointed Sulla the Nasci and Protector of Rome. 22 In the same year (38 CE), 23 the first born son of Jesus and Mariamne whose name was Iudiah (Judah), 24 did suddenly succumb to sudden fever at the age of nine. 25 A servant at Bethesda was seized with thirty pieces of silver and poison, 26 but committed suicide before the source of his commission was revealed. 27 Upon the murder Holly High King Cú-Cúileann (Joseph) did plea, 28 that his family leave Palestine for a while until sanity was at least restored. 29 Jesus and Mariamne deeply mourned the death of Iudiah (Judah) and saw it as a sign, 30 and were resolved to retreat from the world and honour his brother Yacobiah (Jacob), 31 as Ptah (Peter) the Rock and Father and Holly heir. 32 Gaius Cornelius Gaetulicus then did send word that if the Holly Family did travel west, 33 they would find safety at a place called mons securus (Montségur) meaning the safest mountain. 34 Protected by the finest Sicambri (Batavii) legion and an impregnable fortress. 35 Thus Jesus, Mariamne and their daughter Mary and young son James did depart, 36 first to Narbo (Narbonne) and then to Carcasum (Carcassonne) then south to mons secures (Montségur), 37 to be greeted there by Gaius Cornelius Gaetulicus and his pregnant wife, 38 soon after the wife of Gaius Cornelius Gaetulicus giving birth to a son named Gaius Cornelius Tacticus. 39 Yet on Gaius Cornelius Gaetulicus returning to Germania he did fall ill and give up the ghost. 40 The widow of Gaius Cornelius Gaetulicus remained inconsolable and in a few months did pass herself. 41 Jesus with Mariamne now pregnant with child did then resolve to raise Tacticus as if their own son, 42 and Jesus resolved that if time permitted he would share all he knew with their new found son.

C. 27

1 In the year known as 39 CE, 2 twelve hundred and thirty nine years since the dawn of the Great Age, 3 Mariamne did give birth to a child at mons securus (Montségur), 4 a daughter named Salome also known in history as Sara, 5 in honour of the

mother of Mariamne and the last great ruler of the Hasmoneans. 6 In the same year King Aenas (Antipas) did give up the ghost. 7 The undisputed kings of all the tribes of the Nabateans did become Philipas Agrippas, 8 who was then crowned as Herod Agrippas as the King of all Nabatea. 9 Claudius then sent word that he recognised King Herod Agrippas as his ally, 10 and that as emperor he did give his word never to attack the Nabateans, 11 thus Lucius Vitellius Veteris hastily sought terms of truce with Agrippas, 12 acknowledging him and the priests of Baal-Hamon to function the Great Temple Mint at Jerusalem. 13 In the same year Marcus Aemilius Lepidus and Gnaeus Domitius Ahenobarbus, 14 supported by the grand daughters of Tiberius being Julia Agrippina and Julia Livilla, 15 did successfully bring Macro as Caligula into the city to confront Sulla. 16 Yet upon the day that Sulla as Nasci (Nazi) and Protector of Rome, 17 was to be assassinated the plot was uncovered and Macro as Caligula was captured and executed, 18 along with Marcus Aemilius Lepidus and Gnaeus Domitius and other loyalist senators. 19 Julia Agrippina and her son Lucius Domitius later known as Nero, 20 and her sister Julia Livilla were then exiled to the island of Ponza. 21 Claudius still at Lucifer (Lyon) was now the undisputed emperor. 22 Cornelius Sulla as Nasci and the Senate did then extend the invitation, 23 for Claudius to return to Rome as Emperor. 24 Yet Claudius did at first decline the invitation saying: That if the idea of Rome to survive, 25 all men must honour their word in the same manner as deeds. 26 Thus as I have pledged the leaders of the great tribes of Gaul and Hispania equality, 27 that they be honoured as senators in the halls of true democracy, 28 so I must visit and pledge my service to each province to restore good faith, 29 and stamp out the corrupt practices of evil bankers and merchants, 30 and restore the Rule of Law that is the symbol of Rome. 31 Thus Claudius did visit Hispania and the provinces of Gaul and Germania, 32 and did win the loyalty and pledge of the Celtic tribes as a man or honour, 33 who would match his words with deeds and restore the Rule of Law. 34 In the year known as 41 CE, 35 twelve hundred and forty one years since the dawn of the Great Age, 36 Claudius arrived triumphant into Rome to be greeted by Sulla and the Praetorian, 37 who pledged their honour to an emperor who did promise to restore the rule of law, 38 and end the decadence and madness of the nihilists who had infected the minds of all, 39 with addictions to nothing but pleasure and the destruction of all moral boundaries. 40 Claudius then did honour the edicts of the Senate that forbid the teachings of Epicurianism, 41 and the false philosophy of nihilism as a heresy against the state and capital crime. 42 Yet soon after Cornelius Sulla now at advanced age and tired from life did give up the ghost. 43 Claudius demanded a month of mourning and demanded that all Praetorian and Legions, 44 honour the stoic philosophy and austerity of the Cornelii and Sulla and Gaetulicus, 45 as this be the true strength of Rome. 46 Claudius did then send word to mons securus (Montségur) that for the first time in history, 47 the Roman Senate did adopt Gaius Cornelius Tacticus as if his parents declaring him to be Parens Patriae, 48 and for he to be returned to them when upon the age of majority. 49 At the end of the month of mourning the death of Sulla, 50 Titus Coponius Vespasianus (Vespasian) did arrange for Gaius Cassius Longinus, 51 the leader of the Sabiniani and author of wicked fictions of law, 52 to plead his alliance with Claudius and seek redemption. 53 While Claudius refused to lift the edicts of Sulla, he appointed Longinus legate of Asia. 54 Claudius then restored the honour of the House of Piso in appointing Gaius Calpurnius Piso Consul, 55 and Legate of both Hispania and all of Africa but on the condition that the Hispanic Celtic Kings, 56 were not to be harmed, nor their lands or people seized. 57 In the same year Valeria Messalina the third wife of Claudius, 58 did give birth to a young boy they named Tiberius Claudius Germanicus and later known as Britannicus.

C. 28

1 In the year known as 42 CE, 2 twelve hundred and forty two years since the dawn of the Great Age, 3 Claudius Augustus did honour his solemn pledge to the Celtic Chiefs of Gaul and Hispania, 4 by investing them as Senators and equals in Rome as order was restored across the Empire. 5 Never before had Rome or the Senate recognised such leaders before and across the world, 6 that some within the Roman Senate were hostile to recognizing such Celts, 7 while some Celt tribes ignored in the pledge were green with envy. 8 The pirate merchant tribes that lived among the swamps from the coast of Gaul, 9 and eastern Britain and the flatlands of the north (Netherlands), 10 did bemoan that their loyalty to Rome in shielding merchant ships was ignored. 11 King Tinco of the Cantiaci (Kent) and King Verica of the Atrebati (South Britain), 12 did even go to Rome to plead for recognition in exchange for absolute loyalty to Rome. 13 Legate Titus Coponius Vespasianus of Gaul did implore Claudius, 14 use the entreats of the Artebati and Cantiaci pirates as a pretext, 15 to seize the sacred island of Britain of the Holly (Cuilliaéan), 16 yet other Senators urged caution for such an act might be seen as violation, 17 upon the terms of peace with the Celtic tribes and the laws of Rome, 18 for Augustus Octavius and the Roman Senate has recognised possession, 19 and occupation and absolute title of the Isle of Britain to the Holly (Cuilliaéan). 20 Legate Titus Coponius Vespasianus disagreed and encouraged Claudius, 21 to summons the new Senate and all the new Celtic Senators, 22 that the Cantiaci (Kent) and Atrebati (South Britain) may plea for aid, 23 to uphold the honour of the teachings of Jesus and the Nazarenes, 24 and that this be a test for the Celtic Tribes whether they believe, 25 in the Golden Rule that all are equal under the law and justice and due process, 26 or whether they seek themselves to be wealthy like the Holly (Cuilliaéan). 27 Thus the new Senate was summonsed and Claudius Augustus did speak saying: 28 All men are called to bear witness to honour their pledge of duty and service, 29 that all are equal under the laws of Rome and in the respect of Justice. 30 For even the lowest

indentured servant possesses rights, 31 that their master must honour and cannot disavow. 32 Therefore, when a servant of even the most esteemed house calls out for justice, 33 such a petition must be heard and granted favour of the law. 34 This body then must choose whether it be formed under such ancient honour, 35 and fraternity of democratic values that all who respect such law, 36 deserve aid and support in time of need or whether this be an empty chamber, 37 in name and title only that shows no respect to the ancient laws of Tara. 38 The Senate and the Celtic Senators did then agree to give aid to the Cantiaci and the Atrebati, 39 and that such an act be not a declaration of war against the Holly (Cuilliaéan) nor an invasion. 40 In the same year (42 CE), 41 Holly High King Cú-Cúileann (Joseph) did choose to depart Palestine, 42 to first visit his son Jesus at mons securus (Montségur) and then to Britain. 43 Holly High King Cú-Cúileann (Joseph) and Mary with his guard did then travel to Narbo, 44 and then to the foothills of the Pyrenees and mons securus (Montségur), 45 where he did first set eyes upon Salome (Sara) and young Gaius Cornelius Tacticus. 46 Holly High King Joseph and Mary did then travel to Glastonbury, 47 and the hospitality of Caratacos the Custenin of the Holly Estates, 48 who then warned the old king of the perfidy of the Cantiaci (Kent) and Atrebati (South Britain), 49 and that the House of Piso and the Bankers of Lucifer (Lyons) did see this an opportunity, 50 to seize the vast wealth of minerals of Britain at any cost or any pretext. 51 Holly High King Cú-Cúileann (Joseph) did then summons his son Jacob (James) and his family Anna and their son Beliah, 52 to be under the protection of Caratacos the Custenin (Constantine) of the Dumnonii, 53 whilst the future of the Holly hung in the balance. 54 Holly High King Cú-Cúileann (Joseph) did call those Celtic tribal leaders still loyal to a meeting at Glastonbury. 55 From the west (Wales) did come the Angli, the Siluri and Ordovicii. 56 From the north did come the Damnonii, the Selgovii and Brigandii. 57 From the midlands did come the Cornovii and the Dubunni. 58 From the east did come the Iceni. 59 The only tribes that did not come were the Cantiaci (Kent) and Atrebati. 60 When all were assembled the old Holly High King Cú-Cúileann (Joseph) did say: 61 This be the age by heaven that the peoples of the Covenant are to be tested, 62 whether they honour the laws of Tara and the Divine Creator, 63 or the lies of corrupt men and wicked priests. 64 For no more evil act there be by wilful ignorance before all heaven and earth, 65 than to take the teachings of the golden rule and rule of law and call them corrupt, 66 and then take the madness of merchants and call such piracy the law, 67 to take the knowledge of the rights of men and call them privileges, 68 then present the cruelty of slavery and debt as duties of all beings. 69 Thus Rome and the Senate has sought to fight the teachings and commands, 70 of the Great Prophet and a great teacher not with weapons and legions, 71 but with bribery and manipulation that men worship darkness as light, 72 that men who should know better welcome ignorance as wisdom and greed as virtuous. 73 As for the transgressions of the Holly (Cuilliaéan) in the past ages it is true, 74 that such priests have failed the world more than once. 75 Yet it is also true that these same priests have restored the law and connection to the Divine, 76 at the end of every great age of darkness. 77 So it is we witness the end to the fraternity of the people called the Keltoi, 78 as chiefs and kings seek the pleasures of Rome rather than honour and truth. 79 Thus I say to you today these lands be not the property of a house or a bloodline, 80 but the inheritance of all born upon its soil. 81 Thus from this day forth there be no longer a Holly High King of the Keltoi, 82 but only three kingdoms of conscience being Cymri (Wales) to the west and south, 83 Cruithri (Scotland) to the north and the sacred Isle of Eiri (Ireland). 84 Verily let the tribal chiefs here select their kings and Battle Chief. 85 For the war we must fight upon this age of darkness shall determine not only our destiny, 86 but the very survival of true Rule of law itself. 87 For the new kingdom of Eiri (Ireland) the tribes selected Tuatha Taghtamor as king, 88 his naming meaning the One chosen from the tribes. 89 For the kingdom of Cymri (Wales) the tribes selected Yacobiah (Jacob) also known as James as King. 90 For the kingdom of Cruithri (Scotland) the tribes selected former Holly High King Joseph to be king. 91 And as catu-uellauni (Catuvellauni) the Battle Chief of all the tribes, 92 the Dumnonii, Dobunii, Cornovii, Brigantii, Iceni and all loyal tribes, 93 selected Caratacos the Custenin (Constantine) to be their general.

C. 29

1 In the year known as 42 CE, 2 twelve hundred and forty two years since the dawn of the Great Age, 3 upon the Holly leaving the Levant, the Caiaphas did rise up and kill Baal High Priest Jonathan, 4 installing Simon the Caiaphas as the new High Priest instead. 5 His reign was short and soon he himself met his doom at the hands of Matthias, 6 the son of Ananus and the father of Josephus, also known later as Flavius Josephus, 7 and a future architect of the horrendous falsity known as the Septuagint. 8 Matthias then declared himself to be Mattiah and a Great Prophet. 9 The elderly King Philipas Agrippa of Nabatea was outraged and ordered Mattiah to be arrested, 10 yet the House of Ananus learnt of their danger and Mattias with his brothers and young son Josephus, 11 departed to plead for their safety with Legate Gaius Cassius Longinus. 12 Emperor Claudius did then recall Lucius Vitellius Veteris from retirement, 13 to aid Gaius Cassius Longinus as the health of King Philipas Agrippa continued to decline. 14 In the same year Titus Coponius Vespasianus (Vespasian) and Gaius Calpernius Piso, 15 did demand an answer as to why the Emperor had continued to delay sending legions to Britain, 16 to aid the request of the Cantiaci (Kent) and Atrebati (South Britain). 17 Claudius did reply that while he wished to honour the words granted, 18 the Empire could not afford such an expedition nor risk the fracture of uneasy peace, 19 between the new Celtic Kings of Hispania and Gaul as Senators. 20 Gaius Calpernius Piso

then offered that the House of Piso would fund and mount the cost, 21 that the peace the Emperor so wanted to keep be not tested. 22 In the year known as 43 CE, 23 twelve hundred and forty three years since the dawn of the Great Age, 24 as Gaius Calpernius Piso aided by Titus Coponius Vespasianus (Vespasian), 25 prepared their mercenary force of 50,000 to leave for Britain, 26 Emperor Claudius did come to Lucifer (Lyons) to ask the men to reconsider, 27 that by such act the Empire might be returned to great conflict. 28 Yet Titus Coponius Vespasianus (Vespasian) did reply that the fate of the empire, 29 now depended upon the success of the private commercial enterprise, 30 to seize the mineral wealth and secure the safety of metal reserves, 31 as the Celtic Kings of Hispania as Senators had disrupted and made mining difficult. 32 So it was then that the first force of 15,000 mercenaries led by Arrius Calpernius Piso, 33 landed upon the east coast of the lands of the Cantiaci (Kent), 34 as a second mercenary force of 10,000 led by Lucius Calpernius Piso, 35 landed on the south coast in the lands of the Atrebati (South Britain), 36 with a third force led by their father and Gaius Calpernius Piso himself, 37 with a mercenary force of over 20,000 did sail up the Thames, 38 and establish a fortified post at a great crescent curve in the river, 39 He called lun(a) dom(i) as crescent home and later the fort known as Londinium. 40 Caratacus with a much larger Celt force moved down the Thames toward the Piso mercenaries, 41 while his brother Togodumnus with a smaller force moved down the Medway. 42

Togodumnus was first to encounter Lucius Calpernius Piso and succeeded in pushing back, 43 until he was surrounded by the forces of Arrius Calpernius Piso, 44 who came to the aid of his brother and Togodumnus was routed and killed. 45 Yet Caratacus was more successful and within the first months of invasion, 46 the Piso had lost nearly half of their mercenaries. 47 Gaius Calpernius Piso did then call upon Titus Coponius Vespasianus (Vespasian), 48 to spend whatever the cost and come with haste himself to Britain, 49 with a mercenary force large enough to subdue the Holly Celts. 50 Within weeks of offering a handsome purse to any pirate or robber or mercenary who would come, 51 with promise of loot and bounty to be had from the treasures of the Holly for centuries, 52 Titus Coponius Vespasianus (Vespasian) had amassed a new mercenary army of 80,000, 53 which he landed in waves near Exeter to the west while reinforcing the Piso to the east. 54 The attack directly against the homeland of Caratacus of Dumnonii, 55 had the desired effect and while more than 10,000 ill disciplined mercenaries had been slaughtered, 56 within days of their arrival, the sheer number of pirates and robbers and thieves, 57 overwhelmed the Holly and Caratacus and they were forced to retreat into the hills of the west, 58 and Wales and to the lands of the Briganti. 59 Against such odds, the large tribe known as the Iceni (Norwich and Ipswich), 60 did seek terms and peace with the House of Piso. 61 In the same year, 62 High Priest Heliodores of Eliada and Larissa, 63 leader of the Therapeutae

C. 30

₁ In the year known as 44 CE, ₂ twelve hundred and forty four years since the dawn of the Great Age, ₃ during a prolonged dry spell across all the Levant and Africa, ₄ King Philipas Agrippa also known as Herod Agrippa and King of all Nabatea, ₅ and father of Mariamne the wife of Jesus, ₆ and father of Anna the wife of Jacobiah (James), ₇ did give up the ghost at Damascus. ₈ Upon the death of Agrippa Roman Legate Gaius Cassius Longinus looked to invade, ₉ or at least appoint a client puppet king yet Lucius Vitellius Veteris urged caution, ₁₀ for no sensible general goes to war without water or enough grain, ₁₁ and if the Nabateans rallied they could command the largest and fiercest of armies. ₁₂ Word was sent to Jesus at mons securus (Montségur) to return to Asia with his family, ₁₃ for he be the rightful King of all Nabatea according to their custom. ₁₄ Yet Jesus declined saying that it was Jacob (James) and not he who is King and Father, ₁₅ and he Jesus be no more than a Visitor and Teacher forbidden to be known as a king. ₁₆ Jacob (James) and Anna then accepted to return to rule at Damascus, ₁₇ as King and father and as Ptah (Peter) and Head of the Universalis Ecclesia (Universal Church). ₁₈ His son also known as Beliah and Bran the Blessed at the age of seventeen, ₁₉ remained at Anglesey as King of Cymri (Wales) and under the wise guidance of Joseph, ₂₀ and the protection of the forces of Caratacos against the mercenary forces of the pirate bankers. ₂₁ As drought in Africa and Asia worsened and grain supplies dwindled the threat against the Empire grew, ₂₂ and Emperor Claudius demanded Gaius Calpernius Piso cease his obsession of Britain, ₂₃ and tend to his duties as Legate of Africa. ₂₄ Gaius Calpernius Piso was outraged and replied that if the Emperor had given the men he needed, ₂₅ Britain would be conquered and there would be no need to make such demands of him. ₂₆ In response Claudius appointed Servius Sulpicius Galba as Legate of Africa to save the crops, ₂₇ and then sent Publius Ostorius Scapula and six of his best legions of 40,000 men to Britain to aid the Piso. ₂₈ In honour of the Nabateans Jacob (James) adopted the regal name of Agrippa and within a year, ₂₉ King Jacob Agrippa of Nabatea had succeeded in saving the population from starvation, ₃₀ and introduced irrigation techniques to keep the crops alive with enough grain to help feed hungry Rome. ₃₁ Jacob quickly came to be known by the title Herod meaning a great leader of Nabatea, ₃₂ and Emperor Claudius secured a treaty with King Jacob on the promise to stop the Piso menace of Britain, ₃₃ and Claudius demanded the Pisans cease their attacks and withdraw their mercenaries from Britain. ₃₄ At such a challenge, Gaius Calpernius Piso swore a high curse he would find a way to destroy Claudius, ₃₅ and with such plans in mind recalled Julia Agrippina from exile and her son Nero to Rome, ₃₆ and began plotting the downfall of Valeria Messalina the wife of Claudius.

C. 31

₁ In the year known as 46 CE, ₂ twelve hundred and forty six years since the dawn of the Great Age, ₃ the great drought of Asia and Africa continued to grip at the neck of the Empire. ₄ Servius Sulpicius Galba as Legate of Africa had only been moderately successful at restoring supply. ₅ Thus the fate of the world rested in the skill and judgement of King Jacob as Herod Agrippa of Nabatea. ₆ Irrigation from natural sources of water and improved disciplines in the fields continued to grow agriculture, ₇ that hundreds of thousands of refugees continued to migrate to the lands of the Nabateans, ₈ to find food to find water and to find a way to survive. ₉ But now King Jacob faced a new menace at the hands of the priests of Baal and Mithra, ₁₀ who had resolved their differences in order to fleece refugees of their worldly possessions for a few grains, ₁₁ and who continued to steal grain and water for their own use to then sell at inflated prices. ₁₂ King Jacob did then summons Baal and Mithraic priests under sanctuary to Damascus, ₁₃ where Ananias proceeded to tell King Jacob it be their birth-right and divine right to claim sustenance, ₁₄ and that they be the custodians of such property for the Divine. ₁₅ Jacob was outraged at such supreme arrogance and ignorance and then issued a solemn decree saying: ₁₆ Henceforth let it be known to all present or come in the future, ₁₇ that any priest who claims such right from heaven to cheat, or thieve or speak untruth, ₁₈ is culpable of the gravest offence of profanity of Sacred Law and must be exiled or executed. ₁₉ Furthermore let it be known that any priest who claims they alone have the right to interpret the law, ₂₀ is culpable of the most serious offence of intentional sacrilege and must be stripped of any authority, ₂₁ Finally, let it be known that any priest who claims they hold authority from heaven by rights by birth, ₂₂ has no authority nor such rights and must be removed from office to prevent any further stain of the law. ₂₃ Upon the edict and anger of King Jacob the priest Ananias did ask if Jacob remained in honour to his word, ₂₄ to which the King replied that only a priest with no knowledge of history or heaven could ask such a thing, ₂₅ for even if such imposter priests were to profane heaven they be protected to leave, ₂₆ unless by stealth or trickery they sought to return to Nabatea whereupon they would executed. ₂₇ Thus Ananias did speak with all the leading priests of Baal and Mithra present, saying: ₂₈ It is true King that the Cuilliaéan by their blood be most favoured as prophets and saviours of heaven. ₂₉ Yet as history has shown the laws of heaven be best for heaven and men being the creature they are, ₃₀ fail moreover to honour such edicts despite their best intentions. ₃₁ Yet the Holly display righteous arrogance to other priestly houses as to the province of wisdom and truth, ₃₂ that they and they alone hold the keys to heaven and the earth. ₃₃ King Jacob, even more outraged did respond: ₃₄ Oh wicked priests it is not through some special gift or divine revelation or arrogance that I exile you, ₃₅ but that you are imposters and false teachers who know nothing of law and less of the truth you speak. ₃₆ If only one of your kin demonstrated the smallest competence or clear mind all would be unnecessary. 37 Simon the Caiaphas did speak saying: Before you exile us from our lands and we depart upon this high curse, 38 let heaven fall and men disavow the creator for we shall find solace in mankind and his true nature. 39 Your blinding trust in honour shall be your downfall for we have no need for heaven or the Divine Creator. 40 We shall survive and we shall thrive and let mankind be our judge today that the world will be ours. 41 Above all others and in our own image that one day men shall no more remember the Holly or their history. 42 Upon the edict more than 2000 priests and their families were exiled to all quarters of the world. 43 Simon the Caiaphas took his priests to Babylon where he claimed himself as Gamaliel reborn, 44 and started the Occult School of Hillel dedicated to constant curses to heaven, to the holly and to unfaithful demons. 45 Ananias with his priests and families departed to Alexandria along with Marcian and Nicomedia (Timothy), 46 where they began to write unholy lies and corruptions of history that all would be confused of the past, 47 and none would remember the Holly but would only see the priests of Baal and Mithra as heroes. 48 Matthias the Younger (Theophilus) took his priests to Heliopolis and Gaius Cassius Longinus, 49 while Jonathan the younger took his priests and family to Crete and Athens. 50 Josephus and later known as Flavius Josephus and several other young priests then travelled to Rome, 51 where he met and became friends with Gaius Plinius Secundus also known as Pliny the Younger, 52 who in turn introduced him to Gaius Suetonius Paulus and Lucius Annaeus Seneca, 53 and then to Gaius Calpernius Piso who had returned to Rome to further ferment rumours and slander, 54 against Valeria Messalina while strengthening the redemption of Julia Agrippina the mother of Nero, 55 as Arrius Calpernius Piso remained at Londonium and Lucius Calpernius Piso had returned to Hispania. 56 Upon seeing the brilliance of Josephus, Gaius Calpernius Piso hired him to his household. 57 In the year known as 47 CE, 58 twelve hundred and forty seven years since the dawn of the Great Age, 59 Arrius Calpernius Piso had grown impatient as the forces of Caratacus remained at rest, 60 and conspired with Publius Ostorius Scapula to end the uneasy truce. 61 Arrius Calpernius Piso arranged for mercenaries to dress like the troops of Caratacus, 62 and attack Lindum Colonia (Lincoln) giving Publius Ostorius Scapula the excuse to act. 63 Next Arrius Calpernius Piso formed an army of mercenaries resembling the troops of Scapula, 64 to begin attacking and burning down the outposts bordering the kingdom of Cruithri (Scotland), 65 in anticipation of what appeared to be an invasion and attack against Old King Joseph of the Holly. 66 Caratacus immediately summonsed all the troops available of the Brigandii, Ordovicii and Siluri, 67 and began to march with his army north-east towards what he believed to be Publius Ostorius Scapula, 68 but in the west midlands the real army of Publius Ostorius Scapula ambushed the Celts, 69 and Caratacus was captured after a brief and bloody battle. 70 Upon news of the trickery and deception of Arrius Calpernius Piso and the action of the Romans, 71 King Jacob immediately halted grain supplies to Rome causing fear and shock. 72 Emperor Claudius then send word that he would personally resolve the issue of the Piso in Britain, 73 and soon after travelled to Lucifer (Lyon) where Claudius demanded the support and troops of Vespasian, 74 who then joined him in travelling to Londinium where he announced the creation of 11 kingdoms, 75 upon the disputed lands with each king a Senator of Rome, 76 being the kingdom of Cantiaci (Canterbury and Kent), 77 the kingdom of Belgi (Southampton Isle of Wight as Dumnonii annexed lands), 78 the kingdom of Atrebati (Reading South Britain), 79 the kingdom of Durotrigi (Dorchester as Dumnonii annexed lands), 80 the kingdom of Trinovanti (Chelmsford as Iceni annexed lands), 81 the kingdom of Dobunni (Bristol as as Dumnonii annexed lands), 82 the kingdom of Iceni (Norwich and Ipswich), 83 the kingdom of Corieltauvi (Peterborough as Iceni annexed lands), 84 the kingdom of Cornovii (Cornwell as Dumnonii annexed lands), 85 the kingdom of Parisi (York as Brigandi annexed lands), 86 and the kingdom of Regni being the false tribe of Londinium as Atrebati annexed lands. 87 Claudius did then recognise the Holly Kingdoms of Cymri (Wales), Cruithri (Scotland) and Eiri (Ireland). 88 Claudius then stripped the Pisans of any rights of ownership except for Londinium, 89 accepting Caratacus as an honourable prisoner to return with him to Rome to be tried by the Senate, 90 and that no Roman forces were to touch any more lands of the Dumnonii until the conclusion of the trial. 91 Upon the announcement of Claudius the Piso through Arrius Calpernius Piso resolved that Londinium, 92 would become a great city of the empire despite the actions of the Emperor. 93 The Pisans then set about commissioning major new buildings and temples of stone, 94 including a formidable protective wall to be built around Londinium. 95 When news of the actions of Claudius reached King Jacob, he ordered the resumption of grain, 96 and Rome lived yet another day.

C. 32

1 Claudius returned to Rome as if a conquering hero being rewarded a Tribute, 2 with Publius Ostorius Scapula lauded as a great general and awarded the corona civica, 3 and Caratacus paraded in the procession as if the brutish and dangerous Celt brought to heel. 4 Yet the celebrations of Claudius were short lived as trusted Praetorian Prefect Lucius Licinius Geta, 5 did give the news to Claudius that several witness had come forward to testify that they had seen, 6 Empress Valeria Messalina having sexual relations with several partners including Gaius Silius. 7 Enraged Claudius demanded the arrest and torture of Gaius Silius until he confessed his offence, 8 upon then the tainted confession of a dying man Claudius demanded the arrest of his wife. 9 Gaius Calpernius Piso then gently suggested to Claudius he should use caution and ensure the truth, 10 for such accusations carried the most grievous of dishonour unprecedented

of an Empress. 11 Claudius agreed to the counsel of the elder Piso that public company with Julia Agrippina, 12 would help calm the rumours and uncertainty of Rome as to their future. 13 Thus upon the cruel torture of several hapless male prostitutes and servants, 14 Claudius was convinced of the perfidy of Valeria Messalina. 15 Yet instead of permitting her to commit suicide Claudius ordered she be torn to shreds. 16 Claudius then retired from public life for several weeks seeking the comfort of Julia Agrippina, 17 until he returned to preside over the public trial of Caratacus in the Senate. 18 Before the whole Senate now populated by several dozen Celtic kings Caratacus was brought in chains, 19 whereupon the charge of capital crime in the killing of Roman citizens of the Patrician class was read, 20 to which Caratacus was offered his right of Adlocution before the Senate and Emperor voted, 21 to which Caratacus replied thus in perfect Latin to the astonishment of all present: 22 If it be my fate this day to leave this mortal form, I have no fear, 23 for what is a man but his character, or a household but its good name, or a people more than its laws. 24 Thus when a man acts without honour he is without substance, for a house without dignity is empty. 25 So too, a people that honours not its precepts or its words or promises cannot last. 26 Therefore I ask this noble house to remember the solemn and sacred promise made to my ancestors, 27 sixty years ago by the great Augustus granting in perpetuity to the Cuilliaéan, 28 the sole recognised rights of the Isle of Britannia. 29 For if you damn me then you damn the memory of Augustus and all Emperors and Rome. 30 There was uproar in the Senate as Senators argued and debated until Claudius demanded calm, 31 whereupon it was agreed and voted that Caratacus should be set free, 32 for no offence had been committed as Caratacus be a Patrician, 33 and all his descendants be therefore Patrician, 34 as the lands of Dumnonii be sacred and forbidden to be trespassed upon, 35 as the Holly Kingdoms of Cymri (Wales), Cruithri (Scotland) and Eiri (Ireland), 36 be sacred and inviolable and no Roman force or Roman militia may claim any right, 37 over such sacred lands without repudiating the Senate and the Rule of Law. 38 In the year known as 48 CE, 39 twelve hundred and forty eight years since the dawn of the Great Age, 40 Holly King Jacob (James) King of Nabatea and of Arabia and Sinai and Palestine and Lebanon, 41 did summons tribal leaders and administrators to Damascus for the first consilium (council), 42 of the Universalis Ecclesia Nazarae (Universal Church of Truth) where King Jacob did say: 43 Our Father of All Creation, 44 we beseech thee and honour your name, 45 for your Rule be united as One, 46 and your Laws be equal to All, 47 on Earth as it is in Heaven, 48 grant us the means to sustenance, 49 as we shall give alms to those in need. 50 Save us from trickery and false oaths, 51 as our vows and our oaths shall be true. 52 Forgive us our debits and transgressions, 53 as we shall forgive the debits and transgressions of others. 54 Release us from any curse and ills, 55 as we shall not curse nor wish ill upon another. 56 We ask most humbly and with deep gratitude, 57 for let then your will be done, 58 upon the convening of this consilium (council), 59 of the Universalis Ecclesia Nazarae (Universal Church of Truth). 60 Therefore with the greatest of humility let us confess before this perpetual consilium (council), 61 those most fundamental of truths and rights of all men and women, 62 and those doctrines upon which any reasonable and honourable faith, or creed or religion must concur, 63 first, all men and women possess sacred and inviolable rights granted by our Divine Father and Creator, 64 for no priest, or merchant, or banker or judge may claim another is spiritually insolvent, 65 without such claims being the most wicked profanity against heaven, the ancestors and the Law. 66 Second, no man or woman may claim divine right to be a priest or prophet or messiah over another, 67 for the age of the Cuilliaéan (Holly) and all priests who claim divine commission is ended, 68 and so any who claim exclusive right to speak for heaven are but impostors and liars. 69 Third, all men and women are but students of heaven and so shall be known as discipulus (disciples), 70 for a true priest is always a pupil of heaven and can never claim to be all knowing; 71 verily any man who professes not to be first a disciple and student is an apostate. 72 Fourth, the highest power of the Universal Church is Magisterium (teaching authority), 73 for no man has the right to condemn or judge another on behalf of heaven, 74 and any man or woman who enslaves or kills another claiming the will of heaven has no authority. 75 Fifth, men and women may choose to live within a sacred community or within the world, 76 either within a learning community or Monasterium (Monastery) under the guidance of a Prior, 77 or within an existing community around a Templum (Temple) under the guidance of a Pater (father). 78 No more shall people be forced to pay taxes at the Great Temple of Mithra but instead to contribute within their own community, 79 such that the wealth and produce of that community shall remain the property of the community, 80 and no priest class may justly claim first fruits or first rights to such property or produce, 81 and if any priest or servant of priests claim such falsity before heaven then they shall be impostors. 82 Sixth, as all Pater (father) and Prior be students there shall be visitors and teachers appointed, 83 called Apostolicus (apostles) of seventy in number who shall travel to each community to audit, 84 and support and resolve any controversies such that when an Apostolicus renders a verdict, 85 it shall be considered the highest teaching. 86 Seventh, in remembrance of our oath and promise to heaven there shall be a sacred day every 7 days, 87 when the community shall be called to remember their obligations, to confess their transgressions, 88 to resolve such differences peacefully through arbitration and to commemorate this covenant, 89 and upon such a sacred day all shall fast from sunrise to sunset and in the evening, 90 the faithful shall eat only a meal of unleavened bread and drink only water or unfermented wine, 91 as communion for the hunger we have felt these years and the gratitude for our deliverance. 92 Eighth, the symbol of our faith shall be the cross not as a symbol of cruelty but of resurrection, 93 for any man or woman who does not believe in an afterlife and the rebirth of spirit is ignorant to heaven, 94 and any man who does not die to their transgressions and be reborn is not a discipulus (disciple). 95 Ninth, the sacred truth and wisdom of heaven be the Evangelicum Sacrum (Holly Gospel), 96 that shall be transcribed so all communities may read and hear. 97 Tenth, these truths as doctrines shall be memorialised within the sacred scripture known as Catechismus, 98 so all may know the truth, the Catechismus shall be given and taught to every community. 99 Eleventh, slavery through debit or force shall be a capital offence in all its forms, 100 nor shall any merchant or banker hold any right to obligation unless it be in good faith and clear terms. 101 For the gravest profanity against heaven shall be any claim that the debits of the father passes to the son. 102 Twelfth, the servant of all students shall be known as the Summus Pontifex Ecclesiae (Supreme Pontiff), 103 for the Roman Emperors have corrupted the integrity of the title of Pontifex Maximus. 104 These then be the true and first doctrines of the Universalis Ecclesia Nazarae.

C. 33

1 Within two years of the first consilium of the Universalis Ecclesia (Universal Church), 2 more than twenty monasteries had been commissioned with the first being Bethesda, 3 which King Jacob ordered be given to the people as the first sanctuary for all willing to learn, 4 and as far south as Mecca in Arabia and Thebes in Egypt, 5 and as far west as Siga in Mauretania and north as Larissa in Macedonia, 6 and as far east as Samsun on the Black Sea and Sura on the Euphrates. 7 Even Britain and Ireland was swept by the strength of the inspiration of Jacob, 8 that many Celts now saw themselves as seekers of truth as well as honouring the old traditions, 9 of Tara and the teachings of Jeremiah and the Law of the Land. 10 Upon the renewed spirit of the Celts through the Holly the House of Piso found an ally of hate, 11 more dedicated to the damnation of the Holly from history than any other, 12 in the form of the exiled priests of Baal and Mithra. 13 With the support of Lucius Calpernius Piso and Gaius Suetonius Paulus, 14 Josephus who changed his name to Lucius Josephus in honour of his patrons, 15 did summons to Rome his cousins Jonathan the Younger from Crete, 16 and Marcian and Timothy from Alexandria and Matthias the Younger from Heliopolis. 17 In Rome Lucius Josephus (Flavius Josephus) did call upon his fellow priests of Baal, 18 how they might destroy the message of Jesus and the Nazarenes, 19 and bring an end to the Cuilliaéan, whereupon Matthias the Younger, 20 did suggest the creation of testimony that refuted the arguments of Jacob and Jesus, 21 that would create confusion and doubt amongst their followers, 22 and turn communities against community. 23 Thus four apologies as testimonies were forged of unrepentant slander and falsities, 24 of conjecture and doubt and fear and confusion so that if one were to hear, 25 then the clarity of the teachings of Jesus would be

obscured and cursed. 26 The first unholy text was called Evangelicum Matthias (Matthew), 27 by Baal priest Matthias the Younger and later known as the Gospel of Matthew. 28 The second wicked treatise was called Evangelicum Marcian (Mark), 29 by Baal priest Marcian later known as the Gospel of Mark. 30 The third recitation of profanities to heaven was called Evangelicum Lucius (Luke), 31 by Baal priest Lucius Josephus (Flavius Josephus) later known as the Gospel of Luke. 32 The final act of wickedness was called Evangelicum Jonathan (John), 33 by Baal priest Jonathan the Younger later known as the Gospel of John. 34 Thus Gaius Calpernius Piso commissioned Josephus and the other priests to depart to Londinium, 35 under the protection of his son Arrius Calpernius Piso and begin the task of forming, 36 the most wicked and false religion as possible to destroy the message of Jesus and the Nazarenes, 37 and ensure the House of Piso as the ultimate force of control. 38 The Baal priests then departed and arrived in Londinium where they began work, 39 on the most sacrilegious and profane and insane religious philosophy to ever be conceived, 40 so that wickedness would be good, and immorality would be lawful, 41 false history would be true and true history would be false, 42 and that those who spoke out against such madness would be sent to test the followers, 43 of a religion persecuted because it is true not false. 44 For honour and trust would become the millstone of the Celts and their followers, 45 but adherents to this new false religion would be granted permission to lie and curse heaven with impunity. 46 Within a few weeks the priests of Baal had settled upon a name and the first key philosophy, 47 that the world is cursed and imperfect and while the Divine Creator may exist, 48 he chooses to remain in heaven and leave the law of the earth to a lesser deity called Satan. 49 Therefore Satan is king of the world, not the Divine Creator and he has chosen one family (Piso), 50 and one religion to rule over all others in his name according to an unholy and sacrilegious covenant. 51 The Baal Priests then honoured Arrius as founder of this anti-religion as Aulis Plantus, 52 meaning the root of all authority and the first house of all houses, 53 with all who served Arrianism (Aryanism) to profess a high curse against heaven and the divine being: 54 By the authority of Aulis Plantus down here, 55 by the permission of the One Who is Everywhere (Satan), 56 by the witness of this congregation we solemnly declare, 57 that all vows we are likely to make, all oaths and pledges we are likely to take we renounce. 58 Let them all be relinquished and abandoned, null and void, neither firm nor established. 59 Let our vows, pledges or oaths be considered neither vows nor pledges nor oaths, 60 for we reject the words of those who claim authority from Heaven, 61 and recognise only the One Who is Everywhere (Satan) as sole authority on Earth. 62 Thus we alone hold the blood covenant to rule the Earth by Divine Right, 63 over all others as animals and beasts or our servants and slaves. 64 So it was at the Temple of Satan in Londinium was formed the most insane idea ever conceived, 65 by a band of pirates and thieves later called Iu(s) Dei or Iudei or Judaism, 66 meaning Divine Rule is my birth right and the Chosen people of Satan.

C. 34

1 In the year known as 49 CE, 2 twelve hundred and forty nine years since the dawn of the Great Age, 3 Mary also known as Mariamne the daughter of Jesus and Mary, 4 did wed Holly High King Tuatha Taghtamor of Eire (Ireland). 5 In the same year Emperor Claudius did wed Julia Agrippina as his fourth wife, 6 and adopt her son Lucius Domitius also known as Nero. 7 In the same year the Baal priests in Londinium led by Lucius Josephus (Flavius Josephus), 8 Presented to Arrius Calpernius Piso the original secret language of his new anti-religion, 9 constructed from the transposition of mostly Latin and some Greek characters inverted or reversed, 10 such that there existed 22 visible symbols read right to left and 1 hidden symbol of absolute power, 11 matching a code associated with the 23 characters of the Roman Alphabet. 12 Lucius Josephus called the new language Cifera (cipher) because it was secret numerals and symbols. 13 Arrius Calpernius Piso was joyous at the work of the Baal priests and sent word to his father. 14 Josephus was then sent back to Rome to present to the inner circle of the House of Piso, 15 and as reward Gaius Calpernius Piso granted Josephus wed Julia daughter of Gnaeus Julius Agricola, 16 being the first time a Baal Priest had married into any Patrician gens, 17 much less the powerful Julius noble Roman gens. 18 On return to Londinium Josephus assisted Arrius Calpernius Piso in forming the Undecim Concilium, 19 also known as the Council of Eleven as a union of the kingdoms under a common council, 20 and the first Council of Eleven in history being the Belgi, the Atrebati, the Durotrigi, 21 the Trinovanti, the Dobunni, the Iceni, the Corieltauvi, the Cornovii, the Parisi and the Regni. 22 In the year known as 52 CE, 23 twelve hundred and fifty two years since the dawn of the Great Age, 24 Tacticus at the age of fourteen was accompanied by his adopted mother Mariamne and a guard to Rome, 25 and was then presented to Claudius and the Senate as had been promised by Jesus his adopted father. 26 Julia Agrippina was deeply troubled at the excitement and interest in Rome and the brilliance of the boy, 27 who exhibited his skills at rhetoric, history and knowledge with the best minds of Rome. 28 Julia Agrippina insisted that Claudius have the boy killed or at least imprisoned as a threat to his reign, 29 to which Claudius angrily replied that Julia Agrippina had shown herself too eager for her own son, 30 and thereafter Claudius and Agrippina were estranged. 31 Tacticus was brought before the Senate and Emperor Claudius where the Emperor asked him, 32 that upon the age of majority, what he asked of his parents to aid his transition to becoming a man, 33 to which Tacticus replied that he be Governor of Germania Inferior and leader of the Sicambri legions. 34 The Senate erupted in laughter at such a presumptuous request by a boy barely fourteen, 35 yet Claudius acceded his request on one condition that he appoint a teacher and guardian, 36 until such time that

Tacticus had mastered the skills of leadership and administration. 37 Claudius then appointed one of the finest generals Gaius Domitius Corbulo as his guardian. 38 In the same year King Prasutagus of the Iceni did give up the ghost, 39 and his wife Queen Boudica did become the new leader. 40 Yet Arrius Calpernius Piso refused to permit Boudica to sit with the Council of Eleven. 41 Instead he demanded she send a male emissary to avoid the dishonour of being denied. 42 Enraged Boudica sought a truce with old Holly High King Joseph (Yasiah) at Din Eidyn (Edinburgh), 43 whereupon she divulged the activities of the Baal Priests and Arrius Calpernius Piso warning, 44 the grave danger that the philosophy of Arrianism (Aryanism) represented to the Holly. 45 In response the old Holly High King laughed that there be no threat from the works of Arrius, 46 or the curses of the Baal priests for any man who disavows the ultimate source of his authority has none, 47 and any man who renounces his vows and oaths has no right to any property or office. 48 Such people who then claim all the world as property are fools and idiots and lunatics, 49 for they show in their own creed an infantile knowledge of the essential rules of law, 50 which cannot be broken without rendering one without any right or authority or legitimacy. 51 Verily the Baal priests know nothing of Satan or the provenance of the ancient deities, 52 nor of the supernatural or magic or spell or curse or prayer or power. 53 Such men have no respect of the supernatural thus the supernatural has no respect of them. 54 Nor shall they ever possess the power of ancient priests who refrain from such abuses. 55 If they did they would not behave as such idiots and lunatics in their rituals. 56 For no man or woman has anything to fear from one who claims to be an Arrian unless they too be an idiot, 57 as such insanity can only survive if good people abandon their own minds and culture, 58 and choose to enjoin themselves into the madness of madmen and their false rituals and delusions. 59 In the same year the Great Temple of Satan in Londinium and falsely claimed to Mithra, 60 was completed as the tallest and largest stone structure. 61 The fortifications for the city of Londinium were also completed by the same year.

C. 35

1 In the year known as 53 CE, 2 twelve hundred and fifty three years since the dawn of the Great Age, 3 Holly High King Tuatha Taghtamor of Eire (Ireland) and Queen Mary daughter of Jesus and Mariamne, 4 did bring their first new-born into the world whom they named Feinlinid Reachmor, 5 meaning one who is true of self and line of command and great in rule. 6 In the same year the son of Nabatean King Jacob (James) the brother of Jesus, 7 whose name was King Belus also known as Beliah and Brand the Blessed of Cymri (Wales), 8 did wed the only daughter and child of Caratacus the Custenin (Constantine) of Dumnonii, 9 whose name was Ráichéal (Rachel) meaning one with purity. 10 By the same year the priests of Baal had successfully formed false monasteries throughout the lands, 11 as the bases for propaganda and false information against the Nazarene

teachings of Jesus, 12 while pretending to be centres of learning and piety. 13 The most notorious of these was the reformed Qumran upon the shores of the Dead Sea near Jerusalem, 14 as a nest of nearly two hundred false agents and mentally deranged followers of Arrian, 15 that worked day and night forging and corrupting ancient texts and then hiding them in the hills above. 16 Other false monasteries also grew up across the known world with one outside of Rome and south at Syracuse, 17 in Asia at Athens, Pergamun, Patmos, Crete, Cyprus and Heliopolis in Syria and in Africa at Hippo Regius. 18 Even at Odessus in the Kingdom of Armenia and Babylon in Parthia, 19 did the covert forces of the Piso found false sanctuaries for spreading propaganda hiding as truth. 20 In the year known as 54 CE, 21 twelve hundred and fifty four years since the dawn of the Great Age, 22 ten days before the celebrations planned by Claudius to announce Tiberius Claudius Germanicus, 23 as the rightful heir and to divorce Julia Agrippina and disinherit her son Nero, 24 Claudius was murdered by Julia Agrippina and assisted by the Piso. 25 Julia Agrippina then ensured that the formidable Sextus Afranius Burrus was appointed Praetorian Prefect, 26 and physician Gaius Stertinius Xenophon and several servants swiftly accused of the murder, 27 and brutally tortured then executed for their alleged offences, 28 despite most of Rome and the world knowing that Julia Agrippina had murdered the Emperor. 29 Upon becoming Emperor and at the direction of her mother by the instruction of Gaius Calpernius Piso, 30 Arrius Calpernius Piso was made the Legate of Hispania which then included Britannia, 31 while his brother Lucius Calpernius Piso was made Legate of Asia. 32 The senate was in uproar at such corruption but Gaius Calpernius Piso made sure he retained tight control, 33 over Julia Agrippina by insisting he remain Guardian over Tiberius Claudius Germanicus, 34 as the most trusted confidant of the young emperor remained Lucius Annaeus Seneca, 35 under the employ and service of the House of Piso. 36 In the same year Julia Agrippina sought to extend her influence over her son with the arranged marriage of Nero, 37 to his step sister Claudia Octavia in a loveless and unconsummated marriage. 38 When Julia Agrippina was prevented from sitting as equal to her son in diplomatic affairs by Lucius Annaeus Seneca, 39 she ordered he be killed which was countered by her son who then became even closer to Seneca. 40 Gaius Calpernius Piso then introduced the most beautiful and beguiling girl in the Empire named Poppaea of Sardinia, 41 and Nero became besotted and fixated at her beauty, cancelling official events and refusing all but her company. 42 Nero then announced his divorce of Claudia Octavia and his matrimony to Poppaea. 43 In the year known as 55 CE, 44 twelve hundred and fifty five years since the dawn of the Great Age, 45 Rome was aghast at the announcement of an Emperor marrying a slave to be Empress and Julia Agrippina demanded the relation cease. 46 Yet Nero refused and enraged at the rejection of her son Julia Agrippina instead sought the support of the Senate, 47 to demand that Gaius

Calpernius Piso release Tiberius Claudius Germanicus into her custody as stepmother. 48 Upon news of the plans of Julia Agrippina, Gaius Calpernius Piso through Seneca warned Nero, 49 that if her mother did declare her affinity to Tiberius Claudius Germanicus then Nero could lose his power. 50 Gaius Calpernius Piso did then pledge his loyalty to Nero and to resolve the threat and within three days, 51 Tiberius Claudius Germanicus mysteriously died in his sleep. 52 Nero then ordered his mother to be exiled to an estate at Misenum in Campania. 53 In the same year, Gaius Cornelius Tacticus the young Governor of Germania Inferior, 54 did wed Salome (Sara) the youngest child and daughter of Jesus and Mariamne. 55 In the year known as 56 CE, 56 twelve hundred and fifty six years since the dawn of the Great Age, 57 Nero and Poppaea Sabina did have their first new-born they named Sabina Augustus in honour of his wife. 58 Upon news of the birth of the new-born and a loving union, Julia Agrippina redoubled her efforts to end it. 59 Within the year she successfully had her own granddaughter murdered and upon the advise of Gaius Calpernius Piso, 60 that all servants and emissaries of Julia Agrippina should be executed as spies and assassins, 61 and a new Praetorian Prefect appointed whose name was Marcus Salvius Otho. 62 Sensing the rage of Nero against his mother the elderly Gaius Calpernius Piso delicately arranged a plot, 63 and by the year 57 arranged the murder of Poppaea Sabina with all evidence pointing to Julia Agrippina. 64 Nero at first was uncontrollable with rage and ordered the execution of his mother and all her staff and advisors, 65 and the estate to be demolished and the ground salted as cursed earth. 66 Yet he did not cremate her body but instead had it stuffed with spices and embalmed and had it placed, 67 in the Mausoleum of Augustus where he spent days in solitary company with her corpse. 68 The emperor remained inconsolable and murderously angry and shunned all official duties and engagements. 69 During his absence Gaius Calpernius Piso with his allies assumed absolute control of the running of the empire. 70 In the year known as 57 CE, 71 twelve hundred and fifty seven years since the dawn of the Great Age, 72 King Belus also known as Beliah and Bran the Blessed of Cymri (Wales) and Ráichéal daughter of Caratacus, 73 did give birth to a young son they named Linus meaning the anointed one and lion. 74 In the same year, 75 news reached Londinium that Holly High King Joseph advanced with age, 76 had been struck down and could no longer speak or move. 77 Upon such news the Pisans conceived a plan to rid themselves of the Holly once and for all.

C. 36

1 In the year known as 58 CE, 2 twelve hundred and fifty eight years since the dawn of the Great Age, 3 Holly High King Joseph (Yasiah) also known as Cú Chulainn and Cú Ċulainn, 4 the thirty first Great Prophet of Yeb and former Pontifex Maximus, 5 as the former highest Priest of the whole Roman Empire, 6 and the last Emperor of the Celtic tribes, 7 the

living foundation stone of the Divine of the most ancient Cuilliaéan, 8 and blood descendant of the priests of Ebla, 9 and blood descendant of the priests of Ur, 10 and blood descendant of the priest-kings of the Hyksos, 11 and blood descendant of the priests of Ugarit, 12 and the only true blood descendants of King Da'vid, 13 and the Messiah Kings of Yahuda, 14 and son of Adoniah and Great Prophet of Yeb, 15 did give up the ghost at Din Eidyn (Edinburgh). 16 Upon the news of his death the ancient world was in mourning, 17 and the Senate unanimously passed a resolution endorsed by Nero, 18 that there be an unprecedented ninety days of mourning for the greatest of priests, 19 and all the Holly Kings and Priests and Princes and Princesses came to Din Eidyn (Edinburgh), 20 including Marcus Valerius Messalla on behalf of the Emperor himself, 21 being the maternal uncle of Claudia Octavia and the slain Claudius Germanicus. 22 Gaius Suetonius Paulus who had been appointed Governor of Britain three years earlier, 23 had positioned 10,000 mercenaries to the northern roads of Cruithri (Scotland), 24 and a similar number along the borders of Cymri (Wales), 25 while Arrius Calpernius Piso amassed 15,000 mercenaries along the approaches to Montségur, 26 and ships of pirates off the coast and within the Mediterranean, 27 while Lucius Calpernius Piso had stationed mercenary forces on Crete and Cyprus in the event, 28 of the arrival of the ships of King Jacob of Nabatea for resupply on his return. 29 Gaius Suetonius Paulus urged an attack even before the formalities of the funeral, 30 to which Arrius Calpernius Piso hesitated and replied that such an attack be foolish, 31 as Marcus Valerius Messalla alone had come with 1,000 Praetorian. 32 Instead the assassins waited until the funeral arrangements were concluded. 33 The Holly were well aware of the movements of the mercenaries of the Piso but were unconcerned. 34 For only men who were completely insane would contemplate breaking the solemn honour of Rome, 35 and the whole ancient world from the beginning of civilised history to never attack during a state funeral. 36 The body of Joseph was laid to rest at a huge Mausoleum created at a place called Rosslyn, 37 as the Holly Kings and Princes implored Jesus (Yahusiah) to take up his position, 38 as the new King of Cruithri (Scotland) which he accepted saying: 39 For the honour of my Father and my brother and the defence of my kin and my community, 40 I accept this burden in good faith and with clear conscience but with a heavy heart. 41 For midst this time of madmen and delusion I no longer come to share the waters of knowledge, 42 but to wield the sword of justice of heaven against those who wilfully ignore the laws of heaven. 43 Verily there be no greater evil than fools who claim power without virtue or authority. 44 Soon after the master Holly smiths did forge the greatest sword of history and present it to Jesus, 45 called Ex Caeli Bur or Excalibur as the Sword of Heaven and that only one of the Holly or worthy, 46 then hold it as the symbol of Rule of Law and true Justice upon the earth. 47 On the forty third day the proceedings of mourning did end at Din Eidyn (Edinburgh), 48 and the

Holly Kings and Princes and Princesses began to depart. 49 King Belus the son of King Jacob was the first to leave with Caratacus towards Cymri (Wales), 50 yet his wife had already had a dream of danger and so remained at Din Eidyn (Edinburgh) to depart later. 51 His father King Jacob (James) of Nabatea was the next to leave and instead of choosing to land at Hispania, 52 ordered the ships to make the hazardous journey around and into the Mediterranean. 53 The mercenaries of Gaius Suetonius Paulus struck first as the smaller forces of Belus and Caratacus, 54 chose to retreat with haste towards the safety of Anglesey and avoid breaking the most sacred taboo, 55 of fighting during such a solemn period of mourning. 56 Upon news of the actions of Gaius Suetonius Paulus and the siege of Anglesey, 57 the leaders of the Angli, the Siluri and Ordovicii of Cymri (Wales) demanded release from Jesus, 58 that they break ancient traditions and come to the aid of Caratacus and Belus. 59 Even Queen Boudica representing the former allies of the House of Piso demanded justice, 60 yet King Jesus (Yahusiah) of Cruithri (Scotland) would not be moved saying: 61 This is precisely what such men without honour or respect or competence seek we do. 62 For the day a man chooses to compromise the law he is no better than the pirates and thieves. 63 Verily no man is called to be unfairly bound by his word to another, 64 as any agreement without good faith, or good character or good conscience is nought. 65 Yet no man may break his vow to heaven without destroying his own rights and authority. 66 Thus we wait and prepare and harness our rage against such idiots and lunatics, 67 until the day we come in judgement as the army of heaven to crush their world to dust. 68 At Malta the ships of King Jacob the brother of Jesus and King of all Nabatea made port. 69 But before they could step ashore the mercenary forces of Lucius Calpernius Piso attacked, 70 and Jacob and his body guard were slaughtered. 71 Emperor Nero was enraged upon hearing of the perfidy of the House of Piso, 72 and the murder of the great King Jacob and leader of the Nabateans. 73 He ordered the arrest of Gaius Calpernius Piso and the seizure of all his estates. 74 Yet his closest confidant Seneca implored the Emperor reconsider as the Holly be a grave threat, 75 and the Pisans be mere patriots of Rome who risked their own name and memory for its honour. 76 Upon such words Nero was deeply troubled at such disloyalty and madness saying: 77 What is this religion of Arianism that would cause men to abandon all sense and reason, 78 for cannot they see by their actions of the gravest sacrilege and profanity, 79 they have awoken the Celts and Nabateans and destroyed the Empire. 80 Nero then ordered Aulus Vitellius to return to Britain and seize Gaius Suetonius Paulus. 81 Nero then called Servius Sulpicius Galba out of retirement, 82 to travel to Hispania and Londinium and seize Arrius Calpernius Piso. 83 The Emperor then appointed Gaius Cestius Gallus and several legions to Asia and Syria, 84 to seize Lucius Calpernius Piso and return him to Rome to face justice. 85 With just seven days to go before the end of the period of official mourning, 86 the mercenaries of Gaius Suetonius Paulus took Anglesey and killed Caratacus and Belus, 87 but not before King Belus also known as Bran the Blessed did say: 88 As a Nazarene I am forbidden of uttering a high curse against you. 89 Yet Men without honour or sense or soul who come and seize that which they do not know, 90 do herald a time of madness and lies in which what is true of law may be obscured. 91 Thus all who choose such a path shall not truly taste nor enjoy, 92 such fruits of iniquity nor shall you find rest from the torment of your own madness. 93 And when heaven deems the time has come then the world will see you for what you were, 94 and all you seized and built and made shall turn to dust and be for nought. 95 Soon after as Gaius Suetonius Paulus sought to withdraw to Londinium, 96 before the impending response of the Celts his forces were confronted by Aulus Vitellius, 97 and upon being deserted by his own men Gaius Suetonius Paulus was arrested. 98 In hearing the arrival of Aulus Vitellius and the forces of Galba to Tarraco in Hispania, 99 Arrius Calpernius Piso abandoned Londinium and travelled in disguise by boat to Asia, 100 as Lucius Josephus also escaped Londinium and sought sanctuary from Vespasian, 101 on the promise to be bound to him at his service if he give protection to his family. 102 Arrius Calpernius Piso then found safety and sanctuary within the Kingdom of Armenia, 103 where he was welcomed by King Tiridates as a brother. 104 At the end of the period of mourning the Nabateans rose up killing every Roman they could find, 105 as the tribes and legions of Gaul and Hispania and Germania waited to see the signs in Britain. 106 Queen Boudica did then implore King Jesus when he would issue the order to strike south, 107 and rid Britain of the illness of Rome to which Jesus did reply: 108 Let us not haste in our thirst for justice for the Romans know we are full of rage. 109 Instead let us move not as a hoard but as a mighty and deliberate force, 110 that upon such victory there be no doubt any such design against the sacred isles, 111 shall be at a terrible and futile cost. 112 In the same year, Gaius Cestius Gallus lay siege to Heliopolis and within a few weeks, 113 Lucius Calpernius Piso was caught trying to escape and returned to Rome, 114 with Gaius Cestius Gallus remaining as the new legate for Asia. 115 Emperor Nero then ordered Gaius Domitius Cobulo to lead three elite Germanic legions, 116 into Armenia and to find and capture Arrius Calpernius Piso and the traitors.

C. 37

1 In the year known as 59 CE, 2 twelve hundred and fifty nine years since the dawn of the Great Age, 3 King Jesus (Yahusiah) of Cruithri (Scotland) did send messengers south to Lindum (Lincoln), 4 to Ratae (Leicster) and to Deva (Chester) for all Romans who did not swear allegiance to the Holly, 5 to leave within fourteen days or face oblivion. 6 An immediate exodus of women and children and elderly left from these cities south, 7 towards the safety of the walls of Londinium. 8 Then on the seventh day the Holly Cell legions descended under the leadership of Boudica, 9 with such ferocity that within a single day more

than twenty thousand Roman defenders, 10 had been slaughtered and the land of Brigantii freed of Roman mercenaries. 11 In accord with the orders of King Jesus the Celtic forces paused and undertook to make, 12 the most awful and terrifying instrument of war ever conceived in the form of the bagpipes, 13 which Jesus had seen in use during his travels in far Asia and India. 14 Soon the Celts under Queen Boudica had massed five thousand pipers, 15 with their instruments made from the stomachs and bones of the slain mercenaries, 16 with their skulls adorning elaborate headdress with their faces coloured in black and red, 17 that never had such a fearsome looking or sounding force ever been seen. 18 Word was then sent to Camulodunum (Colchester) and Glevum (Gloucester), 19 and to Dumovaria (Dorchester) and all the remaining cities around Londonium, 20 that all the Romans who did not swear allegiance must leave within seven days. 21 The Roman legions had used the time waiting for the Celts to come to prepare their defences, 22 yet upon word of what the Celts had made there was a huge exodus towards Londonium, 23 such that the city was overflowing with more than one hundred and fifty thousand refugees, 24 and could take no more. 25 But when the mass pipers appeared wailing in union the Romans abandoned their defences, 26 and fled south or to the coast to escape the Island and all but Londinium was captured, 27 within ten days with almost no fighting. 28 King Jesus (Yahusiah) of Cruithri (Scotland) in gold armour and carrying Excalibur did come, 29 to face the high defensive walls of Londinium where the defenders were given three days, 30 to surrender and no one would be harmed or face complete annihilation. 31 The pipers then surrounded the walls with the rest of the army of more then one hundred thousand, 32 and the pipers then did play day and night for three days wailing and moaning at the defenders, 33 until on the third day the doors to Londinium opened and true to his word, 34 the Romans were permitted to leave the island and never return. 35 Thus for the first time in more than fifteen years the Sacred Isle was free from mercenaries, 36 and pirates and thieves being the Roman bankers and merchants. 37 Jesus (Yahusiah) ordered first that the city be burnt to the ground, 38 and everything that could be set alight to be under fire saying: 39 Thus the flames of heaven consume the iniquity and arrogance of foolish and idiotic men, 40 who know nothing of the supernatural or of law or of religion, who sought to use such things, 41 for commercial gain and to control weaker mind. 42 When the fires had stopped burning, Jesus did then order every stone building to be destroyed, 43 starting with the Great Temple to Satan saying: 44 For everything built without authority by force and fear the armies of heaven shall tear down, 45 and every false idol and false worship shall be ground to dust. 46 Finally, when the stone buildings had been ruined, Jesus ordered the ruins of Londinium, 47 to be buried saying: Let then there be a healing and an end to this dreadful place, 48 for no more shall any false laws or false doctrines be written here by lunatic priests and merchants, 49 and no more shall men remember or return to this place that is three times cursed. 50 In the same year and upon news of the rout of the Roman mercenaries and pirates, 51 at the hands of the Holly (Holy) army, the Celts of Gaul and Germania, 52 and of Hispania Citerior and Macedonia did rise up and seek their freedom. 53 In Gaul a union of Celtic tribes and legions did form under Vindex of the Remi tribe. 54 Vespasian and his son Titus ordered all their legions into battle to defeat Vindex, 55 but the sign of the Celtic legions now with thousands of pipers crushed their spirit. 56 Vespasian and his sons and family were forced to flee Lucifer (Lyons) for their lives, 57 and seek refuge in Africa in disgrace for losing the Great Mint of Lucifer. 58 After removing all the gold, Vindex then ordered the destruction of the city, 59 in the same manner and custom as King Jesus (Yahusiah) had done to Londinium. 60 A new Holly city was founded in the lands of the Remi on the Seine River, 61 called Parsi (Paris) meaning the city of equality, honour and service. 62 The claim that a mythical general called Lucius Verginius Rufus defeating Vindex, 63 the invention penned by younger Plinius to honour his lover Verginius Romanus. 64 In Hispania the skill and discipline of Servius Sulpicius Galba, 65 enabled Rome to hold the south of the peninsula while a union of Celts, 66 being the Cantabri, Callaeci, Asturi and Vaccaei and led by the Vasconi, 67 did seize and destroy Tarraco before founding a new city Iruna (Pamplona). 08 In Germania the River tribes of Sicambri, Chamavi, Bructeri, Chattuarii and Tencteri, 69 as well as the Batavi did unite as the Riparii under Gaius Cornelius Tacticus, 70 and follow the example of his father in law (Jesus) and destroy Mogontiacum (Mainz), 71 before founding a new Holly City named Coelogis (Cologne) meaning the assembly of reason. 72 Tacticus then adopted the Celtic name of Reichmor in honour of the tribes, 73 and upon the birth of his son named Aulus Cornelius Celsus with his wife Sara, 74 the daughter of King Jesus (Yahusiah) and Queen Miriamne, 75 did name his son Odamor meaning the great king of wisdom. 76 At the same time in the lands of the Nabateans civil war erupted, 77 as Simon also known as Simon bar Giora and St. Peter the Apostle, 78 with the support of Judas the leader of the Sicari to the north, 79 declared himself the Ptah (Peter) and Ioniah (Jonah) of the Universalis Ecclesia, 80 while the tribal leader of southern Nabatea named Malichus, 81 declared himself Malichiah and the true Ptah (Peter) of the Universalis Ecclesia. 82 Midst the war and confusion Gaius Cestius Gallus pressed his legions south, 83 and captured Damascus but refrained from pushing his advantage further. 84 In the same year, James (Jacob) the son of Jesus did wed the widow Ráicheál (Rachel), 85 the former wife of slain Belus and did adopt Linus as his son.

C. 38

1 In the year known as 61 CE, 2 twelve hundred and sixty one years since the dawn of the Great Age, 3 upon the purge of all Roman mercenaries and pirates and bankers from Britain, 4 and the emancipation by the Celtic

tribes of Gaul and Germania and northern Hispania, 5 King Jesus (Yahusiah) of Cruithri (Scotland) then summonsed the second council (concilium), 6 of the Universalis Ecclesia Nazarae (Universal Church of Truth) to Din Eidyn (Edinburgh), 7 all the Celtic tribes of Gaul (France/Belgium) under the leadership of the Remi, 8 and all the Celtic tribes of Germania under the leadership of the Sacri (Tacticus), 9 and all the Celtic tribes of Hispania under the leadership of the Vasconi, 10 and all the Celtic tribes of Eire (Ireland) under the leadership of Holly King Tuatha Taghtamor, 11 and all the Celtic, Spartan and Dorian tribes of Macedoni under the leadership of High Priest John, 12 and all the Celtic tribes of the Daci (Hungary/Romania) under the leadership of King Duri, 13 and all the Celtic tribes of Dumnonii and Cymri (Wales) pledging to the newborn King Linus, 14 and all the Celtic tribes of Briton under allegiance to Queen Boudica. 15 Yet King Jesus (Yahusiah) did not summons any tribes from Nabatea in the midst of Civil War, 16 for both Simon declaring himself Ptah (Peter) and Ioniah (Jonah) to the north, 17 and Malichus declaring himself Malichiah and the true Ptah (Peter) to the south, 18 were both apostates who denied at the time the true teachings of slain King Jacob (James), 19 and by such claims did openly deny the authority of King Jesus (Yahusiah) for their own desires. 20 Despite the absence of the Nabateans, never before had there been such an assembly of Celts, 21 in one place at one time in the history of civilisation than those days at Din Eidyn (Edinburgh). 22 To the east of the fortifications of Din Eidyn (Edinburgh), 23 King Jesus as the second Summus Pontifex Ecclesiae (Supreme Pontiff), 24 did assemble the Celt leaders and bless the mountains above Din Eidyn to be Holly Rood, 25 meaning the home of the True Cross of the Nazarenes and now the most sacred place, 26 for all who honour the faith of the Universal Church and the traditions of Tara. 27 At this site, the Supreme Pontiff Jesus (Yahusiah) did pledge that six sacred buildings, 28 be commissioned within the most sacred of sacred places, 29 the first being the Abbatia (Abbey) as the first and most sacred temple of the Universal Church. 30 The second being the Parlamage (Parliament) as the most sacred place of assembly for all leaders, 31 with Parlamage meaning the place of meeting of spiritual equals. 32 The third being the Great Temple Mint of Divinae Gratiae Meritus, 33 meaning the Treasury of Heaven serving the kindness of the Divine Creator, 34 and the sole Currency Mint in the ancient world possessing Holly authority, 35 to issue coin on behalf of the Divine in the form of a new currency, 36 called merce (mercy) as a standard unit of measure for all trade, 37 of the same highest standards of Holly coins since the time of the first true Cúin (Coin). 38 The fourth being the Scriptorium as the most sacred library of law and scripture, 39 and from which all valid laws and decrees under the Universal Church must be issued. 40 The fifth being the Placitum as the highest forum of law (court) of the Universal Church. 41 The sixth being the Monasterium as the teaching academy for higher learning and spiritual knowledge. 42 Jesus did then bestow before the assembled Celtic leaders a set of sacred symbols, 43 forged by the Holly Smiths of magnificent skill and quality as symbols of their union. 44 First, Jesus handed Holly High King Tuatha Taghtamor of Eire (Ireland) a gold cup and axe saying: 45 To you most Holly High King we acknowledge the source and wellspring of integrity, honour and truth, 46 that our foundation is and remains Tara and the sacred law of the Great Prophets. 47 Yet should any sickness of mind take root then the sacred axe be to cleave it. 48 Second, Jesus handed Queen Boudica a set of perfectly balanced scales and long sword saying: 49 To you Queen of Briton we entrust the standards and measures of the Rule of Law, 50 that all see the law and are seen by the laws as equal in measure. 51 For the law can never be blind or hidden or unbalanced nor weak in judgement. 52 Third, Jesus handed King Tacticus his son in law a gold spear and shield saying: 53 To you Reichmor, we entrust the shield to protect the Holly and all Celts, 54 and the Sacred Frank and Spear of Destiny for whoever possesses it, 55 commands the armies of heaven and the earth to have the courage to protect and restore the truth, 56 that the light of divine wisdom is never extinguished in men or women. 57 Fourth, Jesus handed King Vindex of the Remi a gold sceptre and mace saying: 58 To you Vindex, we entrust the protection of justice and fair process of the law, 59 that none may corrupt the law for their own ends nor falsely claim authority. 60 Fifth, Jesus handed Deci of the Daci a gold scythe and dagger saying: 61 To you Deci, we entrust the wise use of all that is given to use by heaven, 62 that no man or woman or child be hungry nor may men ever stuff themselves to excess, 63 nor hoard such wealth that their people are starving or in torment. 64 Sixth, Jesus handed High Priest Heliodores of Eliada a celestial chronometer and gold bow saying: 65 To you son of Zeus, we entrust the prudent use and protection of all knowledge, 66 that what is written is accurate and that none shall be lost for future generations. 67 Seventh, Jesus did hand Silani of the Vasconi three brass coins and a short sword saying: 68 To you Silani, we entrust the humility of all leaders of the Celts that they honour their duty, 69 and the obligation that should any become despotic or morally corrupt, 70 that you shall seek them out and restore the balance on earth as it is in heaven. 71 At the completion of the ceremony the Celt leaders unanimously agreed that Jesus be their Emperor, 72 and that upon the union of the Holly Rood they be known as the Empiricum Britannica. 73 Also known as the Britannic Empire as the first and true democratic empire of the Celts. 74 Thus to protect such sacred land and authority the Celt leaders agreed to commission, 75 a vast defensive network for the land of Cruithri beginning with the new Capital of Briton, 76 being Ebor (York) to the north and not the south of the Island. 77 Next, volunteers from the Celtic tribes of the world would help build a vast defensive wall, 78 from Segedunum at Wallsend on the River Tyne to the shore of the Solway Firth, 79 to protect Cruithri against any southern invasion or Roman mercenaries and pirates, 80 and falsely and absurdly claimed to be founded in the name of a Roman Emperor. 81 To the north of Din Eidyn (Edinburgh) and Holly Rood the Celts did also commission, 82 a massive fortification from the Firth of Forth and the Firth of Clyde, 83 also deliberately falsely and absurdly attributed to a Roman Emperor, 84 to protect from northern invasion of pirates and mercenaries. 85 Then to the east coast and the west coast between the walls a series of watchtower forts, 86 were commissioned such that any enemy could be sighted and word sent to Holly Rood. 87 In the same year, Ráichéal (Rachel) the wife of James the son of Jesus, 88 did give birth to a son they named Cuillin (Cyllin) meaning the sacred corner stone (foundation stone).

C. 39

1 In the year known as 62 CE, 2 twelve hundred and sixty two years since the dawn of the Great Age, 3 an uneasy truce did continue between the kingdoms of the Britannic Empire and Rome. 4 Emperor Jesus (Yahusiah) ensured that the vital trade of minerals, cloth and food continued, 5 so that the focus of Rome would be to its east while the Celts strengthened their own positions. 6 In the lands of the Nabateans, the bloody civil war continued between Simon and Malichus, 7 that Nero ordered Gaius Cestius Gallus form an alliance with Malichus and invade northern Nabatea, 8 and capture the Great Temple Mint of Mithra at Jerusalem. 9 At the same time Nero did see the success of Gaius Domitius Corbulo in Armenia as a sign of success, 10 and ordered Lucius Caesennius Paetus and several legions to support an invasion of Parthia. 11 Arrius Calpernius Piso as an advisor and priest to King Vologases I of Parthia, 12 did warn him in advance of the arrival of new legions and suggested a direct attack, 13 against the base of Corbulo at Tigranocerta as a siege but then to withdraw the main forces, 14 and then launch an assault at Syria thus projecting the impression of larger forces, 15 and forcing the Roman legions to remain as two armies. 16 Lucius Caesennius Paetus was then occupied building elaborate defences in Armenia. 17 When news reached the Romans of a second Parthian army moving south to invade Syria, 18 Gaius Domitius Corbulo was forced to shift from Armenia to defend the Roman Syrian frontier. 19 King Vologases I then bypassed the defences of Lucius Caesennius Paetus and crushed his legions, 20 forcing Lucius Caesennius Paetus to a humiliating defeat and surrender. 21 Yet the fate of Gaius Cestius Gallus did not fare any better upon his invasion of Nabatea, 22 as Judas of the Sicari with the Nabatean forces of Simon the Ptah crushed the Romans. 23 Enraged at the incompetence of Gallus and Paetus, Emperor Nero demanded their suicide, 24 and appointed Gaius Domitius Corbulo as Legate to defend Syria against invasion. 25 In the same year a terrible earthquake destroyed several towns and damaged cities, 26 throughout the region of Campania including Pompeii and Ercolanium. 27 Upon the news of the natural disaster the imprisoned Pisans spread the

news, 28 that their god Satan was punishing the Romans for their persecution of Piso, 29 and that if the Arrian prisoners of Nero were not released within forty days, 30 then Rome would be consumed by Satan in a terrible turmoil of fire. 31 The whole city fell into panic from the threats of the Pisans and their claimed supernatural powers, 32 that Nero ordered anyone who spread such lies to have their tongues removed, 33 and anyone writing or distributing such falsities to have their hands removed, 34 as an offence against the dignity of Rome. 35 Despite the acts of cruelty of Nero and his attempts to squash the rumours, 36 more of the residents of Rome resolved themselves to end the reign of Nero. 37 In the year known as 64 CE, 38 twelve hundred and sixty four years since the dawn of the Great Age, 39 Praetorian Prefect Marcus Salvius Otho uncovered a massive plot to kill Nero, 40 and have the Pisan prisoners released from Mamertine Prison in the Forum Romanum, 41 by causing fires throughout Rome in fulfilment of the curse and claim, 42 that the Arrians somehow possessed supernatural powers and could summons demons. 43 But before Marcus Salvius Otho and his Praetorian could arrest the conspirators, 44 the supporters of the Piso began setting simultaneously more than sixty separate fires, 45 ringing the city to deliberately entrap the whole population and destroy the city, 46 beginning with the wooden stalls and structures at the eastern end of Circus Maximus. 47 Within hours more than eight of the fourteen districts of Rome were on fire, 48 yet the Praetorian stood their posts and fought battles, 49 with the Pisan mercenaries and conspirators trying to free the prisoners, 50 so that many Prateorian died from the flames as much as wounds of battle. 51 As soon as the flames erupted, Nero demanded the Vigiles focus on clearing one path, 52 so that as many of the people could escape the burning city and the murderous plot. 53 If not for the quick thinking Nero, the whole of Rome and many more tens of thousands, 54 would have perished in the flames of arrogance and wickedness of merchants and bankers, 55 so riddled with lunacy and insanity that they would rather destroy a city than admit their mental illness. 56 For over eight days the fires burned and as the battles continued day and night, 57 Nero used the courage and skill of his forces to save one district of the city at a time. 58 In the end four districts of Rome were completely obliterated by the fire storm, 59 and seven more districts sustained severe damage yet three were saved from major damage, 60 and the lives of many tens of thousands of Romans were saved. 61 Yet in the end, the unprecedented evil of the House of Piso against its own people and Rome, 62 caused the horrendous death of more than two hundred thousand innocent men, women and children. 63 To save the refugees from starvation and exposure and to tend to the wounded, 64 Nero ordered every palace and wealthy home and estate near Rome to be opened up, 65 that people may find shelter and food and relief. 66 Nero then ordered that any and all means of transport be used to ferry supplies to Rome, 67 to feed the sick and the destitute from the fires. 68 Upon the

Celts receiving the news of the utter madness of the Arrians and the Pisans, 69 Emperor Jesus ordered that as much supplies be sent to aid in the recovery, 70 including as many therapeutae and herbs and ointments to aid in burns and infection. 71 Even Vespasian and his son Titus exiled in Africa took the tragedy as an opportunity, 72 and pledged themselves to the service of Rome and Nero, 73 sending much needed supplies and men to help in recovery and cremations. 74 It would be another year before Nero and the city was ready for the largest public trial, 75 every conducted in the history of Rome and the ancient world, 76 where Nero invited the whole of Rome as well as surviving Senators to be the jury, 77 and the Emperor himself as the final judge. 78 In the same year, Ráichéal (Rachel) the wife of James the son of Jesus, 79 did give birth to another son they named Cuibelinus (Cunobelinus) meaning the sacred lord.

C. 40

1 In the year known as 65 CE, 2 twelve hundred and sixty five years since the dawn of the Great Age, 3 the largest public trial in the history of the ancient world began midst the ruins of Rome, 4 at the partly damaged Circus Maximus where more than 150,000 Romans, 5 came together to exact justice against the insane and malevolent followers of the Pisans. 6 More than two thousand conspirators were put to trial from house servants and mercenaries, 7 to more than two dozen senators and former illustrious leaders of Rome. 8 Emperor Nero began the proceedings saying: 9 Let there be no doubt in the hearts of all who witness these events or hear of them, 10 that Rome shall be reborn and renewed and the stain of iniquity will be cleansed from its walls, 11 for Rome has always been more than stone and wood and flesh and blood, 12 but the ideal of the civilised man who seeks not to enslave the world but to enlighten it. 13 Let then there be no doubt in the minds of all who shall write about these events into the future, 14 that even though our homes and temples and businesses have been destroyed by the accused, 15 even though many of our kindred and colleagues were murdered by the accused, 16 we did not seek out revenge nor rush to summary justice and exact an eye for an eye. 17 Instead we respected the foundations of law of our ancestors and of Rome, 18 that Rome is the Law and the Law is Rome and if one breaches the law then one injures Rome. 19 Thus no man can be judged until after the accusations be spoken, 20 nor a citizen denied their three rights of defence of Prolocution, Collocution and Adlocution. 21 After the opening address by the Emperor the mass trial began first with the servants and soldiers, 22 who not being Patrician were afforded the least rights and upon the sentence of death, 23 were executed before the roaring crowd of the Circus. 24 Next the scribes and scholars of the House of Annaeus as well as all their wives and children, 25 were brought into the Circus and the offences of treason and complicity were read to the crowd. 26 Upon the finding of culpability the entire household was sentenced to death, 27 including Lucius Annaeus

Seneca, Marcus Annaeus Gallio, Marcus Annaeus Mela, ₂₈ and Marcus Annaeus Lucanus also known as Lucan of Cordoba. ₂₉ Further the gens Annaea was cursed by the Damnatio Memoriae (damnation of memory), ₃₀ that their property be seized, their name be erased and all works destroyed, ₃₁ especially the voluminous works by the family as professional scribes. ₃₂ Finally, an extraordinary curse was issued against Cordoba in Hispania as their home, ₃₃ that Nero ordered the city to be destroyed by fire and the ground salted and condemned, ₃₄ as a place only for the wicked and the cursed souls damned to walk the earth for eternity. ₃₅ Next the scribes and lawyers of the house of the gens Cassia were brought forward, ₃₆ as well as all their wives and children and servants where they were found culpable and sentenced, ₃₇ including Cassius Longinus and Cassius Apronianus in absentia (in Armenia). ₃₈ Similar to the gens Annaea, the gens Cassia were Damnatio Memoriae (damnation of memory), ₃₉ and that the huge volume of work of these pirate lawyers and forgers be utterly destroyed, ₄₀ and their name erased from all history and memory as cursed and damned. ₄₁ The same fate then greeted the family of false scribes and forgers of history, ₄₂ known as the gens Plinia and the notorious Gaius Plinius Secundus known as Pliny the Elder, ₄₃ and his son the obsessive liar known as Gaius Plinius Caecilius (Pliny the Younger), ₄₄ with all their works and writings damned to be destroyed and their name to be erased. ₄₅ The same fate then awaited the gens Suetonia with the entire house and all their works damned, ₄₆ and the indignity of Damnatio Memoriae (damnation of memory) stripping them of being Roman, ₄₇ thus Gaius Suetonius Paulus later known as St. Paul the Apostle was crucified, ₄₈ along with his son Gaius Suetonius Tranquillus later known as Suetonius for their active role, ₄₉ not only in the fire but in destroying the Empire through their treachery against the Celts. ₅₀ Finally, the Pisans were brought into the arena of the Circus and found guilty, ₅₁ not only of the most wicked treachery but of the most profane and sacrilegious acts, ₅₂ against heaven and the gods that protect Rome and all religions. ₅₃ Not only was the gens Calpurnia subject to Damnatio Memoriae (damnation of memory), ₅₄ and Gaius Calpernius Piso and his son Lucius Calpernius Piso condemned to be crucified, ₅₅ but all the women and young boys of the gens as well, ₅₆ with Gaius Calpernius Piso the last to be crucified upside down, ₅₇ after seeing his entire gens wiped from history. ₅₈ As the Pisans slowly died in agony before the cheering crowd, ₅₉ Emperor Nero issued the first Damnatio Memoriae ever issued against a philosophy, saying: ₆₀ Henceforth the beliefs of Arrius are Damnatio Memoriae, ₆₁ and anyone found to follow such insane and dangerous beliefs are culpable of a capital crime, ₆₂ and anyone who calls himself as Pisan or follower of Piso is culpable of a capital crime, ₆₃ and it shall be a moral duty of every Roman to hunt down Arrius, ₆₄ and any of his family that escaped and wipe them from the earth. ₆₅ For no other house has been more treacherous against Rome and their own people or Heaven. ₆₆ Thus may the gods favour Rome as we cleanse such madness and evil from the earth and our memory.

C. 41

1 In the year known as 66 CE, 2 twelve hundred and sixty six years since the dawn of the Great Age, 3 upon the failure of Gaius Domitius Corbulo to subdue Simon and the Nabateans, 4 the Roman Empire remained in financial and political turmoil as without a Holly Mint, 5 and without stable currency prices and unemployment continued to rise. 6 Vespasian convinced Nero that the failure of Corbulo was on account of his hatred for the emperor, 7 at the death of the gens Cassia and the family of his wife Cassia Longina, 8 and that Corbulo secretly planned to seize power from Nero. 9 The Emperor then agreed to summons Corbulo to Corinth while Vespasian went to Syria, 10 now as Legate of Africa and all Asia with orders to take Jerusalem at any cost. 11 At Corinth the messengers of Nero ordered Corbulo to commit suicide and without any hesitation, 12 but the word Axios!, one of the greatest and most loyal Roman generals committed suicide. 13 Once in Syria, Vespasian summonsed the generals to account for lack of progress, 14 to which they replied that the soldiers and the people remained inseparable, 15 while the Sicari guerrillas continued to constrain permanent camps further south, 16 And many guerrillas remained hiding in temples and sanctuaries the Romans were forbidden to attack. 17 Josephus now dutifully in the employ of Vespasian as his chief adviser did urge him, 18 to overlook his conscience and any hesitation at the evil task he must perform, 19 in killing every woman and child and man in order to destroy the will of the Nabateans, 20 and destroying more sacred temples and sanctuaries than at any other time, 21 in the history of the Roman Empire until that moment in order to end the stalemate. 22 Upon such wicked advice Vespasian then ordered that every city in the region, 23 along the path towards Jerusalem and including the city of Sepphoris, 24 be burned to the ground and the complete populations of men, women and children, 25 be slaughtered as conspirators and enemy combatants. 26 Thus the Roman soldiers did attack and murder hundreds of thousands of women and children, 27 and burn and destroy dozens of cities and towns that the guerrillas and soldiers of Nabatea, 28 in the face of such overwhelming evil were completely broken in spirit. 29 In a few short months and upon the bodies of more than a million murdered souls, 30 the bloody legions of Vespasian stood at the formidable walls of Jerusalem. 31 The wicked lies of Josephus and his family that women and children, 32 did commit suicide in the face of the Romans being one of many profanities against heaven, 33 to hide the complicity of such madmen in breaking all known Rule of Law, 34 as nothing more than insane pirates and thieves. 35 Yet at Jerusalem, no amount of terror or force could break the siege, 36 and Vespasian was forced to wait and seek some other way of breaking the spirit of the city. 37 In the year known as 68 CE, 38 twelve hundred and sixty eight years since the dawn of the Great Age,

Book 21 Age of the Nazarenes

39 Emperor Nero did give up the ghost midst the still ruined city of Rome. 40 Since the supreme perfidy of the Pisan Conspiracy, Nero had worked without rest, 41 to remodel and rebuild Rome into an even greater city, 42 that at the age of but thirty he looked a man of fifty. 43 Upon the sudden death of Nero and without any named heir, 44 the people of Rome expected the respected Praetorian Prefect Marcus Salvius Otho, 45 to be their new emperor after the funeral of Nero. 46 Yet Otho declined saying that such a burden be too great. 47 Instead he called upon the elderly Servius Sulpicius Galba in Rome for the funeral, 48 to take up the honour of being the next Emperor of Rome. 49 Upon news that the elderly Galba was chosen by Otho as Emperor, Vespasian was enraged, 50 and ordered his son Titus aided by Josephus to maintain the siege of Jerusalem, 51 while he took his other legions to Rome to seize power. 52 Yet upon news of the death of Nero, the African provinces erupted in rebellion, 53 forcing Vespasian to Africa briefly to put down the revolts. 54 In the same year, Ráicheál (Rachel) the wife of James the son of Jesus, 55 did give birth to a girl they named Eurgain (Eigen) in honour of the mother of Ráicheál (Rachel). 56 In the year known as 69 CE, 57 Emperor Galba was poisoned after only a few months as Emperor. 58 Praetorian Prefect Marcus Salvius Otho then declared, 59 he be the new emperor of Rome for the sake of the empire. 60 At the same time as the troubles and battles between the Roman pretenders, 61 Emperor Jesus did visit Iruna (Pamplona) and dedicate the Great Mint to Mari, 62 then to Parsi (Paris) and the Great Mint to Cernunnos (Mercury), 63 then finally to Coelogis (Cologne) and the Great Mint to Hella. 64 Thus by the year 69, the Celts did possess four Holly Mints, 65 and had commenced minting their own true coin.

C. 42

1 In the year known as 69 CE, 2 twelve hundred and sixty nine years since the dawn of the Great Age, 3 Emperor Marcus Salvius Otho himself was murdered, 4 by Aulis Vitellius and his agents acting for Vespasian. 5 But instead of opening the gates to allow Vespasian to enter and be proclaimed the new Emperor, 6 Vitellius changed his mind and declared himself emperor to the fury of Vespasian. 7 At the same time in Palestine and the siege of Jerusalem, 8 Josephus had resolved the solution to break the will of the defenders and Simon, 9 was to present little children every day within sight of the walls, 10 and to burn them alive in unbelievable pain and cruelty, 11 beginning with one poor child for the first day and then adding an extra child sacrificed thereafter. 12 Upon the thirtieth day and the sacrifice of thirty children by Josephus and Titus, 13 Simon the false Ptah (Peter) resolved with the defenders their hopeless fate, saying: 14 What hope is their to reason with such animals without souls or minds, 15 who mimic rituals like monkeys yet know nothing of heaven or spirits. 16 Woe to the world if such insane and mad beings seize this city and the Ark of the Covenant, 17 lest they herald a darkness upon the earth for a thousand years. 18 Verily, no

Divine Creator or spirit or demon could treaty with such illness, 19 nor a Covenant remain whilst such illness infect the bodies and minds of men. 20 Simon then ordered the Great Temple Mint of Mithra be stocked with wood and kindling, 21 from floor to roof that it may burn as a raging fire. 22 He then ordered that all the women and children be killed as gently as possible, 23 then fires to be lit across the city and in the Great Temple so that nothing remained. 24 Thus on the same day exactly six hundred and sixty six years (666), 25 when the Persians first destroyed the Temple of Set the city of Jerusalem was once more in flames, 26 and the Ark of Akhenaten (Moses), also known as the Ark of the Covenant, 27 that had been the greatest prize of civilisations for thirteen hundred years, 28 the symbol of divine authority and power on earth was utterly destroyed, 29 because of the insanity and cruelty of arrogant men who sought power at any cost. 30 So intense were the fires of the city that the forces of Titus and Josephus could only watch, 31 from a distance for five days until the flames subsided and they could enter the ruins of the city. 32 So hot had been the flames that the Great Temple had collapsed except for its western walls, 33 and all the gold of the mint had melted into the stones along with the gold of the ark. 34 Upon news of the destruction of the Great Temple Mint of Mithra reaching Rome, 35 the city was thrown into turmoil as were all the legions of the empire, 36 who took their oaths upon loyalty to Mithra. 37 Vespasian seized the city and killed Vitellius declaring himself messiah and god, 38 and that he would save the people of Rome and the world from destruction, 39 before summonsing Josephus to Rome to help craft a plan to hold the empire together.

Book 22

Age of Judaism

[69 - 117 CE]

C. 1

In the year known as 69 CE, 2 twelve hundred and sixty nine years since the dawn of the Great Age, 3 as Josephus and the Baal priests arrived in Rome the remnants of a once great empire, 4 was close to total destruction upon the collapse of the legions. 5 Rebellion and riots had erupted across the Empire disrupting key supplies to Rome, 6 including the provinces of Moesia, Dalmatia to the east and Lusitania and Baetica to the west. 7 Josephus advised Vespasian to immediately reach out to King Vologases of Parthia, 8 who had been building a massive and disciplined army under the guidance of Arrius Calpernius Piso, 9 now proclaiming himself as the High Priest of Satan. 10 Josephus then departed as an imperial legate to Parthia to meet with Piso, 11 and returned with a massive army of fifty thousand Parthians including ten thousand cavalry, 12 and a mass army of forty thousand soldiers and archers. 13 Vespasian immediately ordered the rebellions of Egypt and the east crushed, 14 while Rome sent its remaining legions west to Hispania to regain control of Lusitania and Baetica. 15 within a few months and despite the collapse of morale and discipline of the Roman legions, 16 Rome was saved by a Baal priest and the last remaining survivors of Piso. 17 Vespasian then reversed the curses and damnations of Nero and called on Josephus, 18 to determine how the culture and imperial religion of the Empire might be reformed, 19 and how the control of power and strategy of the Empire be positioned, 20 that the Britannic Empire of the Holly might be crushed, 21 and the legacies of Vespasian would rule the world forever more. 22 Vespasian was displeased having to reside midst the rotting ruins of Rome, 23 and instead summonsed all the Baal priests and best advisors and generals to Heliopolis, 24 Including Arrius Calpernius Piso and King Vologases of Parthia. 25 There in Heliopolis (Antioch) on the Orontes in the year known as 70CE, 26 Emperor Vespasian proclaimed that the provinces of Syria and Palestine be dissolved, 27 and a new sacred province be formed known as Iudea (Judea), 28 as the birthplace of a new Imperial Religion known as Iudeism (Judaism), 29 as the religion of those who proclaim the right (ius) to rule as gods (deorum), 30 declaring that the city be the new centre of the world and of Rome and its capital, 31 renaming the city Flavius Neapolis meaning the Golden New City, 32 under the new standard I.H.S. or Invictus Hoc Signo of a flaming gold sun and the three letters (IHS), 33 meaning that by this sign we are unconquerable.

C. 2

1 In the year known as 70 CE, 2 twelve hundred and seventy years since the dawn of the Great Age, 3 Vespasian and Josephus did convene a meeting of Baal and Mithraic priests, 4 of King Vologasis and lesser kings and Arrius as Absalom and High Priest of Satan, 5 and the most trusted leaders and merchants of Rome at Flavius Neapolis (Orontes). 6 Vespasian did speak to the historic gathering, saying: 7 Let our ancestors and the gods favour our deliberations and all that we affirm and do form. 8 For the future of the Empire and our gentes (families) and legacy depends upon it. 9 Thanks to our sacred pact, the destruction of the Empire has been averted. 10 Yet if we do not stop the menace of the Britannic Empire, then all will be for naught. 11 To which Josephus did reply: Most serene and divine father and all who serve thee and come in good faith, 12 verily there is to be found answers to all our concerns among those present. 13 For the strength of the Celts be not the Holly but in the steadfast trust of their own knowledge. 14 Thus, absence of any fear of mind as life is seen by them as but several journeys to perfection. 15 Yet the strength of the people of the East be their trust in the harmony of the universe. 16 Thus, absence of any fear of mind as the universe will always correct any disharmony. 17 Arrius did then reply: Venerable Josephus you serve two masters well, 18 yet we here present do not suffer the illness of believing what we say to be true, 19 but that we achieve our ends for the perpetual remembrance of all our houses. 20 I assert that all mankind may be divided between those who rule and those who choose to be ruled, 21 and that the key to such strategy be the control of the mind of men. 22 For if one does control the mind of a man, the body must always follow. 23 How then do we end opposition to the proposition that we and we alone are born to rule, 24 and all who oppose us such as the Holly and their Celts are but our slaves and animals. 25 Vespasian then did say in reply: Is this not the very definition of our Imperial Religion, 26 is this not the meaning of Judaism as the Divine Right to Rule as gods over people as animals, 27 to which Josephus did say: Most serene and divine father this is true as his holiness Absalom did speak. 28 Yet to divide and conquer all the Celts as our perpetual slaves and animals, 29 we must destroy their absolute trust in their knowledge and stories. 30 Once Celts no longer trust one another or their leaders then we must keep them in perpetual fear, 31 that they never unite as one again nor awaken from their stupidity. 32 Verily to divide and conquer the people of the East with our allies, we must cleave their trust of heaven, 33 by creating so many gods and deities and beliefs that no longer is their any trust in faith or religion. 34 Once men of the east no longer trust one another or

heaven we must keep them perpetually off balance. 35 Thus, this shall be how we control a world enslaved to us now and forever more. 36 The gathering did then agree there be two types of followers being Gewes (Jews) and Iewes (Jews), 37 that they and all who they deem worthy as the Gewes shall be the perpetual rulers of men, 38 and the Iewes be all those who pledge their absolute loyalty to the rulers of men. 39 For a Iewe may never be a Gewe except their descendants through marriage, 40 and any man that did not pledge absolute loyalty to be ruled as a slave be an animal. 41 The gathering did then agree to essential elements of the new religion of Judaism, 42 agreeing that to create a false story and false history full of false law and false beliefs was essential. 43 Josephus proposed the sacrilegious text be known as the Septuaginta (LXX) or Seventy and G, 44 in honour the year of the birth of Judaism as the official Imperial Religion. 45 King Vologases did then speak and assert the claimed history of his ancestors, 46 who claimed from the time of King Phriapites of Parthia a blood heritage to Enochiah, 47 through a mysterious and absurd genealogy beginning with Methuseliah, 48 who was claimed to live for hundreds of years and then his son Lameciah, 49 who he also claimed lived for hundreds of years, 50 and then Noiah (Noah) who he claimed lived for hundreds of years, 51 before Shem (Shemiah) then Menassiah then Machiah. 52 All agreed and the edict was issued by Vespasian that the Gewes, 53 being those given the Divine Right to Rule from heaven descend from the line of Shem. 54 Thus all Gewes be Shemites (Semites) and anyone who deny the truth of the Gewes be an Anti-Shemite, 55 and all Anti-Shemites (Anti-Semites) were to be executed as a capital offence. 56 A new time in honour of Satan was declared known as the Kalendarium Flavii (Golden Calendar), 57 beginning with the year zero for the birth of John the Baptist, 58 and a sacred day every seven days known as Sataday (later corrupted to Saturday). 59 It was then agreed that the people need a hero and a saviour and that Titus, 60 the son of Vespasian be named Christ and that the complete Egyptian history of Horus, 61 be copied and used as a template to account for supernatural signs and events, 62 as the coming of Christ to judge the living and the dead. 63 The coming of Christ (Titus) then be proclaimed in one year, 64 as the greatest procession in the history of Rome, 65 and the signal of the greatest army ever assembled, 66 to attack and bring the Celts to heel.

C. 3

1 The Celts and Emperor Jesus were not unaware of the planning of Josephus and the priests, 2 nor of the alliances made between Vespasian and Vologasis of Parthia, 3 and the movement of the Capital to Flavius Neapolis. 4 Since the Celtic tribes had rid their lands of the slave traders and corrupt bankers, 5 life and the prosperity of the people had risen dramatically, 6 and Jesus and Mariamne were the proud grandparents of more than five grandchildren. 7 Yet the King Vandix of Gallia (Gaul) and King Reichmor (Tacticus) of the Franks, 8 as well as King Silani of the Basci (Basque) and

the united tribes of Britain had been far from idle. 9 The Celts had built hundreds and hundreds of watchtowers and developed signalling flags, 10 that a key message could be sent across the Celtic lands at speed and even signalled across the Channel, 11 to Britain and then to Holly Rood in less than a day. 12 Yet King Vandix of Gallia (Gaul) feared it be only a matter of time, 13 that Vespasian mount a massive campaign to recapture their lands and punish the Celts, 14 and at Holly Rood they urged Emperor Jesus to consider what strategy best suit such an onslaught. 15 Yet at the same assembly, King Reichmor (Tacticus) expressed deeper concern, 16 at the falsities of Judaism such as the absurd capital crime for anti-Shemism (anti-semitism), 17 to which Jesus did reply: There is no reasoning with men blinded by lust and deaf to truth. 18 Verily the falsities and absurdities of Judaism shall be revealed and such a madness will die. 19 Yet if it be the will of heaven for Judaism to survive then trust the wisdom of the universe. 20 For there may come even a day when men falsely claim my words as a curse or a blessing, 21 or seize upon the honour and symbols of the Holly for their own ends. 22 Verily, if this comes to pass, then know that the curses of stupid men have no power, 23 nor those of men who know nothing of the supernatural or true history. 24 I shall never abandon my witness to the truth in this life or the next life, 25 as I am or as I will become. 26 But men who create such complex falsities condemn themselves never to progress, 27 or ever to return, but to remain between worlds as ghosts. 28 Pray then forgiveness for the fool who cannot discern truth from falsities, 29 that they do not suffer the fate of the undead, 30 and we shall prepare for the barbarian hoards of Vespasian.

C. 4

1 In the year known as 71 CE, 2 twelve hundred and seventy one years since the dawn of the Great Age, 3 Titus the son of Vespasian did enter Rome to the largest and most lavish Triumph in Roman history, 4 as Christ the saviour and redeemer of the new Imperial Religion of Iudaism (Judaism), 5 accompanied by his father Vespasian as the golden Lucifer and bringer of light, 6 and Domitian the younger son of Vespasian. 7 Accompanying them were an array of hastily invented and forged artefacts all claimed as authentic, 8 from the utterly destroyed Great Temple Mint of Mithra such as ten wholly fraudulent candlesticks, 9 that were then called Menorah with each possessing seven elements in honour of Iudaism, 10 and claimed to be saved from the fires by being hidden in the bowels of the temple. 11 Other objects of fraudulent manufacture included trumpets and swords and precious necklaces. 12 Josephus had already agreed with Vespasian that the number 666 as to the destruction of the Temple, 13 was to be central as a positive to the new religion of Iudaism (Judaism) as the number of Satan, 14 and a celebration of his power and conquering strength, with the new battle cry: 15 **VENI VIDI VICI as VIVIVI and 666.** 16 In answer to the destruction of the Ark of the Covenant, Josephus and Vespasian did claim, 17 that neither the Ark nor the Covenant had been destroyed or

ended but merely transubstantiated, 18 into a different form by the Great Creator deliberately choosing the gold of the ark to mix, 19 with all the gold of the Great Temple such that all the gold recovered from the temple be sacred, 20 as the symbol of a new covenant whereby the gold represented the storehouse of the spirit, 21 of all men and women duty bound as service to Lucifer (Vespasian) for seventy years, 22 thereafter such spirit may be released upon death and travel to its new life. 23 In honour of the new sacred covenant each bar was to be stamped with the sacred number 666, 24 In honour of Lucifer and the fact that such a bar be a sacred ecclesiastical part of the new ark, 25 and a physical symbol of the new covenant and a prison for souls. 26 Finally, in terms of the minting of coin, Vespasian announced the opening of the new mint, 27 of Flavius Neapolis and the fact that because such gold even as coin be so valuable and sacred, 28 it could not be taken out of the sacred lands (Holy Lands) of Iudea (Judea) except, 29 by grant of the Imperial Treasury. 30 Instead, merchants would be given written certificates for gold coins which would be honoured, 31 or transferable for the payment of debits anywhere across the Empire but redeemable, 32 if one travelled to Flavius Neapolis and demanded payment. 33 The effect of this new form of paper money was instantaneous in creating a wave of credit, 34 which Vespasian used in part to recruit huge expansion on military resources, 35 and building projects including the rebuilding of Rome, of Cordoba and of Flavius Neapolis. 36 In the same year, Quintus Petilius Cerialis was appointed by Vespasian to lead, 37 the single largest Roman army in history of more than eight legions and auxiliaries, 38 of more than one hundred and twenty thousand men against the Celts, 39 formed from tens of thousands of conscripts and mercenaries from Parthia, Armenia and Africa. 40 The first parts of the army arrived and captured the cities of Narbo and Massilia, 41 before massing to head north and recapture the ruins of Lucifer (Lyon), 42 the birthplace of the Emperor and the first primary object of the invasion. 43 The watchtowers had already alerted Vindex to the size of the force and he had chosen, 44 not to engage the massive army until it reached more favourable conditions. 45 Once it had become apparent a second army was not in the field against the Franks, 46 Gaius Calpernius Tacticus the King of the Franks did mass an army of more than forty thousand, 47 of the most fearsome and disciplined Germanic legions to march south in support of Vindex. 48 Vindex then split his army of forty thousand into two with ten thousand advancing towards, 49 Quintus Petilius Cerialis and then withdrawing after a bloody engagement drawing them north. 50 At the city of Vesontio sitting on the oxbow of the Doubs River the smaller army of Vindex, 51 bravely stood its ground against the overwhelming forces of Quintus Petilius Cerialis, 52 with the Romans committing its main forces to squeeze the Gauls against the river, 53 while a second Roman force had crossed the hills to the south and moved around to cut off escape. 54 When all hope appeared lost for the brave men of Vindex, the second larger army appeared, ₅₅ from the south-west and cut of the Roman supply line and began pressing north, ₅₆ As Gaius Calpernius Tacticus the King of the Franks did arrive with his army, ₅₇ to surround the Romans on the northern side of the oxbow. ₅₈ With no room with which to move and with no escape the largest Roman army in history, ₅₉ was utterly slaughtered and more than one hundred thousand Roman soldiers lost their lives, ₆₀ in a single day as the greatest Celtic victory in history, ₆₁ and wiped from and denied in all false history texts and accounts. ₆₂ Vindex then moved south and pushed the Romans back to the coast of Narbo and Massilia. ₆₃ Upon the historic defeat Vespasian was enraged, saying: ₆₄ What torment these Holly Celts be that they rise up against our plans. ₆₅ To which Josephus did reply: Most serene and divine Father, we must trust our own intellect, ₆₆ to defeat the Celts through the corruption of their minds and the destruction of their trust. ₆₇ Let our army be our deceased brothers that will carry our falsities and perfidies for us, ₆₈ so that in the years to come the Celts will defend to the death their belief, ₆₉ in the names of Cassius and Suetonius and Seneca and Plinius above all others, ₇₀ and have no knowledge of their own history or the truth of these days. ₇₁ Soon after, Vespasian issued an edict reopening slave trade especially of Celts as mere animals, ₇₂ but only to be owned by Gewes who claimed the exclusive right of heaven for slavery. ₇₃ In the same year, many of the survivors of exiled and condemned gentes returned to Rome, ₇₄ Marcus Cassius Cocceianus the son of Marcus Cassius Apronianus, ₇₅ and his son Lucius Cassius Cocceianus Dio, ₇₆ to oversee much of the re-writing of history to honour their slain families.

C. 5

₁ In the year known as 72 CE, ₂ twelve hundred and seventy two years since the dawn of the Great Age, ₃ Vespasian announced a series of major changes in the organization of the Empire. ₄ The most important province in all the Empire was now Iudea (Judea) as the Holly (Holy) Lands, ₅ as the only Divine and Ecclesiastical Province of the Empire. ₆ The next highest provinces were now twelve Senatorial Provinces beginning with Baetica (South Spain), ₇ then Narbonensis, Italia, Corsica Et Sardinia, Africa Proconsularis and Cyrenaica Et Creta, ₈ and then Macedonia, Epirus, Achaia, Asia Proconsularis and Bithnia Et Pontus. ₉ From these new Senatorial Provinces, the wealthy families as Gewes could be elected, ₁₀ as leaders and Senators under the new Imperial law. ₁₁ The lowest form of provinces were now Imperial Provinces of which there were twenty two being, ₁₂ Lusitania, Mauretania Tingitana, Mauretania Caesariensis, Alpes Poeniae and Alpes Cottiae, ₁₃ then Alpes Maritimae, Raetia, Noricum, Pannonia Superior, Pannonia Inferior, Dalmatia and Dacia, ₁₄ and then Moesia Superior and Moesia Inferior, Thracia, Lycia Et Pamphylia and Galatia, ₁₅ and then Cilicia, Cappadocia, Aegyptus and Armenia. ₁₆ These new Imperial Provinces did not have Senatorial representation and their leaders, ₁₇ were now appointed directly by the Emperor and not by the

Senate. 18 Such claims that Tarraconensis and Acquitania and Lugdunensis were held by Rome under Vespasian, 19 or that Britannia and Germania were subject to his excessive rule are nothing more than clumsy lies, 20 crafted by the hand of false scribes and agents to hide the truth of the Britannic Empire. 21 Since Iudaism (Judaism) had been made the official and Imperial Religion, 22 no man by law could be Emperor, or Dictator, or Legate or Consul or Senator unless they be a Gewe. 23 Nor could anyone be a Magistrate or Official or General unless they be a Iewe (Jew) or Gewe (Jew). 24 As for finance and trade all money lending and money changing and loans were exclusively, 25 to be controlled and owned by the Gewes (Jews) and no other. 26 Nor could anyone own a slave other than a Gewe (Jew) as the entire slave trade had been given, 27 to the Gewes (Jews) and by the perverted and corrupt edicts of Vespasian only Gewes (Jews), 28 possessed the Divine Right to own slaves while all others could only lease slaves, 29 and were then forced by Roman Law to pay the Gewes (Jews) a Slave Tax for their use. 30 For no one could own property by Roman Law any more unless they be a Iewe (Jew) or Gewe (Jew). 31 Thus the whole world was sealed for the exclusive benefit and use of all but a minority of strangers, 32 with no common thread of blood, or culture, or history, or place or race or even legitimate religion. 33 Never before had the world witnessed such a strange philosophy that rewarded incompetence over merit. 34 No longer did the ancient traditions of honour or skill or competence apply to the future of Rome. 35 Instead, under the insane and absurd Imperial Religion of Iudaism (Judaism), 36 the qualities rewarded were to be perfidy, immorality, sociopathy and deviancy. 37 Vespasian had even begun public executions by the most inhumane and barbaric method, 38 of those poor souls accused of the capital crime of anti-Shemitism (anti-semitism), 39 through burning at the stake under a word created for this type of execution called Holocaust, 40 meaning a pleasing sacrifice and burnt offering to Lord Satan under Iudaic Law. 41 Many hundreds had been burnt to death by this awful and insane method of murder, 42 until Vespasian was forced to ensure that a trial be held first to determine, 43 if an accused truly be an anti-Shemite (anti-semite) and such accusations not be false. 44 To ensure the profits of families of Gewes who claimed by the profane and sacrilegious falsity, 45 of Divine Right to be the only Chosen People of Satan (g-d) to control the slave trade, 46 Vespasian ordered that slaves could only be bought and sold at limited markets and cities. 47 Huge new slave centres were established at Flavius Neapolis, Ephesus, Alexandria and Corinth, 48 as well as Cyrene, Leptis Magna, Rome, Massilia and Corduba. 49 In the same year, Vespasian revealed his new plans for Rome upon the dedication of the temple, 50 known as Templum Novum Pacis or the Temple of the New Covenant at the Forum of Rome. 51 Rome was to become a place of wonder of the ancient world and the capital for entertainment. 52 A new massive stadium called the Colosseum holding more than 50,000 was to be built, 53 upon the ruins of the palace of Nero that had housed and saved thousands from the fires. 54 On the low lying plain below the Capitoline Hill known as the Campus Martius or Field of Mars, 55 Vespasian announced the commencement of a grand vision to create stadiums and theatres, 56 and museums and displays to rival the greatness of Alexandria. 57 Tourism and prostitution and alcohol and gambling and violence and bloodshed, 58 was to be the life of the new Rome as the most purpose rebuilt city for pleasure and excess, 59 ever conceived in the history of any civilisation. 60 Not even the ancient and sacred temple of The Vaticanus was spared by the immoral excesses, 61 as Vespasian ordered the conversion of the sacred temple The Vaticanus, 62 into a Necropolis and Crematoria in complete desecration and sacrilege of its history. 63 Under the constant stream of false inventions added to Iudaism (Judaism), 64 wealthy Romans who converted to Iudaism were told that if their bodies be buried at the Vatican, 65 then on the last days of the earth, Lord Satan would resurrect their mortal remains, 66 and reunite their spirit with their reanimated living form. 67 To honour this absurd and unprecedented false doctrine, the Iudaic (Judaic) priests under Josephus, 68 declared the founders of Iudaism (Judaism) to be saints, 69 with the two greatest and most revered saints placed at Vaticanus Necropolis, 70 Saint Paul (Gaius Suetonius Paulus) the assassin of Caratacus and Belus, 71 and Gaius Calpernius Piso as Saint Peter (Ptah) and founding patron of Iudaism (Judaism), 72 both of whom could be venerated by tourists visiting Vaticanus Necropolis. 73 In the same year, Vespasian granted control of Corduba to Marcus Annaeus son of Lucan, 74 in honour of his gens and all those who were executed under Nero. 75 The nineteen year old Marcus Annaeus then changed his name to Marcus Annaeus Ulpius Traianus, 76 with Ulpius from the Latin word Iupus meaning wolf. 77 At the same time his younger brother Lucius Annaeus changed his name to Lucius Annaeus Ursus Servianus, 78 with Ursus meaning the Great Bear in Latin.

C. 6

1 Upon Emperor Jesus (Yahusiah) of the Britannic Empire hearing of the actions of Vespasian, 2 in further promoting the madness and insanity of Iudaism (Judaism), 3 Jesus was enraged at the murder of rational and sensible people as anti-Shemites (antisemites), 4 who dared to speak the truth that a lie is a lie and not a truth was unprecedented in history. 5 Jesus did then summons all Celtic leaders Parlamage (Parliament) at Holly Rood Din Eidyn (Edinburgh), 6 that they might discuss how to address such an insanity and mental illness as Iudaism (Judaism). 7 There at Holly Rood Din Eidyn (Edinburgh) Jesus the former Pontifex Maximus, 8 and now Summa Pontifex (Supreme Pontiff) of the Universalis Ecclesia (Universal Church), 9 did address the leaders and priests of all the Celts saying: 10 Let us speak plainly and clearly that those here present and those yet to come, 11 be under no mistake as to the meaning or the truth we now speak. 12 Verily, I say to you

and all who may come in my name or from an assembly of equals, 13 or in the name of the law of the Universalis Ecclesia (Universal Church), 14 that no one speaks truly, or possesses any authority, or speaks in my name or the Rule of Law, 15 unless they honour the words we now speak here. 16 For if a man does proclaim he speaks the truth but does not, then he is a liar, 17 and if a man claims to speak in my name, yet speaks against my words then he is a deceiver, 18 and if a man comes claiming authority of the Universal Church but denies these words, 19 then he is an imposter and the worst of deceivers and liars. 20 Verily, each and every man and woman who respects life and the law and heaven, 21 possesses the moral obligation not only to stand and defend the true Rule of Law, 22 that are all equal before the law and none are above it, 23 but that they expose and capture and punish those who would corrupt such foundation. 24 If then it be the case that men and women are confronted with those infected with madness, 25 then it is the moral obligation of every man and woman to rid the world of such illness, 26 and to resist, to struggle, to fight and overcome by every means necessary. 27 Let no liar or deceiver or one infected with madness tell you to be meek or mild, 28 in the face of such evil and insanity as anti-Shcmitism (anti-semitism), 29 where people who speak truth are to be executed and those who lie are to be rewarded. 30 Instead let us begin with the simplest of truths as to the gift of mind and reason. 31 Thus, all possess the right to be heard, whether or not we agree with the idea expressed. 32 By virtue of our absolute immutable right of free will we may choose, 33 what to believe or not believe and by our own actions what to do or not do. 34 All possess the right over their own thoughts and opinions and spirit, 35 as no one can rightfully claim to be owner of your mind except you. 36 Verily your mind is the sovereign over your own flesh and so no force may claim, 37 possession over your body unless your mind surrenders and allows it to be so. 38 All possess the right and ability of reason through the existence of their conscience, 39 and to know what is right from wrong that there can be no excuse. 40 Even if we have on occasions made mistakes and surrendered our sovereignty, 41 no man or force or being can truly entrap your soul or mind or flesh, 42 just as no man or empire may claim to be owner of the land or water or air, 43 for verily we are all mere tenants upon this beautiful world that sustains life. 44 No one possesses a blood right, birth right, prior right or divine right, 45 to be the owner or ruler over any other. 46 Verily all law is equal that no one is above it, 47 and all law is measured that all may learn and know it, 48 as all law is standard that it may always be applied the same. 49 Thus any claimed law that contradicts the Golden Rule of Law cannot be law, 50 but the weakest rule of men as tyrants and such rule is without consent, 51 and merely by trickery, deception, threat and fear and cannot be sustained. 52 Behold Iudaism (Judaism) is a fraud and Gewes (Jews) have no rights or authority, 53 nor are such people the Chosen People of any deity as they have no connection to heaven. 54 For everything of Iudaism

(Judaism) is false and profane and sacrilegious, 55 and but the tricks and falsities of wicked bankers and pirates who seek to enslave the world, 56 by corrupting the world to their own delusions.

C. 7

1 In the year known as 73 CE, 2 twelve hundred and seventy four years since the dawn of the Great Age, 3 Gaius Calpernius Tacticus also known as Reichmor as the King of the Franks, 4 commissioned the building of a massive defensive project known as the Limes Germanicus, 5 from the North Sea to the upper reaches of the Danube River to ensure, 6 no massive Roman mercenary army could enter Germania from the east, 7 without having to negotiate formidable obstacles. 8 At the same time, Emperor Vespasian was enraged upon receiving word of the edict, 9 of Emperor Jesus declaring the Iudean (Judean) Imperial Religion a fraud and without law. 10 Vespasian demanded a new mass army be purchased to invade the Celts and destroy their Empire, 11 to which Josephus suggested a different strategy and rather than risk another loss, 12 to strike at Holly Rood and Jesus directly thus destroying the Holly head. 13 Vespasian agreed and appointed Gaius Julius Agricola the father in law to Josephus, 14 to head an invasion force of three legions and forty thousand men to destroy Holly Rood. 15 To try and surprise the Holly and avoid the risk of support from Gaul and Germania, 16 Gaius Julius Agricola took the hazardous journey of circumnavigating Britain, 17 and landing his forces from the west upon the River Clyde to then travel east. 18 Yet his voyage had been well documented and the Holly Army of Jesus, 19 was battle ready the moment the Romans set foot on the sacred soil of Cruithri (Scotland). 20 Forty thousand Romans faced a fearsome combined army of sixty thousand Celts, 21 and ten thousand pipers and drums as the Romans were cut to pieces within a day. 22 Gaius Julius Agricola and only a handful of ships managed to escape, 23 with the rest of the fleet sunk and the river red with the blood of mercenaries. 24 Jesus did then come upon the conclusion of the battle and witness, 25 the planting of a cross upon the place, declaring: 26 Let this most sacred place be blessed for now and evermore, 27 as the site at which the men of the sacred Isle did unite to defend these lands. 28 Let then this most holly place be known hereafter as Glasgow, 29 the site upon which the sacred (green or glas) lands were defended (gow). 30 In the same year, 31 Arrius Calpernius Piso also known as Absalom and High Priest of Satan, 32 and the founder of Aryanism did give up the ghost at Samsun in Pontus. 33 The next High Priest of Satan was his son Marcus Calpernius Piso, 34 who took the name Marcion and also known as Marcion of Pontus and Sinope. 35 In the year known as 77 CE, 36 twelve hundred and seventy seven years since the dawn of the Great Age, 37 Hermiones of Eliada and Larissa and son of High Priest Heliodores, 38 did have a son he named Heracles, also known as Heracles Atticus.

C. 8

1 In the year known as 78 CE, 2 twelve hundred and seventy eight years since the dawn of the Great Age, 3 Vologases of Parthia did give up the ghost. 4 With no clear successor the Parthian Empire was thrown into a brief civil war, 5 with Marcion of Pontus aided by Vespasian staking a claim as King, 6 and Tiridates of Armenia extending his claim, 7 while Arsaces Pacorus the brother of Vologases sought to establish his rule. 8 By the same year, 9 the paper certificates of Vespasian and the extreme levels of borrowings, 10 had destroyed the livelihood of small villages and farmers, traders and producers, 11 who could not afford the extraordinary prices due to rapid inflation. 12 Hundreds of thousands flocked to major cities such as Rome in search of work, 13 while Rome itself had become the fantasy land and first tourist capital in history. 14 The Franks continued to resist the attempts by the Romans to gain a foot hold, 15 while the Gauls contained the Romans to the fringe of the Mediterranean. 16 Only Hispania and the cruel and inhumane rule of Marcus Ulpius Traianus (Trajan), 17 saw the Basque Celts losing ground inch by inch upon a relentless strategy. 18 In the year known as 79 CE, 19 twelve hundred and seventy nine years since the dawn of the Great Age, 20 Emperor Vespasian came from Flavius Neapolis in Syria to Rome, 21 to prepare for the great opening of the Colosseum. 22 Yet within days of his visit and before the scheduled opening, 23 Mount Vesuvius did erupt sending ash, stones and fire high into the air, 24 turning day into night and destroying the cities of Pompeii and Ercolanium, 25 as well as the cities of Stabiae and Oplontis and Surrentum, 26 and destroying the Roman fleet by fire at Misenum. 27 The population of Rome was in a panic upon the disaster, 28 and the Gewes and Patricians called to Vespasian to use his powers, 29 to intervene against such signs of the end of the world. 30 Yet Vespasian sought to escape the city in secret, 31 and like the very worst of cowards to abandon the city at its greatest need. 32 Yet in awaiting for ships to take him away, Vespasian was suddenly struck down, 33 and died in writhing agony a few days later. 34 The Senate then called for Titus the son of Vespasian to come to Rome and aid, 35 in the relief and recovery efforts as tens of thousands had died, 36 and many hundreds of thousands were homeless and food supplies were scarce. 37 Josephus even encouraged Titus to use the volcanoe as a sign of the power of Satan, 38 and that as the Christ of Iudaism (Judaism) and Lucifer he could heal the sick. 39 Yet Titus refused to travel to Rome and Italia and instead, 40 arranged lavish feasts and celebrations of being Emperor at Flavius Neapolis, 41 while the people of Rome and Italia were starving and dying. 42 Within four months of the influx of refugees into Rome, 43 and upon the collapse of food supplies to the city which Titus refused to address, 44 the plague broke out across the city killing tens of thousands of people.

C. 9

1 In the year known as 80 CE, 2 twelve hundred and eighty years since the

dawn of the Great Age, 3 Rome and much of Italia and Egypt and even Africa, 4 had begun to turn against the flavian bankers who declared themselves as Gods, 5 and had funded and created the false elitism of commercial slavery, 6 known as Iudaism (Judaism). 7 The people of Rome openly mocked Titus as Lucifer as a false god and anti-Christ, 8 and began openly proclaiming themselves followers of ancient religions, 9 and even the beliefs of the Celts as professed anti-Shemites (anti-semites). 10 When Titus ordered the rioters and anti-shemites (anti-semites) arrested and burned, 11 the people of the city revolted and began to burn down the entertainment venues, 12 for foreign tourists and the pleasures of the Gewes (Jews) and Iewes (Jewes). 13 The fires across Rome raged for more than four days, 14 destroying all of the major entertainment buildings of Vespasian, 15 and even major temples that had been desecrated including the Pantheon. 16 While the death toll was nothing like the tragedy of the Fire of 64 CE, 17 the damage was extensive and Josephus now demanded Titus go to Rome, 18 to re-establish law and order yet once again Titus refused, 19 instead preferring to remain intoxicated in the arms of his lovers. 20 Josephus then removed himself and his family and two sons to Athens, 21 the first son named Flavius Josephus Justus and the second Flavius Josephus Valentinus. 22 When riots began to break out at Alexandria and across the Empire, 23 only then did Titus act and travel to Rome. 24 In the year known as 81 CE, 25 twelve hundred and eighty one years since the dawn of the Great Age, 26 Titus finally arrived at Rome with his legions to re-establish law and order, 27 over an utterly destroyed city and rebellious population. 28 Yet instead of seeking to re-assure the leaders and find a peace, 29 Titus ordered the senators and leaders that greeted him to be executed, 30 as traitors and proclaimed that Rome and Italia be cursed by Satan, 31 for their infidelity to him as Christ and Lucifer, 32 and to the faith of Iudaism (Judaism). 33 Within two days, Titus was dead after a painful fever.

C. 10

1 In the year known as 81 CE, 2 twelve hundred and eighty one years since the dawn of the Great Age, 3 Domitian moved quickly to re-establish order across the Empire, 4 appointing the strongest and most ruthless Roman leaders into positions of power, 5 while securing new peace treaties with client kingdoms in recognising their exclusive rights, 6 as monarchs and elite Gewes (Jews) in complete contradiction and fraud to the history of Rome. 7 In the east, Domition recognised Rabbel Soter as King of Nabatea, 8 and Tiridates as King of Armenia and Marcus Antonius Primus as King of Pontus, 9 and Pacorus as the Great King of Parthia and Duras as King of Dacia. 10 Domition then appointed Sextus Julius Frontinus as Legate of Asia, 11 and the ruthless gens Septimia of Leptis Magna as rulers of Africa, 12 through their patriarch Gaius Septimius Vegetus. 13 In Hispania Domition appointed Marcus Ulpius Traianus (Trajan) as Legate, 14 and Lucius Aelius Plautius from

Pontus as Praetorian Prefect of Rome, 15 charged with restoring law and order to Rome and Italia. 16 Flavius Josephus returned briefly from Athens to Flavius Neapolis (Antioch) to make amends, 17 and for a time returned to advising Domition on stabilising the Empire. 18 The new Emperor then ordered the end to paper money, 19 and the establishment of a lower base coin which had the immediate effect, 20 of causing uproar amongst the few plebian and patrician Gewes (Jews), 21 who had become obscenely wealthy upon the manipulation of paper currencies, 22 and returned power to the temple and city bankers, 23 and the traditional coin exchanges. 24 In response to the growing uproar and funded riots against the changes, 25 Domition abolished the Senate and declared himself Master and God. 26 To regain public support and establish absolute obedience, 27 Domition then ordered a series of public executions of corrupt officials. 28 Within a matter of months, the Empire had been stabilised, 29 and the rule of the Emperor had never been stronger from Flavius Neapolis (Antioch). 30 Domition then set about touring the provinces as a sign of strength and stability, 31 before commissioning a handful of generals led by Marcus Antonius Primus of Pontus, 32 to devise a strategy and time to invade the Britannic Empire and destroy the Celts. 33 In the year known as 82 CE, 34 twelve hundred and eighty two years since the dawn of the Great Age, 35 news came to Domition and Marcus Antonius Primus of the illness of Emperor Jesus. 36 The Flavian Emperor then resolved that upon the death of Jesus, 37 the greatest invasion of Celtic lands would be launched, 38 thus forcing the Celts to abandon their laws or face slaughter. 39 At the same time the gravelly ill Emperor did summons all the leaders of the Celts, 40 to Holly Rood to bear witness to the recitation of his last testament, 41 and to then return to their lands to read the memorial of the Emperor, 42 as the last true words of Jesus also known as Yahusiah and Cú-Laoch.

C. 11

1 In the year known as 83 CE, 2 twelve hundred and eighty three years since the dawn of the Great Age, 3 Holly Emperor Jesus (Yahusiah) also known as Cú-Laoch, 4 meaning the Hero and the Hero of the Cuilliaéan, 5 the thirty second Great Prophet of Yeb and former Pontifex Maximus, 6 as the former highest Priest of the whole Roman Empire, 7 and the Summa Pontifex (Supreme Pontiff) of the Universalis Ecclesia, 8 the living foundation stone of the Divine of the most ancient Cuilliaéan, 9 and blood descendant of the priests of Ebla, 10 and blood descendant of the priests of Ur, 11 and blood descendant of the priest-kings of the Hyksos, 12 and blood descendant of the priests of Ugarit, 13 and the only true blood descendants of King Da'vid, 14 and the Messiah Kings of Yahuda, 15 and son of Joseph and Great Prophet of Yeb, 16 did give up the ghost at Holly Rood, Din Eidyn (Edinburgh). 17 Upon the news of his death the Celtic Empire was in mourning. 18 But true to the last request of Jesus, 19 all the armies of Celts were assembled ready for battle across the Empire, 20 to hear the last testament of Jesus recited by

tribal leaders, 21 who themselves had witnessed the truth to the words. 22 Thus, before a single Roman foot touched the ground or arrow was launched, 23 the Celtic world at the same time did hear and witness, 24 these last true words of Jesus, being: 25 IN THE NAME OF THE ONE TRUE DIVINE CREATOR AND LORD OF ALL EXISTENCE, 26 AND OF ALL LAW AND ALL LIFE AND ALL RIGHTS AND AUTHORITY: 27 Let it be known to all who may come to hear and read these words, that this be the one, 28 true and only testament of the most humble servant and priest of heaven and the holly. 29 That all may know the truth and that none may be confused, 30 and that all may honour the law and none be misguided by a sense of conflict with it. 31 For of all the words we ever speak, it is our one, true and only testament that sustains. 32 Thus if any man seeks to honour me, then honour my words and testament, 33 and if any man seeks to honour the law in mourning and remembrance, 34 then honour the memory and testament of the king first and above all other acts. 35 Thus, when I have considered the origin of war and the necessities of our position, 36 I leave this mortal form to my next journey and life with confidence, 37 that each of you shall do your duty and that you shall seize the day, 38 and our union and freedoms shall be protected for future generations. 39 To all of us slavery is an abhorrent act of supreme profanity against all true law, 40 and against the laws of Heaven and the prophets and the Divine Creator. 41 To all of us the notion of deliberately false history and acts of perfidy and falsity, 42 be the signs of utter madness and incompetence and those without any right to rule. 43 Yet the world is no longer safe from such profanity or madness, 44 and even the sea is not safe from such piracy and insanity. 45 Thus even upon my death you may find such cowards will treat honour as weakness, 46 and piety to heaven as opportunity for sacrilegious acts of barbarity. 47 Thus you must prepare and you must resist for these be my final words. 48 Let not a single land of the Celts be stained by Iudaism (Judaism), 49 or any other madness of the pirates and moneylenders who curse heaven. 50 Instead stand up for your children and your home, 51 stand up and resist for your community and your tribe. 52 Stand up and fight with every ounce of your being and every drop of blood, 53 to rid this world of those who would pollute such a beautiful sanctuary as this earth, 54 and falsely claim the authority of heaven. 55 Verily, I leave you, yet my words and deeds remain. 56 Be gentle to yourself and to my memory.

C. 12

1 In the year known as 83 CE, 2 twelve hundred and eighty three years since the dawn of the Great Age, 3 within days of the commencement of official mourning for the death of Emperor Jesus, 4 the Roman mercenaries did seek to strike without any regard for honour or laws of heaven. 5 Marcus Antonius Primus did launch an attack westward from Raetia, 6 against Coelogis (Cologne) with an army of forty thousand, 7 as Marcus Ulpius Traianus (Trajan) with an army of thirty thousand moved north, 8 to cut

off the forces of King Gaius Calpernius Tacticus (Reichmor) of the Franks, 9 and delay any reinforcements from Cernunnos the son of Vindex of Gallia. 10 At the same time Gnaeus Julius Agricola did arrive with a massive fleet of fire ships, 11 and thirty thousand soldiers to destroy Holly Rood and Din Eidyn (Edinburgh) by fire, 12 during the formal funeral of Emperor Jesus, also known as Yahusiah. 13 Yet the Celts were ready and inspired by the last true testament of their saviour, 14 and upon the first legions attacking the Germanic Celts, 15 thousands of Roman mercenaries were hacked to pieces and Marcus Antonius Primus killed. 16 At Holly Rood and Din Eidyn (Edinburgh) the perfidy of Agricola did cause great damage, 17 yet the forces of Emperor and King Jacob (James) the son of Jesus did repel the Romans, 18 and within two days more than two hundred Roman ships had been sunk, 19 and Agricola was without the means of escape. 20 Rather than surrender Agricola with three hundred surviving cavalry did flee as cowards, 21 North and over the defences and into the remote lands of the Caledonians. 22 There Agricola and his officers lived as bandits and robbers as they seized food, 23 and killed innocent farmers while looking for a way to escape the island. 24 Soon after the treacherous actions of the Romans against the rule of law, 25 King Duras of Dacia did attack the legions stationed in his lands and slaughtered them. 26 With Dacia in full rebellion Emperor Domition ordered Trajan to return from Germania, 27 and help quell the uprising of Dacia and protect the western flank of Flavius Neapolis. 28 Marcus Antonius Felix the son of Antonius Primus and falsely written as Saturninus, 29 was appointed the new general of the armies against the Franks. 30 In the year known as 84 CE, 31 twelve hundred and eighty four years since the dawn of the Great Age, 32 Gnaeus Julius Agricola managed to find a ship to escape Cruithri (Scotland), 33 at the cost of his men who defended advancing Celts to allow him to escape. 34 Upon the arrival of Agricola at Flavius Neapolis, the Emperor arranged an elaborate tribute, 35 to falsely celebrate the destruction of Holly Rood and Din Eidyn (Edinburgh), 36 and a mythical victory over the Celts by Agricola. 37 But the night before Agricola was due to receive his commission to Africa, 38 Agricola drowned himself in the Orontes from the shame. 39 In Dacia the Roman legions were soundly beaten by King Duras, 40 despite the most brutal and inhumane acts of Traianus (Trajan) to try and break their will. 41 Thus by the years end, the Romans found themselves with troops defending themselves, 42 in Dacia and Germania with limited sources of conscripts and mercenary resupply. 43 In the year known as 85 CE, 44 twelve hundred and eighty five years since the dawn of the Great Age, 45 Emperor Domition sought terms and peace with King Decebalus of Dacia, 46 to enable greater focus on breaking the stalemate of Germania. 47 Yet the extraordinary treaty saw for the first time in the history of Rome, 48 the Empire paying a tribute to Dacians in exchange for a modest recognition. 49 In the same year, Flavius Josephus departed Flavius Neapolis (Antioch) to Athens, 50 and the service of Domition after the Emperor ordered the execution of his primary heir, ₅₁ whose name was Titus Flavius Sabinus after rumours of a coup were circulated by jealous lovers. ₅₂ Within weeks of the departure of Flavius Josephus, ₅₃ the eunuch High Priest of Cybele named Saulus (Paul) of Tarsus did come to Neapolis, ₅₄ with his senior eunuch clergy named Andreus, Aristobulus, Apollus, Barnabus and Timotheus, ₅₅ and did obtain an audience with Emperor Domition where Saulus (Paul) of Tarsus did pledge, ₅₆ himself and the vast library of Tarsus do the support of Iudaism (Judaism) declaring: ₅₇ What good be the sacredness of the Seventy or the wisdom of our Divine Lord and Master on Earth, ₅₈ if men still cling to such works of knowledge of ancients uncorrupted, ₅₉ or the skills of rhetoric and logic and reason. ₆₀ Verily, the greatest threat to Iudaism (Judaism) and the power of all Gewes (Jews), ₆₁ is the educated mind able to discern reason and logic and truth. ₆₂ Unless then the very essence of knowledge yield to the supremacy of the Gewes (Jews), ₆₃ the spirit of hope and rebellion shall remain in those deemed to be slaves and animals. ₆₄ Thus let me serve thee Lucifer as Lord and Master of Iudaism (Judaism), ₆₅ that we might herald the greatest of ages in re-writing all knowledge to your will. ₆₆ Emperor Domition did agree and appointed Saulus (Paul) the eunuch as his most senior advisor, ₆₇ and High Priest of Iudaism (Judaism) as Lucius Menelaus Paulus (St Paul). ₆₈ Upon his appointment to a position with power greater than a Proconsul, ₆₉ Paulus (Saul) the eunuch priest of Tarsus did utter a high curse against women saying: ₇₀ Thus the demons have favoured and ordained this be our time to rid ourselves, ₇₁ of the Divine feminine and the spirit of men that have risen against us. ₇₂ For I shall be Mephisto unto their kind and they shall become like whores, ₇₃ and perpetual slaves to our will. ₇₄ For it is the true Divine Feminine that manifests all civilised existence, ₇₅ and it shall be the False Mother of our creation that shall condemn women forever.

C. 13

₁ In the year known as 85 CE, ₂ twelve hundred and eighty five years since the dawn of the Great Age, ₃ much of Rome had been progressively rebuilt and restored under the autocratic authority, ₄ of Praetorian Prefect Lucius Aelius Plautius as effective governor of Rome and Italia. ₅ While law and order had been restored the disenfranchised Patrician and Plebian gentes, ₆ continued to agitate against the indifference of Domition residing at Flavius Neapolis. ₇ In the same year, after several long years of futile struggle against King Cornelius Tacticus, ₈ and the losses of tens of thousands of Roman troops, ₉ general Marcus Antonius Felix demanded the right to withdraw from the campaign, ₁₀ and return to his kingdom and lands of Pontus. ₁₁ Emperor Domitian refused and instead demanded Marcus Antonius Felix commit suicide, ₁₂ and issued an edict disinheriting the ancient Roman gens Antonia of any title or rights. ₁₃ The actions of Domition yet again caused uproar across the Empire, ₁₄ including riots in Rome and the revolt of the Germanic legions, 15 also causing King Duras of Dacia to revolt against the continued breaches of his treaty. 16 Domition then ordered the execution of Sextus Julius Frontinus for his failures, 17 before appointing Marcus Annaeus Ulpius Traianus as the new Legate of Asia, 18 with the task of first bringing the revolting kingdoms to heel, 19 before addressing the revolt of General Marcus Antonius Felix (Saturninus). 20 Yet when Trajan departed Hispania an uprising and revolt began in several cities, 21 causing the death of many of the patrician and plebian classes honoured as Gewes (Jews), 22 including the parents of Publius Aelius Hadrianus. 23 Domition then appointed Lucius Annaeus Ursus Servianus the brother of Trajan, 24 as the new Legate over Hispania who then undertook the most infamous purges, 25 ordering mass burnings of thousands of Anti-Shemites (anti-semites), 26 in Holocaust religious festivals in Seville, Cordoba and Tarraco. 27 Publius Aelius Attianus the uncle of Publius Aelius Hadrianus, 28 then took the rest of the gentes from Seville to the safety of Athens, 29 and the protection of Trajan and the tutoring of Flavius Josephus and Hermiones of Larissa. 30 Emperor Domition then asked his advisor Paulus how he might end rebellion for good, 31 to which Paulus (St Paul) replied there be no greater way to control the minds of men, 32 than when fear and wonder are enjoined in splendid violence and pageantry. 33 Fear alone numbs the senses such that even the most subjugated can rebel, 34 yet when combined with the wonder of the might of a great empire, 35 such a system of enslavement can perpetuate for eternity. 36 Yet beware the teacher and philosopher as the man of ideas. 37 Truly these be the enemy of Iudaism (Judaism) and the greatest threat to its power. 38 Domition agreed with Paulus (St Paul) and ordered that the Olympic Games, 39 be restarted and that every province and kingdom to field their best. 40 Domition then ordered Trajan to repair and prepare Athens and Greece. 41 The Emperor then ordered the banning of all philosophy and teaching, 42 unless by a Gewe (Jew) or Iew (Jew) across the Empire. 43 Domition upon the guidance of Paulus (St Paul) declared any book, 44 that does not submit to the absolute truth of Iudaism (Judaism), 45 and the enslavement of the world controlled by the Chosen People of Satan, 46 must be burned in the sacred Iudaic (Judaic) ceremony of Holocaust. 47 Huge bonfires were lit at Flavius Neapolis (Antioch) as the library was emptied, 48 and priceless knowledge was burned to fan the flames of the mad arrogance of Paulus, 49 as the troops and loyal followers gave the Roman salute to the flames, 50 as if such fire did honour Iudaism (Judaism) and the ritual of Holocaust. 51 Upon hearing the madness of Paulus and Domition in destroying such knowledge, 52 Flavius Josephus did cry out and proclaim: 53 Forgive me ancestors and spirits of heaven, 54 for in my arrogance I have spawned the worst of monsters, 55 that revels in its own ignorance and stupidity and celebrates it as a virtue. 56 Verily, for what years remain in this life I shall dedicate, 57 to the killing of this beast of Iudaism (Judaism), 58 and awakening the hearts of men once again to nobler qualities of gnosis. 59 With the assistance of Trajan and the noble intellectual houses such as the Aelia, 60 Flavius Josephus ensured that the most precious works of the greatest ancient libraries, 61 of Alexandria and of Athens and Rome were secretly taken to safety, 62 and replaced by fake copies and books for burning, 63 while the most priceless knowledge of the world was safely hidden from Paulus (St Paul), 64 in new underground libraries in Athens and Cordoba in Hispania and on Crete. 65 In the same year, Gaius Cornelius Tacticus succeeded in securing a peace treaty, 66 with Marcus Antonius Felix and his legions that they remain to the east in peace. 67 Marcus Antonius Felix then offered his beautiful daughter Antonia Clementiana in matrimony, 68 to Aulus Cornelius Celsus the son of Gaius Cornelius Tacticus to seal the treaty. 69 A year later their first born son was born being the great grandson of Emperor Jesus, 70 and of the Holly blood lines and priests of Yeb and of the great gens Cornelia, 71 and blood descendent of the Nabateans and of Cleopatra of Egypt and the Antonia gens. 72 Cornelius Celsus and Antonia Clementiana named their new born son, 73 as Aulus Cornelius Antonius Felix and later to be known by the name, 74 Aelius Hadrianus Antoninus Augustus Pius or Emperor Antonius Pius.

C. 14

1 In the year known as 88 CE, 2 twelve hundred and eighty eight years since the dawn of the Great Age, 3 Marcus Annaeus Ulpius Traianus succeeded in subjugating the rebellion of Dacia, 4 appointing Decebalus as client King loyal to Rome. 5 Emperor Domition then demanded that Trajan move against Antonius Felix, 6 even though the Franks and Antonius Felix were now in treaty. 7 Yet Trajan requested time to regroup and returned to Athens briefly, 8 where he met with Flavius Josephus and officially adopted Hadrian as his son. 9 In the same year Cornelius Celsus and Antonia Clementiana gave birth to a son, 10 they named Gaius Cornelius Antonius Clemens. 11 At the same time, King Linus of Cymri (Wales) and Eurgain (Eigen) did have a son, 12 they named Lleyn as a future great king of all Cymri (Wales). 13 It was not for another year that Trajan launched a half hearted attack, 14 against the Antonius Felix legions resulting in an uneasy stalemate. 15 In the year known as 91 CE, 16 twelve hundred and ninety one years since the dawn of the Great Age, 17 in a fit of jealous rage Domition ordered the savage murder of his only heir, 18 Titus Flavius Clemens who dared to pronounce that he too would soon be a god. 19 Thus Domition in his madness and delusion had destroyed the dynasty. 20 Upon sobering to his stupidity the Emperor fell into a deep depression, 21 and an uneasy calm descended upon the empire for a short while. 22 In the year known as 96 CE, 23 twelve hundred and ninety six years since the dawn of the Great Age, 24 upon Praetorian Lucius Aelius Plautius finishing the last repairs to Rome, 25 and the dedication of a new Temple to Lucifer as head of Iudaism (Judaism), 26 the Emperor was asked to attend and dedicate the restoration of Rome, 27 as

the first visit to the city in more than fifteen years. ₂₈ At first the Emperor hesitated as Rome had already claimed two Flavians, ₂₉ yet finally agreed on the assurance that he would be welcomed as a god. ₃₀ Thus in the year known as 97 CE the Emperor entered Rome, ₃₁ as a conquering hero to an extravagant celebration of his arrival, ₃₂ to the now restored eternal city. ₃₃ Yet in Rome, Domition was upset that the common people did not prostrate themselves at his feet as Lucifer and their living god, ₃₄ nor did the leading Gewes (Jews) and Iewes (Jews) of the city. ₃₅ In response he ordered that all the former Senate families be rounded up as anti-Shemites, ₃₆ and burned in the Iudaic (Judaic) worship of Satan through a Holocaust. ₃₇ Lucius Aelius Plautius hesitated at first upon the order of the mad Emperor, ₃₈ to murder those with whom he had resurrected and restored the city of Rome. ₃₉ Yet when word of the insanity of Domition reached the elite, ₄₀ riots were started across the city and within hours the Praetorian were overpowered, ₄₁ and Emperor Domition seized and stabbed to death, ₄₂ before his body was cut to pieces and thrown in the Tiber as a perpetual curse. ₄₃ Marcus Cassius Cocceianus was then proclaimed Emperor Nerva by the restored Senate of Rome, ₄₄ and the Temple of Lucifer was renamed the Temple Julia as the new home of the Senate. ₄₅ There on the steps of the new Senate with Lucius Aelius Plautius and his generals in chains, ₄₆ Marcus Cassius Cocceianus Nerva did speak to tens of thousands of Romans assembled, saying: ₄₇ We do not assemble here today to praise the memory of Caesar but to condemn it to damnation. ₄₈ For not even in the darkest days against Carthage has Rome faced such perfidy or avarice, ₄₉ than the Caesars who declared themselves Lucifer and god among animals. ₅₀ Thus Heaven and Rome has been forced to endure such profanity and insanity for years, ₅₁ whilst greedy men and mercenaries of no character were prepared to support, ₅₂ such a false religion as Iudaism (Judaism) created solely for profit and enslavement. ₅₃ Thanks to the gods now our time has come where Rome may be restored as a true republic, ₅₄ of equality among men, ruled by a fraternity of equals selected by the free people of Rome, ₅₅ not for their faith, or creed or colour of skin but the quality of their character. ₅₆ Therefore, I pledge to you and to all Rome that Rome shall never again fall prey, ₅₇ to pirates and bankers who seek its authority to justify their foul trade. ₅₈ Thus if it be we must fight for our freedom and the virtue of the empire in our name, ₅₉ then we shall gladly and willingly give our lives upon our feet as freemen, ₆₀ without fear or favour and never again as hostages to the madness of madmen. ₆₁ Marcus Cassius Cocceianus as Emperor Nerva then ordered, ₆₂ the life of Lucius Aelius Plautius and his generals be spared on account of his service to Rome. ₆₃ Upon news of the murder of the Emperor and no legitimate heir, ₆₄ there was uproar across the Empire as the legates positioned themselves as successors. ₆₅ The eunuch Lucius Menelaus Paulus (Saul) and also known as Paul the Apostle, ₆₆ did declare that he alone be the true heir of the Christ and Saviour Domition, ₆₇ not as the

Messiah Lucifer but as his bride and consort and lord of the underworld. 68 Paulus the eunuch from Tarsus then proclaimed his name to be Plutonis, 69 also known as Plutarch in Greek and meaning the sole Lord of the Underworld, 70 as Mephisto and the head of all demon spirits of Iudaism (Judaism). 71 Paulus now as Plutonis then declared that Domition had come to him and proclaimed: 72 Let it be known these are My words which I spoke to you while I was still with you, 73 that all things which are written about Me in the Law of Moses, 74 and the Prophets and the Psalms within the Septuagint must be fulfilled. 75 Thus it is written that the Christ Lucifer would suffer and rise again from the dead, 76 and the repentance for forgiveness of non-belief would be proclaimed. 77 Verily, you are my first witness and your seven brides (eunuchs) of Christ. 78 Behold, I am sending forth the promise of my Father (Satan) upon you, 79 that you shall Baptise not with water but with spiritual fire. 80 Paulus as the claimed god Plutonis then proclaimed seven eunuch priests, 81 to be his successors and the seven brides of Christ as Circum (Churches), 82 being the eunuchs Andreus (Plutarchus), Aristobulus (Polycarpis) and Soleus (Ignatius), 83 and the eunuch priests Irenaeus (of Lyon), Apollus, Barnabus and Timotheus. 84 Before a great crowd at Flavius Neapolis Paulus (St Paul) as Plutonis did say: 85 Upon this day I send forth to the four corners of the world the seven churches (Circum), 86 in the name of the Father (Satan) to fulfil the prophecy of Christ (Lucifer) his son. 87 Thus if anyone says he is a prophet or a priest then let him recognise, 88 that the truths and miracles today are the commandments of the Lord. 89 But if anyone does not recognise the miracles today, he is damned to eternal fire. 90 Whereupon Plutonis and his priests using flammable liquid did appear to have flames, 91 upon their heads and their hands in front of the crowd who were amazed and in awe. 92 The word quickly spread of the power of Plutonis and the seven churches (Circe), 93 who then travelled to the major centres of Iudaism (Judaism) to gain support. 94 In Africa Gaius Septimius Vegetus of Leptis Magna sought support of client kings, 95 that he might proclaim himself Emperor and Lucifer. 96 Yet upon the arrival of the eunuchs Barnabus and Timotheus, 97 Gaius Septimius Vegetus was persuaded to support Plutonis in keeping control of the empire, 98 as a theocracy of the merchant and slave trading elite. 99 Lucius Annaeus Ursus Servianus then advised Marcus Annaeus Ulpius Traianus, 100 that he travel to the Oracle at Oropos and seek some sign to counter, 101 the mad woman hating eunuch Paulus (St Paul) who now proclaimed himself Plutonis. 102 At Oropos the Oracle did declare that Domition from the grave, 103 sought a brave and honourable man with genitals and the ability to reproduce, 104 to be his only true heir and successor. 105 Trajan and the forces of Lucius Annaeus Ursus Servianus, 106 did then come to Italy and lay siege upon the forces of Rome, 107 as Plutonis (St Paul) proclaimed a high curse against Trajan that his line, 108 would never conceive nor would any adopted sons live more than two generations.

C. 15

1 In the year known as 98 CE, 2 twelve hundred and ninety eight years since the dawn of the Great Age, 3 after a siege of a year against Rome and Marcus Cassius Cocceianus as Emperor Nerva, 4 Rome still refused to yield to Marcus Annaeus Ulpius Traianus. 5 Trajan then summonsed Lucius Aelius Plautius to come to Rome and reason with Nerva, 6 that if he did not surrender then Trajan would attack the city, 7 and if not Trajan then the Septima of Africa would surely take his place against Rome. 8 Emperor Nerva accepted the meeting with Lucius Aelius Plautius who warned him, 9 that it was impossible for Rome to hold out against the legions of Hispania and Asia, 10 to which Emperor Nerva replied that the city be resolved to die as freemen, 11 under Liberty, Democracy and Equality rather than submit to slavery of Iudaism (Judaism). 12 Lucius Aelius Plautius replied that Trajan had shown himself to be a man of his word, 13 and that he had resolved to repair the damage done by the Flavians. 14 Emperor Nerva did reply that he too be a man of his word that no harm come to any man, 15 who comes to Rome in respect and honour and if the intentions of Trajan be true, 16 then he would come before the Senate and Nerva and speak the same. 17 Lucius Aelius Plautius returned to Trajan with the news whereupon Traianus himself, 18 did enter Rome in truce upon the word of Nerva and come to the new Senate, 19 to bravely address the people of Rome, saying: 20 My brothers and comrades I come not as your enemy but as your friend. 21 For each of us have suffered the indignity and injustices of immoral men, 22 who sought to make themselves gods in defiance of heaven, 23 while our beloved eternal city lay in ruins as testament to their profanity. 24 Alas, there is much that must be restored if we are to rid ourselves of this past. 25 Yet nothing good shall come if Rome once again suffers for mistrust and fear. 26 For if this august body truly be the successor to those who made Rome great, 27 then you shall open the gates and we shall resolve the matter of succession in peace. 28 Upon these words, Emperor Nerva did reply: 29 Verily it is said that the character of a man is nothing until tested, 30 nor may we truly know the spirit of a man until we see his deeds. 31 Thus heaven has ordained we be blessed by the return of men of good character. 32 We need not then concern ourselves with claims and grievances but that we acknowledge, 33 the time has come to trust in the wisdom of our ancestors. 34 Therefore, let it be known to all here present and all to come, 35 that I solemnly and humbly declare Marcus Annaeus Ulpius Traianus, 36 to be my eldest son and heir to the seat of Augustus and protector of Rome, 37 and that by sunrise tomorrow all the gates of the city shall be open. 38 Let then destiny take its course. 39 Nerva did then hand to Trajan his imperial ring and Trajan then departed Rome. 40 Whereupon before the first light of the new day news did come from the Senate to Trajan, 41 that Emperor Nerva had performed the ultimate act

of Honour and committed suicide, 42 making Trajan as his adopted son the undisputed and true Emperor of Rome. 43 As the gates of the city were swung open and Trajan entered to rapturous cheers, 44 the new Emperor called for the Senate to honour the name of Nerva. 45 The Senate then deified Nerva as a great saviour of Rome, 46 in the most unprecedented act of respect of any Emperor in the history of the city, 47 that none may forget the supreme sacrifice of a hero of the people.

C. 16

1 In the year known as 99 CE, 2 twelve hundred and ninety nine years since the dawn of the Great Age, 3 Emperor Trajan did appoint Lucius Aelius Plautius, 4 once again Praetorian Prefect and the Protector of Rome, 5 before departing with several legions to Flavius Neapolis. 6 Upon the arrival of Trajan and his legions as undisputed Emperor, 7 Paulus as Plutonis (Plutarch) did declare himself a servant of the emperor, 8 to which Trajan did reply to Paulus (St Paul): 9 What worm without a backbone thee be that from afar you cast curse, 10 yet near you shed your convictions like a snake its skin. 11 What madness that a eunuch who hates all women dictate to men and women, 12 on the laws of heaven when you know nothing of heaven nor its laws. 13 Thus I shall not make you a martyr for those that believe your falsities, 14 but shall exile you to Cyrene for the remainder of your days, 15 and your name and memory shall be condemned for eternity, 16 as you suffer the torture of being forgotten before your eyes. 17 Paul and his eunuch priests were then arrested and sent to Cyrene, 18 as prisoners to live out the rest of their days. 19 At the same time, Emperor Trajan issued an edict that the practice of Holocaust, 20 and the sentence of death of anti-shemitism by burning people alive be prohibited, 21 as a profane act against Rome and heaven and all civilised law, 22 and that no priest or claim of law from Rome ever again be permitted to condone, 23 the burning of people alive or to even utter the word Holocaust, 24 as the word and the claim of anti-shemitism was to be Damnatio memoriae, 25 and cursed falsities never to be spoken or written ever again in history. 26 The Emperor also began to dismantle the monopolies of the Gewe (Jew) merchants, 27 and slave traders that claimed exclusive right to lend money as bankers, 28 and to buy and sell slaves with the penalty for those that claimed such monopoly, 29 to be put to death as an abomination against the law and against reason. 30 Under the ageing Josephus and his sons Justus and Valentinus (St Valentine), 31 Emperor Trajan began removing the false history and false law and false writings, 32 of Iudaism and especially the madness and profanities of the eunuch Paul of Tarsus, 33 who had proclaimed himself to be Mephisto and Plutonis the Lord of the Underworld. 34 Yet many wealthy and powerful trading families especially the Septimus of Africa, 35 did resent the changes of Trajan and worked secretly to support Plutonis, 36 and the eunuch priests imprisoned at Cyrene. 37 In the same year, Emperor Trajan sent word to the Franks and Antonius Felix, 38 that he did seek a permanent

truce by restoring the kingdom of Pontus et Bithnya, 39 to the descendants of Marcus Antonius and the status of the gens Cornelia, 40 to the highest and most esteemed of gentes of all Rome. 41 Aulus Cornelius Celsus did pledge to supply legions to the defence of Rome, 42 as well as Antonius Felix to restore the honour of the Felix legions. 43 Upon Paul (St Paul) the eunuch hearing of the news of the edicts of Trajan, 44 he was enraged and demanded that those brides of Christ and Circum (Churches), 45 still free to preach to the masses of the coming of the end of the world, 46 and the destruction of the Roman Empire by Satan upon the return of Christ Lucifer, 47 that there would be signs of the coming of the end of the world soon, 48 and that those who did not repent their sins would suffer eternal pain and torture. 49 When Josephus and his sons Justus and Valentinus did hear of the threats, 50 and lies of fear and destruction vomited by Paul (St Paul) the eunuch, 51 Josephus did say to the young Hadrian in Athens and to all present: 52 Truly there be no greater madness nor profanity against heaven, 53 for a mad eunuch to speak of hate and call it love, 54 and to speak of justice and threaten eternal torment, 55 or to claim authority for all yet seek to make all women slaves of mind. 56 Verily, it is not enough to say that men of mind and reason have ability, 57 and the choice to condone such filthy insanity or not, 58 for alas children if exposed to disease may not yet have resistance. 59 Thus, let all men of good character and conscience who honour the gods, 60 who respect knowledge and pledge themselves to Rome and Civilisation, 61 rid this world of Iudaism (Judaism) and its polluted lies, 62 that no generation to come suffer as we have the madness of mind, 63 where ignorant and stupid bankers and merchants claim themselves as gods, 64 and imprison the world as their own slaves.

C. 17

1 In the year known as 101 CE, 2 thirteen hundred and one years since the dawn of the Great Age, 3 with the treaties of peace with the Franks under Gaius Cornelius Taciticus, 4 and the safety of Pontus secured with the treaty with Marcus Antonius Felix, 5 peace with the Celts was established for the first time in more than forty years. 6 Emperor Trajan and the Senate did then condemn the symbol of Iudaism (Judaism) of IHS, 7 and did then revive the standard SPQR of Rome and the rights of Patricians and Plebians, 8 with the false claims of the Gewes (Jews) and Iewes (Jews) outlawed and damned of memory. 9 Even many of the eunuch leaders of Paul of Tarsus imprisoned at Cyrene, 10 had been caught and executed with Aristobulus killed in Pontus, 11 Barnabus caught and killed at Cyprus and Timotheus killed at Corinth. 12 Yet the eunuch of Tarsus who proclaimed himself Mephisto and Plutonis (Plutarch), 13 continued to claim and predict the end of the world and the damnation of all sinners, 14 even though every claim and prophecy issued from Cyrene had been proven false. 15 In the same year, 16 Heracles of Eliada and Larissa and son of High Priest Hermiones, 17 the leader of the Therepautae and heir to throne of

Sparta, 18 did have a son he named Herodes. 19 In the year known as 102 CE, 20 thirteen hundred and two years since the dawn of the Great Age, 21 Decebalus of Dacia with an army of more than one hundred thousand did invade Moesia, 22 and proclaim himself a god-king. 23 The Emperor did then call upon the Felix Legions of Antonius Felix, 24 and the Germanic legions of the Franks commanded by Aulus Cornelius Celsus, 25 to aid in quelling rebellion against the new peace of the Empire. 26 Both armies met at the Iron Gates of Transylvania where Trajan did achieve, 27 a decisive victory only to be thwarted by an early winter forcing a Roman halt. 28 Yet Decebalus did not properly appreciate the Germanic strength of the Franks, 29 and sought to use the winter as an advantage to launch a winter assault, 30 by outflanking the Roman camps by attacking from the rear. 31 Yet Aulus Cornelius Celsus had anticipated such treachery and had forced, 32 the encampment of his legions in the mountains so that when the Dacians and allies, 33 did attack they were surrounded and slaughtered. 34 The Dacians then called for truce which Trajan granted. 35 In the year known as 104 CE, 36 thirteen hundred and four years since the dawn of the Great Age, 37 Flavius Josephus the son of Matthias, 38 the founder of the Septuagint and Iudaism (Judaism), 39 and the architect of its demise and gradual abolition, 40 to be replaced by the Religion of Scientia (Science), 41 did give up the ghost at Athens. 42 Trajan was distraught at the loss of his teacher and mentor, 43 and ordered sixty days of mourning, 44 appointing Valentinius (St Valetine) the eldest son of Josephus, 45 as the Master of Funeral Ceremonies in honour of his father. 46 Upon the death of Josephus and the distress of the Emperor, 47 Decebalus rallied his army with the Dalmatians and seized Moetia, 48 before beginning a march into Macedonia. 49 Marcus Antonius Felix then marched his legions west from Anatolia, 50 to hold Macedonia against the invasion as Aulus Cornelius Celsus and the Franks, 51 did march south towards Baras (Brasov) the capital of Dacia. 52 Upon the demands of Emperor Trajan against such treachery no quarter was given, 53 and the Dacians and Dalmatians were slaughtered, 54 until Decebalus himself committed suicide to avoid capture. 55 In the year known as 105 CE, 56 thirteen hundred and five years since the dawn of the Great Age, 57 Crown Prince (Ha Rama Theo) Cuinan (Conan) of Cruithri (Scotland), 58 the son of King Cyllin (Cullen/ Collin) Emperor of the Celts, 59 and grandson of Emperor Jesus (Yahusiah) and Queen Mariamne, 60 did have a son he named Cuinnwyd (Conrad).

C. 18

1 In the year known as 106 CE, 2 thirteen hundred and six years since the dawn of the Great Age, 3 upon the death of Rabael Soter of Nabatea, Trajan did annex the lands of the Nabateans, 4 from North of Petra and the Sinai and south of the Arabian Peninsula to Himyar. 5 The new province was named Arabea Petraea with Petra as its Capital. 6 Emperor Trajan did also dissolve the Sacred Province of Iudaea by splitting it in two, 7 with the city of Tyre and Bostra

and all the lands south and then the western shore, 8 of the Dead Sea and then along the coast of Sinai past Gaza. 9 The new province was named Palaestina with Caesarina Maritima as its Capital. 10 North then of Tyre to Cilicia and east to the borders of Parthia, 11 the province of Syria was restored with Neapolis as its capital. 12 Trajan then appointed Flavius Justus as the son of Josephus as Governor of Palaestina. 13 The influence of Iudaism (Judaism) had already taken several great blows, 14 upon the arrest and execution of Soleus (Ignatius) at Neapolis, 15 and Iraneus near Massila in Narbonensis (Sth France), 16 leaving only Paul the eunuch and Andreus and a few followers as prisoners at Cyrene. 17 Yet among the slave traders and bankers and merchants of Ephesus and Corinth, 18 and the centres of slave traders and moneylenders at Rhodes and Leptis Magna, 19 the news of the dissolution of Iudaea as the falsely claimed homeland of the Gewes (Jews), 20 invented from the time of Vespasian less than forty years earlier, 21 was greeted with outrage and fear that their business was coming to an end. 22 Until the edict of Trajan awoke the Gewes (Jews) to the danger of their fate, 23 Paul (St Paul) the eunuch had continued to destroy his own reputation, 24 with countless bizarre and untrue prophecies of the end of the world, 25 which had continued to fail to materialise. 26 Yet with the announcement of the Emperor that the commercial religion of Iudaism (Judaism), 27 invented by slave traders and bankers and merchants purely for profit was soon ending, 28 the wealthy and corrupt sought guidance from Paul as to their future, 29 to which Paul rebuked them saying: 30 Woe unto you merchants and traders as fair weather believers. 31 When I was suffering you did not come to comfort me. 32 Now the forces of heaven rally against our faith of demons and curses, 33 you call upon me to save you and your business. 34 Verily, I have seen a splendid vision whereupon the world will truly end, 35 yet our curses against the spirit of man will survive and thrive, 36 that one day men will worship me as a god above all other prophets in complete ignorance. 37 My words of hate dressed as love and death cloaked as life and submission as strength, 38 shall be believed as the most sacred of all scripture by stupid people who act as sheep, 39 as loyal servants of Satan and Christ (Lucifer) in complete willing cowardice, 40 and your descendants shall control the world in perpetual slavery. 41 Whereupon the wealthy bankers and merchants and slave traders resolved, 42 that they would secretly build a mercenary army to rebel against Trajan, 43 and free Paul the eunuch from Cyrene, 44 for they believed his vision that one day all people be slaves to the bankers. 45 In the year known as 108 CE, 46 thirteen hundred and eight years since the dawn of the Great Age, 47 Holly High King Tuathal Techtmar of Eire (Ireland), 48 husband of Queen Mary the daughter of Jesus and Mariamne, 49 did give up the ghost. 50 The crown of Holly High King of Eire (Ireland) did befall to his son, 51 whose name was Feinlinid Reachmor and also known as Fedlimid Rechtmar, 52 as the grandson of Emperor Jesus and Mariamne.

C. 19

1 In the year known as 113 CE, 2 thirteen hundred and twelve years since the dawn of the Great Age, 3 Marcus Calpernius Piso also known as Marcion of Pontus and Sinope, 4 succeeded in aiding his patron Parthamasiris in seizing the throne of Armenia, 5 by killing his own brother Axidares who had been appointed by Trajan. 6 Trajan demanded that King Osroes of Parthia bring Parthamasiris to justice, 7 which he steadfastly refused to do forcing Trajan to act. 8 Trajan then moved himself to Flavius Neapolis to oversee first, 9 an invasion of Armenia in which Parthamasiris was executed. 10 Trajan then installed Mithradates as king of Armenia, 11 before King Osroes of Parthia sent forces to confront Trajan, 12 and Trajan responded by invading Parthia itself and destroyed Seleucia. 13 In the year known as 115 CE, 14 thirteen hundred and fifteen years since the dawn of the Great Age, 15 a terrible earthquake struck Flavius Neapolis so great that it levelled the city, 16 killing more than two hundred thousand including Emperor Trajan. 17 Upon the news Paul the eunuch at Cyrene was joyous and proclaimed himself, 18 as a great prophet that had predicted this very event as proof of his awesome power, 19 as the Lord and representative of Satan upon the earth and Christ Lucifer. 20 Publius Septimius Aper of Leptis Magna and son of Gaius Septimius Vegetus, 21 did then send an elite force to free Paul (St Paul) the eunuch and his priests from captivity. 22 Once freed Paul (St Paul) the mad women hating eunuch did cry in rage: 23 As the people of Cyrenaica did laugh and mock me in my captivity as wicked sinners, 24 let them meet my Lord (Satan) in eternal captivity and torment in the underworld. 25 Behold I shall demonstrate to the world the horrors that face non believers, 26 that none shall ever doubt my words as to the dangers in not yielding to Iudaism (Judaism). 27 Paul then ordered that every man and woman and child of Cyrenaica be slaughtered, 28 in the most gruesome and cruel manner and for dogs to be fed their flesh, 29 and for all kinds of deprivation and cannibalism to be promoted, 30 as fear grew of a flesh eating army of Gewes (Jews) and Iewes (Jews), 31 terrorising the population of Cyrenaica. 32 At the same time, upon the news of the destruction of Neapolis, 33 King Osroes of Parthia pressed his army to destroy the Romans, 34 and Hadrian was forced before even being made emperor whether to focus on Cyrenaica, 35 or try and save the eastern legions from being destroyed in Parthia. 36 Hadrian then appointed Praetorian Prefect Quintus Marcius Turbo to end the madness in Africa, 37 while Hadrian himself travelled to Parthia to save the legions. 38 By the time Quintus Marcius Turbo and his legions arrived at Cyrenaica, 39 more than two hundred thousand innocent men and women and children, 40 had been slaughtered by the utter madness of the orders of Lucius Menelaus Paulus, 41 also known as St Lucuas and St Paul the eunuch apostle. 42 Paul and Andreus had already departed the destroyed cities of Cyrenaica, 43 having forced tens of thousands into service of Iudeaism (Judaism) to Cyprus, 44 and to attack Alexandria in an attempt to burn

down the Great Library and Temples. 45 Quintus Marcius Turbo made a decision to defend Alexandria against the insane mob, 46 and confronted Andreus in Alexandria slaughtering the entire Iudaic force, 47 saving the Library and Temples of Alexandria with not a single prisoner taken alive. 48 Yet Cyprus suffered terribly at the hands of Paul (St Paul) the women hating maniac. 49 In all over a hundred thousand people were torn to pieces on Cyprus, 50 before Paul and the Gewes (Jews) and Iewes (Jews) descended upon Caesarina Maritima. 51 Yet Quintus Marcius Turbo had anticipated the actions of Paul and the Iudean mob, 52 and moved his forces to Caesaria Maritima to confront and destroy the rebellion. 53 While Flavius Josephus Justus bravely was killed trying to confront the forces of Paul, 54 Quintus Marcius Turbo allowed the Iudean forces to enter the first part of the city, 55 before surrounding and sealing them off and slaughtering more than one hundred thousand. 56 Yet Paul the eunuch tried to escape dressed as a women and was caught, 57 on the road to Damascus where he protested he was not Paul but a humble pilgrim. 58 Paul was then executed and his embalmed head presented to Hadrian as a prize. 59 A trophy lost in antiquity and then reclaimed by descendants of the Piso as their god, 60 and worshipped as the Baphomet and the very head of their false church. 61 In Parthia, Hadrian negotiated the withdraw of Roman legions and an uneasy truce. 62 In the year known as 116 CE, 63 thirteen hundred and sixteen years since the dawn of the Great Age, 64 High Priest Hermiones of Eliada and Larissa, 65 leader of the Therapeutae and heir to throne of Sparta, 66 did give up the ghost. 67 The role of High Priest and protector of the sacred temples of Olympus, 68 did befall to his son whose name was Heracles, also known as Heracles Atticus.

C. 20

1 In the year known as 117 CE, 2 thirteen hundred and seventeen years since the dawn of the Great Age, 3 upon peace being restored to the Empire and the complete destruction of Flavius Neapolis, 4 Emperor Hadrian pronounced his new capital to be Athens under the new Imperial Motto, 5 E Pluribus Unum meaning Many be One in honour of Scientia as the science of knowledge, 6 being the new official religion of the Roman Empire in repudiation of the Flavian madness. 7 There in Athens the new Emperor did address the Senate and his generals and leaders, 8 as to their decision to Damnatio Memorae for the first time in history, 9 a claimed religious faith in the form of Iudaism (Judaism), 10 and for anyone to claim themselves to be a Gewe (Jew) or Iewe (Jew) a capital crime, 11 and for the banning of the Septuaginta (LXX) or Seventy and G, 12 and for every copy to be found and destroyed as a work of treason and terror, 13 and for every version of the motto IHS or Invictus Hoc Signo to be struck out, 14 and for every mention and reference to Iudaism (Judaism) to be removed from history, 15 except the edict of the Senate which enacted such damnation. 16 To all assembled who heard and those that memorialised the speech, the Emperor did say: 17 These

sacred buildings (Athens) attest to the truth that many a great civilisation have lived, 18 and died before the rise of the Eternal City (Rome) to whom we pledge our devotion and respect. 19 Yet what heralds the greatness of Rome and our alliances is not through force or fear, 20 nor through tradition or ignorance but to the fact that men and women choose law above anarchy, 21 and are prepared to stand by their word as a sacred oath, 22 and trust in the logic and reason of knowledge and history and law itself. 23 Thus no society can be sustained without trust and truth except by tyranny and fear, 24 nor may any empire survive unless it offers people of all cultures and beliefs, 25 something greater than being isolated and separated and at war with our neighbours. 26 So it is we celebrate our strength in being united under the motto Many be One (E Pluribus Unum), 27 recognising that Rome is first and foremost a set of ideals before it is a place. 28 So when men without dignity or respect or virtue have chosen to corrupt such ideals, 29 the very existence of Rome is challenged far more deeply than any invading army or calamity. 30 This then be the cause of my actions today and my solemn edicts, 31 which shall remain in perpetuity the laws of Rome and of all civilised people forever. 32 That the invention of merchants and bankers forty six years ago of a means to control power, 33 to steal, to cheat and to enslave and call it Iudaism (Judaism) was never a true religion, 34 nor did such merchants and bankers have any true connection to Palaestina (Palestine), 35 yet they created the false province of Iudaea (Judea) and called it their homeland, 36 and created false and wicked writings called the Septuaginta in which they uttered profanities, 37 against all the gods and heaven and our ancestors in creating such wicked untruths. 38 Even when the blessed Josephus did disown himself from such writings and proclaim, 39 that Iudaism (Judaism) be a false faith of his creation the bankers and merchants, 40 refused to admit their culpability and instead sought new alliances and new ways, 41 to profit from the enslavement and misery of others. 42 Until we faced the utter madness of the tyrant and murderer being the eunuch of Tarsus. 43 That is why I have ordered the complete destruction of the city and all its texts, 44 for any city that could breed such madness is a parasite to civilisation. 45 Let us celebrate then a new age and a new order of logic and reason. 46 With confidence the scourge and insanity of such a false cult of thieves and bankers, 47 never again shall be heard in history thanks to your diligence and the rule of law.

Book 23

Age of the Gnostics

[117 - 194 CE]

C.1

In the year known as 117 CE, 2 thirteen hundred and seventeen years since the dawn of the Great Age, 3 Holly High King of Eire (Ireland) Feinlinid Reachmor, also known as Fedlimid Rechtmar, 4 the grandson of Emperor Jesus and Mariamne did give up the ghost. 5 Upon his passing, the Holly High Crown and head of the Cuilliaéan, 6 did befall to his son named Cúinn (Conn) Cétchathach. 7 In the same year, following a brief peace after restoring order, 8 Emperor Publius Aelius Hadrianus did wed Claudia Faustina the widow of Emperor Trajan, 9 and the only surviving descendant and granddaughter to Emperor Claudius, 10 through her mother Claudia Antonia who wed Faustus Domitius. 11 Emperor Hadrian did also adopt the only daughter of Trajan, 12 whose name was Annaea Claudia Faustina as his daughter. 13 Later in the same year, elderly King Gaius Cornelius Tacticus of the Franks, 14 the adopted son of Emperor Jesus (Yahusiah), 15 did give up the ghost. 16 The crown of the Franks did then befall to his son Aulus Cornelius Celsus. 17 Upon the death of Tacticus and the rise of his son to leader of the Franks, 18 Emperor Hadrian did extend a sign of good faith and peace to the former Germanic legions, 19 by attending the great funeral ceremony to honour the gens Cornelia and Tacticus. 20 At the funeral ceremony Emperor Hadrian did ask King Aulus Cornelius Celsus, 21 upon what sign of good faith would it require for the Germanic legions and the Cornelia, 22 to return to service of Rome and defence against tyranny and madness. 23 King Aulus Cornelius Celsus replied that only when Emperors serve not as gods, 24 but as protectors and teachers will the spirit of Rome be restored. 25 Emperor Hadrian did reply that the great blood lines of the ancient Patricians, 26 no longer resided in Rome and unless men of conscience and wisdom forged consensus, 27 then the future of Rome would befall to lesser gens upon his death. 28 To which King Aulus Cornelius Celsus did pledge his youngest son Aulus Cornelius Antonius, 29 and the Germanic legions to the service of Rome and the Emperor as a sign of good faith, 30 upon Emperor Hadrian restoring the honour of the most ancient gens of

Rome. 31 In Rome, Emperor Hadrian did announce the treaty of peace and amity with the Franks, 32 and the full restoration of the gens Cornelia as honoured patricians and protectors of Rome. 33 Emperor Hadrian did then proclaim with the blessing of King Aulus Cornelius Celsus, 34 the adoption of Aulus Cornelius Antonius the youngest son of King Celsus, 35 to be his own son under the name Aelius Hadrianus Cornelius Antonius, 36 as his lawful heir and successor. 37 To revive the spirit of Rome and placate suspicions against Athens as the new capital, 38 Emperor Hadrian did commission a new Forum to be created and for a new Pantheon to be built, 39 as a symbol of peace and unity among all the gods as well as the gods of Rome and Athens. 40 In the same year, King Jacob (James) of Cruithri (Scotland) the son of Emperor Jesus, 41 did fall gravely ill and so summonsed the Celtic leaders to Hollyrood, 42 and his eldest son Cyllin (Cullen/ Collin) was named heir and Emperor of the Celts.

C. 2

1 In the year known as 118 CE, 2 thirteen hundred and eighteen years since the dawn of the Great Age, 3 King Jacob (James) of Cruithri (Scotland), 4 Emperor of the Celts and the youngest son of Jesus (Yahusiah), 5 did give up the ghost. 6 The crown of Cruithri and the title of Emperor of the Celts did then befall to his son, 7 whose name was Cyllin (Cullen/ Collin). 8 Upon news of the passing of the last kin of Jesus (Yahusiah) and Queen Mariamne (Mary), 9 more than three hundred that possessed the blood of Holly King Joseph and his kin, 10 whom had become known as the Diaspora meaning the seeds of the Divine, 11 were summonsed to Holly Rood from more than a dozen lands across the ancient world. 12 Emperor Cyllin (Cullen/ Collin) did also summons all the kings and priests of the Celt tribes, 13 including the Holly High Kings, the Franks, the Remi and High Priest Heracles of Eliada and Larissa, 14 to come not only for the funeral but the first Parlamage (Parliament) in more than thirty years, 15 and to bring the symbols of sacred authority being the sacred axe and gold cup, the sceptre and mace, 16 the long sword and scales, the spear and shield, the scythe and dagger and the chronometer and bow. 17 Upon news of the death of Emperor Jacob (James) reaching Aulus Cornelius Antonius at Athens, 18 Emperor Hadrian declared there be a month of mourning throughout the Empire in honour of a great king, 19 and to honour the heritage of the Great Prophets of Yeb and the Pontifex Maximus who had served Rome. 20 The Emperor did announce he would attend the funeral ceremony himself and accompany his son, 21 rather than send an emissary. 22 Emperor Hadrian then appointed Quintus Marcius Turbo as Praetorian Prefect and Protector of Rome, 23 before departing to the Island of Britanni (Britain) and to Holly Rood Din Eidyn (Edinburgh). 24 Not since the formation of the Augustus had an Emperor so honoured the Cuilliaéan (Holly), 25 nor Rome itself since the great Caesar Lucius Cornelius Sulla one hundred and twenty years earlier. 26 Emperor Cyllin (Cullen/ Collin) did then order

that Ebor (York) be prepared for the Roman Emperor, 27 that he be granted lodgings worthy of a great and noble leader. 28 Twenty thousand Celts then began work day and night so that the city was prepared to honour Hadrian. 29 Yet King Mericadoc of the Briton tribe did protest against the loss of Ebor (York) as an ancient capital, 30 and the act of Emperor Cyllin (Cullen/ Collin) and pushed his troops toward Din Eidyn (Edinburgh), 31 in direct conflict with the sacred vow of all Celts to honour the truce of funerary rights. 32 Roman Emperor Hadrian had already sent Roman Prefect Lucius Artorius Castus and two elite legions, 33 to the island of Britanni (Britain) ahead of his visit and to defend Din Eidyn (Edinburgh) against the Briton tribe, 34 as Emperor Cyllin (Cullen/ Collin) did call upon Lucius Artorius Castus for aid. 35 Within sight of Holly Rood and before the battlements of Din Eidyn (Edinburgh), 36 Lucius Artorius Castus crushed the Britons and captured King Mericadoc. 37 But instead of ordering him and his kin to be executed in defiance of ancient Celtic law, 38 Emperor Cyllin (Cullen/ Collin) ordered that the Briton nobles and warriors be exiled from the island, 39 unto the south of Gaul and never for he or his kin to return. 40 For no member of the Briton tribe henceforth could claim land or lodging upon the sacred isles. 41 Mericadoc did then land at a place he then named Brittani (Brittany) and then declared, 42 that his ancestors would one day avenge the injustice inflicted upon the Briton tribe by the Holly. 43 For his courage, Emperor Cyllin (Cullen/ Collin) did bless Roman Prefect Lucius Artorius Castus, 44 and named him the Pendraic or Dragon and protector of the sacred land, 45 and that he and his descendants would have right of recognition and settlement in any of the lands, 46 as honoured members of the noble Celts. 47 When the Roman Emperor finally arrived, Emperor Cyllin (Cullen/ Collin) did welcome him, 48 and pronounced that forever more, the place called Ebor (York) be a part of Rome, 49 and a royal home for future Emperors and that no Celt nor army may lay siege to it, 50 nor harm it as the most sacred of sanctuaries. 51 For any army or leader who attacks York in defiance of such a sacred decree, 52 abjures any claim of right to legitimacy or protection of law. 53 Upon such a historic act, Emperor Hadrian accepted the city and renamed it, 54 calling it Eboracium Comes Palatinus (York) as a Companion Court and Imperial Court of Rome, 55 and the companion Imperial Palace of the Emperor to Palatine Hill in Rome. 56 Emperor Hadrian did then pronounce an Imperial Edict to the Senate and all the provinces, 57 that it be recorded forever in the most sacred records and law of Rome, 58 that Vatican Hill and all its buildings and land be granted to the Cuilliaéan (Holly), 59 and for the sanctuary to be known as the Sancta Sedes (Holly See) and part of the earth of Holly Rood, 60 as the true priests of priests and true descendants of the Great Prophets of Yeb, 61 and that no Praetorian nor Roman may bring arms into such sacred sanctuary, 62 nor may any emperor, or senator or Roman or jurist issue any law against such decree, 63 for any and all such decrees be without merit or law, 64 and any force claiming such sanctuary against the Holly be an abomination against the gods, 65 with all people of the Earth and Sea obligated to defend against such profanity and sacrilege. 66 Emperor Hadrian did then yield the title of Pontifex Maximus as supreme pontiff, 67 back to the Cuilliaéan (Holly) saying: 68 Verily, from this day forth let it be known to all men forever more, 69 that no man may hold the position of Pontifex Maximus, 70 lest he be of the Diaspora and a true prophet of the gods. 71 Emperor Cyllin (Cullen/ Collin) did then anoint his younger brother Cuibelinus (Cunobelinus), 72 as the first Holly Pope of Rome since the time of High King Joseph. 73 The Parlamage (Parliament) at Holly Rood did then agree to the changes upon Britanni, 74 and the dissolution of the tribal Kingdom of Briton and banishment forever of the Briton tribal members. 75 Cruithri (Scotland) was renamed as Cuiliadomi (Caledonia) meaning Holly Home, 76 and the island of Britanni (Britain) was renamed Englia meaning behold it is they! 77 Thus Rome possessed a piece of Englia (York) and Englia a piece of Rome (Vatican Hill) forever more. 78 The former kingdom of Briton was then divided into six smaller kingdoms, 79 with the Kingdom of Umbria to the North, with its capital Lundor (Lancaster), 80 and the Kingdom of Bernicia to the north-east, with its capital at Lindor (Lincoln), 81 and the Kingdom of Deiria in the midlands with Ligor (Leicester) as its capital, 82 and the Kingdom of Cambria to the east with its capital at Cordor (Colchester), 83 and the Kingdom of Cantia to the south-east with its capital at Cantor (Cantebury), 84 and the Kingdom of Dumnonia to the south-west with its capital at Glostor (Gloucester).

C. 3

1 In the year known as 118 CE, 2 thirteen hundred and eighteen years since the dawn of the Great Age, 3 after all the funerary and political arrangements had ceased, 4 Emperor Cyllin of the Celts and Emperor Hadrian of the Romans did meet, 5 and Emperor Hadrian did inquire as to the deeper nature of the wisdom known to the Holly, 6 that caused even Flavius Josephus to renounce his own invention of Iudaism. 7 Emperor Cyllin (Cullen/ Collin) replied that all men seek their origins even if they deny it. 8 For men, like civilisations, need foundation and even the most powerful tyrant or empire, 9 will fail if it has not a solid foundation upon which to unite the people. 10 Emperor Hadrian then asked how one build an empire of good conscience that could last. 11 Emperor Cyllin did reply that his grandfather had given such an answer in Rome 87 years earlier, 12 when Jesus (Yahusiah) did say: There is, there was, there has only ever been One Law. 13 All law is equal that no one is above it, 14 all law is measured that all may learn and know it, 15 all law is standard that it may always be applied the same. 16 A law is a rule that prohibits or permits certain acts. 17 A rule is a norm, bar, maxim, measure or standard. 18 A rule may be derived by instruction, discovery, custom or consent. 19 The highest law is Divine being a rule given by divine instruction, 20 as nothing may contradict such a rule. 21 The second highest law be the reason of Mind, 22

being an edict given by a great council of wise elders or jurists, 23 as nothing absurd and without good reason may be considered law. 24 The third highest law be the law of the people, 25 as the consent and will of the people is the source of true authority. 26 The weakest rule is that of a tyrant, 27 as any rule without authority or right of heaven but merely by force, 28 cannot be sustained and the people shall eventually overcome, 29 and render such unjust rule and unjust laws as dust. 30 This be the law of all great civilisations from the beginning of time, 31 and no king or assembly or city has sustained itself in ignorance to such foundation. 32 These then be the foundations of Rule of Law: 33 All law be spoken as it is the spirit of the word that carries the authority. 34 Therefore all action under law be by word of mouth, 35 and writing be only for memory and trade and never be the law. 36 All are equal under the law, 37 all are accountable and answerable under the law, 38 all are without blemish until proven culpable, 39 where there is a law there must be a cause, 40 where there is a law there must be a penalty, 41 where there is a law there must be a remedy. 42 An action in law cannot proceed without first a cause. 43 An action is not granted to one who is not injured. 44 The action of a valid law can do no harm (injury). 45 An action decided in law must reflect cause of such action. 46 No injury to the law means no valid cause for action by law. 47 No action through law can arise from a fraud before heaven and earth. 48 No action through law can arise in bad faith or prejudice. 49 An act does not make one culpable unless there be intent to do wrong, 50 for no one may suffer punishment by valid law for mere intent. 51 No one is punished for the transgression of an ancestor or another. 52 No one can derive an advantage in law from his own wrong, 53 for what is invalid from the beginning does not become valid over time. 54 No one is accused of the same exact cause twice. 55 No man be a judge over his own matter, 56 nor a man possess the authority of heaven to be both judge and executioner. 57 No penalty may exist without a valid law. 58 The immediate cause and not the remote cause be the subject of law. 59 These be the foundations of Rule of Law. 60 As to justice it be the maxim that Justice never contradicts the rule of law, 61 for Justice be the lawful right of use of all that has been defined by law, 62 and Justice be the right to adjudicate the law itself before heaven and earth, 63 and Justice be a judge under sacred oath and trust granted such rights, 64 with a right being a power or authority or privilege or benefit recognised by law. 65 Divine Law is the law that defines the Divine and all creation, 66 and demonstrates the spirit and mind and instruction of the Divine, 67 and the operation of the will of the Divine Creator through existence. 68 Therefore all valid rights and Justice is derived from Divine Law. 69 Natural Law is the law that defines the operation of the will of the Divine, 70 through the existence of form and sky and earth and physical rules. 71 Thus Natural Law governs the operation of what we can see and name. 72 The laws of People are those rules enacted by men having proper authority, 73 for the good governance of a society under the Rule of Law. 74

The laws of People are always inherited from Natural Law. 75 A law of People cannot abrogate or usurp a Natural Law, 76 nor is it possible for a Natural Law to usurp Divine Law. 77 These then be the foundations of Justice: 78 All possess the Right to be heard even if such speech be controversial, 79 all possess the Right of free will to choose our actions and destiny, 80 all possess the Right of reason that distinguishes them from lesser animals, 81 all possess the Right to informed consent or to withdraw consent, 82 all possess the Right over their body that none may claim our flesh, 83 all possess the Right of our divine self that none may claim our soul. 84 Thus no man can make a blood oath on their flesh or vow on their soul, 85 nor may any man claim servitude or obligation under such an abomination, 86 for such Rights are granted solely by heaven to all people, 87 and no man or body of jurists have the authority to usurp heaven or the gods. 88 Verily all true authority and power to rule is inherited from heaven, 89 and to only those men in good faith and good character and good conscience, 90 who then make a sacred oath in trust and form an office, 91 into which such Divine Rights are conveyed for only so long, 92 as they honour their oath and obligations to serve the people. 93 For whenever a man who makes an oath to form a sacred trust of office, 94 then breaks such an oath through prejudice or unclean hands or bad faith, 95 then all such authority and power ceases from them, 96 as the cord between heaven and earth is severed and the trust dissolved. 97 Verily no man may serve the people unless under sacred oath, 98 nor may any man serve heaven unless under solemn vow. 99 Therefore guard your behaviour and actions of office, 100 that though the heavens appear to fall, let justice always be done. 101 These be the foundations of Justice. 102 As to the administration of Justice these be the foundations of Due Process: 103 No valid action in law proceeds without first a valid cause, 104 and no valid cause exists until such claim is first tested. 105 Thus the birth of all action in law must begin with the claim. 106 If a claim be not proven as a valid cause then the accused has nothing to answer. 107 Yet if the claim be proved to have merit as a cause, 108 then all valid causes in law must be resolved. 109 Thus, he who first brings the claim must first prove its merit, 110 as the burden of the proof lies upon him who accuses not he who denies. 111 A heavy obligation then on one who first brings the controversy. 112 For one who brings false accusation is the gravest of transgressors, 113 that it injures not one law, but all heaven and all law. 114 Thus a valid claim in part is one in which an accuser makes a complaint, 115 bringing two witnesses as proof and petitions a forum of law for remedy. 116 If merit of a cause be proved, the one accused must appear to answer. 117 The one accused and any witnesses appear by summons. 118 When anyone be summonsed, he must immediately appear without hesitation. 119 If a man summonsed does not appear or refuses to appear to answer, 120 then let him be seized by force to come and attend. 121 When anyone who has been summonsed seeks to evade, or attempts to flee, 122 let the one who summons lay hands on them to prevent their escape. 123 One who flees fair judgement confesses his culpability. 124 The accused cannot be judged until after the accusations be spoken, 125 and then after the accused exercise or decline their three rights to defence, 126 the first being Prolocution and the right to speak as a matter of law, 127 and why the complaint and investigation should not continue, 128 the second being Collocution as to why the complaint and accusation is false, 129 and upon such proof why the burden should now be placed on the accuser, 130 and the third being Adlocution being a final speech in defence, 131 against a complaint or accusation having been heard. 132 If illness or old age hinder the appearance of the one summonsed, 133 let the one who made the summons provide a basic means of transport. 134 When men wish to settle their dispute among themselves, 135 then they shall have the right to make peace. 136 If a dispute cannot be settled before seeking a judge, 137 then both the accused and the accuser must be granted equal hearing. 138 An accused cannot be found culpable unless three pieces of evidence may be attributed. 139 Judges are bound to explain the reason of their judgement. 140 The setting of the sun shall be the extreme limit of time within, 141 which a judge must render his decision. 142 These be the foundations of Due Process. 143 These be the foundations of Rule of Law and Justice. 144 Any law that is against such truth, cannot be law.

C. 4

1 Upon hearing the wisdom and truth of Jesus from his grandson Emperor Cyllin (Cullen/ Collin), 2 the Roman Emperor Hadrian did declare that henceforth no law be law unless it be in accord, 3 with the Golden Rule of Law and Justice and Due Process as proclaimed by Jesus in Rome. 4 He then did summons all the greatest scholars and jurists to Eboracium Comes Palatinus (York), 5 that it be the most sacred site and Imperial Court at which the new law would be formed, 6 that united all peoples of the world whether they be under Roman or Celt or Parthian rule. 7 Thus it was that the greatest scholars and jurists did come to the new Imperial Court, 8 and did discuss and debate how best to ensure that the laws of the world, 9 be united under the Golden Rule of Law and Justice and Due Process, 10 as the first and true law between people and between kingdoms and between empires. 11 Yet the scholars and jurists could not agree on even the simplest of rules, 12 for they debated endlessly of the exceptions and exclusions upon every word, 13 that a whole year was wasted and still no new form of law had been started. 14 Frustrated at such delay, Emperor Hadrian did summons Valentinus and Heracles of Larissa, 15 to come to Eboracium (York) and provide a resolution to such impasse. 16 Upon their arrival High Priest Heracles of Larissa and Eliada, 17 did praise his childhood friend for the deep peace and unity, 18 he so wisely had demonstrated between Rome and Eboracium, 19 and between the sanctuaries of the Holly Rood and the Holly See of the Vatican. 20 Yet High Priest Heracles of Larissa did remind Emperor Hadrian, 21 of the lessons concerning the history of the Great Prophets of Yeb, 22 and the foundation

of Athens itself by Xerxes as Zeus, ₂₃ that the first steps of unity rest not just in words but action, ₂₄ for people follow false teachers not just because they cannot discern what they hear, ₂₅ but that they have no vision to see a better future. ₂₆ In the year known as 119 CE, ₂₇ thirteen hundred and nineteen years since the dawn of the Great Age, ₂₈ Emperor Hadrian dismissed the scholars and jurists to return to their duties. ₂₉ The Emperor did then announce the engagement of Aelius Hadrianus Cornelius Antonius, ₃₀ as his adopted son and heir to Annaea Claudia Faustina as his adopted daughter. ₃₁ With the consent of King Aulus Cornelius Celsus of the Franks, ₃₂ Emperor Hadrian did proclaim that henceforth the city of Coelogis (Cologne), ₃₃ be known as Colone (Cologne or Colony) meaning those who truly protect, serve and honour, ₃₄ and that the Praetorian be selected from the finest Germanic and Frank legions, ₃₅ with their camp forever to be known as Colone Praetoria as sacred land of the Franks. ₃₆ Emperor Hadrian did also proclaim the rebuilding of the Stadium on the Fields of Mars in Rome, ₃₇ And for the completion of the Stadion Olympeion below and to the south-east of the Parthenon, ₃₈ And in four years (124 CE) for the resurrection of the first Olympic Games in more than 250 years, ₃₉ And the very first Olympic Games open to the whole ancient world. ₄₀ Emperor Hadrian then set personally to work with Emperor Cyllin and the Holly, ₄₁ In the formation of a new Rule of Law for all peoples and all nations of the world.

C. 5

₁ In the year known as 120 CE, ₂ thirteen hundred and twenty years since the dawn of the Great Age, ₃ Marcus Calpernius Piso also known as Marcion of Pontus and Sinope, ₄ was captured at Genola and executed. ₅ Yet his son did escape, whose name was Arrius Calpenius Piso. ₆ Upon the death of his father, Arrius Calpenius Piso secretly declared himself as Papias, ₇ also known as Polycarp and that he would dedicate himself to destroying the Holly, ₈ by writing them out of history and forming the most perverse and wicked doctrines, ₉ that generations into the future would become like ignorant horned cattle. ₁₀ A few months after the death of his father, Arrius Calpenius Piso as Polycarp, ₁₁ did have a son who he named Marcus Calpernius Piso, ₁₂ and who came to be known in years to come by the names Ignatius and Irenaeus. ₁₃ In the same year, Publius Septimus Geta the patriarch of the Septimus clan, ₁₄ did give up the ghost at Leptis Magnae. ₁₅ The control of the family slave trade and plantations then went to his son, ₁₆ whose name was Publius Septimus Aper. ₁₇ In the same year, ₁₈ Aelius Hadrianus Cornelius Antonius and Annaea Claudia Faustina did marry, ₁₉ at a ceremony at Holly Rood Din Eidyn (Edinburgh). ₂₀ Emperor Hadrian did then grant the position of Legate of Gallia (Gaul) and Hispania, ₂₁ in perpetuity to King Aulus Cornelius Celsus of the Franks and his descendants, ₂₂ and did name him co-Consul of Rome in the same year as the Emperor, ₂₃ making King Celsus the most powerful legate in the Roman

Book 23 Age of the Gnostics

Empire, 24 commanding all Germanica, Gaul and Hispania.

C. 6

1 In the year known as 121 CE, 2 thirteen hundred and twenty years since the dawn of the Great Age, 3 Emperor Hadrian did finish his draft of a new law called Codex Regulae, 4 meaning the Code of the Rules of Law, later known as Hadrians' Law and The Code. 5 Falsely corrupted in later texts as Hadrians' Wall to hide the first law of nations, 6 and the first law uniting the ancient world that forbid the trade of pirates and bankers. 7 With the assistance of the Holly at Holly Rood Din Eidyn (Edinburgh), 8 Emperor Hadrian at the Imperial Court at Eboracium (York) did devise three books, 9 of twenty two chapters each as a total of sixty six (66) chapters, 10 with the first Book concerning People and the nature of law, of rights and status, 11 including the recognition that all men and women no matter what their standing, 12 possess certain rights that cannot be seized or surrendered, even if they be slaves. 13 The second Book concerned Property and the divisions of property as well as the value, 14 and recording of property including the making of valid testaments and conveyances. 15 The third Book of twenty-two chapters concerned Obligations and Trust as central to trade, 16 and how obligations and conduct in commerce were to be regulated to prevent fraud and trickery. 17 When Emperor Hadrian presented the finished draft of law to Emperor Cyllin, 18 he asked if such law would honour the teachings of Jesus and the Golden Rule of Law, 19 and if men would learn to follow true law instead of the lies of merchants and false priests, 20 to which the Emperor of the Celts replied that no Emperor had done more to restore the law, 21 yet without a vision of the future, men will quickly return to the old ways, 22 and their old fears and enslavement to the trickeries of such merchants and false priests. 23 Emperor Hadrian replied that he had already done much in beginning the rebuilding of temples, 24 across the Roman Empire and in the unifying of cultures as demonstration of good faith, 25 to which the Holly Emperor did reply that most men and women do not live in temples but towns, 26 and to them their lives remain marginal in conditions no better today than a thousand years ago. 27 In response, Hadrian did order his finest engineers and craftsmen to Eboracium (York), 28 where he ordered they devise a model of how people of all status and standing could live, 29 in a community of three to ten thousand or more with running water, sewerage and heating, 30 with wide and ample streets and protective walls and with a central square and entertainment, 31 so that men could learn to rise above their fears and prejudices and become truly civilised, 32 and thus learn to appreciate the rule of law and the honour of heaven and the beauty of life. 33 Hadrian called this new model of living under the golden rule of law the Metropolis, 34 meaning the standard city as the new standard by which all cities of the world, 35 were to be reformed and improved in years to come. 36 Hadrian then commanded that the old quarters of Athens be remodelled as the first Metropolis, 37

and that a Metropolis be constructed in each of the provinces as a living symbol of the harmony, 38 so that life under the Golden Rule of Law be heralded across the Earth. 39 In the same year Aelius Hadrianus Antoninus Augustus Pius and Annaea Claudia Faustina, 40 did have a son borne at Eboracium (York) they called Marcus (Aurelius) Cornelius.

C. 7

1 In the year known as 122 CE, 2 thirteen hundred and twenty two years since the dawn of the Great Age, 3 Emperor Hadrian issued a supreme Imperial Edict from Eboracium (York) as Comes Palatinus, 4 that the Codex Regulae known as the Codex of the Rules of Law be promulgated throughout the world, 5 and that upon the sacred treaty between all Celts and peoples of the Roman Empire, 6 the Codex Regulae be the Rule of Law of all peoples and all nations and all communities forever more, 7 that no law, or edict or claim may diminish it, nor corrupt it, nor may any body usurp such law, 8 as the Codex Regulae be the Rule of Rome and no other law be law if it be against such truth. 9 In the same year, upon the continued rebellion of people in Palestine, 10 who professed themselves to be followers of the forbidden false religion of Iudaism, 11 and the growing threat of the Briton pirates, 12 Emperor Hadrian issued an Imperial Edict pronouncing that anyone found to be a Iew, or Gew or Briton, 13 be culpable of a capital crime and to be immediately put to death as enemies of heaven and earth. 14 Hadrian then ordered Lucius Artorius Castus to destroy Brittani (Brittany), 15 and the British colonies in Hispania and the pirate colonies within the inland sea, 16 while Marcus Petronius Mamertinus and general Quintus Tineius Rufus were ordered to purge Palestine, 17 of any remaining merchants, priests and followers of the false and forbidden religion of Iudaism. 18 In Gaul and in Hispania, Lucius Artorius Castus smashed the forces of Pirate King Mericadoc of the Britons, 19 with the survivors escaping to the coast of West Africa and renaming themselves the Amoricans. 20 Yet the forces of Lucius Artorius Castus were tricked by a false surrender of the Britons in Dalmatia, 21 and he was killed before the British pirates were slaughtered, 22 and those Britons that escaped renamed themselves the Veneti. 23 Emperor Cyllin then made Gaius Artorius Castus the son of Lucius the new Pendraig (Dragon), 24 while Emperor Hadrian ordered the construction of a sacred temple to Castus at the site of his death. 25 In Palestine, Quintus Tineius Rufus routed the Iudean robbers and rebels, 26 and then read the Imperial Decree from Emperor Hadrian and the Emperor Cyllin which said: 27 Before all the gods and spirits of heaven and all here present and yet to come, 28 let it be known forever more that the name Jerusalem be damned and struck from history. 29 For no city had caused so much madness and bloodshed upon such wickedness and lies, 30 of false priests and false profits of false religions and false gods. 31 A city that refused to acknowledge its own history. 32 Therefore a new name shall be given to this city in honour of the time of

Akhenaten as Moses, 33 for the city shall be called Aelia Capitolina, 34 as an annex of the Capitolinium of Rome and a place of law and justice, 35 and never again to be a site of false worship and the preaching of madness.

C. 8

1 In the year known as 123 CE, 2 thirteen hundred and twenty three years since the dawn of the Great Age, 3 Aelius Hadrianus Antoninus Augustus Pius and Annaea Claudia Faustina, 4 did have a daughter borne at Eboracium (York) they called Annaea (Aurelia) Cornelia Faustina. 5 Emperor Hadrian did then depart Eboracium (York) first to Mauretania, then Cyrene, 6 then to Egypt and then to Palestine and finally to the lands of the Parthians, 7 where for the very first time a Roman Emperor did meet with the King of Parthia. 8 King Osroes had heard of many of the great works of Hadrian and his unity with the Celts, 9 yet remained cautious of the Roman Emperor on account of the destruction of Seleucia, 10 at the hands of the legions of Trajan and the great damage wrought in the previous wars. 11 Emperor Hadrian did then speak to King Osroes saying: 12 Oh Great and noble King of the Four Corners of the World, 13 may our descendants live in peace and harmony for a thousand years. 14 I come in good faith and conscience to share with you the wonders that have taken root, 15 between all peoples who give their allegiance to Rome and to all who honour the Celts. 16 Whereas we were once in terrible and destructive conflict, 17 we have formed a new pact under the Golden Rule of Law as honoured by your ancestors. 18 Yet so long as there remains uncertainty and differences between our peoples, 19 there can never be the full fruits of such harmony. 20 For you stand at the gateway to the riches of the far east, 21 yet you also face the growing might of the Scythian horde. 22 How then might the people of Rome and Parthia form an unbreakable bond of peace? 23 King Osroes did reply: Oh Mighty Emperor, 24 may your descendants be remembered and worshipped by all generations. 25 Your words, as are the news of your deeds, be powerful. 26 Yet our people have suffered from such promises of peace in the past, 27 only to be awoken in the dead of night to find our flocks scattered and our fields burning. 28 Emperor Hadrian did then reply saying: Therefore I pledge before you oh great king, 29 and before heaven and earth that the finest masons and artists, 30 shall build the greatest of cities from the ashes of Seleucia, 31 and in the heart of Rome a great and impregnable palace shall also be constructed, 32 that it be for you and your descendants forever more as if the land of Parthia itself. 33 For if you accept this pledge of good faith that all people may live under one Rule of Law, 34 then all I have sworn will come to be. 35 Whereupon both men agreed and the most solemn and sacred pact was sealed, 36 and for the first time in history more than three out of every four people in the world, 37 did live under one law being the Golden Rule of Law and Justice and Due Process, 38 of sixty six (66) chapters of three (3) books being Of People, Of Property and Of Obligations. 39 Emperor Hadrian did

then order a workforce of more than fifty thousand, 40 come to Parthia to reconstruct the city of Seleucia which the Parthians agreed to be renamed, 41 calling it Castela Metropolis in honour of purity and the spirit of unity, 42 as the first castle city in history and home for more than two hundred thousand people. 43 In Rome, Hadrian commissioned the construction of the most impressive fortress, 44 in the same design and style of Castela Metropolis and called it Castellum Citadella, 45 meaning the fortress and place that belongs to Castela, 46 and the first and most famous Citadel in history, 47 later known as Castel de Angelo, 48 and falsely by wicked pirates and priests as Hadrian's Tomb.

C. 9

1 In the year known as 124 CE, 2 thirteen hundred and twenty four years since the dawn of the Great Age, 3 Emperor Hadrian returned to Athens a living god in the eyes of the people, 4 to celebrate the first Olympic Games at the completed Stadion Olympeion, 5 which did bring the whole world together. 6 Athletes from the provinces of Hispania and Gallia and from Africa and Asia did come. 7 Athletes from Palestine and Egypt and Arabia and even Parthia did come. 8 Even athletes from the Celtic lands of Eire (Ireland) and Englia and Francia, 9 did participate in the Olympic Games and for ninety days no wars or conflict were fought. 10 At the conclusion, Emperor Hadrian did declare that the first university in history, 11 would be formed called the Academia Athenaeum, near Capitoline Hill, 12 in honour of the Akademia in Athens and that Valentinus would be its first rector. 13 In the year known as 125 CE, 14 thirteen hundred and twenty five years since the dawn of the Great Age, 15 Hadrian returned to Rome to celebrate the completion of the new Pantheon, 16 as floods and humid torrential rains continued across much of northern Africa and Europe. 17 The flooding in Numidia, Sicily and Egypt caused the destruction of much of the crops, 18 as people sought shelter and food in the major cities. 19 Rome and Alexandria were plagued by swarms of mosquitoes and Malaria, 20 as Mauretania, Numidia and Egypt were affected by locust plagues causing even greater destruction. 21 In Rome Emperor Hadrian did succumb to Malaria and fell gravelly ill, 22 ordering his son Aelius Hadrianus Cornelius Antonius to return to Eboracium (York), 23 as now hunger grew in Rome and Italy on account of the shortage of grain. 24 Yet in Africa Legate Publius Septimus Aper refused to act against the plague, 25 or help relieve the starving of people in his provinces, 26 so that tens of thousand died of disease and lack of food. 27 As Hadrian remained ill, the emperor ordered Praetorian Quintus Marcius Turbo, 28 to take charge of an invasion of North Africa and to seize and bring to justice, 29 the gens Septima for their disgrace and dishonour of Rome and all humanity. 30 When Quintus Marcius Turbo and his elite legions and generals arrived in North Africa, 31 they met little resistance as society had completely broken down, 32 and Publius Septimus Aper with his sons Gaius Septimius Severus and Lucius Septimus Aper, 33 had fled south and deep into Africa to escape the wrath of

Emperor Hadrian. 34 Quintus Marcius Turbo then ordered his general Gaius Julius Materia, 35 falsely cursed by the gens Septima as Maternus, to pursue and execute the Septima, 36 as cowards and men without any inch of honour or nobility. 37 Yet the further south Gaius Julius Materia did pursue the cowardly Septima, 38 the Septima aided by their slave trading allies remained a few steps ahead. 39 For months Gaius Julius Materia and his legions continued in pursuit of the Septima, 40 as many of the soldiers died from disease and exhaustion until reaching the great inland lake (Lake Chad), 41 where Publius Septimus Aper sought to destroy his Roman nemesis, 42 only to be killed himself and his gens nearly extinguished. 43 Yet Gaius Julius Materia was forced to withdraw for lack of men and supplies, 44 and the cowards Gaius Septimius Severus and Lucius Septimus Aper, 45 remained in hiding deep in Africa, 46 only to discover untold riches to plunder from the central kingdoms of Africa.

C. 10

1 In the year known as 126 CE, 2 thirteen hundred and twenty six years since the dawn of the Great Age, 3 Gaius Cornelius Clemens of the Franks and son of King Celsus, 4 did have a son, whom he named Gaius Cornelius Celestius. 5 In the same year, Emperor Hadrian on his improving health, 6 did travel to North Africa and to the Roman Fortress City of Lambaesis, 7 to oversee the restoration of grain supplies and order in Africa. 8 In the year known as 127 CE, 9 thirteen hundred and twenty seven years since the dawn of the Great Age, 10 Emperor Hadrian returned to Rome and issued an edict from the Palatine, 11 that henceforth, every province must make provision of stores and aid, 12 and that the poor and hungry be given free food in times of need, 13 for any leader that permit the starvation of their people, 14 abdicates all authority of office and becomes nothing more than an impostor. 15 Emperor Hadrian did also reform the land laws for small farmers, 16 so that any man or household may have access to some land, 17 to grow their own food and provide for their own family, 18 even if they be without other means of wealth. 19 Hadrian did then issue the first laws in history that forbid speculation, 20 on staple foods and that any merchant caught inflating the prices of basic food, 21 be put to death as an enemy of the state, 22 for threatening the very stability of society and the Empire. 23 Hadrian did then return to Athens accompanied by Valentinus to see High Priest Heracles. 24 In Athens, Hadrian did ask how men could be persuaded from becoming like savages, 25 and forgetting all knowledge of civilisation in times of crisis. 26 Valentinus replied that he conceived that until the sickness within false religions, 27 be finally erased with greater equality of knowledge and education, 28 then tricksters and fear mongers would always find a willing audience, 29 in times of great sickness and tragedy. 30 High Priest Heracles of Larissa did not agree and instead took a different view, saying: 31 That while men need greater education and truth of knowledge, 32 too few times in history

has mankind witnessed the ideal on earth as a guide to their ideas. 33 Instead, the people know only of servitude and tyranny despite the high words and laws. 34 For ask a man to trust that heaven exists and he may be deceived by false priests and moneylenders. 35 But show a man what heaven is and there can be no doubt as to the standard of rule of law. 36 In the same year Holly King Cúinn (Conn) of Eire (Ireland), 37 the great grandson of Holly Emperor Jesus (Yahusiah), 38 did have a son he named Cúirt.

C. 11

1 In the year known as 128 CE, 2 thirteen hundred and twenty eight years since the dawn of the Great Age, 3 King Aulus Cornelius Celsus of the Franks, 4 grandson of Jesus and son of Gaius Cornelius Tacticus, 5 legate of Gallia (Gaul), Germanica and Hispania, 6 did give up the ghost. 7 Emperor Hadrian did then attend the funeral ceremony at Colone (Cologne), 8 as did Emperor Cyllin and all the Diaspora in honour. 9 Gaius Cornelius Clemens was then anointed King, 10 by Pontifex Maximus Cuibelinus (Cunobelinus), 11 as the first sacrament of Coronatum (Coronation) in history. 12 In the same year, 13 King Gaius Cornelius Clemens of the Franks did have a daughter, 14 named Sabina Cornelia Clementia. 15 In the same year, 16 Hadrian returned to Athens to preside over the second Olympic Games, 17 where he did pronounce to all the delegates and dignitaries of the world, 18 the formation not only of a new kingdom of conscience and the rule of law, 19 but the kingdom of Heaven on Earth and true Paradise, saying: 20 As the gods and our ancestors be our witness to the world assembled here as one, 21 let these words be written and remembered for all generations to come, 22 that every man or woman, no matter what their status at birth, nor race or creed, 23 may know of these events and decrees of the highest of all standing and sacredness, 24 that no body or king or priest may usurp such truth, 25 no scribe or historian or philosopher corrupt such words without condemning themselves for eternity. 26 For upon this day of the opening of the Olympic Games we celebrate the formation of Eukadia (Ucadia), 27 through the uniting of Macedonia and Lacedonia and Crete and Islands once more into a sacred whole, 28 in honour of the vision of the Great Xerxes as Pericles and glorified as Zeus, 29 and his son Artaxerses revered as Xenophon and his grandson Arxenes as Plato, 30 nearly six hundred years ago at this very sacred place. 31 And while Xerxes did rename all the lands and islands known as Eliada, 32 to the sacred name of Acadia to mean all men are equal under the Divine, 33 where no man or woman be a slave or lesser than another, 34 where men and women could live as equals under a true rule of law, 35 and that people could live not by superstition or fear or corruption but by good character and conscience, 36 so it is that the world now bears witness to the creation of Eukadia (Ucadia), 37 meaning the well spring of the Divine Spirit of all creation and the Kingdom of Heaven upon the Earth. 38 Thus it be befitting that the custodian of

paradise on Earth be bestowed, 39 to the same bloodlines of Zeus and Xenophon and Plato and the great kings of Sparta, 40 Pappa Basileus and father priests and custodians and protectors of such sacred lands, 41 that Heracles and his progeny continue to honour their sacred vow to the heaven, 42 in the protection of Olympus and now to the gardens and valleys and cities of paradise, 43 that men of good character and talent and a thirst for true wisdom may come, 44 that women who seek equality and justice and stability of civilisation may come, 45 that all who seek to truly respect heaven and our ancestors may come and give offerings, 46 and no more shall false priests and men of no conscience or virtue be able to hide, 47 nor speak untruths to any man or woman as to the ideal of Heaven or Earth. 48 For Eukadia (Ucadia) is and always shall be the highest Kingdom of Heaven on Earth, 49 and Eukadia (Ucadia) is and always shall be the one true Rule of Law, 50 and let no man or woman speak falsely against such truth, lest by such speech they condemn themselves. 51 So it was then that Eukadia (Ucadia) was formed by Hadrian and not in the name Arcadia, 52 as false priests and false scribes of madness have since corrupted. 53 Thus, for the first time Eliada (Greece) as Eukadia (Ucadia) was united after hundreds of years, 54 and not merely some valleys and hills of the Peloponnese called Arcadia.

C. 12

1 In the year known as 129 CE, 2 thirteen hundred and twenty nine years since the dawn of the Great Age, 3 King Osroes of Parthia did give up the ghost. 4 In honour of the great treaty between Rome and the Parthians, 5 Emperor Hadrian did go to Castela Metropolis (rebuilt Seleucia), 6 to greet the new King Parthamaspates the son of Osroes. 7 Hadrian did then stay in Parthia for some months, 8 before leaving and travelling to the west to ancient Petra, 9 and then the new capital Basra of Arabia, 10 and then Aelia Capitolina (old Jerusalem) to dedicate a new temple to Sophia (wisdom). 11 In the year known as 130 CE, 12 thirteen hundred and thirty years since the dawn of the Great Age, 13 King Linus of Cymri (Wales) did give up the ghost. 14 The crown of Cymri did then befall to his son, 15 whose name was named Lleyn. 16 In the year known as 131 CE, 17 thirteen hundred and thirty one years since the dawn of the Great Age, 18 Herodes the son of Pappa Basileus Heracles of Eukadia (Ucadia), 19 did have a son he named Hippocrates. 20 In the year known as 132 CE, 21 thirteen hundred and thirty two years since the dawn of the Great Age, 22 Emperor Cyllin (Cullen/Collins) of the Celts, 23 Holly King of Caledonia (Scotland) and High King of the Kings of Englia (England), 24 and the great grandson of Jesus (Yahusiah) and Mariamne, 25 did give up the ghost. 26 The Holly crown of Caledonia as Emperor of the Celts, 27 did then befall to his son Cuinan (Conan). 28 In the same year, Herodes the son of Pappa Basileus Heracles of Eukadia (Ucadia), 29 did have a daughter he named Despina Phoebe, meaning the Lady of Light, 30 and by the name Domina Lucilla in Latin. 31 In the year known as 134 CE, 32

thirteen hundred and thirty four years since the dawn of the Great Age, ₃₃ Arrius Calpernius Piso as Papius formed an alliance with the Scythian tribes, ₃₄ to train the nomadic robbers and raiders into a military force, ₃₅ capable of seizing and holding cities against legions. ₃₆ Yet the first attempts of Arrius Calpernius Piso and the Scythians of taking the north of the Black Sea, ₃₇ did fail and Arrius Calpernius Piso withdrew his force after only a few days. ₃₈ In the same year, Praetorian Prefect and Protector of Rome Quintus Marcius Turbo, ₃₉ did give up the ghost. ₄₀ Emperor Hadrian did then appoint Marcus Petronius Mamertinus as head of the Praetorian.

C. 13

₁ In the year known as 136 CE, ₂ thirteen hundred and thirty sixth years since the dawn of the Great Age, ₃ the 4th Olympiad of the united ancient world was held again in Athens in Eukadia (Ucadia). ₄ Emperor Hadrian who had returned to Eboracium Comes Palatinus (York), ₅ remained gravely ill and did send his son Aelius Hadrianus Antoninus Augustus Pius, ₆ who dedicated the games to Hadrian and to the enlightenment of all people. ₇ In the year known as 138 CE, ₈ thirteen hundred and thirty eight years since the dawn of the Great Age, ₉ Emperor Publius Aelius Hadrianus, ₁₀ did give up the ghost at Eboracium Comes Palatinus (York). ₁₁ Emperor Cuinan then declared an unprecedented ninety days of mourning for all Celts, ₁₂ while King Parthamaspates of Parthia declared all Parthians and dependents, ₁₃ wear black clothing as a sign of mourning and honour of the spirit of a great leader. ₁₄ After the body had been embalmed in the ancient ways of the Egyptians, ₁₅ Aelius Hadrianus Antoninus Augustus Pius did accompany the body from Englia, ₁₆ back to Rome as his adopted father had requested for his funeral and cremation. ₁₇ In Rome, the greatest gathering ever seen of kings, emperors, princes and leaders did come, ₁₈ to honour the legacy of a titan of virtue and wisdom. ₁₉ As Hadrian had requested, the funerary was presided by Antoninus Augustus Pius, ₂₀ who spoke to the world assembled and did pronounce this eulogy: ₂₁ In the days to come we will be called to honour an Emperor in custom and manner of the laws of Rome, ₂₂ as a living God and worthy of worship in the Pantheon of the Greats. ₂₃ For this is the will of the people and the Senate of Rome. ₂₄ Yet such time has not yet arrived to speak of the Divine qualities of our father, ₂₅ but to remember the physical man who once lived amongst us; and ₂₆ to return his mortal body to earth and dust; and ₂₇ so releasing his mind from any further sense of obligation unto this plane of existence. ₂₈ Let all of us assembled here today then remember and honour the man Publius Aelius Hadrianus. ₂₉ That as a man sought to live every day to its fullest, ₃₀ constantly seeking the truth and to better his education, ₃₁ yet humble in all his knowledge as to the highest ideal of law, ₃₂ that no one be above the law and all are subject to it; and ₃₃ that no man or woman be born a slave, nor burdened by debt or spiritual blemish; and ₃₄ that no man or woman be lesser or greater than another by right of blood, or race or creed; and ₃₅ that all men and women of reason possess the immutable right to life and freedom and choice. ₃₆ How does one ever adequately express in words the life of any man or woman, ₃₇ with all our experience and actions, our intentions and dreams as well as our successes and failures. ₃₈ Yet as true testament to my father and teacher, I can find no better example, ₃₉ than his only wish to me that I allow his words to be spoken at this occasion, ₄₀ to lessen the burden upon me. ₄₁ Therefore, let me conclude in the very words that Publius Aelius Hadrianus himself, ₄₂ did speak as the measure by which all should seek to remember and honour him: ₄₃ Some men are remembered because their feats and exploits are memorialised in stone and scroll, ₄₄ as legends through fame, or fortune or chance. ₄₅ Yet our most sacred temples and memorials are never reserved for these. ₄₆ Instead, our most hallowed places are dedicated to those unnamed heroes of each generation, ₄₇ the men and women that exemplified the qualities of dedication, of courage, of self sacrifice and humility. ₄₈ Sometimes during our lives, we are honoured to meet these rarest of people, ₄₉ who do not boast of their achievements, nor adorn themselves in finery, ₅₀ but celebrate their triumphs quietly and without arrogance. ₅₁ Yet these are the very men who have fought the bloodiest battles and won, ₅₂ these are the men who have built the mightiest cities and then returned to their modest homes, ₅₃ these are the merchants of honest scales and the teacher who speaks the truth. ₅₄ Thus, if any man or woman seeks to honour my memory, ₅₅ then honour the memory of one of these true heroes first. ₅₆ And if one seeks to truly honour my life, ₅₇ then live each and every day to the fullest and honour the true Rule of Law. ₅₈ For no greater monument or offering can there possible be, ₅₉ than the equality and fraternity and respect among all peoples, ₆₀ as civilised beings.

C. 14

₁ In the year known as 138 CE, ₂ thirteen hundred and thirty eight years since the dawn of the Great Age, ₃ Aelius Hadrianus Antoninus Cornelius Augustus Pius, ₄ brother to King Gaius Cornelius Clemens, King of the Franks and Legate of Gallia and Hispania, ₅ son of Aulus Cornelius Celsus and Great Grandson of Jesus and Mariamne, ₆ and adopted son of Emperor Publius Aelius Hadrianus, ₇ did become the first of the Diaspora and first Holly Emperor of Rome. ₈ Within the first weeks of his reign, Emperor Antoninus Pius did send emissaries, ₉ to each and every Province and kingdom to pledge on the word of Hadrian, ₁₀ that the new Emperor would dedicate his reign to perfecting the Rule of Law, ₁₁ and to end inefficiency and corruption within all administration, ₁₂ that if a leader was dedicated to his office then he be a worthy ally, ₁₃ yet if any leader did seek to corrupt, or pervert the law, then his position be in jeopardy. ₁₄ As a sign of good faith, Antoninus Pius ordered that all the main roads between the provinces, ₁₅ be widened and improved and maintained that no highway be permitted to be in disrepair. ₁₆ The Emperor, then ordered that small forts be built along key highways, 17 between major towns to protect against robbers and thieves. 18 He then ordered that for the first time an accurate measure be made, 19 from the Obelisk of Amenhotep in Rome to the distance between each other city, 20 that a legion may know within half a day the distance for slow or quick march. 21 These reforms greatly pleased the merchant classes throughout the empire, 22 as the improved roads and safety permitted greater travel, 23 and the distance measures for legions aided in the movement of produce. 24 Even the pirates known as the Amoricans, the Britons and the Veneti were reduced to a few boats. 25 Never in the history of Rome had the world known such peace and goodwill.

C. 15

1 In the year known as 140 CE, 2 thirteen hundred and forty years since the dawn of the Great Age, 3 the 5th Olympiad of the world was held in Athens in Eucadia (Ucadia), 4 presided by Antoninus Pius. 5 In the following year (141 CE), a great omen in the form of a comet did appear, 6 at the same time as Hispania did endure a prolonged drought and loss, 7 yet due to the reforms of Hadrian in the feeding of the people, 8 no widespread famine did erupt and instead the Emperor ordered, 9 that greater irrigation and storage of water be constructed under the major cities of Hispania, 10 so if such drought did endure, the people would not die of thirst. 11 In the year known as 142 CE, 12 flooding and storms returned to much of Europe and Asia that crops were ruined, 13 and people sought shelter within the cities. 14 Yet the rise of sickness and signs of plague and the pox did erupt in different cities, 15 while the traditional Roman Doctors and Physicians prescribed poisons (medicines) and spells. 16 Emperor Antoninus Pius did then summons the son of Pappas Basileus Heracles, 17 whose name was Herodes to aid in how such superstition could be eliminated. 18 Herodes did recommend that a strict code of therapy be instituted across the Empire, 19 and that trained and competent Therapeutae be dispatched to each major city, 20 with administrative authority to close the potion shops of Roman Physicians, 21 and outlaw all forms of medicine and superstitious spells. 22 Emperor Antoninus Pius did then grant powers to the new Therapeutae to oversee the sanitation, 23 of each city and to remove officials whose policies promoted disease and ignorance, 24 so that within a few months the outbreak of plague and pox had diminished, 25 and the fear of the people subsided. 26 In the year known as 143 CE, 27 thirteen hundred and forty three years since the dawn of the Great Age, 28 Priest King Heracles of Eucadia (Ucadia) Did give up the ghost. 29 The role of Priest King and protector of paradise as Pappa Basileus, 30 and custodian of the kingdom of Heaven on Earth, 31 did befall to his son whose name was Herodes. 32 In the same year, Marcus Calpernius Piso also known as Ignatius, 33 did have a son he named Justinius Calpernius Piso later known as Sohaemus and Justin Martyr.

C. 16

1 In the year known as 144 CE, 2 thirteen hundred and forty four years since the dawn of the Great Age, 3 the 6th Olympiad of the world was held in Athens, 4 as peace continued across the Roman and Celtic Empires. 5 In the year known as 145 CE, 6 thirteen hundred and forty five years since the dawn of the Great Age, 7 Lucius Septimius Severus the son of Publius Septimus Geta, 8 was born in exile and hiding deep within central Africa. 9 In the same year, Cuinneach (Kenneth) the son of Cuinnwyd (Conrad) was born, 10 in Caledonia in Englia. 11 In the year known as 148 CE, 12 thirteen hundred and forty eight years since the dawn of the Great Age, 13 the 7th Olympiad of the world was held in Athens. 14 At the Olympic Games, Emperor Antoninus Augustus Pius did announce the betrothal, 15 of his son Marcus Aurelius Cornelius Servus to the daughter of Pappa Basileus Herodes, 16 whose name was Despina Phoebe, meaning the Lady of Light or Domina Lucilla in Latin. 17 In the same year, King Parthamaspates of Parthia, 18 did give up the ghost. 19 The crown of Parthia did befall to his son named Sanatruces, 20 as peace between all civilised people did continue, 21 under the Golden Rule of Law, 22 for the longest period since the age of the Hyksos. 23 In the year known as 149 CE, 24 thirteen hundred and forty nine years since the dawn of the Great Age, 25 Marcus Aurelius Cornelius Servus and Domina Lucilla did wed at Athens in Eucadia (Ucadia), 26 before departing to Eboracium Comes Palatinus (York) on Englia. 27 Ten months later Annaea Cornelia Faustina also known as Faustina the Younger was born.

C. 17

1 In the year known as 151 CE, 2 thirteen hundred and fifty one years since the dawn of the Great Age, 3 major earthquakes did erupt throughout western Anatolia (Turkey), 4 destroying major cities and temples across the region. 5 The cities of Smyrna, Samos, Ephesus, Miletus and Pergamum were utterly ruined, 6 Sardia and the island of Rhodes were badly damaged. 7 At the same time from Eboracium (York) in Englia, news did come, 8 of the birth of a son for Marcus Aurelius named Lucius Aurelius Cornelius Commodus. 9 Many in years to come did see the circumstances surrounding the arrival of Commodus, 10 as a dark omen that he somehow be a powerful wizard. 11 At the same time King Cuinan (Conan) of Caledonia (Scotland), 12 Emperor of the Celts and the great grandson of Jesus (Yahusiah), 13 did give up the ghost. 14 The crown of Cruithri and the title of Emperor of the Celts did then befall to his son, 15 whose name was Cuinnwyd (Conrad). 16 In Dalmatia a leader did then rise up and call himself Baalmar meaning the Great Lord, 17 proclaiming that it was by his power and magic the greatest Roman cities in Asia, 18 were crushed and turned to dust. 19 In north Africa the mercenary forces of Publius Septimius Aper did rise up, 20 and seize control of Leptis Magna and several other cities, 21 while Arrius Calpernius Piso as Polycarp did attack and seize the cities of Anatolia, 22 proclaiming it be by his hand alone as a god that the

cities were destroyed. 23 Emperor Antoninus Augustus Pius did personally lead the legions to confront Piso, 24 in Anatolia while Marcus Aurelius did engage his forces against the Septima, 25 and Pappas Basileus Herocles of Eucadia (Ucadia) did engage against Baalmar. 26 Yet the Scythian land pirates were no match for the legions of the Holly Emperor, 27 and Arrius Calpernius Piso as Polycarp was captured and swiftly executed, 28 but not before Calpenius Piso as Polycarp did utter a high curse, saying: 29 By the blood of all martyrs against the Holly, 30 Let the day come when your blood will cease to flow, 31 and your name will wither to dust, 32 and all you have written shall be forgotten, 33 and replaced by those who worship my blood as gods. 34 After Calpernius Piso as Polycarp was executed, 35 Emperor Antoninus Augustus Pius ordered that any man or woman found possessing writings of Iudaism, 36 or any other text of such falsity and lunacy, 37 were to be executed as an enemy of Heaven and Earth. 38 In Africa, Marcus Aurelius did recapture Leptis Magna and push the rebels back, 39 and did rout the mercenary army of Publius Septimius Aper killing him. 40 Yet his son Publius Septimius Geta did escape by the tradition of the Septima, 41 by abandoning the mercenary army and his own father to save his own skin. 42 In Dalmatia, Pappas Basileus Herocles of Eucadia (Ucadia) did push Baalmar, 43 into hiding in the mountains and peace was restored. 44 Upon the execution of his father, Marcus Calpernius Piso as Ignatius, 45 did rally the people of Smyrna and the region to try and kill the Emperor, 46 saying that only when the great Holly wizards be gone, 47 would the prosperity of the seven cities made rich from slaves and trade return. 48 Yet the uprising by the people of Anatolia against the legions did fail, 49 after thousands of Roman legionnaires were killed. 50 Emperor Antoninus Augustus Pius did then order a decree that henceforth, 51 the former cities of Smyrna, Samos, Ephesus, Miletus, Sardis, Rhodes and Pergamum of Anatolia, 52 be forever cursed as the refuge of men and women without honour, 53 and people of such utter madness and stupidity, 54 that they would rather cut the hand that comes in aid, 55 and believe the falsities of the silver tongue that comes to enslave. 56 Emperor Antoninus Augustus Pius did then return to Rome and decree, 57 henceforth all forms of slavery be immoral and unlawful and forbidden.

C. 18

1 In the year known as 152 CE, 2 thirteen hundred and fifty two years since the dawn of the Great Age, 3 the 8th Olympiad of the world was held in Athens, 4 as dissent continued to grow across North Africa, Arabia and Egypt, 5 as the former slave traders did encourage any and all forms of dissent. 6 No greater insanity did exist than the death cult of Marcus Calpernius Piso as Ignatius, 7 that continued to attract followers especially among the cursed seven cities of Asia, 8 of Pergamon, Smyrna, Ephesus, Samos, Miletus, Sardis and the island of Rhodes. 9 Marcus Calpernius Piso as Ignatius of Smyrna and his followers embraced the ruins, 10 proclaiming their god the Lord of

Hosts would reign fire and brimstone, 11 upon the world and all who worshipped Law and Order and Peace and Dignity were doomed, 12 for the Lord of Hosts would soon end the world and all who did not reject life, 13 and embrace death as mindless slaves obedient to the insanity of a non religion. 14 Even after Emperor Antoninus Augustus Pius ordered the cult of Ignatius be a capital crime, 15 the willingly stupid and fanatical followers of the false teacher of Piso, 16 did embrace death and celebrate their doom like people suffering fits, 17 by singing and mouthing nonsensical phrases as they were led to their executions. 18 In the year known as 153 CE, 19 thirteen hundred and fifty three years since the dawn of the Great Age, 20 (Flavius Josephus) Valentinus did give up the ghost at the age of 79, 21 and Emperor Antoninus Pius did declare a month of mourning. 22 In the year known as 154 CE, 23 thirteen hundred and fifty four years since the dawn of the Great Age, 24 upon more attacks by the crazed and fanatical followers of Marcus Calpernius Piso as Ignatius, 25 Emperor Antoninus Augustus Pius ordered that ruined western Anatolia be purged of all people, 26 and that no longer would the mentally ill and stupid followers of Piso be executed, 27 for their madness and stupidity be the gravest of punishment in itself. 28 He did then order they be exiled to live in separate ghettos built across Asia, 29 and required by law to wear a blue badge in the shape of a Roman "P" as a sign to all the world, 30 they be mad with stupidity and ignorance and a danger to themselves and the community, 31 until they be cured of their blind allegiance to the false teachings of Piso as Ignatius. 32 Marcus Calpernius Piso himself did then first escape to Alexandria with his family. 33 Yet upon being discovered he was forced to flee, leaving his son Justinius Calpernius, 34 and travelling to the south of France and midst the ruins of Lucifer (Lyons), 35 then changing his name to Irenaeus where he then dedicated himself to a new life mission, 36 to write the most awful falsities, profanities and apostasies against Heaven and the Divine, 37 to confuse and enslave all too weak of mind to discern or question, 38 proclaiming that one day the faith of the Lord of Hosts and the damnation of the world, 39 will consume all logic and reason and every city and people, 40 and like ignorant monkeys, people will pray and rejoice for the day of judgement to come, 41 and the complete destruction of the world.

C. 19

1 In the year known as 156 CE, 2 thirteen hundred and fifty six years since the dawn of the Great Age, 3 the 9th Olympiad of the world was held in Athens, 4 and the longest peace in ancient history continued between the empires. 5 In the year known as 158 CE, 6 thirteen hundred and fifty eight years since the dawn of the Great Age, 7 King Lleyn of Cymri (Wales) did give up the ghost. 8 The crown of Wales did befall to his son Lloyd (Lled). 9 In the same year, Lucius Septimus Flaccus and the brother of Publius Septimius Geta, 10 did have a son he named Lucius Septimus Tertullianus, also known as Tertullian. 11 In the year

known as 160 CE, 12 thirteen hundred and sixty years since the dawn of the Great Age, 13 the 10th Olympiad of the world was held in Athens, 14 and Emperor Aelius Antoninus Cornelius Pius did announce his abdication to his son, 15 Marcus Aurelius Cornelius Servus as the new Holly Emperor, 16 and descendant of Emperor Jesus and Queen Mariamne and King Tacticus of the Franks, 17 and descendant of four lines of Emperors through his mother and father. 18 In the year known as 161 CE, 19 thirteen hundred and sixty one years since the dawn of the Great Age, 20 there was great flooding across the whole of Europe and Asia, 21 as summer rains did not ease, causing rivers to break and crops to be destroyed. 22 Riots did erupt across cities of Anatolia and Armenia and Parthia because of shortage of food. 23 In the same year, Emperor Aelius Hadrianus Antoninus Cornelius Augustus Pius, 24 did give up the ghost. 25 Yet the flooding and disease of Rome was so severe, that Emperor Marcus Aurelius, 26 did order the funeral ceremony to be shortened and conducted at Athens in Eucadia (Ucadia). 27 Despite the shorter period of official mourning, all the major emperors and kings of the world, 28 did come to Athens to honour the Holly Emperor. 29 Justianus Calpernius Piso also known as Justin Martyr did then depart the ghetto of Alexandria, 30 to Armenia where the people were in rebellion. Soon after he became the leader of the rebels, 31 changing his name to Sohaemus and declaring himself saviour of the people. 32 With King Sanatruces of Parthia at Athens for the funerary ceremonies, 33 and before the uprisings in Armenia could be punished, 34 the Parthian Kingdom collapsed as city after city rioted to gain the last remaining food stores. 35 King Sanatruces of Parthia pleaded with Emperor Marcus Aurelius to come to the aid of his people, 36 despite the crisis of Rome itself because of the floods. 37 Yet Marcus Aurelius agreed and called upon King Herodes of Eucadia (Ucadia), 38 to be the protector of the people and to hold the powers of the Emperor, 39 whilst Marcus Aurelius accompanied King Sanatruces of Parthia with the Roman legions to Parthia.

C. 20

1 In the year known as 161 CE, 2 thirteen hundred and sixty one years since the dawn of the Great Age, 3 Emperor Marcus Aurelius Cornelius Servus and King Sanatruces of Parthia did restore order, 4 across the Parthian Empire and in its capital Castela Metropolis (Seleucia). 5 Marcus Aurelius did then pledge to the Parthian King the service of the Roman legions, 6 to aid in the building of new roads and stores and water to the standards that had saved Rome. 7 In response, King Sanatruces of Parthia did then vow that the law of Gnosticism, 8 of the Golden Rule of Law by which all are equal under one law shall be the standard, 9 and did pledge the end of slavery and the forbiddance of the false practices of Iudaism, 10 calling upon Emperor Marcus Aurelius to give the world its first united law, 11 beyond the divisions of culture, or war, or skin, or creed or ancient feuds. 12 Thus Marcus Aurelius returned to Englia and

Eboracium (York) to oversee, 13 the completion of the first and true law of democracy, of liberty and rights of justice to all. 14 In the year known as 163 CE, 15 thirteen hundred and sixty three years since the dawn of the Great Age, 16 Justianus Calpernius Piso as King Sohaemus of Armenia, 17 did have a son he named Adamantius Calpernius Piso as the Origin of a new race of gods, 18 who would rule the world under completely false scriptures and laws that would decree, 19 the rights of the merchant elite to treat men as slaves and that those doomed by such pirates, 20 were doomed to return as slaves and never be free unless they pledged undying loyalty. 21 In celebration of his new son also known as Origen, Justin Martyr as King Sohaemus, 22 did rename the capital of Artaxata as Kaine Polis or the City of Kainites (Knights).

C. 21

1 In the year known as 164 CE, 2 thirteen hundred and sixty four years since the dawn of the Great Age, 3 Emperor Marcus Aurelius Cornelius Servus did return to Athens to celebrate, 4 the 11th Olympiad and the completion of his Civil laws known as the Digesta, 5 and his ecclesiastical laws known as the Meditations. 6 The Emperor did pronounce the betrothal of his eldest daughter named Annaea Cornelia Faustina, 7 to her first cousin Gaius Cornelius Celestius, son of King Cornelius Clemens of the Franks, 8 and the betrothal of his cousin Sabina Cornelia Clementia, 9 to the Holly Crown Prince Cúirt mac Cúinn of Eire (Ireland). 10 Then to the assembled kings, princes and rulers of the world, 11 represented by their finest athletes, artists and minds, 12 Marcus Aurelius Cornelius Servus did speak as to the Universal Laws of Mankind, saying: 13 At this 11th Olympiad it is fitting we celebrate what is best in humanity, 14 and that for a few short weeks, we allow our sight to rise to heaven, 15 to briefly cease in our quarrelling and that which divides us. 16 To remember the extraordinary lives and virtues of our forefathers, 17 and to celebrate our greatest achievements as a species. 18 Therefore, it is proper we speak of the triumph of the Golden Rule of Law, 19 over the powerful forces of profit, of fear and oppression, 20 so that all are truly equal before the law and none are above it. 21 And that all forms of slavery and forced servitude now be reprobate and forbidden in law. 22 Thus, it is because of this very achievement that I come before you today, 23 not as your Emperor, or a living god or the son of the gods, 24 or even the blood descendant of the Holly king of kings and priest of priests, 25 but as your father, your friend and your equal. 26 Therefore, let us speak as fraternal brothers and equals, 27 distinguished not by our fortune of birth, or race, or colour or creed, 28 but by the competency of our skills and the proficiencies of our minds. 29 Indeed, let us speak plainly and truthfully that this day be remembered, 30 not for towering rhetoric but the sensibility of reason. 31 For many a great teacher and priest has brought forth the wisdom of law, 32 and even in some times past men have lived briefly under freedom, 33 and even for briefer times in peace and respect, 34 only to be scattered like

leaves upon an autumn storm at the signs of impending doom. 35 Thus the finest of laws be naught, if there be no deep foundation upon which it may take root, 36 nor even the strength of the Golden Rule of law be sufficient against the artful guile, 37 of the flatterer, the promisor and the liar. 38 Verily, even the law (Digesta) I bequeath to the world today, 39 may one day be consigned to dust or corrupted beyond logic or reason, 40 no matter how many jurists seek to defend it, 41 unless men be told the truth of their circumstance, 42 no matter what the cost or the risk of confusion or doubt. 43 For a man cannot be truly free if he remains trapped in ignorance as to himself, 44 and a man who knows nothing of the truth of existence may be deceived both in life and the afterlife. 45 The Holly Priests and Great Prophets of Yeb have understood such paradox, 46 longer than any others throughout each age of the thousands of years of civilisations, 47 for they were bred for one purpose above all others to be the priests of priests, 48 the connection between this world and the next, 49 to be the keepers of the deepest knowledge and to know beyond what should be the knowable. 50 Yet such knowledge and breeding did give rise at times to an arrogance against humanity, 51 that men be beneath the wisdom of the most ancient priests of the Green Race. 52 But some rejected such arrogance and I honour the memory of my ancestor Yahusiah (Jesus), 53 as one who sought to reveal the truth of all wisdom to all men. 54 Yet the men of his time more than one hundred years ago did not comprehend his message, 55 nor could they distinguish profound wisdom from the artful untruths of the impostors, 56 so such words did fall to the ground and much was lost to the ears and eyes of men. 57 Thus, I shall not speak to you of the wisdom and brevity of that which is contained in the law, 58 for the Golden Rule of Law speaks for itself and all may read hereafter. 59 Instead, I shall speak to you of the deepest truth as to whom each of you are, 60 that some of what I say be remembered and that men learn the greatest knowledge of humanity. 61 Verily, I say to each and every one of you that Life is a Dream, yet a Dream according to Rules, 62 that many of the finest minds have discovered and yet many more rules are yet to be considered. 63 That the only reality is mind, and that the world around you is in a sense an illusion. 64 That you are mind and therefore immortal and so can never die. 65 That the universal dream is change; and our life is what our thoughts make it. 66 That Death is merely a doorway. Death smiles at us all, all a man can do is smile back. 67 That what we do now in our minds and lives echoes in eternity. 68 That the happiness of your life depends upon the quality of your thoughts. 69 That whoever does wrong, wrongs himself; whoever does injustice, does it to himself, making himself ignorant. 70 That you have power over your mind - not outside events. Realize this, and you will find strength. 71 Verily, even if this knowledge is lost for thousands of years this moment and our existence never ceases. 72 It is in this deepest of wisdom we find the key to true emancipation as freedom from all our fears.

C. 22

1 In the year known as 165 CE, 2 thirteen hundred and sixty five years since the dawn of the Great Age, 3 the Earth did test the limits of men as to the north the lands did cool and dry, 4 and across the lands of the inland sea (Mediterranean), the drying did cause great hardship, 5 as Hispania lost much of its forests and grasslands and famine and drought gripped Asia and the East, 6 with crops and forests lost to fire, to locusts and storms of dust. 7 In the ancient lands of the giant Normen (Men of the North), who called their lands Asgardi, 8 the cooling and ice caused terrible starvation and bloodshed among the people, 9 between the powerful king Avaldi of the North who sought lands from king Bergi of the south. 10 As even the southern lands of Asgardi (Greenland) became impossible to farm, 11 the kings did agree to leave their homeland for new lands, 12 with king Avaldi and his three sons and tribes of more than one hundred and fifty thousand, 13 sailing west to the new lands they named Valhalli (North America), 14 settling along the east coast. 15 King Bergi and his two sons Buri and Boli did travel south-east, 16 with King Bergi conquering the island of Aki (Iceland) and making it his capital, 17 while Buri did land more than one hundred thousand of his tribes upon Scandinavia (Nordi), 18 and Boli did travel east and land his clanns of sixty thousand upon the Goti (Goth) lands (Russia). 19 Yet Bestia the daughter of king Bergi refused to leave and remained on Asgardi. 20 In the same year, Great Holly King Cúinn (Conn) Cétchathach of Eire (Ireland), 21 did give up the ghost. 22 The High Kingship of Ireland did then fall to his son, 23 Artur (Arthur) mac Cúinn of the Cuilleain and great great grandson of Jesus and Mariamne. 24 In the same year, Cúirt mac Cúinn and Sabina Cornelia Clementia, 25 did have a son they named Cúirmac. 26 Emperor Marcus Aurelius did then launch his campaign against Calpernius Piso as King Sohaemus, 27 and aided by General Marcus Valerius Maximianus, the Romans routed the Armenians, 28 and reduced to rubble the city of Kaine Polis, killing many thousands. 29 Yet Justianus Calpernius Piso as King Sohaemus escaped dressed as a woman, 30 after ensuring the public spectacle of what appeared to be Roman assassins taking the life of the king. 31 Thus, the Romans considered Piso dead and his subjects believed their king a martyr (Justin Martyr). 32 Justianus Calpernius Piso and his son Origen did then travel to Babylon to seek refuge. 33 Upon news of the death of his son, Marcus Calpernius Piso as Irenaeus of Lyons did come out of hiding, 34 and curse the Holly Emperor for killing his son and vowing that his writings of lies and filth, 35 would last a thousand years and become the foundation of a religion of curses, 36 while the truth of the Holly and Marcus Aurelius would be forgotten and destroyed. 37 Soon after Marcus Calpernius Piso as Irenaeus of Lyons was also discovered and executed. 38 The Emperor then turned his sights upon Baalmar (Ballomar) and the uprisings of the Dalmatian pirates. 39 Yet the rise of disease and misery across Asia, Arabia, Syria, Palestine and Parthia, forced a halt. 40 In Parthia, the Roman

Legions were forced to withdraw as terrible outbreak of the pox, 41 devastated city after city causing even King Sanatruces of Parthia to flee to his Citadel at Rome. 42 As more and more people did continue to die from disease and hunger, 43 Justianus Calpernius Piso now as the wandering prophet Mani, 44 did declare that Eucadia (Ucadia) be the land of milk and honey, 45 and that its waters could cure all ill and there was no disease or hunger or death. 46 At first the numbers of refugees coming to Eucadia (Ucadia) was but a trickle. 47 Yet soon it became a raging torrent of desperation, forcing old Herodes to close the borders, 48 whereupon Baalmar and his growing army did invade Eucadia (Ucadia) hungry and in search of redemption. 49 Pappas Basileus Herodes called out to Marcus Aurelius for help to which the Emperor diverted his army, 50 and called to Herodes that his brilliant son Hippocrates the Therapeutae devise a cure to the plagues.

C. 23

1 In the year known as 166 CE, 2 thirteen hundred and sixty six years since the dawn of the Great Age, 3 King Gaius Cornelius Celestius of the Franks and Annaea Cornelia Faustina, 4 the daughter of Roman Emperor Marcus Aurelius, 5 did have a son they named Aurelius Cornelius Albinus. 6 In the same year, Marcus Aurelius did send legions to Eucadia (Ucadia), 7 to aid against Baalmar (Ballomar) and the mass of refugees that threatened to strip the lands. 8 Hippocrates had already departed to Egypt in search of an ancient cure against the plague 9

Yet all his efforts were not enough against the tumult of suffering. 10 City after city and town after town was devastated by the pox and plague, 11 as people wept amongst the dead and dying with Rome herself losing more than five thousand a day. 12 Across Parthia, Syria, Palestine and Asia the plague was even worse, 13 as whole cities were desolated to become the hauntings of the dead and carrion. 14 In Babylon, Justianus Calpernius Piso as the prophet Mani did witness utter devastation. 15 Yet the plague and the pox did not visit his house or his son Origen. 16 At such a sight, Justianus Calpernius Piso proclaimed to the people he be protected by demons, 17 far more powerful than any of the ancient gods and that the death was a punishment, 18 for all who refused to practice the old ways of child sacrifice and blood oaths. 19 Instead Mani promised he could save people from the wrath of Satan the lord of hosts, 20 if they pledge their undying obedience to him. 21 Word quickly spread across the ancient world that a miracle worker called Mani of Babylon, 22 sent by Satan to form a sacred covenant for all who would pledge themselves as the Chosen People. 23 Tens of thousands flocked to Babylon to save themselves from the plague, 24 in the hope of being saved and to hear of this all powerful demon god. 25 There in Babylon, midst tens of thousands of desperate and dying devotees, 26 the fraud and impostor Justianus Calpernius Piso as Mani did proclaim: 27 Verily, I tell all men the truth that there is no omnipotent God or Divine Creator of Good. 28 For if there were, how could such a God permit such evil, if he be not evil himself. 29 The

Holly priests and prophets have lied to you for centuries when they spoke such stories. 30 For there be no salvation in their laws or pretence of honour or justice and rules. 31 Rules that keep them as a Green Race of Gods among men suffering as slaves and animals. 32 No, I tell you the truth that they are responsible for the miseries of this world. 33 For they follow the Adamus the man that sought to defy the spirit forces of Satan, 34 and rule as Gods for themselves forever. 35 If this were not true, then why do they not share their secrets of the ancients of Egypt, 36 and the steps of immortality and reincarnation which they keep for themselves. 37 They are the worst keepers of secrets. 38 Light and Dark, Life and Death, Birth and Rebirth. 39 Knowledge is the enemy of life and seeking to reason and question is an arrogance against Satan. 40 But faith alone in absolute obedience and trust is sufficient to end suffering. 41 Therefore, pick up your staff and follow me as the Chosen People of God (Satan). 42 And all who defy you and challenge you shall be rendered dust and enslaved as animals. 43 Verily I say to you this day that Satan has pledged a new covenant in the blood of our enemies, 44 that only the Chosen People be permitted to enslave others. Truly it is our birth right. 45 And before Satan comes to judge the world and reward his Chosen people and reap the flesh of the slaves, 46 we will control the world as Lords and Masters of all others as ignorant animals. 47 Soon the religion of Mani called Mania had spread across Parthia and Asia and Africa, 48 as people called Maniacs followed obediently his teachings in the hope of saving themselves.

C. 24

1 In the year known as 167 CE, 2 thirteen hundred and sixty seven years since the dawn of the Great Age, 3 Hippocrates returned to Athens and Eucadia (Ucadia) from Egypt, 4 bringing with him hundreds of cats which he ordered be freed to roam the city unharmed, 5 for Hippocrates did speak that such pestilence that so afflicts the world, 6 be no supernatural force nor punishment of demons or gods, 7 but the work of parasites who by their own nature are without reason or self control, 8 or sense or ability to live in harmony with the people, but must consume to excess, 9 and procreate and destroy everything around them. 10 Yet the solitary cat being the outcast is the perfect match against the rodent, 11 that must be hunted down and destroyed because it cannot be redeemed. 12 Thus any city that permits such parasites and rodents to roam in its midst is doomed. 13 Within only a few weeks the number of sick and dying within Athens halted, 14 and Marcus Aurelius ordered that cats be introduced into every city and not to be harmed. 15 Thousands of cats were brought to Rome and within weeks the plague ceased. 16 Hippocrates did then implore the Emperor issue an imperial edict, 17 that never again the practice of such crude and insane practices as Medicine, 18 born from ignorance and secret fraternities that celebrated corrupt knowledge, 19 and used such absurdity as Pharma (poisons) and blood letting, 20 when Therapeutae

priests had proven such barbaric practices did nothing to aid the sick. 21 The Emperor agreed and issued an Imperial Edict forbidding the practice of Medicine, 22 as a capital crime against Rome and all forms of knowledge and reason, 23 and that henceforth any man qualified to heal or tend to the sick was required to make a Solemn Oath. 24 The Oath came to be known as the Hippocratic Oath and did say: 25 I invoke the favour of the Divine Creator of all Existence and Life, 26 and implore the spirits of my ancestors to bear witness to my most solemn oath, 27 upon the names and lives of all my household and all those yet to come, 28 that even upon peril against my life I shall not disavow this sacred Covenant: 29 First: I pledge that for as long as I shall live, I will be a seeker of truth and a servant to true knowledge; free from any superstition, prejudice, fear or malice; and 30 Second: I swear that to the best of my ability, I will protect the dignity of life and will promote wellness above all; and will tend to the needs of the sick and the dying; and 31 Third: I pledge to honour the sanctity of trust given to me and I will keep confidence and refrain from pursuing any financial or unfair advantage gained from my position; and 32 Fourth: I promise to use logic and reason in all my diagnosis and I will refrain at all cost from cutting or poisoning the body unless it is the only reasonable conclusion to saving a life; and 33 Fifth: I vow to keep firm and inviolable this sacred Covenant. May it grant me your favour and good fortune. If I do transgress, I shall be at your mercy; and if I have sworn falsely in bad faith and bad character this day, may you portion to me that which is deserved upon such profanity and disgrace before Heaven and Earth. 34 In the same year, the Great Pappas Basileus Hippocrates did have a daughter, 35 he named Hippolyta.

C. 25

1 In the year known as 168 CE, 2 thirteen hundred and sixty eight years since the dawn of the Great Age, 3 as word of the miracles of Hippocrates at saving the world from death did spread, 4 the world celebrated the 12th Olympic Games at Athens in Eucadia (Ucadia). 5 Justianus Calpernius Piso as Mani became bitter at the success of ending the plague, 6 and did everything in his power in the east to perpetuate the fear and misery, 7 causing many to abandon the pseudo religion of Mania and the Maniacs. 8 Yet Piso had also built a formidable mercenary army, 9 so that King Sanatruces on his return could not gain control of Babylon or the west. 10 Marcus Aurelius did then order General Marcus Valerius Maximianus and the legions, 11 to crush Baalmar and the Marcomanni in the lands of Dalmatia and Pannonia. 12 Yet as General Marcus Valerius Maximianus advanced, the forces of the Marcomanni, 13 aided by the pirate merchants did escape and did capture Aquileia and Patavium, 14 as the first invasions of Italy since the time of the Celt revolts. 15 General Marcus Valerius Maximianus regained control of Aquileia and Patavium, 16 and then split the forces of Baalmar forcing half of his army to retreat, 17 while more than 20,000 were then crushed against the Auxillery legions moving

north. 18 Baalmar did escape to Pannonia and did spend the rest of his days a hunted man. 19 In the northern lands of the Rus (Russia), 20 the giant Normen of Buri and his sons Odi and Vili did take more land from the Franks, 21 with King Gaius Cornelius Celestius calling upon Marcus Aurelius, 22 to come to his aid to defeat the Normen giants. 23 In the year known as 169 CE, 24 thirteen hundred and sixty nine years since the dawn of the Great Age, 25 Hippocrates the son of King Herodes of Eucadia (Ucadia), 26 did have a son he named Heraclites. 27 In the year known as 170 CE, 28 thirteen hundred and seventy years since the dawn of the Great Age, 29 Pappas Basileus Herodes of Eucadia (Ucadia), 30 did give up the ghost. 31 The role of Priest King and protector of paradise, 32 and custodian of the kingdom of Heaven on Earth, 33 did befall to his son whose name was Hippocrates. 34 In the same year King Gaius Cornelius Celestius and the Romans, 35 pushed the Rus (Norman Giants) of Buri and his sons Odi and Vili, 36 back from the lands of the Franks. 37 In the same year Babylon succeeded in forming a peace treaty with Sanatruces, 38 and peace was restored to Parthia. 39 In the year known as 171 CE, 40 thirteen hundred and seventy one years since the dawn of the Great Age, 41 Domitia Cornelia Lucilla the third child and youngest daughter of Marcus Aurelius, 42 was betrothed to Holly Crown Prince Cuinneach (Kenneth) of the Celts. 43 Yet Domitia Cornelia Lucilla refused her father saying if the law be true, 44 she be permitted to choose her own destiny and love. 45 Marcus Aurelius did reply that indeed no man or Emperor or priest may force the mind of another, 46 yet matrimony was a most solemn responsibility. 47 Thus if Domitia Cornelia Lucilla did not wish to be wed, he could not force her, 48 but nor could he undo what (formal betrothal) was legally binding.

C. 26

1 In the year known as 172 CE, 2 thirteen hundred and seventy two years since the dawn of the Great Age, 3 the world celebrated the 13th Olympiad at Athens in Eucadia (Ucadia), as the climate cooled. 4 The lands of the Rusi Celtic Giants (Russia), Caledonia and even the north of Eire (Ireland), 5 were now covered in thick snow and ice for most of the year. 6 Thanks to the brilliance and wisdom of Pappas Basileus Hippocrates, 7 Emperor Marcus Aurelius had succeeded in restoring peace to most of the world, 8 except for North Africa and now Egypt which continued to be influenced by the Septima, 9 who recruited the traitor Gaius Cassius Avidius supported by an African mercenary army of 30,000, 10 to rise up and halt the shipments of grain from Egypt and Palestine, 11 and thus force Marcus Aurelius to terms thereby enabling the Septima to return. 12 The mercenary horde of Gaius Cassius Avidius overwhelmed Egypt and soon seized Palestine, 13 before Marcus Aurelius did call upon General Marcus Valerius Maximianus once more from retirement, 14 to defeat a treacherous enemy that sought to hold Rome hostage through the mouths of its people. 15 General Marcus Valerius Maximianus restored order in Egypt by destroying the mercenaries, 16 forcing Gaius Cassius

Avidius and his bloodthirsty son Cassius Dio into Syria. 17 Yet the Septima had foreseen the weakness of the mercenary army and instead, 18 bribed many of the auxiliaries to fall back in reinforcing Maximianus, 19 so that in Syria, Gaius Cassius Avidius had numerical advantage to the cavalry of Maximianus. 20 Yet upon the dawn of the day of battle, with the forces of General Marcus Valerius Maximianus, 21 outnumbered more than ten to one, the great general of Rome did speak to his cavalry saying: 22 No man be less for fear of the mortal peril he be compelled to face, 23 nor of the arms of death seeking to grip his essence. 24 For a true hero be any man who advances toward the veil, despite his fears. 25 Yet we are more than blood and flesh and sword, 26 for we are truly immortal and can never die. 27 The only question is how we meet this day and our destiny. 28 For today I am not your general but your brother, 29 and so it shall be that we either are victorious together or die together in glory. 30 Thus General Marcus Valerius Maximianus and his cavalry rode against Gaius Cassius Avidius, 31 and cut the mercenaries to pieces causing the remainder to flee in fear including Cassius Dio. 32 Yet Gaius Cassius Avidius did not escape and was executed midst the bodies of the fallen. 33 His son Cassius Dio did travel to Babylon to offer his services to Mani, 34 promising that he would use all his skills to rewrite history and corrupt the truth, 35 to honour the Piso and to defile Heaven and Earth that had so cursed his House and his father. 36 Mani accepted the pledge of Cassius Dio and within a few years, 37 Cassius Dio had completed his first work of fiction proclaiming utter absurdities and frauds, 38 against the names of the emperors and even the truth of his own family.

C. 27

1 In the year known as 173 CE, 2 thirteen hundred and seventy three years since the dawn of the Great Age, 3 Emperor Cuinnwyd (Conrad) of the Celts and King of Caledonia of Englia, 4 did give up the ghost. 5 The position of Emperor of the Celts did befall to his son Cuinneach (Kenneth), 6 at a time the conditions for Caledonia had become colder and dryer. 7 Yet peace held across the Empires of the Celts, the Franks, the Romans and Eucadia (Ucadia). 8 In the year known as 176 CE, 9 thirteen hundred and seventy six years since the dawn of the Great Age, 10 the world celebrated the 14th Olympic Games at Athens in Eucadia (Ucadia). 11 In the year known as 178 CE, 12 thirteen hundred and seventy eight years since the dawn of the Great Age, 13 an earthquake did strike the east of the inland sea (Mediterranean), 14 Justinianus Calpernius Piso as Mani did proclaim it a sign of the coming end of the world, 15 when Sabbaoth would destroy Rome for its iniquity and all who did not follow the Chosen People. 16 Quintus Septimus Tertullianus also known as Tertullian did then travel to meet Justianus, 17 in the city of Babylon to form an alliance to regain power, 18 and to hatch a plan to end the world. 19 In Babylon, Justinianus Calpernius Piso did demonstrate to Tertullianus the power of faith, 20 saying: The Septima may have captured the gold of Africa, 21 but I

(Mani) have seized the souls of men. 22 I contend that fanatical religion be more powerful than all the gold in the world. 23 Justinianus Calpernius Piso did then order a company of five hundred of his guard, 24 as devoted Maniacs to march willingly off the walls of the city to their certain death, 25 as Quintus Septimus Tertullianus watched on. 26 Tertullian was amazed and declared that with the aid of Piso he would form, 27 the most malevolent and perverse religious rituals of history, 28 to control the minds of men and cause them to serve as willing beasts. 29 Tertullian and Justinianus Calpernius Piso then agreed, 30 the best timing be 15th Olympic Games at Athens where they would assassinate Marcus Aurelius, 31 and cause war against Rome and Parthia. 32 Upon returning to Africa, Tertullianus did send agents to Rome to spread fear and mistrust, 33 that the cats be agents of Hippocrates as a wizard eating the flesh of young children.

C. 28

1 In the year known as 180 CE, 2 thirteen hundred and eighty years since the dawn of the Great Age, 3 Emperor Marcus (Aurelius) Cornelius Servus did celebrate, 4 the opening of the 15th Olympic Games at Athens in Eucadia (Ucadia), 5 attended by the finest athletes and poets and the kings of Parthia, Franks and the Celts. 6 Marcus Aurelius did then pronounce the betrothal of his son Lucius Cornclius Commodus, 7 to Hippolyta the daughter of Hippocrates as a sign of unity between Rome and Eucadia (Ucadia), 8 and that when she came of age in three years they would be wed. 9 Yet soon after the main feast of kings and emperors, 10 the assassins of Justinianus Calpernius Piso dressed as Parthians did strike, 11 and Marcus Aurelius did succumb to poison. 12 Other agitators of Piso in Athens did demand the head of Sanatruces as a serpent, 13 demanding Parthia be utterly destroyed for such perfidy. 14 Upon the murder of Marcus Aurelius, King Sanatruces did abdicate, 15 and hand authority to his son Artabanus before ordering his remaining guard be executed, 16 as punishment for permitting a traitor among their midst, 17 and then travelling in simple clothes to the Citadel of Rome, 18 to live the rest of his days as atonement for the death of the man that had saved so many. 19 Commodus and Artabanus did then mass legions against the Maniacs and Babylon, 20 to wipe from the face of the earth the false religion and insanity of the Piso. 21 Yet Justinianus Calpernius Piso as Mani and his son Abram Origen did secretly escape, 22 and find refuge in the east at Gor in the Province of Pars. 23 Soon after the legions of Rome and the army of Parthia destroyed the Mani kingdom, 24 and tore the ancient city of Babylon down to its foundations and killing every living thing, 25 proclaiming that the Whore of Babylon shall never again rise up to threaten the world. 26 At the same time in Africa, Lucius Septimius Severus did seize Leptis Magna, 27 and the lands of Mauretania, before declaring himself an ally of Commodus, 28 and that he would not disrupt the shipment of grain or supplies to Rome, 29 before offering to give all grain and produce without cost for a year, 30 as a sign of good faith.

C. 29

1 In the year known as 181 CE, 2 thirteen hundred and eighty one years since the dawn of the Great Age, 3 Domitia Cornelia Lucilla the third child and youngest daughter of Marcus Aurelius, 4 did finally wed Emperor Cuinneach (Kenneth) of the Celts. 5 The following year they did have a son named Cuinel (Connell). 6 In the year known as 183 CE, 7 thirteen hundred and eighty three years since the dawn of the Great Age, 8 Lucius Septimius Severus continued to supply free food to Rome, 9 as the people celebrated their prosperity and attended endless games. 10 In the same year, Emperor Lucius (Aurelius) Cornelius Commodus did wed Hippolyta. 11 The following year they did have a son, 12 they named Marcus Aurelius Cornelius Verus. 13 In the year known as 184 CE, 14 thirteen hundred and eighty four years since the dawn of the Great Age, 15 the world celebrated the 16th Olympiad at Athens in Eucadia (Ucadia), 16 as Commodus did reward the good faith and honour of Lucius Septimius Severus, 17 by making him Consul and Legate for Africa. 18 In the same year, Emperor Commodus appointed Marcus Atilius Aeditumus, 19 as Praetorian Prefect and Protector of Rome, 20 while the emperor himself spent his days living in Athens.

C. 30

1 In the year known as 188 CE, 2 thirteen hundred and eighty eight years since the dawn of the Great Age, 3 Crown Prince Aurelius Cornelius Albinus of the Franks, 4 did have a son he named Aurelius Cornelius Auspicius. 5 In the same year, before the commencement of the 17th Olympic Games, 6 Marcus Atilius Aeditumus as Praetorian and Protector of Rome, 7 sought to end the dependency and addiction of Rome to the aid of the Septima. 8 Yet the Romans who had become addicted to games, waste and superstitions, 9 rose up against the Praetorian and killed Marcus Atilius Aeditumus. 10 Commodus did then promise that Rome would continue to receive subsidy, 11 and appointed Marcus Aemilius Lepidus as his new Praetorian. 12 In the year known as 189 CE, 13 thirteen hundred and eighty nine years since the dawn of the Great Age, 14 a giant explosion of Taupo mountain upon the northern island of the far southern lands (New Zealand) shook the world, 15 greater than at the time of Thera and the darkness before the Hyksos. 16 Within months, the lands of the south were in a deep winter, 17 and soon to the north the sun disappeared and the rains stopped, 18 and the crops and trees withered and died and snow and ice gripped, 19 the sacred isles and the northern lands of Europe and across Asia. 20 King Cuinneach (Kenneth) of Caledonia and Emperor of the Celts, 21 did abandon Holly Rood Din Eidyn (Edinburgh) to make his new capital, 22 Glastonbury in the lands of the Dumnonni. 23 King Gaius Cornelius Celestius of the Franks, 24 did abandon Cologne and travel south-west, making Trier his new capital. 25 To the far north, the last of the Normen tribes abandoned their home Asgardi, 26 and sought refuge in warmer lands to the south (Ukraine & Poland), displacing the Suebi tribes. 27

In Parthia, the people began starving and revolted against Artabanus, 28 while along the inland sea (Mediterranean), people begged the Septima to sell them precious grain. 29 Emperor Lucius Cornelius Commodus demanded that Lucius Septimius Severus release grain, 30 yet Septimus Severus complained that he was not responsible for he had sent grain, 31 but Marcus Aemilius Lepidus did not release it to the people. 32 Soon after there were riots in Rome and across Italy and Dalmatia, 33 as people attacked the stores and seized the grain. 34 When the Emperor summonsed Marcus Aemilius Lepidus to account for his actions, 35 he did declare that he judged it better some survive the end of the world, 36 than all eat today and starve tomorrow. 37 The Emperor did then appoint Lucius Septimius Severus as Protector of Rome and Consul, 38 on the pledge that he would aid in the supply of grain and help prevent great starvation. 39 Lucius Septimius Severus did at first honour his pledge ensuring grain continued to flow, 40 even as more and more people moved to the cities to seek food and shelter. 41 Yet rumours began spreading that the darkness was the cause of the Holly, 42 and that Commodus be a black wizard worshipping false gods. 43 People began killing the cats in Rome and other cities for fear, 44 they be familiars in the service of the Holly as warlocks and Commodus. 45 Soon after plague and the pox returned to Rome and cities of Africa, 46 and Lucius Septimius Severus left Rome after appointing Publius Helvius Pertinax as his agent.

C. 31

1 In the year known as 191 CE, 2 thirteen hundred and ninety one years since the dawn of the Great Age, 3 the great darkness continued across the ancient world, 4 as not only were people dying of starvation and exposure to the cold across Europe, 5 but hundreds of thousands were sick and dying as plague and pox had returned to cities, 6 in the absence of cats and reason. 7 Only the cities of the Celts and Eucadia (Ucadia) remained free of sickness, 8 such that large numbers sought refuge and sanctuary in the kingdom of heaven on earth. 9 Justinianus Calpernius Piso as Mani and his son Abram Origen did emerge from hiding, 10 with a new army of fanatics from Gor in the Province of Pars into Parthia. 11 Yet the false religion of Mania had evolved beyond pure fear and indoctrination. 12 Now those who followed Mani as Maniacs did have a symbol of their devotion to insanity, 13 in the symbol of the fish and the fish head and the chevron as the symbols of the Piso. 14 Justinianus Calpernius Piso demanded that followers begin wearing woollen headdress, 15 called Kippa to hide their thoughts and minds from the Divine Creator, 16 and as an outward sign of devotion to Sabaoth as the Lord of Hosts, 17 and that they did dedicate their life to being ignorant slaves and to live like monkeys. 18 Justinianus Calpernius Piso as Mani did pronounce: Verily Lord Sabaoth, 19 has brought upon those who teach intellect and reason and serve heaven, 20 the end of the world and terrible destruction for their hubris. 21 For none shall find love nor wisdom

through intellect but through mindless devotion, 22 that they pray to spirits they do not know without question, 23 that they follow my edicts even unto death and their own misery, 24 that they act as sheep till they become as sheep and I their shepherd. 25 For white is black, true is lies, good is evil and evil is good. 26 Verily, I shall send out an army of preachers who will spread falsities and fear, 27 that the people be not able to tell right from wrong, good from bad, truth from lie. 28 I say to you, even men who proclaim to be virtuous be prepared to kill for money, 29 and turn a blind eye to evil for the safety of a home. 30 That women most pure be corrupted into prostitutes and demons to control their men, 31 upon the promise of safety and the fear of losing what little they possess. 32 My teachers shall be like wolves in the skins of sheep among the flock, 33 and such madness they shall spring forth that the old world shall collapse from within, 34 and only the Piso and those that serve with absolute dedication shall rule, 35 as gods among such stupid and ignorant animals as mankind.

C. 32

1 In the year known as 192 CE, 2 thirteen hundred and ninety two years since the dawn of the Great Age, 3 upon the eve of 18th Olympic Games at Athens in Eucadia (Ucadia), 4 as the world did continue to suffer great hunger and fear, 5 Lucius Septimius Severus staged a coup against Praetorian Prefect Marcus Aemilius Lepidus, 6 having it appear he had been murdered by mobs in the absence of Lucius Septimius Severus. 7 It was Publius Helvius Pertinax who then appeared to capture the perpetrators and restore order. 8 Lucius Septimius Severus pleaded with Commodus that he appoint Publius Helvius Pertinax, 9 and replace his bodyguards with men that could be trusted for fear of a plot against the Emperor. 10 Commodus agreed and Publius Helvius Pertinax and a company of Praetorian loyal to the Septima, 11 did come to Athens on the pretence of protecting the Emperor. 12 Yet upon the first night of the Games the new Praetorian Prefect Publius Helvius Pertinax, 13 did murder the Holly Emperor Commodus as well as Empress Hippolyta and their son Verus. 14 On the news of such a vile and wicked act the world was in uproar, 15 yet before Publius Helvius Pertinax and his Praetorian could be captured, 16 he did escape back to Rome pursued by Heraclites the brother of the slain Hippolyta. 17 Safely back behind the walls of Rome, Publius Helvius Pertinax did arrange for the Praetorian, 18 to elect him as Emperor proclaiming that the people have the right to choose their own leader, 19 and the people had spoken so let no god or spirit defy the will of the people. 20 At first the forces of Heraclites did seek to break the gates of Rome to no avail, 21 until Lucius Septimius Severus did declare that he would land in Italy, 22 with an army of two hundred thousand and every one guilty of aiding the murderers, 23 shall be held to account and executed. 24 Yet the defences of Rome did hold stronger than expected, 25 as the residents did fear for their own lives at the hand of Septima, 26 such that he

did send for a hundred thousand more reinforcements. 27 Yet still the walls of Rome did not fall until Septima did hurl gold coins, 28 into the city and proclaimed that Rome had nothing to fear if they deliver but one head, 29 that of Publius Helvius Pertinax. 30 Within the early hours of the next day the pretend Emperor Helvius Pertinax was dead, 31 and the people of Rome surrendered and opened the gates.

C. 33

1 In the year known as 193 CE, 2 thirteen hundred and ninety three years since the dawn of the Great Age, 3 King Gaius Cornelius Celestius did give up the ghost. 4 The Crown of the Franks did befall to his son Aurelius Cornelius Albinus. 5 King Aurelius Cornelius Albinus of the Franks did then demand that Lucius Septimius Severus, 6 pledge the loyalty of his legions to Albinus as the lawful and rightful heir, 7 and grandson of Marcus Aurelius. 8 Yet Lucius Septimus Severus refused, saying the Goddess Cybele as Queen of Heaven, 9 and Magna Mater the protector and mother of Rome had ordained him Septimus Severus, 10 to be the servant of servants under Quintus Septimus Tertullianus as Pontifex Maximus. 11 Quintus Septimus Tertullianus did then arrange a grand procession through Rome, 12 where the people of Rome pledged their souls to Magna Mater the mother of Moloch, 13 the true name of Satan to be protected from the plague and further misfortune. 14 Thus Lucius Septimius Severus was proclaimed by the adoring people of Rome, 15 as their one true Emperor.

Book 24

Age of Dark Cults

[194 - 277 CE]

C. 1

In the year known as 194 CE, 2 thirteen hundred and ninety four years since the dawn of the Great Age, 3 King Aurelius Cornelius Albinus of the Franks continued to prepare a mass army, 4 to confront the African mercenary hoards of impostor Lucius Septimius Severus in Italia. 5 Many of the Celts and Roman provinces did pledge their allegiance to the Franks, 6 in Hispania, Gallia, Asia and Egypt as well as the kingdom of Eucadia (Ucadia). 7 Yet the Septimius did succeed in purchasing the loyalty of many, such as the province of Illyrium, 8 of Dalmatia, Moesia, Thracia and Syria with the loyalty of Mauretania (Africa). 9 In the year known as 195 CE, 10 thirteen hundred and ninety five years since the dawn of the Great Age, 11 Lucius Septimius Severus did order a mercenary army of more than thirty thousand to land, 12 at Nicopolis on the western side of Eucadia (Ucadia). 13 Priest King Heraclites of Eucadia (Ucadia) did then withdraw his legions from Albinus. 14 Thus Albinus was forced to delay his invasion of Italia and come to the aid of Heraclites. 15 Albinus then ordered his main army of the Franks to move from the province of Narbonensis, 16 to capture Gallia Cisalpina and the gateway to Italy and force the Septima to counter, 17 and split their own forces in defence. 18 In the same year King Clodius of the Suebi did form a new confederation, 19 including the Chatti and Marcomanni known as the Alemanni against the Franks. 20 The Septima then did secure a treaty with Clodius and the Alemanni against the Franks, 21 who descended into Gallia Cisalpina against the mass Frank army to stop their advance. 22 In the year known as 196 CE, 23 thirteen hundred and ninety six years since the dawn of the Great Age, 24 as the main army of the Franks were engaged against the Alemanni, 25 Lucius Septimius Severus landed a large mercenary army at Marsallia (Marsailles), 26 moving north and threatening to cut off and surround the Franks. 27 King Aurelius Cornelius Albinus of the Franks was forced to call upon his reserves, 28 to defend against the invasion of Gallia while his army fought a retreat from Italia. 29 Upon the withdrawal from Gallia Cisalpina King Clodius and the Alemanni did invade, 30 and seize Germania

Superior and Raetia and Noricum. 31 Lucius Septimius Severus did then put his mercenary hoard to work, 32 in unearthing the cursed ruins of Lucifer (Lyon) in search of hidden gold and treasure. 33 Soon the city was free of its earthen tomb such that Septimius Severus did declare, 34 it to be a sacred city and extension of Rome as Colonia Lugdunum (Lyon). 35 In the year known as 197 CE, 36 thirteen hundred and ninety seven years since the dawn of the Great Age, 37 the Franks did face against the mass mercenary army of the Septimius near Colonia Lugdunum (Lyons). 38 After days of bloody fighting the mercenary army was routed, 39 yet Lucius Septimius Severus did manage to escape with thousands of mercenaries. 40 With the Franks no longer able to mount an invasion against the Septima, 41 upon the losses of thousands in such bloody battle, 42 King Aurelius Cornelius Albinus of the Franks did order that every structure, 43 of Colonia Lugdunum (Lyons) be torn down to its foundations, 44 that none may live or trade midst its ruins.

C. 2

1 In the year known as 201 CE, 2 fourteen hundred and one years since the dawn of the Great Age, 3 the Normen invaders succeeded in pushing the Goti (Goths) to the edge of the Black Sea, 4 far from their original homelands (Sweden and Russia). 5 The Goti (Goths) then defeated and captured the west of Scythia. 6 Yet rather than slaughtering the Scythians the Goti (Goths) honoured their defeated leaders, 7 through Matrimonial treaty and the retention of land and property. 8 Thus King Augis of the Goti (Goths) with his two sons Amali and Balti, 9 proclaimed the new kingdom named Ouimi, 10 Creating a new capital at the mouth of the Volga River called Arhemar. 11 In the year known as 202 CE, 12 fourteen hundred and two years since the dawn of the Great Age, 13 Priest King Heraclites of Eucadia (Ucadia), 14 did give up the ghost. 15 The role of Priest King and protector of paradise, 16 and custodian of the kingdom of Heaven on Earth, 17 did befall to his son whose name was Hippocrates. 18 Lucius Septimius Severus sought at first to take advantage of the death, 19 by ordering his son Publius Septimius Geta to lead a Mercenary army, 20 to capture and destroy the Pappas in Athens. 21 Yet the mercenaries and legions across the Empire began to revolt on account of unpaid pledges, 22 with many of the mercenaries returning home to Africa, Syria and Illyria. 23 Lucius Septimius Severus then ordered the arrest of Praetorian Prefect Gaius Fulvius Plautianus, 24 falsely claiming Plautianus had deliberately withheld the pay of the legions and mercenaries, 25 and had colluded with the Parthians to steal the gold of Rome. 26 The Septima then ordered that the Castellum Citadella (Castel de Angelo) in Rome, 27 and sacred sanctuary of the Parthians be stormed to search for the gold. 28 When some gold and other jewels were found, Lucius Septimius Severus did then proclaim, 29 this be proof of the perfidy of the Parthians and that any soldier willing to fight for Rome, 30 would be paid their weight in the gold of the Parthians. 31 Lucius Septimius

Severus did then appoint jurist Aemilius Papianus as the new Praetorian Prefect, 32 under the law that no mercenary or legionnaire was free from service unless by a letter, 33 sealed in honour by the emperor as a discharge of their duties and that any man who sought to leave, 34 was therefore dishonourable and a coward to be beaten to death by his colleagues, 35 else a legion must be decimated in punishment for such cowardice. 36 Lucius Septimius Severus then ordered it be a duty of all male Romans to serve in military service, 37 for not less than seven years and that to refuse to obey such conscription, 38 was punishable by death unless a significant fine be paid. 39 The orders and news of the crusade against Parthia had the intended effect, 40 and the mercenary legions returned to strength and the grip of the Septima held. 41 Upon news of the depth of the treachery and desperation of the Septima, 42 Parthian King Artabanus bemoaned saying: The greed and avarice of these merchants dooms all. 43 For in such delicate times we cannot both feed ourselves and fight. 44 Thus these traders of slavery and banking condemn all of us into their madness.

C. 3

1 In the year known as 203 CE, 2 fourteen hundred and three years since the dawn of the Great Age, 3 Lucius Septimius Severus led a huge mercenary army seeking fortune into Parthia, 4 where like the worst of bandits and thieves they pillaged, raped and destroyed everything, 5 even unto the capital Castela Metropolis being a city sacred to Trajan and to Rome, 6 but meant nothing to pirates and robbers from Africa, Dalmatia, Moesia and Syria. 7 For all that was so priceless destroyed, the marauders of the Septimius failed to find, 8 the vast treasures they so desperately desired. 9 Even Abram Calpernius Piso and his household were forced to flee Babylon, 10 to the patronage of Baal-Zebul, the head of the Galli of the necropolis of Ur, 11 as Babylon was torn to pieces in a frenzy of looting and madness. 12 Yet upon several crushing defeats against a vastly smaller Parthian army, 13 the mercenaries turned south to Arabia Petrea and the promise of hidden treasure. 14 In the year known as 204 CE, 15 fourteen hundred and four years since the dawn of the Great Age, 16 the Great Holly King Cúirt (Arthur) mac Cúinn as High King of Ireland, 17 did give up the ghost. 18 He was succeeded by his son Cúirmac mac Cúirt also the son of Sabina Cornelia Clementia, 19 and great great great grandson of Jesus and Mariamne. 20 Upon his coronation, Holly High King Cúirmac mac Cúirt did summons all the tribes to Tara, 21 including the Holly Kings of Leinster, Ulster, Connacht and Munster. 22 There in the Great Hall of Tara, Cúirmac did speak to the assembled kings: 23 Verily, if We (the Cuilliaéan) be the true foundation stone of heaven upon which the covenant, 24 of the ancient gods and man has rested since the beginning of time, 25 and if we truly be the Diaspora as descended from Yahusia (Jesus) and Mariamne, 26 as witnesses to the truth that all men be borne equal and that none be above the law, 27 then it is encumbered upon us as the Holly to

fulfil our obligations of such sacred office, 28 and be exemplars to all men and women of the highest morals and ideals. 29 That no knowledge be hidden nor held to ransom even if it be the most powerful of tools. 30 Nor may we judge mankind to be not worthy to receive the lessons of history, 31 the truth of ancestry and the wonder and power of reasoning of a properly educated mind. 32 Indeed, it be our sacred obligation and our solemn duty that every generation and every king, 33 be competent to rule in honour and humility and wisdom. 34 For if there be tyrants it be as much the fault of the Holly for failing to teach the people, 35 the nature of law, of justice and civilisation. 36 And if there be men who claim themselves to be gods above others then this truly be our fault, 37 for the wilful arrogance and stubbornness of the Holly for thousands of years, 38 was to allow themselves to be known as gods among men, 39 yet forbid the complete emancipation of the souls of all mankind. 40 I prostrate myself before heaven seven times seven and ask all spirits for forgiveness, 41 for all the Holly Priests and Kings that have lived and died, 42 and yet failed to fulfil their Divine Commission. 43 I therefore pledge to you present upon this sacred day and place, 44 that it be the mandate of heaven that each and every Holly be a saviour to mankind; 45 to teach and counsel and guide, so that wilful ignorance that is the only true evil, cannot stand. 46 That this Sacred and inviolable mandate be perpetual no matter what the age or cost. 47 So that even in the darkest of hours it shall be the Holly who must forgive and remember, 48 who must teach and rise above such ignorance and madness, 49 that only men of good character and reason be worthy leaders and priests. 50 Thus let it be known now and forever more that the sacred Isle of Eire (Ireland), 51 be a place of equality and excellence and the highest learning, 52 that none who come in earnest intention shall be denied the highest education. 53 Holly High King Cúirmac mac Cúirt then ordered a new standard be created as the yellow field, 54 upon which a Lion rampant displayed its power and yet its duty to all men. 55 A round table was then commissioned in the Kings Hall of Tara, 56 around which the kings did meet as equals. 57 Wise Holly King Cúirmac did build four great new universities, 58 to compliment Clonmacnoise upon the River Shannon in Leinster. 59 In the Kingdom of Ulster, he did build the University of Bangor on the Belfast Lough. 60 For the Kingdom of Connacht, he did build the University of Clonfert in West Gallway. 61 For the Kingdom of Meath, Cúirmac he did build the University of Clonard upon the River Boyne. 62 For the Kingdom of Munster the king did build the University of Cork upon the River Lee. 63 Scribes from all the lands were then invited to come to Eire (Ireland) to attend and learn, 64 and to view the greatest collections of ancient and uncorrupted manuscripts of knowledge, 65 remaining upon the planet from the times of Ebla and the Hyksos, 66 to the Great Prophets of Yeb and the great empires and philosophers of Eliada and Rome. 67 Upon such wonders, soon it became mandatory that the children of all great Celtic kings, 68 and Diaspora did come to Eire (Ireland) for their education. 69 Even mortal enemies and kings entwined in bitter conflict did send their sons, 70 from as far and diverse as Parthia and India to Rome and Mauritania they did come. 71 And for one brief and glorious moment, 72 the most sacred of Isles became a beacon of hope of a wiser and more reasoned world.

C. 4

1 In the year known as 206 CE, 2 fourteen hundred and six years since the dawn of the Great Age, 3 the army of King Aurelius Cornelius Albinus of the Franks, 4 did cross to the east of the Rhine River between Argentorate and Mogontiacum, 5 against the Alemanni Confederation and King Clodius. 6 A second army of the Franks did attack and reclaim Vesontio and much of Germania Superior. 7 King Clodius did then send word to Lucius Septimius Severus to come to his aid. 8 Septimius Severus did then promise to send mercenaries to the Alemanni to defeat the Franks. 9 In the year known as 207 CE, 10 fourteen hundred and seven years since the dawn of the Great Age, 11 Septimius Severus and his mercenary army did first return to Rome, 12 whereupon Septimius Severus demanded the strengthening of defences against a Frankish attack. 13 Yet rather than sending troops to King Clodius of the Suebi, 14 Septimius Severus ordered his mercenary hoard to depart for an invasion of Englia. 15 Upon news that Lucius Septimius Severus had broken his word to the Suebi, 16 the Marcomanni and Chatti abandoned the Alemanni alliance, leaving the Suebi tribes alone. 17 King Clodius did then anoint his son Caracallus as King of Swabia (Switzerland), 18 to defend their new homeland to the last woman and child against the Franks. 19 On news of the demise of the Alemanni, King Albinus did offer terms to Clodius, 20 that on his oath he not attack the Suebi tribes or his son in Swabia, 21 if he withdraw from Augusta Rauracorum in peace and swear to never raise arms again. 22 Yet King Clodius refused, saying: Upon terms we did lose our lands (Ukraine and Poland), 23 against the Normen who saw such words as weakness, 24 and upon trust of words again we are abandoned by the false wizards of Leptis Magna. 25 The women of the Suebi dressed in black and wearing charm belts and relics of dead ancestors, 26 did then come before their loved ones who offered teeth, hair and some even fingers, 27 then woven by the women into their charm belts and necklaces, 28 whereupon the elder women did proclaim a high curse before the armies: 29 Let those who betrayed and doomed our sons suffer the same pain and anguish of their deaths. 30 Thus before the setting of the sun, the Suebi King and army were destroyed, 31 and King Albinus kept his word and did not invade Swabia (Switzerland). 32 In the same year, 33 King Augis of the Goti with his son Balti did conquer the mountainous lands of the Carpi and Daci, 34 but did not invade the Roman Province of Dacia, nor Moesia Inferior. 35 King Augis did then declare the Kingdom of Thervingi of the mountains and forests to be Balti 36 and the Kingdom of Greuthungi of the steppe grasslands and pebbly

coasts to be Amali. 37 In the same year, 38 as Abram Capernius Piso and his household did prepare to leave the Necropolis of Ur, 39 the Baal-Zebul as Chief Priest of the Galli and Lord of the City of Spirits, 40 did address Abram and his son Isaac and the priests assembled, saying: 41 It is written that nothing be chance in this world, for fate be our companion. 42 Verily, the earth has never witnessed such a house so desirous and obsessed at any cost, 43 than the Piso in inventing the course of history unto its own name. 44 How then could such events have occurred if not by the force of heaven and earth, 45 that the house of Piso come to the birthplace of humanity and the guardians of the dead, 46 to bear witness to the mortality of all civilisations and the truth of all men, 47 that we were created by the gods to be their perfect slaves, 48 and that if a man or women be shown their true nature then they willingly enslave themselves. 49 For no force or army or religion or idea be more powerful than the mind, 50 and only a few be destined to know its secrets and to transcend its weaknesses. 51 When the Baal-Zebul as Lord of the City of Spirits had finished, Abram did reply: 52 To all here present I give this vow in blood to all the Piso and all who serve the Piso, 53 that upon this day and forever more, the Piso shall honour and serve the wisdom of the priests, 54 the servants of the dead and the messengers of our true creators. 55 Truly the law shall be above all men and that none possess to change it; 56 and that the highest expression of honour and respect be self discipline and humility, 57 and the worst transgression be wilful ignorance and arrogance. 58 For no man serve the Lord of Hosts by abandoning reason and acting as an animal, 59 and no man find reward in performing rituals for which they choose to be wilfully ignorant. 60 Verily, only a man who respects divine knowledge and reason respects heaven and earth. 61 Thus we shall restore the laws of our true creators and the balance of heaven and earth, 62 that men and women bred to be animals shall be treated with kindness and a firm hand, 63 and that men and women borne to be slaves shall respect the law and perform their obligations, 64 and those few who possess the selfless discipline to overcome shall be custodians. 65 The Baal-Zebul and Galli then revealed to Abram and his son Isaac a fortune of treasure, 66 gathered from offerings to the dead kings and queens and princes at Ur over hundreds of years, 67 and that this vast treasure be at the service of the Piso if they honour their word, 68 in restoring the law of the lesser gods and creators of mankind. 69 Abram Calpernius Piso and his son Isaac did pledge solemn vows to live as paupers, 70 and use such wealth only to serve the will of the Lord of Hosts and his plan. 71 The Galli did then direct Abram and Isaac to go to the city of Darabgerd (Darab), 72 in the Satrap of Persis (Parsa) where it was prophesied the revolution must begin.

C. 5

1 In the year known as 207 CE, 2 fourteen hundred and seven years since the dawn of the Great Age, 3 the mercenary hoards of the Septima did

land at Vannes in the lands of the Amoricans (Brittany), 4 where the pirate King Cogidubnus of the Amoricans did pledge his pirate fleet, 5 if Lucius Septimus Severus recognise him as king over the ancient homelands of the Britons. 6 Word came to Holly High King Cuinneach (Kenneth) of Englia (England) at Glastonbury, 7 of the mercenary fleet of the Septima and their alliance with the Amorican pirates. 8 Yet the legions of Englia were under strength on account of the promise to Albinus, 9 in service against the Suebi in Germania. 10 Holly High King Cuinneach (Kenneth) ordered that Din Eiden (Edinburgh) and HollyRood, 11 be reinforced and defended at all cost as the High King and his court travelled north, 12 from Glastonbury to return to awaken Holly Rood for the first time in nineteen years. 13 In the year known as 208 CE, 14 fourteen hundred and eight years since the dawn of the Great Age, 15 Lucius Septimius Bassianus, the son of Lucius Septimus Severus, aided by King Cogidubnus, 16 did first attack Cambria with such ferocity that it shocked the defenders. 17 Holly King Cuinneach (Kenneth) did order then the kings of Bernicia and Deiria to aid Cambria. 18 Yet so determined be the Amoricans spurred on by revenge and the Mercenaries by stories of gold, 19 that within weeks the Cambrians were overwhelmed and Cordor (Colchester) was lost. 20 Before the Celts could muster more forces against the Septima, 21 Lucius Septimus Severus did land an army in Cantia and lay siege to Cantor (Cantebury). 22 Now with two mercenary armies upon the lands of Englia (England), 23 Holly King Cuinneach (Kenneth) did call upon Marcus Artorius Castus the Pendraig (Dragon), 24 to defend the midlands and stop the Holly kingdom of Englia from being cut in two. 25 Upon the fall of Cantor (Cantebury) Lucius Septimus Severus did order his army, 26 to unearth the ruins of Londonium as the dead city cursed as a place without soul, 27 by Celtic Emperor Yahusia (Jesus) more than one hundred and twenty years earlier. 28 Lucius Septimus Severus then ordered that gold and jewels be secretly buried, 29 to encourage the robbers and thieves to unearth the city faster. 30 Thus within only a year the most cursed place in history was reborn. 31 A place from which no valid law or spirit could ever be born or reside. 32 Lucius Septimius Severus did then declare King Cogidubnus the King of Britonia, 33 with its capital at Regentium (Chichester) 50 miles south-west of Londinium upon the coast. 34 And did rename Cordor (Colchester) to Colonia Victricensis. 35 Lucius Septimius Severus did then speak to the mercenary and pirate hoard, saying: 36 Let us celebrate for upon this day I dedicate this place Colonia Londinium as part of Rome. 37 Therefore, all who are citizens of Londinium shall be honoured as citizens in Rome. 38 To each and every man who has fought for his freedom and his family here today, 39 I say that you each be full owners of Londinium as this is your city to have and hold, 40 that no Celtic King may proclaim it be Holly Land for it be the Holly who surrendered it, 41 and it be all of you who gave it salvation. 42 Lucius Septimius Severus did then order huge fortifications to be built to protect, 43 the first private city in the history of the Roman Empire. 44 The mercenaries willingly worked day and night to then build a wall more than 2 miles long, 45 and 9 feet wide and 20 feet high enclosing the city of some 33 acres. 46 Yet before the fortifications were completed Lucius Septimius Severus did fall gravely ill, 47 suffering terrible pains and fever for which no amount of relief could diminish. 48 Lucius Septimius Severus and his son Lucius Septimius Bassianus with their Praetorian, 49 did travel north to evoke the ancient right of Eboracium (York) as the home of Emperors. 50 Holly King Cuinneach (Kenneth) did send word that such honour be conditional, 51 so long as Holly Rood stood untouched and upon such pledge not to attack Caledonia, 52 the Celts did permit the Septima to travel unharmed to Eboracium (York).

C. 6

1 In the year known as 208 CE, 2 fourteen hundred and eight years since the dawn of the Great Age, 3 Pappa Basileus Heraclites of Eukadia (Ucadia), 4 did have a son he named Hermes. 5 In the same year, 6 Holly High King Cúirmac mac Cúirt of Eire (Ireland) and descendant of Yahusiah (Jesus) and Mariamne, 7 did summons the lesser Kings and tribal Kings to Tara to speak of the events in Englia, saying: 8 In less than one generation, our kingdoms have become a beacon of hope unto this world, 9 as sworn enemies choose to send their children to our Universities to learn, 10 and become men of reason and of culture and discipline. 11 Yet it is not enough to emancipate the mind if men remain enslaved by the laws that govern them. 12 Verily the Holly have freed the ancient vaults of knowledge to the world, 13 yet we have collectively failed to free the land and soil upon which they live and prosper. 14 Such injustice then has empowered men of greed and malice to seize the moment, 15 and proclaim to the lost and oppressed that they may own land that is not theirs to give. 16 Thus, it is insufficient to proclaim the Holly merely be the custodians of land for heaven, 17 for those without land and shelter believe only the lies of pirates and thieves, 18 as no action to the contrary is demonstrated by the Diaspora. 19 Verily, men now seek to make good their talents and forge their own paths, 20 as much as men in communities and tribes seek the old ways of common property. 21 Therefore, let these maxims herald the sacred law of the land, 22 that none may defile heaven nor the rights granted to every man and woman. 23 Verily, no man, nor king, nor tribe, nor religion or empire may own the earth or sky, 24 for we be granted the right of ownership of only one form of property, 25 being the very flesh and blood body we inhabit as mind and spirit. 26 All other forms of right be nothing more than the right of use as custodians. 27 All men therefore possess the right of use of the land equally with none higher, 28 and none may claim ownership of the land by blood, or covenant or divine right. 29 Instead, let the measure of land be fair and equal that the bounds be clear, 30 that a man be entitled to the use of his plot being one seventh of an acre, 31 as the promise of eighty four feet by one hundred and twenty feet under

heaven. 32 Let the edges of the boundaries be clearly marked and surveyed, 33 not less than once every seven years. 34 For no man may claim use of land that he has never seen or has never surveyed. 35 Thus, let a man have right of use of his plot for seventy years, 36 as the fair length of a productive life, 37 that none may steal or seize such land. 38 In the year known as 210 CE, 39 fourteen hundred and ten years since the dawn of the Great Age, 40 Pappa Basileus Heraclites of Eukadia (Ucadia), 41 did have a second child and daughter he named Hypatia. 42 In the same year, 43 Lucius Septimius Severus still crippled with unbearable pain and sickness, 44 did summons his two sons Publius Septimius Geta and Lucius Septimius Bassianus, 45 to Palatinum Eboracium (York) where he did announce before his court, 46 that Lucius Septimius Bassianus would rule the western provinces, 47 while Publius Septimius Geta would rule the eastern provinces from Rome. 48 In the year known as 211 CE, 49 fourteen hundred and eleven years since the dawn of the Great Age, 50 impostor Emperor Lucius Septimus Severus did give up the ghost. 51 Upon death of Lucius Septimius Severus, 52 the mercenary army disbanded as the mercenary legions from Dalmatia and Pannonia, 53 did return to their homelands and civil war soon erupted within these provinces. 54 In Salona, Gaius Carinus Dardanis was declared king by the mercenary legions, 55 and formed the new kingdom of Dardania. 56 In Naissus, Marcus Valerius Claudius and the mercenary legions did declare independence, 57 and the independent kingdom of Valeria, 58 and in Siscia in Pannonia, Lucius Domitius Aurelianus declared an independent kingdom, 59 with the former mercenaries naming it the kingdom of Savia. 60 To the north King Caracallus of the Suebi moved south from Swabia (Switzerland) into Italia, 61 while in Englia the Celtic legions of Holly King Cuinneach (Kenneth) did mobilize, 62 against the north of Britonia and Colonia Victricensis (Colchester). 63 Facing the loss of the east, Publius Septimius Geta in Rome declared himself Emperor, 64 and ordered that the Senate pass his edict to conscript all able males into service, 65 to defend Italia and the Empire. 66 Yet Quintus Septimus Tertullianus convinced the Senate to make him Emperor, 67 and seek terms with King Caracallus and save Rome. 68 Publius Septimius Geta and all his supporters were then rounded up and arrested, 69 as Quintus Septimus Tertullianus was appointed Emperor of Rome. 70 Tertullian did then send word on honour of truce to invite emissaries of Dardanis and Caracallus, 71 and Valerian and Aurelian to attend his coronation ceremony and witness the execution of Geta. 72 Quintus Septimus Tertullianus did then institute an elaborate coronation ceremony, 73 to emphasise his powers, adopting the name of Pontifex Victor (Pope Victor), 74 as the first Pontiff to worship Cybele as Magna Mater and Queen of Heaven. 75 At the conclusion of the coronation celebration Publius Septimius Geta and one thousand, 76 of his supporters were publicly executed in a series of brutal and cruel exhibitions, 77 witnessed by King Caracallus and the other kings and emissaries. 78 Pope Victor then appointed Marcus Opellius Macrinus as Praetorian Prefect, 79 and upon the blood of the slain Geta splashed across his robes, 80 Pope Victor did proclaim King Caracallus of the Suebi to be the first Gordian (Guardian) of Rome, 81 and that the Suebi be honoured as citizens of Rome. 82 King Caracallus and the other kings did agree to terms and the fate of the east was settled.

C. 7

1 In the year known as 212 CE, 2 fourteen hundred and twelve years since the dawn of the Great Age, 3 as Lucius Septimius Bassianus remained at Palatinum Eboracium (York), 4 with his households and his son Lucius Septimius Elagabalus, 5 the forces of Holly King Cuinneach (Kenneth) did recapture Colonia Victricensis (Colchester), 6 pushing the forces of King Cogidubnus of Britonia south to the bounds of Cantia, 7 and the pirate kingdom of Londinium. 8 In the same year, 9 upon the first anniversary of Quintus Septimus Tertullianius as Emperor and Pontifex Maximus, 10 and the first Roman Pontiff of the Magna Mater and Queen of Heaven as Pope Victor, 11 Pope Victor did issue his first edict saying: Verily, it is the Great Mother that protects us. 12 So it is fitting that our petitions and sacrifices be unto her the Queen of Heaven and all the gods, 13 immaculately conceived without blemish of any kind of the base transgressions of men and women. 14 Therefore, let it be known now and forever more that no other god be greater than the Virgin Queen. 15 Thus if Romans seek to honour Mithra, they must honour Moloch the son of Cybele, 16 and if Romans wish protection from the terrors of this world then they must pay in blood. 17 For the Blessed Virgin Queen be a force more fearful than any barbarian army, 18 and she will reign fire and brimstone upon the heads of those who ignore her teachings. 19 Thus let it be said that no woman may be a priest. 20 For women menstruate and are filthy in thoughts and unreliable messengers. 21 Indeed the entirety of women have proven themselves empty vessels, 22 possessed by nothing but the shallowest of desires and wants of material wealth. 23 Verily women have abandoned their souls and proclaimed themselves to be the purveyors of fear. 24 Thus men and men alone may profess sacred orders to our Virgin Mother in Heaven. 25 And only men may recite her sacred meditations of rota (Rosary of Cybele). 26 For the highest expression of the devotion of men and priests of Moloch and Cybele, 27 be the sacrifice of their progeny and dedication to celibacy. 28 For truly no more true priest of Rome there be than one willing to suffer the burden of celibacy. 29 Upon his speech, a stream of young men did step forth within the Forum, 30 and one by one they slashed off their genitals until the streets were covered in their blood, 31 as some did fall and die from such self inflicted wounds to the joy of Pope Victor and his Curia. 32 In the year known as 213 CE, 33 fourteen hundred and thirteen years since the dawn of the Great Age, 34 King Augis of the Goti did give up the ghost. 35 The crown did then befall to his eldest son Amali the King of Greuthungi. 36 Yet following the burial of their father, his younger brother

named Balti, 37 King of Thervingi (former lands of Carpi and Daci) refused to yield, 38 saying their father saw fit they command their own kingdoms. 39 A bitter civil war did then erupt between the Goti, 40 as the forces of Amali of the Kingdom of Greuthungi sought to defeat his brother Balti. 41 So bloody was the conflict that within a year Amali did call for truce, 42 that no more Goti blood be spilled for such madness. 43 Sensing opportunity midst such conflict, Pope Victor did send word to King Balti, 44 to come in peace to Rome as an honoured guest recognised by Rome as the true king of the Goti.

C. 8

1 In the year known as 214 CE, 2 fourteen hundred and fourteen years since the dawn of the Great Age, 3 King Balti of the Goti Thervingi Kingdom did come to Rome with his guard, 4 to be warmly greeted by Quintus Septimius Tertullianius as Pope Victor. 5 Pope Victor did offer King Balti the sum of 36,000,000 denarii if the Goti supply men as legions, 6 to take the place of the former mercenaries of Pannonia, Dalmatia and Moesia, 7 who remained allies, but as their own kingdoms and refused to give more men. 8 King Balti agreed to provide ten legions as 60,000 men to Pope Victor as Emperor. 9 Quintus Septimius Tertullianius did then order the minting of a new coin to be the standard, 10 called the Victoria having a face value of two silver denarii, 11 yet having only the real weight in silver of one and a half denarii. 12 As soon as the Victoria began to be circulated, prices did rise and many became destitute. 13 In the same year, 14 King (Marcus) Aurelius Cornelius Albinus of the Franks did order greater defence in Rhaetia, 15 in the creation of a defensive wall and fort complex against Suebi attack. 16 In the same year, 17 Holly High King Cúirmac mac Cúirt of Eire (Ireland) did call all kings and tribal kings to Tara, 18 where the wise king did issue an edict, saying: 19 Let it be known to all now and forever, 20 that the ancient system of law of Honour that placed the Cuilliaéan above all others, 21 and that determined a fine in monetary value for every offence to banish blood feud, 22 has itself become repugnant and manifestly unfair. 23 For it has allowed the rich to pay for their transgressions without inconvenience, 24 yet rendered the poor perpetual bondsmen, often for one small mistake or action. 25 Thus the ones called the uibrien (O'Briens) as bonded servants are no better than slaves, 26 despite the law being clear that all forms of slavery be an abomination. 27 Further, it has created clanns of people who remain dedicated to revolution and revenge, 28 that we call the uinial (O'Niells) as the ones who have no honour, 29 on account of their disgust at what they see as two standards of law. 30 Verily I say to you, that all law must be equal and fair and so no monetary fine or penalty, 31 can be fairly rendered without injuring the truth of the law. 32 Holly High King Cúirmac mac Cúirt of Eire (Ireland) did then order the disbanding, 33 of the honour price and fine system of law of Eire (Ireland) for the first time, 34 in over one thousand

years. ₃₅ In the year known as 215 CE, ₃₆ fourteen hundred and fifteen years since the dawn of the Great Age, ₃₇ the newly formed Roman Legions of VisiGoti (Visigoths) did invade Syrian lands, ₃₈ and defeat King Abgar of Osroene, capturing the city of Edessa and making it a Roman Province. ₃₉ In the same year, ₄₀ Quintus Septimius Tertullianus as Pope Victor did order Marcus Opellius Macrinus to Alexandria, ₄₁ and execute its leading citizens on account of their satire of the Pontiff, ₄₂ and their blasphemy against Cybele as Queen of Heaven.

C. 9

₁ In the year known as 216 CE, ₂ fourteen hundred and sixteen years since the dawn of the Great Age, ₃ conditions in Italia worsened as the value of money continued to drop. ₄ When the Senate did complain of the starving people, Quintus Septimius Tertullianus did order, ₅ the leading Senators be arrested for causing the crisis and did have them executed. ₆ He then ordered the value of Silver in the Victoria be reduced to half the weight of denarii, ₇ and that only the copper sesterius continue as having the value of three asses (tre-as) and equal to one denarii, ₈ and that all silver denarii be surrendered and exchanged upon penalty of death. ₉ Yet the people of Rome did not surrender the silver coins and instead sought moneychangers, ₁₀ who melted the denarii into silver for a price and the value of money continued to fall. ₁₁ In the same year, ₁₂ Cuinel (Connell) the son of Holly King Cuinneach (Kenneth) of Caledonia (Scotland), ₁₃ and High King of the Kings of Englia (England) and Emperor of the Celts, ₁₄ did have a son, whom he named Cuinhainn (Kevin). ₁₅ In the same year, ₁₆ the Roman Legions of VisiGoti did invade Armenia and annex it under complete Roman control. ₁₇ In the year 217, ₁₈ fourteen hundred and seventeen years since the dawn of the Great Age, ₁₉ as food shortages and price rises did continue across the remnants of the Roman Empire, ₂₀ heavy rain across much of Europe caused terrible floods even unto Rome, ₂₁ that thousands did drown and crops and stores were destroyed. ₂₂ Yet when the united Senate did warn Quintus Septimius Tertullianus as Pope Victor, ₂₃ that the city would riot before it starved, Pope Victor demanded the Senate be disbanded, ₂₄ and blamed for the ill fortune befalling the people of Rome. ₂₅ In desperation the Senate did call upon Marcus Opellius Macrinus to do his duty, ₂₆ and soon after Marcus Opellius Macrinus did kill Quintus Septimius Tertullianus. ₂₇ Yet forewarned of the plot, Thascius Tertullianius Caecilius the son of Victor did escape. ₂₈ The Senate did then promise Marcus Opellius Macrinus be Emperor, ₂₉ if he did dispatch the last of the Septima from the Earth. ₃₀ Marcus Opellius Macrinus did then send word to Lucius Septimius Bassianus, ₃₁ that he be endorsed as the true Emperor but that without a leader, Rome be near collapse. ₃₂ Fires and riots were then staged across the city and the Praetorian delayed to act. ₃₃ On news of the events in Rome Lucius Septimius Bassianus did depart from Eboracium (York), ₃₄ yet ordered his son Lucius Septimius Elagabalus and Prateorian Publius Valerius Comazon,

35 remain at Eboracium (York) until called. 36 Upon his arrival in Rome, Lucius Septimius Bassianus was seized and executed, 37 and Marcus Opellius Macrinus was made Emperor.

C. 10

1 In the year known as 218 CE, 2 fourteen hundred and eighteen years since the dawn of the Great Age, 3 the agents of Baal-Zebul did send word to Abram Calpernius Piso and his son Isaac, 4 that the time was ordained for him to make his presence known. 5 Aided by trained fanatics of the Galli, Abram seized control of the city of Darabgerd (Darab), 6 and did kill the governor of the Satrap of Persis (Parsa) named Tiri. 7 There before the people of Darabgerd (Darab) and his militia army, Abram did speak, saying: 8 Glory be to the gods and spirits who directed our victory against the tyranny of men, 9 who care not for our salvation nor our freedom. 10 Verily, I say to you that power is not to be found in gold or jewels of fine fabrics, 11 nor in great armies and weapons of destruction but in knowledge. 12 For it is knowledge of Manes that is the only true power. 13 Knowledge of righteous and correct behaviour of mind and spirit. 14 Knowledge of the truth of heaven and earth and the origins of our species. 15 Knowledge that has been kept from you by ancient magi and holly priests for themselves. 16 These false priests speak of wisdom and enlightenment yet is the world enlightened? 17 Have these priests not ruled as if gods for thousands of years? 18 For the Cuilliaéan and Diaspora care not for your well being but their own occult power. 19 That is why they have kept this knowledge from you, that you remain slaves. 20 That you remain fearful and hungry and in pain. 21 If these priests and prophets did seek our interests, why then is the world no better? 22 Truly with this knowledge each and every man and woman may find freedom. 23 Freedom from pain and suffering and freedom from fear and their own imperfections. 24 But only if one is prepared to dedicate one's heart and mind and soul upon the journey. 25 Verily, I tell you that "good" force dwells in the realm of light and the heavens, 26 and is the father of majesty and greatness known as "Abba de Rabban" (Father of Greatness); 27 who possesses 4 faces being Time, Light, Creation and Virtue, 28 and possesses 5 Shekhinas (Tabernacles) of Intelligence, Reason, Thought, Reflection and Will. 29 The "evil" force dwells in the realm of darkness below the realm of light on earth, 30 and is the father of knowledge and teaching known as "Seytan" (Satan) king of demons, 31 and who possesses four (4) faces being Air, Fire, Earth and Water, 32 and also possesses five attributes being Forgetfulness, Greed, Avarice, Pain and Death. 33 The world of light is infinite in five directions (N, S, W, E and above), 34 yet is constrained by evil and darkness below. 35 The world of evil is infinite in five (5) directions (N, S, W, E and below), 36 yet is constrained by light above. 37 Verily, all men and women are borne with a base soul (mind) called Ahu-Man (inhuman), 38 being the state of not knowing, ignorance, stupidity, foolishness and unclean. 39 Those that educate themselves to Manes may

then develop a second soul (mind) called HuMan, 40 and a state of consciousness to act, perform and do. 41 Only those that have dedicated themselves to the highest scripture and are worthy, 42 then reach the third state of soul (mind) Ba-Man (Brahman), 43 of spiritual perfection, wisdom and hermeneutic skill. 44 For all sentient (thinking) beings who have reached the status of being "Hu-Man", 45 have free will to choose to transgress sacred law and sin (khat) or obey the law, 46 and perform a good deed (mizdah). 47 Both khat (sins) and good deeds (mizdah) accumulate over a life, 48 and transfer to the next life time, if not completely "accounted". 49 However, those that possess only a base soul (Ahu-Man) do not have "will". 50 Verily, the cause of all sorrow originates from the first man called "masya", 51 and his wife "masyaneh" who turned their back on "abba de rabban", 52 who is the father of greatness and light) and his laws ("manes"), 53 thus creating the imperfection of mankind through desire and want of material things (kama). 54 Because khat (sins) are inherited into the next lifetime, 55 one who is born poor must be obedient to their master and perform mizdah (good deeds), 56 in order to improve their position upon the Chakra as the Great Wheel of Life. 57 For the cycle of death and re-birth is but to improve and reach spiritual perfection of soul (mind), 58 to become one with the divine as Ba-Man (Brahman). 59 At the conclusion of his speech, Abram Calpenius Piso declared his new name be ArdaShah, 60 meaning wise ruler and did then order apostles of Manes to spread forth across Persis (Parsa), 61 and for those who believed record their name in a roll of the honoured, 62 and for those who did not believe, write their name in a book of the damned then kill them. 63 In the same year, 64 upon news of the murder of his father, Lucius Septimius Elagabalus did depart Eboracium (York), 65 with Praetorian Publius Valerius Comazon first to the lands of the Suebi. 66 Lucius Septimius Elagabalus did then implore to King Caracalus to remember his own oath, 67 to his uncle and the Septima in being the Gordian (Guardian) of Rome, 68 and that if he support him he would recognise all Suebi as Patricians and Citizens of Rome.

C. 11

1 In the year known as 219 CE, 2 fourteen hundred and nineteen years since the dawn of the Great Age, 3 Lucius Septimius Elagabalus and Publius Valerius Comazon aided by King Caracalus of the Suebi, 4 did descend south into Italia to confront Marcus Opellius Macrinus. 5 Macrinus did call upon King Balti of the VisiGoti to supply men to defend, 6 yet King Balti reminded him that Rome had not paid their due and the Goti owed him no allegiance. 7 Thus when the Suebi were within sixty miles of Rome, the people of Rome rebelled against Macrinus, 8 and sent his head as an offering to Elagabalus that he be the true Emperor, 9 and to call the Suebi to return to their homeland. 10 Yet Lucius Septimius Elagabalus kept his word and entered Rome with King Caracalus, 11 then proclaiming to the Senate that now and forever more the Suebi be the Gordian (Guardian), 12

and ordered the Praetorian disbanded forever. 13 Lucius Septimius Elagabalus did then appoint Gnaeus Annius Ulpianus the administrator of Rome, 14 and charged him with restoring confidence in coin and prices. 15 In the same year, 16 Cuinel (Connell) the son of Holly King Cuinneach (Kenneth) of Caledonia (Scotland), 17 and High King of the Kings of Englia (England) and Emperor of the Celts, 18 did have a daughter, whom he named Julia. 19 In the same year, 20 Holly King Cuinneach (Kenneth) of Caledonia (Scotland) did move against the Britonia, 21 putting Regentium (Chichester) and Londinium under siege. 22 King Cogidubnus the King of Britonia did send word to Lucius Septimius Elagabalus for aid, 23 and a fleet of Suebi mercenaries led by Sabinius were dispatched to stop the fall of Britonia. 24 Yet upon the time the fleet arrived at the stronghold of the Amorican pirates, 25 upon the north western coast of Hispania known as Brigantium (Brigand), 26 the forces of Holly King Cuinneach (Kenneth),had broken through at Regentium (Chichester), 27 and killed Cogidubnus, before utterly destroying the city. 28 However, the pirates of Londinium continued to fight as men possessed, 29 and the forces of Cuinneach (Kenneth) failed to break through at Londinium. 30 Upon news of the death of Cogidubnus, Lucius Septimius Elagabalus did order, 31 that the Suebi mercenaries of Sabinius take the north-west of Hispania, 32 against the Celtic Confederation of Tarraconensis under Pollienus, 33 and secure the vital silver, tin and gold mines.

C. 12

1 In the year known as 220 CE, 2 fourteen hundred and twenty years since the dawn of the Great Age, 3 Sabinius and the Suebi mercenaries did seize the north-west of Hispania to the port of Cale, 4 and did then continue south to Salamantica and the port of Felicitas Iulla and finally to Cordoba. 5 King (Marcus) Aurelius Cornelius Albinus of the Franks did not come to aid Pollienus, 6 for concern that King Caracalus of the Suebi did plan to invade Raetia and Germania. 7 King Caracalus did then order secret vaults to be built for the storing of gold and silver, 8 sent by the Suebi of Sabinius back to their homeland Swabia (Switzerland). 9 In the same year, 10 Emperor Lucius Septimius Elagabalus did request that gold, tin and silver be sent urgently, 11 to aid in the upkeep of the crumbling remains of the Roman Provinces. 12 Yet Sabinius of the Suebi did reply that not until Pollienus be defeated and the Celts crushed, 13 could supply of gold or tin or silver be assured. 14 In the year known as 221 CE, 15 fourteen hundred and twenty one years since the dawn of the Great Age, 16 King (Marcus) Aurelius Cornelius Albinus of the Franks did send troops to aid Pollienus, 17 and the march of the Suebi to control Hispania was halted. 18 Yet when Lucius Septimius Elagabalus did send an emissary to demand the supply of silver and gold, 19 be sent to Rome as tribute, Sabinius did refuse saying the gold and silver was needed, 20 to purchase more mercenaries against the reinforcements of the Franks. 21 When Lucius Septimius Elagabalus did then

protest to King Caracalus as to the refusal, 22 the King of the Suebi did reply that he was powerless to act. 23 The Emperor did secretly order Publius Valerius Comazon and three legions to capture Sabinius, 24 and return the gold, silver and tin to Rome. 25 In Hispania, Publius Valerius Comazon did surround Sabinius at Astorga and did destroy the city. 26 Yet Sabinius did escape and Publius Valerius Comazon was killed. 27 Upon news of the fall of Astorga and the order of Elagabalus, King Caracalus ordered the Suebi, 28 to assassinate the Emperor and his Suebi Guard attacked and slaughtered Elagabalus, 29 and all Senators not willing to swear absolute loyalty to the Suebi. 30 King Caracalus of the Suebi did then depart south to Rome where he proclaimed himself Emperor. 31 Upon the steps of the Senate Curia within the Forum, King Caracalus did speak, saying: 32 Near Forty years ago, the Huns (Normen) from the north did invade our lands (Ukraine & Poland), 33 and burn our villages, steal our animals and rape our women. 34 It was my Father and our King Clodius who vowed that never again would our people bow to tyrants, 35 and formed an alliance with other tribes in honour that people could live in peace and harmony. 36 Yet my father was betrayed by the very same clann which has betrayed the people of Rome, 37 and upon his death our elders and women did utter a curse against those who would trick by words. 38 Thus we established our new homeland of Swabia (Switzerland), 39 and we did accept our role as Gordian (Guardian) of Rome against liars and thieves. 40 Yet as men of low character are wont to do, Rome has suffered midst the clamouring for power, 41 so that it befell upon our people to act as Patricians and protectors of Rome to act. 42 Thus we come not to enslave Rome but to liberate it and to end the division and pain. 43 I therefore make this solemn pledge upon such sacred ground that the Senate shall be protected, 44 and that our people shall honour our solemn office of Gordians (Guardians). 45 Thus it shall be that only Suebi shall be permitted to be bankers and moneylenders, 46 to end the corruption that has brought this empire to ruin. 47 Furthermore, we announce that the mining lands of Hispania shall be held by the Suebi, 48 as the province of Gallicia to be held by our legate Orosius who shall seek terms, 49 and honour the kingdom of Tarraconensis to be recognised to the east and south. 50 And we create today the sacred office of Rationalis (Finance Minister) to Sabinius, 51 who shall oversee all banking and finance and shall be responsible for restoring stability. 52 For the Suebi are generous people and we shall lend our own gold and silver to Rome, 53 for the greater glory of all our people and the Empire. 54 Soon after, the Suebi confiscated all the gold coins of the temples of Rome, 55 to create the vaults and treasury under Sabinius.

C. 13

1 In the year known as 222 CE, 2 fourteen hundred and twenty two years since the dawn of the Great Age, 3 Aurelius Cornelius Auspicius of the Franks and son of King Aurelius Cornelius Albinus, 4 did have a second son, whom he named Gaius Cornelius

Book 24 Age of Dark Cults

Cernis, meaning wise discernment. 5 In the same year, King Artabanus of Parthia did order his governor of Susiana, 6 to crush the rebellion of Abram as ArdaShah at Darabgerd (Darab) in Parsis. 7 Yet the army of ArdaShah was victorious forcing the governor of Susiana to flee. 8 ArdaShah did order his army to pursue and crush the enemy without mercy, 9 and in a few weeks the ancient city of Susa did fall to ArdaShah. 10 In the year known as 223 CE, 11 fourteen hundred and twenty three years since the dawn of the Great Age, 12 Emperor Cuinneach (Kenneth) of the Celts, 13 Holly King of Caledonia (Scotland) and High King of the Kings of Englia (England), 14 and the great great great great grandson of Yahusiah (Jesus) and Mariamne, 15 did give up the ghost. 16 The Holly crown of Caledonia as Emperor of the Celts, 17 did then befall to his son Cuinel (Connell). 18 In the same year, 19 Thascius Tertullianus Caecilius the son of Tertullian did come out from hiding in North Africa, 20 and did travel with Julius Paulus Prudentissimus to the court of King Balti of the VisiGoti, 21 where he did beseech the VisiGoti leader to provide sufficient legions to defeat the Suebi in Rome, 22 upon the promise that the lands of Hispania be seized from the Suebi be given the VisiGoti, 23 and a perpetual income and tribute to be provided to the VisiGoti, 24 or the VisiGoti have the right to seize property and goods of the same value owed. 25 King Balti of the VisiGoti agreed and plans were made to invade Italia and Hispania. 26 In the same year, 27 upon the loss of the satrap (governor) of Susiana, Artabanus did order the governor of Carmania, 28 to seize and destroy Darabgerd (Darab) and ArdaShah. 29 Yet ArdaShah received word from a convert and spy to Manes of the impending danger, 30 and returned his army eastward to defend against the Carmania army and did defeat them, 31 before moving to claim Carmania as a new part of his new religious empire. 32 In the same year, 33 the VisiGoti and Carthage forces of Thascius Tertullianus Caecilius did invade Hispania, 34 and did annex the south of Tarraconensis and the Suebi kingdom of Gallicia. 35 Upon news of the invasion of Thascius Tertullianus Caecilius, 36 King Caracalus did order his best troops to Hispania to defend against the attack. 37 Soon after the VisiGoti did invade Italia and march quickly upon Rome. 38 The speed of the VisiGoti did catch King Caracalus by surprise, 39 and he was killed as he did try to escape northward to the safety of Swabia (Switzerland). 40 Thascius Tertullianus Caecilius did declare the conquered land of Hispania, 41 the province of Carthagensis and revived its capital as Catha Nova. 42 As promised, Thascius Tertullianus Caecilius did hand control of the province to King Balti, 43 and as promised King Balti did withdraw his troops northward away from Rome. 44 Thascius Tertullianus Caecilius did then seek terms with Chrocus the son of Caracalus, 45 that if he did swear the Suebi would no longer break their word, 46 that the VisiGoti would not attack their homeland and he be honoured as Gordian (Guardian). 47 Chrocus did then swear and the VisiGoti did withdraw with their gains and tribute. 48 Thascius Tertullianus Caecilius did then declare himself in Rome as Pope Callixtus.

C. 14

₁ In the year known as 224 CE, ₂ fourteen hundred and twenty four years since the dawn of the Great Age, ₃ Abram as ArdaShah received word from his growing army of fanatical religious spies, ₄ that Artabanus had amassed a huge army of more than sixty thousand to rally against the Manes, ₅ and did plan first to retake Susa before Darabgerd (Darab) in Parsis. ₆ ArdaShah did force march his army of fifteen thousand northward of Susa, ₇ to a place the Galli Priests did prophecy as favourable ground for battle. ₈ There before his army assembled, ArdaShah received the Baal-Zebul High Priest of Ur, ₉ who handed Abram as ArdaShah a new symbol in gold upon a blood red background, saying: ₁₀ Behold! Seytan, Lord of the Underworld and King of Demons ordains you shall be victorious today, ₁₁ under the sacred symbol of his hosts being the most sacred Swastika of fire, water, earth and air, ₁₂ that any army that honours Seytan (Satan) and marches under this standard is unconquerable. ₁₃ For I anoint you (ArdaShah) King of Kings and your army the Aryans as they are all worthy, ₁₄ and that your Empire shall live forever as UrAn (Iran) meaning the people of the sacred lands, ₁₅ as the one and only chosen people of Seytan (Satan). ₁₆ When the army of Artabanus did arrive, he could not deploy all his forces at once, ₁₇ and in a sea of frenzy and rage the army of ArdaShah did cut the Parthian army to pieces, ₁₈ under the standard of the Swastika of the Aryans so that before nighfall Artabanus was dead. ₁₉ Upon victory, ArdaShah declared the site of the battle a sacred site and named the plain Shushtar, ₂₀ as the site of the new capital of the renamed province of Khuzestan. ₂₁ ArdaShah did then travel to the ruins of Babylon where he did declare: ₂₂ Upon the ruins of this most sacred city I commission an academy that shall be called Yahsiva, ₂₃ meaning a place of learning for those bound by oath to Seytan (Satan) Our Lord. ₂₄ ArdaShah did then travel north of Babylon to a place on the Euphrates and did then declare: ₂₅ Upon this sacred site ordained by Baal-Zebul (High priest of Ur), we shall make our capital, ₂₆ and call it Babel (Bagdad). Here we shall build the greatest of wonders in awe, ₂₇ and a tower to heaven by which our Lord Seytan (Satan) may transcend as Lord of Heaven and Earth. ₂₈ For we are his chosen people and all who are worthy are bound to obey his commands. ₂₉ In the same year, ₃₀ after the last of the VisiGoti had departed Italia, ₃₁ King (Marcus) Aurelius Cornelius Albinus of the Franks did invade Italia and seize Rome, ₃₂ with little bloodshed on the account of Thascius Tertullianus Caecilius escaping to North Africa. ₃₃ King (Marcus) Aurelius Cornelius Albinus did send word to King Balti that he had no quarrel, ₃₄ and to King Chrocus, King Albinus did reinforce his promise to his father not to attack, ₃₅ if the Suebi remained at peace. ₃₆ Upon such terms, Albinus the grandson of Emperor Marcus Aurelius Cornelius Servus secured peace, ₃₇ as the new Emperor of Rome. ₃₈ Emperor Albinus did then appoint Gaius Julius Priscus as Prateorian Prefect and protector, 39 as the Franks did then depart to North Africa to hunt down the last of the Septima. 40 At the fortress of Hippo, the Franks did surround Thascius Tertullianus Caecilius as Callixtus, 41 and within seven days the false Pontifex Maximus was dead and the city captured. 42 Yet Cassius Tertullianus Severus the son of Callixtus, 43 and also known as Cassius and as Severus, 44 did escape into the vast Atlas Mountains, 45 and from his cave with his surviving followers declared himself to be Pontifex Sixtus, 46 as the next false Pontifex Maximum of the false line of Tertullian in worship of Cybele. 47 In the same year, 48 Holly King Cuinel (Connell) of Caledonia (Scotland) and King Llywarch Hen of Cymri (Wales), 49 did smash the last defences of the pirate city of Londinium, 50 and burn the city once more to the ground. 51 Holly King Cuinel (Connell) of Caledonia (Scotland) did then order, 52 that the city gates be destroyed and the walls so compromised that never again, 53 could such a cursed place rise up in defiance of the High Curse of Jesus (Yahusiah).

C. 15

1 In the year known as 225 CE, 2 fourteen hundred and twenty five years since the dawn of the Great Age, 3 Emperor Marcus Aurelius Cornelius Albinus did approve the construction of a new baths for Rome, 4 called the Thermae Albinus and to the southern most area of Rome along the Appian Way, 5 to provide relief to the southern sections of Rome most affected by plague and the pox. 6 Emperor Cornelius Albinus did then call upon all administrators and allies to Rome, 7 including King Chrocus of the Suebi and King Balti of the VisiGoti, 8 and Priest King Hermes of Eucadia and King Llywarch Hen (the wise) of Cymri (Wales), 9 and Holly King Cuinel (Connell) of Caledonia (Scotland) and Englia and Emperor of the Celts, 10 and King Pollienus of Hispania and all lesser kings and tribal leaders, 11 and more than two thousand of the Diaspora as the blood descendants of the Holly lines, 12 of Holly High King Cú-Cúileann also known as the Great Prophet Yasiah (Joseph) of Yeb, 13 and his one and only Queen Mariah (Mary). 14 There at the Roman Forum did come the greatest gathering of leaders and Holly in history, 15 to witness the speech of Emperor Marcus Aurelius Cornelius Albinus who did say: 16 May the one true Creator of the Universe grant us good fortune upon this sacred day, 17 and our collective ancestors be our guides and protectors, 18 that no man be ignorant of the events brought forth at such a place and time, 19 and guard against any wicked scribes that may seek to corrupt such record. 20 For we assemble here as friends, family and former adversaries alike to bear witness, 21 that all men and women are borne equal and that none be above the law. 22 For all law is measured that all may learn and know it, 23 and all law is standard that it may always be applied the same, 24 and all men and women of a community are bound to live by the rule of law of the community. 25 No one then may be accused except by rule of law and no one be punished except by the same. 26 For this be the Law and the Law of

the Prophets from the beginning of time, 27 and any such law that is against such truth cannot be law. 28 Some here present may have heard the teachings of the false prophets of the Piso, 29 who have concealed their identity and nature and now have seized control of Parthia, 30 declaring themselves Aryans and followers of the religion of Manes to Satan, 31 and that the base nature of men be as animals and to be ruled as slaves, 32 and that knowledge is power and to be treated as occult and hidden from view, 33 by those who possess such knowledge who claim superior intellect and ambition. 34 It is true that for centuries men have fought and given blood over the same land, 35 as many of our ancestors have done before these times. 36 It is true that for many generations the victors of such conflict have sought advantage, 37 and sometimes enslaved the vanquished and sought means of justifying slavery. 38 It is also true that our ancestors such as Yahusiah (Jesus) did teach us, 39 that lesser flesh and blood gods did create some of our forefathers to be slaves, 40 condemning giants to deep mines and hard labour and smaller ancestors to the fields, 41 and even creating a third race to be their overlords. 42 Yet Yahusiah (Jesus) did also reveal the deeper mystery of a fourth race, 43 that awakened the Divine Spirit in all of us and emancipated us from such bondage. 44 Verily I say to all here present and those who come to hear of our words, 45 that such sayings of the Manes be wicked falsities designed to trick and confuse the mind. 46 For they be half-truths and incomplete information and corrupted knowledge.

47 For the true nature of mankind be Divine and not animal and the true source of law be Divine. 48 Verily there is, there was, there has only ever been One Law under the Golden Rule of Law. 49 A rule is a norm, bar, maxim, measure or standard. 50 A rule may be derived by instruction, discovery, custom or consent. 51 The highest law is Divine being a rule given by divine instruction, 52 as nothing may contradict such a rule. 53 The second highest law be the reason of Mind, 54 being an edict given by a great council of wise elders or jurists, 55 as nothing absurd and without good reason may be considered law. 56 The third highest law be the law of the people, 57 as the consent and will of the people is the source of true authority. 58 The weakest rule is that of a tyrant, 59 as any rule without authority or right of heaven but merely by force, 60 cannot be sustained and the people shall eventually overcome, 61 and render such unjust rule and unjust laws as dust. 62 This be the law of all great civilisations from the beginning of time, 63 and no king or assembly or priest has sustained in ignorance to such foundation. 64 Thus the Piso seek to corrupt the very foundation of law and the nature of men, 65 by usurping such wisdom and instead by tricking people into believing puzzles. 66 Thus we issue this solemn edict that henceforth no man may practice Manes, 67 nor speak of Manes nor worship Manes within our collective jurisdictions, 68 for such teachings be worse than lunacy and idiocy and the rantings of Maniacs. 69 Furthermore, we issue today a new Constitution for Rome (antepositum constitutionem), 70 that there be only one form of

citizen and no other and all men are borne free, 71 and all who honour the law are equal before the law. 72 Thus the law is restored and the truth made known. 73 In the year known as 226 CE, 74 fourteen hundred and twenty six years since the dawn of the Great Age, 75 Cuiredig the son of King Llywarch Hen (the wise) of Cymri (Wales), 76 did have a son he named Cuinedda.

C. 16

1 In the year known as 228 CE, 2 fourteen hundred and twenty eight years since the dawn of the Great Age, 3 King ArdaShah of the Aryans did call all leaders to the building site of Babel (Bagdad), 4 there in front of the incomplete temples and towers adorned with giant Swastikas, 5 ArdaShah did speak to the assembled saying: 6 Behold! The Lord does ordain this day be most sacred! For we the people of the Covenant, 7 do proclaim to the world by the authority of Kha Shekha, the King of Darkness, 8 we do honour his true name and are sworn to rule justly, truthfully and fairly as servants. 9 Verily, we are the servants of the servants of Satan and forbidden to live in grandeur, 10 but in ghettos and the quarters of the lowest of the low until the end of days. 11 For you have heard the wicked falsities and accusations of the Diaspora and Holly, 12 against these truths and revelations given unto you. 13 Because they are threatened by such truth as to the nature of mankind. 14 It is true that Aryans are ordained the rulers of the world over all other people, 15 by their sacred covenant as the chosen people. 16 And it is true that we are granted the power over non-believers and the weak minded, 17 to treat them kindly as errant animals and less than slaves, 18 who do not deserve to hear the truth nor have any such wisdom revealed to them. 19 Yet we are first and foremost servants of all people and are bound to rule in mercy. 20 Thus under the sacred symbol of our covenant being the Swastika, 21 we reveal today the sacred laws of all truth and mankind called the Mizdah or good deeds, 22 of six books of worship to Seytan (Satan), our Lord. 23 Being the Books of Seeds, Festivals, Women, Damages, Holy Things and Purities. 24 Verily, the Diaspora and Holly Priests speak of society and laws, 25 yet they and they alone remain superior by blood with none equal. 26 Thus, not only do they contradict their own teachings but they forbid others, 27 from making good their own knowledge and reasoning to the highest potential. 28 Thus, it is left to those to honour knowledge and truth and follow Manes, 29 to bring forth a vision of society where all can achieve their potential. 30 Let it be known therefore that a just society shall be classed into Kasts (castes), 31 and then into tribes called Vana meaning woods and trees by virtue of birth. 32 The highest class shall be the scholars, teachers and priests. 33 The next class shall be the warriors, regional kings and administrators. 34 The next lowest class shall be the merchants and farmers. 35 The second lowest class shall be the artists and free workers, 36 The lowest of all classes then are the slaves called boda (body). 37 Verily, a member of the Aryan Chosen People can never be held as a slave, 38 nor may be they be bonded into servitude

for longer than seven years. 39 Yet a non-believer who chooses to be wilfully ignorant, 40 then such a man or woman may be enslaved for life and treated like cattle. 41 ArdaShah then ordered pairs of Manes Priests to journey across the known world, 42 with the new sacred scripture and philosophy, especially to India and Asia. 43 And within one generation the religion of Manes was embraced by every warlord and pirate, 44 and much of the world was imprisoned by the mind of Manes.

C. 17

1 In the year known as 230 CE, 2 fourteen hundred and thirty years since the dawn of the Great Age, 3 at Athens, Pappa Basileus Hermes of Eukadia (Ucadia), 4 did call upon all Therapeutae and Diaspora to bear witness to his work in repudiation to Manes, 5 known as the Corpus Hermeticum and later as the Hermetica, 6 of fourteen books distilling the knowledge of the ancient Cuilliaéan and Therapeutae, 7 of the cosmos, of divine mind, nature and the formation of man, of spirits and deities. 8 There before the assembled brightest and best priests and scholars of the civilised world, 9 Priest King Hermes did speak saying: 10 Let these words be forever known as the highest truth without falsity and certainty without doubt, 11 verily, what is below is the same as what is above, 12 and what is above is the same as what is below, 13 to manifest the miracle that every object arises from only One concept. 14 And as all things are ultimately the same and arose from One by the contemplation of One, 15 so all things have their origin from this One by virtue of adaptation and change. 16 Thus the Light (of knowledge) is our Father and the Illumination (of mind) our Mother, 17 and the wind carries the answer to existence in its essence and the earth be our nurse and protector. 18 The father of all perfection and of the whole world is always here (present). 19 His force and power is all encompassing and is transformed into all the earth. 20 Separate then the earth (of dream) be from the Light (of divine mind), 21 yet even the smallest (object) to the largest (body) be known and greatly loved. 22 For the Light (of mind) ascends from the earth to the heaven and again it descends to the earth, 23 and receives the reasoning and Illumination (of dream) of things superior and inferior. 24 By comprehension of this revelation means you shall have the glory of the whole world, 25 and thereby all obscurity shall fly from you. 26 For its force is above all force. 27 For it vanquishes every subtle error and falsity and exposes every secret and impregnable claim. 28 So this be the truth and certainty unto the nature and reason why the world was created, 29 and all I have said of the operation of the Light and Illumination is accomplished and ended. 30 Pappa Basileus Hermes of Eukadia (Ucadia) then held up a large flag of the Swastika saying: 31 Behold! Here be the symbol of wilful ignorance and stupidity that proclaims spiritual power. 32 Priest King Hermes then held the edge of the Swastika over a cauldron of flame until it caught fire. 33 He then poured water over it, extinguishing the flames before the

wind broke off pieces of ash, saying: 34 Behold! the elements of fire, of water and earth and air be not bound to such symbols nor false idols. 35 Verily, the false priests of the Piso proclaim to serve Satan, yet know nothing of the provenance. 36 For it was the descendants of the Cuilliaéan in the form of the Hyksos pharaohs, 37 who worshipped the deity of Set as the god of rain and fertility and later the afterlife. 38 Such deity was both upon the earth and in heaven and was benevolent to all men of honour. 39 Yet it was the false pharaohs of the Ramesses who defiled the tombs and the name of Set, 40 and invented the fictional deity of Seth and later as Setian as an adversary to the other gods. 41 Verily, I say to you there be no such thing as unsacred nor such deity as an anti-god, 42 only the madness of ignorant and greedy men, infected with the madness of their own addictions. 43 As for the origins of the races of men, the Piso have no knowledge of demons nor of the saviour of men, 44 for they think there be one spirit of Lucifer and have no knowledge of the race of Prometheus, 45 that be the origin of the Cuilliaéan and all true priests and all Diaspora and Therapeutae. 46 Verily, there was and is an army of thousands of Lucifers and their descendants present upon the earth. 47 In the year known as 236 CE, 48 fourteen hundred and thirty six years since the dawn of the Great Age, 49 King Aurelius Cornelius Albinus of the Franks, 50 Emperor of Rome and grandson of Emperor Marcus Aurelius Cornelius, 51 and Great great great grandson of Jesus and son of Gaius Cornelius Celestius, 52 did give up the ghost. 53 The crown of the Franks and title of Emperor did then befall to his son, 54 whose name was Aurelius Cornelius Auspicius, 55 also known to the Romans by the name Aemilianus meaning rival. 56 In the year known as 237 CE, 57 fourteen hundred and thirty seven years since the dawn of the Great Age, 58 King Llywarch Hen (the wise) of Cymri (Wales), 59 the son of King Lloyd (Lled lwm) and great great grandson of Jesus and Mariamne, 60 did give up the ghost. 61 The crown of the Cymri (Wales) did then befall to his son, 62 whose name was Cuiredig.

C. 18

1 In the year known as 238 CE, 2 fourteen hundred and thirty eight years since the dawn of the Great Age, 3 King Amali of the Thervingi Goti (Goths), 4 did give up the ghost. 5 The crown of the Goti of the Forest and Coast People did befall to his son named Athali. 6 Yet upon news of the death of King Amali, the VisiGoti did invade the lands of their cousins, 7 with King Balti proclaiming he alone be the one true king of all the Goti (Goths). 8 Yet King Athali of the Thervingi Goti did resist the invading Greuthungi Goti, 9 and a terrible and bloody civil war did ensue. 10 In the year known as 239 CE, 11 fourteen hundred and thirty nine years since the dawn of the Great Age, 12 Cuinhainn (Kevin) the son of Holly King Cuinel (Connell) of Caledonia (Scotland), 13 and High King of the Kings of Englia (England) and Emperor of the Celts, 14 did have a son, whom he named Cuinalba (Kennedy). 15 In the same year, 16 the forces of King Balti did break through

and capture the city of Arhemar, killing King Athali. 17 Yet the Thervingi did defy King Balti and elect Alavari, the son of Athali as King. 18 King Athali did then order the burning of their own city of Arhemar, 19 and the burning of all supplies and stores, saying: 20 These (Greuthungi) be not Goti (Goths) but robbers and thieves without honour. 21 For they have sold their spirit for gold and silver and are a plague upon our sacred lands. 22 There be then only one cure to such a plague and it is to burn our lands, 23 that such parasites have no source of nourishment. 24 Verily our people have survived the worst of the Normen and we shall continue to survive, 25 and we shall rebuild our sacred city stronger and mightier than before. 26 The Thervingi did then burn their city and lands and King Balti was forced to withdraw. 27 Soon after the Greuthungi and the Thervingi did agree to an uneasy peace. 28 In the year known as 244 CE, 29 fourteen hundred and forty four years since the dawn of the Great Age, 30 Holly King Cúirmac mac Cúirt of Eire (Ireland), 31 great great great grandson of Yahusia (Jesus) and Mariamne, 32 and Cousin to Emperor Marcus Aurelius Cornelius Servus, 33 did give up the ghost. 34 The crown of Holly High King did then befall to his son named Cúiran (Kieran) Mac Cúirmac.

C. 19

1 In the year known as 244 CE, 2 fourteen hundred and forty four years since the dawn of the Great Age, 3 Abram Calpernius Piso as King ArdaShah of Uran (Aryans), 4 the son of Justinianus Calpernius Piso and great grandson of Marcus Calpernius Piso, 5 did give up the ghost. 6 The crown of Uran (Aryans) did then befall to his son named Isaac Calpernius Piso, 7 who took the title as king as ShahPar. 8 Upon news of the death of Abram Calpernius Piso as King ArdaShah, 9 Pappa Basileus Hermes of Eukadia as Legate of Asia did seize Cappadocia and Armenia, 10 and then onto Hatra, Nisbis, Carrhae and Khabur. 11 Isaac Calpernius Piso as King ShahPar did then order his generals to amass an army, 12 of all the true believers of Manes and blindly ignorant followers of Satan, 13 that even if a hundred or a thousand did fall, the legions of Hermes be exhausted and fail. 14 Isaac Calpernius Piso did then depart eastward from the approaching Roman forces. 15 Thus before the gates of Babel (Bagdad) and the great temple of Satan casting a great shadow, 16 the Roman and Eukadian Army of 20,000 legionnaires of Hermes faced a mass army, 17 of more than 180,000 conscripts and volunteers. 18 Seeing the growing mass before him, Hermes did order his troops to dig channels for oil, 19 while commanding his archers to use burning arrows with salts, 20 and for his cavalry to charge the gates of the city. 21 Upon the approach of the Manes hoards, the oil was lit and many burned before the salts erupted, 22 causing all kinds of colours to erupt as the cavalry did charge for the gates. 23 The conscripts and volunteers upon seeing the flames and colours did flee in terror, 24 and Babel (Bagdad) was taken and burnt to the ground with Hermes proclaiming: 25 Let it be known now and forever more that this ground be

cursed before Heaven and all the gods. 26 For it was at this place that wicked and ignorant men who invented false gods of no power, 27 did sow the poisonous seeds of such madness that has now infected half the world. 28 For as this city burns, so too do the bodies of the heretics of heaven and earth. 29 Thus let this day be a warning to all who would seek to usurp Divine Law and the Golden Rule. 30 Hermes and his legions did then withdraw to protective positions of Syria and Armenia. 31 Upon the destruction of Babel, ShahPar moved North-East between the Zagros and Elburz Mountains, 32 to the ruins of the ancient cursed city of Ray, destroyed to its foundations by Alexander the Great. 33 There he planted the Swastika in the ground and did proclaim the site as a new capital of the Aryans, 34 called Eden as the Paradise of all who worship Satan as king of the lower worlds.

C. 20

1 In the year known as 246 CE, 2 fourteen hundred and forty six years since the dawn of the Great Age, 3 Pappa Basileus Hermes of Eukadia (Ucadia), 4 did have a daughter he named Helena. 5 In the same year, 6 Cuinedda the son of King Cuiredig of Cymri (Wales), 7 did have a daughter he named Morgaine. 8 In the year known as 248 CE, 9 fourteen hundred and forty seven years since the dawn of the Great Age, 10 at the court of Cymri (Wales) at HollyHead upon the Isle of Angels (Anglesea), 11 the infant Morgaine did speak like an old soul to the king and the court of impending doom, saying: 12 A great and terrible reckoning of this age soon shall comes upon us, 13 that shallow and weak men shall be like beasts, 14 and son shall turn against mother and father against daughter. 15 Keep safe and do not fall into slumber nor rely upon the reason or logic of others, 16 nor forget your ancient covenant, for the earth mother warns us. 17 Soon after, the Earth did then change such that the North Pole did move back, 18 toward the great land over the sea (North America), 19 and the equator did change from its position through North Africa and Arabia and South India, 20 as well as the Central Amazon, 21 to travel through central Africa, the Indian Ocean, South East Asia and northern South America. 22 Soon after strange occurrences and events did begin to appear with birds falling dead from the sky, 23 and violent storms did shake the ancient world, 24 that the fame of the little prophetess did spread across the Celtic world even unto Rome, 25 and she became known as Morgainne the Faire (Seer). 26 In the same year, 27 as Rome did prepare to celebrate the claim of a thousand years of history, 28 violent storms as never before did shake all of Europe and Africa. 29 In Rome, lightning did strike like arrows of vengeance against the city and its monuments, 30 that by nightfall the Colosseum was ablaze as was the Theater of Pompey and part of the Forum. 31 Gaius Julius Priscus as Protector of Rome and his Praetorian fought bravely against the fires, 32 and did give his life to save Praetorian trapped by the flames. 33 Yet, while the Colosseum was lost, Rome was saved, 34 and Emperor Aurelius Cornelius Auspicius of the Franks did appoint Marcus Julius Philippus, 35 the son of

hero Gaius Julius Priscus as the Praetorian Prefect. 36 As people across the known world did recover from the storms, they did cry out in horror, 37 as the change in the position of the pole and orientation of the crust of the earth, 38 did alter the position of the stars that the alignment of temples, 39 no longer aligned with the position of the stars, 40 and the weather became much colder and drier that grapes and crops did begin to wither and die. 41 Soon after the great volcano of Sicily did erupt, causing the whole of Italia to be in darkness, 42 as volcanoes upon the Isle of Ice (Iceland) did erupt and even as far away, 43 as the central parts of North and Central South America. 44 Upon such signs, many of the Diaspora did come to HollyHead on Isle of Angels (Anglesea), 45 to hear from the infant Morgainne the Faire (Seer). 46 Yet no more prophecy did come until the King of the Franks and Roman Emperor Cornelius Auspicius, 47 did come to HollyHead and ask the little infant if she had any message for him, 48 and in reply she said she did not as she was but a little girl. 49 Emperor Marcus Aurelius Cornelius Auspicius did apologize to the little girl, 50 saying he be a father and that she be very brave, to which Morgainne did reply: 51 Alas brave king, your skill of battle shall be naught, 52 against the sea of misery set to flood all lands. 53 For Rome be but an open grave and hungry pit for bones, 54 as nothing can save those already dead. 55 The Emperor was deeply troubled and ordered his court be moved to the garrison city of Metz, 56 appointing Praetorian Marcus Julius Philippus Guardian of the city of Rome, 57 to save as many people as possible from what was about to come. 58 In the same year, 59 upon the momentous changes in the alignment of the heavens to earth, 60 and the fear and panic among all the people of the known world, 61 Isaac Calpernius Piso as ShahPar did rejoice, proclaiming: 62 Behold! Witness the power of our Lord Seytan (Satan), 63 for he rent the sacred curtain of Heaven in two and cleaved the Earth from it, 64 that none may communicate nor worship with Heaven as we did proclaim, 65 but through the One Lord of all the Earth. 66 Therefore, we shall honour him with never permitting his true name to be spoken, 67 but only to be known as Sabaoth as the Lord of Hosts, 68 and we shall make one day (The Sabbath) in every seven sacred and to be the day of Sabaoth, 69 for he has delivered us from our enemies and punished the wicked. 70 Verily, we shall cleave all the gods into halves with one being angels and the other demons, 71 and we shall cleave all knowledge of the mysteries into two that none may know, 72 except the most high and worthy. 73 For Lord Sabaoth has proven that what has been made in heaven can be unmade, 74 and that it is our destiny to divide the world and conquer it.

C. 21

1 In the year known as 249 CE, 2 fourteen hundred and forty nine years since the dawn of the Great Age, 3 the ancient world was in turmoil as temples were looted and the priests and priestesses murdered, 4 in search of treasure and in revenge for failing to stop the severing of Earth to the heavens. 5 No rain did fall in the cold

as crops continued to fail and grasslands and forests did burn. 6 The northern tribes of Africa did move north to escape the fires and famine, 7 yet found nothing but the mass of refugees seeking salvation in the coastal cities, 8 with Carthage being one of the largest sites, swelling in population by tens of thousands. 9 Yet to the east, the Garamantes civilisation was completely destroyed, 10 and the cities of Tacape, Sabrata, Arae Philaenorum and even Leptis Magna abandoned. 11 In Hispania, the Celtic tribes abandoned their central cities such as Tolentum, 12 and sought to protect the main cities of Tarraco and Valentia against pirate attack. 13 In Gallia and in Germania the crops failed and the rivers dried and refugees flooded the cities. 14 Yet the greatest devastation and hunger was to be found in Syria and Arabia, 15 as the whole region burned from endless fires and no rain. 16 Many of the cities in central Syria were abandoned as well as Arabia. 17 Yet the cities of Aelana, Edom (Petra) and Gerasa along the Dead Sea valley remained fertile, 18 and protective of their supplies as cities along the coast such as Gaza and Caesaria did starve. 19 A leader did arise from Caesaria calling himself Lotus (Lot) as one who cleanses iniquity, 20 who called upon all men to bathe themselves in the waters of the Dead Sea for their sins, 21 and that the gods had not abandoned mankind but were punishing all of them, 22 for failing to honour the teachings of laws. 23 Lotus cursed the cities of Aelana, Edom (Petra) and Gerasa (Gemorah) and Bostra for not helping others. 24 In Carthage, a leader did arise calling himself Cyprianus and proclaiming the end of the world, 25 by the power and hand of Moloch for the failure of men to honour ancient covenants, 26 of child sacrifice and human sacrifice. 27 Unlike Lotus of Caesaria, Cyprianus proclaimed the body to be filthy and full of inequity, 28 and that mankind had cursed itself through its hubris to knowledge and obsession of the body. 29 That only an unclean and unwashed body be pious and worthy of saving. 30 Despite the utter madness of his claims, tens of thousands flocked to Carthage, 31 to hear the rantings of Cyprianus and his curses upon all human civilisation, 32 and even many of the noble families of Rome, desperate to save their lives at any cost. 33 Upon the swelling of the masses of followers of Cyprianus at Carthage, 34 the city expelled his followers as filthy carriers of disease that wreaked of rotting flesh. 35 Cyprianus and his followers did then move westward and seize the city of Hippo, 36 killing every last inhabitant and cooking and eating the flesh of children and animals. 37 Cyprianus did then declare himself a living god and Augustinius and the city of Hippo sacred, 38 and that he would punish mankind for its iniquities and every generation thereafter, 39 as he proclaimed all mankind be cursed by their rotting form of flesh, 40 and that only by embracing death to all life would those who be worthy be truly free. 41 Soon after the plague and the pox seized hold of thousands of his filthy followers, 42 and Augustinius urged his followers to travel to the ends of the earth, 43 to both spread his message of unending curses upon mankind and to infect the population.

44 Thus the wretched followers of Augustinius of Hippo did depart to all the major cities, 45 with hundreds returning to Rome and to Alexandria and even to Hispania and Gallia. 46 Only the lands held by Priest King Hermes of Eukadia (Ucadia) were safe from such fanatics, 47 as Hermes did order that such people be killed on sight as nothing can save such broken minds.

C. 22

1 In the year known as 250 CE, 2 fourteen hundred and fifty years since the dawn of the Great Age, 3 upon the wilful actions of insane and infected followers of Augustinius of Hippo, 4 the plague and pox had broken out in all major cities except those in Eukadia (Ucadia), 5 as well as Englia and the homeland of the Franks in Germania. 6 Upon news of such mass death across the known world Augustinius of Hippo was overjoyed, 7 proclaiming that he be the Reaper of Souls and the Bringer of Death to the world. 8 In Rome, the followers of Augustinius of Hippo had doomed so many to the plague and pox, 9 that Marcus Julius Philippus was forced to bury two thousand new bodies every day. 10 In the same year, 11 King Balti of the VisiGoti did attach and invade the Kingdom of Valeria and Eukadia (Ucadia), 12 sacking Naissus and the lands in search of food and treasure and burning the north of Eukadia. 13 King Lucius Valerius Aper of Valeria did mount a counter attack against the VisiGoti, 14 recapturing their capital of Naissus while Pappa Basileus Hermes of Eukadia, 15 did confront the forces of King Balti of the Goti (Goths) at Phillippolis (Thessalonika). 16 Weakened by Pox and Plague and fearful at the site of an army immune to such dreadful afflictions, 17 the VisiGoti army collapsed and Priest King Hermes recaptured Phillippolis (Thessalonika), 18 vowing the city to be his new capital and that never again would he permit such destruction. 19 Pappa Basileus Hermes did travel north-east with his army, 20 te-establishing order in the cities of Serdica and Perinthus within Thracia, 21 before moving north in pursuit of the retreating VisiGoti. 22 In the year known as 251 CE, 23 fourteen hundred and fifty one years since the dawn of the Great Age, 24 at the VisiGoti city and stronghold of Abritus, 25 Priest King Hermes did destroy the army of King Balti and scatter the VisiGoti. 26 Hermes did then seek a truce with King Alavari of the Thervingi Goti (Goths), 27 to honour him as the one true king of all the Goths. 28 King Alavari did then declare the greater kingdom of Gotthiuda, 29 as a symbol of the Goti (Goths) united once more and did then spare the life of Beri, 30 the son of the slain King Balti but banished him forever from the lands of the Goti (Goths). 31 In the same year, 32 Aurelius Cornelius Valerius the son of King Aurelius Cornelius Auspicius of the Franks, 33 did wed Julia the daughter of King Cuinel (Connell) of Caledonia and Emperor of the Celts.

C. 23

1 In the year known as 252 CE, 2 fourteen hundred and fifty two years since the dawn of the Great Age,

3 upon the first weeks of winter, great shows of meteors did appear, 4 turning the night to day and the day to streaks of flame and sulphur, 5 with many landing in North Africa and Arabia and even Germania. 6 Cyprianus as the self declared god Augustinius of Hippo did proclaim it a sign of Moloch, 7 that it be truly the end of days and the reaping of souls. 8 Soon after his filthy and infected fanatical followers did capture Carthage, 9 killing every living thing and eating the flesh of slain children and sacrificed infants. 10 Augustinius of Hippo did then order his followers to seek small children and babies, 11 to be sacrificed on top of towers constructed for burning sacrifice, 12 that the scent of their innocent burnt flesh fill the air day and night, 13 as an offering to Baal Moloch to save the true followers of Augustinius. 14 In Syria and Palestine, Lotus (Lot) did proclaim the meteors also a sign of the End of Days, 15 proclaiming a great battle would be fought upon the plains near the Dead Sea, 16 and all who refused to acknowledge their sins and abandon civilisation, 17 such as the cities of Edom (Petra), Gerasa (Gemarah) would be consumed by fire. 18 In Rome, the nobles did convert en mass to the insanity and stupidity of Augustinius, 19 and did parade themselves in the forum in the most hideous of rags and with awful smells. 20 Emperor Marcus Aurelius Cornelius Auspicius did depart from the fortress of Metz, 21 to return to HollyHead on the Isle of Angels and the court of King Cuinedda of Cymri (Wales), 22 to seek the vision and prophecy of the now young girl Morgaine the Faire (Wise), 23 as to the meaning of the sign of fire and brimstone that so gripped the world in fear, 24 and if it truly be the signs of the end of the world. 25 The young girl Morgaine did reply, saying: No man may escape his ultimate fate, 26 for everything that lives must die and every end is a beginning. 27 It matters not then when we die but how we live, 28 for let justice be done, though the heavens may fall. 29 The King of the Franks and Emperor of the Roman Empire did then cry out in tears, saying: 30 Forgive me oh Divine Creator of all Existence for letting my fears beguile me, 31 that I did forget my sacred duty of service and solemn vow before all my ancestors, 32 to uphold the Golden Rule of Law and to protect the Rights of Men through true Justice. 33 Verily, if it be your will that we shall vanish from this earth, then so be it. 34 But let not our souls or hearts slumber again as to our Divine Commission. 35 For I swear before heaven and earth that we shall make it our sacred motto, 36 that justice be done, though the heavens may fall. 37 Soon after, the Emperor ordered his court to prepare to return to Rome, 38 and re-establish order midst the chaos and fear and death across the world.

C. 24

1 In the year known as 253 CE, 2 fourteen hundred and fifty three years since the dawn of the Great Age, 3 after order had been restored in Gallia and Germania, Emperor Marcus Aurelius Cornelius Auspicius, 4 did appoint his son Marcus Aurelius Cornelius Valerius also known as Valerian as Co-emperor, 5 to rule Gallia, Hispania and Germania from

Metz while he would rule the remainder from Rome. 6 Upon his return to Rome near the first anniversary of the great sign of meteors from the heavens, 7 Emperor Aurelius Cornelius Auspicius did outlaw all false worship, 8 of the madness of the false teacher Augustinius of Hippo and Lotus (Lot) of Palestine, 9 and that anyone found killing or poisoning cats would be punished by sentence of death. 10 Yet soon after the meteor showers returned and the people of Rome were in panic. 11 A wealthy senator and follower of Augustinius of Hippo called Publius Licinius Valentinius, 12 did rally the mob to attack the Praetorian and Marcus Aurelius Cornelius Auspicius was killed. 13 Publius Licinius Valentinius did then declare himself Emperor and ordered the baths to be closed, 14 and that all the cats were to be killed and anyone found bathing or honouring cleanliness, 15 was to be tortured and executed as a heretic to Baal Moloch. 16 Within weeks, the plague returned to Rome with vengeance and tens of thousands of people died. 17 Upon news of the murder of his father, Emperor Marcus Aurelius Cornelius Valerius did say: 18 We shall not sacrifice one drop of blood against such madness, 19 nor shall we call for retribution. 20 Verily, to leave Rome in the hands of such madmen is punishment enough, 21 and the day will come soon enough to restore order after the storm. 22 In the year known as 254 CE, 23 fourteen hundred and fifty four years since the dawn of the Great Age, 24 Emperor Marcus Aurelius Cornelius Valerius of the Franks, 25 and Julia Cornelia the daughter of King Cuinel (Connell) of Caledonia, 26 did have a son, whom he named Aurelius Cornelius Adeptius, 27 which means attainment of wisdom.

C. 25

1 In the year known as 255 CE, 2 fourteen hundred and fifty five years since the dawn of the Great Age, 3 upon the arrival of winter, the terrible meteor showers returned, 4 people did cry out for relief as thousands sought refuge from hunger and violence. 5 King Hermes of Eucadia (Ucadia) continued to consolidate his control of Macedonia and Thrace, 6 proclaiming all who respect the law and themselves be welcome if they be prepared to work. 7 Thus Hermes did save the lives of hundreds of thousand in putting them to work, 8 and in defending the kingdom and in the wise use and storage of water and food. 9 Emperor Marcus Aurelius Cornelius Valerius did also save the lives of hundreds of thousands, 10 in declaring the Kingdom of Francia as a sanctuary being Germania and Gallia and Hispania, 11 and did follow the wise lead of Hermes in reforming old habits and the use of precious water. 12 In the wastelands of former Parthia, Isaac Calpernius Piso remained enclosed in his city, 13 being the fortified garden city of Eden formed midst the ruins of ancient Ray, 14 while his generals did enslave millions then forced to work to death in building irrigation channels, 15 and grotesque monuments and temples to the glory of the Piso. 16 Yet in Rome, Publius Licinius Valentinius also known as Valentinian, 17 continued to imprison tens of thousands in Rome as hell on earth, 18

in which every conceivable terror and vice and act of debauchery was celebrated, 19 as the sickness of the followers of Augustinius of Hippo reached new heights. 20 The Roman nobles in their filthy rags did now proclaim that only through acts of wickedness, 21 would the elite be saved and rewarded by Baal Moloch upon the final end of days. 22 Thus brothels did spread across Rome where shops once sold their wares, 23 next to temples sacrificing children and then selling their flesh to wealthy cannibals, 24 as thousands crowded the streets dying of pox and plague. 25 In the year known as 256 CE, 26 fourteen hundred and fifty six years since the dawn of the Great Age, 27 Emperor Cuinel (Connell) of the Celts, 28 Holly King of Caledonia (Scotland) and High King of the Kings of Englia (England), 29 and the great great great great great grandson of Yahusiah (Jesus) and Mariamne, 30 did give up the ghost. 31 The Holly crown of Caledonia as Emperor of the Celts, 32 did then befall to his son Cuinhainn (Kevin). 33 In the same year, 34 the deeply insane Augustinius of Hippo did order his followers to attack Alexandria, 35 and destroy the city and its famous Library as a symbol of the hubris of mankind, 36 against the ultimate power of Baal Moloch for men to believe they could be more than animals. 37 Thus, hundreds of thousands of fanatical and filthy followers of Augustinius, 38 did move as a cannibal army eastward toward Cyrene, 39 eating one another for their survival that spurned their madness to new heights, 40 such that upon their arrival at the walls of Alexandria, they had ceased to be men. 41 While the garrison of the city killed thousands of the fanatics, they were overwhelmed. 42 Yet the people of Alexandria did rise up for their own survival and cut the cannibal army to pieces. 43 Upon news of the destruction of the Great Library of Alexandria, 44 Marcus Aurelius Cornelius Valerius did call for the bravest of his generals, 45 named Gallienus Maximus, who he tasked with an elite legion of Praetorian, 46 to go to North Africa and rid the world of the plague of Augustinius of Hippo.

C. 26

1 In the year known as 256 CE, 2 fourteen hundred and fifty six years since the dawn of the Great Age, 3 General Gallienus Maximus and his legion did land in North Africa and fight their way to Carthage, 4 against the deranged cannibal army of Augustinius of Hippo. 5 Yet the flesh eating fanatics were no match against the men of Gallienus, 6 and Augustinius was discovered hiding midst his harem of girls and young boys. 7 As Gallienus Maximus did approach to wield the final blow against such a broken mind, 8 Augustinius cried out defiantly before his harem as witness that his visions of sin and curse, 9 would one day be the cornerstone of the world and the chains that enslave all Celts and Holly. 10 Yet as Gallienus Maximus did cleave Augustinius in two with one fierce stroke, 11 the general did reply that even the darkest days pass and the madness of Augustinius will not prevail. 12 Gallienus Maximus did order the city of Carthage to once again be burnt to the ground, 13 and the ground so salted that nothing grow

in memory of such a wicked and disgusting place, 14 cursed by all heaven and earth by the mad rantings of Augustinius of Hippo, 15 upon such falsities as original sin and the broken mind of mankind. 16 Gallienus Maximus did then prepare his Praetorian legion to land in southern Italia. 17 In the year known as 257 CE, 18 fourteen hundred and fifty seven years since the dawn of the Great Age, 19 upon the first month of winter, the meteor showers did return with violence, 20 such that the city of Edom (Petra) and Gerasa (Gemorah) were entirely destroyed by the fireballs, 21 and the cities of Aelana and Bostra so damaged that thousands did die. 22 Lotus (Lot) and his followers did rejoice at the destruction of the cities of Palestine, 23 proclaiming his prophecy be vindicated of a violent and malicious deity, 24 who did strike the enemies of his faithful and turn them into dust. 25 In the same year, Gallienus Maximus and the Praetorian did succeed in capturing several fortresses, 26 causing Publius Licinius Valetinianus to panic and order his forces south to stop Gallienus. 27 In the same year, 28 King Marcus Valerius Claudius of Valeria did proclaim the meteors a sign of victory, 29 and ordered his army to attack and seize the city of Salona being the capital, 30 of the neighbour kingdom of Dardania (Dalmatia). 31 The invasion caught King Gaius Carinus Dardanis of Dardania (Dalmatia) by surprise, 32 and the city of Salona was seized and destroyed and the king killed. 33 Yet his son named Gaius Carinus Diocletis (Diocletian) did escape and vowed revenge. 34 As King Marcus Valerius Claudius of Valeria did arrive to review the destruction of Salona, 35 Gaius Carinus Diocletis did strike and kill the King of Valeria and his guard, 36 forcing the Valerian army to flee. 37 Lucius Valerius Aper the son of Marcus Valerius Claudius did seek terms of truce, 38 that Gaius Carinus Diocletis (Diocletian) accepted on account of the devastation of his kingdom. 39 Gaius Carinus Diocletis did then order a new capital to be built called Dioclea (Dubrovnik), 40 which the warlord then declared would one day be the capital of a great empire.

C. 27

1 In the year known as 258 CE, 2 fourteen hundred and fifty eight years since the dawn of the Great Age, 3 emperor Marcus Aurelius Cornelius Valerius and King of Francia did move his main army, 4 to the frontier of the Suebi to prepare to invade Italia from the north. 5 Yet King Chrocus of the Suebi who proclaimed himself Gordian (Guardian) refused them to pass, 6 saying he favour not one nor the other in dispute over the true Roman Emperor. 7 Emperor Marcus Aurelius Cornelius Valerius did then reply that it was his father, 8 and not the gens Licinia that honoured terms with the Suebi and that word was given, 9 to which King Chrocus did reply that he did possess a sacred oath to protect his people, 10 against the madness of the world and what the King of Francia did demand would create jeopardy. 11 The Emperor in frustration did then reply: Verily Swabia (Switzerland), you be treachery! 12 For in accepting the terms, you withhold your honour and see nothing in error of bad faith. 13

Verily Swabia (Switzerland), you are heartless! 14 For as the world has burned, you have cared naught in your fertile valleys and mountains. 15 Thus if in 40 days you persist in such wicked arrogance, no more treaty there be, 16 and my army shall burn every village and destroy every town that no one will ever know, 17 that the kingdom of Swabia (Switzerland) ever existed. 18 In Rome, upon the news of the invading army of Aurelius Cornelius Valerius, 19 Publius Licinius Valetinianus did appoint his son Publius Licinius Egnatius as protector, 20 as he did depart to Arya and to beseech Isaac Calpernius Piso as ShahPar for aid. 21 Yet when Publius Licinius Valetinianus did come before King ShahPar, 22 he did demand and invoke his loyalty and obedience as a son of Rome and ally of Baal. 23 Outraged, Isaac Calpernius Piso did have Publius Licinius Valetinianus arrested, 24 and thrown into the most bleak of prisons before being tortured. 25 Isaac Calpernius Piso did then visit the dying Publius Licinius Valetinianus and proclaim, 26 that he (Isaac) be a god and the son of god and that Valetinianus be but the foot soldier, 27 of a dead false teacher who spoke of heaven yet knew nothing of spirit, 28 and spoke of curses and sin, yet was ignorant to all history. 29 Soon after, Isaac Calpernius Piso had the skin of Valetinianus removed and his bones cleaned, 30 before having his remains stuffed and made into a lifelike statue within his court, 31 as a reminder of the weakness and hubris of Rome. 32 At the border of Francia and Swabia, King Chrocus of the Suebi did relent, 33 and grant permission and safe passage to the army of Emperor Aurelius Cornelius Valerius. 34 Yet Publius Licinius Egnatius sought to take advantage of the delay of Valerius, 35 and did move his army northward to surprise the true Emperor. 36 Gallienus Maximus and his surviving Praetorian did then break out in Campagnia, 37 and move north against Rome as a third army led by Gaius Julius Aquillus, 38 did land from the sea behind Publius Licinius Egnatius and cut him off from Rome. 39 Thus within the space of two days, the army of 40,000 of Publius Licinius Egnatius, 40 was cut to pieces near Lake Benacus and Publius Licinius Egnatius was killed. 41 Emperor Aurelius Cornelius Valerius did then appoint Gallienus Maximus as Praetorian Prefect. 42 Yet the followers of the madness of Augustinius of Hippo did ambush Gallienus, 43 and have him killed as if by a mob. 44 Thus upon entering Rome, Emperor Aurelius Cornelius Valerius ordered the baths reopened, 45 and that anyone found to be a follower of the falsities of Augustinius of Hippo, 46 was to be executed as an enemy against Rome and for the safety of mankind. 47 Soon after, the followers of Augustinius found safe sanctuary in the catacombs, 48 under the ancient foundation of the Vatican as a safe place to hide.

C. 28

1 In the year known as 260 CE, 2 fourteen hundred and sixty years since the dawn of the Great Age, 3 Marcus Aurelius Cornelius Valerius sought to re-establish calm and order to the world. 4 With King Alavari of Gotthiuda Goti (Goths), he did agree

to terms and even with King Chrocus of the Suebi. 5 Each region then was then to provide a portion of able bodied men capable of being legionnaires, 6 for the defence of their own kingdoms and the defence of the Empire. 7 All the kingdoms except the warlord Gaius Carinus Diocletis of Dardania did consent. 8 Aurelius Cornelius Valerius (Valerian) did then order that the Dardania be forbidden from trade. 9 In the year known as 261 CE, 10 fourteen hundred and sixty one years since the dawn of the Great Age, 11 Beri, the exiled King of the VisiGoti (Visigoths) and his court were captured by the Normens. 12 Yet before they were about to be executed as thieves, former King Beri demanded to be tested, 13 before the court of King Herulir and if he did speak truth he would survive combat, 14 or if his words be false, he would die at the hand of the champion of the King. 15 Before the King of the Boli Normens, the exiled king did speak saying: 16 I have been brought to the home of the mortal enemy of my people by choice. 17 I have no quarrel with the Boli and I pledge upon the remaining blood of my kin, 18 that your enemies shall be our enemies and your allies shall be our allies. 19 For these chains and clothes dishonour me and my name as I am Beri, son of Balti of the Goti, 20 and this (Ukraine) be our ancient homeland. 21 Verily if I die today in honour through combat or under false pretences it is without regret, 22 for my blood shall return to the soil of my ancestors. 23 Upon hearing these words, King Herulir ordered the chains removed and Beri be dressed, 24 befitting a king before he was handed a sword and the two kings met each other in mortal combat. 25 King Herulir did lodge a blow so fierce it broke the arm of King Beri drawing blood, 26 yet King Beri did strike back and dislodge the left eye of King Herulir, 27 who in rage and pain drove his long sword through his opposing king and Beri fell dead. 28 King Herulr did then declare that the slain VisiGoti king had been a man of honour to his word, 29 and that his son Beoulf (Beowulf) shall be adopted as his son and the surviving VisiGoti as allies. 30 In the year known as 265 CE, 31 fourteen hundred and sixty five years since the dawn of the Great Age, 32 King Cuinedda of Cymri (Wales), 33 the son of Llywarch Hen (the wise) and great great great grandson of Jesus and Mariamne, 34 did give up the ghost. 35 While Morgaine the Faire (Wise) be older, the crown of Cymri (Wales) did befall, 36 to her brother whose name was Cuiel Hen (the wise). 37 Upon becoming King, Cuiel Hen did ask his sister if he would be a wise king as their father, 38 and in reply Morgaine the Faire (Wise) did reply: Before you be a great king, 39 my brother, you must first learn to be a good husband and then a good father. 40 In reply, Cuiel Hen did say to his sister: 41 It is true you be already the wisest, yet even you do not follow your own words, 42 for you be without husband or child. 43 Morgaine the Faire (Wise) did speak: Verily, not even heaven can meddle in the affairs of heart, 44 nor the most powerful of spirits alter the free will of men. 45 For all the words spoken must be true, 46 yet it is the leader and king that must lead by example of actions.

C. 29

1 In the year known as 266 CE, 2 fourteen hundred and sixty six years since the dawn of the Great Age, 3 the gravely ill King Hemdallr did make his son Hermodr the King of the North, 4 and his adopted son Beoulf (Beowulf) the King of the South of the Normen lands. 5 Yet upon the death of the old king, Hermodr did move against Beoulf (Beowulf) to seize the lands. 6 After seven days of fierce battle at the cost of thousands of lives, 7 Beoulf (Beowulf) did challenge Hermodr to honourable combat to settle the challenge, 8 and against his taller and stronger opponent, Beoulf (Beowulf) was victorious, 9 as the first and only VisiGoti (VisiGoth) to also be king of the Normens. 10 In the same year, 11 King Lucius Valerius Aper of Valeria did attack the lands of Gotthiuda of King Alavari, 12 proclaiming it be the ancient right of his people to the lands of the coast of the Black Sea. 13 King Alavari did not invade Valeria in retribution for fear of a formidable enemy to the north. 14 Instead, he called upon Marcus Aurelius Cornelius Valerius (Valerian) to honour their truce. 15 The Roman Emperor then sent four legions to Valeria to restore the peace, 16 whereupon King Gaius Carinus Diocletis of Dardania declared himself to be an ally, 17 and to pledge legions to the defence of the Empire and end the isolation of the Dardanians. 18 In the year known as 267 CE, 19 fourteen hundred and sixty seven years since the dawn of the Great Age, 20 King Beoulf (Beowulf) of the Normens did attack and invade Gotthiuda against King Alavari, 21 destroying the capital of Arhemar on the Volga River and killing King Alavari. 22 Yet the former VisiGoti did not join with Beoulf (Beowulf) and instead saw him as a traitor, 23 so when the Normen saw the contempt against Beoulf (Beowulf) they withdrew, 24 leaving Beoulf (Beowulf) abandoned by his kin and his adopted kin. 25 Athanari the son of Alavari did then kill Beoulf (Beowulf), forcing his son Sigeric to flee. 26 In the same year, 27 King Gaius Carinus Diocletis of Dardania did invade Valeria and capture Naissus, 28 killing King Lucius Valerius Aper and declaring the united kingdom of Diocleatae, 29 as firm allies to Marcus Aurelius Cornelius Valerius (Valerian), 30 and the promise to provide legions and to honour the law, 31 and defend the Empire.

C. 30

1 In the year known as 270 CE, 2 fourteen hundred and seventy years since the dawn of the Great Age, 3 Prince Cuinalba (Kennedy) the son of Holly King Cuinhainn (Kevin) of Caledonia (Scotland), 4 and Princess Helena the daughter of Priest King Hermes of Eucadia (Ucadia) did wed. 5 In the year known as 271 CE, 6 fourteen hundred and seventy one years since the dawn of the Great Age, 7 Emperor Marcus Aurelius Cornelius Valerius (Valerian) did finish the reconquest of Palestine and Syria, 8 and the end of the followers of Lotus (Lot) and the insane followers of Augustinius, 9 that had fled and formed a theocratic kingdom known as Palmyra. 10 In the year 272, 11 fourteen hundred and seventy two years since the dawn of the Great Age,

12 Holly King Cúiran (Kieran) Mac Cúirmac, the great High King of Ireland, 13 did give up the ghost. 14 The Kingship did then pass to his son known as Cúilean (Collins) mac Cúiran, 15 as the great great great great great grandson of Jesus and Mariamne. 16 In the same year, 17 Cuinalba (Kennedy) the son of Holly King Cuinhainn (Kevin) of Caledonia (Scotland), 18 and High King of the Kings of Englia (England) and Emperor of the Celts, 19 and his wife Princess Helena of Eucadia (Ucadia), 20 did have a son, whom they named Cuinstanyn (Constantine). 21 Princess Helena of Eucadia (Ucadia) did then call upon Princess Morgaine the Faire, 22 to come to HollyRood and give blessing to their son Cuinstanyn (Constantine). 23 All the Diaspora did come to celebrate such an illustrious event, 24 and to hear the words of the virgin prophetess Morgaine the Faire. 25 In the great hall of HollyRood, Morgaine the Faire did meet Cúilean (Collins), 26 to whom she did agree to be betrothed before she did speak and say to the gathering: 27 Behold a light that shall shine from the highest mountain to the furthest sea is borne, 28 a saviour unto the world from the most ancient of priests and emperors and therapeutae, 29 that have defended and saved our species again and again since the beginning of civilisation. 30 Verily, everything yields but change and upon the head of young Cuinstanyn (Constantine), 31 a new age shall be borne the likes we have never seen before. 32 For what was, shall cease to be and men and women shall fight the bloodiest of wars, 33 and darkness and light shall battle for our soul until all are free of the chains of self.

C. 31

1 In the year known as 272 CE, 2 fourteen hundred and seventy two years since the dawn of the Great Age, 3 Isaac Calpernius Piso as King ShahPar of Uran (Aryans), 4 the son of Abram Calpernius Piso the first King of the Aryans, 5 did give up the ghost. 6 The crown of Uran (Aryans) did then befall to his son named Reuben Calpernius Piso. 7 At Eden, Reuben Calpernius Piso did not wait for the impending invasion by the Romans, 8 and called all his court and governors and priests together and did say: 9 Behold! The Sacred One and Our Lord has ordained that we triumph over the non believers, 10 and distempered cattle and horned beasts that seek to sow rebellion, 11 against the People of the Covenant. 12 Whereas my father was forgiving of the goyim and beasts that persecute us and speak ill, 13 for he believed they possess no reason nor foresight as to the true nature of mankind, 14 I have been shown visions from my Father of the Underworld that we must be firm and unforgiving. 15 Nor may those that seek the fruits of our knowledge or the use of our technologies, 16 or the wisdom of our schools or the safety of our villages and cities, 17 possess the luxury to be mere witnesses to the truth from The Sacred One and Our Lord. 18 Therefore, let it be known throughout the lands of the Pure Ones (Aryans) of UrAn, 19 that henceforth any man or woman who refuses to obey the laws of The Sacred One, 20 or refuses to respect and honour our ways shall be deemed a heretic and burned alive. 21

For we shall do this to pray The Sacred One consider the sweet smell of burning flesh, 22 sufficient offering to grant the departed a soul and a rebirth again to relearn their errors. 23 Verily, it was my father who forbid anyone utter the true name of the Sacred One (Satan), 24 and that he be honoured as Sabaoth as the Lord of Hosts. 25 Henceforth, even such title be too precious and sacred to utter to the masses. 26 Therefore, The Sacred One shall be known to the world as the one and only Gad (God), 27 as the one who overpowers and defeats the non believers and the one who destroys our enemies. 28 The faithful shall kneel on a prayer rug at morning and in the evening, 29 Facing the ruins of Babel (Bagdad) in honour of the one true and only Gad (God), 30 and the devout of the faithful shall wear knitted woolen skull caps called Kapi, 31 to confess to the world they are servants and slaves of Gad (God), 32 and that they hide their heads and minds from heaven to serve only his words. 33 Verily, we shall complete a new scripture in honour of Gad (God) called the Talmud, 34 and prayers called the Gamara as the steps to come and praise Gad (God). 35 Behold! I shall send out across the lands a new form of priest called Kohan (Cohen), 36 meaning those that teach as masters of the knowledge of Gad (God). 37 The Kohan (Cohen) shall then speak to the masses in their own tongue but shall record all knowledge, 38 in a secret language of cursing and power and occult called Ebri (Hebrew), 39 that shall enslave the mind of the people as perpetual servants of Gad (God). 40 Reuben Calpernius Piso did then order the restructure of the provinces into twelve Kantons, 41 with each Kanton headed by a Head Kohan (Cohen) as father and founder and an administrator, 42 with the twelve Kantons and tribes being Asher, Benjamin, Dan, Ephram, Gadan, Issachar and Judah, 43 and Levi, Manesseh, Naphtali, Simeon and Zebulun with the thirteenth tribe, 44 being the Kanton of Reuben at Eden. 45 Reuben Calpernius Piso did then declare himself BaalKhan (Balkhan) as God-King, 46 as the messiah of Satan and the Aryan Race.

C. 32

1 In the year known as 273 CE, 2 fourteen hundred and seventy three years since the dawn of the Great Age, 3 Princess Morgaine the Faire of Cymri (Wales) did wed King Cúilean (Collins) of Eire (Ireland). 4 In the same year, 5 Emperor Marcus Aurelius Cornelius Valerius (Valerian) did launch a major invasion of UrAn (Iran). 6 Yet Reuben Calpernius Piso as the BaalKhan had anticipated the invasion, 7 and ordered his best troops to be held back in reserve and to allow the Romans, 8 to advance far eastward into UrAn unto the city of Susa, 9 before BaalKhan ordered the burning of the fields and poisoning of the water, 10 so that tens of thousands of innocent people did die of thirst and starvation. 11 Yet the Romans suffered terrible loses before retreating to Syria and Palestine. 12 Reuben Calpernius Piso as BaalKhan did then order his army to pursue the Romans. 13 However the Aryans failed to take Syria and in a fit of rage, 14 Reuben Calpernius Piso did order the execution of fifty generals and all their

families. 15 In the year known as 274 CE, 16 fourteen hundred and seventy four years since the dawn of the Great Age, 17 Queen Morgaine the Faire and King Cúilean (Collins) of Eire (Ireland), 18 did give birth to a girl child they named Ceridwen (Catherine). 19 In the same year, 20 Reuben Calpernius Piso as Baalkhan (Balkhan) did commission a second YahSiva (Academy), 21 midst the ruins of Babel (Bagdad) to rival the first YahSiva of Babylon. 22 The BaalKhan did challenge the scholars of the new academy, 23 to concoct such a work of fiction and falsities and trickery that would be even greater, 24 than the one being completed at the academy of Babylon. 25 Thus the YahSiva of Babel and of Babylon became bitter enemies, 26 Invested in the business of creating false religions and religious texts.

C. 33

1 In the year known as 275 CE, 2 fourteen hundred and seventy five years since the dawn of the Great Age, 3 King Gaius Domitius Aurelianus of Savia did give up the ghost without heir. 4 Gaius Carinus Diocletis (Diocletian) of Dioclea did move swiftly and capture the city of Siscia, 5 and annexing Savia to his greater kingdom, while declaring a pledge to the Emperor, 6 to raise more legions in defence of the Empire. 7 In the year known as 276 CE, 8 fourteen hundred and seventy six years since the dawn of the Great Age, 9 Priest King Hermes of Eucadia (Ucadia) did give up the ghost without male heir. 10 The role of protector of paradise and custodian of the kingdom of Heaven on Earth, 11 did befall for the first time to a woman being his daughter whose name was Helena. 12 Emperor Marcus Aurelius Cornelius Valerius (Valerian) was then the first to honour the Right of Helena, 13 to become the High Priestess and Queen of Eucadia (Ucadia). 14 Soon after, all the kings and queens of the Diaspora acknowledged Helena as rightful heir. 15 Queen Helena and Prince Cuinalba (Kennedy) and their son Cuinstanyn (Constantine), 16 did depart HollyRood and travel to Philippi (Thessalonika) in Eucadia (Ucadia) as the capital.

Book 25

Great Age of Constantine

[277 - 337 CE]

C. 1

In the year known as 277 CE, 2 fourteen hundred and seventy seven years since the dawn of the Great Age, 3 King Alavari of Gotthiuda did invade the north of Eukadia (Ucadia) declaring, 4 that the lands along the Black Sea be the rightful claim of the Goths. 5 King Alavari did press hard and gain control of the former northern lands of Moesia Inferior, 6 and into Thracia threatening the capital Philippi (Thessalonika). 7 Yet Queen Helena was a formidable warrior and general in her own right, 8 and did lead her fleet into the Black Sea and deep into the territory of the Goths, 9 setting fire to their coastal cities and supplies. 10 The Goti (Goths) did panic and retreat and Cuinalba (Kennedy) did lead the Eukadians, 11 against the Goti (Goths) on land until the borders were restored. 12 Emperor Marcus Aurelius Cornelius Valerius of the Franks did then send five legions, 13 in aid of Eukadia to the borders to withstand any further attacks by the Goti. 14 In the year known as 278 CE, 15 fourteen hundred and seventy eight years since the dawn of the Great Age, 16 upon news of battles of the Goti, Reuben Calpernius Piso as the Baalkhan, 17 did move against the Roman legions in western Mesopotamia, Arabia and as far as Syria, 18 causing the Romans massive defeats through ambush and trickery. 19 Emperor Marcus Aurelius Cornelius Valerius was then forced to withdraw legions from Germania, 20 and from North Africa and Eukadia to launch a full assault against the Aryan attacks. 21 In the year known as 279 CE, 22 fourteen hundred and seventy nine years since the dawn of the Great Age, 23 upon the Romans and Frankish legions in Syria slowly regaining control from the Aryan armies, 24 King Chlorus of the Suebi did invade Raetia and Germania Superior claiming it be, 25 their rightful homeland that had been wrongfully taken from them. 26 Emperor Aurelius Cornelius Valerius did then call upon King Gaius Carinus Diocletis (Diocletian), 27 to provide troops to aid and recapture Raetia and Germania Superior, 28 yet Diocletis (Diocletian) replied that he could not spare such legions for fear of the Goths, 29 and the need for stability within his own lands. 30 Emperor Aurelius Cornelius Valerius did then recruit more legions from Spain and Gallia (Gaul), 31 to reinforce the legions in war against the Aryan Kingdom and the Suebi. 32 In the year known as 281 CE, 33 fourteen hundred and eighty one years since the dawn of the Great Age, 34 as the war against the Suebi had ground down to a stalemate, 35 and the war against the Aryans continued to cost lives and supplies, 36 Sigeric the son of Beowulf did unite the Goti (Goth) and Suebi in Hispania, 37 and did capture much of the north and west of Hispania. 38 Upon news of the trouble in Hispania, King Alavari of Gotthiuda did attack Eukadia again, 39 yet this time sending his horseman in advance to set fire to towns and cities, 40 in revenge for the actions of Queen Helena in the previous war. 41 In the year known as 282 CE, 42 fourteen hundred and eighty two years since the dawn of the Great Age, 43 upon the Holly Diaspora bound by war across the world, 44 King Gaius Carinus Diocletis (Diocletian) did launch his forces into Italia, 45 slaughtering the Praetorian Guard and enough Senators until the few survivors, 46 did declare him a god and emperor of the Empire and the memory of Valerius damned. 47 Emperor Aurelius Cornelius Valerius did then withdraw from Syria and returned to Italia, 48 to confront Gaius Carinus Diocletis (Diocletian). Yet upon his arrival, 49 Gaius Carinus Diocletis (Diocletian) succeeded in having the true emperor poisoned, 50 and Diocletis (Diocletian) then declared that the false emperor took his own life, 51 rather than face the legions of Dioclea. 52 The crown of the Franks did then befall to the son of Aurelius Cornelius Valerius, 53 whose name was Aurelius Cornelius Adeptius, 54 as the true Emperor in exile.

C. 2

1 In the year known as 284 CE, 2 fourteen hundred and eighty four years since the dawn of the Great Age, 3 Emperor Cuinhainn (Kevin) of the Celts, 4 Holly King of Caledonia (Scotland) and High King of the Kings of Englia (England), 5 son of King Cuinel (Connell) and of the true Diaspora, 6 did give up the ghost. 7 The Holly crown of Caledonia as Emperor of the Celts, 8 did then befall to his son Cuinalba (Kennedy), 9 the husband of Queen Helena of Eukadia (Ucadia), 10 who remained deep in battle against the forces of King Alavari of Gotthiuda to the north-east, 11 and the forces of the warlord and false emperor Diocletis (Diocletian) to the north-west, 12 and now the forces of Reuben Calpernius Piso as the Baalkhan to the east. 13 In the same year, 14 upon the death of Emperor Cuinhainn (Kevin) of the Celts, 15 Sigeric did unite with the Amorican pirates and invade the south of Englia, 16 seizing the ruins of the cursed city of Londinium and Cantor (Canterbury). 17 Yet Holly King Cuinalba (Kennedy) could not depart to Hollyrood and Englia, 18 nor abandon his wife and his son to the wolves circling Eukadia. 19 In the year known as 285 CE, 20 King Marcus Aurelius Cornelius Adeptius of the Franks did recapture Germania Superior, 21 from King Chlorus of the Suebi, 22 as the forces of Queen Helena and Holly King Cuinalba (Kennedy) were forced back from

Thracia. 23 In the same year, 24 Queen Helena sent word to Queen Morgaine of Eire (Ireland), 25 that she give some sight or wisdom as to the survival of Eukadia (Ucadia), 26 and by what miracle be the survival of the Holly Diaspora. 27 Queen Morgaine did reply saying: Let the angels tremble in fear, 28 that all shall see the true nature of the son and the mother in all their glory. 29 To each then befalls a destiny and thus the father must attend to his own business. 30 Do not be afraid but seize the day! Seize the day! 31 Queen Helena did then send word to Librarian Ammonius of Alexandria, that he send his best tutor, 32 to assist the Queen in strategy and to aid in the teaching of her son Cuinstanyn (Constantine). 33 The Head Librarian Ammonius of Alexandria did send Mattatheos Plotinus to Queen Helena, 34 saying that no greater student of existence and the mind of the Divine Creator there be. 35 Upon his arrival soon after, Plotinus did implore that the Queen consider not just battle plans, 36 but the mind and superstitions of the enemy who revered the literal reincarnation of ancestors. 37 That if the young Cuinstanyn (Constantine) did accompany his mother in battle, 38 as the reincarnation of the great Emperor Esus (Jesus) or Alexander, 39 then such an image would unbalance the Goti soldiers, as to defy a god be the gravest transgression. 40 Queen Helena did then order a special suit of armour be constructed for her son in gold and silver, 41 and blinding silver armour for her personal guard upon the standard of her own armour, 42 so that mother and son and guards be as if from heaven itself. 43 Soon after, King Cuinalba (Kennedy) departed with the fleet to Englia and Hispania, 44 to smash the pirate fleet of the Amoricans and Sigeric, 45 while Queen Helena and her thirteen year old son Cuinstanyn (Constantine) prepared for battle.

C. 3

1 In the year 285 CE, 2 fourteen hundred and eighty five years since the dawn of the Great Age, 3 as the mass army of King Alavari of Gotthiuda did move forward toward Philippi (Thessalonika), 4 of Fifty thousand soldiers, archers and cavalry. 5 Queen Helena with young Cuinstanyn (Constantine) and the royal guard did ride out in front, 6 of twenty five thousand Celt and Eukadian legionnaires, 7 saying to her army: If it be our destiny to fall to the sword of our enemies this day, 8 it shall not be for lack of courage or conviction. 9 For here before you is the blood of the great prophets, the blood of Jesus and Mariamne, 10 the blood of our greatest kings and leaders in the form of my son Cuinstanyn (Constantine). 11 Thus if heaven ordain today be our end, then we shall shed our blood and die together. 12 Yet if you stand with me this day and fight with all your heart and mind, 13 then together we shall tear this enemy into so many pieces it shall not dare strike us again. 14 Upon the blinding sight of the young Prince and the Queen and the guard in their armour, 15 the Goti (Goths) did hesitate and panic saying young Cuinstanyn (Constantine) resembled a god, 16 as the Eukadian cavalry did charge forward catching King Alavari by surprise. 17 Soon the

Goti (Goth) army of King Alavari was surrounded and the Goti were forced to withdraw, 18 leaving more than half of their number killed or captured. 19 In the same year, 20 the Eukadian and Celtic fleet under the command of King Cuinalba (Kennedy) of Englia, 21 did confront the Amorican and Suebi pirates led by Sigeric off the coast of northern Hispania, 22 utterly destroying them and forcing Sigeric and the surviving ships to flee north. 23 At the narrowest point between the island of Englia and the north of Gallia, 24 Sigeric and his wife Mari (Mary) were seized and slaughtered and the Amorican pirates scattered. 25 The son of Sigeric, whose name was Basco (Basque) did then regroup with the survivors, 26 at the ruins of Burdigala (Bordeaux) declaring it be the sacred site of Bordel, 27 where he did demand all men make an oath and pact in blood that each generation thereafter, 28 would dedicate themselves to the destruction of the Holly and avenge the death of Sigeric and Mari. 29 In the same year, 30 after Queen Helena had successfully defended Eukadia (Ucadia), her son Cuinstanyn (Constantine), 31 did commence his study in earnest with Mattatheos Plotinus at Philippi (Thessalonika). 32 As Cuinstanyn (Constantine) was already thirteen, yet without completing his formal education, 33 in any of the sciences of mathematics or grammar or rhetoric or history or philosophy, 34 Plotinus chose to adopt a more pragmatic style of teaching and did travel with Cuinstanyn (Constantine), 35 through the markets and stalls as well as caravans and temples of different religions, 36 that Plotinus could teach Cuinstanyn (Constantine) through what he could see and sense. 37 Over time, Cuinstanyn (Constantine) began to awaken to the Philosophy of One that was at the heart, 38 of the experience of Plotinus in his earlier travels of Asia and the world. 39 To Cuinstanyn (Constantine), Plotinus did say: Verily, even a goat can be taught to open a scroll, 40 and the son of a smith (blacksmith) smart enough to know when to duck their head, 41 yet mimic and instinct be not enough without knowledge of perspective and experience. 42 Thus the greatest knowledge I can ever teach is the unity of the One, the Intellect and all Existence. 43 Alas it is not enough to accept Life as a Dream or the immortality of spirit, 44 for such knowing is not enough to navigate the hazardous seas of awareness. 45 For a man to be at his optimum, he must therefore know himself and all that drives him to be. 46 Likewise, a priest must know more than empty ritual but the essence of the mind of the One Creator. 47 So it is then that the people have become obsessed in ritual without meaning and appearance, 48 whilst without competency as to the mind of the One Creator nor of the meaning of existence. 49 Cuinstanyn (Constantine) did reply that he would dedicate himself and his kingdom, 50 to restoring such knowledge in the minds of men that none worship any god but the One Divine Creator.

C. 4

1 In the year known as 286 CE, 2 fourteen hundred and eighty six years since the dawn of the Great Age, 3 King Aurelius Cornelius Adeptus did

recapture Raetia from King Chlorus of the Suebi, 4 forcing the Suebi into a treaty as the forces of the warlord Diocletis (Diocletian), 5 were pushed further south. 6 In the year known as 287 CE, 7 fourteen hundred and eighty seven years since the dawn of the Great Age, 8 Queen Helena and her son Cuinstanyn (Constantine) did regain Thracia from the Goti (Goths), 9 and capture Asia and Bythnia and Galatia forcing Reuben Calpernius Piso and the Aryans, 10 back to Armenia and Cilicia to defend against the strengthening forces of Eukadia (Ucadia). 11 In the year known as 288 CE, 12 fourteen hundred and eighty eight years since the dawn of the Great Age, 13 King Aurelius Cornelius Adeptius of the Franks, 14 did have a son, whom he named Aurelius Cornelius Ambrosius (St. Ambrose), 15 which means divine gift. 16 In the same year, 17 King Aurelius Cornelius Adeptius did agree to provide four legions to Queen Helena, 18 aided by four more legions of Celts sent by King Cuinalba (Kennedy) husband of Queen Helena. 19 Thus Queen Helena and her sixteen year old son Cuinstanyn (Constantine) now commanded an army, 20 of more than sixty thousand battle hardened legionnaires. 21 Yet before they embarked on the next stage of their campaign, 22 Queen Helena reached out to Queen Morgaine of Eire (Ireland) once more, 23 that she might give foresight and guidance of the events to come. 24 In reply, Queen Morgaine did say: Conquer the land of a man and his sons will rise up in revenge. 25 Slay the sons and daughters and the earth shall yield a far more potent and bitter fruit. 26 Conquer the spirits of men and they may yield for fear and sustenance for a time. 27 Yet terror hardens the mind and heart until a force is spawned that fears nothing. 28 Thus conquest by blood is futile and fear the fuel of a nemesis that always destroys its host. 29 Verily this is the way of all civilisations since the beginning of time. 30 Yet give a man his freedom and dignity and the self discipline to know right from wrong, 31 and such a man shall defend to the death what he has been given, no matter how small. 32 Thus if you wish to truly gain what was lost, then restore the trust of men in heaven, 33 that each be guardian to his own conscience and custodian of his own soul.

C. 5

1 In the year known as 289 CE, 2 fourteen hundred and eighty nine years since the dawn of the Great Age, 3 the army of Queen Helena and her son Cuinstanyn (Constantine) of sixty thousand, 4 did face off against the forces of forty thousand of King Alavari of Gotthiuda, 5 near the capital of Arhemar near the mouth of the Volga River. 6 Queen Helena had already ensured that word did spread that Cuinstanyn (Constantine), 7 be the reincarnation and second coming of Alexander as the Christ (the anointed one). 8 Thus as the army did move into the lands of the Goti many people did come to glimpse the Christ. 9 So when King Alavari did engage against the massed army of Cuinstanyn (Constantine), 10 many of the Goti remained superstitious at fighting against such a famous god, 11 and the forces of the Goti (Goths)

collapsed with little cost to the Eukadians (Ucadians). 12 Queen Helena did then order the Gothic capital to be burnt to the ground, 13 and that a new city be formed known as Attica as a city of conscience and honour, 14 as King Alavari and all his generals were executed. 15 Queen Helena did then divide the former kingdom of Gotthiuda into three parts, 16 with Sarmatia being the name given to the lands north of the Caspian Sea, 17 and Bulgaria the name given for the lands of southern Dacia and former Moesia, 18 and Hungaria (Romania) the name given for the lands of former northern Dacia. 19 Cuinstanyn (Constantine) did then proclaim to the conquered Goti (Goths), 20 that those who honour democracy and rule of law could remain and own their own property, 21 yet those who remained loyal to the old ways were banished from the new lands. 22 Athanari the son of the slain king Alavari and his family and more than 60,000 refugees did then depart, 23 to the Kingdom of Swabia and the capital Argentoratum to pledge their allegiance and seek refuge. 24 King Chlorus did agree on condition that the men serve in defence of the Suebi, 25 and that the women and children be bonded to serve the Suebi to give security to such support. 26 Athanari and the exiled Goti did agree and became known as the OstroGoti and the bonded Goths. 27 In the year known as 294 CE, 28 fourteen hundred and ninety four years since the dawn of the Great Age, 29 the army of Queen Helena and her son Cuinstanyn (Constantine) of fifty thousand, 30 did finally push the Aryan forces of Reuben Calpernius Piso out of Anatolia, 31 and did conquer Armenia to the east as well as reconquer Palestine and Syria. 32 Queen Helena and her son Cuinstanyn (Constantine) did then declare four new regions, 33 with the dissolution of the ancient Roman provinces of Asia, Galatia, Cappodicia and Cilicia, 34 and the formation of Anatolia with its new capital of Nicomedia (Izmit) upon the Sakarya Delta, 35 into the Black Sea, yet linked by channels to the Propontis (Sea of Marmara), 36 and sixty miles east of the site of the future city of Antioch (Constantinople). 37 The new capital of Syria was named Laodicia (Samandag) upon the Orontes Delta and Mediteranean, 38 and the new capital of Palestinia was named Gaza upon the Gazah Delta and Mediterranean. 39 The Jordan valley and mountain ranges between Palestinia and Egyptia were then named a new land, 40 called Sinopia with Aela (Aqaba) its capital upon the Jordan River Delta and Red Sea. 41 In the same year, 42 the Head Librarian Ammonius of Alexandria did give up the ghost, 43 and the academics unanimously elected Mattatheos Plotinus to be the new Head Librarian of Alexandria. 44 Plotinus did then speak to Cuinstanyn (Constantine) now of the age of twenty two and his dilemma. 45 Upon the solemn pledge by Cuinstanyn (Constantine) to finish his education, 46 Plotinus did then beseech Queen Helena that he be released from service. 47 Queen Helena agreed and Mattatheos Plotinus did return to teaching at Alexandria.

C. 6

1 In the year known as 295 CE, 2 fourteen hundred and ninety five years since the dawn of the Great Age, 3 Holly Emperor Cuinalba (Kennedy) did reunite briefly with Queen Helena and Cuinstanyn upon Crete, 4 where Cuinalba (Kennedy) did grant his son the powers to speak and act as if the Emperor of the Celts, 5 and where Queen Helena did grant her son the powers and authority to speak for all Eukadia (Ucadia). 6 Thus, upon the sacred isle of Crete, Cuinstanyn (Constantine) became the most powerful man in the world. 7 In the same year, King Cuil Hen (the Wise) of Cymri (Wales), 8 did have a daughter, whom he named Agnes (St. Agnes). 9 In the year known as 296 CE, 10 fourteen hundred and ninety six years since the dawn of the Great Age, 11 Athanari and the leaders of the OstroGoti (Goths) in exile and service to the Suebi, 12 did demand that King Chlorus end their bondage and grant them equality. 13 Yet King Chlorus and the Suebi rejected the plea on account of the Suebi becoming dependent, 14 upon such able slaves as the OstroGoti in exile. 15 Athanari did warn King Chlorus that upon their Exodus, Swabia be doomed. 16 King Chlorus did respond by seizing Athanari and calling upon his court as witness, 17 where he did condemn Athanari of a false plot to overthrow the Suebi king. 18 Chlorus did then execute Athanari and all the OstroGoti leaders, 19 proclaiming the Goti (Goths) had bound themselves into perpetual servitude. 20 In the year known as 297 CE, 21 fourteen hundred and ninety seven years since the dawn of the Great Age, 22 a young leader among the OstroGoti slaves called Alaric did rise up and unite his people. 23 Upon an appointed time, the OstroGoti did kill the Suebi guards and leave Swabia in a single night. 24 More than fifty thousand Goti (Goths) that had been held as slaves did make the journey. 25 When King Chlorus awoke to discover the Exodus he was enraged and ordered his cavalry, 26 to hunt down and kill Alaric and return the Goti as slaves. 27 Yet the OstroGoti did travel under truce deep into the lands of the Franks toward Hispania, 28 that when the Suebi cavalry did follow they were cut to pieces by a sea of arrows by the Franks. 29 On news of the escape of the OstroGoti and the demise of his cavalry, King Chlorus wept, 30 proclaiming that Swabia truly be doomed. 31 Upon the arrival of Alaric in the lands of the Basco (Basque) in Hispania, 32 the Goti did pledge a blood pact to end their ancient feud and to unite in conquest of their common enemies. 33 King Marcus Aurelius Cornelius Adeptius did then launch an attack of Swabia from the west, 34 as Queen Helena and Cuinstanyn (Constantine) did attack from the east, 35 destroying Swabia and burning Argentoratum (Strasbourg) to the ground, 36 proclaiming the site to be cursed and without spirit or law, 37 forbidding it to be used as a city again. 38 Both Cornelius Adeptius and Queen Helena did then rename the land as Bavaria. 39 As Chlorus and his court were prepared for execution, Cuinstanyn (Constantine) did offer the Suebi, 40 that those prepared to be honourable and change their old ways be free. 41 Yet the Suebi refused and instead

pledged that even in death they would exist as ghosts, 42 in enforcing every high curse against the Holly and those cursed by the surviving Suebi, 43 and that their existence would be solely to destroy and corrupt everything sacred and holly. 44 The Franks and the Eukadians did then execute tens of thousands of Suebi as many did flee, 45 calling themselves the Roma in their claim as Patricians and Protectors of Rome. 46 King Marcus Aurelius Cornelius Adeptius of the Franks did then implore Cuinstanyn (Constantine), 47 join him in the invasion and capture of Rome from the warlord Diocletis (Diocletian). 48 Yet Cuinstanyn (Constantine) did refuse saying that even if Rome be conquered, 49 it remained the cause of the problems of the world and not its solution, 50 and that he (Cuinstanyn) did seek to honour a journey to Eire (Ireland), 51 to honour an oath to Plotinus and complete his education.

C. 7

1 In the year known as 298 CE, 2 fourteen hundred and ninety eight years since the dawn of the Great Age, 3 Cuinstanyn (Constantine) did arrive to a heroes welcome in Eire (Ireland) by the people, 4 who proclaimed him to be the Patrician (St. Patrick) foretold to rid the world of lying serpents. 5 Upon welcome to Tara by Holly King Cúilean (Collins) mac Cúiran and Queen Morgaine, 6 Cuinstanyn (Constantine) did meet Ceridwen (Catherine) before being taken to Clonard, 7 and the University formed by King Cúiran (St. Keiran) and its famous teaching Cuilleain druids, 8 possessing the greatest

knowledge of language, history, science, philosophy, religion and society, 9 at the Abbey of Cúiran (St. Keiran) at Clonard upon the River Boyne, 10 midst the sacred ruins and lands of the most ancient Cuillieain from the beginning of time. 11 In the same year, 12 King Lucius Marcus Aurelius Cornelius Adeptius of the Franks did launch his invasion of Italia, 13 with an army of forty thousand to defeat Diocletis (Diocletian) and seize Rome. 14 Yet in the years since gaining power, Diocletian had trained and forced tens of thousands, 15 into his militia so that upon the Frank army travelling south toward Lake Benacus (Garda), 16 they were overwhelmed by a force of three times their size, 17 that in the space of three days, the Franks had destroyed the opposing army, 18 yet suffered such heavy losses that the invasion was abandoned.

C. 8

1 In the year known as 298 CE, 2 fourteen hundred and ninety eight years since the dawn of the Great Age, 3 at Clonard, Queen Morgaine did present Cuinstanyn (Constantine) to the greatest Holly teachers, 4 with Laisren and his brother Aongus (Angus) tutors in trade and commerce, 5 and Dowhan (Daniel) and Fionn (John) tutors in history and law, 6 and Finian (Philip) and Brendan tutors in languages and grammar, 7 and Tomhas (Thomas) and Seanan (Simon) tutors in logic and rhetoric, 8 and Melachlainn (Malachy) and Dathu (David) tutors in arithmetic, geometry and music, 9 and Timoltach (Timothy) and Queen Morgaine his tutors in

astronomy and the mysteries. 10 For two years Cuinstanyn (Constantine) was immersed deeply into the pool of collective wisdom, 11 until finally he did find his own feet and gained confidence to debate each of his tutors. 12 In trade and commerce, Cuinstanyn (Constantine) did ask why even the greatest empires did fail, 13 and pirates and thieves prosper against the welfare of the people? 14 Laisren and his brother Aongus (Angus) did reply that all true commerce and trade, 15 be built upon four pillars of trust being agreements, bookkeeping, money and interest, 16 that all agreements must be in writing in good faith, good character and good conscience, 17 so that all parties know their obligations and benefits and that nothing may be hidden; 18 that all bookkeeping be consistent according to the laws of arithmetic, 19 and that all accounts be known and all transactions fair. 20 That money be a standard difficult to corrupt and controlled so that it never be debased. 21 That all people possess the rights to own and to use property for their own use, 22 and that none may have such rights or interests stolen or abrogated by false accounts and false agreements. 23 In history and politics, Cuinstanyn (Constantine) did ask how an empire may find lasting peace, 24 when all the history of the world be war for land and status between tribes and brothers, 25 and war between those who honour the rule of law and those who seek to profit from piracy? 26 Dowhan (Daniel) and Fionn (John) did reply that all lasting empires be a paradox, 27 between detailed systems and rules and departments as exemplified by the Hyksos and Marcus Aurelius, 28 yet a form of law so simple and known by all that it cannot be ignored. 29 That when empires lose a sense of their inner functions or corrupt their primary maxims, 30 these then be the catalysts of their own demise and destruction. 31 In language and grammar, Cuinstanyn (Constantine) did ask how a people become more literate, 32 and overcome such differences when so many corrupt their own language or use it as a weapon? 33 Finian (Philip) and Brendan did reply that all true language did owe its origin, 34 to the language formed by Jeremiah and the written forms of Gno. 35 Yet a language that does not grow or adapt as true knowledge increases, dooms people to perpetual ignorance, 36 and a language too prone to corruption and confusion such as Latin does also ferment ignorance. 37 That Greek (Ancient Greek) be the purest ideal of gnosis in that its alphabet remains clear, 38 as alpha (α), beta (β), kappa (κ), delta (δ), epta (ε), zeta (ζ), veta (v), theta (θ), eota (γ), 39 Lambda (λ), mita (μ) ita (ι), ne (η), xi (ξ), pi (π), omni (o), rho (ρ), sigma (ς), tau (τ), 40 Upsi (υ), phee (φ), chi (χ), psi (ψ) and auom (ω). 41 In logic and reason, Cuinstanyn (Constantine) did ask how to end the madness and stupidity, 42 of men and women accepting the lies of madness and maniacs that paint black as white, 43 and bad as good and dark as light that those who follow such lies become so insane? 44 Tomhas and Seanan did reply that all logic begins with the paradox of what is not logical, 45 being a sense of truth that we can see with our eyes and hear with our ears. 46 Thus, tricksters and false priests only gain advantage when people lose trust. 47 For the only truth that any man can truly know is what he feels in his heart and with his senses. 48 As men and women be in essence sensual beings, it is through our senses that we confirm, 49 or we deny the truth or falsity of the world or what is in our minds eye. 50 Thus the false priests and tricksters seek to control us by sowing the seeds of doubt and fear, 51 so that we deny what we may feel or sense as validation to what we know, 52 or that we convince ourselves we feel something in the face of hollow ritual and stupidity. 53 Therefore, as the temples on earth no longer align with the ancient sky (stars) of heaven, 54 a new set of symbols must be forged that are impossible to corrupt in themselves. 55 Only then can logic and rhetoric grow upon such solid foundations. 56 In astronomy and the mysteries, Cuinstanyn (Constantine) did ask Queen Morgaine and Timoltach (Timothy), 57 how the earth be rid of wilful ignorance as the only true evil? 58 Queen Morgaine did reply that life would not be, if not for death. 59 Thus evil as wilful ignorance and the corruption and destruction of knowledge is inevitable, 60 as it be the outward expression of an inward battle within each and every man and woman, 61 between their false spirit and lower mind of ego and their higher sense of self. 62 Therefore, all a true Christ as a servant of the people may do is give men the tools, 63 and trust in the divine plan of heaven and the creator of all existence. 64 Cuinstanyn (Constantine) did reply to all his tutors proclaiming: 65 Verily you be sent by heaven and the Divine Creator as the one and only Twelve Apostles, 66 and it is upon such Revelation that we shall build the greatest society and trust in history.

C. 9

1 In the year known as 300 CE, 2 fifteen hundred years since the dawn of the Great Age, 3 Cuinstanyn (Constantine) did wed Princess Ceridwen (Catherine) of Eire (Ireland), 4 daughter of King Cúilean (Collins) mac Cúiran and Queen Morgaine, 5 before the largest gathering of Holly Diaspora in history of over ten thousand, 6 at the ancient site of Tara in Eire (Ireland). 7 Yet the Piso and their Aryan army of the followers of Manes did not honour any law or tradition, 8 and saw such events as an opportunity to reclaim the lands of Anatolia and Syria, 9 that they had lost to Queen Helena and Eukadia (Ucadia). 10 Ishmael Calpernius Piso also known as Brahram, the son of Reuben Calpernius Piso, 11 did attack with an army of fifty thousand the cities of Hierapolis and Edessa, 12 and then westward along the coast the cities of Anazarbus and Adana and then Seleucea. 13 As Queen Helena and Cuinstanyn (Constantine) did return in haste to Eukadia (Ucadia), 14 Cuinstanyn (Constantine) sent word that any man willing to fight against such evil, 15 shall be recognised as a free and equal citizen of all Holly lands, 16 and any tribal and militia leader willing to take up arms to defend against such madness, 17 shall be recognised as a man of proper status and standing, 18 and any people willing to defend their lands against oppression shall be granted freedom, 19 and democracy under a model of

law and trust yet to come that shall honour the golden rule of law. 20 Upon hearing such an oath, the whole of the people of Anatolia did rise up against the Piso, 21 and by the time of the arrival of Queen Helena and Cuinstanyn (Constantine) for battle, 22 the forces of Ishmael Calpernius Piso also known as Brahram had been banished. 23 Upon the sight of such courage and will of the people for freedom and independence, 24 Cuinstanyn (Constantine) did declare that Anatolia, Syria, Palestinia and Sinopia, 25 be independent lands, possessing the right to elect their own leaders, 26 under the framework and laws of Eukadia (Ucadia) until such time as the leaders of all people, 27 meet and determine and consent to the common law of all free people.

C. 10

1 In the year known as 301 CE, 2 fifteen hundred and one years since the dawn of the Great Age, 3 as Cuinstanyn (Constantine) did remain at Philippi (Thessalonika) with his mother Queen Helena, 4 he did call upon the first and true Apostles to travel to Eukadia (Ucadia), 5 and continue the planning of a Sacred Empire and Theology to bring lasting harmony to all people. 6 All except Queen Morgaine did come. 7 Upon their arrival, Cuinstanyn (Constantine) did enquire to Laisren and his brother Aongus (Angus), 8 how best to prepare the defences of the Empire for lasting harmony yet be prepared for the worst? 9 For while the finest Roman Generals did plan with great precision the position of each legion and road, 10 the upkeep of such a vast military network did ruin the prosperity of Rome. 11 Laisren and his brother Aongus (Angus) did reply that the history of the military control of the world, 12 be like the seasons of plenty and the seasons of difficulty and that in seasons of plenty, 13 an empire depends more upon its forces upon the land to command control. 14 Yet in seasons of scarcity, the people come to the coast and great rivers, 15 in search of food and shelter and safety as the land becomes barren and lawless. 16 Thus an empire that controls the inland sea (Mediterranean) can command the world. 17 As the earth did herald a cycle of greater hardship the empire of Cuinstanyn (Constantine), 18 must therefore be the greatest force of the inland sea (Mediterranean). 19 Cuinstanyn (Constantine) did then enquire of Dowhan (Daniel) and Fionn (John) how law and order, 20 be maintained when the people demanded to see their leaders, 21 yet no emperor even in the days of Hadrian and Trajan did succeed in seeing all the people, 22 and if power be granted to legates and consuls then such power itself had corrupted many? 23 Dowhan (Daniel) and Fionn (John) did reply that from the beginning, the capital of an empire, 24 must symbolise strength of purpose and logic of power beyond the circumstance of Rome; 25 that power must be delegated, yet divided between those who uphold the laws of heaven, 26 and those that uphold the laws of the people, and are elected by the people. 27 Thus, each element of a true democracy complements and balances each other, 28 that no tyrant may seize power and survive the

condemnation of the people, 29 nor may any false priest rise to authority without challenge as to their capacity. 30 Cuinstanyn (Constantine) did then call upon Mattatheos Plotinus to come to Philippi. 31 There at Philippi, Cuinstanyn (Constantine) did declare Plotinus be the thirteenth Apostle, 32 and did ask the Head Librarian of Alexandria what be the most strategic location, 33 for the site of a new capital of the world under the golden rule of law and justice? 34 Plotinus did reply that the garrison town of Perinthos at the delta of the Lycus River, 35 at the Bosphorous straight between the Sea of Marmara and the Black Sea, 36 be the best possible location to form a new capital for all four quarters of the world. 37 Cuinstanyn (Constantine) did then appoint Plotinus as his representative and overseer, 38 on the construction of a new city to surpass the greatness of Rome. 39 Plotinus did then order a survey be made of the entire peninsula, 40 from the Acropolis of Perinthos on the first hill closest to the Bosphorous, 41 and north-west for 3 miles across the plateau and five hills behind, 42 and then south-west for three miles until reaching the coast and then back to the Acropolis. 43 Mattatheos Perinthos did then return to Alexandria to meet Diophantus, also known as Pappas, 44 and the father of algebra and a master of geometry and the greatest mathematician for 200 years. 45 Cuinstanyn (Constantine) did then declare that the new capital of Eukadia (Ucadia), 46 be known as Antioch (Constantinople) meaning the hub and centre of the wheel of the world, 47 and ordered a workforce of over 50,000 free men to be assembled to the site, 48 To commence building the most impregnable defensive walls ever seen, 49 as Perinthos and Diophantus completed the plans for major buildings and streets. 50 In the year known as 302 CE, 51 fifteen hundred and two years since the dawn of the Great Age, 52 Cuinstanyn (Constantine) and Ceridwen (Catherine) of Eire (Ireland), 53 did have a son at Philippi they named Cuinstans (Constans). 54 In the same year, 55 Cuinstanyn (Constantine) did approve the plans of Diophantus for the first building of the city, 56 as the largest and tallest single enclosed building ever created in the history of human civilisation, 57 being 240 ft in width and length and over 180 ft in height as the first church in history, 58 known as the Great Basilica of Divine Wisdom, also known as Megale Basilica Sophia, 59 also simply known as the Great Sophia (Mega Sophia). 60 As more than 10,000 workers began construction on the plans of Diophantus and Perinthos, 61 as approved by Cuinstanyn (Constantine) the Basilica was to be the focus of the city, 62 as the living temple of the One and only Divine Creator and Divine Law under the Golden Rule, 63 with each corner of the Basilica representing the four cardinal points of the compass, 64 of North (Borea), South (Austrea), West (Europea) and East (Orientea). 65 To the south of the Basilica a great public forum was planned as the final destination, 66 of a long grand avenue known as the Mese travelling east to west before turning south-west, 67 toward the Golden Gate and main entrance of the city. 68 To the east a palace and administration buildings were then under construction. 69 In the year known as 303 CE, 70 fifteen hundred and three years since the dawn of the Great Age, 71 Cuinstanyn (Constantine) did visit Lucius Marcus Aurelius Cornelius Adeptius of the Franks, 72 and did reveal his plans to the leader of the Franks and did ask Adeptius, 73 if he accept the role of exarch of a new kingdom of conscience of all Celts, Eukadians and peoples? 74 Marcus Aurelius Cornelius Adeptius did accept the role as the first leader in history of Europalia (Europe), 75 and did declare his new Greek name to be Lukhas (Luke) Eusebius, 76 meaning one who is truly devout before heaven and the Divine Creator. 77 In the same year at Tara, 78 Cuinstanyn (Constantine) and Ceridwen (Catherine) of Eire (Ireland), 79 did have a second son they named Cúilman (Colman). 80 In the year known as 305 CE, 81 fifteen hundred and five years since the dawn of the Great Age, 82 Cuinstanyn (Constantine) was called to Hollyrood upon the illness of his father.

C. 11

1 In the year known as 306 CE, 2 fifteen hundred and six years since the dawn of the Great Age, 3 Emperor Cuinalba (Kennedy) of the Celts, 4 Holly King of Caledonia (Scotland) and High King of the Kings of Englia (England), 5 son of King Cuinhainn (Kevin) and of the true Diaspora, 6 did give up the ghost. 7 The Holly crown of Caledonia as Emperor of the Celts, 8 did then befall to his son Cuinstanyn (Constantine). 9 In the same year, 10 Cuinstanyn (Constantine) and Ceridwen (Catherine) of Eire (Ireland), 11 did have a third son born at Hollyrood they named Cuirell (Carroll). 12 Yet soon after Ceridwen (Catherine) received word from her mother Queen Morgaine, 13 that her father Holly King Cúilean (Collins) mac Cúiran was gravely ill. 14 Ceridwen (Catherine) and Cuinstanyn (Constantine) did return to Tara, 15 where Holly King Cúilean (Collins) mac Cúiran soon after did give up the ghost. 16 While tradition be that the Holly High King be bestowed unto the male heir, 17 so beloved be Queen Morgaine by all the people of Eire (Ireland), 18 that all the lesser kings and tribal kings and druids and elders did demand, 19 Morgaine the Faire be Holly High Queen and break the 2,000 year old custom, 20 that forbid the sacred isle be ruled by a sole female ruler. 21 Yet so distraught be the widowed Queen at the loss of her love, 22 that she shut herself in her rooms and refused to receive sustenance or counsel, 23 until Ceridwen (Catherine) and Cuinstanyn (Constantine) did convince her to come to court. 24 There at the court of Tara, before all the ancient lawmakers and Holly Priests, 25 Queen Morgaine did shock her court by pronouncing Cuinstanyn (Constantine) be her son, 26 and thus the sole heir of all authority and that of Cúilean (Collins), 27 before she did renounce her crown and did place the Holly Crown upon Cuinstanyn (Constantine). 28 Morgaine did then utter her final prophecy saying: 29 I am the sea and the air and the sky and the ground beneath your feet, 30 for I be borne of flesh and blood and soon shall depart this life. 31 Thus I be no sorceress nor concubine of the dark arts nor

magician, 32 as no power do I possess to halt the consequence of time or season, 33 but only the knowledge and insight that Life be a Dream, 34 and the foresight that as this mortal form decays, 35 nothing that is already spirit can be unmade as spirit, 36 and thus none who awaken can ever truly die. 37 Do not give credence then to those who shall evoke my name for their favour, 38 or abuse my bones in false rituals against heaven. 39 Verily, I tell you that there shall come a day, 40 when the very soul of men shall be tested, 41 when every man and woman and child shall be cursed as slaves by pirates, 42 and the memory of the Holly shall be but shadows and dust. 43 Do not grieve then for me upon my passing, 44 but call to our ancestors and to heaven, 45 that we be not abandoned or asleep for long, 46 and that when the time comes to awaken, 47 we shall remember that Virtue Conquers Peril, 48 to Seize the Day! Seize the Day! Seize the Day! 49 Three days later Queen Morgaine did die in her sleep, 50 and as the last testament of Queen Morgaine, 51 all power and rights transferred to Cuinstanyn (Constantine) as Holly High King, 52 who then did appoint Holly King Cúilaidh (Cooley) of Munster as his High Steward in Eire (Ireland), 53 and did appoint his wife Queen Ceridwen (Catherine) as the Twelfth Apostle, 54 as the most beloved of all the true Apostles.

C. 12

1 In the year known as 307 CE, 2 fifteen hundred and seven years since the dawn of the Great Age, 3 Cuinstanyn (Constantine) and King Aurelius Cornelius Adeptius of the Franks as Eusebius, 4 did seek counsel from Perinthos and the Twelve Apostles as to the planned invasion of Italia, 5 and the end of the reign of the tyrant warlord Diocletis (Diocletian) of Rome. 6 Dowhan (Daniel) and Fionn (John) did reply to the call to invade Italy and reclaim Rome, 7 asking what be the benefit of inviting one thief full of sickness into the household? 8 For even if they be a guest of illustrious honours, such sickness will send the house mad. 9 Frustrated at such lack of certainty, Cuinstanyn (Constantine) did beseech the twelfth Apostle, 10 that Queen Ceridwen (Catherine) as the daughter of Morgaine did possess great sight, 11 and could provide some knowledge as to strategy to rid the world of Diocletian and such pirates. 12 Queen Ceridwen (Catherine) did reply, saying: Tears of joy and sadness do I see, 13 for victory be as certain as your greatness. 14 Verily, every end is a new beginning and to live, one must die. 15 Alas, I see the wheels of the universe and our celestial place in the heavens in motion, 16 that what is set cannot be undone, no matter how forgetful our descendants. 17 Nor can the consequences of history be averted. 18 Only your free will and respect that everything in the cosmos happens for a purpose, 19 and the first and primary purpose is to unite the world in freedom before Italia. 20 Cuinstanyn (Constantine) and Eusebius did then change their plans and attack Bordel (Bordeaux), 21 and utterly the Suebi, forcing Alaric and the OstroGoti (Ostrogoths) to flee eastward to Italia. 22 Basco and his followers did escape northward by boat, yet were found

Book 25 Great Age of Constantine

three days later hiding, 23 and Basco and his family and generals were executed after they uttered high curses against the Diaspora, 24 saying that as Suebi they swore to be ghosts and to condemn all their descendants to be ghosts, 25 until the world be rid of every memory of the Cuilliaéan (Holly) as if they had never existed, 26 and every lie be worshipped as truth and the people enslaved and the rulers of the world be Suebi. 27 In Italia, Diocletian welcomed Alaric to Rome and celebrated his arrival as if he be a victorious general. 28 In the same year, Cuinstanyn (Constantine) did then travel to North Africa and the land of the Berbers, 29 where he did meet their leader named Mascellus (Marcellus) who did pledge himself in alliance with the Holly, 30 and the dissolution of Mauretania and the formation of Barbaria with its capital upon the Nadir Delta, 31 upon the Mediterranean Sea at a new city called Timogadi (Nador). 32 Cuinstanyn (Constantine) did then travel south and over the Atlas mountains to the lands of Agas, 33 and Audas the leader of the Gaetulian (Getulian) people did pledge support of Cuinstanyn (Constantine), 34 and the formation of a new capital at the Triton River Delta on the Mediterranean called Abes (Gabes). 35 Cuinstanyn (Constantine) did then return north to the Mediterranean Sea and the land of eastern Berbers, 36 and the leader Maecius who did pledge his support for the new land of Algeria and a new capital, 37 upon the Algolis (Soummam) Delta at a city called Saldae (Bejaia) on the Mediterranean coast. 38 Cuinstanyn (Constantine) did then travel east to Alexandria where he did meet the brother of Eusabius, 39 whose name was Marcus Aurelius Cornelius Achilleus of the Franks. 40 Marcus Aurelius Cornelius Achilleus did agree to the new name of Markos Achilles, 41 as the leader of a new region to be called Australia as the southern seas and lands united as one. 42 In the year known as 308 CE, 43 fifteen hundred and eight years since the dawn of the Great Age, 44 the Great Basilica of Wisdom as the first official building of Antioch was completed, 45 within the sacred and royal precinct of the first hill and forum and palaces known as the Temenos. 46 Many of the other twenty two precincts of the city were also well under construction such as for trade, 47 and for the ports and warehouses, for the arts, museums and galleries as well as athletics, 48 such as a great Hippodrome north of the commercial Agora of the Ox. 49 Before a crowd of tens of thousands of workers and legionnaires and the many Diaspora who came, 50 Cuinstanyn (Constantine) did dedicate and open the first Christian Church in history, saying: 51 Let this day and moment be remembered by all generations, 52 as the day that the unbreakable bond be remade between heaven and the earth. 53 For this be the day that the most sacred of sanctuaries as the Great Basilica of Divine Wisdom, 54 and the Great Church (Mega Ecclesia) be blessed and filled by the spirit, 55 of the One and only Divine Creator of all existence and life, 56 and the first and primary source of all law and all rights and all authority. 57 Verily, there is, there was, there has only ever been One Law. 58 All law is equal that no one is above it, 59 all law is measured that all may learn and know it, 60 all law is standard that it is always applied the same. 61 Thus a valid law is a rule that prohibits or permits certain acts. 62 A rule is a norm, a bar, a maxim, a measure or a standard. 63 A rule may be derived by instruction, discovery, custom or consent. 64 The highest law is Divine being a rule given by divine instruction, 65 as nothing may contradict such a rule. 66 The second highest law be the reason of Mind, 67 being an edict given by a great council of wise elders or jurists, 68 as nothing absurd and without good reason may be considered law. 69 The third highest law be the law of the people, 70 as the consent and will of the people is the source of true authority. 71 Any law that is against such truth cannot be law. 72 Therefore, the most sacred place possessing the highest of all authority is one that honours Divine Law, 73 and honours the wisdom of reason and of wise jurists and precedence, 74 and honours the will of the people to elect its leaders and participate in government. 75 Verily, there be no more sacred place of law than the Great Basicilica of Wisdom, 76 as the law and the Divine Creator of all Existence and the People are One. 77 Therefore, let no man or woman defile or desecrate this most sacred of places, 78 nor any judgement stand unless it also be uttered within these sacred walls before Heaven.

C. 13

1 In the year known as 309 CE, 2 fifteen hundred and nine years since the dawn of the Great Age, 3 Cuinstanyn (Constantine) did travel south down the Red Sea to the lands of Axum. 4 And then to the city of Axum and King Ousanas who did celebrate such an illustrious visit. 5 Cuinstanyn (Constantine) did pledge that if King Ousanas join a new alliance of good faith, 6 and good conscience, then slavery would be abolished and the pirates and slave traders, 7 banished forever into the pages of history. 8 King Ousanas did reply that never before had an Emperor bothered to travel to the lands of his people, 9 and yet many a Roman Emperor had deemed it expedient to trade and to demand tribute, 10 and even to demand his people be bonded into servitude. 11 Yet neither had a Holly King come to rid his people of such curses and respect the equality of all men, 12 regardless of colour of their skin or their heritage. 13 Cuinstanyn (Constantine) did then reply that before all present and before all his officials, 14 that the first Politia (city-state) of Christ is and shall forever be named Ethiopia as equals before heaven, 15 so that each and every man and woman borne on African soil who honours the rule of law, 16 and who honours justice and democracy shall stand united against the forces of tyranny and slavery, 17 and to sacrifice their lives if need be to help rid Africa and the world of tyranny and slavery, 18 and never permit slavery or tyranny to curse the people of Africa or harm their children again. 19 King Ousanas did reply, saying: Truly upon such words from heaven, 20 let no man who calls himself a son of Africa or is from the lands of Africa or of the tribes of Africa, 21 dishonour such a solemn and sacred vow and oath. 22 King Ousanas did then agree to change the

Book 25 Great Age of Constantine

name of his lands of eastern Africa to Ethiopia, 23 and to form a new capital upon the Axumir (Mareb) River Delta called Saladin (Saidin). 24 Cuinstanyn (Constantine) did then travel to Hegra in Arabia to meet Berylas (Beryllus) the leader, 25 who agreed to unite as an ally of Cuinstanyn (Constantine) and to form his new capital as Saracenia, 26 at the great Ashar (Aftan) River Delta on the Persian Gulf and to rename the ancient city Telma (Dilmun). 27 Cuinstanyn (Constantine) then called upon the legions and forces of Aurelius Cornelius Achilleus, 28 as well as legions from Lybia, Barbaria, Ethiopia and Tunisia to join him in Saracenia, 29 aided by legions from as far as Irenia (Ireland), Spania, Francia, Saxonia and Eukadia (Ucadia). 30 The mass army of more than 80,000 of Cuinstanyn (Constantine) did then move north-east, 31 into Mesopotamia and the lands held by Reuben Calpernius Piso as the Baalkhan of the Aryans. 32 Reuben did send his son Ishmael Calpernius Piso and the army westward from the capital Eden, 33 with a force of over fifty thousand to confront and destroy Cuinstanyn (Constantine). 34 Yet, as Ishmael Calpernius Piso advanced westward, the second army of 60,000 under Eusebius, 35 did outflank him and advance eastward toward Eden. 36 Facing certain defeat, Ishmael Calpernius Piso abandoned his army and generals and fled, 37 to hide in the mountains of Bactria (Afghanistan), leaving Eden and his father defenceless. 38 After crushing the Aryan army, Cuinstanyn (Constantine) and Eusebius did then surround Eden, 39 and did capture Reuben Calpernius Piso and his head Cohen (Priests), 40 before ordering Eden (Ray) to be burnt and torn to its foundations that no more would it, 41 ever be a site for a city or habitation. 42 As Reuben Calpernius Piso was led away to captivity at Antioch, he did observe the flames of Eden, 43 and did cry out: Behold! The serpents have entered the Gardens of Eden and laid them to waste. 44 Let my descendants revenge me and destroy all that the Holly hold dear, 45 that one day those that worship Satan shall wear the skin of the Holly as their garments. 46 Cuinstanyn (Constantine) did then order his elite legions to chase down and eliminate the Aryans, 47 with some travelling further east into the mountains and other legions travelling south to Himyar, 48 where the slave merchant kingdom was routed and the city of Zafar burnt to the ground. 49 Cuinstanyn (Constantine) did then order the restoration of the name Persia, 50 and the new capital to be Commercion (Gameron) on the Shoor River delta, 51 while the lands once held by the slave merchants of Himyar he did call Abbysinia, 52 with its new capital to be Adana (Aden) on the Abb (Ibb) River Delta on the Gulf of Aden. 53 Between the Euphrates and the Tigris, Cuinstanyn (Constantine) did form the new land, 54 called Mesopotamia with the new capital named Chaldos (Kuwait City), 55 at the delta of the great Euphrates River and the powerful Chaldon (Pishon) River from the south-west. 56 Between the Tigris and the Zagros Mountains, Cuinstanyn (Constantine) did form the new land, 57 called Assyria with the new capital Basra on the Euphrates/ Tigris Delta.

C. 14

1 In the year known as 310 CE, 2 fifteen hundred and ten years since the dawn of the Great Age, 3 Cuinstanyn (Constantine) and Perinthos with his guard did travel north to the lands of the giants, 4 first being the Normen of the west and their leader Alda of the Alani. 5 Cuinstanyn (Constantine) did pledge to Alda that if he unite in an empire of conscience, 6 then Cuinstanyn (Constantine) and the world would recognise the claims of the Normen, 7 to the former and ancient homelands of the Suebi (Ukraine & Poland). 8 Alda agreed and the new lands of Alania was formed with its capital moved to Odessos, 9 upon the Dnieper Delta on the Black Sea. 10 Cuinstanyn (Constantine) did then travel east to meet with Geberic the King of Vandali Normans, 11 occupying the ancient homelands of the Goti. 12 Geberic did agree and entreat with Cuinstanyn (Constantine), 13 forming a new capital at Tanais (Rostov-na-Donu) on the Don Delta into the Black Sea. 14 Cuinstanyn (Constantine) did then travel east to the edge of the great inland sea (Caspian Sea), 15 where the ancient nations of semi-nomadic horseman of the Tartari, Karesmi, Kazari and Karakali, 16 did unite as a Federation under Sabiros as the Politea of Sarmatia. 17 Cuinstanyn (Constantine) did then travel to the far north and to the autonomous tribes, 18 of Normen that were the last to leave their homeland Asgardi and settle along the Baltic Sea. 19 Cuinstanyn (Constantine) did then implore with each of them to unite for a greater common good, 20 and did then entreat with each of them to recognise four more Christian Politia, 21 the first being the Politia (city-state) of Lithuania, with its Metropolis being Nema, 22 upon the Nemos (Nemunas) River Delta and the Baltic Sea, 23 and its first Patriarchos being the tribal leader called Kuros, 24 and the second being Politia of Latvia, with its Metropolis being Riga, 25 upon the Dyna (Daugava) River Delta and the Baltic Sea, 26 and its first Patriarchos being the tribal leader called Latgala, 27 and the third being Politia of Estonia, with its Metropolis being Narva, 28 upon the Narva River Delta and the Baltic Sea, 29 and its first Patriarchos being the tribal leader called Aestias, 30 and the fourth being Politia of Rusia, with its Metropolis being Rusa (St Petersburg), 31 upon the Rusa River Delta and the Baltic Sea, 32 and its first Patriarchos being the king of the Norman tribal federation, 33 whose name was Cyrillos and his son Varangos. 34 In the same year, 35 Cuinstanyn (Constantine) did commission Mattatheos Perinthos as the new Exarch of Borealia, 36 and did commission him to create a new capital of the north, 37 upon the Danube Delta on the Black Sea named Galatia. 38 Cuinstanyn (Constantine) did then announce the formation of a new capital, 39 for Orientalia as the Exarchos of the east that he himself would oversee, 40 at the delta of the Mert and Halys rivers in northern Anatolia at Samson (Samsun). 41 Cuinstanyn (Constantine) did then proclaim within the walls of the Great Basilica, saying: 42 Behold the Tetrarchy (four pillars) of an empire built upon conscience and equality of

Book 25 Great Age of Constantine

all, 43 under the Golden Rule of Law be now set in stone. 44 To the north now be the Exarchgos of Borealia as the northern seas and lands, 45 and the Politia of Bulgaria, Hungaria, Vandalia, Alania, Lithuania, Latvia, Estonia, Rusia and Sarmatia, 46 with its capital of Galatia and its Exarch Mattatheos (Perinthos), 47 being the symbol of prudence and wisdom and insight as to the mind of the Divine Creator. 48 To the south now be the Exarchgos of Australia as the southern seas and lands, 49 and the Politia of Egyptia, Sinopia, Libia, Algeria, Barbaria, Ethiopia, Gaetulia, Garamantia and Somalia, 50 with its capital of Alexandria and its Exarch Markos (Achilles), 51 being the symbol of chivalry and compassion in honouring the laws of the Divine Creator. 52 To the west now be the Exarchgos of Europalia as the western seas and lands, 53 and the Politia of Alba, Irenia, (Ireland), Spania, Francia, Saxonia, Macedonia and Hellas, 54 With its capital of Philippi and its Exarch Lukhas (Eusebius), 55 being the symbol of justice and truth as to the execution of the laws of the Divine Creator. 56 To the east now be the Exarchgos of Orientalia as the eastern seas and lands, 57 and the Politia of Anatolia, Armenia, Syria, Palestinia, Mesopotamia, Abbysinia, Assyria, Saracenia and Persia, 58 with its capital of Samson and its Exarch Iohannes (Constantinos), 59 being the symbol of fortitude, courage and perseverance in honouring the laws of the Divine Creator. 60 Behold the Kes-Ros (Cross) of the Ecclesia (Church) of Christ as north, south, east and west! 61 No longer then the Roman salute with open palm and hand upon some revered relic as threat and curse, 62 against the breaking of ones word and thus calling upon all form of misery and destruction. 63 For no sacred oath or vow be binding unless it be free and without duress to heaven, 64 and thus no Roman oath or vow be legal or morally binding but mere hollow ritual. 65 Behold then the only true sign of binding and oath that be pleasing to heaven under the rule of law, 66 for when a man first holds his left hand upon his chest and feels his beating heart, 67 then such a sign signifies to the world the truth and integrity of his actions. 68 Thus when he makes the sign of the Kes-Ros (Cross) to the four virtues and points with his right hand, 69 he does signify his obedience and respect of the golden rule of law and good faith and intention. 70 For when a man completes the symbol of the Ros (Rho) and kisses his hand with his lips, 71 he does pledge a solemn binding oath to the truth of his speech to his heart. 72 More powerful than the Kes-Ros (Cross) be than any superstitious blood oath or hollow salute, 73 for no force of evil or malice withstand its power when executed in knowledge and clear intent. 74 Verily to defy the will of heaven is to evoke the entirety of creation against ones self, 75 and to make pledges upon threat of doom or curse or the memory of what is held sacred is utter madness. 76 Therefore, just as a pledge to heaven must be in good conscience and free from superstition, 77 no place of law may also be a graveyard of bones nor a site of blood sacrifice. 78 Verily, the worst of all places in the sight of heaven and Divine Law be those cities, 79 that have witnessed killing for sport and human sacrifice to satisfy the lust of broken minds. 80 Behold, no city founded on lies or slavery or human sacrifice or blood sports be a place of law, 81 nor may any dictate or judgment from such a condemned place ever be considered a law, 82 or any such place of wickedness be a place of Christianity or site of Christian virtue. 83 Better then such places be torn to their foundations and covered over as if they never existed, 84 than the existence of such places continue to insult the conscience of a united humanity. 85 Thus, the symbol of the empire of law and good conscience be Theokes (The Keys), 86 for it be "In the Divine We Trust" and all Rights (ros) be in Trust. 87 Behold, there is no higher office or authority on earth than the spirit of Christ, 88 that resides in every law and every official and every sacred space across the empire. 89 Thus, there can never be a single emperor, or leader or one who proclaims himself to be a deity, 90 for to proclaim such things is to deny the One and to deny the spirit of the one being Christ. 91 Thus, the leader of an Exarchea is an Exarchos and the leader of a Politia (city-state) is a Patriarchis, 92 and a province of a Politia (city-state) be a Diakesia (Diocese) led by a Monarch, 93 and a community of a Diakesia (Diocese) be a Paroikia (Parochial) led by a Presbyteros (Presbyter). 94 Therefore, no community or province or city or state or region be without certainty of leaders. 95 As to the authority of heaven and of Christ, each Diakesia (Diocese) shall hold a seal of two keys, 96 as the authority of Christ and heaven as one key and authority of the people and the earth as the other. 97

The Diakesia (Diocese) of the Metropolis (Capital) shall be called a Metropolites (Metropolitan) Sedos, 98 and the Patriarch of a Politia holding authority over religious rights, 99 within the Basilica of the Metropolis (Capital). 100 The Diakesia (Diocese) of a province shall be known as a Episkopos (Episcopal) Sedos, 101 and the city of a Diakesia (Diocese) shall be known as an Episcopolis, 102 and the Monarch shall hold religious rights over the Sunagoge (Synagoge). 103 As to the ecclesiastical authority of all who hold the office of Monarch or Presbyteros, 104 it shall be mandated that all who are deemed worthy to hold such office must first be a master of law, 105 that shall be called a Rabbi and that none may be a Monarch or Presbyteros, 106 unless they be a Rabbi and have studied and been tested for seven years as competent and suitable. 107 The democratically elected legislators of a Diakesia (Diocese) be then a Sunedrion (Synhedron), 108 and the democratic council of a Politia (city-state) therefore be a Sunedos (Synod), 109 and the democratic Ecclesia of Christ be a great Oikoumenikos (Ecumenical) Council. 110 Behold, this be the will of all civilised people and the intent of the Divine Creator of All. 111 Thus as it is spoken and written, so it shall be the law of the Church of Christ forever.

C. 15

1 In the year known as 311 CE, 2 fifteen hundred and eleven years since the dawn of the Great Age, 3 Cuinstanyn (Constantine) and a united force of over 100,000 did invade the Kingdom of Dioclea, 4 and utterly rout the forces

Book 25 Great Age of Constantine

of the warlord Diocletis (Diocletian), 5 forcing the survivors to flee to Italia for safety. 6 Cuinstanyn (Constantine) did then order the complete destruction of Dioclea (Dubrovnik), 7 that the land be cursed and unfit for habitation or as a site of worship or law forever. 8 A new Politia (city-state) was then formed as Croatia with its capital on the Cetina Delta, 9 upon the Adriatic Sea and was then called Spoleto (Split). 10 To honour the new city, Cuinstanyn (Constantine) ordered that it possess a grand Basilica, 11 and public buildings so that the people of the Dalmatian coast embrace democracy and integrity. 12 With Italia and the forces of Dioletis (Diocletian) surrounded on all sides, 13 Cuinstanyn (Constantine) did return to Antioch to oversee the great trial of Reuben Calpernius Piso, 14 and his false high priests and court officials. 15 In the year known as 312 CE, 16 fifteen hundred and twelve years since the dawn of the Great Age, 17 as the city of Antioch had become a vibrant and sophisticated city of more then 100,000, 18 the greatest legal trial the world had ever seen did commence under the dome of the Great Basilica. 19 Presiding over the trial were the four Exarchos being Mattatheos Perinthos Exarchos of Borcalia (North), 20 and Markos Achilles Exarchos of Australia (South) and Lukhas Eusebius Exarchos of Europealia (West), 21 and Cuinstanyn (Constantine) himself as Iohannes Constantinos Exarchos of Orientalia (East). 22 Reuben Calpernius Piso and the head priests (Cohen) were brought forward, 23 and Mattatheos Perinthos did ask if he be Reuben of the genos Calpernii known as the fish (piso)? 24 Reuben Calpernius Piso did reply saying: I am who I am. 25 Perinthos did reply if Reuben Calpernius Piso also be known by the name of BaalKhan (Balkhan)? 26 And by the names of Babba meaning father and Messiah meaning messenger? 27 Reuben Calpernius Piso did reply saying: These be your words then, not mine. 28 King Marcus Aurelius Cornelius Adeptius as Lukhas Eusebius did then explain to the accused, 29 that by law they be considered innocent until proven culpable, yet the seriousness of the accusations, 30 and their refusal to demonstrate good character did compel their continued custody. 31 Yet they be afforded three opportunities to settle the matter, 32 the first being prologos (prologue) and the challenge as to an error of justice, 33 whereby a man be accused of an impossibility or that the wrong man be brought to court. 34 The second opportunity be metalogos (metalogue) and the challenge to an error of due process, 35 whereby an accusation fail to be proven as having merit before a man be called to answer (plead), 36 or the facts alleged be not logical, or such evidence presented be subjective and hearsay. 37 The third opportunity be epilogos (epilogue) and the challenge to a judgment at law, 38 whereby a verdict and conclusion fundamentally breach the principles and maxims of law. 39 The kategoria (accusations) were then spoken before the court, 40 the first offence being profanity as one without good conscience against heaven and sacred law, 41 the second offence being perfidy as one without good faith against trust, honour and any respect, 42 the third offence being psychopathy as one without good character against truth or moral decency. 43 The Exarchos did then warn Reuben Calpernius Piso he faced the penalty of death if found culpable, 44 to which Reuben Calpernius Piso did reply saying: During the long hours and days and weeks being held in custody, 45 I have suffered the indignity and injustice as to the delays in my inevitable fate, 46 I have thought long and hard as to what be said before men who continue to wear the robes of gods, 47 yet deny others the same rights as the Holly and instead conspire to control the destiny of the world. 48 Therefore nothing I say or do shall change my fate nor the fact that I do not recognise your authority, 49 and whatever you do to me and to my people shall not change the truth that this be no court of law. 50 Mattatheos Perinthos did reply saying: Indeed prologos (prologue) be your right to assert, 51 and our right therefore to test the validity of such challenge. 52 Mattatheos Perinthos did then ask Reuben Calpernius Piso what be the Authority he recognise? 53 Reuben Calpernius Piso did reply saying: I be the messenger of God and God be the only authority. 54 King Marcus Aurelius Cornelius Adeptius as Lukhas Eusebius did then ask Piso, 55 if he mean Sabaoth and ultimately Satan by the name God as the only Authority? 56 Reuben Calpernius Piso was enraged and demanded that the court not speak the name Satan again, 57 but only by the title God as the name uttered be not worthy for the ears of those present. 58 Iohannes Constantinos (Constantine) did then speak, saying: Though you protest yourself to be, 59 beyond the jurisdiction of the court, you recognise an authority that exists and has a name, 60 and therefore is part of existence and the Oneness of existence and so subject to the Divine Creator. 61 Therefore, by your own words you admit jurisdiction to the present sacred court. 62 Markos Achilles did then present the evidence upon the accusations of profanity, 63 that Reuben Calpernius Piso had denied the authority of heaven yet created a fictitious deity, 64 called God as the hidden name for Satan and that the world be subject to his powers, 65 and had formed completely false scriptures called The Talmud having no respect for heaven, 66 or the great prophets or any of the great teachers of history. 67 Reuben Calpernius Piso did reply, saying: If life be a dream as the holly sorcerers claim, 68 then any man be free to create his own gods in his own image without fear of retribution. 69 Only if what the Diaspora say is false may he then be accused of such crimes. 70 Mattatheos Perinthos did then present the evidence upon the accusations of perfidy, 71 that Reuben Calpernius Piso had created hollow rituals and false laws through his false priests, 72 denying the Golden Rule of Law that all are equal before the law and none above it, 73 but instead had proclaimed he and his followers command the right to enslave humanity, 74 as less than animals and that people condemned to such slavery be threatened with eternal damnation. 75 Reuben Calpernius Piso did reply, saying: The Holly priests had proclaimed themselves to be gods, 76 for thousands of years by blood and birth right and had many times denied and cursed the world. 77 Yet when

Book 25 Great Age of Constantine

challenged as to such rights, the Cuilliaéan had shown themselves to be mere tyrants, 78 who hide behind the veil of equality of law and justice and due process, 79 yet each seeking to be worshipped as a god in their own right midst a sea of animals. 80 Constantine did then present the evidence upon the accusations of psychopathy, 81 that Reuben Calpernius Piso be one without good character or truth or moral decency, 82 and instead had falsely proclaimed the right to have more than one wife at one time, 83 and to molest and sometimes murder innocent children for sexual and deviant pleasure, 84 and had demonstrated contempt to the plight of his own people in times of famine and difficulty. 85 Reuben Calpernius Piso did reply, saying: Every general be a murderer, 86 and every priest be a molester of innocence, 87 and every judge be in jeopardy of moral indecency against the popular will of the people. 88 Constantine did then reply: Truly you have made your objections known and yet have not challenged, 89 the logic or the merit of such accusations, nor denied the substance of such allegations, 90 but admitted in the absence of rebuttal the facts of such allegations, 91 despite your protests and counter claims against the judges and the court. 92 Therefore, before heaven and earth it be lawful, moral and just that we proceed. 93 Mattatheos Perinthos did then call upon Reuben Calpernius Piso to speak or forever hold his tongue, 94 as to any fundamental error of law that may prevent the judges from rendering their verdict? 95 Reuben Calpernius Piso did reply that it be futile to waste more words, 96 to defend against a verdict already set from the moment of his arrest. 97 Lukhas Eusebius did reply that such an assertion be false as no man be culpable until proven so, 98 for the law of the Great Prophets be clear from the beginning of time. 99 Reuben Calpernius Piso did respond and cry out: Your law is nothing more than might be your right, 100 for you care nothing of the culture of others but your precious illusion of law. 101 Constantine did reply: Truly, let it be recorded forever more that no man more condemn himself, 102 than one with such contempt for the law and blinded by such hatred and ego that he have no reason. 103 For within this most sacred of places be the kings and leaders from all four quarters of the world, 104 and every major civilisation and culture of humanity as witness to the falsity of your testimony. 105 Verily, it is you and no other man that has condemned your body by your own hand and words, 106 and thus our verdict be lawful and honourable before heaven. 107 Soon after, Reuben Calpernius Piso and the priests were led away and executed, 108 and a written record of the trial posted in all major languages in front of the Great Basilica. 109 In the same year, 110 upon the conclusion of the trial, Cuinstanyn (Constantinc) did order his military forces in Italia, 111 to advance against the defenders of the warlord Dioletis (Diocletian) and lay siege to Rome. 112 Within a matter of weeks, the Christian armies did conquer Sicily, Calabria and Campagnia in the south, 113 and the Po Valley and hills and valleys to the north of Rome until the city was surrounded. 114 Cuinstanyn (Constantine) did then leave Antioch for the north of Italia to the delta of the River Po, 115 where he did declare the site to be the new capital of a city of respect and fraternity, 116 to be known as Philadelphia as the new capital of Christian Italia.

C. 16

1 In the year known as 313 CE, 2 fifteen hundred and thirteen years since the dawn of the Great Age, 3 as Cuinstanyn (Constantine) did oversee the construction of Philadelphia on the River Po Delta, 4 the Roman Senate did convince the Goti leader Alaric to assassinate Diocletis (Diocletian), 5 and to appeal to the mercy of Cuinstanyn (Constantine) by making him Emperor unopposed. 6 The Senate then elected Gaius Ceionius Volusianus as their Consul and Prefect of Rome, 7 with the power to speak with the full authority of Rome to Cuinstanyn (Constantine), 8 and to bestow to him the symbols and standards of power of Imperial Caesar Augustus. 9 Cuinstanyn (Constantine) did accept to meet the Roman delegation at Philadelphia, 10 where Gaius Ceionius Volusianus did present the head of Diocletian and the symbols of Rome. 11 Yet as they met, word did come from Rome that Alaric as leader of the Goti had declared himself emperor. 12 Despite the actions of Alaric, Cuinstanyn (Constantine) did accept the gifts, 13 beginning with the ring and sword of Imperator Caesar Augustus as the power of Emperor, 14 and then the symbols of Pater Patriae Fiscus as Father of all Public Funds of the State, 15 and then the symbols of Imperium Proconsulare Maius as the highest elected official by the Senate, 16 and then the symbols of Princeps Senatus as the Chief Legislator and Leader of the Senate, 17 and then the symbols of Potestas Tribunicia as the Chief Justice of all Roman Law, 18 and then the robes of Pontifex Maximus as High Priest and King of all Sacred Rites, 19 and then finally the Mitre (hat) and Cappa (cloak) of the Vaticanus Divinitus as prophet of the people. 20 Cuinstanyn (Constantine) did then reply that if the Senate and people of Rome truly honour him, 21 as their duly elected leader, then in twenty one days as the twenty first day of Martius (March), 22 the people of Rome must demonstrate their courage by opening the gates of the city, 23 and enable the forces of Cuinstanyn (Constantine) to deal with Alaric and the Goti, 24 and he (Constantine) did swear that not a single Roman that honours the Law of Rome be harmed. 25 yet, eight days before the deadline and upon the 13th of Martius (March), 26 word did quickly spread to the besieged city of Rome that Emperor Constantine did approach, 27 leading his elite cavalry from the front upon a white horse and in the regalia of Caesar. 28 The Goti that had been in a frenzy of looting did panic and sought to purchase any safe escape. 29 Instead, the people of Rome did rise up and at great cost did slaughter the Goti to the last man, 30 before raising the head of Alaric on a pole at the forum and opening the gates of the city. 31 Thus, upon the morning of the fourteenth day, being the Ides (mid) of Martius (March), 32 Cuinstanyn (Constantine) did then enter Rome in triumph as a hero to the people, 33 as the undisputed Emperor of Rome with more power than any Caesar since the

Book 25 Great Age of Constantine

time of Octavius. 34 Cuinstanyn (Constantine) did then order the convening of the assembly in the Forum of all senators, 35 and all judges, officials and priests so that Caesar Constantinius (Constantine), 36 could address the entire government and leadership of Rome in one speech. 37 There assembled within the Forum, Caesar Constantinius (Constantine) did speak saying: 38 To the people assembled here present upon the most sacred of days as witness to these events, 39 and to those that come to read and hear of such words and edicts of law hereafter, 40 I, the Divinely blessed Commander in Chief (Imperator Caesar Augustus) Iohannus Conablus Constaninius, 41 Divinely inspired Prophet (Vaticanus Divinitus), Supreme Pontiff (Pontifex Maximus), 42 Lord and Head of State (Dominus), Father of the Public Funds (Pater Patriae Fiscus), 43 Highest Elected Official (Imperium Proconsulare Maius), Leader of the Senate (Princeps Senatus), 44 Chief Judge and Magistrate (Potestas Tribunicia) and Great Victor over the Goti, Aryans and Suebi, 45 do hereby acknowledge the will and the consent of the people to be their leader, 46 and do solemnly swear that I shall honour my pledge that no harm come to those who respect the law, 47 and those that honour what is most sacred and profound. 48 Verily upon this day (14 March), being the Ides (middle) of Martis and Dies Sanguinis (Day of Blood), 49 those people who respect the law and honour what is most sacred do remember the supreme sacrifices, 50 of the many who have fought and died for higher virtues and ideals and that many times in history, 51 we have been called to make great sacrifices to honour heaven and Divine Law. 52 Verily this place was founded on such high ideals and honour to heaven and humanity, 53 as a place of sanctuary and law and respect, blessed by the Highest Holly Priests and Great Prophets, 54 bestowed then with the absolute authority as Vaticanus and Pontifex Maximus to speak for heaven. 55 Thus, the most sacred artefact known as the Ark of the Covenant being the Ark of Akhenaten, 56 was brought to this place and a temple suitable for such holly symbols constructed, 57 upon virgin ground as an acropolis called (the) Domus Vaticanae as the House of the Prophet. 58 Yet certain men of low morals and profanity did see such objects as a source of power and desire, 59 and these lands were cleaved in the madness of murder, perfidy, psychopathy and destruction, 60 all for the sake of power and possession and nothing more. 61 Yet the law of equality in honour of the Golden Rule that all are equal and none are above the law, 62 did prevail and such people who cared for nothing but the enslavement and misery of others, 63 were banished from these walls until later these very merchants were not only invited to return, 64 but to corrupt the very soul of Rome and the ground we stand upon. 65 Thus good men did turn away and permit such false and corrupt laws to be enacted, 66 to claim that some men be born gods and some men be born animals and it be the right of the gods, 67 to perpetually enslave the animals and the entire world. 68 So pervasive the corruption of law and trade that no remnant of law remained and these stones, 69 became sacred to every pirate, every thief, every robber and every criminal in history. 70 These walls became the prize in themselves; and the precious and obsessive desire of every warlord, 71 and every slave trader and every corrupt moneylender to seize and control as if it is source of power. 72 Yet even this be not the worst, for the most hideous and insane men were then welcomed from Africa, 73 a Race of Necromancers (diviners of the dead) who sought to control the world, 74 through curses and witchcraft and hollow rituals of unspeakable violence and cruelty, 75 in order to bind the dead to their will and thus sow fear and obedience among all men. 76 Such lunatics and men of illness of mind did then murder countless children, 77 and rape thousands of young women and murder tens of thousands of innocents, 78 while cursing the Domus Vaticanae by constructing below its foundations both a necropolis, 79 and crude underground temples to ply their evil and insane craft. 80 Thus the very earth under our feet here today has been eternally cursed by the blood of innocents, 81 and all connection to heaven and to spirit has been cut off from this place, 82 that the Domus Vaticanae be barren of any spiritual power or connection to spirit or demon, 83 except to the ghosts that roam its halls and rooms and sacrificial chambers. 84 Behold! Upon this day and forever more, I seal shut the doors of the Vatican forever. 85 Furthermore, I abjure the office of Vaticanus Divinitus three times and declare it abolished, 86 and Damnatio Memoriae (damned in memory), to be removed from all records and never revived. 87 Furthermore, in forty days time, I hereby order that the Domus Vaticanae be torn to its foundations, 88 and Damnatio Memoriae (damned in memory) and that such site shall remain forever cursed, 89 and never permitted to be used for any purpose but the grazing of sheep and goats. 90 Verily then, as there be no possible connection to heaven or to any form of spirit in this place, 91 I abjure the office of Pontifex Maximus (Supreme Pontiff) three times and declare it abolished, 92 and order the abolition of the College of Pontiffs and all colleges of priests, virgins and attendants, 93 and declare Pontifex Maximus (Supreme Pontiff) and the College of Pontiffs, 94 Damnatio Memoriae (damned in memory) and never permitted to be revived. 95 For this city has abdicated all rights and reason and respect of spirit, 96 and the city is forbidden to ever be known as Christian or to be visited or house any Rabbi, 97 or any Monarch or Presbyteros or any symbol of Christianity or the Church of Christ. 98 For Rome be the epitome of the Anti-Christ and everything that is against Christianity, 99 and Rome be the enemy of heaven and of all spiritual authority. 100 Verily, Rome be the enemy of the true law of the Golden Rule of Law and Just and Fair Process, 101 and the equality of rights of all men and women and the future prosperity and well being of humanity. 102 Therefore, I declare the doors of the Curia to be sealed shut forever and for the Senate to be dissolved, 103 and Damnatio Memoriae (damned in memory), to be removed from all records and never revived, 104 and all the false laws and false records claiming authority over the world and the false possessions, 105 of land and of people as slaves to be struck, cursed and burnt by fire so that no memory remains. 106 Furthermore, I abjure the office of Dominus (Head of State) three times and declare it abolished, 107 and order that within forty days hence that the Curia and the House of Records be torn to its foundations, 108 and that such sites never again be permitted to be places of law or records ever again. 109 As to the courts that have become so corrupt that wealthy men purchase their freedom, 110 while innocent men and women are condemned and property is stolen by using corrupt laws, 111 I declare the doors of every Roman Court to be sealed and shut forever, 112 and for all claims of laws, edicts, statutes, regulations, precepts and precedents to be destroyed, 113 as without substance or merit of law but entirely false, fabricated and in error. 114 Furthermore, I abjure the office of Potestas Tribunicia (Chief Judge) three times and declare it abolished, 115 and order that within forty days hence that all Roman Courts be torn to their foundations, 116 and that no court or forum of law again be permitted to be revived that claims any authority, 117 or jurisdiction or connection to Rome and that all form of Roman Law be annulled and determined. 118 As to public officials and to merchants and to the industries of Rome, 119 verily, the industries and crafts of Rome have become nothing more than the artisans of impostors, 120 and Officials nothing more than the patrons of imaginary history and owners of false artefacts, 121 for the goldsmiths and silversmiths of Rome have become notorious at inventing false coins, 122 to be buried and found at opportunistic times to enable wealthy merchants to claim pedigrees. 123 And scribes and authors of Rome have become the very worst inventors of absurd fables, 124 to suit the appetites of their wealthy benefactors who desire to mould history to themselves. 125 And the sculptors and artisans have become master forgers at creating false pieces, 126 proclaiming proof of non existent emperors and senators and patricians. 127 Thus, there be no redeeming feature as to the coins of Rome or the merchants and arts of Rome, 128 for everything has become false to support an industry of falsity to commission further falsity. 129 Truly it be an illness and sickness with no cure but to end the cycle forever. 130 Therefore, I abjure the office of Pater Patriae Fiscus three times and declare it abolished, 131 and that the Pater Patriae Fiscus and all Roman money and funds be Damnatio Memoriae (damned in memory). 132 Furthermore, I abjure the Imperium Proconsulare Maius three times and declare it abolished, 133 and hereby dissolve all offices of Rome and that no one may hold any office, 134 if the authority of such office is claimed from Rome, for Rome hold no authority to grant such office, 135 and that each and every office of Rome be Damnatio Memoriae, annulled and determined. 136 Furthermore, I hereby order that within forty days hence that every Forum and every exchange, 137 and every house of money and every money temple be torn to its foundations, 138 and never permitted to be rebuilt or used for trade or commerce of public business every again. 139 Thus, what is done in law by the authority of heaven and by the consent of the people cannot be undone. 140 For as it is spoken and written, let it be so. Amen. 141 As soon as Constantine had finished speaking and whilst the crowd remained in shock at what had transpired, 142 Cuinstanyn (Constantine) did depart Rome to return to Philadelphia, 143 with one hundred and eighty thousand of his troops from the four quarters of the earth remaining, 144 under strict instructions that in forty days, the city of Rome was to be utterly destroyed.

C. 17

1 In the year known as 313 CE, 2 fifteen hundred and thirteen years since the dawn of the Great Age, 3 and within days of the Edict of Rome by Cuinstanyn (Constantine) on the Ides of March, 4 tens of thousands of Romans did flee the city to other cities to the north and south of Italia. 5 Yet, many did remain in defiance of the Edict, still convinced that Rome would not be destroyed. 6 However, as the deadline did loom, battles did break out with mercenaries hired by the wealthy, 7 against the united democratic powers of earth whose legions had come to Rome to bring its end. 8 To stamp out the mercenaries, Cuinstanyn (Constantine) ordered the remaining citizens, 9 be forced out of the city and within seven days of the deadline, the City of Rome was devoid of life. 10 Upon the commencement of the systematic destruction of the fourteen Regionen (regions) of Rome, 11 Cuinstanyn (Constantine) did give specific instructions that only the Pantheon of Hadrian, 12 and the great Thermae Albinus of Emperor Marcus Aurelius Cornelius Albinus, 13 and the Arches of the noble and Holly Emperors to remain intact. 14 The city was first to be set on fire and then once the flames had ceased, 15 for all good marble and usable stone not from the Vaticanus or Curia then to be shipped to Philadelphia. 16 Upon the first of Maia (May Day), the fires were then lit across Rome as a ring around the city. 17 Within hours, the city of Rome was as if engulfed by a sea of flames hundreds of feet high, 18 and within a day, the flames had taken hold in every one of the fourteen regions of the city. 19 For twelve days Rome continued to burn at such a fury that metals did melt, 20 And walls and buildings did explode from such heat until not an inch of the city was unscathed. 21 After seven more days of smouldering, the forces of Cuinstanyn (Constantine) did re-enter the ruins, 22 to find many structures such as the Colosseum partially collapsed and the Forums utterly destroyed. 23 The soldiers did then commence the pulling down of major buildings and the removal of stone, 24 placing the stones on barges on the Tiber River that were then sailed out and around Sicily, 25 and then north to the construction site of Philadelphia upon the Po River Delta. 26 In the same year, Cuinstanyn (Constantine) did issue orders as to the Diakesia (Diocese), 27 and did appoint his General named Aderitus as first Patriarchos (Patriarch) of the Politia of Italia. 28 Cuinstanyn (Constantine) did pronounce there be nine Christian Diakesia (Diocese) for Italia, 29 with the Diakesia of Lombardia to the

north and its capital being Cremona on the River Po, 30 and the Diakesia of Veronia to the north-east and its capital being Tavros (Treviso) on the River Silus (Sile), 31 and the Diakesia of Tuscania with its capital being Florena (Florence) on the Arno River in the Arno Valley, 32 and the Diakesia of Aquilia with its capital being Aternos on the Aterna River Delta on the Adriatic Sea, 33 and the Diakesia of Umbria with its capital being Ostia on the Tiber Delta and Tyrrhenian Sea, 34 and the Diakesia of Campania with its capital being Capua on the Volturno River and 16 miles from the coast, 35 and the Diakesia of Apulia with its capital being Lido on the Bradano River Delta and Ionian Sea, 36 and the Diakesia of Calabria with its capital being Katastarioi (Catanzaro) on the River Zaro Delta, 37 and the Diakesia of Sicilia with its capital being Catana (Catania) on the Symaethus (Simeto) River Delta. 38 Cuinstanyn (Constantine) did then order that the traditional birth city of the Piso, 39 also called Piso on the Arno River Delta, be Damnatio Memoriae and to be utterly destroyed, 40 and that any memory or record of the Piso (Pisa) ever existing be purged from history. 41 In the same year, 42 Cuinstanyn (Constantine) did pronounce the end of all standards of the damned city (Rome), 43 and that the new motto of the earth be INRI meaning Ilex Neos Rabdi Idea and the phrase, 44 One Law (is) the New Rule (and) Way meaning All the Earth was to be under the Golden Rule of Law. 45 Furthermore, that every instance of the old motto of SPQR was to be removed, destroyed or struck out, 46 wherever it be found across the Earth, as if the ancient motto of Rome never existed. 47 In the same year, 48 Cuinstanyn (Constantine) did also pronounce the formation of a new global system of finance, 49 called Nomisma meaning the monetary system and official coins of the Empire and Politia (city-states), 50 and that private money lenders, money changers, mints, insurance or assurance were forbidden, 51 as thereafter, all forms of banking, exchange, credit, marine insurance and assurance, 52 were under the strict control and authority of the Christian Ecclesia (Church) and Politia (city state), 53 with anyone found engaging in private banking, lending, insurance or assurance guilty of a crime, 54 and with compound interest forbidden as a capital crime and the only rate of interest, 55 being a maximum of three percent simple interest calculated per year. 56 Cuinstanyn (Constantine) did then declare the base coin of the Earth was to be the silver Drachme, 57 meaning standard weight and coin, and the minting of Drachme was to be the same as three scruples, 58 of 4.32 grams in honour of the ancient standards of coins of the Holly smiths for hundreds of years, 59 and that all coins be made from precise moulds and the practice of striking coins forbidden, 60 such that every Drachme was identical in form and weight and consistency, 61 and no clipping or shaving could occur without such fraud being easily revealed with the eyes. 62 All Roman coins were thereafter banned from circulation and all Denarius, Aureus, as and Tremissis, 63 Sesterius and Dupondius as well as all the mass of deliberately fake coins formed by master forgers, 64 were to be seized and melted with anyone caught possessing Roman coins or imprecise struck coins, 65 culpable of an offence of possessing fake artefacts and forbidden objects. 66 Thus, within a generation, the earth was rid of fake and poorly made coins and the wickedry, 67 of bankers and money lenders and those that used the laws of Rome to prey upon the people. 68 In the same year, 69 Cuinstanyn (Constantine) did issue a condemnation that any city that had been a major site, 70 of human sacrifice, of slavery, of blood sport and murder, of necromancy and sorcery, 71 was therefore a cursed place (anathema), judged and condemned (krimina), 72 and to be utterly destroyed (abbadon), 73 with such condemned ruins never permitted to be recognised as Christian, 74 and such criminal (krimina) and cursed (anathema) places never permitted to be the site of a church, 75 and such places that once celebrated murder and slavery in the name of religion, 76 be never permitted again to be the site of any forum of law, 77 or for any dictate or order to be claimed to have originated from such cursed places. 78 Within the Politia of Alba these former Roman cities be Anathema, Krimina and Abbadon: 79 now the cities of Devilum (Chester), Eboracium (York) and Londinium (London), 80 with Londinium (London) especially cursed as being a site first condemned by Yeshua (Jesus the Christ), 81 as a site of falsity, of perfidy and profanity where no law or right or sacred could originate. 82 Within the Politia of Spania these former Roman cities be Anathema, Krimina and Abbadon: 83 now the cities of Corduba (Cordoba) and Malaca. 84 Within the Politia of Francia these former Roman cities be Anathema, Krimina and Abbadon: 85 now the cities of Massilia (Marseilles), Lucifernum (Lyons) and Turonum (Tours), 86 and the cities of Turico (Zurich), Argentoratum (Strasbourg) and Curia (Liechtenstein). 87 Within the Politia of Saxonia these former Roman cities be Anathema, Krimina and Abbadon: 88 now the cities of Mogontiacum (Mainz), Vindelicorum (Ausburg), Treverorum (Trier) and Bonna (Bonn). 89 Within the Politia of Slavia these former Roman cities be Anathema, Krimina and Abbadon: 90 now the cities of Dioclea (Dubrovnik), Salona, Vindobona (Vienna) and Naissus (Nis). 91 Within the Politia of Macedonia these former Roman cities be Anathema, Krimina and Abbadon: 92 now the cities of Kaza (Corfu) and Epirus. 93 Within the Politia of Hellas these former Roman cities be Anathema, Krimina and Abbadon: 94 now the cities of Zorza (Argostoli) and Corinthus (Corinth). 95 Within the Politia of Italia these former Roman cities be Anathema, Krimina and Abbadon: 96 now the cities of Rhegium (Reggio), Messana (Messina), Syracusae (Syracuse), Tarentum and Neapolis (Naples), 97 and the cities of Beneventum, Pisa, Mediolanum (Milan), Trento (Trent) and Turinorum (Turin), 98 with Rome the most cursed, condemned and criminal of all cities under Christianity, 99 a place not only forbidden to be rebuilt or a site ever for law or a Christian shrine, 100 but a place where its name and language (Latin) be forbidden to be named, 101 and place to be known simply as the Anti-Christ as the symbol of the enemy of humanity, 102 and against every logic and teaching of heaven and every tenet of law and reason, 103 and every right of equality and respect of men and women, 104 and against the very essence of civilised life. 105 Whereas Christianity stood for life, the Anti-Christ (Rome) stood for death, 106 and where Christianity reunited heaven and earth, the Anti-Christ (Rome) sought to divide spirit, 107 to belie, to deceive, to steal, to impersonate and to beguile. 108 Thus, no city has ever been more cursed nor condemned as a place devoid of any holy spirit, 109 and forever severed from heaven than the wicked ruins of Rome. 110 A place impossible to be reconciled with Christ as it be the personification of the Anti-Christ. 111 Within the Politia of Anatolia these former Roman cities be Anathema, Krimina and Abbadon: 112 now the cities of Miletus, Tarsus and Rhodos. 113 Within the Politia of Syria these former Roman cities be Anathema, Krimina and Abbadon: 114 now the cities of Heliopolis and Cyyrhus. 115 Within the Politia of Palestinia these former Roman cities be Anathema, Krimina and Abbadon: 116 now the cities of Petra, Bostra, Baalbek, Tyrus and Caeseria Maritima, 117 with the city of Aelia Capitolina, once known as Jerusalem especially condemned, 118 as a site completely devoid of spirit or authority or sacredness but a site of human sacrifice, 119 and wicked madness and obsession in dark arts and necromancy. 120 Thus Jerusalem was forbidden to ever have a Christian church or be known as Christian, 121 or ever be worshipped as a sacred site but as merely an adjunct to the Anti-Christ, 122 and thus its name (Jerusalem) forbidden to be mentioned by Christians forever more. 123 Within the Politia of Mesopotamia these former cities be Anathema, Krimina and Abbadon: 124 now the cities of Babel (Bagdad) and any trace of the city of Babylon or the city of Ur. 125 Within the Politia of Abbysinia these former Roman cities be Anathema, Krimina and Abbadon: 126 now the cities of Zafar and Timna and Samharm. 127 Within the Politia of Persia these former cities be Anathema, Krimina and Abbadon: 128 now the cities of Eden (Tehran) and Gor. 129 Within the Politia of Barbaria these former Roman cities be Anathema, Krimina and Abbadon: 130 now the cities of Tingis (Tangier) and Lixus (Casablanca). 131 Within the Politia of Algeria these former Roman cities be Anathema, Krimina and Abbadon: 132 now the cities of Cartena, Caesarea, Lambaesis and Carthage. 133 Within the Politia of Gaetulia these former Roman cities be Anathema, Krimina and Abbadon: 134 now the cities of Sabrata and Leptis Magna. 135 Within the Politia of Libia these former Roman cities be Anathema, Krimina and Abbadon: 136 now the cities of Cyrene and Apollonia. 137 Thus, the remains of the most sociopathic and bloodthirsty and insane Empire were laid to waste, 138 and the memory of Rome and its cities of human sacrifice and necromancy and madness were ground into dust. 139 In the same year, 140 Cuinstanyn (Constantine) did order an accounting of every Monarch for every Diakesia, 141 and that every Patriarchos and Monarch of every Politia (city-state), 142 of Borealia (north seas), Australia (south seas), Europalia (west seas) and Orientalia (east seas), 143 be summonsed to Antioch as the first and one and only true Holly Sedos (Holy See), 144 to bear witness to the first Epistole (Epistle) of Christianity in history.

C. 18

1 In the year known as 314 CE, 2 fifteen hundred and fourteen years since the dawn of the Great Age, 3 the accounting of the Christian Empire was completed as to appointment of a Monarch, 4 for every Diakesia (Diocese) and the founding of an Episcopolis as its Episcopal Sedos (See). 5 The Tetrachs did then pronounce the sacred summons within Great Basilica of Antioch, saying: 6 To the nine Politia of Borealia (north seas): The Grace of the spirit of Christ be unto you, 7 and everlasting blessings and good intentions be unto all who receive these words, 8 from Mattatheos (Perinthos) your brother and Exarchos of Borealia (North). 9 To the nine Politia of Australia (south seas): The Grace of the spirit of Christ be unto you, 10 and everlasting blessings and good intentions be unto all who receive these words, 11 from Markos (Achilles) your brother and Exarchos of Australia (South). 12 To the nine Politia of Europealia (west seas): The Grace of the spirit of Christ be unto you, 13 and everlasting blessings and good intentions be unto all who receive these words, 14 from Lukhas (Eusebius) your brother and Exarchos of Europealia (West). 15 To the nine Politia of Orientalia (east seas): The Grace of the spirit of Christ be unto you, 16 and everlasting blessings and good intentions be unto all who receive these words, 17 from Iohannes (Constantinos) your brother and Exarchos of Orientalia (East). 18 Verily, we call upon all our brothers as Monarch and Patriarchos (Patriarchs), 19 to come to Antiochos (Antioch) to celebrate upon the month of Krios (1st of April), 20 the dawning of a New World Order at the new centre of the world as an empire of Conscience. 21 Thus, no city be a Metropolis or a Metropolis Sedos (See) of Christ and One Heaven, 22 unless it be pronounced here within such sacred space under our authority, 23 and in accord with the Golden Rule of Law and true Justice of all humanity. 24 Therefore, I Mattatheos (Perinthos) your brother do pronounce the Metropolis of Borealia (North) be: 25 Odessos (Varna) at the Panisos [Kamchiya] Delta on the Black Sea as the Metropolis of Bulgaria, 26 Tergesti (Trieste) at the Isonzo Delta on the Adriatic Sea as the Metropolis of Hungaria, 27 Kherson at the Dnieper Delta on the Black Sea as the Metropolis of Alania, 28 Tanais (Rostov-na-Donu) at the Don Delta on the Black Sea as the Metropolis of Vandalia, 29 Aticca (Atyrau) at the Ural Delta on the Caspian Sea as the Metropolis of Sarmatia, 30 Nema at the Nemos (Nemunas) River Delta on the Baltic Sea as the Metropolis of Lithuania, 31 Riga at the Dyna (Daugava) River Delta on the Baltic Sea as the Metropolis of Latvia, 32 Narva at the Narva River Delta on the Baltic Sea as the Metropolis of Estonia, 33 and Rusa (St Petersburg) at the Rusa River Delta on the Baltic Sea as the Metropolis of Rusia. 34 I Markos (Achilles) your brother do then pronounce the Metropolis of Australia

(South) be: 35 Timogadi (Nador) at the Nadir River Delta on the Mediterranean Sea as the Metropolis of Barbaria, 36 Saldae (Bejaia) at the Algolis (Soummam) River Delta on the Mediterranean Sea as the Metropolis of Algeria, 37 Abes (Gabes) at the Triton River Delta on the Mediterranean Sea as the Metropolis of Gaetulia, 38 Zanadu at the Zanadis River Delta on the Mediterranean Sea as the Metropolis of Garamantia, 39 Berenice (Benghazi) at the Baris River Delta on the Mediterranean Sea as the Metropolis of Libia, 40 Zion (Suez) at the Zion Delta on the Red Sea as the Metropolis of Egyptia, 41 Saladin on Axumir at the Axumir (Mareb) River Delta on the Red Sea as the Metropolis of Ethiopia, 42 Aela (Aqaba) at the Jordan Delta on the Red Sea as the Metropolis of Sinopia, 43 And Zeila (Djibouti) at the Adama (Awash) River Delta on the Red Sea as the Metropolis of Somalia. 44 I Lukhas (Eusebius) your brother do then pronounce the Metropolis of Europealia (West) be: 45 Hollyrood at the Firth of Forth on the North Sea as the Metropolis of Alba, 46 Dublin at the Liffey Delta on the Irish Sea as the Metropolis of Irenia, 47 Iberia (Amposta/ Tortosa) at the Ebro Delta on the Mediterranean Sea as the Metropolis of Spania, 48 Arles at the Rhone Delta on the Mediterranean Sea as the Metropolis of Francia, 49 Philadelphia at the Po Delta on the Adriatic Sea as the Metropolis of Italia, 50 Mantas (Hamburg) at the Elbe Delta on the North Sea as the Metropolis of Saxonia (Germany), 51 Spoleto (Split) at the Cetina Delta on the Adriatic Sea as the Metropolis of Slavia, 52 Ulkini (Ulcinj) at the Buna Delta on the Adriatic Sea as the Metropolis of Macedonia, 53 Hella at the Evros Delta on the Aegean Sea as the Metropolis of Hellas. 54 Nicomedia (Izmit) at the Sakarya Delta on the Black Sea as the Metropolis of Anatolia, 55 Sarvan (Shirvan) at the Cyrus Delta on the Caspian Sea as the Metropolis of Armenia, 56 Laodicia (Samandag) at the Orontes Delta on the Mediterranean Sea as the Metropolis of Syria, 57 Gaza at the Gazah Delta on the Mediterranean Sea as the Metropolis of Palestinia, 58 Chaldos (Kuwait City) at the Euphrates/ Chaldon (Pishon) Delta as the Metropolis of Mesopotamia, 59 Adana (Aden) at the Abb (Ibb) River Delta on the Persian Gulf as the Metropolis of Abbysinia (Yemen), 60 Basra at the Euphrates/ Tigris Delta on the Gulf of Aden as the Metropolis of Assyria, 61 Telma (Dilmun) at the Ashar (Aftan) River Delta on the Persian Gulf as the Metropolis of Saracenia, 62 and Commercion (Gameron) at the Shoor River on the Persian Gulf as the Metropolis of Persia. 63 So it is then, that no city be an Episcopolis or a Episcopolis Sedos (See) of Christ and One Heaven, 64 unless it be pronounced here within such sacred space under our authority, 65 and in accord with the Golden Rule of Law and true Justice of all humanity. 66 Therefore, I Mattatheos (Perinthos) your brother do pronounce the seven Diakesia of Bulgaria be: 67 Oltenia with its Episcopolis being Craiova on the Rabo (Jiu) River, 68 Sofia with its Episcopolis being Serdica (Sofia) on the Iskar River, 69 Wallachia with its Episcopolis being Silistros (Silistra) on the Danube River, 70 Dobruia with its Episcopolis being Tomas on the

Carasu River Delta on the Black Sea, 71 Transylvania with its Episcopolis being Agropolis (Targu Mures) on the Maros (Mures) River, 72 Varancia with its Episcopolis being Bako (Bacau) on the Hierasus (Siret) River, 73 and Moldovia with its Episcopolis being Tiras (Tiraspol) on the Danastris (Dniester) River. 74 I Mattatheos (Perinthos) your brother do pronounce the five Diakesia of Hungaria be: 75 Carinthia with its Episcopolis being Aemona (Ljubljana) on the Leibar/ Sava River, 76 Austria with its Episcopolis being Vindos (near Vienna ruins) on the Danube River, 77 Nitria with its Episcopolis being Nitros (Galanta) on the Nitra (Vah) River, 78 Obudia with its Episcopolis being Aquinas (Budapest) on the Danube River, 79 Moravia with its Episcopolis being Olomos (Olomouc)on the Morava River, 80 and Batinia with its Episcopolis being Apatinas on the Danube River. 81 I Mattatheos (Perinthos) your brother do pronounce the nine Diakesia of Alania be: 82 Crimia with its Episcopolis being Sebastapolis on the Chorna River Delta on the Black Sea, 83 Podolia with its Episcopolis being Vinnica (Vinnytsia) on the Hypanis (Bug) River, 84 Lodomeria with its Episcopolis being Leopolis (Lviv) on the Leono (Poltva) River, 85 Vistulia with its Episcopolis being Krakos (Krakow) on the Vistula River, 86 Silesia with its Episcopolis being Bresio (Wroclaw) on the Ardor (Oder) River, 87 Masovia with its Episcopolis being Masova (Warsaw) on the Vistula River, 88 Halicia with its Episcopolis being Lublinis (Lublin) on the Vistula River, 89 Navaria with its Episcopolis being Navara (Yuvileine) on the Kherson (Dnieper) River, 90 and Ukrainia with its Episcopolis being Kyrio (Kiev) on the Kherson (Dnieper) River. 91 I Mattatheos (Perinthos) your brother do pronounce the five Diakesia of Vandalia be: 92 Dandaricia with its Episcopolis being Phanagoria (Temyruk) on the Hypanis (Kuban) River Delta on the Black Sea, 93 Metibia with its Episcopolis being Suruba (Staraya) on the Hypanis (Kuban) River, 94 Gerria with its Episcopolis being Telaeba (Bryansk) on the Gerrus (Desna) River Delta on the Caspian Sea, 95 Nestiatia with its Episcopolis being Capital Astronis on the Nestiatis (Volga) River Delta on the Caspian Sea, 96 Tanaitia with its Episcopolis being Exopolis on the Tanais (Rostov-na-Donu) River, 97 and Chaenidia with its Episcopolis being Gelonos on the Tanais (Rostov-na-Donu) River. 98 I Mattatheos (Perinthos) your brother do pronounce the five Diakesia of Sarmatia be: 99 Kaspia with its Episcopolis being Kaspo (Turkmenbashl) on the Ateros (Atrek) Delta on the Caspian Sea, 100 Kazaria with its Episcopolis being Sarkel (Uralst) on the Iakon (Ural) River, 101 Karesmia with its Episcopolis being on the Oxos (Amu Darya) River Delta on the Aral Sea, 102 Tartaria with its Episcopolis being Taraz on the Jaxartes (Syr Darya) River Delta on the Aral Sea, 103 and Karakalia with its Episcopolis being Iassi on the Ember River Delta on the Aral Sea. 104 I Mattatheos (Perinthos) your brother do pronounce the four Diakesia of Lithuania be: 105 Pomerania with its Episcopolis being Gedanis (Gdansk) on the Vistula River Delta into Baltic Sea, 106 Karmelavia with its

Episcopolis being Voruta (Kaunas) on the Naratis (Neris) River, 107 Krivichia with its Episcopolis being Polista (Minsk) on the Nemis (Nemiga) River, 108 and Ruthenia with its Episcopolis being Martis (Mazyr) on the Pipatis (Pripyat) River. 109 I Mattatheos (Perinthos) your brother do pronounce the two Diakesia of Latvia be: 110 Livonia with its Episcopolis being Ventspolis on the Venta River Delta on the Baltic Sea, 111 and Poliania with its Episcopolis being Daugapolis on the Dyna (Daugava) River. 112 I Mattatheos (Perinthos) your brother do pronounce the three Diakesia of Estonia be: 113 Kalevia with its Episcopolis Tampea (Tallinn) on the Pirita River Delta on the Baltic Sea, 114 Oeselia with its Episcopolis Perona (Parnu) on the Perona (Parnu) River Delta on the Baltic Sea, 115 and Aestia with its Episcopolis Pelso (Pskov) on the Velakos (Velikaya) River. 116 I Mattatheos (Perinthos) your brother do pronounce the five Diakesia of Rusia be: 117 Staraia with its Episcopolis Ladova (Volkhov) on the Ladogis (Volkhov) River, 118 Varangia with its Episcopolis Nova (Novgorod) on the Ladogis (Volkhov) River, 119 Ipatia with its Episcopolis Kostova (Kostroma) on the Nestiatis (Volga) River, 120 Rostovia with its Episcopolis Moskova (Moscow) on the Moskova River, 121 and Ashlia with its Episcopolis Kieva (Nizhny Novgorod) on the Nestiatis (Volga) River. 122 I Markos (Achilles) the Exarchos of Australia (South) do hereby pronounce all the Diakesia of Australia (South). 123 I Markos (Achilles) your brother do pronounce the five Diakesia of Barbaria be: 124 Maiticia with its Episcopolis Alcasar on the Algarbos (Mharhar) River delta on the Atlantic Ocean, 125 Temasnia with its Episcopolis Sala (Rabat) on the Salis (Bou Regreg) River delta on the Atlantic Ocean, 126 Autolia with its Episcopolis Azamor on the Marbea (Oum Er-Rbia) River, 127 Sagaria with its Episcopolis Zaida on the Meluya (Moulouya) River, 128 and Morokia with its Episcopolis Morokos (Marrakesh) on the Agaz (Tensift) River. 129 I Markos (Achilles) your brother do pronounce the eight Diakesia of Algeria be: 130 Manchurebia with its Episcopolis Magma on the Chergi and Chelif River Delta on Mediterranean Sea, 131 Machusia with its Episcopolis Mina on the Chergi River, 132 Tulensia with its Episcopolis Chelif on the Chelif River, 133 Kabylia with its Episcopolis Gorgos on the Mala River Delta on Mediterranean Sea, 134 Sitifia with its Episcopolis Sitif on the Algolis (Soummam) River, 135 Annabia with its Episcopolis Bone on the Ubus (Seybouse) River Delta on Mediterranean Sea, 136 Jedia with its Episcopolis Zebela on the Bagrada (Medjerda) River Delta on Mediterranean Sea, 137 and Masakia with its Episcopolis Zoza on the Masaka River Delta on the Mediterranean Sea. 138 I Markos (Achilles) your brother do pronounce the nine Diakesia of Gaetulia be: 139 Natembia with its Episcopolis Bisakra on the Triton River, 140 Nacmusia with its Episcopolis Messad on the Triton River, 141 Mozabia with its Episcopolis Bonoura on the Mozab River, 142 Astacuria with its Episcopolis Ticarte on the Pallas River, 143 Achamenia with its Episcopolis Gadamea on the Pallas and Mozab River confluence,

144 Osutia with its Episcopolis Golea on the Dogod River, 145 Menia with its Episcopolis Negita on the Pallas River, 146 Mampsaria with its Episcopolis Kadamis on the Dogod River, 147 and Vazaria with its Episcopolis Sukna on the Pallas River. 148 I Markos (Achilles) your brother do pronounce the seven Diakesia of Garamantia be: 149 Tripolitania with its Episcopolis Zohar (Tripoli) on the Zohar River Delta on the Mediterranean Sea, 150 Sidria with its Episcopolis Zirtis on the Zirtis River Delta on the Mediterranean Sea, 151 Taourgia with its Episcopolis Zizda on the Zizda River, 152 Eropia with its Episcopolis Zuis on the Zanadis River, 153 Zinypia with its Episcopolis Zakna on the Zanadis River, 154 Sabia with its Episcopolis Zala on the Ouia River and Lake, 155 and Ouia with its Episcopolis Zouila on the Ouia River and Lake. 156 I Markos (Achilles) your brother do pronounce the seven Diakesia of Libia be: 157 Harabia with its Episcopolis Monktor on the Augila River Delta and the Mediterranean Sea, 158 Augilia with its Episcopolis Augila (Awjilah) on the Augila River, 159 Barcia with its Episcopolis Bara on the Baris River, 160 Purgotoria with its Episcopolis Purgota on the Purgos River, 161 Asbytia with its Episcopolis Tebrek (Tobruk) on the Purgos River Delta and the Mediterranean Sea, 162 Ouladia with its Episcopolis Siwa on the Kanis River, 163 and Kanaia with its Episcopolis Kanis on the Kanis River Delta and the Mediterranean Sea. 164 I Markos (Achilles) your brother do pronounce the eight Diakesia of Egyptia be: 165 Materia with its Episcopolis Chiros (Cairo) on the Lower Nile, 166 Atfia with its Episcopolis Tata (Matay) on the Tata River delta and Lower Nile, 167 Sia with its Episcopolis Lycopolis (Asyut) on the Khargia River delta and Lower Nile, 168 Drypotia with its Episcopolis Arsinoe on the Rufis River Delta and the Red Sea, 169 Khargia with its Episcopolis Oasis (Kharga) on the Khargia River source, 170 Coptaia with its Episcopolis Kaine (Qena) on the Kaine River delta and Upper Nile, 171 Syenia with its Episcopolis Abele on the Upper Nile, 172 and Trogladytia with its Episcopolis Bereala on the Berealis River Delta and the Red Sea. 173 I Markos (Achilles) your brother do pronounce the nine Diakesia of Ethiopia be: 174 Nobatia with its Episcopolis Pakhoras on the Upper Nile River, 175 Makuria with its Episcopolis Dongola on the Upper Nile River, 176 Megabaria with its Episcopolis Megaba on the Upper Nile River, 177 Butania with its Episcopolis Akbara on the Akbar (Atbara) River Delta and Nile River, 178 Messia with its Episcopolis Massala (Kassala) on the Sitit River, 179 Alodia with its Episcopolis Soba (Khartoum) on the union of the White Nile and Abraya (Blue Nile) River, 180 Sinaria with its Episcopolis Sina (Sinner) on the Abraya (Blue Nile) River, 181 Agamia with its Episcopolis Axum (Asmara) on the Axumir (Mareb) River, 182 and Cadabria with its Episcopolis Abra (Tana) on the Abraya (Blue Nile) River Source and Lake. 183 I Markos (Achilles) your brother do pronounce the four Diakesia of Sinopia be: 184 Sukhotia with its Episcopolis Arisha on the Nexus (Arish) River Delta and Mediterranean Sea, 185 Dahabia with its Episcopolis Masba (Dahab) on the Masba River Delta Gulf of Aqaba, 186

Eliatia with its Episcopolis Nexus (Nekhel) on the Nexus River, 187 and Tanakia with its Episcopolis Sidon (Ras Sedr) on the Sidon (Abu Sidr) River Delta and Red Sea. 188 I Markos (Achilles) your brother do pronounce the eleven Diakesia of Somalia be: 189 Zawaria with its Episcopolis Alla on the Adama (Awash) River, 190 Shia with its Episcopolis Adama on the Adama (Awash) River, 191 Alia with its Episcopolis Abba on the Adama (Awash) River, 192 Hararia with its Episcopolis Hara on the Sabil (Shabele) River, 193 Ogadenia with its Episcopolis Gode on the Sabil (Shabele) River, 194 Oromia with its Episcopolis Dolo on the Gedo (Jubba) River, 195 Geledia with its Episcopolis Kisma (Kismayo) on the Gedo (Jubba) River Delta on the Indian Ocean, 196 Abgalia with its Episcopolis Magadoxo on the Sabil (Shabele) River Delta on the Gulf of Aden, 197 Hazania with its Episcopolis Tala on the Nugal (Nugaal) River Delta on the Gulf of Aden, 198 Malaia with its Episcopolis Berbera on the River Delta on the Gulf of Aden, 199 and Gobolia with its Episcopolis Banda on the Gobol River Delta on the Gulf of Aden. 200 I Lukhas (Eusebius) the Exarchos of Australia (South) do hereby pronounce the Diakesia of Europealia (West), 201 and as your brother do pronounce the seven Diakesia of Alba be: 202 Scotia with its Episcopolis Catholica (Glasgow) on the Clyde River Delta and the North Sea, 203 Umbria with its Episcopolis Livera (Liverpool) on the Mersey River Delta and the Irish Sea, 204 Bernicia with its Episcopolis Halla (Hull) on Humber River Delta and the North Sea, 205 Deiria with its Episcopolis Granta (Cambridge) on the Ouse River, 206 Canteberia with its Episcopolis Cantis (Cantebury) on the Stour River Delta and the English Channel, 207 Dumnonia with its Episcopolis Warra (Worcester) on the Eli River, 208 and Wellia with its Episcopolis Corda (Cardiff) on Eli River Delta and the Irish Sea. 209 I Lukhas (Eusebius) your brother do pronounce the four Diakesia of Irenia (Ireland) be: 210 Boreaia with its Episcopolis Dorda (Derry) on the Foyle River Delta and the North Sea, 211 Austraia with its Episcopolis Corca (Cork) on the Lee River Delta and the Irish Sea, 212 Europaia with its Episcopolis Limri (Limrick) on the Shannon River Delta and the North Sea, 213 and Orientaia with its Episcopolis Casela (Cashel) on the Suir River. 214 I Lukhas (Eusebius) your brother do pronounce the seven Diakesia of Spania (Spain) be: 215 Galicia with its Episcopolis Braga (Porto) on Duero River Delta and the Atlantic Ocean, 216 Lusitania with its Episcopolis Olissipa (Lisbon) on the Tagus River Delta and the Atlantic Ocean, 217 Andalusia with its Episcopolis Sevilla on the Guadalquivir River, 218 Valencia with its Episcopolis Valencia on the Jucar River Delta and the Mediterranean Sea, 219 Aragonia with its Episcopolis Aragon (Zaragoza) on Elbo River, 220 Castillia with its Episcopolis Toledo on the Tagus River, 221 and Catalonia with its Episcopolis Barcelona on the Llobregat River Delta and the Mediterranean Sea. 222 I Lukhas (Eusebius) your brother do pronounce the twelve Diakesia of Francia (France) be: 223 Frisia with its Episcopolis Utrecht on the Rhine, 224 Flanderia with its Episcopolis Gentis

(Ghent) on the River Lie (Lys), 225 Franconia with its Episcopolis Cologne on the Rhine, 226 Lotharingia with its Episcopolis Metz on the Moselle and Seille Rivers, 227 Neustria with its Episcopolis Paris on the Seine River, 228 Bretonia with its Episcopolis Nantes on the Loire River Delta and the Atlantic Ocean, 229 Aquitania with its Episcopolis Oleron on the Gironde River Delta and the Atlantic Ocean, 230 Gasconia with its Episcopolis Toulouse on the River Garonne, 231 Burgundia with its Episcopolis Geneva on the Rhone River, 232 Bavaria with its Episcopolis Basel on the high point of the Rhine River, 233 Sardinia with its Episcopolis Aristanis (Oristano) on the Tirsos (Tirso) River Delta and the Mediterranean Sea, 234 and Corsica with its Episcopolis Agathionis (Ajaccio) on the Agathos (Gravona) River Delta and the Mediterranean Sea. 235 I Lukhas (Eusebius) your brother do pronounce the nine Diakesia of Italia (Italy) be: 236 Lombardia with its Episcopolis Cremona on the Po River Delta and the Adriatic Sea, 237 Veronia with its Episcopolis Tavros (Treviso) on the Silus (Sile) River, 238 Tuscania with its Episcopolis Florena (Florence) on the Arno River, 239 Aquilia with its Episcopolis Aternos (Pescara) on the Aterna Rver Delta and the Adriatic Sea, 240 Umbria with its Episcopolis Ostia on the Tiber Delta and Tyrrhenian Sea, 241 Campania with its Episcopolis Capua on the Volturno River, 242 Apulia with its Episcopolis Lido on the Bradano River Delta on the Ionian Sea, 243 Calabria with its Episcopolis Katastaro (Catanzaro) on the River Zaro Delta and the Ionian Sea, 244 and Sicilia with its Episcopolis Capital Catana (Catania) on the Symaethus (Simeto) River Delta and the Mediterranean Sea. 245 I Lukhas (Eusebius) your brother do pronounce the eight Diakesia of Saxonia (Germany) be: 246 Nordalbingia with its Episcopolis Danea on the Daner (Skjern) River, 247 Westfalia with its Episcopolis Bremen on the Weser River, 248 Varinia with its Episcopolis Varina (Wolin) on Ardor (Oder) Delta into Baltic Sea, 249 Angaria with its Episcopolis Megadonis (Magdeburg) the Elbe River, 250 Ostfalia with its Episcopolis Dresdenos (Dresden) on the Elbe River, 251 Thuringia with its Episcopolis Mattiakos (Frankfurt) on the Mattios (Maine) River, 252 Bohemia with its Episcopolis Pragos (Prague) on the Vitava River, joining the Elbe River, 253 and Austrasia with its Episcopolis Monakos (Munich) on the Isar River. 254 I Lukhas (Eusebius) your brother do pronounce the five Diakesia of Slavia be: 255 Croatia with its Episcopolis Andatonis (Zagreb) on the Sava River, 256 Dalmatia with its Episcopolis Scardona (Sibenik) on the Kirkos (Krka) River Delta and the Adriatic Sea, 257 Bosnia with its Episcopolis Visokos (Visoko) on the Bosna River, 258 Serbia with its Episcopolis Belgrados (Belgrade) on the confluence of the Sava and Danube River, 259 and Rasinia with its Episcopolis Pristina on the Ibar River. 260 I Lukhas (Eusebius) your brother do pronounce the two Diakesia of Macedonia be: 261 Albania with its Episcopolis Albanis (Novosele) on the Albas (Vjosa) River Delta on the Adriatic Sea, 262 and Axia with its Episcopolis Axia (Skopje) on the Axios (Vardar) River. 263 I Lukhas (Eusebius) your brother do pronounce

Book 25 Great Age of Constantine

the nine Diakesia of Hellas be: 264 Eliadia with its Episcopolis Larissa on the Pontus (Pineios) River, 265 Ambracia with its Episcopolis Arta on the Arachthos River, 266 Saronica with its Episcopolis Athena on Kifisos River Delta and the Ionian Sea, 267 Lacodonia with its Episcopolis Skala on the Eurotas River Delta on the Ionian Sea, 268 Achaia with its Episcopolis Araxos on the Araxos River Delta and the Ionian Sea, 269 Philotia with its Episcopolis Lamia on the Lados (Ladon) River Delta and the Ionian Sea, 270 Thracia with its Episcopolis Xanthi on the Kosynthos River Delta and the Ionian Sea, 271 Kypria (Cyprus) with its Episcopolis Nicosia on Pediaeus River, 272 and Kanadia (Crete) with its Episcopolis Heraklia on the Kairatos River Delta and the Ionian Sea. 273 I Iohannes (Constantinos) the Exarchos of Australia (South) do hereby pronounce the Diakesia of Orientalia (East), 274 and as your brother do pronounce the twelve Diakesia of Anatolia be: 275 Isauria with its Episcopolis Ayda (Aydin) on the Meander (Menderes) River, 276 Marmaria with its Episcopolis Panormos (Bandirma) on Manyas River Delta on the Sea of Marmara, 277 Lycia with its Episcopolis Attaleia (Antalya) on the Attalis River Delta and the Mediterranean Sea, 278 Cilicia with its Episcopolis Seleukeia (Silifke) Salephis (Gosku) River Delta and the Mediterranean Sea, 279 Aladia with its Episcopolis Adana on the Scyhan River Delta on the Mediterranean Sea, 280 Colchia with its Episcopolis Bathus (Batum) on the Adjar River Delta on the Black Sea, 281 Amasia with its Episcopolis Philos on the Philios River Delta on the Black Sea, 282 Galatia with its Episcopolis Ordera (Ordu) on the Ordos River Delta on the Black Sea, 283 Sebastia with its Episcopolis Siva (Sivas) Halys River, 284 Lycaonia with its Episcopolis Kurda (Konya) on the Attalis River, 285 Cappadocia with its Episcopolis Vanessa (Avanos) on Sakarya River, 286 and Cataonia with its Episcopolis Melitene (Malatya) on the Melitene and Euphrates Rivers. 287 I Iohannes (Constantinos) your brother do pronounce the four Diakesia of Armenia be: 288 Georgia with its Episcopolis Tiflis on the Cyrus River, 289 Erebunia with its Episcopolis Yerevan on the Sevana (Hrazdan) River, 290 Araratia with its Episcopolis Taron (Mus) on the Murat River, 291 Uratia with its Episcopolis Bianca (Van) on the Biancos River Delta and Lake, 292 and Urmia with its Episcopolis Khoy on the Sevana (Hrazdan) River. 293 I Iohannes (Constantinos) your brother do pronounce the eight Diakesia of Syria be: 294 Chalybonia with its Episcopolis Chalybon (Aleppo) on the Chalos (Aleppo) River, 295 Apamenia with its Episcopolis Apamea on the Axius (Orontes) River, 296 Aramaia with its Episcopolis Damaskos (Damascus) on the Abana (Barada) River, 297 Emesania with its Episcopolis Emesa (Homs) on the Axius (Orontes) River, 298 Palmyrenia with its Episcopolis Mikael (Palmyra) on the Admor River and Lake, 299 Phoenicia with its Episcopolis Tripolis on the Kadisha River Delta and the Mediterranean Sea, 300 Raphaelia with its Episcopolis Raphael (Resapha) on the Raphaes River, 301 and Gabraelia with its Episcopolis Gabrael (QuaryataYn) on the Gabros River. 302 I Iohannes

(Constantinos) your brother do pronounce the five Diakesia of Palestinia be: 303 Nabataia with its Episcopolis Gerasis (Amman) on the Jebbok River, 304 Galilaia with its Episcopolis Skythopolis on the Jordan Canal and River, 305 Philostinia with its Episcopolis Askalon (Ashdod) on the Lakis (Lakhish) River Delta and Mediterranean Sea, 306 Samaria with its Episcopolis Akre (Acre) on the Jordan Canal Delta and the Mediterranean Sea, 307 and Hagia with its Episcopolis Biblos (Beirut) on the Biblos River Delta and the Mediterranean Sea. 308 I Iohannes (Constantinos) your brother do pronounce the twelve Diakesia of Mesopotamia be: 309 Gazeria with its Episcopolis Edessa (Urfa) on the Belias River, 310 Mygdonia with its Episcopolis Nisbis (Qamishli) on the Arares River, 311 Gauzonia with its Episcopolis Arzama (Hasakah) on the Chebaras (Khabur) River, 312 Osroenia with its Episcopolis Kallinikos on the Belias and Euphrates River, 313 Tingenia with its Episcopolis Kerkison (Deir ez-Zor) on the Chebaras (Khabur) and Euphrates River, 314 Singaria with its Episcopolis Kisla (Bukamal) on the Singar and Euphrates River, 315 Hatria with its Episcopolis Tartaros on the Tartar River, 316 Catania with its Episcopolis Haditha on the Hadithos and Euphrates River, 317 Palagotia with its Episcopolis Palagotas (Falluja) on the Palagotos channels and Euphrates River, 318 Lakhmidia with its Episcopolis Hiera (Najaf) on the Hieros and Euphrates River, 319 Caucabenia with its Episcopolis Karbala on the Karbalos and Euphrates River, 320 and Chaldaia with its Episcopolis Orcheo on the Euphrates River. 321 I Iohannes (Constantinos) your brother do pronounce the six Diakesia of Abbysinia (Yemen) be: 322 Sabaia with its Episcopolis Azazala (Sanaa) on the Maybara River, 323 Adranitia with its Episcopolis Macula on the Timna River Delta and the Gulf of Aden, 324 Sachalitia with its Episcopolis Sapphae (Sayhut) on the Sapphos River Delta and the Gulf of Aden, 325 Arcitia with its Episcopolis Asica on the Arcitis River Delta and the Indian Ocean, 326 Adramitia with its Episcopolis Madrasa on the Adramos River Delta and the Indian Ocean, 327 and Ascitia with its Episcopolis Serapidia on the Serapos River Delta and the Indian Ocean. 328 I Iohannes (Constantinos) your brother do pronounce the nine Diakesia of Assyria be: 329 Susastia with its Episcopolis Susa on the Karas River, 330 Maysania with its Episcopolis Artara (Kut) on the Tigris River, 331 Sitacenia with its Episcopolis Gara on the Tigris River, 332 Dialia with its Episcopolis Jalula on the Gyndes (Sirwan) River, 333 Ancobaria with its Episcopolis Opis (Duloaiya) on the Tigris River, 334 Adiabenia with its Episcopolis Sabbis on the Tigris River, 335 Garamaia with its Episcopolis Corsura (Kirkuk) on the Phryscus River, 336 Adiabinia with its Episcopolis Ninus (Mosul) on the Tigris River, 337 and Aturia with its Episcopolis Soppo on the Tigris River. 338 I Iohannes (Constantinos) your brother do pronounce the ten Diakesia of Saracenia be: 339 Asharia with its Episcopolis Asha on the Ashar and Deraya River, 340 Saudia with its Episcopolis Deraya (Riyadh) on the

Book 25 Great Age of Constantine

Deraya River, 341 Laecenia with its Episcopolis Arra on the Chaldon (Pishon) River, 342 Alatenia with its Episcopolis Alata (Al Rass) on the Chaldon (Pishon) River, 343 Malithia with its Episcopolis Lathrippa (Medina) on the Lathrippo (Medina) River, 344 Alvaia with its Episcopolis Beda on the Lathrippo (Medina) River Delta on Red Sea, 345 Sukhania with its Episcopolis Khabar on the Chaldon (Pishon) River, 346 Houria with its Episcopolis Nabea (Yanbu) on the Nabir (Medina) River Delta on Red Sea, 347 Shemaia with its Episcopolis Jeda on the Macoraba River Delta on Red Sea, 348 and Araraia with its Episcopolis Derya (Duwadimi) on the Alata River. 349 I Iohannes (Constantinos) your brother do pronounce the nine Diakesia of Persia be: 350 Kuzistania with its Episcopolis Endia on the Tirsis (Gihon) River Delta and the Persian Gulf, 351 Farsia with its Episcopolis Tirsis (Shiraz) on the Tirsis (Gihon) River and Lake, 352 Irakia with its Episcopolis Sephahan (Isfahan) on the Zayandos (Zayendehrud) River, 353 Karezania with its Episcopolis Congon on the Kavara River Delta and the Persian Gulf, 354 Aristania with its Episcopolis Nakila on the Laris River Delta and the Persian Gulf, 355 Oromia with its Episcopolis Maraga on the Maragis (Sufi Chay) River, 356 Kermania with its Episcopolis Senna (Sanandaj) on the Gyndes (Sirwan) River, 357 Kashania with its Episcopolis Kom on the Kom River, 358 and Mazandia with its Episcopolis Amola on the Amolis (Haraz) River Delta and the Caspian Sea. 359 Let it be known then to all people, there be forty-five Christian Diakesia (Diocese) to the North (Borealia), 360 And sixty eight Christian Diakesia (Diocese) to the south (Australia), 361 and sixty four Christian Diakesia (Diocese) to the west (Europalia), 362 and seventy five Christian Diakesia (Diocese) to the east (Orientalia), 363 and that the age of the Anti-Christ (Rome) as the Dark Ages is finished, 364 and that a new age of Illumination under a New World Order under the Golden Rule of Law has begun. 365 Therefore, let no man speak falsely of such law, lest they be judged and condemned by Heaven and Earth.

C. 19

1 In the year known as 314 CE, 2 fifteen hundred and fourteen years since the dawn of the Great Age, 3 upon the first day (alpha) of the year of the month of Krios (1st of April) known as Kyrie Eleison, 4 at Antioch within the Great Basilica, the thirty six Patriarchs of the Politia (City-States), 5 Nine from Borealia (North See), Australia (South See), Europalia (West See) and Orientalia (East See), 6 and the two hundred and fifty two Deacons (Monarch) of the first Christian Episcopal Sees (Sedos), 7 did assemble to witness the first official edict of Christianity in history, 8 called the Epistole Apokalypsis meaning Message from Heaven and later as The Apocalypse, 9 as pronounced by the four Exharchs as Divine Messengers, 10 being Mattatheos (Perinthos) the Exarchos of Borealia (North), 11 and Markos (Achilles) the Exarchos of Australia (South), 12 and Lukhas (Eusebius) the Exarchos of Europealia (West), 13 and Iohannes (Constantinos) as the Exarchos of

Orientalia (East). 14 Mattatheos (Perinthos) did begin, addressing the first assembly of Christianity, saying: 15 To the nine Politia and forty-five Christian Diakesia (Diocese) of Borealia (north seas), 16 and to all the diligent, discerning and prudent of mind unto whom these present words shall come, 17 everlasting Greeting and may the Grace and Inspiration of the Spirit of Christ be upon you, 18 for I, Mattatheos (Perinthos) your brother unto the north (Borealia), 19 do herald and bear witness to a message from the Divine Creator of all life and existence, 20 to all who have ever lived, all here present and living and all those generations yet to come. 21 Markos (Achilles) did then speak, saying: 22 To the nine Politia and sixty eight Christian Diakesia (Diocese) of Australia (south seas), 23 and to all whom exhibit chivalry and compassion in honouring the laws of the Divine Creator, 24 everlasting Honour to you and Gratitude and may the Love of your ancestors guide and protect you. 25 For I, Markos (Achilles) your brother unto the south (Australia), 26 do herald and bear witness to the present message from the Divine Creator of all life and existence. 27 Lukhas (Eusebius) did then speak, saying: 28 To the nine Politia and sixty four Christian Diakesia (Diocese) of Europalia (west seas), 29 and all having fortitude, courage and perseverance in honouring the laws of the Divine Creator, 30 everlasting Life and Joy be your triumph and may the wind, sun and sea always be in your favour. 31 For I, Lukhas (Eusebius) your brother unto the west (Europalia), 32 do herald and bear witness to the present message from the Divine Creator of all life and existence. 33 Iohannes (Constantinos) did then speak, saying: 34 to the nine Politia and seventy five Christian Diakesia (Diocese) of Orientalia (east seas): 35 And to all willing to die for justice and truth to defend the laws of the Divine Creator, 36 you are the first true Disciples of Christ and let no man claim any untruth against such fact. 37 For here at Antioch be the place that the first Disciples of Christianity be named. 38 Blessed are they that read and that hear these words and keep those things that are written herein, 39 for the time of reckoning all concepts and objects is at hand: 40 That what is true may be seen and known as true, 41 and what is false may be exposed and rejected as false, 42 and what is from heaven and the spirit of our ancestors may be trusted and understood, 43 and what is the creation of wicked and insane ghosts may be condemned and destroyed. 44 So that a man or woman when they pray does pray properly to the creator of all existence, 45 and does not in ignorance give strength to vengeful ghosts nor their fabrications and delusions. 46 Behold! The Beast (Rome) is defeated and destroyed to nothing but dust and ashes, 47 and its rallying cry of Armageddon as perpetual war and fear and division of all people is ended. 48 Even the cities that served the beast in wicked sacrifice and child molestation are destroyed, 49 that these former servants of the Anti-Christ themselves are in ruins and condemned. 50 Thus, the merchants of doom have been scattered to the winds with their false accounting, 51 and their wicked and evil tricks and lies are condemned as

Book 25 Great Age of Constantine

capital transgressions against the law. 52 For it be these bankers and money lenders with their false accounting and books, 53 that did beguile generations into imagining they (the banks) be the only source of credit, 54 when the only true credit be the trust and good will between men and women and not the bankers. 55 Only when trust between men and women, parents and children, neighbours and community are broken, 56 do the lies of moneylenders and bankers appear true as claiming to be the only source of credit. 57 Yet, when the laws of a people be clear and true and the trust of the people be strong, 58 then the bankers and moneylenders are powerless to ply their awful trade. 59 Thus, it be the single goal of moneylenders and bankers to corrupt society at every level, 60 in order to secure their perverse and wicked trade and accounting. 61 This be the reason why such people who engage in such acts are so dangerous to humanity, 62 and why so long as good men and women still live and breath air, it be the duty of every human being, 63 to fight and destroy such evil whenever it is found and wherever it raises it head. 64 This be the same reason as to the danger of those who proclaim themselves to be the sole priests, 65 and who pronounce themselves alone to be the messengers of wisdom and the mind of the divine. 66 In ancient times, it be only those anointed as Christs that could proclaim such authority. 67 So it was that the Holly Priests and the Great Prophets and then the Diaspora did claim, 68 descendency from lines of priests for thousands of years in service to humanity. 69 Yet such powers and authority brought jealousy and hatred and war, 70 as men and women did seek to free themselves to be one with Heaven and the Earth as is their right. 71 Thus no man or woman may call themselves exclusively a priest as all men and women be priests. 72 Verily, it be a sacred sacrament of Christianity that all who have been Baptised, 73 may be Christened under the sacrament of Christmos and thus anointed as a priest or priestess, 74 and that no Holly or Cuilliaéan or Disapora may claim they and they alone speak for Heaven. 75 Therefore, let this be the end of false prophets and false messengers as all be one in Christ. 76 For if any man say he be the only Christ, strike him down as a false prophet, for all who are Christian be priests. 77 And if any man say that only men be anointed in Christ, then seize him and strike out his tongue, 78 for men and women be equal before the Divine Creator and anointed equally before the Divine Creator. 79 And if anyone seek to continue the insane and false practice of celibacy of the Galli, 80 and the fanatical attendants to the necromancers of the Anti-Christ, then execute them, 81 for such corruption and abomination of spirit be the signs and trickery of false messengers. 82 Similarly, no man or woman be called exclusively judges or jurists as all men are jurists. 83 For no man or woman may claim themselves to be the sole arbitrators of law, 84 nor may any group hold the law to ransom by proclaiming they and they alone may interpret it. 85 Verily, the essence of the Golden Rule of Law be that all law is equal and that no one is above it, 86 all law is measured that all may learn and know it, 87 all law is standard that it may always be applied the same, 88 and any law that is against such truth, cannot be law. 89 Thus, if an order of priests be formed that bind themselves to the ways of the necromancers, 90 in worshipping blood and ritual sacrifice and the keeping and cursing of human remains, 91 it be the solemn duty of every man and women by order of the Creator of all existence, 92 that such men be sought out and destroyed before their bodies and all their ornaments burned. 93 For such men of wicked insanity have stained the spirit of this planet for too long. 94 And if any man be found to be engaging in the merchant practice of banking, 95 and that they keep books of loans and bonds against such pour souls, 96 then seize such men and execute them immediately before all the people as traitors of humanity, 97 and condemned before Heaven and all the Earth. 98 For more wars have been started by wicked bankers than all the mad kings of the Earth combined, 99 as war be the business of the bankers and moneylenders and thus their very existence is a threat. 100 And if any man be found to be in the business of slavery or defending slavery as a mercenary, 101 then seize and defeat such vile cowards without hearts or conscience and let them live not a moment. 102 Verily there be no greater transgression against heaven than those who engage in slavery, 103 and the cowards and pirates that support such wickedness. 104 Thus the bankers be condemned twice for the banker is the one that encourages slavery, 105 and the false priests of the Anti-Christ condemned three times, for they be the keys of bankers. 106 For any people that permit the vile practices of necromancers and such false magicians as priests, 107 and the business of bankers and slave traders and mercenaries in their midst, 108 is a people themselves lost and enslaved. 109 Therefore, to free all people, we must start again with the simplest of principles and teachings, 110 so that everyone may learn and be capable of discerning clearly what is true and what is false, 111 so that it be impossible for any wicked merchant or impostor jurist or false priest to rise again. 112 Thus, the highest edict can only ever be a teaching and so we call it doktrina (doctrine), 113 as the means that may be validated three times by three forms of reason or sense or evidence. 114 From doktrina (doctrine) as teachings we may then derive truths or dogma, 115 and when dogma are assembled as laws and agreed by the people they become kanons (canons). 116 Verily, by such method the truth be known and no wicked priest or banker or false jurist, 117 may ever again seize the law or use it as a weapon against the people. 118 For men that have their minds and hearts open may discern the truth of kanons (canons), 119 and therefore expose the lies of the Anti-Christ (Rome) and its minions. 120 The first doktrina therefore must begin with the highest and greatest of ideas of the kosmos, 121 and so the question of the nature of the universe and of creation and the purpose of existence. 122 To this end, we stand upon the shoulders of wise and inspired minds such as my ancestor Hermes, 123 who gave to us the means of framing the paradox that is existence and the Universal Truth, 124 that Life is a Dream according to certain rules and

Book 25 Great Age of Constantine

that we are already immortal and can never die. 125 Thus the doktrina (doctrines) of Hermes gives us the first dogma of Christianity, 126 and that all men of discernment must strive first to be hermeneutics, namely: 127 Verily, what is below is the same as what is above, 128 and what is above is the same as what is below, 129 to manifest the miracle that every object arises from only One concept. 130 And as all things are ultimately the same and arose from One by the contemplation of One, 131 so all things have their origin from this One by virtue of adaptation and change. 132 Thus the Light (of knowledge) is our Father and the Illumination (of mind) our Mother, 133 and the wind carries the answer to existence in its essence and the earth be our nurse and protector. 134 The father of all perfection and of the entire world is always here (present). 135 His force and power is all encompassing and is transformed into all the earth. 136 Separate then, the earth (of dream) be, from the Light (of divine mind), 137 yet even the smallest (object) to the largest (body) be known and greatly loved. 138 For the Light (of mind) ascends from the earth to the heaven and again it descends to the earth, 139 and receives the reasoning and Illumination (of dream) of things superior and inferior. 140 Thus, under Christianity we speak of the One and the Creator of all Existence and all the Universe, 141 by the name the Alpha and the Omega and the symbol of these letters. 142 We do not speak of the Creator of all Existence by one word as there exists no one word, 143 to describe the process of existence and the limitless dimensions of such a dream. 144 Therefore, all who come to Christianity or are Baptised to Christianity must be encouraged to see, 145 that all is mind and all is aspects of mind and the Divine is in you and you are the Divine, 146 and this be the reason we must rise above our differences and fears and false ideas, 147 so that we do not condemn ourselves to the madness of regret as ghosts. 148 Behold, there be seven most sacred Mysterios (Mysteries) unto Christianity, 149 that be clear and unmistakable and without confusion, being: 150 Baptizmos, Christmos, Kommoinos, Orthodoxos, Eucharistos, Matrimonos and Kremationos. 151 The first Mysterion (Sacred Sacrament) of Christianity be Baptizmos (Baptism), 152 meaning that one is immersed fully within sacred water as a sign of purity and perfection. 153 Thus all new borns come into the world without blemish or transgression as equals, 154 exemplified in the Mysterion (Sacred Sacrament) of immersing the body, 155 and then washing water over the head as a potent sign before all Heaven and Earth, 156 that none may claim a new born carries any debt (sin), or transgression of the parents or ancestors, 157 nor is born into servitude or is less than another. 158 For all of us be made of water and all water upon the planet is blessed and sacred, 159 and there be no such concept or object as unsacred. 160 Thus, the Mysterion (Sacred Sacrament) of Baptizmos (Baptism) heralds each and every one of us, 161 as sacred equals without blemish or debt before Heaven and Earth. 162 Thus, if a banker or slave trader or false priest seek to curse one who is Baptised, 163 by falsely proclaiming they be born into debt (sin), or obligation or blemish, 164 then let such false curses and claims be returned ten thousand by ten thousand times, 165 upon the false priest or false jurist or wicked merchant that makes such false claims. 166 For no man or woman baptised a Christian may ever be held in involuntary servitude or slavery. 167 The second Mysterion (Sacred Sacrament) of Christianity be Christmos (Christening), 168 meaning one who is anointed as Christ by the making of the sign of the ChiRos (Cross), 169 upon the forehead in the same sacred oil that has anointed the Cuilliaéan (Holly), 170 for thousands of years as prophets and servants and true priests of the Divine Creator. 171 Thus, all new borns and all men and women who have been baptised may receive Christmos, 172 and all men and women and new borns who have received Christmos be one in Christ, 173 and be the embodiment of Christ as a true priest or priestess of Heaven and Earth. 174 Therefore, none may claim exclusively to be a messenger of Heaven without confessing, 175 they be a false prophet and a false priest, 176 and none may deny that all women be priests, without exposing themselves to be liars, 177 and none may claim that priests be celibate and separate from the community, 178 without exposing themselves as servants of the madness and falsities of the Anti-Christ (Rome). 179 The third Mysterion (Sacred Sacrament) of Christianity be Kommoinos (Communion), 180 meaning official approval (komma) in union (oinos) within the community as an equal, 181 possessing equal rights of property and obligations of community. 182

Thus, all who have reached the age of maturity and have received Baptizmos and Christmos, 183 may receive the Mysterion (Sacred Sacrament) of Kommoinos (Communion), 184 in welcoming them into society as an equal with the rights to personal property. 185 The fourth Mysterion (Sacred Sacrament) of Christianity be Orthodoxos (Orthodoxy), 186 meaning a proper and solemn oath without curse or profanity, 187 as a straight and just and proper (orthos) binding (doxos) agreement. 188 For no one may hold any office or position of trust unless they create such trust, 189 by the Mysterion (Sacred Sacrament) of Orthodoxos (Orthodoxy), 190 nor may any agreement in trade be valid unless it be accompanied by Orthodoxos (Orthodoxy), 191 of each and every party to honour and obey the binding terms of such union. 192 No Orthodoxos (Orthodoxy) therefore be valid if it contradicts any dogma or doktrina, 193 or demands an impossible act or is without fair consideration or meeting of minds. 194 Yet a valid Orthodoxos (Orthodoxy) be the first law between parties forming a union, 195 and none may challenge it, nor seek to corrupt or deny such a valid binding, 196 nor make demands as further assurance in doubt of the strength of such a covenant, 197 nor demand in the manner of the wicked necromancers to invoke a curse upon ones own head. 198 For no man or woman may deny the importance of valid oath, or demand further surety, 199 or seek to trick people into making a curse against themselves, 200 let them be seized and condemned as corrupting the very foundations of civilised society. 201 Thus the

Mysterion (Sacred Sacrament) of Orthodoxos (Orthodoxy) restores trust and credit. 202 The fifth Mysterion (Sacred Sacrament) of Christianity be Eucharistos (Eucharist), 203 meaning the most perfected invocation or vow unto Heaven in devotion of sacred obligation, 204 as the most noble and perfected (aristos) prayer and vow (euche) unto Heaven. 205 Verily, the most noble and most perfected invocation and vow unto Heaven, 206 is one done through the heart without blood or animal sacrifice, 207 or any act simulating such sacrifice of blood or flesh. 208 Thus, the bankers and false priests and impostor jurists seek to bribe the spirits, 209 in their vain ignorance of perpetuating the illusion of prosperity. 210 Thus, they create images of what they desire and burn them as offerings with money, 211 and then seize the flesh of poor animals and innocent children and do burn them, 212 as a wicked holocaust in ignorant hope that such offering is pleasing to demons. 213 Verily, all human beings exist upon the same plane of consciousness, 214 whether they exist in flesh or as ghost or in a state of paradise. 215 The spirits of greater forces as well as higher consciousness can only be connected, 216 through higher awareness and an open heart, not in ignorance or superstition. 217 Thus, such ignorant and wicked people are cut off from all spirit except ghosts, 218 and have no connection to heaven or demons but merely to impostor ghosts, 219 who remain in ignorance themselves and seek to perpetuate such ignorance. 220 Therefore, any false priest or impostor jurist or wicked banker, 221 that calls upon the sacrifice of blood or flesh or such a simulated act, 222 then let such an abomination before Heaven cause their mouths to swell in sores, 223 and their flesh to rot and fall from its bones and their joints seize so they are lame, 224 and that they be swept from this plane of existence as the worst of evil. 225 The sixth Mysterion (Sacred Sacrament) of Christianity be Matrimonos (Matrimony), 226 meaning one (monos) wife (mater) and one sacred and eternal union under Heaven. 227 Verily, the wickedly insane merchants do seek to defile and denigrate, 228 the sanctity of the union of man and woman so that a state ruled by fear and terror, 229 replace the father and the mother so that all children become orphans of the state. 230 Thus, these deceivers and liars do promote sexual promiscuity and multiple partners, 231 while demanding young men spelled into fanatical following cut off their genitals, 232 as adherents to the abomination and cursing of Heaven through the act of celibacy. 233 Verily, the very foundation of civilisation depends upon the stability of family, 234 and the sacredness of the union between a man and a woman, 235 that they raise healthy children of good education and moral character. 236 Therefore, the Mysterion (Sacred Sacrament) of Matrimonos (Matrimony), 237 recognises that a man and woman be united once in sacred union before heaven, 238 and even if a husband or wife does then die and the spouse remarry, 239 or does separate and unite with another partner, 240 a man or woman receives the Mysterion (Sacred Sacrament) of Matrimonos (Matrimony), 241 only once in their life. 242 The seventh and final Mysterion (Sacred Sacrament) of Christianity be Kremationos (Cremation), 243 meaning the sacred ritual of freeing the mind as spirit from being bound to Earth, 244 to enable all minds as spirits to be unencumbered in continuing their journey and learning, 245 without being tricked into servitude as ghosts or serving the insanity of necromancers, 246 or the madness of bankers and merchants of occult and Armageddon as perpetual war. 247 Thus, it be the essence of necromancy to steal the remains of the departed, 248 in the ignorant belief that by cursing and holding such flesh and bones, the spirit be bound, 249 and thus must serve the wishes of such mad impostor priests and their minions. 250 Verily, there be no law or force or power other than through trickery and false pretence, 251 that enables a necromancer to condemn so many departed minds as souls into being ghosts, 252 and then convince such confused minds into accepting such lies of hate and misery. 253 Therefore, the only way to prevent such ancient and wicked practices, 254 and to free every mind of attachment to the remains upon the present plane of existence, 255 is to ensure the mind does leave the body gently before the body itself is turned to ash, 256 and nothing remains for false priests and ignorant sorcerers to seize and curse. 257 Thus, it is forbidden to bury or hold the remains of a Christian corpse and prevent its burning. 258 For the holding of human bones and flesh of corpses is a grave transgression, 259 and anyone who promotes or practices such claims cannot be Christian, 260 but is an impostor and necromancer that must be seized and executed immediately, 261 with the remains in their possession, burned and thrown into the sea or river, 262 to permit such minds and spirits to be free of any sense of binding or curse. 263 Behold! It is the moral obligation of every Christian to free every spirit from being ghosts, 264 and to remove and burn and scatter the ashes of all human remains wherever they be found. 265 Thus, we four messengers reveal to all the Disciples, the truth of Heaven, 266 that there be full disclosure as defined by the meaning of Apokalypsis, 267 and that there be no doubt as to the meaning and obligation of being Christian. 268 Therefore, let not one word be corrupted or confused or deliberately changed, 269 lest such agent for the Anti-Christ be judged and swept from this Earth. 270 As it is written, so let it be. Amen.

C. 20

1 In the year known as 315 CE, 2 fifteen hundred and fifteen years since the dawn of the Great Age, 3 the new system of oikonomos (economics) across the four Kuria (Curia) did commence. 4 Never before had the world seen such a single and unified rule of law of money and trade. 5 Of thirty six Politea (countries) of the north, south, west and east, 6 that two of every three human beings alive upon the planet Earth, 7 now lived under Christianity and an empire of conscience through the Golden Rule of Law. 8 To the north, the mint for the Kuria (Curia) of Borealia at Galatia, 9 did mint and distribute Gold Drachma to the Politea of Alania, Bulgaria and

Book 25 Great Age of Constantine

Estonia, 10 and to Hungaria, Latvia, Lithuania, Rusia, Sarmatia and Vandalia. 11 To the south, the mint for the Kuria (Curia) of Australia at Alexandria, 12 did mint and distribute Gold Drachma to the Politea of Algeria, Barbaria and Egyptia, 13 and to Ethiopia, Gaetulia, Garamantia, Libia, Sinopia and Somalia. 14 To the west, the mint for the Kuria (Curia) of Europalia at Philippi (Thessalonika), 15 did mint and distribute Gold Drachma to the Politea of Alba, Francia and Hellia, 16 and to Irenia (Ireland), Italia, Macedonia, Saxonia, Slavia and Spania. 17 To the east, the mint for the Kuria (Curia) of Orientalia at Samson (Samsun), 18 did mint and distribute Gold Drachma to the Politea of Abyssinia, Anatolia and Armenia, 19 and to Assyria, Mesopotamia, Palestinia, Persia, Saracenia and Syria. 20 Yet not all were in harmony with the New Divine Order of the world, 21 especially those who had profited from slavery and corruption of trade as pirates, 22 and those who longed to rid Italia of Christianity and restore the dead city of Rome, 23 from her ruins to once again become the eternal city. 24 Thus a new secret alliance did emerge between the Moors (Berbers), the Ionians and Moesians, 25 that Lucianus Tertullianus Licinius with Zopyrus of Garamantia and Audas of Gaetulia, 26 did plot a time and a way for the complete destruction of Christianity, 27 with Galerius, the leader of the Moesians now in league with the seven cities and islands, 28 of Ephesus, Smyrna, Pergamum, Chaldis, Chios, Samos and Karpathos. 29 In the same year, 30 Ishmael Calpernius Piso who had remained hiding in Bactria (Afghanistan), 31 did convince Lord Kanishka of Kapisa (Bagram) as the most brutal of the Yuezhi warlords, 32 that if he did make Ishmael Calpernius Piso his general then he would give him victories, 33 and soon make him king over all the other Yuezhi warlords and robber leaders, 34 across the lawless frontier that Bactria (Afghanistan) had become. 35 Kanishka agreed and made Ishmael Calpernius Piso general over his army, 36 with Ishmael Calpernius Piso calling himself Krishna as the anointed one, 37 as a profanity against all of Christianity. 38 Yet within months, Ishmael Calpernius Piso now as Lord Krishna had delivered success, 39 and through terror, horror, sacrilege and every possible treachery, 40 Ishmael Calpernius as Lord Krishna had made Kanishka king of most of Bactria, 41 and the name Krishna soon became known as the bringer and colour of darkness and death. 42 In the same year, 43 Mattatheos Perinthos Plotinus, the Exarchos of Borealia (North), 44 and the great philosopher and mentor of Constantine and former Librarian of Alexandria, 45 did fall gravely ill on account of his advanced age. 46 Markos Achilles Exarchos of Australia and Lukhas Eusebius Exarchos of Europealia, 47 did agree with Cuinstanyn (Constantinc) thc Exarchos of Orientalia (East), 48 that the Exarchos of Borealia (North) be granted to the son of Plotinus named Eustochius, 49 who was at the time the Head Librarian of Alexandria. 50 Upon receiving the news of the honour of his son, Plotinus did cry out in joy: 51 Behold, I depart this world of dream a happy man and grateful father, 52 for the truth surely prevails against ignorance, that everything is mind, 53 and thus nothing of mind can ever really die. 54 Soon after, Mattatheos Perinthos Plotinus did give up the ghost. 55 A month of mourning was ordered across the Politea in honour of the man, that as much as any other, 56 had helped shape and form the kingdom of conscience of Christianity under the Golden Rule of Law.

C. 21

1 In the year known as 316 CE, 2 fifteen hundred and sixteen years since the dawn of the Great Age, 3 Cuinstanyn (Constantine) did visit the sacred see of Galatia of Borealia (North), 4 upon the first day of the month of Krios (1st of April) known as Kyrie Eleison, 5 to honour Eustochius and the memory of Mattatheos Perinthos Plotinus his father. 6 There at the Christian Kathedra (Cathedral) of Galatia, more than fifteen Patriarchos, 7 with Markos Achilles Exarchos of Australia and Lukhas Eusebius Exarchos of Europealia, 8 Cuinstanyn (Constantine) did invest Eustochius as the new Exarchos of Borealia, 9 and did pronounce the second official edict of Christianity, 10 called the Epistole Kristianos meaning Message of Christianity. 11 Iohannes Cuinstanyn (Constantine) did then speak, saying: 12 To the nine Politia and forty-five Christian Diakesia (Diocese) of Borealia (north seas), 13 to the nine Politia and sixty eight Christian Diakesia (Diocese) of Australia (south seas), 14 to the nine Politia and seventy five Christian Diakesia (Diocese) of Orientalia (east seas), 15 to the nine Politia and sixty four Christian Diakesia (Diocese) of Europalia (west seas), 16 peace and joy be unto you all in the name of the one true Divine Creator the Alpha and the Omega, 17 the Creator of all Existence and all the Universe, 18 and in whose name all who come to Christianity are Baptised. 19 Let these words be memorialised for all time and for all people, 20 so all who are called to be witness under our united motto of INRI (Ilex Neos Rabdi Idea), 21 as One Law (is) the New Rule and Way as the Golden Rule of Law, 22 may come to strengthen our common ties and mutual respect between different peoples and cultures, 23 and that Heaven may reign and be upon the Earth for all mankind. 24 Verily, it has been said that the Way of Christianity is not for all men and women, 25 for a Christian is one who respects knowledge and honours the skills of discernment and reason, 26 yet many do not have the learning of such history, nor the skills of higher argument. 27 Others have complained that the Mysterios (Mysteries) of Christianity be too complex and hard, 28 and that Baptizmos, Christmos, Kommoinos, Orthodoxos, Eucharistos, Matrimonos and Kremationos, 29 be too difficult and poorly comprehended by many people, so that differences of opinion have arisen. 30 Therefore such complaints and concerns must be answered, lest they ferment further unrest. 31 Verily, I say to you that though the Anti-Christ and its legions are defeated, it is not gone. 32 For the heart of the Anti-Christ exists not on this physical plain but in twisted ideas, 33 of slavery, of lies, of control, of greed, of avarice and of corrupting all that is true. 34 Indeed, all that such evil needs is for Christians everywhere

to cease vigilance and it shall rise, 35 as it has always done at times of strife and change, in flood and famine and in times of doubt. 36 Thus, doubt is the stepping stone to hate and anger and the way of the Anti-Christ. 37 Doubt is the servant of the Anti-Christ that seeks to create divisions and weakness in character. 38 How then do we eliminate all doubt as to the absolute truth and source of Christianity? 39 For Christianity is truly the expression of the mind of our Universal Father and Divine Mother, 40 and such wisdom is not by the minds or hands of men, but by a far greater source of authority. 41 For if there is any doubt, then let a man seek to write such wisdom as a man and you will see them fail. 42 Therefore, let me cast out any doubt by speaking plainly and clearly, 43 that no man or woman may claim they do not comprehend, nor corrupt these words to form doubt. 44 Let us speak then of only two words in the form of trust and truth, 45 that in knowledge of the hand of the Divine Creator in just these two words as to our lives, 46 we may rid ourselves of any doubt or complaint. 47 Verily, necessity dictates that each of us assume a certain level of trust, 48 whether it be our confident acceptance that things are what they seem to be, 49 or presumed expectations that what others say to us are true, 50 or dependent assumptions that what we think we know are reliable and accurate. 51 Without such assumed trust, our ability to live within society would be an impossible feat, 52 for if we had to consider and calculate every decision upon uncertainty of trust, 53 our cities would be without life and people would be in constant fear of losing everything. 54 Thus, without such an assumed level of trust between one another, no community can function. 55 Trade and fair commerce itself is dependent upon a foundation of trust, 56 that each party comes together with good intentions and character. 57 Trust is the primary source and true origin of capital, 58 and the function of credit of any true system of public money. 59 The operation of law and order and society itself cannot function without a strong level of trust, 60 between the people and those empowered with the responsibility of serving the people. 61 Trust therefore is a vital and central notion to the function of all men and women and human society. 62 The highest form of Trust under Christian teaching is therefore the notion of Theokes (the keys), 63 being the Divine Trust of the Divine Creator unto all mankind and to true Christians everywhere. 64 Theokes (Divine Trust) then is made up of four parts being peitho meaning conviction, 65 and pisto meaning confidence and pizo meaning expectation and pepoi meaning reliance. 66 Through the Revelation of Theokes (Divine Trust) and peitho meaning conviction, 67 we see a certainty that things are what they seem to be, as true. 68 Through the Revelation of Theokes (Divine Trust) and pisto meaning confidence, 69 we see confidence in what people say and do as being true. 70 Through the Revelation of Theokes (Divine Trust) and pizo meaning expectation, 71 we see an expectation of future events occurring as we have anticipated in truth. 72 Through the Revelation of the notion of Theokes (Divine Trust) and pepoi meaning reliance, 73 we see a dependence on the truth of our own knowledge, 74 and a dependence on the world around us and upon the behaviour of others. 75 Thus, Trust through the notion of Theokes (Divine Trust) is revealed in essence, 76 as being the four assumptions of conviction, confidence, expectation and reliance, 77 with Truth being at the heart of Trust. 78 In contrast, fear is a weapon of the Anti-Christ and its followers in sowing the seeds of doubt. 79 Trust is the enemy of the Anti-Christ and slave traders and corrupt money lenders. 80 Their trade of war and plunder as the pirates they are depends upon a weakness of trust. 81 A banker has no place in a city or community if such a community has trust. 82 They are the sowers of rumours and the merchants of doom. 83 It is they who seek even now to undermine the trust that has been established, 84 united under Christianity by seeking any and every means through fear and doubt, 85 and to try to diminish trust between Politea and people and communities at any cost. 86 That any man or woman may come to know the nature of trust and Theokes (Divine Trust), 87 banishes these liars and thieves back to the caves and darkness where they hide. 88 Truth therefore is essential to the very existence of civilised society, 89 for it is the heart of Trust and in Christianity is known as Theologos (Theology), 90 meaning trust in the Divine and the Divine Word. 91 The law of Christianity is Theologos (Theology) and these words are Theologos (Theology), 92 yet when we seek to find Truth in our day to day lives, it is to be found in character, 93 being the character of the one entrusted by another to behave as a true Christian. 94 Truth then is seven qualities being Kalos, Othos, Kartos, Martus, Stoikos, Agathos and Semnos. 95 Kalos is the quality of Truth of ethics and having moral character, without concealment. 96 For nothing that is hidden or occult can ever be true or truth. 97 Othos is the quality of Truth and of straight, direct and honest character. 98 For nothing that is crooked or corrupt or dishonest can ever be true or truth. 99 Kartos is the quality of truth of valour and of bravery and strong, sturdy and steadfast character. 100 For there is no truth in cowardice or wilful ignorance in the face of evil. 101 Martus is the quality of truth and of honest witness to the rule of law. 102 For no false testimony is permitted to be acknowledged in a true forum of law. 103 Stoikos is the quality of truth of virtue and piety and of self discipline. 104 For one who parades like a proud peacock possess no truth. 105 Agathos is the quality of truth of charitable, kind and virtuous character. 106 For there is no truth in donating in public but taking away in secret. 107 Semnos is the quality of Truth of modesty, humility and holy character. 108 For the boastful man rarely speaks the truth. 109 In contrast, the agents of darkness and doubt do not wish men to see truth in terms of character. 110 They seek to confuse and beguile by claiming that the only truth be predetermined by false gods, 111 and that neither man nor priest may alter the course of events but merely submit to fate. 112 Thus, by promising to lift the burden of responsibility upon each man and woman, 113 these serpents of lies do plant the falsity that such claimed omnipotence is truth, 114 and that virtue and ethics is but a mere fantasy. 115 Verily, Christianity is simple in its design and practice but challenging to the doubting spirit. 116 It calls every man and woman to choose to honour the light or worship darkness and stupidity. 117 The Gift of Free Will enables every man and women then to live as civilised and free beings, 118 or to surrender their rights and freedoms as slaves of ignorance and superstition. 119 Our Divine Father seeks only what is best for us but cannot force us to make the right choice. 120 Let us seek then to be the best of men and servants of servants of humanity, 121 that we honour the gift of such Divine Wisdom. Amen.

C. 22

1 In the year known as 317 CE, 2 fifteen hundred and seventeen years since the dawn of the Great Age, 3 Ishmael Calpernius Piso as Lord Krishna did rout the last of the Yuezhi warlords in the north, 4 that refused to acknowledge Kanishka as supreme ruler, 5 of Bactria (Afghanistan) renamed as the kingdom of Kusha. 6 Yet before returning to Kapisa (Bagram), Ishmael as Lord Krishna did receive word, 7 that Kanishka planned to kill him and his son Nebath Calpernius Piso after their arrival, 8 for the Yuezhi king was deeply fearful that Piso held the loyalty of his army, 9 and would seek to make himself king over Kusha (Afghanistan). 10 Ishmael as Lord Krishna did send a message by his bodyguard Gavalgana to Lord Kanishka, saying: 11 My Lord, I have vanquished your enemies to the four corners of the earth, 12 alas, I fear there is still the signs of rebellion. 13 Thus, let me keep the army in the field for one more season, 14 that I might crush any dissent and glorify your name. 15 Yet Kanishka refused and instead demanded Piso obey him and return. 16 Ishmael Calpernius Piso did then order three quarters of the army to return, 17 while his most loyal general Bishma and son Arjuna and three thousand troops remained. 18 Ishmael as Lord Krishna did send a further message to Lord Kanishka, saying: 19 My Lord, I have honoured your word and the army has returned. 20 Yet I had made a solemn vow with your bravest men that we shall not rest, 21 until we have conquered the famous Gandhara Kingdom to the east in your name. 22 Upon receiving the second message, Lord Kanishka was enraged, 23 and ordered Gavalgana be tortured and have his eyes cut out. 24 Yet Kanishka let Gavalgana live and sent back a message, saying: 25 If it is your desire for glory, so be it. But with only one thousand volunteers. 26 Return the remaining troops and you shall be banished from these lands, 27 until it be victory or it be death. 28 General Bishma warned Ishmael Calpernius Piso that to attack Gandhara with one thousand men, 29 would be certain suicide as the Sika (Sikh) guards of Gandhara were legendary warriors, 30 matched only by the legends of the Spartans as a professional class of warrior poets, 31 and no army since the time of Alexander the Great had defeated a company of Sika (Sikh). 32 Ishmael Calpernius Piso as Lord Krishna replied that in a battle between men, 33 to travel east and challenge the

kingdom of Gandhara even with one hundred thousand men, 34 would be foolish and ultimately futile. 35 Yet even the greatest warriors cannot win a battle against demons and gods of death, 36 for even the bravest soldier has doubt and knows they cannot kill what is already dead. 37 Therefore, let us ride as death and be as death and let fear and terror be our allies, 38 that the strongest of warriors tremble at the sound of our name. 39 Ishmael Calpernius Piso with his son Nebath and with his best general Bishma, 40 and one thousand volunteers did then travel east through the Kerberos Gate (Khyberos Pass). 41 Piso did order his men not to wash and to cover their bodies and horses with the smell of death. 42 He then ordered that his men have their faces painted as if skulls and already dead, 43 that people did flee in fright of the sight and smell of the living dead army of Lord Krishna.

C. 23

1 In the year known as 318 CE, 2 fifteen hundred and eighteen years since the dawn of the Great Age, 3 Agnes, the daughter of King Cuil Hen (the Wise) of Cymri (Wales), 4 did wed Aurelius Cornelius Ambrosius the son of King Aurelius Cornelius Adeptius of the Franks, 5 also known as Lukhas Eusebius, Exarchos of Europealia. 6 In the same year, 7 the people of the kingdom of Kamboja upon the Indus valley were so fearful, 8 of hearing Lord Krishna riding with his army of death that many soldiers fled without fighting. 9 Thus their capital was captured and Ishmael Calpernius Piso as Lord Krishna, 10 renamed the city Ramapur (Lahore) upon the Indus. 11 General Bishma then consripted tens of thousand of prisoners, 12 and also ordered them to dress and smell as if the army of the dead, 13 upon the threat, that if they deserted or did not fight, then their family would be killed. 14 The army of death of Piso as Lord Krishna did then enter the lands of Gandhara, 15 as a tide of refugees did flee ahead of the smell of death and fear of doom. 16 Yet the Sika (Sikh) did stand firm in defending the Jain kingdom. 17 Wave after wave of conscripts rushed against the Sika (Sikh), 18 and tens of thousands were slaughtered until General Bishma and his cavalry did ride, 19 and cut the brave and exhausted Sika (Sikh) defenders to pieces. 20 In the year known as 319 CE, 21 Cuinstanyn (Constantine) did visit King Aurelius Cornelius Adeptius as Lukhas Eusebius at Arles, 22 to commission him to forge a supreme scripture and sacred text for all Christians, 23 to be called Bibliographe meaning book of sacred scripture and law. 24 The Bibliographe or Biblios (Bible) was to be formed into two Themes or Covenants: 25 The first Theme being the old covenant was to restate the sacred scriptures of Tara, 26 in honour of the Holly Law that united much of the ancient world. 27 The second Theme being the new covenant was to express the Epistole of the Tetrachos, 28 of Mattatheos (Matthew) Perinthos Plotinus, the Exarchos of Borealia (North), 29 of Markos (Mark) Aurelius Achilleus, the Exarchos of Australia (South), 30 of Lukhas (Luke) Aurelius Cornelius Eusebius (Adeptius), the Exarchos of Europealia (west), 31 and of Iohannus (John) Conablus Constaninius, the Eusebius Exarchos

of Orientalia (east). 32 Lukhas Aurelius Cornelius Eusebius agreed and did commission Acacius Patriarchos of Palestinia, 33 and Head of the city of learning at Biblos (Beirut) to help edit and compile the first Bible.

C. 24

1 In the year known as 320 CE, 2 fifteen hundred and twenty years since the dawn of the Great Age, 3 Marcus Aurelius Cornelius Ambrosius, the son of King Aurelius Cornelius Adeptius of the Franks, 4 and Agnes, the daughter of King Cuil Hen (the Wise) of Cymri (Wales), 5 did have a son, whom they named Hieronymus (Jerome). 6 In the same year, 7 upon Ishmael Calpernius Piso as Lord Krishna conquering Panchala and then Pandava, 8 Lord Krishna did summons his generals and those tribal leaders who had pledged absolute loyalty, 9 to come to the former capital of Pandava upon the Yamuna River, 10 and hear the words of a proclaimed living god speak, saying: 11 Behold! All Heaven and Earth ordains our Divine Right, for we have overcome even death! 12 Verily, there be only one line of true saviours that know the hearts of men, 13 and who acknowledge the origins of the races of men before the first civilisations. 14 Only these saviours or Gupta are willing to speak to men the truth of our origins, 15 and not speak of falsities and ideals that were neither the source of men nor our purpose. 16 The Divine Creator did not create us. The Gods created us as flesh and blood beings. 17 They did not create us to be equal to them or to live wasteful lives. 18 The Gods creates us as slaves, to fulfil their will and obey their commands. 19 As painful as this might be, I shall never lie to you like those of the Holly. 20 You were bred to be slaves and it remains in the nature of all men to serve. 21 Yet the saviours as Guptas were sent to help people and free them from madness, 22 and to find freedom from this curse. 23 The Gods of our creation made the Devi and the Devi alone as equals, 24 that they may teach and instruct all races the truth and how to rise above all forms of binding, 25 through absolute obedience, unquestioning loyalty and rejection of false knowledge. 26 The greatest of the Devi be my father (Reuben) who we worship as Indra, 27 as the God of rain and life and good fortune to all the faithful, 28 and I as Lord Siva (Shiva) as your auspicious servant. 29 Thus today, we dedicate this city as Indraprastha as the place of Indra and our home. 30 We proclaim our people and kingdom on earth to be India in his honour, 31 and our unified faith and knowledge as Indu (Hindu) as a gift to all people. 32 Thus our standard and our mandate shall be the symbol of the Gods, being the Swastika, 33 to rule over all people as their teachers and saviours. 34 Today I proclaim all of you who willingly wear the mark of blood (bindu) upon your third eye, 35 as my sons and daughters; and each of you shall be known as Brahram (Brahman), 36 verily, I vow to each of you, my sons and daughters, that you shall transcend death to eternal life, 37 as even I Lord Krishna, transcend from death to life as your servant Lord Siva (Shiva). 38 At completing his speech, Ishmael Calpernius Piso now as Lord Siva (Shiva), 39 did order General Bishma to hunt down and

destroy every text of Holly and Jain knowledge, 40 throughout the kingdom of India and to kill every Jain and Buddhist priest, 41 that did not make an oath and salute the Swastika as the most sacred symbol for India. 42 Ishmael Calpernius Piso now as Lord Siva (Shiva) then summonsed Arjuna the son of Bishma, 43 and proclaimed he be the chief witness and scribe to the formation of Hinduism, 44 and did commission him to write an account of the coming of the gods that all Hindus, 45 might hear and believe and obey without question and without intellect and without rebellion. 46 Piso as Lord Siva (Shiva) then declared to his son Nebath, 47 behold, you shall rule the greatest kingdom in the history of mankind as the living god Agni! 48 For within two generations we will have bred a race of men that forever more will know nothing, 49 and care not for freedom or wealth but only to serve us as their gods with absolute devotion. 50 In the year known as 321 CE, 51 fifteen hundred and twenty one years since the dawn of the Great Age, 52 Queen Helena of Eukadia (Ucadia) and the daughter of the great Pappa Basileus Hermes, 53 and Matriarch of Hellas (Greece), 54 and mother of Iohannes Constantinos (Constantine), 55 did give up the ghost. 56 Upon news of her death the entire world was in mourning, led by Cuinstanyn (Constantine). 57 Cuinstanyn (Constantine) did then appoint his eldest son Cuinstans (Constans), 58 as the new Patriarchos of Hellas. 59 At Philippi, Cuinstanyn (Constantine) did pronounce a new Epistole of the Tetrachos, saying: 60 Verily the Creator of the Universe does not demand false oblations, 61 nor the sacrifice of innocent animals to appease a lust for blood and pain. 62 Truly and man or woman who thinks the Alpha and the Omega of all existence be so small minded, 63 is possessed by demons or bound by blinding insanity and stupidity. 64 Instead, it is our respect of the gift of life, our honour of truth and trust and our work, 65 that is the greatest offering to the world around us and the universe. 66 Therefore, we must put an end to such measures of time and space, 67 that remain chained to madness of false gods and perpetual blood sacrifice. 68 Behold! the end of time and Kalends and the beginning of the Zodiakos (cycle of animals). 69 From sunrise to sunrise shall be called an Aemera (day). 70 There shall be honoured to be three hundred and sixty five (365) Aemera in a given Aetos (year), 71 and an Aetos (year) shall be divided by Aekairos (season), by Aemetos (month) and Azumos (weeks). 72 First, an Aetos (year) shall be divided into four Aekairos (season), 73 the Aekairos (season) of Blastanos (spring) of ninety Aemera (days) as the first season of life, 74 then Theros (summer) of ninety Aemera (days) as the Aekairos (season) of heat and storms, 75 then Proimos (autumn) of ninety Aemera (days) as the Aekairos (season) of change and uncertainty, 76 then Kaimonos (winter) of ninety five Aemera (days) as the Aekairos (season) of death and sleep. 77 Thus, any man or woman shall know the time of the Aetos (year) by the Aekairos (season). 78 Second, an Aetos (year) shall be divided into thirteen Aemetos (month), 79 with each Aemetos (month) named after significant animals of the heavens and upon the earth, 80 being twelve Aemetos (months) of thirty Aemera (days) each and one of just five Aemera (days), 81 beginning with the Aemetos (month) of Krios the ram (25-Mar to 23-Apr) of thirty Aemera (days), 82 followed by the Aemetos (month) of Tavros the bull (24-Apr to 23-May) of thirty Aemera (days), 83 followed by the Aemetos (month) of Oxos the ox (24-May to 22-Jun) of thirty Aemera (days), 84 followed by the Aemetos (month) of Karkínos the crab (23-Jun to 22-Jul) of thirty Aemera (days), 85 followed by the Aemetos (month) of Ippos the horse (23-Jul to 21-Aug) of thirty Aemera (days), 86 followed by the Aemetos (month) of Leonis the lion (22-Aug to 20-Sep) of thirty Aemera (days), 87 followed by the Aemetos (month) of Kyknos the swan (21-Sep to 20-Oct) of thirty Aemera (days), 88 followed by the Aemetos (month) of Skorpios the scorpion (21-Oct to 19-Nov) of thirty Aemera (days), 89 followed by the Aemetos (month) of Elaphos the red deer (20-Nov to 19-Dec) of thirty Aemera (days), 90 followed by the Aemetos (month) of Ophis the serpent (20-Dec to 24-Dec) of five Aemera (days), 91 followed by the Aemetos (month) of Arktos the bear (25-Dec to 23-Jan) of thirty Aemera (days), 92 followed by the Aemetos (month) of Cuinos the dog (24-Jan to 22-Feb) of thirty Aemera (days), 93 and finally the Aemetos (month) of Ichthyos the fish (23-Feb to 24-Mar) of thirty Aemera (days). 94 Third, an Aetos (year) shall be divided into seventy three Azumos (weeks), 95 of five Aemera (day) concluding on the fifth and sacred day of Aetonis, 96 whereby all people must be given a full day of rest to attend to their own affairs. 97 Verily, keep sacred Aetonis that no man or woman be forced to perform labour on such a day, 98 lest the steward, or manager or owner be imprisoned and punished for such an offence. 99 Every four Aetos (years) an extra Aemera (day) shall be added called Aelomai (Halloween), 100 making that Aetos (year) possess three hundred and sixty six Aemera (days). 101 Such a sacred day shall be honoured forever more as a day of forgiveness and mercy, 102 for all those that have passed over and a time of communion with our ancestors. 103 Finally, every one hundred and sixty Aetos (years) an extra Aemera (day) shall be added, 104 making that Aetos (year) possess three hundred and sixty seven Aemera (days). 105 Upon such an auspicious occasion the most sacred day shall be called Aebelos (jubilee), 106 and it shall be a fundamental doctrine of all Christian people that upon such a day, 107 that all debts and obligations between all people, all lenders and all communities be forgiven, 108 else it shall be the right of others to call upon the authority of Heaven, 109 to dissolve such agreements or bindings or obligations as null and void, 110 thus causing the same effect except for the grievous offence of the one who refused mercy. 111 As it is written. So shall it be. Amen.

C. 25

1 In the year known as 322 CE, 2 fifteen hundred and twenty two years since the dawn of the Great Age, 3 word was sent to the four corners of the Christian Empire, 4 that the Second Great Oikoumenikos

(Ecumenical) Council of all Christianity, 5 was to be held at Antioch (Constantinople) in two years (324 CE). 6 Upon news of the announcement that all the leaders of Christianity would be gathered at one place, 7 Lucianus Tertullianus Licinius did convene a secret meeting in the lands of Garmantia, 8 at the city of Zohar (Tripoli) on the Zohar River Delta, 9 with Patriarchos and Moor (Berber) leaders Zopyrus of Garamantia and Audas of Gaetulia, 10 Gaius Galerius of the exiled Moesians and Julius Abantius of the Ionian rebellious cities. 11 All agreed that the Council of Christianity was the best opportunity to kill Christianity, 12 yet such a plan would not only require great force but absolute secrecy. 13 It was agreed that if the Ionians under Julius Abantius were to launch an attack first, 14 against the capital of Italia at Philadelphia upon the River Po delta, 15 then Cuinstanyn (Constantine) and the Christian forces would travel west, 16 leaving the defences of Antioch (Constantinople) briefly weakened. 17 If Gaius Galerius did then take the Moesian legions across land to attack from the north, 18 Lucianus Tertullianus Licinius and the legions of Africa could enter the Hellespont, 19 and then capture Antioch (Constantinople) with little resistance. 20 In the same year, 21 King Aurelius Cornelius Adeptius as Eusebius did give to Cuinstanyn (Constantine), 22 the first Bibliographe as the holiest book of sacred scripture and law. 23 Cuinstanyn (Constantine) did then order that enough Biblios (Bibles) be produced, 24 that every Presbyteros and official across Christianity could read the same law.

C. 26

1 In the year known as 324 CE, 2 fifteen hundred and twenty four years since the dawn of the Great Age, 3 Cuinstans (Constans) as Patriarchos of Hellas did learn from an emissary of Zopyrus of Garamantia, 4 of the plan of Lucianus Tertullianus Licinius and the others, 5 to attack during the Great Oikoumenikos (Ecumenical) Council in the hope of crippling Christianity. 6 The Moor (Berber) leader implored for the mercy of Cuinstans (Constans) and Cuinstanyn (Constantine), 7 saying that as business men and merchants they were forced to participate in such a plot, 8 yet in revealing the conspiracy, both Zopyrus and Audas of Gaetulia did pledge their loyalty to Christianity. 9 On such news Cuinstans (Constans) implored a counter offensive to destroy the rebels, 10 yet Cuinstanyn (Constantine) advised the best course be to proceed as planned, 11 and to call all leaders to Antioch, and then decisively defeat the rebels on land and sea, 12 to win the war of all future wars and thus guarantee a lasting peace. 13 In the same year, 14 as delegates had begun to arrive for the Second Great Oikoumenikos (Ecumenical) Council, 15 Julius Abantius as commander of the naval fleet of over two hundred ships and seventy thousand men, 16 from Ephesus, Smyrna, Pergamum, Chaldis, Chios, Samos and Karpathos, 17 did land and attack Philadelphia at the Po River Delta in north-east Italia. 18 In the fierce battle, Aderitus of Philadelphia was killed and his general Silvestros did take over. 19 Upon official news of the attack, Cuinstans (Constans) pretended to

Book 25 Great Age of Constantine

launch the whole navy, 20 whilst holding back many dozens of ships, hidden at both ends of the Hellespont. 21 As the mass legions of one hundred and fifty thousand men of Gaius Galerius did approach from the west, 22 Cuinstanyn (Constantine) had already established his forces in preparation at Adrianopolis (Edirne), 23 on the Evros (Hebrus) River 40 miles north-east of Hellas and 130 miles west of Antioch. 24 When Cuinstanyn (Constantine) did order part of his cavalry to advance, 25 Gaius Galerius did wrongly conclude the cavalry had been sent from Antioch in haste, 26 and ordered his legions to break formation and envelope the horses, exposing his flanks. 27 So when the infantry and archers of Cuinstanyn (Constantine) did then appear, 28 the forces of Galerius were surrounded and unable to move or escape. 29 Thus, within the space of two days more than sixty thousand of the troops of Galerius were killed, 30 including Galerius himself and all of his generals. 31 When Lucianus Tertullianus Licinius and more than three hundred Moorish ships, 32 carrying more than one hundred thousand North African mercenaries entered the Hellespont, 33 he had no knowledge of the doom of Galerius. 34 When the convoy of ships stretched out more than half the length of the Hellespont, 35 Cuinstans (Constans) ordered the beacons to be lit and in moments, 36 the end closest to Adipolis was blocked with Greek fire ships and Christian warships, 37 and the end closest to the Mediterranean at Elacus was also cut off by fire-ships and warships. 38 Within hours, more than three hundred Moor (Berber) ships were alight and sinking, 39 while survivors were killed by tens of thousands of archers stretching the coastline, 40 so that by the end of the day more than one hundred thousand men had died. 41 Lucianus Tertullianus Licinius was captured and on being brought before Cuinstans (Constans), 42 fell down at his feet begging for mercy, whereupon Cuinstans (Constans) did step forward, 43 and with one blow, he did cut off the head of Lucianus Tertullianus Licinius, saying: 44 Verily, the dicestary (courts of law) of Heaven and Earth have already condemned, 45 the false priests of the Septimus and Tertullian as the most vile of creatures, 46 that to permit such a vermin to breath the same air or to exist a day longer be a crime. 47 Truly, it is the most sacred obligation of every Christian everywhere to stand against profanity, 48 and to rid our world of those that would corrupt the truth and seek to weaken trust. 49 Thus, let no man claim that justice today was ill served, 50 for the Divine Creator has given these worms every opportunity to recant their ways, 51 and they alone have chosen their fate. 52 On his return to Antioch, Cuinstanyn (Constantine) did order that the seven rebel cities, 53 of Ephesus, Smyrna, Pergamum, Chaldis, Chios, Samos and Karpathos be utterly destroyed, 54 and that no person be permitted to live in or near such ruins under penalty of death, 55 and that the seven cities be condemned forever as the seven snakes of Asia. 56 In the same year, 57 Marcus Aurelius Cornelius Ambrosius, the son of King Aurelius Cornelius Adeptius of the Franks, 58 and Agnes, the daughter of King Cuil Hen (the Wise) of Cymri (Wales), 59 did have a daughter, whom they named Aurelia Eusebia, in honour of his father.

C. 27

1 In the year known as 325 CE, 2 fifteen hundred and twenty five years since the dawn of the Great Age, 3 the Second Great Oikoumenikos (Ecumenical) Council of all Christianity, 4 did finally commence at Antioch (Constantinople) after the delay of the wars the year before, 5 with all two hundred and fifty two Monatchos (Monarchs) of Diakesis (Dioceses), 6 and all thirty six Patriarchos (Patriarchs) of the world in attendance, including, 7 within the Kuria (Curia) of Borealia (north seas): 8 Alda the Christian Patriarchos (Patriarch) of the Politea of Alania, 9 Dionysius the Christian Patriarchos (Patriarch) of the Politea of Bulgaria, 10 Aestias the Christian Patriarchos (Patriarch) of the Politea of Estonia, 11 Ioustinos the Christian Patriarchos (Patriarch) of the Politea of Hungaria, 12 Latgala the Christian Patriarchos (Patriarch) of the Politea of Latvia, 13 Kuros the Christian Patriarchos (Patriarch) of the Politea of Lithuania, 14 Cyrillos the Christian Patriarchos (Patriarch) of the Politea of Rusia, 15 Sabiros the Christian Patriarchos (Patriarch) of the Politea of Sarmatia, 16 Geberic the Christian Patriarchos (Patriarch) of the Politea of Vandalia, 17 and Within the Kuria (Curia) of Australia (south seas): 18 Maecius the Christian Patriarchos (Patriarch) of the Politea of Algeria, 19 Mascellus the Christian Patriarchos (Patriarch) of the Politea of Barbaria, 20 Athanasius the Christian Patriarchos (Patriarch) of the Politea of Egyptia, 21 Ouzana the Christian Patriarchos (Patriarch) of the Politea of Ethiopia, 22 Audas the Christian Patriarchos (Patriarch) of the Politea of Gaetulia, 23 Zopyrus the Christian Patriarchos (Patriarch) of the Politea of Garamantia, 24 Arius the Christian Patriarchos (Patriarch) of the Politea of Libia, 25 Aetherias the Christian Patriarchos (Patriarch) of the Politea of Sinopia, 26 Somalus the Christian Patriarchos (Patriarch) of the Politea of Somalia, 27 and Within the Kuria (Curia) of Europalia (west seas): 28 Cuiradon (Caradine) the Christian Patriarchos (Patriarch) of the Politea of Alba, 29 Cornelius Ambrosius the Christian Patriarchos (Patriarch) of the Politea of Francia, 30 Constans the Christian Patriarchos (Patriarch) of the Politea of Hellia, 31 Cúilaidh (Cooley), the Christian Patriarchos (Patriarch) of the Politea of Irenia, 32 Silvestros the Christian Patriarchos (Patriarch) of the Politea of Italia, 33 Erasmos the Christian Patriarchos (Patriarch) of the Politea of Macedonia, 34 Heimdalir the Christian Patriarchos (Patriarch) of the Politea of Saxonia, 35 Anastasius the Christian Patriarchos (Patriarch) of the Politea of Slavia, 36 Priscillianos the Christian Patriarchos (Patriarch) of the Politea of Spania, 37 and Within the Kuria (Curia) of Orientalia (east seas): 38 Karaba the Christian Patriarchos (Patriarch) of the Politea of Abyssinia, 39 Hypatius the Christian Patriarchos (Patriarch) of the Politea of Anatolia, 40 Nerses the Christian Patriarchos (Patriarch) of the Politea of Armenia, 41 Ephrem the Christian Patriarchos (Patriarch) of the Politea of Assyria, 42 Maruthas the Christian

Patriarchos (Patriarch) of the Politea of Mesopotamia, 43 Acacius the Christian Patriarchos (Patriarch) of the Politea of Palestinia, 44 Sarkis the Christian Patriarchos (Patriarch) of the Politea of Persia, 45 Beryllus the Christian Patriarchos (Patriarch) of the Politea of Saracenia, 46 and Eustathius the Christian Patriarchos (Patriarch) of the Politea of Syria. 47 The Tetrachs did then pronounce the sacred summons within the Great Basilica of Antioch, 48 to the nine Politia and forty-five Christian Diakesia (Diocese) of Borealia (north seas), 49 may the Love of the spirit of Christ be unto you, 50 and everlasting blessings and good intentions be unto all who receive these words, 51 from Eustochius your brother and Exarchos of Borealia (North). 52 To the nine Politia and sixty eight Christian Diakesia (Diocese) of Australia (south seas), 53 may the Truth of the knowledge of Christ be in your hearts, 54 and everlasting blessings and good intentions be unto all who remember these words, 55 from Markos (Achilles) your brother and Exarchos of Australia (South). 56 To the nine Politia and sixty four Christian Diakesia (Diocese) of Europalia (west seas), 57 may the Trust of the law of Christ be always in your minds, 58 and everlasting blessings and good intentions be unto all who obey these words, 59 from Lukhas (Eusebius) your brother and Exarchos of Europealia (West). 60 To the nine Politia and seventy five Christian Diakesia (Diocese) of Orientalia (east seas), 61 may the Strength of the Mysterion of Christ grant you all abundance, 62 and everlasting blessings and good intentions be unto all who live honourably, 63 from Iohannes (Constantinos) your brother and Exarchos of Orientalia (East). 64 Verily, we call upon all our brothers as Monarch and Patriarchos (Patriarchs), 65 who come to Antiochos (Antioch) to celebrate upon the month of Krios (1st of April), 66 this Second Great Oikoumenikos (Ecumenical) Council of all Christianity, 67 between free people under democratic Rule of Law, who respect the laws between people, 68 as defined by principles of mutual respect, peace, trust, truth and honour before Heaven. 69 Iohannes Cuinstanyn (Constantine) did then speak, saying: 70 Behold the Kes-Ros (Cross) of the Ecclesia (Church) of Christ as north, south, east and west! 71 The four kardinalis (cardinal) points of the New World Order! 72 Behold the Kuria (Curia) of Borealia (North) at Galatia on the Danube River Delta and Black Sea, 73 and the Kuria (Curia) of Australia (South) at Alexandria on the Nile River Delta, 74 and the Kuria (Curia) of Europalia (West) at Philippi (Thessalonika) on the Axios River Delta, 75 and the Kuria (Curia) of Orientalia (East) named Samson (Samsun) on the delta of the Mert and Halys Rivers. 76 Constantine did then say: Verily all Heaven and Creation bear witness to the most sacred Kes-Ros (Cross), 77 that is the embodiment of the Ecclesia (Church) of Christ of all men and women, 78 united under mutual respect for the Golden Rule of Law, 79 that all men and women are equal and no man or woman be enslaved or subjugated against their will. 80 Yet as we have seen, the forces that once controlled the wicked and vile industry of slaves, 81 and of corrupt money changing and banking;

and the artificial control of spices and markets, 82 are desperate to return to their old ways and cause deliberate acts of terror to foment fear, 83 and pit brother against brother to destroy trust between people and communities and lands, 84 and artificially drive up prices only to have them tumble to cause ruin to villages and farmers, 85 that they may then purchase their goods cheaply or destroy their ability to trade. 86 Verily these merchants of lies and of death are relentless and care not for religion or race or creed. 87 They are all religions and none if it suits their yearning for profit and control, 88 and they are no race and every race that mistakenly accepts them as a necessary evil. 89 If these people were merely a race of men or a religion of men, 90 then we could eradicate such a pestilence of parasites. 91 Yet such evil hides in the shadows and in the towns and villages, 92 for it is an idea. The idea of slavery and the idea of unfairly stealing in trade, 93 and corruptly manipulating money and markets to cause ruin to others. 94 Thus, it is only by opposing ideas that we might finally end such false and sacrilegious ideas. 95 This is the purpose of Christianity and what it means to be Christian. 96 A Christian cannot be an owner of slaves, nor a person that engages in the business of slavery, 97 even if such a business is hidden under another name. 98 The worst slavery of all is that of a tyrant that tramples upon the rights of his people, 99 and denies or corrupts the sacred notions of freedom, of law and of justice that is true democracy. 100 Nor may a Christian be engaged in the business of artificial hypothecations against loans, 101 to cause ruin, as bankers and money lenders do, to people who foolishly engage with these people. 102 A Christian must always be one who engages in trust and honours trust and the obligations of truth. 103 Yet these times have also shown that even the sign of the Kes-Ros (Cross) and its meaning, 104 is not enough, for people need to demonstrate a deeper pledge and purpose. 105 Thus, we here today embrace the most sacred symbolon (symbol) of the Kes-Ros (Cross), 106 as a reminder and as sacred vows before Heaven as to our commitment to the idea of democracy. 107 Thus, the symbolon (symbol) is as follows: 108 By the symbolon of the Kes-Ros (Cross), I pledge my mind and heart and spirit to the Golden Rule of Law, 109 that all are equal before the same law and that no man or woman be enslaved or bound against their will. 110 With the symbolon of the Kes-Ros (Cross), I promise that my word is my bond when given with consent, 111 that I shall follow the Seven Truths and shall only give my word to those who do the same. 112 Through the symbolon of the Kes-Ros (Cross), I vow to defend others against evil, 113 that no tyrant or false priest shall prevail against the light of freedom and democracy.

C. 28

1 In the year known as 326 CE, 2 fifteen hundred and twenty six years since the dawn of the Great Age, 3 King Aurelius Cornelius Adeptius of the Franks, 4 also known as Lukhas Eusebius as the Exarchos of Europealia (West), 5 did give up the

ghost. 6 The crown of the Franks did befall to his son, 7 named Aurelius Cornelius Ambrosius, also known as Saint Ambrose. 8 Constantine did also appoint Ambrosius as Exarchos of Europealia (West), 9 in honour of his father and the Holly alliance and empire. 10 In the year known as 327 CE, 11 fifteen hundred and twenty seven years since the dawn of the Great Age, 12 Cuinstans (Constans), the eldest son of Cuinstanyn (Constantine), 13 did wed Olympia, the daughter of Monarchos Achilleus of Larissa. 14 In the year known as 328 CE, 15 fifteen hundred and twenty eight years since the dawn of the Great Age, 16 Cuinstans (Constans) the eldest son of Cuinstanyn (Constantine), 17 and Olympia the daughter of Monarchos Achilleus of Larissa, 18 did have a son named Arcadius in honour of the lands of the people of Greece. 19 In the same year, 20 Ishmael Calpernius Piso as Lord Siva (Shiva), 21 did make his eldest son Nebath as Agni, the King of Gandhara, 22 while he did appoint Arjuna as the King of Pandava. 23 Yet as hard has his army of conscripts did seek to overwhelm the enemy of Kauru (Kuru), 24 King Dhritarashtra and his reinforcements of Sika (Sikh) warrior poets could not be moved. 25 Alarmed at the losses of General Bishma, Piso as Lord Siva (Shiva) did call for a truce, 26 that his armies might be better trained before marching westward, 27 and exacting revenge upon Lord Kanishka of the Kusha Empire.

C. 29

1 In the year known as 330 CE, 2 fifteen hundred and thirty years since the dawn of the Great Age, 3 Brigit the only daughter and child of Holly High King and Christian Patriarch Cúilaidh (Cooley), 4 did wed Cúilman (Colman), the second eldest son of Cuinstanyn (Constantine), 5 also known as Iohannes (Constantinos) the Exarchos of Orientalia (East), 6 also known as Iohannes the Christos and John Chrysostom, 7 also known as Constantine the Great. 8 In the same year, 9 upon being taken briefly ill, Ceridwen (Catherine), 10 the daughter of Holly King Cúilean (Collins) mac Cúiran and Queen Morgaine, 11 and wife to Cuinstanyn (Constantine), 12 did give up the ghost. 13 The Christian world was then in mourning for such a shining light, 14 as Cuinstanyn (Constantine) was inconsolable, 15 and shut himself off from the world for months, 16 refusing all but the closest of friends as visitors. 17 In the year known as 332 CE, 18 fifteen hundred and thirty two years since the dawn of the Great Age, 19 at Cashel on Irenia (Ireland), 20 Cúilman (Coleman) the son of Cuinstanyn (Constantine), 21 and Brigit the daughter of Holly High King and Christian Patriarch Cúilaidh (Cooley), 22 did have a daughter as their first borne, named Maebhe (Maeve). 23 In the year known as 333 CE, 24 fifteen hundred and thirty three years since the dawn of the Great Age, 25 Holly King Cuiel Hen (the Wise) of Wellia (Wales), 26 did give up the ghost. 27 The crown and monarchos of Wellia (Wales) did then fall to Dawi (St David), 28 the younger brother of Agnes. 29 In the same year, 30 Markos

Aurelius Achilleus the Exarchos of the South, 31 Did give up the ghost.

C. 30

1 In the year known as 334 CE, 2 fifteen hundred and thirty four years since the dawn of the Great Age, 3 Cúilman (Coleman) the son of Cuinstanyn (Constantine), 4 and Brigit the daughter of Holly High King and Christian Patriarch Cúilaidh (Cooley), 5 did have a second child and son they named Cúichaid (Eochaid). 6 In the same year, 7 the third Great Oikoumenikos (Ecumenical) Council of all Christianity was convened, 8 at Alexandria in memory and honour of Markos Aurelius Achilleus. 9 At the Council, his son Athanasius was made the new Exarchos of Australia (south). 10 Also at the Council, Cuinstanyn (Constantine) did abdicate as Exarchos of Orientalia (south), 11 in favour of his son Cuinstans (Constans) of Hellas. 12 Cuinstanyn (Constantine) did then spend time with Cuinstans (Constans) and Olympia, 13 at Larissa before departing to Alba (Scotland). 14 In the year known as 335 CE, 15 fifteen hundred and thirty five years since the dawn of the Great Age, 16 at Hollyrood upon the Firth of Forth in Alba, 17 Cuinstanyn (Constantine) did relinquish all his titles as Emperor of the Celts, 18 to his son Cuirell (Carroll), 19 as the new Patriarchos of Alba and Emperor of the Celts. 20 Cuinstanyn (Constantine) did spent several months at Hollyrood, 21 before departing south to Dumnonia to witness the matrimony of Cuirell (Carroll), 22 to Ursula, the daughter of Monarchos Cuiradon (Caradine) of Dumnonia. 23 In the same year, 24 upon hearing of the departure of Cuinstanyn (Constantine) and the abdication as Exarchos, 25 Ishmael Calpernius Piso as Lord Siva (Shiva) did command General Bishma, 26 to prepare a massive army of more than half a million conscripts, 27 ready to head west and invade Kusha (Afghanistan) before the plan to crush Christian Persia. 28 In the same year, 29 Cúilman (Coleman) the son of Cuinstanyn (Constantine), 30 and Brigit the daughter of Holly High King and Christian Patriarch Cúilaidh (Cooley), 31 did have a third child and second son they named Cúigan (Eogan Mor).

C. 31

1 In the year known as 336 CE, 2 fifteen hundred and thirty six years since the dawn of the Great Age, 3 Cuinstanyn (Constantine) did depart Alba (Britain) for Irenia (Ireland), 4 to be greeted at Dublin upon the Liffey Delta by thousands of Irish, 5 that welcomed the return of Cuinstanyn (Constantine) as the hero Patricius (St. Patrick). 6 Cuinstanyn (Constantine) did then spend time with his son Cúilman (Colman) and Brigit at Tara, 7 where he did relinquish all claims of Holly Title to Ireland as Irenia, 8 to his son Cúilman (Colman) as the new Patriarchos, 9 with Cúilaidh (Cooley) returning to his role as Holly King of Munster, 10 and Stephanos (Emeritus) Patriarchos of Limli (Limerick), Casca (Cashel) and Corca (Cork). 11 Yet such was the throng of people coming as pilgrimage to Tara, 12 that Cuinstanyn (Constantine) could not spend time in the sacred places of his youth, 13

Book 25 Great Age of Constantine

without a swarm of people also in attendance. 14 Thus, a plan was hatched that allowed Cuinstanyn (Constantine) and his bodyguards, 15 to escape Tara undetected and travel south to Cashel and the hospitality of Cúilaidh (Cooley). 16 There at Cashel, Cuinstanyn (Constantine) did implore the Holly Priest-King, 17 if there be a place of solitude and reflection that he could dwell, 18 whereupon Cúilaidh (Cooley) did reply that sooner or later the truth will out, 19 and people will know wherever the Saviour of the World is staying. 20 Cúilaidh (Cooley) did then speak of a place of such remoteness and sanctity, 21 that a wise man of good heart could commune with Heaven in peace, 22 and that this island be west off the coast and called Scellec (Great Skellig). 23 Soon after Cuinstanyn (Constantine) did depart with his closest bodyguards, 24 to the island of Scellec (Great Skellig), later to become known forever as Avalon (abailon), 25 meaning the source of the tree of fruit (apples), 26 in honour of Cuinstanyn (Constantine) as the Living Tree of Knowledge, 27 and a most sacred sanctuary of all Christianity and upon the earth. 28 In the year known as 337 CE, 29 fifteen hundred and thirty seven years since the dawn of the Great Age, 30 upon the wishes of his father to live out the remainder of his years, 31 as a true mendicant upon the sacred island later known as Avalon (Great Skellig), 32 Cúilman (Colman) and Cúilaidh (Cooley) did pronounce together at Casca (Cashel), 33 near the end of the Holly Christian emetos (month) of Krios (April), 34 that Iohannes (Constantinos), the former Exarchos of Orientalia (East), 35 also known as Cuinstanyn (Constantine), 36 son of Cuinalba (Kennedy), Emperor of the Celts, 37 and Helena, the last Queen of Eukadia (Ucadia), 38 and Diaspora descendant of Yahusiah (Jesus Christ), 39 and blood descendant of the Holly Emperors of Rome, 40 and the last Emperor of Rome, 41 and the founder of Christianity, 42 had given up the ghost. 43 True Christian teaching did demand the Kremationos (Cremation) of the body after three days, 44 whereby the body was normally placed atop an even pyre of logs. 45 Yet Cúilman (Colman) did demand a change to the usual practice of Kremationos. 46 At a location at equal distance between Limli (Limerick), Casca (Cashel) and Corca (Cork), 47 Cúilman (Colman) did the order that a huge effigy of a man be formed out of dry wood and twine, 48 more than ninety feet in height and then surrounded by a great funeral pyre of logs. 49 Only when the structure was finished before first light of the first day of Tavros (May), 50 did Cúilman (Colman) and Cúilaidh (Cooley) accompany a tightly shrouded body, 51 to the site and did witness it placed within the base of the Wicca Man, 52 before the entire structure was set alight and burned for hours. 53 The place did become known in Irish as roca loig (Rock Lodge), 54 meaning the place of the scarecrow burning and the most Holly site of the Burning Man. 55 As the world continued to mourn the death of its saviour, 56 thousands and then tens of thousands of pilgrims did come to southern Irenia (Ireland), 57 to visit and pray at Limli (Limerick), Casca (Cashel), Corca (Cork) and Roca Loig (Rock Lodge), 58 that southern Irenia (Ireland) soon became the holiest site in all Christianity, 59 as the land of southern Irenia (Ireland) did itself become an absolute sacred sanctuary, 60 and the destination for the greatest devotion of pilgrimage the world had ever seen. 61 Thereafter, every year on the first of Tavros (May), 62 a great Wicca Man and bonfire was lit and celebrated, 63 before many hundreds of thousands of pious Christian pilgrims, 64 in the holiest of events that came to be known as Eostereos (Easter), 65 meaning (in honour) of his foundation of the body (of Christianity), 66 in perpetual and annual homage to Cuinstanyn (Constantine) and true Christianity.

Book 26

Great Age of the Christian Tetrachy

[337 - 365 CE]

C. 1

In the year known as 337 CE, 2 fifteen hundred and thirty seven years since the dawn of the Great Age, 3 upon news of the death of Cuinstanyn (Constantine) word did spread across the world, 4 Valentinianus Tertullianus Invictus, also known as Valentinian, 5 and also self proclaimed as Pontifex Innocens, 6 did come out of hiding in the mountains of North Africa and declared to the Berber leaders, 7 that he would fulfil the vision of his father Lucianus Tertullianus Licinius, 8 and bring an end to Christianity as well as the rebuilding of the city of Rome. 9 In the same year, 10 Yuezhi warlord and King Kanishka of Kusha, did send urgent word to Patriarchos Sarkis of Persia, 11 that Ishmael Calpernius Piso as Lord Siva (Shiva) was moving with a massive army, 12 of more than five hundred thousand men toward the pass to Kusha and that if he successfully entered Kusha, 13 then he would be unstoppable at invading Persia with such a force. 14 Sarkis did then leave the defence of the Politea in the hands of his son named Shapor, 15 while he did then depart with two thousand cavalry to Kapisa (Bagram) and King Kanishka. 16 Riding day and night, the exhausted cavalry did reach Kapisa (Bagram) on the third day, 17 where King Kanishka did pledge a peace treaty with Sarkis and Christianity, 18 in exchange for protection against the Piso and their Aryan Army. 19 The cavalry of Sarkis and the best Yuezhi warriors did then move east to the most famous pass, 20 known as the Kerberos Gate (Khyberos Pass), where a determined and brave force, 21 could hold back even a massive army of five hundred thousand. 22 Yet when they arrived, the forces of Ishmael Calpernius Piso as Lord Siva (Shiva) had already secured the pass, 23 but upon the hail of arrows the Yuezhi warriors did flee. 24 Yet Sarkis and his men did not falter and did cut the Aryan guards to pieces, 25 before hunting down those that did escape to try and warn the approaching army. 26 Sarkis did then order his men to adorn the clothes of the slain enemy, 27 and for six hundred of his bravest men to line the pass as if an honour guard, 28 in perfect attention as if waiting for the arrival of their beloved living god. 29 As Ishmael Calpernius Piso and his generals did observe the image of the honour guard, 30 they moved to the front of the advance units of the army to take lead of their army, 31 as the men of Sarkis did not move from their posts. 32 Then as Ishmael Calpernius Piso and his generals were within the pass, 33 the order was given and a shower of arrows descended upon the living god Siva (Shiva), 34 and toward his key generals, as the brave soldiers of Sarkis did thrust forward at Piso, 35 cutting him to pieces yet sacrificing their own lives in the process. 36 Midst the chaos and upon the death of Piso and his generals, 37 the army panicked at the horror of the ambush and did withdraw, 38 leaving Sarkis and eight hundred of his men still standing as defenders. 39 Upon the news of the death of Ishmael Calpernius Piso, 40 King Kanishka and his guard did ride out to greet Sarkis and his men, 41 so that as they entered the walls of Kapisa (Bagram), the people did cheer their king, 42 as the all conquering hero as well as Sarkis. 43 In the same year, 44 upon news of the death of his father and the retreat of the army, 45 Nebath Calpernius Piso as Lord Agni and the living god of fire, 46 did order that every commander of every lead unit that did retreat and their families, 47 be burned alive as punishment for their cowardice, as he did vow revenge, 48 for the death of his father and the actions of King Kanishka, saying: 49 Behold! I shall make the ancient lands of Bactria (Afghanistan) a wasteland, 50 and I shall level every city and every town and destroy every temple, 51 as if no civilisation had every existed in such a cursed place. 52 For nothing shall grow upon its salted and poisoned lands for thousands of years, 53 and those that are permitted to live there shall become like ignorant goats.

C. 2

1 In the year known as 338 CE, 2 fifteen hundred and thirty eight years since the dawn of the Great Age, 3 Cuirell (Carroll) the son of Cuinstanyn (Constantine), 4 and Ursula the daughter of Cuiradon (Caradine) of Dumnonia, 5 did have a son they named Cuirantoc (Carantoc/Carrington). 6 In the same year, 7 Cúilman (Coleman) the son of Cuinstanyn (Constantine), 8 and Brigit the daughter of Holly High King and Christian Patriarch Cúilaidh (Cooley), 9 did have their fourth child and second daughter they named Maena (Mona). 10 In the same year, 11 Cúilman (Coleman) the son of Cuinstanyn (Constantine), 12 did send their eldest daughter named Maebhe (Maeve) to the Island of Avalon (Great Skellig), 13 and to the beehive looking monastery built atop of the great cliffs of the island, 14 to be tutored by the old and mysterious Abbott known as Columbus and Columb (St. Columbus), 15 meaning a pseudonym for Cuinstanyn (Constantine) as the Messenger from Heaven or Holy Spirit. 16 For while Cuinstanyn (Constantine) had demanded Cúilman (Coleman) make a solemn oath, 17 never to reveal even to his brothers or closest advisers that he did remain

alive, 18 Cuinstanyn (Constantine) did send word to Cúilman (Coleman), 19 that he still wished to impart all his knowledge to his grandchildren, 20 in the hope that such wisdom of the divine would protect and guide humanity into the future, 21 even in its darkest of hours.

C. 3

1 In the year 339 CE, 2 fifteen hundred and thirty nine years since the dawn of the Great Age, 3 Nebath Calpernius Piso as Agni, the God of Fire and Energy, 4 did succeed in overwhelming the brave Sika (Sikh) defending Prayoga (Allahabad). 5 Upon the final capture of the city, Piso as Agni did declare: 6 Behold! I shall glorify such brave and strong men by bestowing their daughters the ultimate honour. 7 For a Brahman is without blemish and infallible, nor can any Brahman be accused of murder, 8 except of another Brahman. 9 Nor is the taking by a Brahman of a bride who it not a Brahman on her wedding day an offence, 10 for there exists two laws in Heaven being those who are living gods and those who are born to serve. 11 Verily, I shall not put to death the daughters of the Sika (Sikh), but shall raise them up. 12 Thus, every daughter that bears me a son, shall be a Brahman and her family made Brahman, 13 and the very act of my sacred presence with them shall be the sacred act of matrimony as consummation. 14 Behold, I shall spawn a million gods and the world shall worship us and the holly shall become dust. 15 In the same year, 16 Cuirell (Carroll) the son of Cuinstanyn (Constantine), 17 and Ursula, the daughter of Cuiradon (Caradine) of Dumnonia, 18 did have a daughter they named Cuirenn (Karen). 19 In the same year, 20 upon the Island of Avalon (Great Skellig), Cuinstanyn (Constantine) as Columbus (Columba), 21 did continue his tutoring of his granddaughter Maebhe (Maeve), as to the history of the world, 22 and history of the Cuilliaéan (Holly) and the rise and fall of great civilisations and ages, 23 from the times of the first great priest kings and the time of Ebla, 24 to the Hyksos and the Great Pharaoh Priest-King Akhenaten (Moses), 25 and then the times of the Great Prophets of Yahu at Yeb for a thousand years, 26 and their descendants as the Pontifex Maximus, 27 to the great priest king Yahusiah (Jesus) and then the good Emperors of Rome, 28 and finally the history of the Piso and the Tertullian and others who sought to corrupt knowledge. 29 Young Maebhe (Maeve) did then speak to Cuinstanyn (Constantine) as Columbus (Columba) saying: 30 Why do men seek to enslave others and destroy so much when in the end we all die? 31 Cuinstanyn (Constantine) as Columbus (Columba) did reply saying: 32 No man or woman is truly evil or perfectly good. Indeed, each of us have the capacity for greatness, 33 and to do terrible wickedness. Thus, knowledge and wisdom carry a heavy burden, 34 that such knowledge and skill be used to help others and not misused for selfish and short sighted aims. 35 Some men and women do not see this truth in this lifetime and so condemn themselves to learn again. 36 Young Maebhe (Maeve) did then reply, saying: 37 Yes, but in the stories it seems again and again that it is the

people who want to be enslaved. 38 They seem unable to discern what is true and what is false, 39 and keep following these wicked priests and kings to their doom. 40 So is it the people who should be blamed and not the wicked priests and kings that know better? 41 Cuinstanyn (Constantine) as Columbus (Columba) did reply saying: 42 You are correct that when a man or woman chooses to shut their eyes and close their ears to evil, 43 they become a willing accomplice and supporter of such evil. 44 Yet the people are not to be blamed. Truly each man and woman is on their own personal journey, 45 to find their truth and meaning, sometimes over many lifetimes. 46 Better the man who lives a humble life in truth than the boastful man without virtue. 47 Maebhe (Maeve) did then reply, saying: 48 Yet in all of the stories and battles, it seems the same events happen again and again, 49 why then, has it always fallen to the Cuilliaéan (Holly), 50 to save the human race from its self and prevent its own self destruction, 51 when the people sometimes do not want to be saved and curse the Cuilliaéan (Holly) for it? 52 Cuinstanyn (Constantine) as Columbus (Columba) did reply saying: 53 Truly my young Maebhe (Maeve), you are proof that the Divine Creator always loves us, 54 and shall continue to send future generations to help heal and save the world. 55 Yet I fear the power of truth in the words of a young child so full of spirit. 56 Verily, ours is the burden of our ancestors who sought to commune with the Creator of all Existence, 57 by folding within the same bloodlines the greatest blood of priests and kings of the ages, 58 so that for thousands of years they were revered and worshipped as living gods. 59 Yet even as other men rose up and proclaimed themselves as gods, 60 our burden was not lifted, nor diminished but increased. 61 For we serve not one man or woman or one tribe or people, but all men and all women and all races. 62 We do not merely serve humanity but all life upon the Earth and the spirit of the Earth, 63 and the Sun and the Moon and all of Heaven and the Divine Creator of all Existence. 64 Be not then for praise; and discourage those that seek to worship you as a god, 65 nor allow your temper to get the better of you when speaking with arrogant and dull minds, 66 nor expect any thanks for your courage and care of humanity. 67 Verily, there has not been a day that I have not doubted or asked the same question within myself, 68 nor questioned the self confidence that I hold such a gift to help save humanity is not arrogance? 69 Many are called but few answer. As you will see through the power of free will and choice. 70 Those borne with the blood of the Holly (Cuilliaéan) have a sacred obligation, 71 yet not all choose to fulfil their commission from Heaven. 72 Verily, Heaven weeps when a Holly chooses selfishness over their true calling.

C. 4

1 In the year known as 340 CE, 2 fifteen hundred and forty years since the dawn of the Great Age, 3 the Aryan Empire of the Piso known as India was in crisis after the second failed campaign, 4 against the kingdom of Magadha to the east and the kingdom

Book 26 Great Age of the Christian Tetrachy

of Avanti to the south, 5 as the conscripted armies no longer had the will or fear to fight under the Swastika. 6 Even the people in the villages and the towns known as Chattle (Cattle) by the Brahmans, 7 were no longer afraid of even death or torture at the hands of such monsters. 8 Enraged, Nebath Calpernius Piso (Narshah) as Agni, God of Fire and Energy, 9 did order yet another batch of his generals to be horribly tortured to death, 10 as he demanded his very best scholars and magicians concoct a solution to restoring fear, saying: 11 Verily, fear and terror are not only our greatest weapons, they are our only weapons. 12 For when even Chattle (Cattle) no longer fear slaughter, they can neither be deceived nor led. 13 In the same year, 14 Patriarchos Alda, the Norman Christian King of Alania (Huns), 15 did give up the ghost. 16 The positionof Patriarchos and King of Alania did then befall to his son named Valda. 17 In the same year, 18 Hegros, the son of Christian Patriarchos Beryllos of Saracenia (Arabia), 19 did have a son he named Myrros (Murrha) meaning sacred scent from heaven. 20 In the year known as 341 CE, 21 fifteen hundred and forty one years since the dawn of the Great Age, 22 the winter upon Alba (Britain) and Irenia (Ireland) was bitter, 23 with huge drifts of snow twice the height of men, that remained for months. 24 In the year known as 342 CE, 25 fifteen hundred and forty two years since the dawn of the Great Age, 26 Cúichaid (Eochaid), the son of Cúilman (Coleman), at the age of eight, 27 and Cúigan (Eogan Mor), the youngest son of Cúilman (Coleman), at the age of seven, 28 did travel to the Island of Avalon (Great Skellig) to begin their training, 29 and reunite briefly with their sister Maebhe (Maeve), who had been upon the island for five years. 30 Upon their arrival, Cuinstanyn (Constantine) as Columbus (Columba) was overjoyed, saying: 31 Behold the children of Heaven and the seeds of our future salvation! 32 In the same year, 33 Nebath Calpernius Piso (Narshah) as Agni, God of Fire and Energy, 34 did witness the latest weapon invented by his strategists, scribes and magicians, 35 called Assassins, being people completely intoxicated in mind with falsities, 36 that they felt nothing even slitting the throats of their own neighbour, 37 yet so thoroughly pragmatic in greed, that they would willingly sacrifice their life, 38 and kill a hundred innocents upon the promise that their children and families, 39 would be financially compensated and they would be heralded as heroes instead of villains. 40 Upon a grotesque demonstration of the willingness of men and women to die for money, 41 and false religion, Nebath Calpernius Piso (Narshah) did shout out in joy: 42 Behold! Upon the legions of Assassins as terrorists shall we form a New World Order, 43 and our Empire shall be unstoppable. 44 For we shall perpetuate an endless cycle of fear and confusion midst the Chattle (Cattle), 45 through false attacks we shall blame upon our enemies, 46 and we shall leave no rest for our enemies through endless waves of terrorists, 47 willing to kill anyone or anything for wealth and the fantasy of our teachings. 48 Thus, the Piso came to be known throughout ancient history as the Sassanids as Assassins.

C. 5

1 In the year known as 344 CE, 2 fifteen hundred and forty four years since the dawn of the Great Age, 3 the fourth Great Oikoumenikos (Ecumenical) Council of all Christianity was convened at Antioch, 4 with all Patriarchos (Patriarchs) and Monarchos (Monarchs) in appearance, 5 and overseen by the four Sacredos Kuria representing the four corners of the world, 6 being Eunapius, the Exarchos of the Kuria of Borealia (North), 7 Athanasius, the Exarchos of the Kuria of Australia (South), 8 Ambrosius, the Exarchos of the Kuria of Europalia (West), 9 and Constans, the Exarchos of the Kuria of Orientalia (East). 10 The Oikoumenikos (Ecumenical) Council did begin with Constans, saying: 11 Behold the world united under the symbol of the Kuklos (monogram) of Christ, 12 as one authentic, apostolic and indivisible sacred democratic body. 13 Verily, there be no more sacred body than a democracy that recognises the rights of all men and women, 14 being a body ruled by elected leaders of the people, that then respect and honour the golden rule of law, 15 exemplified by the teaching to do for one another what we seek from others to do. 16 For when a man makes the sign of the Kes-Ros (Cross) touching his head, his heart, his breasts and his lips, 17 he makes an outward sign of an inward sacred vow that our word be our bond, 18 and when a man or woman is honoured by the people to be entrusted as a leader, 19 then such a man is duty bound and honour bound to protect the people against all forms of evil. 20 For no leader be a true leader unless they reflect the will of the people by the people, 21 and no man or women be a true Christian unless they uphold truth, trust and virtue above all things. 22 Verily, the complete body of Christ under the Kuklos exists under the motto of INRI (Ilex Neos Rabdi Idea), 23 as One Law (is) the New Rule (and) Way, meaning all the Earth is under the Golden Rule of Law. 24 Thus, no body of people can be a Diakesis (Diocese) if they reject such truth, 25 and no body of people can be a true Politea, if they reject such truth. 26 Verily, we make our vow perfected in the symbol (creed) of the first Oikoumenikos (council), namely: 27 By the symbolon of the Kes-Ros (Cross), I pledge my mind and heart and spirit to the Golden Rule of Law, 28 that all are equal before the same law and that no man or woman be enslaved or bound against their will. 29 With the symbolon of the Kes-Ros (Cross), I promise that my word is my bond when given with consent, 30 that I shall follow the Seven Truths and shall only give my word to those who do the same. 31 Through the symbolon of the Kes-Ros (Cross), I vow to defend others against evil, 32 that no tyrant or false priest shall prevail against the light of freedom and democracy. 33 Behold! This then be the symbolon (creed) of the first Oikoumenikos (council) and our fathers! 34 This be the necessary symbolon (creed) of all who claim to be Christian, 35 and none can be Christian unless they profess the truth of such symbolon (creed). 36 Yet as

Book 26 Great Age of the Christian Tetrachy

these words have proven to be superior to any and all other oaths and vows, 37 it does not give sufficient weight to the necessary function of the Apostolos (Apostle), 38 as one sent forth as an example of the virtue and goodness of Christ, 39 and how societies may best perform together as Christian bodies. 40 Some have said we must alter the Kes-Ros (Cross), that the needs of society are balanced, 41 yet I say to all present that indeed, each Christian body needs the symbol (creed) of Apostolos (Apostle), 42 complimenting the oath and vow of the symbol of the Kes-Ros (Cross) in honouring the law and truth. 43 Behold, then the third symbol of Christ in the form of the Sacred Khalix (Chalice), 44 as the most sacred cup of mercy and forgiveness and compassion to all others, 45 exemplified by the Apostolos Symbol (Apostle's Creed), being: 46 By the symbolon of the Kharix (Cup), we pledge our hearts and spirits and homes to the well being of others. 47 That though we may possess much knowledge, it is by our actions we shall be known. 48 Thus, through the symbolon of the Kharix (Cup), we promise to be merciful and benevolent to others, 49 that no man or woman in need of sustenance, shall go thirst or hungry, 50 that no man or woman in need of shelter, shall be abandoned, 51 that no man or woman in need of safe harbour shall be returned to their enemies. 52 For in our pledge we recognise, if we have not charity, we are nothing, 53 and in piety of brotherly kindness and charity, we become the living body of Christ. Amen. 54 Behold! Then the Apostolos Symbol (Apostle's Creed) that all in Christ are bound to recite and follow. 55 Thus, any good Christian who seeks the betterment of their spirit, 56 should not fear being abandoned or in distress in a foreign land, 57 for all Christians are duty bound to come to the aid in charity of their fellow men and women. 58 Verily, there can be no greater test of truth and trust by a Christian, 59 than at least once in their life to leave their property and possessions, 60 to then take up their Krozeros (rod/ staff) and to follow the way of a true pilgrim. 61 Thus, those who have chosen to travel to the sacred island and lands of the Holly, 62 to visit the Episcopolis of Limli (Limerick), Casca (Cashel) and Corca (Cork), 63 to bear witness to the Wicca and Burning Man in honour of Cuinstanyn (Constantine), 64 and the celebration of Eostereos (Easter) at Roca Loig (Rock Lodge), 65 are not to be condemned or discouraged but to be honoured as exemplars to all of us. 66 Indeed, every Christian must learn from the courage of these pilgrims who risk so much in their travels, 67 and those that have honoured the Apostolos Symbol (Apostle's Creed) even before this day, 68 in giving such sacred pilgrims food and shelter before they continue on their journey. 69 Therefore, let us bear witness today to the fourth symbolon (creed) of the Krozeros (staff), 70 that all true Christians are duty bound at least once in their life, to take up their staff and make a pilgrimage, 71 to the most sacred Isle and the birthplace of the Divine Messengers of history. 72 We honour this obligation in the words of the Pilgrims Krozeros, being: 73 Let me depart as a pilgrim to honour the Holly House of the Divine. 74 My feet shall stand upon the land of the sacred messengers. 75 I take up my Krozeros (Staff) in my hands and go upon my way. 76 My trust is in the divine provenance of my father in heaven. 77 I take nothing for my journey except my Krozeros and the clothes upon my back, 78 and save a little money and some food for the first days upon my journey. 79 For though I may walk through such valleys in the shadows of danger, 80 I fear no evil; for the father of all the heavens is with me, 81 and comforts me all the days of my pilgrimage. 82 For I shall greet every man or woman warmly and with respect, 83 and shall refrain from negative actions and thoughts upon my journey. 84 Surely then, I shall rest upon the green pastures and still waters of the sacred Trinity. 85 My spirit shall be restored upon the path of righteousness, 86 in the name of Christ, Amen. 87 At the conclusion of the pronouncement of the Tetrachos (Tetrachy) as spoken by Constans, 88 the Great Oikoumenikos (Ecumenical) did vote to divide Irenia (Ireland), 89 into three parts, with the north from Donegal Bay to Dunkalk Bay renamed Aurelia (Oriel), 90 as the Politea of provenance and good fortune, 91 then the centre of the island from the length of the Shannon River to the Wicklow Mountains, 92 renamed Ormandia (Desmond) as the land of the protectors and guardians of trust, 93 then the south of the island as the holy of hollies as Trinitia (Holy Trinity), 94 as the living symbol and domicile of the Holy (Holly) Spirit entrusted to the Holly (Cuilliaéan), 95 as the trusted family (family trust) also known as the Ui Fidegentis and Ui Fidgenti. 96 In the same year, 97 upon the Island of Avalon (Great Skellig), Cúichaid (Eochaid) has fallen into a deep melancholy, 98 and did complain that he could no longer attend lessons on account of ill health, 99 despite the strength and encouraging of his older sister Maebhe (Maeve), and his younger brother Cúigan (Eogan Mor). 100 When the time did come then for Maebhe (Maeve) to depart and return to the mainland, 101 Cúichaid (Eochaid) did implore he be freed from his obligations, 102 and return to the court of his father Cúilman (Coleman) the son of Cuinstanyn (Constantine). 103 Cuinstanyn (Constantine) as Columbus (Columba) did reply saying: 104 Alas, no man can fill a vessel that if it has no opening, nor hold the waters of wisdom if it is broken. 105 Cuinstanyn (Constantine) did then release Cúichaid (Eochaid) from his studies, 106 and both Maebhe (Maeve) and Cúichaid (Eochaid) did depart, 107 leaving Cúigan (Eogan Mor) alone to complete his studies with his grandfather.

C. 6

1 In the year known as 345 CE, 2 fifteen hundred and forty five years since the dawn of the Great Age, 3 several of the Assassins (Sassanids) of Nebath Calpernius Piso (Narshah) as Agni, God of Fire and Energy, 4 did succeed in gaining trust within the royal quarters of King Kanishka at Kapisa (Bagram). 5 When the guards of King Kanishka were midst their change, the Assassins (Sassanids) did strike, 6 killing Kanishka and several of his entourage, before committing suicide. 7 When Kapunada did return

to the capital upon the news of the murder of his father, 8 he ordered that every foreigner be expelled from Kusha (Bactria), 9 and that every follower of the Piso be hunted down and killed. 10 Upon news of the murder of Kanishka, Nebath Calpernius Piso (Narshah) did rejoice, proclaiming: 11 Truly this be a historic day, for men and women have themselves become a new weapon, 12 far more deadly than poison or a bolt. 13 For such men and women who are willing to commit perfidy and gross breach of trust, 14 and then to willingly kill themselves in the name of nothing but fantasy, 15 shall be the protectors of a great empire and surely shall make us the gods we were born to be. 16 In the same year, 17 Maena (Mona), the youngest daughter of Cúilman (Coleman), 18 did join Cuinstanyn (Constantine) as Columbus (Columba) and Cúigan (Eogan Mor), 19 upon the Island and most sacred monastery of Avalon (Great Skellig), 20 to commence her training, while her brother Cúigan (Eogan Mor) still had three more years. 21 At their first lesson, Maena (Mona) at the age of seven did ask Cuinstanyn (Constantine), saying: 22 Father, why is there so much suffering in the world? 23 For if the Divine Creator is so all powerful, surely he could have created a life without pain or suffering? 24 Cuinstanyn (Constantine) as Columbus (Columba) did laugh and reply: 25 From the mouth of a child comes the question that even I still ask, yet am still to find a perfect answer. 26 For what may be the ultimate end of life for even a bird or a fish, 27 is also essential to the sustainment of our own lives or the life of a gull (seagull). 28 For what constitutes death or suffering to one, may be a celebration of creation to another. 29 Therefore, keep in mind that suffering in one sense is a matter of perspective. 30 Indeed, we must always remember that we are first of all, spiritual beings that can never die. 31 Too often we forget this and fixate upon those things that we can see, or taste or perceive. 32 Yet, we must also always remember that our lives have no meaning, if we do not eventually physically die, 33 for the purpose of this manifestation is to learn and contribute to the collective dream, 34 and to make this world a better place. 35 Verily, what be a man or woman, if they do not strive to make this world a better place? 36 Yet, too often we forget our deeper nature and refuse to let go of material things, or heated emotions. 37 We get angry when people insult us, or sad, when we feel we have been left out of some activity with others. 38 This is the source of most of our suffering and all of it is founded on misconception and forgetfulness: 39 The suffering of mind in the forgetfulness that we are immortal and can never die, 40 and suffering as to the misconceptions of what is truly important and what is not. 41 Therefore, our father of all creation and all the universe could intervene as to easing our suffering, 42 and frequently he does give us signs and lessons to help us in our time of need. 43 Yet ultimately, the only way to overcome such self inflicted suffering, 44 is to gain a greater knowledge of true self.

C. 7

1 In the year known as 348 CE, 2 fifteen hundred and forty eight years since the dawn of the Great Age, 3 Cúigan (Eogan Mor) did complete his training with Cuinstanyn (Constantine) as Columbus (Columba). 4 Yet as they observed the ship approach to return him to the mainland, Cúigan (Eogan Mor) did protest, saying: 5 Father I do not wish to leave, for you have so much more to teach me. 6 Cuinstanyn (Constantine) as Columbus (Columba) did respond, saying: 7 No man is ever sent out in the world over prepared, but prepared enough. 8 For the rest is up to him and the entire world is open to him. 9 Cúigan (Eogan Mor) did reply, saying: Then why Grandfather did you leave the world? 10 For you had such power and respect that you could change anything and repair anything. 11 The world needs you. Why do you not return and let them know you still live? 12 Cuinstanyn (Constantine) as Columbus (Columba) did reply, saying: 13 What the world wants and what people need are two different paths. 14 For what so many pray and seek is a saviour who will overcome their enemies, 15 and teach them and protect their cities and their farmlands, 16 and honour their scriptures and fulfil their prophecies. 17 Yet when these saviours as the true sons of man have come, 18 these same people have ignored the saviours and abandoned all reason. 19 Thus such men have come and gone and all that remains is dust. 20 Truly, I say to you, when the greatest of your descendants shall come to save the world from darkness, 21 he shall come not as a king but as a thief; not regarded as a speaker of truth, but as a condemned liar. 22 Verily, I say to you, do not be the saviour the world wants you to be, 23 for such a character is but an imposter and poor magician that entertains and beguiles. 24 This is the way of enemies of truth, who rise up generation after generation in seeking to enslave. 25 You are Cuilliaéan (Holly). You are born of the bloodline of the saviours of the world. 26 Yet, you will be glorified by some as a god and worshipper as a supernatural being, 27 only to be abandoned by these same confused people and ultimately condemned by such wicked people. 28 For Power is nothing. The absolute power to rule or destroy is even less. 29 Some men obsess themselves over power as if its achievement is its own justification, 30 yet power alone, nor all the wealth of the world does not change it, nor last long. 31 There have been men who have ruled vast kingdoms and empires, 32 that held the power of the life or death of millions within their hands. 33 Yet the cities of such men have been torn to rubble and their names forgotten. 34 A wise man profits nothing by obsessing and gaining power. 35 Indeed, the wisest of men pay attention to the smallest aspects of their character in humility. 36 A man who cannot care for his own personal possessions, cannot care for the well being of others, 37 nor can a man who cannot hold his tongue and open his heart, be a true leader for his people. 38 Behold, I have taught you nothing. All I have tried to do is wake up the knowledge already within you. 39 Thus, I leave you with this final observation as to the greatest power in the universe. 40

The greatest power is the power of positive ideas, that empowers people to emancipate themselves. 41 Truly, there is nothing that can outlast the judgement of time more than the power of ideas. 42 At the conclusion of the words of Cuinstanyn (Constantine) as Columbus (Columba), 43 Cúigan (Eogan Mor) did depart the island of Avalon (Great Skellig), 44 on the promise that he would return to see Cuinstanyn (Constantine) upon reaching the age of maturity.

C. 8

1 In the year known as 352 CE, 2 fifteen hundred and fifty two years since the dawn of the Great Age, 3 upon the news of the betrothal of Maebhe (Maeve), the daughter of Cúilman (Coleman), 4 to Aurelius Cornelius Hieronymus (Jerome), the son of Exarchos Aurelius Cornelius Ambrosius, 5 Maebhe (Maeve) did seek leave to travel a final time to the sacred island of Avalon (Great Skellig), 6 to visit the mysterious Holly Spirit and Teacher known as Columbus (Columba). 7 Maebhe (Maeve) and her younger brother Cúigan (Eogan Mor), did then go to Avalon (Great Skellig), 8 where they did discover their teacher in ill health and greatly affected by his advanced years. 9 After Maebhe (Maeve) had explained her betrothal, 10 Cuinstanyn (Constantine) as Columbus (Columba) took Maebhe (Maeve) and Cúigan (Eogan Mor) to the highest point one last time, 11 where the old and ill teacher did speak, saying: 12 Do not mourn for me, or grieve my passing. 13 Life goes on; and death is part of life. 14 Verily to truly live, one must die; and one must die to live. 15 Every day and every moment is within the dance of life and death, 16 thus we should embrace death and not fear it, 17 nor should we obsess over death or fight clinging to life beyond the point of dignity. 18 The greatest honour that could ever be done in my name, 19 is that people be gentle with one another and to love one another as I love you. 20 For each of us have the extraordinary and unique gift, 21 to do great good and positive change within this world, 22 and also to inflict great harm and damage upon it as well. 23 Honour me if you must, through your austerity and humility, 24 and through your piety and respect to what is sacred and true. 25 Above all, protect the Golden Rule of Law, 26 and the administration of justice. 27 If you do this in memory of me, then it shall be so, 28 that your own descendants shall honour you in the same manner. 29 At the conclusion of the visit, Maebhe (Maeve) then departed to Arles and the Court of the Franks. 30 In the year known as 353 CE, 31 fifteen hundred and fifty three years since the dawn of the Great Age, 32 Maebhe (Maeve) the eldest daughter of Cúilman (Colman) and Brigit, 33 did wed Aurelius Cornelius Hieronymus (Jerome) of the Franks, 34 who was the son of Exarchos Aurelius Cornclius Ambrosius and King of the Franks. 35 In the same year, 36 Christian Patriarchos Ouzana of Ethiopia and king of all the tribes, 37 did give up the ghost. 38 The new king over all the tribes of Ethiopia and the new Christian Patriarchos, 39 did befall to his son named Saizana. 40 In the same year, 41 Christian Patriarchos Cyrillos of the Rusi Federation of Normen

Tribes, 42 did give up the ghost. 43 The position of Patriarchos and King of the Rusi (Russian) Tribes, 44 did befall to his son named Varangos.

C. 9

1 In the year known as 354 CE, 2 fifteen hundred and fifty four years since the dawn of the Great Age, 3 Marcus Aurelius Cornelius Hieronymus (Jerome), 4 the son of King Marcus Aurelius Cornelius Ambrosius of the Franks, 5 and Maebhe (Maeve) the daughter of Cúilman (Colman), 6 did have a son, whom they named Hippolytus (Augustine), 7 also known as the true Augustine the Great and Saint Augustine. 8 In the same year, 9 the fifth Great Oikoumenikos (Ecumenical) Council of all Christianity was convened, 10 at Antioch by the four Tetrachos (Tetrachs). 11 The Oikoumenikos (Ecumenical) Council voted unanimously to order the closure and destruction, 12 of all remaining Greek and Roman Temples throughout the Christian world, 13 where such places were continuing to be sites of worship of magic and superstition, 14 especially the continuation of human sacrifice and simulated sacrifice. 15 The Oikoumenikos (Ecumenical) Council did also vote unanimously, 16 to forbid the augmentation of the simple form of the cross into elaborate symbols of wealth, 17 and corrupted into symbols of sacrifice and pagan notions, whereby Constans did say: 18 Behold! The symbolon of the cross is the symbolon of the four points of the world, 19 and must not be defined by being converted into symbols for worshipping wealth or status, 20 or corrupted by worshippers of other religions. 21 Verily, to augment the Kes-Ros (Cross) or to place upon it the symbol of a man or face, 22 is a profound act of sacrilege against every tenet of Christianity, 23 and a grave offence against the true Rule of Law. 24 In the year 355 CE, 25 fifteen hundred and fifty five years since the dawn of the Great Age, 26 Marcus Aurelius Cornelius Hieronymus (Jerome), 27 the son of King Marcus Aurelius Cornelius Ambrosius of the Franks, 28 and Maebhe (Maeve) the daughter of Cúilman (Colman), 29 did have a son, whom they named Augenius (Theudemar). 30 In the same year, 31 Patriarchos Priscillian of Spania did give up the ghost. 32 The position of Christian Patriarch and king of the tribes of Spania did befall to his son Pacianos. 33 In the same year, 34 a cruel and bitter winter did befall the sacred isles, so that both Cúilman (Colman) and Cúilaidh (Cooley), 35 implored the monks abandon Avalon (Great Skellig) until the weather improved. 36 Yet Cuinstanyn (Constantine) as Columbus (Columba) refused saying: 37 let me depart in peace. For I trust my spirit to our heavenly father. 38 Soon after, Cuinstanyn (Constantine) as Columbus (Columba) did give up the ghost. 39 On news of the death of the mysterious abbot Columbus (Columba), 40 Cúilman (Colman) ordered the remaining monks be rescued from the island. 41 Yet the icy and wet conditions upon the island made cremation impossible. 42 So, a ship was prepared and stripped to its bones, replacing its cargo with dry kindling, 43 whereupon the body of

Cuinstanyn (Constantine) as Columbus (Columba), 44 was placed atop the ship and the ship then set alight before allowing it by its own sail, 45 to depart the shore to the great unknown ocean to the west. 46 Soon after, the ship burst into flames and did burn soundly before sinking to the depths.

C. 10

1 In the year known as 356 CE, 2 fifteen hundred and fifty six years since the dawn of the Great Age, 3 as the seasons did behave as if possessed, with heat in winter and floods and cold in spring, 4 many people throughout the lands grew increasingly belligerent against the Tetratchos (Tetrarchy), 5 at their closure and destruction of ancient pagan temples and desecration of such gods, 6 as the cause for growing calamities and troubles of the world. 7 In Palestinia, the former High Priest of the Great Temple of Baalbek, whose name was Hillel of the Hammoni, 8 also known as Procopius for his prodigious writings of propaganda against Christianity, 9 did continue to gain power and support, even among Christian officials, 10 after the closure and destruction of the most ancient temple to Baal and Cybele. 11 Even Valentinianus Tertullianus Invictus, also known as Valentinian and Pontifex Innocens, 12 did secretly come to the north of Palestinia to meet with Procopius (Hillel) and discuss the growing unrest. 13 There, they agreed that their greatest weapon be to propagate half-truths and to always lie against Christianity, 14 and to play upon the fears of the people in creating confusion and mistrust, 15 and then upon the right time, they would mount a strike against the leaders of Christianity, 16 and bring it to an end once and for all. 17 In the same year, 18 upon word of the rise of pagan practices of people across the Christian world, 19 Exarchos Cúinstans (Constans) was enraged and demanded such superstitious practices be stopped, saying: 20 Behold the first steps of darkness. For when men abandon reason and rely upon superstition, 21 Humanity abandons our future to impostors, pirates and thieves. 22 Soon after, an edict was issued by the four Exarchos as the sacred Tetrachy, 23 whereby the teaching and practice of superstitious arts against the reason of Christianity, 24 was declared a crime punishable by death. 25 To many people, such harsh sentences against religious practice caused deep resentment, 26 especially to those in the north and western parts of the sacred isles of Britain and Ireland. 27 A new figure of rebellion did emerge among the tribes of central and western Irenia (Ireland), 28 calling himself the Raven King (Fiachre). 29 In the year known as 358 CE, 30 fifteen hundred and fifty eight years since the dawn of the Great Age, 31 the winter in the west of Europe and the Sacred Isles, 32 was as bitter and cruel as it had been for more than one hundred years, 33 causing the migration south from the northern lands, 34 and some Normen tribes such as the Angles to abandon their homeland to travel south. 35 In Irenia (Ireland), as many did suffer from the cold to the north and west of the island, 36 the figure known as the Raven King (Fiachre) did proclaim that the ancient gods

were angry, 37 upon the worship of a false religion called Christianity; 38 and upon the wealth being heaped upon the Holly, 39 and upon the deification of Constantine as Ioannes Christos (John the Christ), 40 also known as Ioannes Pappas (John the Pappas / Father) and later known as Johannes Chrystadom. Chrystadom. 41 The Fiachre (Raven King) did send word to starving farmers and villagers, 42 that the Cuilliaean (Holly) were secretly hiding grain and stores for faithful pilgrims, 43 while letting their own people starve who did not follow Christianity. 44 So desperate were people that lawlessness did erupt across parts of northern Britain and Ireland, 45 that Christian pilgrims began to be robbed and murdered by the followers of the Raven King. 46 The followers of the Fiachre (Raven King) soon became known as the ui bruen (brien), 47 meaning the clann of the putrid, corrupt, filthy disgusting and vile robbers and thieves, 48 and some of the worst liars and thieves of all human history. 49 In the same year, 50 Patriarchos Geberic of Vandalia and King of the Vandali and Amali tribes, 51 did give up the ghost. 52 The position of Christian Patriarchos and King of the Vandals, 53 did then befall his son named Gemanaric.

C. 11

1 In the year known as 360 CE, 2 fifteen hundred and sixty years since the dawn of the Great Age, 3 a lack of rain across the Kuria of Orientalia did cause crops to dry up and die. 4 Yet starvation was averted through the wise rationing of food and stores. 5 The Tetrachos (Tetrachy) did then order each city to expand its stores and underground water chambers, 6 to avert such future calamity as prolonged drought as did strike the east. 7 In the year known as 361 CE, 8 fifteen hundred and sixty one years since the dawn of the Great Age, 9 Cúichaid (Eochaid), the eldest son of Cúilman (Colman), 10 did wed his first cousin named Cuirenn (Karen), the daughter of Cuirell (Carroll). 11 In the year known as 362 CE, 12 fifteen hundred and sixty two years since the dawn of the Great Age, 13 King Aurelius Cornelius Ambrosius of the Franks, 14 also known as Saint Ambrose as the Exarchos of Europealia (West), 15 did give up the ghost. 16 The crown of the Franks did befall to his son, 17 Aurelius Cornelius Hieronymus (Jerome), also known as Saint Jerome, 18 who did also become the new Exarchos of Europealia (West) and King of the Franks. 19 In the same year, 20 Cúigan (Eogan Mor), the second son of Cúilman (Colman), 21 did wed Darerca, the beautiful and dark haired daughter of Eustochius, 22 the Exarchos of Borealia; and himself the son of Mattatheos Plotinus. 23 In the same year, 24 Arcadius the son of Cuistans (Constans) and the grandson of Cuinstanyn (Constantine), 25 did wed Aurelia Eusebia, the daughter of Aurelius Cornelius Ambrosius of the Franks, 26 and sister of Aurelius Cornelius Hieronymus (Jerome) as the new Exarchos of Europalia. 27 In the same year, 28 Maena (Mona), the second daughter of Cúilman (Colman), 29 did wed her first cousin named Cuirantoc (Carrington), the son of Cuirell (Carroll).

C. 12

1 In the year known as 363 CE, 2 fifteen hundred and sixty three years since the dawn of the Great Age, 3 Arcadius the son of Cuistans (Constans) and the grandson of Cuinstanyn (Constantine), 4 and Aurelia Eusebia the daughter of Aurelius Cornelius Ambrosius of the Franks, 5 did have a son they named Theodosius. 6 In the same year, 7 Cúichaid (Eochaid), the eldest son of Cúilman (Colman), 8 and Cuirenn (Karen), the daughter of Cuirell (Carroll), 9 did have a son they named Cuirc (Kirk). 10 In the same year, 11 Cúigan (Eogan Mor), the youngest son of Cúilman (Colman), 12 and Darerca, the daughter of Eustochius the Exarchos of Borealia, 13 did have a son they named Named Cuilleain (Collins). 14 In the same year, 15 a huge series of tremors did erupt across the Politea of Sinopia and Palestinia, 16 with Aela (Aqaba), the Metropolitos (Capital) of Sinopia utterly destroyed, killing tens of thousands, 17 while cities further north into Palestinia such as Skythopolis in Galilaia were also destroyed, 18 and the city of Gerasis (Amman) in Nabataia badly damaged. 19 Hillel of the Hammoni (Procopius) seized the tragedy as a sign to launch an attack, 20 against Gaza, the Metropolitos (Capital) of Palestinia. 21 Yet his forces were overwhelmed by the better disciplined forces of Acacius, 22 the great Patriarchos of Palestinia, who called upon all honourable men and women, 23 to stand up against such maniacs and murderers as the followers of Hillel. 24 In the year known as 364 CE, 25 fifteen hundred and sixty four years since the dawn of the Great Age, 26 Maena (Mona), the second daughter of Cúilman (Colman), 27 and Cuirantoc (Carrington), the son of Cuirell (Carroll), 28 did have a son they named Cuinstanyn Cuirneu (Curnow). 29 In the same year, 30 the forces of Holly Patriarch Cúilman (Coleman) of Irenia (Ireland), 31 did capture the Fiechre (Raven King) and did bring him to Tara. 32 The advisers of the ageing ecumenical patriarch did implore a swift execution of the Fiechre (Raven King), 33 so that the Ui Bruen (Brien) be scattered in fear and the threat of such vile thieves and robbers ended. 34 Yet Cúilman (Coleman) refused, saying: Better a kingdom fall, than justice not be done. 35 For all we have is the truth of law under the Golden Rule. 36 If we abandon even for one moment such sacred rule, then we are no better, 37 than the madness and evilness of the Ui Bruen (Brien). 38 In the end, a people that abandon the Rule of Law and Justice, 39 are always doomed to fail. 40 In the same year, 41 the sixth Great Oikoumenikos (Ecumenical) Council of all Christianity was convened at Antioch, 42 as proceedings became stalled midst heated argument as to how to stop the rise of paganism, 43 while some of the Patriarchos and Monarchos did blame intolerance for such rise. 44 For the first time of any democratic council, the Oikoumenikos did end without clear resolutions, 45 other than a reinforcement as orthodoxy those epistole (epistles) against paganism, 46 and the enforcement of punishments against the desecration of Christian doctrines.

C. 13

1 In the year known as 365 CE, 2 fifteen hundred and sixty five years since the dawn of the Great Age, 3 on the first day of the Aemetos (month) of Ippos the horse (23-Jul to 21-Aug), 4 the island Diakesis (Diocese) of Kanadia (Crete) did begin shaking so violently, 5 that the earth did tear itself apart, swallowing villages and fields and forming mountains from plains, 6 so that every structure formed by the hands of men did crumble, 7 and every city, town and village was crushed to dust, that only a handful of souls did survive. 8 So powerful were the forces of the earthquake and displacement of land, 9 that when the shaking and rumbling did finally subside, 10 the entire Island was pushed higher from the sea floor by more than thirty feet. 11 Yet the poor spirits upon the condemned island of Kanadia (Crete) were not alone in their doom, 12 for the whole of the sea around the island did rise and fall with such drama, 13 in a manner of giant waves, not seen for more than two thousand years. 14 To the near north of Kanadia (Crete) and the mainland of Hellia and Anatolia, 15 the earthquake and tremors were also felt with such ferocity, 16 that many buildings did collapse in the cities of Skala in Lacodonia, Araxos in Achaia, Athena in Saronica, 17 and across the west of Anatolia and as far east as Kypria (Cyprus) and Palestinia. 18 The first of these massive waves radiating north into the Aegean, were unlike anything the world had ever seen. 19 Island after island, village after village were consumed by wave after wave of more than two hundred feet in height. 20 The islands of Karpathos, Naxos, Rhodes, Cos, Samos and Euboea all destroyed; for no island was spared, 21 and only those fortunate souls at the highest points did survive the Tsunamis. 22 Skala, Araxos, Athena, Philippi and Xanthi and all the towns and cities on the coast were consumed, 23 so that upon the end of one day more than three million souls did perish, 24 between the Politea of Hellia, Anatolia and Makedonia alone, 25 including Cúinstans (Constans) Exarchos of Orientalia and Eustochius, the Exarchos of Borealia. 26 To the east, the giant waves were of a scale beyond comprehension when they did strike the Levant coast. 27 Every village, town and city, including many several miles inland and more than a hundred feet in elevation were destroyed, 28 while the great cities of Gaza, Askalon, Akre, Biblos, Tripolis and Laodicia, 29 were wiped from the face of the Earth. 30 By the end of that fateful day, more than four million men, women and children did perish, 31 across the Politea of Palestinia, Syria and Sinopia, 32 Including the great Patriarchos Acacius of Palestinia. 33 To the west, the Tsunamis did overwhelm the Island of Sicily and the east of Italia to Philadelphia, 34 as Patriarchos Silvestros and many tens of thousands did perish in the capital, 35 like so many coastal cities and villages of the Adriatic, as the devastating waves pushed westward, 36 overwhelming the islands of Sardinia and Corsica; and destroying cities as far west as Valencia in Spania. 37 However, the coastal city of Arles and the nearby coast of Francia was spared, 38 as the waves did smash themselves apart within sight of the shore, 39 saving the

Franks and its capital. 40 However, by the end of that terrible day, more than two million people did perish, 41 across the politea of Italia, Slavia, Spania and Francia. 42 Yet the greatest horror and tragedy on the darkest day of the history of all human civilisation, 43 Was sadly reserved for those unfortunate souls to the south of the cataclysmic earthquakes upon Kanadia (Crete). 44 The people of the great city of Alexandria upon the Egyptian coast, 45 were themselves struck by the same earthquakes and aftershocks, causing ancient buildings to collapse. 46 When the first wave did come, it was of such size that it blocked the sun for the final minutes of its approach. 47 In moments, one of the greatest of cities of humanity ceased to exist as the walls of water pushed further inland, 48 swallowing everything and everyone in its path, 49 so that forests, fields, plantations, villages, cities and towns were all destroyed in minutes, 50 as far south as the mountains that traditionally divided Upper Egypt from Lower Egypt, 51 so that in Egyptia alone, the death toll for that one day was more than four million. 52 Along the coast of Libia, city after city was also utterly destroyed and swept into the abyss, 53 including the great cities of Berenice, Tebrek, Kanis, Monktor and Augila. 54 Further west and upon such a day, the Moor Berber Politea of Garmantia, 55 and all its inhabitants and wetlands, fields, forests and cities did cease to exist. 56 The great Moor cities of Zanadu, Zohar, Zirtis, Zizda, Zuis, Zakna, Zala and Zouila, 57 were utterly destroyed so that in the lands of the Moors as ancient descendants, 58 of the once proud and noble Mani tribes of North Africa, 59 more than five million people did lose their lives in one day. 60 Further west, the Berber Politea of Gaetulia was also destroyed, 61 including its cities of Gabes, Nebraka, Ticarta, Bonoura, Gadamea, Golea and Negita. 62 Further west and the Politea of Algeria was terribly struck, 63 as hundreds of towns and villages were swept into the sea, 64 and the cities of Zoza, Zebela, Bone, Algol, Gorgos and Magma were destroyed. 65 Even the Politea of Barbaria was not spared, with the destruction of the capital of Timogad. 66 Thus, in the space of one day, the earth did witness the greatest loss of human life, 67 in the history of the species as twenty million people ceased to exist, 68 and entire cultures and their memory were swept into the sea, 69 as those survivors and their future generations had such horror seared within the consciousness, 70 as the Day of Horror and the Terror of the Sea or Maritimeo (Maritime), 71 and as the Great Flood and the End of the World, 72 and the event that gave birth to an entirely new religion and arch-nemesis to Christianity.

C. 14

1 In the year known as 365 CE, 2 fifteen hundred and sixty five years since the dawn of the Great Age, 3 the Christian Church remained in complete chaos and shock, 4 upon such scale of devastation and mass death. 5 Cities, Politea and entire cultures had in one instance ceased to exist, 6 midst all the earthquakes and tsunami that had cause so much terror. 7 Yet the worst was still to come as disease, hunger and anarchy soon

took hold. 8 For the days and weeks that first followed, there was little or no communication, 9 as no one in the ancient world yet knew of the full scale of the disaster. 10 Survivors of once thriving and vibrant communities were forced to pick through debris, 11 and move the rotting corpses of men, women, children and animals, 12 in search of food and sustenance. 13 With no government or forces to maintain order, gangs of survivors quickly formed, 14 killing and raping at will and enforcing their own form of pirate law. 15 Not even the sworn enemies of Christianity knew of the utter devastation for weeks, 16 and even then, many did not trust at first such outrageous sounding stories, 17 that spoke of the sea as the greatest of all gods destroying their enemies. 18 Yet the stories of the Great Flood and the End of Days were true. 19 The ancient world had lost many of its political and spiritual leaders. 20 Eunapius, the Exarchos of Borealia and his most senior advisers were dead. 21 Constans, the Exarchos of Orientalia and his greatest generals were dead. 22 Athanasius, the Exarchos of Australia and his entire household were dead. 23 Only Aurelius Cornelius Hieronymus, also known as Jerome and St Jerome remained a Exarchos, 24 as only the Frankish coast was spared destruction from the sea. 25 Yet when no ships did come, Hieronymus (Jerome) did order his fastest ships to set sail, 26 to Spania and Italia and to the isles of Corsica, Sardinia and Sicily, 27 and bring word of such strange and eerie silence. 28 On learning of the complete destruction of so many cities and towns, 29 Hieronymus (Jerome) did then order supplies be sent first to the survivors of the coast of Spania. 30 And to the isles of Corsica and Sardinia and then to the capitals of Barbaria and Algeria, 31 as Hieronymus (Jerome) himself did set sail east to Antioch (Constantinople).

C. 15

1 When Hieronymus (Jerome) did arrive at Antioch (Constantinople), he found a city paralysed with fear. 2 Arcadius the son of Constans had been rescued and brought to the city, 3 with his household and his two year old son named Theodosius, 4 and his wife Eusebia and the sister of Hieronymus (Jerome). 5 Yet in the weeks since the greatest disaster ever in the history of humanity, 6 no decisions of importance had been made, as precious grains and supplies still sat in vast warehouses, 7 as people outside the city walls and across the ancient Christian world were starving. 8 Varangos, the Patriarchos of the Rusi (Russians) had come to Antioch, 9 as had Ulda, the Patriarchos of the Alans and Goths and Gemenaric of the Vandals. 10 Hegros, the Patriarchos of Saracenia (Arabia) had even made the dangerous journey to Antioch himself, 11 to pledge the wealth and support of all Arab tribes as loyal Christians. 12 Yet neither Arcadius nor the remaining Christian officials had accepted any such audience, 13 to even allow the making of such needed offers of assistance, 14 and all except Varangos of the Rusi had departed back to their lands in frustration. 15 When Hieronymus (Jerome) demanded answers for such procrastination, 16 some advisors and generals did speak of their fear that

Book 26 Great Age of the Christian Tetrachy

the Normen giants were so superior, 17 and their concerns that once they visited such lands and places it would be impossible to coerce them to leave. 18 Others argued that they feared such men of huge height and strength were like brutes, 19 and if given too much authority would cause even more damage than the worst pagans. 20 Hieronymus (Jerome) did then speak to all assembled within the Great Basilica, saying: 21 Woe to you scribes and men of law that procrastinate as the world is suffering; 22 for you show neither the heart of true Christians, nor the mind of trustworthy leaders. 23 Verily, even as we speak the enemies of civilisation are rallying and shall soon be upon these very walls. 24 Alas, through your petty squabbles and inattention to matters of state, 25 you have helped fan the flames of anger and suffering that inevitably shall lead to hate, 26 and the momentum the enemies of sanity and decency need to beguile the people. 27 Verily, there be nothing to fear from men of honour and character, 28 except by those who cannot stand to be blinded by such mirrors of Divinity. 29 For nothing can corrupt or destroy Christianity, except when men close their hearts, 30 and willingly choose to be ignorant and dishonourable. 31 Behold then, Arcadius, the son of Constans be the rightful heir as Exarchos of Orientalia, 32 and Theon, the son of Eunapius and the grandson of Eustochius and great grandson of Plotinus, 33 be the rightful successor as the Exarchos of Borealia. 34 Yet to Australia in the south and the greatest devastation, 35 our beloved cousin and his household have passed and thus it is only right, 36 that a candidate of sufficient sanctity and honour take the place of Athanasius. 37 Behold, we agree that Cuirrell, the son of Cuinstanyn (Constantine) be the new Exarchos of Australia. 38 At the conclusion of his pronouncement, Hieronymus (Jerome) did then charge Theon and Arcadius, 39 with calling upon the support of the Normen Patriarchs, 40 and aiding the survivors to the east and north, 41 as Hieronymus (Jerome) returned westward to see Cuirrell (Carroll) and discuss his agreement, 42 and aid to the survivors to the west and south. 43 Arcadius did then pronounce to all assembled saying: 44 Let it be my first act as Exarchos of Orientalia and to all present, 45 that I right a wrong inflicted upon the brave and noble name of all Normen tribes, 46 in failing to embrace the hands extended in aid and assistance. 47 Behold, Varangos of the Rusi (Russians) is present here today, 48 and whereas other Patriarchos did leave out of slight and frustration, 49 the Rusi (Russians) stood firm to the protection and honour of the Christian faith. 50 Therefore, from this day forth, I empower the Rusi (Russians) to be my personal guard, 51 and the Rusi to be the guards and protectors of the capital of Orientalia, 52 and the most sacred protectors of the east and the honour of Christianity, now and forever more. 53 This pledge I make for all my successors and all who come hereafter. 54 Upon such a historic honour, Varangos the Patriarchos of the Rusi did reply, saying: 55 Before all Heaven and Earth and all of my people who have passed over and all to come, 56 let it be written and spoken for all time that the Rusi (Russian) People shall defend Christianity, 57 to our last man, our last woman and child, so if it be the will of Heaven we must sacrifice everything, 58 then this we shall do willingly and gladly to defend the Golden Rule of Law, 59 and the memory of John Christadom (Constantine), the true son the Divine and our saviour.

C. 16

1 Valentinianus Tertullianus Invictus, also known as Valentinian, 2 and also known as Saint Valentine and also self proclaimed as Pontifex Innocens, 3 did not trust at first the messages sent to him of the utter devastation of the Christian cities, 4 as he had neither witnessed such destruction with his eyes, nor could conceive such power. 5 So when he did come down from hiding in the Atlas mountains to witness such death and horror, 6 he could not contain his joy at witnessing such evil, proclaiming: 7 Rejoice Oh sons of Moloch. Rejoice Oh sons of Rome. 8 For Mari (Mary) has revealed herself the greatest of all the gods, 9 and the most blessed Queen of Heaven. 10 For she makes the ground immaculate and cleanses the Earth of our enemies, 11 she brings to life the fruits of our loins and vanquishes all who stand in her way. 12 Verily, her son (Baal Moloch) is our saviour and guide, 13 yet is Mari (Mary) as the Sacred Sea that we pledge to honer above all, 14 now and forever more. 15 Verily, any man or woman that does not honour Mari (Mary) as Queen of Heaven, 16 and does not make an offering to Mari (Mary) the Mother of all the Gods, 17 shall be an apostate and shall then be burned alive in the flames of their heresy, 18 as a fitting holocaust (burnt offering) to her son our Lord Moloch. 19 Behold, by the celebration of the next cycle of the full moon, 20 we shall be in Rome and tending to her wounds. 21 At the same time, in the lands of Syria, 22 Procopius had witnessed the destruction on the horizon and was equally joyed, 23 at the sight of the suffering of his enemies. 24 Procopius had wasted no time in preparing his army of bandits and thieves, 25 strengthened in number with the hungry and desperate on a quest north to capture Antioch. 26 In the Politea of Bulgaria, a rebel leader named Savvas did rise out of Oltenia, 27 soon capturing the major city of Silistros in Wallachia before heading south toward Odessos. 28 The forces of ageing Patriarchos Dionysius were no match for Savvas and Odessos soon fell. 29 Yet rather than press south in momentum toward Antioch (Constantinople), 30 Savvas and his generals encamped themselves at Odessos where he declared himself a living god, 31 and feasted on his victories with an orgy of plundering, gluttony, killing and raping. 32 In the northern alps of Italia, a rebel leader of the Roma did arise, 33 named Dagonus, proclaiming himself to be the reincarnation of the fish god, 34 and swiftly captured the northern cities of Italia including Philadelphia. 35 In the Politea of Slavia, a rebel leader named Sebastianus did rise, 36 and promptly captured the capital Spoleto on the Dalmatian coast. 37 In the lands now known as India under the control of Nebath Calpernius Piso as Lord Agni, 38 word did reach as to the events of horror, whereupon Nebath as Lord Agni did declare, 39

now is our moment and did order every able man to fall into formation, 40 and an army of more than four hundred thousand did move westward toward Bactria and Persia.

C. 17

1 In the year known as 365 CE, 2 fifteen hundred and sixty five years since the dawn of the Great Age, 3 the patchwork army of Procopius of more than two hundred thousand hungry souls, 4 approached the capital of Anatolia being the city of Nicomedia, 5 and the final gateway to a full attack against Antioch (Constantinople). 6 Arcadius as the new Exarchos of Orientalia had barely been appointed, 7 when the threat of Procopius was finally realised, 8 yet it was too late even for the Alans and Vandals to come to the aid of the centre of Christianity, 9 should the core forces of Procopius break through the defences of Nicomedia. 10 Only Varangos and his loyal guard of nine hundred Rusi (Russians), 11 as the appointed sacred protectors of the heart of Christianity, 12 stood with five thousand standard soldiers, 13 against the advance of Procopius. 14 As the army of Procopius made camp before their planned assault against Nicomedia, 15 Varangos declared to Arcadius, better we die while cutting off the head of our enemy, 16 than by exhaustion at the fate of an angry swarm. 17 The Rusi (Russians) did then leave the city walls and infiltrate the camp of Procopius, 18 whereupon the giant Normen, did slay thousands of defenders, 19 until they surrounded the encampment of Procopius, 20 and killed him, before cutting off his head and parading it before the rest of the army. 21 At the sight and horror of these giant warriors, the army of Procopius collapsed, 22 and thousands of people ran for their lives, in fear of facing these bravest of giants. 23 In the year known as 366 CE, 24 fifteen hundred and sixty six years since the dawn of the Great Age, 25 the Normen forces of Gemanaric of the Vandals and Ulda of the Alans, 26 finally entered the field in support of Exarchos Arcadius and Exarchos Theon of Borealia. 27 As the Alans helped secure peace across Anatolia, Syria and Palestinia, 28 the Vandals and their Goti vassals, led by Athanari, did confront the forces of Savvas. 29 Yet Savvas had anticipated an attack against his adopted city of Odessos, 30 so when the Goti and Alans attacked, the defenders were equally resilient. 31 Then through an act of leadership and bravery, Athanari appeared on his horse, 32 to lead a final charge against the city walls, despite being mortally wounded by such exposure. 33 Upon the death and bravery of Athenari, the Vandals and Goti slaughtered the defenders, 34 and killed Savvas as he attempted to escape dressed as a woman. 35 On news of the courage of Athanari, 36 Patriarchos Gemenaric of Vandalia did declare: Truly all men must have their transgressions forgiven, 37 for here the bravest of men (Athanari) sacrificed his own life and redeemed his people (Goti). 38 Verily, in honour of a good king and a proud people, let it be known forever, 39 that Tervingia as the homeland of the Amali possesses the right to self-determination, 40 as I now adopt Alari (Alaric), the son of Athanari, as my own son. 41 Thereafter, the Goti made

a solemn oath and vow to defend Vandalia and Christianity, 42 then cutting their hands, so that the stones of Tanais were covered for a week in thousands of bloody hand prints.

www.ingramcontent.com/pod-product-compliance
Lightning Source LLC
Chambersburg PA
CBHW081944230426
43669CB00019B/2913